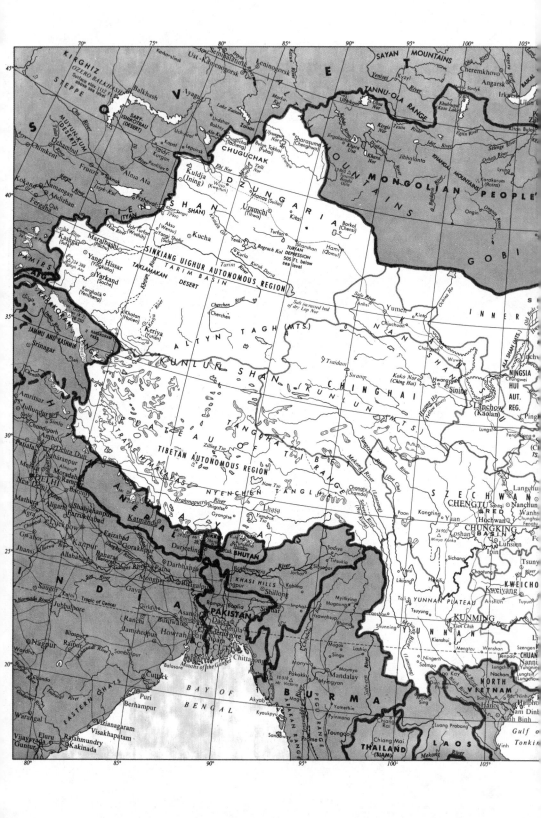

CHINA   Political Map

Names of cities over 1,000,000 are capitalized
National capitals   PEKING
Secondary capitals   SIAN
Secondary Boundaries   Railroads

0 50 100 200 300 400 500 Miles
0 100 200 300 400 500 600 700 800 Kilometers

COPYRIGHT BY
RAND McNALLY & COMPANY
MADE IN U.S.A.

Longitude East of Greenwich   115°

THE CENTER FOR CHINESE STUDIES at the University of California, Berkeley, supported by the Ford Foundation, the Institute of International Studies (University of California, Berkeley), and the State of California, is the unifying organization for social science and interdisciplinary research on contemporary China.

IDEOLOGY AND ORGANIZATION IN COMMUNIST CHINA

SECOND EDITION, ENLARGED

FRANZ SCHURMANN

UNIVERSITY OF CALIFORNIA PRESS

BERKELEY, LOS ANGELES, LONDON

SECOND EDITION, ENLARGED

University of California Press
Berkeley and Los Angeles, California

University of California Press, Ltd.
London, England

ISBN: 0-520-01151-1 (cloth)
0-520-01553-8 (paper)

Library of Congress Catalog Card Number 68-26124

Printed in the United States of America

5 6 7 8 9 0

TO

SSB

AND

L

34364

PREFACE TO THE SECOND EDITION

THE continuing interest in this book, prompted the University of California Press to urge me to prepare a second edition sooner than I had intended. That extraordinary event known as the Great Proletarian Cultural Revolution, which came as a surprise to almost everyone in the field, called into question many analyses of China done by the growing corps of scholars of contemporary China. Had our concepts and categories of analysis been wrong? Had we somehow failed to see the essence of China because of our Western outlook? A reexamination of all that we had done seemed called for.

Since several reviewers of my book pointed out that it dealt largely with the 1950's, I decided to add a supplement on China's ideology, organization, and society during the 1960's. I have not done any special research, other than what I do normally as a student concerned with China—read the newspapers, the Red Guard tabloids, and articles on China written by journalists and scholars. In December 1967, it seemed to me that the Cultural Revolution was subsiding, and that therefore I could attempt an evaluation, and with that, try to link the currents of the Cultural Revolution with those of the period from 1961 to 1966. The supplement does not treat the Cultural Revolution separately, but generally discusses it in the context of the history of the entire period from 1961 to 1967.

I must say that, by and large, the writing of the supplement has not induced me to discard the analytical tools I used in writing the book. I have changed some earlier views, for example in regard to differences between "professional" and "expert," which I earlier regarded as identical. Most important of all has been my awareness that ideology and organization are not so all-powerful as I had thought them to be. Chinese society, particularly in the form of its social classes, is asserting itself against the state, and showing that it cannot be manipulated at will. I do not see this so much as the reappearance of traditional forces as the assertion of human beings, individually and collectively, against the impersonal power of an immense organizational structure. Chairman Mao took a great risk in unleashing the masses against those in power. He did so for his own political reasons, but in the process loosened up a society which had for years been tightly controlled.

When I completed the first edition, the Vietnam war had just begun. It did not yet seem that world peace was threatened. Today, the threat of a greater war looms, and the possibilities of Chinese involvement can not be excluded. I do not believe that the Cultural Revolution itself was caused by the growing war clouds, but its violence and urgency were. The Chinese have always believed that one day they would again be emmeshed in a major war, but they were surprised at the rapidity of the escalation of the Vietnam war. I have written about the importance of whether the environment be defined as one of change or stability (pp. 235-236). Most scholars in the field, I believe, came increasingly to assume that, because world peace was assured, the environment surrounding China could only be one of stability, and that, therefore, it was Mao Tse-tung's willful determination to keep the revolution alive which turned an environment of stability into one of change. But the chief cause for turning the environment into one of change and now of crisis is the Vietnam war.

I wish to thank, in particular, Joseph Anderson Shih, Gene Hsiao, Michel Oksenberg, and Donald Klein for their help in ferreting out errors in the first edition; the second edition has been accordingly revised.

F. S.

February, 1968

PREFACE TO THE
FIRST EDITION ————————

THE WRITING of this book has been, like the Chinese Revolution, a long process climaxed by an act. The process has been the development of a manner of thinking about Communist China in particular, and about ideology and organization in general; the act has been writing it down in final form. Both process and act have taken place through human and intellectual experiences which have affected me as scholastic cogitation and library reading alone could never do. In this brief preface I can only mention a few friends and colleagues who have contributed to these experiences.

Much of my work was done at the Union Research Institute in Hong Kong, where knowledge and friendship have been generously offered to me. The many days of talking with Joseph Anderson Shih were for me not only a basic education on Communist China, but a path into the minds and feelings of Chinese individuals. Many other friends at U.R.I. were always ready to offer a helping hand: Maria Yen, Ho Chen-ya, Robert Hsi, Chao Yung-ch'ing, Jefferson Chen, Richard Diao, Chen Chien-jen, Chen I-lai, Wang Shu-chieh, and many others. I cannot begin to name the many other scholars, refugees, journalists, officials, whose thoughts contributed much to my own thinking during the time spent in Hong Kong.

In Berkeley, I wish to thank, in particular, Gregory Grossman, who always was ready to help me regarding Soviet problems; our Comparative Communism group has been a major source of ideas for this book. At the Center for Chinese Studies, I wish to thank the late Tsi-an Hsia, whose kindness and brilliance are much missed. Gene Hsiao, Joyce Kallgren, and John S. Service have been sources of steady intellectual, and

Rose Fox of steady moral and technical, support. Without the work of my research assistant, Hung Chow, much of the material used would never have been gathered.

The act of writing could never have been completed without months of friendly struggle with Max Knight of the Editorial Department of the University of California Press. I wish to thank the Press for its patience with the many revisions made in the manuscript.

Outside of Berkeley, I wish to thank the members of our national seminar on Communist China: Doak Barnett, Alexander Eckstein, Richard Moorsteen, Jerome Cohen, Ezra Vogel, and others. Many of their ideas and insights have found their way into this book.

Since research began in 1957, I have enjoyed numerous sources of institutional support. At Berkeley, the Institute of International Studies, the Center for Chinese Studies, and the Institute of Social Sciences have been consistent in their support. The John Simon Guggenheim Foundation and the American Council of Learned Societies made the year's stay in Hong Kong (1960-1961) possible. The Committee on the Economy of China of the Social Science Research Council gave me a year to work on industrial management in Communist China; for this, I wish to thank Walter Galenson.

Choh-ming Li was generously helpful during his tenure as Chairman of the Center for Chinese Studies; he made the Center into one of the leading research institutions on Communist China in the Western world.

Shih-hsiang Chen and Philip Selznick gave personal and intellectual support during the most difficult time of the writing of this book.

My two departments, Sociology and History (University of California, Berkeley), have always been willing to grant me leaves of absence to work on the book. Intellectual stimulation came, in particular, from my colleagues Joseph Levenson, Philip Selznick, S. M. Lipset, and Reinhard Bendix.

In most cases, references are to the original sources; translations from the Chinese, Russian, and Japanese are my own. Where terminological renderings are not standard, I have supplied my own.

Romanization follows the Wade-Giles system, but hyphens in words have been omitted following current usage in Mainland China.

In Communist China, the "Liberation" was the end of one phase in China's history and the beginning of another. I feel a sense of liberation now that the writing is over, but I also know that the future will lead to new roads of thought.

F. S.

Berkeley, California
August, 1965

CONTENTS

GLOSSARY

chengchih kuashuai	政治掛帥	Politics Takes Command: the main slogan of the Great Leap Forward
ch'echien	車間	shop; operational unit in a factory, like the Russian *tsekh*
chengchih-pu	政治部	political department; branch-type Party agencies, originally only in the army, but now also in finance, trade, communications, and industry
chengts'e	政策	specific policy; as contrasted with *fangchen*
chiench'a	監察	control; in the sense of after-the-fact investigation
chienjen	兼任	double position or role; such as a Party secretary who is also a factory director
chien-tang	建黨	Party construction; organizational development of the Party

chientu	監督	supervision; before-the-fact control, as contrasted with *chi-ench'a*
chihshih fentzu	知識份子	intellectuals; called "elements" instead of "class"
chihtu	制度	system; institutionalized methods
chihyüan	職員	functionary; general term for all white-collar workers in a factory, also specific term for clerical personnel
chingch'ang wenting	經常穩定	stabilization; policy term of the mid-1950's
chishu shenpi-hua	技術神秘化	fetishism of technology; term widely used during the Great Leap Forward
ch'iyeh, ch'iyeh-hua	企業,企業化	enterprise, "enterprization"; basic-level unit in industry and commerce, making into an enterprise
ch'üanli hsiafang	權力下放	downward transfer of authority; official designation of decentralization II
chungyang	中央	center; Party and state agencies in Peking
-chuyi	主義	-ism; suffix for what we call pure ideology, also for doctrinaire attitudes
fangchen	方針	general policy. See *chengts'e*
fangfa	方法	methods; operational practices
fanshen	翻身	reversal of social status; from an oppressed to a master class
fayen	發言	speaking out; individual expression in discussion sessions
fenhsi	分析	analysis; through use of ideology
hsiafang	下放	sending or transfer down; of persons or authority to lower units, e.g., factories and villages

hsiang	鄉	lowest geographical unit of state administration; equal, in general, to what was formerly called administrative village
hsiaotsu	小組	small group or team; the lowest-level work group
hsingcheng	行政	administration or management; in a corporate, not functional sense
huchi-ching	戶籍警	census policeman; in fact, a "neighborhood cop"
huihsiang	回鄉	return-to-the-village movement; early 1960's, distinct from *hsiafang*
ichang-chih	一長制	one-man management
ichi-chih-chang	一技之長	master-of-one-technique; opposite of *tomienshou*
ichien	意見	opinion. See *t'aolun*
ilantzu	一籃子	controlling everything; such as the Party in a factory; pejorative word
jenmin	人民	the people; excludes state and class enemies. See *kuomin*
kanpu	幹部	cadre
kuan	官	official; traditional term, used largely in a pejorative sense
kuanli-chü	管理局	administrative bureau, which administers other agencies and enterprises but does not manage them operationally
kungjen	工人	blue-collar worker. See *chih-yüan*
kungshe	公社	commune
kungtso	工作	work; operations
kungtso-tui	工作隊	operations squad; sent out for special tasks
kuochia	國家	the state; the formal instruments of rule
kuomin	國民	all people within the nation (except counter-revolutionaries and traitors); broader than *jenmin*

k'uota 擴大 — enlarged; as in Party meetings, includes individuals outside the regular meeting group

lalung 拉攏 — pulling into; pejorative term for recruiting into a clique

lilun 理論 — theory, particularly of Marxism-Leninism

lingtao 領導 — leadership; rule, command

lingtao kanpu 領導幹部 — leadership cadres; any Party or state cadre who holds executive position at any level

luhsien 路線 — line; as in general line of socialist construction, policy in the broadest sense. See *fangchen* and *chengts'e*

maotun 矛盾 — contradiction

mingyü chuhsi 名譽主席 — honorary chairman; Party post reserved for Mao Tse-tung

mintsu 民族 — nationality, race, as "Chinese" or Han, Tibetan, Mongolian, Uighur, and so on; sometimes also "nation"

mou 畝 — unit of land; one-sixth of an acre, sometimes written *mu*

neihang 內行 — professionals; implying experience in a particular organizational unit

neipu t'ungpao 內部通報 — internal communications; within given organizational channels

p'ai 派 — clique; pejorative term

p'aich'u chikuan 派出機關 — extended agency; such as an office of a central agency set up in a regional area but not under the latter's jurisdiction

p'aich'uso 派出所 — branch police station; lowest unit of the police

pao 包 — contractual agreement with a body of workers for a volume of output for which a lump sum is paid before or after completion, normally used in combination with other words, such as *pao-ch'an, paokung*

paopan 包辦   doing everything; such as the Party directing all operations, cf. *ilantzu*

penwei chuyi 本位主義   literally "vested-interestism" or "departmentalism"; corresponds to Russian *vedomst-vennost'*; concern only with one's organizational unit

pienchih 編制   table of ranks; particularly of cadres, like the Russian *nomenklatura*

pingshe 併社   amalgamation of APC's

pumen 部門   branch; as in branch-type agency, like the Russian *otrasi'*, also branch of the economy

pu-t'och'an kanpu 不脫產幹部   having a leadership or administrative role, but doing one's regular work at the same time

shihwu chuyi 事務主義   operationalism; pejorative term meaning excessive concern with routine business or operations

shuofu 說服   persuasion; particularly of opponents in discussion

sufan 肅反   abbreviation for *ch'ingsu fan-koming fentzu*; purge of counter-revolutionaries, specifically for movement during latter half of 1955

szuhsiang 思想   thought; specifically ideological thought of an individual

szuhsiang kaitsao 思想改造   thought reform; ideological process and method of changing identity

tangan 檔案   dossier; of each individual with facts and evaluations kept by Party, police, and other agencies

tangtsu	黨組	Party fraction; that is, "leading Party members' group" directing state agencies
tanshih	但是	but; implying importance of what follows rather than of what preceded
t'aolun	討論	discussion in meetings, where opinions are revealed, juxtaposed, and resolved
tatzupao	大字報	wall newspapers or bulletins; common way of expressing opinions
t'ech'üan	特權	special powers or privileges; pejorative term
tifang	地方	regional or local; normally counterposed to *chungyang*
tifang chuyi		"localism"; corresponds to Russian *mestnichestvo;* meaning concern only with one's geographical area
tomienshou	多面手	jack-of-all-trades; the ideal worker of the Great Leap Forward, cf. *ichi-chih-chang*
tot'ou lingtao	多頭領導	multi-headed leadership; multiple sources of command
toucheng	鬥爭	struggle; conflict with opponents in battle or in discussion, also used as a verb
tsengch'an chiehyüeh	增產節約	increase production and economize; generally indicates campaign to economize and stabilize.
tsofa	作法	methods; in contrast to *fangfa,* specifically implies behavior and action
tzuli kengsheng	自力更生	self-reliance; old term revived by the Communists, first appears in 1957

ts'un 村 — village; normally indicates the natural village

tzu-shang erh hsia, 自上而下 *tzu-hsia erh shang* 自下而上 — From Top down, from Bottom up; meaning action impulses coming both from top and bottom

waihang 外行 — nonprofessionals; implying someone coming from the outside into an organizational unit

wenchien 文件 — documents; ideological material on which discussion is based

yinti chihyi 因地制宜 — Do the Best According to Local Conditions; common slogan of the Great Leap Forward when decentralization, local self-reliance, and native methods were stressed

yüantse 原則 — principle; specifically of doctrine, word commonly used by the Chinese in the Sino-Soviet ideological exchange

yünniang 醞釀 — distillation; fermentation, the preparation of mood and opinions leading to introduction of a policy or resolution of a question

CHRONOLOGY

THE STRUGGLE TO POWER (1920-1949)

1920-1922	THE FORMATIVE PERIOD
Spring 1920	Comintern envoys arrive in China
August 1920	Chinese Socialist Youth League established
July 1921	Founding and first congress of the Chinese Communist party, in Shanghai
October 1921	Hunan branch of the Party established
July 1922	Second congress of the Chinese Communist Party, in Canton
1923-1927	PERIOD OF NATIONALIST-COMMUNIST COLLABORATION
June 1923	Third congress of the Chinese Communist party, in Canton, resolution on collaboration with the Nationalists
February 1924	Founding of the national railroad-workers union
January 1925	Fourth congress of the Chinese Communist party, in Canton
May 1925	The May 30th Movement against foreign imperialism breaks out in Shanghai
March 1926	Anti-Communist coup by Chiang Kai-shek in Canton; peasant leagues arise in various parts of China

July 1926	Northern Expedition begins, led by the Nationalists
April 1927	Break of right-wing Nationalists with left-wing Nationalists and Communists; anti-Communist terror in Shanghai and Peking; fifth congress of the Chinese Communist party, in Wuhan
1927-1934	KIANGSI SOVIET PERIOD
September 1927	Autumn harvest insurrection in Hunan
November 1927	Soviets set up by Mao Tse-tung in Hunan
April-May 1928	Fourth Route Army organized by Mao Tse-tung and Chu Teh in Chingkangshan
July- September 1928	Sixth congress of the Chinese Communist party, in Moscow
August- December 1928	Soviets set up in Hunan, Kiangsi, and Fukien
November 1931	The Chinese Soviet Republic established with capital at Juichin, Kiangsi province
February 1932	The Chinese Soviet Republic declares war on Japan
October 1934	Communists set out on their Long March
1935-1946	THE YENAN PERIOD
January 1935	Tsunyi conference, in Kweichow, conflict of Mao Tse-tung with Chang Kuo-t'ao begins
August 1935	Communists proclaim united front against Japan
October 1935	New base established in Shensi, centered on Yenan
December 1936	Sian incident, abduction of Chiang Kai-shek
July 1937	Outbreak of Sino-Japanese war; establishment of United Front between Communists and Nationalists
April 1939	Renewed clashes between Communists and Nationalists
January 1941	New Fourth Route Army defeated by Nationalists
February 1942	Party rectification movement begins
January 1943	Cooperativization movement begins
April-June 1945	Seventh congress of the Chinese Communist party, in Yenan
August 1945	War with Japan ends
October 1945	Renewed clashes between Communists and Nationalists
1946-1949	THE CIVIL WAR
May 1946	Communists issue a directive on land reform
July 1946	The civil war begins
September 1946	Draft outline of a national land law adopted by the Communists
March 1947	Yenan occupied by Nationalists
October 1947	Communists announce radical new land law
February 1948	Party rectification, attempts to halt excesses

April 1948	Communists reoccupy Yenan
August 1948	North China People's Government formed
November 1948	Communists take Mukden
January 1949	Communists take Peking .
August 1949	Trade pact signed between USSR and Manchuria; Manchurian People's Government is formed
September 1949	The People's Political Consultative Conference meets in Peking to elect a Central People's Government

THE PEOPLE'S REPUBLIC OF CHINA (1949 TO THE PRESENT)

1949-1952	PERIOD OF RECONSTRUCTION AND TRANSITION
October 1949	The "Liberation"; the Central People's Government is established
November 1949	Nationalists flee to Taiwan
December 1949	The Government Affairs Council establishes six Large Administrative Regions; Mao Tse-tung visits Moscow
January-December 1950	Series of government directives on economic problems; maritime customs (January); a unified financial and economic policy (February); taxation of state enterprises (February); inflation (February); commerce (March); supply allocation (March); food storage (March); treasury (March); labor relations in private enterprises (April); grain prices (September); rural taxation (September); contract system in agencies, enterprises, and cooperatives (October); suppression of speculation (November); financial inspection (December); private enterprises (December)
February 1950	Sino-Soviet Pact of Friendship and Alliance, and trade agreement; industrial responsibility system introduced into Manchuria
April 1950	Marriage law promulgated
June 1950	Land-reform law adopted, radical reform modified and orderly procedures introduced
August 1950	Resolution of the Government Affairs Council on class categories of peasants
October 1950	China enters the Korean War
March-July 1951	Further government directives on economic problems: labor insurance (March); budgets (March); production and reconstruction in state industries (April); allocation of economic powers between center and regions (May); founding of Agricultural Bank (July); evaluation of fixed assets in state enterprises (July).

May 1951	Thought reform carried out among writers
October 1951	Publication of Volume I of *Selected Works of Mao Tse-tung*
November 1951- Summer 1952	*Sanfan* (Three-Anti) and *Wufan* (Five-Anti) movements
October 1952	Land reform completed; first national agricultural work conference
Autumn 1952	Eight criteria for Party membership adopted
November 1952	State Planning Commission established, headed by Kao Kang
December 1952	Democratic reform of private business completed; Chou En-lai announces 1953 as beginning of China's First Five-Year Plan; Soviets return Central Manchurian Railroad to China
1953-1957	THE PERIOD OF THE FIRST FIVE-YEAR PLAN
1953-1954	The struggle for centralization
February 1953	Central Committee adopts resolution on formation of mutual-aid teams
March 1953	Stalin dies
March- September 1953	National and local elections for a National People's Congress
July 1953	Korean Armistice; responsibility system officially introduced into industry
September 1953	Ch'en Yün's financial-economic report criticized
December 1953	Resolution of the Central Committee on the development of Agricultural Producers Cooperatives (APC's)
December 1953- Summer 1954	Sporadic articles on one-man management
February 1954	The Fourth Plenum
April 1954	The announcement of the Harbin system of control work
June 1954	The Large Administrative Regions abolished
September 1954	First National People's Congress; proclamation of constitution; setting up of State Council; communique on fulfillment of the State Plan for 1953; People's Bank of China officially reconfirmed; Li Fu-ch'un named head of State Planning Commission; provisional statutes on joint state-private owned industry; Mao Tse-tung and Khrushchev confer in Peking with display of Sino-Soviet amity
1955-1956	The drive forward
February 1955	New currency issued
March 1955	National delegates meeting of the Chinese Communist party announces the expulsion of Kao

Kang and Jao Shu-shih; purge of pro-Kao individuals in Manchuria begins; first national conference on village organizational work of the Chinese Communist party is held to step up rural Party recruitment

Summer-
Autumn 1955   *Sufan* movement against disloyal elements, particularly in the bureaucracy; drive launched to fulfill the targets of the First Five-Year Plan; partial demobilization of the army

July 1955   National People's Congress ratifies the First Five-Year Plan, adopts Yellow River development plan, and conscription law; Mao Tse-tung's report to a Party meeting on agricultural cooperativization (not published until October)

October 1955   Sixth Plenum; decision to implement cooperativization; provisional rules on the work of the State Planning Commission

December 1955-
Spring 1956   "High tide" of cooperativization movement; "administrative simplification"; "socialist reform" of private business intensified

January 1956   Twelve-Year Program for the development of agriculture announced at a supreme state meeting addressed by Mao Tse-tung

February 1956   Twentieth Party congress of the Soviet Communist party

April 1956   Special Politburo meeting in which Mao speaks on "The Ten Great Relationships"; reversal of the "high tide" and inauguration of stabilization policy

1956-1957   The period of stabilization

May 1956   Hundred Flowers policy announced by Lu Ting-i

June 1956   Wage reform; National People's Congress adopts model statutes for higher-stage APC's

July 1956   One-man management openly criticized

September 1956   Eighth Party congress; Central Committee directives on consolidating the APC's; resolutions on the Second Five-Year Plan

October 1956   Hungarian revolt

February 1957   Mao's speech on internal contradictions within the people (not published until June)

March 1957   Ch'en Yün speaks on "increase production and economize," indicating continuing commitment to stabilization policy

April 1957   Central Committee announces beginning of rectification movement; Agricultural Bank abolished

May 1957	Three weeks of free expression by intellectuals; directives from the Central Committee on "increasing production and economizing"
June 1957	Anti-rightist campaign begins; State Council issues directives on "increasing production and economizing"
August 1957	*Hsiafang* movement begins with cadres being sent to factories and villages; later extended to intellectuals; socialist education movement begins in rural areas
September 1957	Central Committee directives indicating continuing consolidation policy regarding the APC's
September-October 1957	Third Plenum: decentralization discussed, twelve-year program for the development of agriculture revived, decision to launch irrigation campaign
October 1957	Sputnik launched; Soviet breakthrough in ICBM field; Sino-Soviet nuclear sharing agreement
November 1957	Mao visits Moscow; new phase of anti-rightist campaign begins, particularly directed against Party rightists; decentralization decisions implemented in new form; water works and irrigation movement intensified
December 1957	Purge of rightists in regional Party organizations, beginning in Chekiang
1958-1960	THE GREAT LEAP FORWARD
1958	The first leap forward
Spring 1958	Decisions to amalgamate APC's
April 1958	Large-scale transfer of central industries to regional jurisdiction
May 1958	Second session of Eighth Party congress; adoption of the general line of socialist construction; Liu Shao-ch'i lays forth new strategy of the Great Leap Forward; nomination of a new Politburo and Central Committee
July 1958	Militarization of the peasantry; labor shortage in face of good harvest; first appearance of communes; Khrushchev flies to Peking
August 1958	Peitaiho enlarged meeting of the Politburo announcing formation of communes; gunfire in Taiwan straits
September 1958	Decision to establish people's militia *(minping)*
December 1958	Sixth Plenum, in Wuhan; retreat on the communes; halting of urban communization; Mao Tse-tung resigns as chairman of the republic
1959	The first retreat
Spring 1959	Consolidation of the communes; stabilization policy

	of "all the country is a single chessboard"
March 1959	Tibetan revolt
August 1959	Eighth Plenum; decision on three-level system of ownership in communes, with the brigade as the major ownership unit; call for "increase production and economize" movement; admission of exaggeration of 1958 crop figures
1960	The second leap forward
September 1959	Camp David meeting between Khrushchev and Eisenhower (turning point in Sino-Soviet relations) ; Khrushchev visits Peking; Marshall P'eng Te-huai and associates dismissed from Ministry of National Defense
Autumn 1959	Renewal of production drive in agriculture and industry, with stress on water conservancy and fertilizer
January-December 1960	*Hsiafang* to villages campaign resumes; urban communization resumed; massive natural disasters; beginning of food crisis; rehabilitation of rightists
April 1960	Twelve-year program for the development of agriculture formally ratified by the National People's Congress
August 1960	Soviet technicians withdrawn from China
September 1960	Intensification of production drives in all economic sectors
October 1960	Publication of Volume IV of the *Selected Works of Mao Tse-tung*
November 1960	*Jenmin jihpao* announces decentralization of communes to the team level; Moscow meeting of 81 Communist parties attended by. Liu Shao-ch'i; worsening of Sino-Soviet relations
January 1961	Ninth Plenum; announcement of full retreat on the economic front; rectification movement aimed at basic-level Party cadres launched "in bits and stages"
1961-present	PERIOD OF RECOVERY AND TRANSITION
1961-1962	Recovery
1961	Priority sequence of agriculture, light industry, and heavy industry proclaimed; liberalization of the economy; "independent operational authority" for management; launching of "return to the [home] village" movement
March 1962	Supreme state conference presided over by Liu Shao-ch'i; National People's Congress; People's Political Consultative Conference
May 1962	National design work conference

June 1962	National accounting work conference
September 1962	Tenth Plenum, attack on "modern revisionism," strengthening of Party solidarity
November 1962	Cuban crisis provokes mass demonstrations in China; Sino-Indian border conflict begins; Li Hsien-nien and seven others added to State Planning Commission
1963 to present	Transition
March 1963	Establishment of a national price commission; national rural areas financial work conference; provisional statutes on accountants; national communications work conference
April 1963	Directive on political work in the People's Liberation Army issued by the Central Committee
July 1963	Sino-Soviet Party talks begin in Moscow; further worsening of Sino-Soviet relations
August 1963	Mao Tse-tung's statements on the civil rights movement in the United States
October 1963	Agricultural Bank established; renewed call in newspaper articles for industrial support of agriculture
December 1963	New regulations on rewards for inventions and technological improvements
Spring 1964	Political departments in finance, trade, communications, and industry established
June 1964	National Congress of the Chinese Communist Youth League held in Peking; beginning of a campaign to train a "revolutionary successor generation"; "working conference" of the Central Committee
October 1964	Fall of Khrushchev; China's first atomic test
December 1964–January 1965	National People's Congress
February 1965	Kosygin visits Peking; escalation of war in Vietnam
March 1965	Chinese-led student demonstrations in Moscow
May 1965	Lo Jui-ch'ing's speech on the twentieth anniversary of V. E. Day
June 1965	All ranks abolished in Chinese army
July 1965	State Capital Construction Commission revived
September 1965	Lin Piao's speech: "Long Live the Victory of the People's War"
October 1965	Anti-Communist coup in Indonesia; China concludes three-year wheat-purchase agreement with Canada
November 1965	Attack on Wu Han is first sign of open political struggle leading to the Cultural Revolution
January 1966	Official beginning of China's Third Five-Year Plan; U. S. resumes bombing of North Vietnam
February 1966	Reported attempts at a "February coup" by anti-Mao forces

March 1966	China refuses to attend Soviet Twenty-third Party Congress
April 1966	Liu Shao-ch'i goes abroad; *Liberation Army Daily* appears as leading organ, temporarily superseding the *People's Daily*
May 1966	Violent attacks on "black gang"; Cultural Revolution begins in the universities of Peking
June 1966	P'eng Chen ousted; Liu Shao-ch'i reportedly in control of Peking, trying to repress the Cultural Revolution; U. S. bombs Hanoi and Haiphong
July 1966	Liu Shao-ch'i announced full support for Vietnam; Mao Tse-tung dramatically reappears after his swim in the Yangtze
August 1966	Eleventh Plenum meets; directive on the Cultural Revolution; gigantic mass meeting in Peking where Mao Tse-tung, Lin Piao, and Chou En-lai appear as the leaders of China; Cultural Revolution bursts forth in full intensity; Red Guards officially formed
September 1966	Mass demonstrations continue; Red Guards attack top Party leaders
October 1966	Chinese students expelled from Russia; China explodes ballistics missile
November 1966	Top Party leaders dragged before the masses
December 1966	Cultural Revolution extended to the factories; anti-Maoists accused of "economism"
January 1967	Strikes and work stoppages in Shanghai and other cities; army becomes directly involved in the Cultural Revolution
February 1967	Proclamation of the "triple alliance"; students urged to return to their classrooms from their long marches through the countryside; revolutionary "power seizures" announced for some provinces; *Pravda* calls for the overthrow of Mao
April 1967	Campaign against Liu Shao-ch'i officially begins; violent fighting in many cities of China; struggle against provincial Party secretaries intensifies, particularly in Szechwan; Canton trade fair opened
June 1967	Reputed anti-Mao uprising in Wuhan, continuing into July; China explodes first hydrogen bomb; riots in Hong Kong
August 1967	Turmoil spreads

September 1967   Mao Tse-tung visits several provinces; policy of
                    "triple alliance" reiterated; attempts to curtail
                    the excesses of the Cultural Revolution; rebuild-
                    ing of organizational networks begins
October 1967   Campaign against "privatism" launched by Mao;
                    mass rally on October 1 with reappearance of
                    many new leaders; turbulence subsides

PROLOGUE

THE CHINESE REVOLUTION is for the latter half of the twentieth century what the Russian Revolution was for the first half. By transforming Chinese society, it has brought a great power into being which proclaims itself the revolutionary and developmental model for the poor countries of the world.

From the eighteenth century to the present, the world has been caught in a wave of revolutions. The industrial revolution in England started a process of economic transformation that has now reached to the farthest corners of the globe. The French Revolution sowed the seeds of a process of political revolution that has given rise to the modern nation-state. The results of these two revolutions have become the goals of the world's new countries: economic development and political integration. Above all, the new countries desire a national economy resting on an industrial-technological basis capable of creating wealth and power, and a national unity which arises from effective political institutions. It is symbolic that these two processes should have different points of origin, for most new countries have discovered that it is difficult to attain both goals simultaneously.

Economic development takes time; we may speak of it as a process of revolution. The British Empire and the world market were brought into being by a long series of developments which finally led to an economic system of great power and creativity. The present world market system, which grew out of the industrial revolution and became global in the nineteenth century, has shown the new countries a road to economic development: linkage to that world market system which will allow them to share in the wealth already created by the old countries. In so doing, they launch their own economic revolutions by becoming a part of a world-wide process of economic revolution.

However, the choice of such a road often prevents the new countries from achieving their other great goal, national unity. Though modern cities, factories, schools, and communications networks arise within their borders, they are usually restricted to a few areas, frequently on their coastlines where they are in close relation to the world's trade routes. The regions of the interior, vital for the creation and maintenance of national unity, benefit little from these developments. Moreover, all the wealth and power of economic development do not give the new countries a sense of national identity through which political integration can be achieved. Thus they are often faced with the choice of ignoring the peoples of the interior and the poor of the cities in order to develop economically within the world-wide context or seeking their support for political integration but thereby sacrificing easily available economic gains.

Though France's history as a nation-state began long before the French Revolution, that revolution gave the people of France a sense of national identity, expressed in the words *patrie, citoyen*, and *français*. The political revolutions that have brought new countries into being in the nineteenth and twentieth centuries have almost without exception sought to create the same sense of national identity in their peoples as the French Revolution did for the people of France. In this sense, many of the political revolutions have succeeded, for they have been able to create unity where earlier it did not exist. However, unity has often been acquired at the cost of economic development, a price which France also paid with its belated industrialization and modernization.

Modern France came into being, not by a process, but an act of revolution which swept away more than an ancient political system; it destroyed an entire social class. The French Revolution was, in effect, a social revolution. Tocqueville, in describing the conditions leading to the French Revolution, makes clear what may be the essence of all social revolutions: an act of destruction willed against a whole ruling class.

Though all new countries of the preceding and the present centuries have participated in the processes of economic and political revolution, not all have undergone social revolution. Germany and Japan, for example, were able to combine the processes of economic development and political integration without a social revolution. Many new countries of this century, however, face the possibility of social revolution as a consequence of their inability to achieve sufficient economic development and political integration. They may have some wealth and power and a sense of national identity, but not enough to still the forces of social revolution.

Revolutionary France is the world's first example of a modern social revolution. In 1917, Russia underwent its social revolution. And, in the late 1940's, it became clear that China had come through its social revolution, marked by the revolutionary struggle of the land reform. China's social revolution had causes deeper than its inability to develop economically and politically, but the shallowness of its economic and political revolutions made the social revolution inevitable.

A series of rebellions began in China toward the end of the eighteenth century, and continued until the advent and final triumph of Chinese communism. In retrospect, we can say that these rebellions began the process of revolution. Generally Buddhist or Taoist in ideology, they combined a revolutionary chiliasm with a hatred of secular authority. They occurred in certain inland areas of the country, many of which took on an endemic rebellious character. The greatest of these rebellions was that of the Taipings (1848-1864). There was much in the Taiping cry *ta-kuan*, smash the officials, which was reminiscent of the murderous hatred of the aristocracy during the French Revolution. The Taipings were crushed, but the process of social revolution did not end. Revolts continued to break out in the inland regions. The Communists succeeded in combining these forces of revolt into a mighty revolutionary movement. The military victories of Chinese communism took place at the same time that a revolutionary struggle was waged on the land against the rural gentry. A whole class was destroyed, not only physically but psychologically. Every act of land reform was climaxed by a drama where the landlord literally "lowered his head" (*tit'ou*) and so symbolically expressed his acceptance of defeat by the people.

All social revolutions are directed against elites, ruling classes. There has been a contemporary revival of interest in elites, for modernization and industrialization are seen as requiring leadership. But the elite concept involves more than leadership. An elite must not only be able to lead men in the organizational structures that criss-cross society, but must have legitimate status at the top levels of a social system. When an elite loses its capacity to lead and the legitimacy of its status, it reaps contempt and hatred from the people. The histories of social revolutions indicate that where an elite constitutes an entire ruling class, hatred can reach intense levels of collective fury.

Why the collective fury should have broken out with such ferocity during the Taiping Rebellion is not clear. The eighteenth century was a period of stability in China, for which it was widely admired in Europe. Toward the end of that century, extreme misery reappeared, but, as Tocqueville indicates, misery is not the cause of revolution. During the Opium War of the early·1840's, China had sustained a stinging defeat at the hands of England. Not only was China as a country humiliated, but, more specifically, those who exercised authority in its name in Kwangtung, an area not far from where the Taiping Rebellion broke out. Whether the defeat China suffered in the Opium War had anything to do with the outbreak of the Taiping Rebellion is a subject for historical inquiry. However, humiliation at the hands of an external enemy who proclaims his moral superiority is particularly subversive to the authority of an elite. If this is paired with ineptness in domestic leadership, the conditions exist for social revolution. The stage is set for the act of class destruction.

China had its political revolution in 1911 and thus became a modern nation-state. The urban bourgeoisie eventually found a role in the emerging republic. But the landed gentry found no real role in the new government. Whether it would have if Chiang Kai-shek had been able to achieve political unity is a matter of dispute. Probably not. Few members of the gentry had much modern education, or much understanding of the great things of the modern world which had an increasing attraction for the people of the country. The outcries of anger against "corrupt officials and lewd politicians, local landlords and inferior literati" began to erupt again. It was inevitable that the Communists, taught to look for revolutionary seeds in the cities, sooner or later would perceive the potential for social revolution in the rural areas. By the 1930's it was clear that China was moving toward a revolution similar to those of France and Russia. Chiang Kai-shek's dream of emulating the German and Japanese examples of nation-building was being gradually shattered. Nevertheless, by 1936 it appeared for a while that Chiang could succeed. The Communists had been reduced to a small band of stragglers holed up in the caves of remote Shensi, and the country enjoyed relative stability and prosperity.

One can argue *ad infinitum* whether the Chinese Revolution would have broken out if the Sino-Japanese war had not started. Even granting the wisdom of retrospection, it seems unlikely that a powerful Japan could have long coexisted with a reunited China, particularly with the mounting demands within China to recover Manchuria and the foreign concessions in China's most advanced regions. There was a growing student movement and a deep dissatisfaction within the corps of younger army officers. The Sino-Japanese war and the United Front between Kuomintang and Communists deflected revolutionary energies in the cities, but created conditions for a new revolutionary outburst on the land. If there had been no war, the revolutionary process would probably have started again within the cities and the Kuomintang. But there *was* war, and it sparked the dormant social revolution in China's rural regions.

France emerged from her revolution as one of the most highly organized countries in the world. The beginnings of political centralization antedate 1789, but the Revolution and the First Empire completed the process. Revolution followed by political centralization is a phenomenon repeated time after time in the wake of the French Revolution. It has been true of all Communist countries ever since the Russian Revolution. One can see it today in the newly emerging countries. Revolutions are followed by the creation of networks of organization.

Social system and organization must be viewed as two different things; a true elite is solidly imbedded in both. When a revolution destroys a social system, it also annihilates its elites. The new revolutionary regime can only pull society together again through organization. Political centralization is one of the forms that postrevolutionary organization has taken.

When a society has experienced political revolution and moves to resurrect organization, it looks for leadership, and naturally turns to its elites. But if its ruling class has lost the capacity to lead, that is, the capacity to strike out in new directions and to get men to follow them on the new road, then organization remains an empty shell. Nothing reveals the nakedness of a ruling class so starkly as its impotence in organization. When a social revolution destroys a social system, it is no longer possible for society to reach out toward its erstwhile elites for leadership, for they have ceased to exist. But the destruction of the social system makes organization more necessary than ever, for otherwise society would disintegrate into chaos. New leaders arise, whose primary qualification is their ability to lead. In time they may turn into a new elite by adding social status to their political positions. The system is reconstituted, but this time on a new basis. Both France and Russia have their elites today, though they are far different from the classes they replaced in the wake of social revolution.

The Manchus, when threatened by the West, did what all rulers do when facing the need to create and staff new organization: they turned to their traditional elite. The tide of social revolution which had erupted with the Taipings had subsided. There was no reason to suspect that the bureaucrats had lost their leadership abilities. The attempt failed. The Kuomintang tried a different approach. The destruction of the monarchy cleared the road for setting up all kinds of new organizational structures. The Kuomintang acquired a strong military streak during the 1920's, and military men have a keen sense of organization. But the Kuomintang persisted in staffing organization with old elites. What was left of the rural gentry moved into inland government positions. The urban bourgeoisie acquired powerful positions in the central government. Chiang Kai-shek, impressed with Germany and Japan, felt that strong military-political organization imposed from the top down, combined with civil government staffed by old and new elites, could accomplish the task of unification. It failed because of the inability of the elites to make civil government work. When the forces of social revolution revived, in the rural areas and within the Kuomintang itself (young army officers and intellectuals), Chiang attempted to suppress them. It was clear by the 1930's that the social revolution had eroded the social system. China needed organization to pull it together again. Chiang realized this, but he never understood that organization needs leaders.

The Communists, however, understood this very well. They recognized the forces of social revolution and made use of them. They not only saw revolution destroying a social system, but actively aided the process. While the revolution was still in the making, they already began to build new structures of military and civil organization. But, in great contrast to the Kuomintang, they knew that new organization needed new leaders. From the beginning of the Yenan period (1935-1946), their main organizational effort concentrated on recruiting and training new leaders. These became the cadres of the revolution and of organization.

The series of rebellions that broke out in China toward the end of the eighteenth century started a process of social revolution that, in some respects, has not yet ended. Tocqueville's suggestion that economic factors were not major causative elements in the French Revolution could be generalized: the immediate factors that lead to acts of class destruction are not economic. Thus, when a country faces social revolution, economic countermeasures alone cannot prevent it. But in a more fundamental sense, the matrix from which revolutionary processes arise is economic. In China, it was not Western imperialism with its new business and industry which created the economic matrix of revolution, because Western enterprise did not come until the latter part of the nineteenth century, whereas the revolutionary process began late in the eighteenth century. Moreover, the impact of Western imperialism was largely confined to the coast and a few select inland regions, whereas the social revolution was an inland phenomenon. Although there was a brief period of revolutionary ferment in the cities during the second and third decades of the twentieth century, which clearly was linked to the economic changes produced by imperialism, the great continuing revolution took place in remote inland regions.

The Communist party was born in Shanghai, but its destiny was in the interior. Ping-ti Ho in his *Studies on the Population of China, 1368-1953* (Harvard University Press, 1959) indicates that far-reaching changes had occurred in China's economic and demographic situation toward the end of the eighteenth century: "The over-all opportunities for gainful employment in the nation began to be reduced amidst continual population increase and technological stagnation" (p. 226). This suggests that the traditional economic fabric had started to disintegrate. But "technological stagnation" is not a phenomenon of nature. It is a manifestation of incapacity on the part of those who hold economic responsibility. In China, the accusation of economic responsibility falls on the shoulders of the gentry. The rebellions that broke out late in the eighteenth century were ferocious, and they were repressed with equal ferocity. That thread of ferocity created a social and psychological climate which ultimately led to the revolutionary terror of the late 1940's. However, it was the ever more evident impotence of the gentry in the face of economic challenges that caused its fall from elite position.

The economic elements that played a part in the genesis of the French Revolution arose from the transformation of post-feudal society, not from the Industrial Revolution, which had just occurred in England. So it was in China. Ping-ti Ho's explanation of the growing tide of misery as due to population increase amidst technological stagnation sketches the terrible problem that has faced all Chinese governments since the end of the eighteenth century. No one has ever been more sensitive to this problem than the present leaders of China who have been trying to create a technological and economic base for Chinese society adequate for its population.

The period of peace and stability which China enjoyed during much of the eighteenth century was very different from a similar period of prosperity a thousand years before during the Sung dynasty. Then a new gentry had appeared on the scene; cities were growing; new ideas came into society. But the eighteenth century was different. The Manchus had allied themselves with an old ruling class that had strong local roots. Cities were mostly stagnant. And, except for a few new political ideas of the early Ch'ing, China's intellectuals had turned into tedious and plodding academics. Rebellion and internal migration in the late eighteenth century were warning signals that something was wrong with the social fabric. Western imperialism led to the rise of new great cities and thus provided new economic opportunities for the rural masses. But the rent in the social fabric had already taken place and could not be healed. The counter revolutionary ferocity of General Tseng Kuo-fan in combatting the revolutionary ferocity of the Taipings created an atmosphere that made the final act of class destruction inevitable. Just as economic improvement in pre-1789 France and pre-1917 Russia failed to stem the tide of revolution, so periodic economic recovery and even progress in pre-1949 China failed to halt the social revolution.

The 1911 upheaval in China destroyed the monarchy and was succeeded by a republic which, in form, was quite modern. But by the 1930's it was evident that more had crumbled than the political system alone. The social fabric had disintegrated in much of rural China, yet the new patterns in the cities were too weak to exercise a commanding force over the country. The disintegration of the traditional economic system which began in the eighteenth century continued without interruption, yet the modern sector could not constitute an effective substitute. In the world of ideas and values, Confucianism was dying. The sharp cry of the intellectuals during the May Fourth Movement, *fan li-chiao,* an untranslatable slogan which in effect announced that the old elite of the country had lost its moral charisma in the eyes of the young, signaled the disintegration of the value system. The Communists saw the trends of history and fought to complete the revolution. In the course of their long struggle, they looked to the future, and began to prepare for it with ideology and organization. When they triumphed, they replaced system by organization, and ethos by ideology.

The French and Russian revolutions were characterized by a seizure of state power which opened the floodgates of the social revolution. The waves of revolution spread outward from Paris and Petrograd to the provinces. Class warfare broke out and sent counterwaves back to the capital which pressed the leaders of the revolution into ever more radical directions. The Chinese Revolution was different. The seizure of state power was the climax of a revolution which began deep in the provinces. The social revolution had been burning for a century and a half. It remained relatively dormant during much of the early twentieth century, but broke out again in the late 1920's. The peasant jacqueries of the Kiangsi period were still reminiscent of the classical rebellions, despite the veneer of Bolshevist ideology. But in Yenan, the Communists began to use the dynamics of revolution and war to build organization. A dual process began to emerge. On the one hand, the drama of class destruction continued, reaching its culmination in the revolutionary terror of the land reform of the late 1940's. On the other hand, the Communists began to create the building blocks of their organizational network, which was to become the basis for their rule over the Chinese mainland after final victory.

The French and Russian revolutions went from the top down. The apex of the political system was smashed with one blow, actually and symbolically, and this led to a disintegration of the social fabric at all points of the system. There were other revolutions from the top down which did not have this effect, because the revolutionary pressures within the social system were not as great. One of them was the Meiji Restoration. The shogunate was overthrown by a basically conservative cabal of feudatories, but soon thereafter leadership passed into the hands of a radical group. One can see the pace of radicalization moving fast during the first years of the Meiji era. A system of social stratification and political order that had taken centuries to construct was obliterated. But there was neither a revolutionary bourgeoisie nor a revolutionary peasantry. The transformation of the political apex did not open the floodgates of social revolution, despite the unsettling rapidity of change.

Why were forces of social revolution comparable to those of France, Russia, and China not present in Japan? There was no absence of peasant discontent during the Tokugawa; there was discontent among a new group of inland merchants who fought against the entrenched privilege of the city bourgeoisie; there was a highly dissatisfied and highly educated body of minor nobility seeking a new role in society. But Japan was yet too feudal, an argument that Tocqueville also invokes to explain the absence of revolutionary pressures in Germany at the end of the eighteenth century. But the French Revolution, like the Russian, was directed against the state and a ruling class closely identified with it. Feudalism had imposed a complex patchwork of social and political relationships on society. Processes of rationalization in France had long before the revolution done away with these patterns, leaving them only as vestiges of an earlier age. Russia and China never knew feudalism in its West European and Japanese senses.

Though China's social revolution was similar to that of France and Russia, it was also different. In the former countries, the ruling classes had lost that intimate involvement with local regions that remained so important in China. The French and Russian aristocracies became court aristocracies, living in cities and drawing their sinecures from their local possessions. The Chinese gentry did not live in the villages, but neither did it live in Peking. The court aristocracy in the nineteenth century was Manchu, an alien race. The 1911 revolution did away with the aristocracy but left the gentry undisturbed. Thus one of the aims of the Taiping Rebellion had been accomplished. But not the other, the destruction of the traditional gentry. In France and Russia, the ruling aristocracies were destroyed by revolutions that seized state power. It was not possible to destroy the Chinese gentry in a similar way. One might say that the Chinese gentry had strong linkages to both state and society. After 1911, it lost its linkages to the state, and, to compensate for this, held on more firmly to its particular interests in society.

This was not the first time that an alien group had come to power leading to a temporary retreat of the gentry from the scene. Most gentry undoubtedly thought that sooner or later the state would require its services again. Indeed, it was not disappointed, for that is precisely what the Kuomintang did. The weakened tie to the state had its advantages, for it immunized the gentry from the constant political changes in Peking and Nanking. On the other hand, heightened commitment to its landed possessions made it more vulnerable to the pressures of social revolution. Revolutions are profoundly influenced by the character of ruling classes. The entrenched localism of gentry power made it inevitable that the Chinese Revolution, in contrast to the revolutions of France and Russia, would come from the outlying areas to the center rather than the reverse, and, moreover, that it would take a long time. The gentry was widely distributed throughout China, and could not be destroyed with one blow. The peculiar conditions of the social situation in China gave the Chinese Revolution a populist character, one which neither Trotsky nor Stalin understood. It retains that character to the present day.

The Chinese Communists claim that their revolution is prototypical for the revolutionary process now burning in the countries of Asia, Africa, and Latin America. They argue that revolution cannot be won by sudden seizures of state power, by occupation of a capital city; they preach the "building-blocks" approach; they argue for revolution as a long-term process; they see capture of state power as the last act in a long drama.

Are they right in their assessment of the world revolutionary situation? Our analysis of revolution suggests that the seeds of social revolution are present when a traditional elite is incapable of exercising leadership in organization and when its status disappears as the result of disintegration of the social system. Thus it loses power and authority. In traditional peasant societies, the elite derives power and authority both from state and society. By society I here mean a localized social system which operates in a district or a region rather than in the country as a whole. The ownership of land usually is an important element in the localized social system. The Chinese Communist doctrine of revolution states that the revolutionaries must strike against such local systems—that it is here where the revolution will be won.

Every old elite tries desperately to maintain its positions in state and society. It will try to staff government with its people, and it will hold tenaciously to its local interests. The lessons of history suggest that it cannot do both. The pressures for land reform force the elite to hold on even more tightly to the reins of government. If a liberal government accedes to demands for land reform, as did Alexander II in Russia, the elite demands in return control of decision-making positions. It is not accidental that the most liberal of bureaucratic administrators often come from the old elite, like Count Witte. On the other hand, if strange people move into government, then the elite must preserve its interests in society. Benito Juarez became president of Mexico, but the caciques maintained a tight grip on the land. The one part of the world that appears to constitute a testing ground of the Chinese thesis is Latin America. Most Latin American countries have old Hispano-Portuguese elites with strong roots on the land and close association with government. Social and economic reform alone will not resolve the problem, for the dispossessed elite will simply move into the cities and into government. This is exactly what emancipation in Russia did. No matter how liberal and reformist the old elite becomes, historical example suggests that revolutionary pressures will rise against it. Land reform may ease revolutionary pressures in the villages, but the presence of a discredited elite in the cities and in the structure of government creates revolutionary pressures in the cities. This would portend a revolution of the French or Russian type. On the other hand, if the elites would rather surrender their hold on government than their grip on the land, a revolution of the Chinese type threatens. The Chinese Communists believe that this will be the pattern of revolution in the coming years.

The Sino-Soviet dispute is not only a conflict between two powers, but one between two different revolutionary models. These two approaches to revolution are reflected in the split that has appeared in revolutionary groups in Latin America. On the one hand, there are the old-line

Communists who maintain their tightly disciplined, centrally organized parties, waiting for the day that a February Revolution will break out. On the other hand, there are the Castroites, spiritually akin to the Chinese, working for a guerrilla war of social revolution on the land.

Can social revolution with all its bloodshed be avoided in Latin America? Marx said that no ruling class departs willingly from the stage of history. Perhaps he is right: the chances of avoiding revolution would appear to be slim. However, the rapid emergence of a liberated peasantry on the land and a new class of technocratic administrators and entrepreneurial managers in the cities could furnish a chance of avoiding social revolution. The old elite, tainted irreparably with ineptness and loss of charisma, would be replaced by younger men of ability, of mixed race reflecting the character of Latin America, and by men who can produce as well as consume. The new men would not only have to have real power, but would have to be visible, to stand out as the true leaders of the country.

After a social revolution has taken place in a country, there no longer exists a ruling class to constitute a source of recruitment for the leadership roles that organization requires. To survive, the revolutionaries need organization. China went through a social revolution in the third century B. C., which led to the disappearance of an old feudal aristocracy. The Ch'in empire emerged from that struggle as the most highly organized political entity known to that time in Chinese history, and armed with an ideology called legalism, which was in fact an ideology of organization. Triumphant revolutionary movements often tend to be military, not only because of the importance of armed struggle, but because armies are by their nature pure organization. The successful revolutionary movement has desperate need for leadership to direct the organization it creates. It recruits leaders from where it can find them. But the type of organization which a revolutionary movement creates in its formative phases, and the kinds of leaders which it recruits, have a decisive influence on the kind of society it builds up after victory.

In Russia, the tight conspiratorial organization of the Bolsheviks, and its direction almost entirely from outside of the Russian social context, influenced the type of organization and leadership that arose after the Russian Revolution. The revolutionary process in Russia had developed for a long time before the October Revolution. However, the Bolshevik party, because of its inability to operate openly in the country, could not become a true mass organization until the eve of the Revolution itself. It was a highly centralized organization with a straight-line chain of command. Though the top leaders were intellectuals (as in China), the Party fighters were men of the working class. Despite the rapid regrowth of bureaucracy during the early 1920's, the new Party men were more managerially than bureaucratically minded. In the early 1920's, workers were put in positions of power to make certain that the proletariat ruled in organization. Subsequently, Stalin made great efforts to create a "workers' intelligentsia." Russia moved in the direction of great organizational centralization. Stalin wanted a phalanx of trained working-class managers to run that organization. Thus revolutionary Russia embarked on a process of political centralization, comparable to that of revolutionary France, but far more thorough. In contrast to the bourgeoisie that came to be the new elite in nineteenth-century France, in Russia organization was increasingly staffed by sons of workers.

The organization and the leaders that came out of the Chinese Revolution were different. Not since 1927 was the Chinese Communist party simply a conspiratorial group aiming to seize state power. In Kiangsi, it was mainly an army riding to power on the waves of a jacquerie. During the Yenan period, it turned into a political-military organization that sought systematically to use the forces of social revolution. The ideal nucleus of that organization was a small armed band that at times fought but at other times tended to agricultural production. The leaders of Communist organization during the Yenan period were the poor young peasants of the villages who centuries earlier had been recruited into defense brigades or roamed the hills as rebels. Out of this group emerged the cadres who led the revolution, fought the battles, took control of the production teams, and finally launched the acts of revolutionary land reform in the later 1940's. The Chinese Communists during the Yenan period wanted leaders first and foremost, and they sought them out wherever they could find them. The young peasant cadres had a military bent; for centuries their predecessors had gone forth to fight. War against the hated Japanese provided fertile ground for organizing. The village elders could not quarrel with the patriotic cause. But, as the land reform shows, the real target was the rural elite. The peasant jacquerie of the early 1930's broke out before the Sino-Japanese war. The revolutionary terror of the late 1940's burst forth after the Japanese had been defeated.

If any group in society is not an elite, it is the poor and the young. They have neither wealth, nor power, nor prestige. In China, the poor and the young peasants became the leaders of the revolution. But leadership could only be actualized in organization. Thus by destroying the social system and replacing it with organization, they created a role for themselves in the new society. What they sought was leadership and power, not status and authority.

The one great organizational product of the Chinese Revolution has been the Chinese Communist party. It is an organization made up of leaders whose one great purpose in life is to lead—at all levels of the structure. In its early years, it was a party of youth. Today, though older, it is still made up largely of workers and peasants. The Party has created an organizational context which gives them a continuing role in society.

Organization, in contrast to a social system, needs conscious efforts to survive. This is all the more so when organization cannot rely on a social system, such as recruiting its leaders from a solidly based status group. In wars, armies survive through the challenges of battle. The end of the war often has a demoralizing effect on military organization, as was the case with the American army after World War II. The Chinese Communists have understood this well, and thus "struggle" (*toucheng*) has become the watchword of the Party. This is not an abstraction, for the constant reappearance of "rectification" keeps the atmosphere of struggle alive, particularly when the leadership role of the Party diminishes. Ideology provides the moral cement that not only arouses commitment but creates the cohesive forces which prevent struggle from turning into disintegration. Cohesion through conflict is a problem with which both Western sociologists and the Chinese Communists have concerned themselves. For the latter, it has been a life and death matter.

When the Chinese Communists triumphed in 1949, there no longer was a social system to which they could turn for support, even if they had wanted to. There was no gentry left, and they distrusted the bourgeoisie. But there was a choice of directions. Should they construct organization along the lines they had developed during the ten years of Yenan or should they emulate the one model they respected above all: the Soviet Union? They chose the latter course, and thus for the first five years of the 1950's, China began rapidly turning into a second Soviet Union. The imposition of bureaucratic organization from the top down proceeded rapidly, symbolized by the elaboration of a vast planning structure. China appeared to be following the road to bureaucratic centralization. If centralization meant the emergence of a new professional elite, the changes in Communist party recruitment in the early 1950's followed the model perfectly. Large numbers of old and new intellectuals were recruited into the Party. Expertise became a prime qualification for Party membership. Untrained rural cadres were dropped from Party rolls. Managers were coming into their own again. A "new class" was in the process of coming into being. But the process was stopped in 1955. The purge of oppositional elements in Manchuria and Shanghai led to the elimination of large numbers of budding apparatchiks. In the summer of 1955 the Party struck against the bureaucracy. And finally collectivization led once again to radicalization.

The evidence indicates that there was a social core to this process. The demobilization of the army in 1955 saw millions of war veterans return to the countryside where they became leaders of the collectivization drive and rural Party cadres. The enormous jump in Party membership went hand in hand with political radicalization and collectivization. Despite the consolidation of 1956 and 1957, the rural Party organization continued to grow. Late in 1957, rectification once again struck the Party and the professionals. While the "regionalization of the Party" was opposed, decentralization nevertheless gave the local Party apparatus great power. When communization was introduced, a great ground swell of enthusiasm came precisely from the young rural cadres. Today, in the declining years of his life, Mao Tse-tung calls for the recruitment of a new generation of Party members from among young workers and peasants. These are the cadres with whom he made the revolution, and these are the young leaders who tried to implement his programs of rural reconstruction. China in the mid-1950's thus veered sharply from the Soviet model of organization which it so assiduously followed during the early 1950's.

China's social revolution has been long. The type of organization that has emerged from it has been much more directly involved with the masses of society than in the Soviet Union. The Chinese peasant, even in remote inland areas, has been drawn into political life. Mao's dream is the transformation of the Chinese peasant into a modern producer. Land reform destroyed the old rural elite. Collectivization deprived the peasant of his ownership over the soil. Communization changed the whole pattern of work organization. Was this the final act of liberation from which a new peasant will emerge? It seems almost inevitable that the forces of bureaucratic centralization will once again make themselves felt in China. It does not seem likely that a political semi-elite of worker and peasant cadres and a social semi-elite of professionals can long coexist in peace. Neither is it likely that the professionals will long be content to do staff work for their Red executives nor that the Red cadres will forgo the chance of acquiring social status through education and professionalization. The lure of education is powerful. If, however, the "new class" emerges after society has been truly transformed, and if the peasant has been brought into the modern world, then Mao's dream will have been realized. Then institutionalization can set in once again. The revolution will then be over. A new society will begin to emerge.

The great challenge of the modern world is the transformation of masses who are outside of that world into individuals who become a part of it. Western capitalism and imperialism have brought about remarkable economic and social development in far-flung parts of the world, but only in a few select locations. Great cities have arisen, but often separated by a deep chasm from their hinterlands. The processes of transformation have not been completed in the Soviet Union, as indicated by Khrushchev's hope for a new Soviet man. Mao Tse-tung preaches that social revolution is a reality in the poor countries, and that political organization must reach out to the most distant and poorest of the masses. From them it will derive the strength to win, and in the course of struggle will transform them. What China offers to the world is a new model of revolution. In France and Russia, the fermenting social revolution gave impetus to the revolutionary parties, but the social revolution itself was not well organized. China preaches the organization of the social revolution itself, and specifically that of the revolution on the land. It also provides a model of postrevolutionary organization based on a cadre-led Party. There already is evidence that the Chinese model, whether by emulation or the force of historical circumstances, is being repeated, notably in Cuba and Algeria.

Despite failures in many areas, the over-all record of Communist China's performance in the past decade and a half has been one of great success. A country wracked by chaos has been transformed into a powerful nation-state. The Chinese have already gone a long way on the road to industrialization and modernization. The Chinese Communist organizational model clearly is not without its demonstration effect. It offers an approach to organization quite different from that of the West or even of the Soviet Union. Its attractions are not so much in the industrial field, where its greatest successes have been achieved with essentially Soviet-type methods, but in organizing a poor backward country, holding it together, preventing bureaucratization, and achieving basic social changes.

It is no coincidence that the origins of Chinese Communist organization have been essentially military, arising from guerrilla-type struggle. All civilized societies have armies, but normally they remain dichotomous to society. Devices are fashioned to keep the wall standing between military organization and civil society. There have been periods in world history when attempts have been made to militarize society, but never with the means available to contemporary society. The old separation of military organization and civil society is breaking down in many parts of the world. This means that a new form of civil organization is challenging both traditional and modern bureaucratic organizations. Political parties in many one-party countries are increasingly taking on a military cast, and are operating according to organizational principles different from those of the Max Weber model. Perhaps the Chinese model of organization is transitional, perhaps it serves a purpose which, once achieved, will lead to bureaucratization. On the other hand, there is enough evidence from stable Western societies to indicate that total routinization is not the fate of all organization. Innovative managerial leaders sometimes suddenly appear again in a context of extreme routinization, and a dormant institution turns back again into active organization. The Chinese have constructed a powerful and effective organization, but one that has built-in deterrents against bureaucratization. In theoretical terms, it constitutes a non-Weberian model of organization.

In the West, there has been an increasing stress on organizational integration during past decades. Present-day managerial ideologies stress cooperation and human relations. Bureaucratization has emerged as a major stabilizing factor in industry. Despite the teachings of Max Weber, there is as yet no certitude that bureaucratization will inevitably lead to stabilization and integration. What appears to me much more plausible is that organization remains Janus-faced, that its rational and integrative aspects remain inherent in it and in contradiction to each other. In China, the Party has evolved as a mechanism to keep contradictions in organization alive, to prevent routinization and excessive bureaucratization. The institutionalization of organization has progressed much farther in the advanced Western countries than in China, but I doubt that one can say that organization has made a decisive transition to institution. Economic competition, for example, demands managerial leadership in contrast to mere bureaucratic expertise. Organization will survive if it retains its leadership capacities and yet rests on a basis of continuity for which bureaucratization can serve as an indicator. As with a true elite, effective organization must perform adequately and also be supported by the social system. This is not a static, but a constantly shifting, conflict-ridden situation. Organization is made up of many parts. There are the tendencies toward routinization and integration that come from the administrative bureaucracy. But there are also countertendencies toward active leadership that come from managers who sense the challenges coming from the outside, and countertendencies of protest that come from below where there is unwillingness to accept routinization on the terms offered.

Even a cursory glance at the writings of the Chinese Communists will reveal their acute concern with problems of organization. In earlier decades, Chinese intellectuals wrote about socialism, anarchism, and the nature of the world and society. This made for an intellectual liveliness that has since disappeared. But few of the intellectual great men of that time had the slightest notion about the true problems of organization. By the time of Yenan, "theory" had been canonized, and the Chinese Communists turned their attention to "practice," namely organization and action. One might say that almost the entire literature of Chinese communism since Yenan has revolved around these two questions.

There is little in the traditional literature of China that prepares the researcher for grappling with Communist China. One can look far and wide in the traditional literature for discussions on leadership, whereas the literature of Communist China often consists of nothing else. In preparing the manuscript of this book, I was repeatedly impressed by how little "Chinese" it appears to be. Where is China in all these processes? Chinese culture has not disappeared, but China's traditional social system has. Revolutionary changes, which began more than a century ago and were brought to completion by the Communists, have profoundly altered the substance and form of Chinese society.

There is indeed a new China—a China of organization. This complex struggle, to create and impose structures of organization on the country, is the subject of this book.

INTRODUCTION

CHINESE COMMUNISM came to power and created the present People's Republic of China through revolutionary struggle. The last decade and a half in China have witnessed a human drama played out by great and small men who have used organized political power for many different ends. They have rebuilt a great country, disciplined its people, improved the conditions of life, and laid the foundations for growth. They have also fought each other, challenged other countries, oppressed their opponents, and imposed suffering on their people. We have not set ourselves the task of describing that human drama. We are concerned with the systematic structures created by these men. Communist China is like a vast building made of different kinds of brick and stone. However it was put together, it stands. What holds it together is ideology and organization.

The key thesis of the Prologue was that ideology and organization have arisen in China because a traditional social system no longer existed to give unity to the society. Sociological theorists have argued at great length about the nature of social systems. Here we can do no more than offer a simple working definition. Systems are "complex unities," or, as sociologists put it, "any patterned collection of elements." [1] Ap-

---

[1] Marion J. Levy, Jr., *The Structure of Society* (Princeton, N. J., 1952), pp. 19-20.

plied to society, the concept "system" designates unified patterns of human interaction.[2] What is important to our working definition is that any social system has core elements. If they are destroyed, then the system ceases to exist. The assumption implies that other elements can be destroyed without affecting the essential unity and existence of the system. Sociologists have also generally made this assumption, and put it in terms of the "functional requisites of society." [3] Further we make the assumption that social systems are self-regulating and self-maintaining. This means that conscious individual effort is not needed to maintain the patterns. The argument on self-regulation is also made by classical economic theory about economic systems. Here self-regulation is assured by the laws of the market.[4]

At certain times in a country's history things change so radically that the old patterns no longer reappear to reconstitute unity. One must therefore ask: what is so central in a social system that its destruction causes the disappearance of the whole system? Sociologists have indicated that the central element of a social system which assures its unity, existence, and self-regulation is "culture." [5] For purposes of our working definition, the designation of "culture" as the central or core element is not a sufficient answer.

It has been suggested that the mark of a true revolution is the destruction of the elite of a social system.[6] The history of the world's great social revolutions bears this out. The climactic moments of social revolutions are the physical and psychological destruction of a ruling elite. What inevitably followed was a radically changed society. The concept "elite" implies the existence of a class of individuals from which flows authority, in its most legitimate sense. Authority is a reciprocal relationship between individuals in which one has the right to command with the assured expectation of compliance on the part of the other.[7] When a ruling group in society loses authority, for whatever reason, it ceases to be an elite.

For our working definition, we shall regard *social elements from which authority flows* as the center or core of any social system. In some

---

2 Talcott Parsons, *The Social System* (Glencoe, Ill., 1951), p. 5.

3 Levy, *op. cit.*, pp. 149 ff.; Robert K. Merton, *Social Theory and Social Structure* (Glencoe, Ill., 1957), pp. 25-37.

4 Karl Polanyi, *The Great Transformation* (Boston, Mass., 1957), pp. 40, 68 ff.

5 Parsons, *op. cit.*, p. 5.

6 Chalmers Johnson, *Revolution and the Social System* (Stanford, Calif., 1964), p. 8.

7 Reinhard Bendix, *Max Weber, An Intellectual Portrait* (Garden City, N. Y., 1962), p. 292.

societies, it is a single recognizable ruling group from which ultimate authority flows. Such a group we will call a true elite.

A true elite may be defined as a social group which enjoys wealth, power, and prestige. It has the relatively largest share of the society's scarce wealth. It exercises command in the various organizational structures that criss-cross society. It gains honor and esteem from the population as a whole.[8] In the instances of revolution which are cited in the Prologue, economic reasons were not the immediate causes for the great acts of destruction practiced against social elites, though they played a crucial part in bringing about the process of revolution. The act of revolution deprives an elite of wealth, power, and prestige. However, examples from history, including that of China, show that when an act of revolution is not complete and only deprives an elite of its wealth, it can subsequently use its power and prestige to reacquire it. An act of revolution to be effective must also destroy the power and prestige of the elite. Since we here are mainly concerned with the act of revolution, we shall only look at power and prestige.[9]

Power can be exercised directly by one man over his subordinate. Some societies, notably feudal, are characterized by highly personalized webs of power relationships. However, in nonfeudal complex societies, power is normally exercised in organization. This brings us to one of the key concepts of this book. Organization has been defined in sociological theory as structures of differentiated roles.[10] In this sense, any group in which roles are differentiated can be described as organization. However, for our working definition, we shall use a narrower formulation: organizations are structures of differentiated roles which require the ordered exercise of power. In these structures, some men command and others obey. Since all societies need the ordered exercise of power, all societies have organization. Every civilized society has complex organizations, ranging from macrosocietal political networks down to the smallest human groupings. Our definition of organization suggests that all organization is ultimately political. Organization requires decisions—decisions require power. Through the structures of organization power is transformed into action.

---

[8] *Ibid.*, pp. 259-260.

[9] Some writers assert that the economy in premodern societies is a subsystem of a larger social system. Thus Polanyi, for example: "The outstanding discovery of recent historical and anthropological research is that man's economy, as a rule, is submerged in his social relationships" (*op. cit.* p. 46). Talcott Parsons and Neil Smelser, in effect, take a similar position even for contemporary society (*Economy and Society* [Glencoe, Ill., 1956]).

[10] Levy, *op. cit.*, p. 165.

Prestige is a somewhat invidious word, normally defined as "blinding or dazzling influence." A more general sociological concept which includes prestige, is status, which Marion Levy defines as the sum total of ideal or institutionalized roles.[11] Men clearly may have low status, from which flows no "blinding or dazzling influence." High status gives rise to prestige, though it need not be as extreme as our definition. We are interested, however, in the relationship Levy asserts between status and role. Levy's formulation states more where status comes from than what it is. We would suggest that status, regardless of where it comes from, is functionally independent of role. It derives directly from the quality of the person and does not relate to what he does, namely his roles. Prestige gives men influence in society, that is, a certain legitimate authority, which they have almost regardless of what they do. Roles are learned, often laboriously. Status is conferred from without. Society gives it and only society can take it away.

Sociological theory asserts the difference of status and role, even though some theorists claim that status arises developmentally from generalized roles. For our purposes, however, the differences are decisive. In effect, organization is a structure of essentially political roles, that is to say defined activities concerned with command and compliance. Organizations may use status, but status is not an inherent part of organization. To expand our working definition further, we assert that status, as a type of authority, is the core element of the social system. High status, in the form of prestige and influence, is generalized authority. It does not depend on specific roles. Organization, on the other hand, is a conscious contrivance with defined roles. Far from being self-regulating, it demands constant effort to maintain it. Routinization and institutionalization may mitigate the intensity of effort but never can do away with a need for it.

In stable societies, organizations are supported by social systems. In turn, social systems need organizations to realize the goals of their members. Nevertheless, no matter how interlocked, the two are different. In some societies, unity of social system and organization exists; in others it does not, or has been broken.[12]

Roles must be filled by individual men. Yet political roles demand special talents. If men cannot exercise leadership, then they are ill-

---

11 *Ibid.*, pp. 157-160.

12 Our distinction between social system and organization is analogous to the well-known distinction of state and society (see Bendix, *op. cit.*, pp. 473 ff.). For our purposes, we use the term "society" in the most comprehensive sense to designate all that is social among a culturally and historically defined body of human beings.

equipped to assume such roles. Leadership talents appear to be generally scarce in society, so that something must be done to make up this lack. This is accomplished essentially in two ways: On the one hand, the power of command is built into the role. Regardless of who exercises the role, some command will flow from it. But leadership requires more than the mechanical exercise of predetermined command—it demands ability to innovate and create. Thus, on the other hand, classes of men exist in society on whom authority in general has been conferred and who have been trained to wield such authority. It is normal for an organization to recruit such men to fill its political roles. Men who have status assume leadership roles in organization. The power they exercise thus rests on a foundation of authority. A reverse process undoubtedly also occurs, as implied in Levy's statements, namely that men acquire status from the generalization of specific roles. These are matters of historical process.

If a recognizable class of men in society enjoy status and power, they have high position in a social system and exercise leadership in organization. If they also command wealth, that class constitutes a true elite. Whether it is command over wealth which gives rise to power and prestige, as Marx argues, or the reverse, as Weber argues, is a matter we cannot discuss here. Suffice it to say that, in traditional China, wealth, particularly in the form of land, was generally the first step on the ladder of social mobility.[13]

Since power is exercised as leadership in organization and status is imbedded in a social system, one can say that a true elite occupies a firm position both in organization and in system. It has roots in the system and acts in organization. It needs both to maintain itself. In turn, this dual position serves to reinforce both system and organization. An elite armed with status makes its role in organization more authoritative. An elite that has organizational power can use it to increase, solidify, and transmit to its progeny the status that it enjoys. We call this "the unity of system and organization." As long as system and organization are functionally interlocked by a true elite, unity and stability prevail in society.

Traditional societies have been characterized by such a unity of system and organization. However, as traditional societies have gone into decline, system and organization have begun to recede from each other. The impact of the West on the non-European countries has resulted in the generation of complex, new structures of organization.

---

13 Ping-ti Ho, *The Ladder of Social Success in Imperial China* (New York, 1962), pp. 41-52.

Indeed, one may even speak of an organizational revolution in the world. Under these conditions, many traditional elites have been unable to carry out the leadership roles demanded by modern organization. The result has been that they have gradually lost authority, even though they could still command the power that their formal organizational roles gave them. But the authority of traditional elites has often been attacked from another direction as well. As the social system begins to disintegrate, the influence, prestige, and status of the elites begin to disappear. Our discussion of the social revolution in China indicates that even before the coming of the West, an assault had been mounted against the traditional social system.

Having distinguished between social system and organization, let us look again at the problem of the core or central elements of a social system, which we have defined as those from which authority flows. First, as sociological theorists have generally recognized, social systems are held together by cultures. For purposes of our working definition, we shall state this more specifically by saying that social systems are held together by an ethos from which values and norms derive. Values and norms have a compelling effect on human behavior and thus constitute a form of authority. Therefore, in order to exercise authority, an individual must have fully internalized these values and norms. Anthropologists call this enculturation; sociologists call it socialization. In contrast, organizations are held together in some instances by laws and rules, and in others by ideology.

We have already identified a second core element, namely a true elite from which authority flows, in the form of high status or prestige. Prestige and influence are collectively imbedded in such an elite or status group. In turn, membership in such a group confers prestige and influence, hence authority. Depending on what kind of society it is, membership may be acquired by achievement or ascription. The counterpart of an elite in organization is its body of leaders. These may or may not coincide with an elite, depending on whether there is or is not a unity of system and organization.

Human relations require behavior, and only individuals can manifest behavior; therefore social systems require ideal individuals. We can now identify a third core element in a social system, namely individuals who, having been thoroughly enculturated and being members of the highest status group, are able to exercise authority. These are what sociologists call "modal personalities." These are the men on whom a society governed by a social system confers status and power. Such ideal individuals are assured of the highest positions in society. However, this is possible only if the ethos, the status group, and the "modal personality" retain full legitimacy in society. Only under this condition can authority flow from them. But if they lose legitimacy, the ideal individuals—no matter how gifted and saintly—find that the social system no longer grants them authority. On the other hand, they may, by these same gifts and saintliness, find it possible to play a leadership role in organization and rise to the top. As we have pointed out, roles can be learned, but status is conferred only by society.

In traditional China, the trinity of ethos, status group, and modal personality was represented by Confucianism, the gentry, and the *pater familias (chiachang)*. By 1949, the revolution had destroyed all three. The assault on Confucianism began around the turn of the century.[14] The great land reform of the late 1940's finished the destruction of the gentry. And as for the *pater familias*, China has undergone a family revolution, which began toward the turn of the century and was completed by the Communists. The new marriage law symbolized the liberation of women and the final destruction of the authority of the *pater familias*.[15]

After many years of Communist rule, there is no evidence that China will ever return to this ancient trinity. There are lingering vestiges of Confucian humanism, but Confucius' "museumification" by the Chinese Communists testifies to its present-day impotence as a living ethos.[16] Despite the recurring attack on "landlord elements," the real rural enemy of the regime is the newly emerging rich peasant, and not the landlord of a past day. The authority of the *pater familias* in the past depended on the suppression of women. If the Communists have succeeded in anything, it has been in bringing women fully into public life. With the traditional trinity of authority gone, the social system itself has disappeared.

The traditional elite of China was attacked from two directions. The coming of modern organization deprived it of its leadership role in society. The erosion of the social system deprived it of its status. All it had left was naked power and naked wealth. The act of class destruction directed against the traditional elite at the time of the land reform in the late 1940's came when its position in a crumbling social system was already undermined.

Social systems take time to build up; once destroyed, long periods

[14] Joseph R. Levenson, *Confucian China and Its Modern Fate* (Berkeley and Los Angeles, 1958 and 1964), I and II.

[15] Marion J. Levy, Jr., *Family Revolution in Modern China* (Cambridge, Mass., 1949).

[16] Joseph R. Levenson, "The Place of Confucius in Communist China," *The China Quarterly*, 12 (October-December 1962), 1-18.

of time must elapse before one can say that a new social system has arisen. During the interval, organization pulls and holds society together. Organization must now do for society what earlier had been done by the social system. It must provide functional equivalents for the elements swept away by the revolution.

We have stated that ethos, status group, and modal personality are core elements of a social system. What are their equivalents in China today? For ethos, ideology has been substituted. A belief system that expressed basic social and human values has been replaced by an ideology that expresses values and goals of sociopolitical action and achievement.

As for status, its functional equivalent today is leadership, specifically in organization. Thus its corporate form is the body of organizational leaders, in particular the Party. However, since a social system may be gradually re-forming in China, leadership is taking on some qualities of status. As we shall point out (p. 51), the body of organizational leaders is turning into a new elite with political status deriving from ideology. However, China also has a second emerging elite with social status deriving from education. If the former are the red cadres, the latter are the professional intellectuals. There has so far been no meshing of the two to constitute a true single elite, functionally comparable to the old gentry. A "new class," in the words of Milovan Djilas, may have arisen in the Soviet Union, but not yet in China.

Who in China today constitutes a functional equivalent to the *pater familias*? The "modal personality" in Communist China is the cadre, the revolutionary leader in organization. He is young, not old; he is a leader, not a conciliator; he operates in the public realm, not in the private. But, the ideal of the cadre is being challenged by another ideal, that of the educated professional. Thus, not only are two elites competing with each other, but two human ideals. The contradiction between these two ideals is, in fact, reflected in the cadre concept, as we shall point out in the Party chapter; the cadre is ideally expected to be both "Red and expert."

It is an immense task to study a structure of ideology and organization which is the functional equivalent of an entire social system. The only approach I could see was to identify certain central areas of concern, and begin the study. The chapters of this book are the central concerns I chose: Ideology, Party, Government, Management, Control, Cities, and Villages.

Ideology, as we have said, is the functional equivalent of the former ethos. Just as the ethos held the social system together, so does ideology hold organization together. When the decision was made to study the ideology, it was quite early apparent that little would be gained by exegesis of the voluminous ideological literature that has appeared in China. Given the Chinese Communist stress on the unity of thought and practice, the only meaningful way to study ideology seemed to be to see how it was used. In the early parts of the chapter on ideology, we introduce some theoretical distinctions useful for the analysis of the ideology as a whole. We have tried to single out the central ideas of the ideology. We end the chapter with a discussion of how ideology was used by the leaders of Communist China to analyze the basic elements (i.e., contradictions) of their society and to develop a program of action that led to the Great Leap Forward.

The Party can be regarded as the postrevolutionary successor to the gentry. Earlier the gentry with its status dominated the life of China; today it is the Party with its leadership. This remarkable organization is a phenomenon China has never known before. It stands as an *alter ego* alongside every unit of political, social, economic, and cultural organization in the country. In the Party chapter we begin with a discussion of the self-conception of the Party, which may be considered a link between our discussion of ideology in the first chapter and our discussions of organization in the later chapters. After describing the Party's growth and development, we discuss it in structural terms, and end with a section on the Party cadre, the new leader in Communist China.

The government of Communist China is new in function as well as structure; it has replaced one that, more often than not, was new only in structure. The chapter on government is relatively short, because material for more detailed study was not available. In this chapter, we are mainly concerned with principles and methods of administration, and the general trends which have led to different concentrations and distributions of power.

The chapters on Party and government deal with structures of organization; the two that follow deal with functions of organization. Management and control have been selected as two important types of organizational function.

Management means leadership; leadership, as we have said, has replaced status as a source of command. Though there were many possible approaches to the study of leadership, we chose management because of its importance for economic development. In the chapter on management we begin again by introducing some theoretical and conceptual distinctions needed for later analysis, both in this and other chapters. We also briefly discuss pre-1949 Chinese business practices, since they have influenced management methods in Communist China. Beginning with this chapter, we treat the subject chronologically. As with the chapters on control, cities, and villages, we trace the development of different policies and methods of management from the "Liberation" through the end of the 1950's. A periodization is apparent in the management chapter, with the two main time periods marked by the First Five-Year Plan and the Great Leap Forward. Our discussion of management deals largely with the command system and has relatively little to say about the economic aspects of management.

Control is an essential counterpart to leadership; we might say that, in Communist China, active organizational controls have supplanted the passive compliance deriving from the traditional authority of the social system. Although the police and legal systems may appear to be obvious organizations to study from the point of view of control, study of the interrelationships between political and economic controls over industrial enterprises promised to reveal more about the nature of control in Communist China than a study of the former. Our discussion in the chapter on control focuses on the changing fortunes of the Ministry of State Control, whose rise and fall shows how control functions in Communist China.

Whereas chapters two through five discuss organization alone, the last two chapters, cities and villages, deal with the imposition of organization on society. These two chapters discuss the reorganization of Chinese society attempted by the Communists.

Though the appearance of Chinese cities has changed greatly in the wake of the revolution, more important have been the changes in social organization. The many associations that once governed the life of city dwellers in China have disappeared; they have been replaced by new forms of social organization, two of which we discuss in the chapter on cities, namely the residents committees and the urban communes.

The last chapter deals with China's most typical form of social organization: the village. The Chinese Revolution was fought and won in the villages, but the end of the revolution did not bring about a transformation of the nature of the village. Though the old gentry elite was destroyed and land was distributed through the land reform, the Chinese Communists only gradually introduced new forms of organization into the village. Since the problems of the village, more so than any others discussed in this book, are rooted in the past, we begin with a brief discussion of certain aspects of traditional village social organization, notably the relationship between state and village, and types of village civil and military organization. We continue, for the Communist period, with a discussion of the three stages of Chinese Communist village policy: land reform, cooperativization, and communization. A theme sounded in this chapter, as well as in others, is that the revolution has continued beyond the "Liberation." We suggest in fact that the social revolution continued down to the time of communization, and that perhaps only now is it being succeeded by the economic revolution.

Forty years after the October Revolution, sociological study of the Soviet Union became possible, because in time new patterns of social organization and stratification had solidified and become visible.[17] That time may now gradually be approaching in China. For example, lines of status differentiation are reappearing in various social and organizational contexts. As indicated, the "intellectuals," the general term for those with higher education, constitute an emerging status group. The Party itself is now more than an organization; it has become an important vehicle for granting political status. Regional differences continue to remain important, indicating that the past has not been completely replaced by the present. There is evidence that new kinship ties are being formed, now that the impact of "liberation" (i.e., the freeing of men from the shackles of the past) has passed. All this would indicate that a social system is slowly beginning to reconstitute itself.

Though a social system may be re-forming, the story of Communist China to this day is still one of organization. Men spend most of their everyday life in organization. During the day, they work in factories, rural production teams, administrative offices, and schools. During the evening, they attend public meetings, rest in public parks, participate in public amusements. Private life takes place mostly within the confines of the small nuclear family; the old three-generational family is difficult to maintain, to a large extent because the smallness of living space does not allow for it. In Communist China, man lives, works, and rests in organization.

It is possible that the seeming reconstitution of the social system may simply be institutionalization; that is, organizational forms and individual behavior are becoming habitual. In traditional China, the social system was realized at the local level—for example, in a rural area cen-

---

[17] Alex Inkeles and Raymond Bauer, *The Soviet Citizen* (Cambridge, Mass., 1959).

tered on a town. The gentry, China's traditional elite, lived in the town and exercised authority over the villagers. A common culture covering the entire society and a state which recruited from the gentry held these many systems together. Since China is today half-Western and half-Chinese, so to speak, there is as yet no single unifying culture. The state today covers all of society through organization, but there is no local community such as that of the traditional social system. As long as local life remains public, that is, a part of China as a whole, there is little likelihood of social systems comparable to the traditional ones emerging. The new social system, if it ever emerges, must be the equivalent of the whole society, or the nation. China, like most modern countries, appears to be so far from a condition of such national integration that one can yet speak of the reappearance of a social system.

After I had completed this book, I realized that I had omitted an important area of organization: the army. By the mid-1960's, it was becoming clear that the Chinese Communists were moving in the direction of creating a new organizational trinity of state, where party, government, and army each played a different, vital, and interrelated role.

The army today consists of two great parts, the regular army known as the People's Liberation Army and the civil militia (*minping*). The latter forms a crucial part of the commune system. The former, although of course constituting China's major defense force, has now entered civil society and plays a vital role in economic administration. During the last few years, so-called political departments, directly modeled on those in the army, have been established throughout the economic and industrial administration. Even more important, there is evidence that former army officers are assuming leadership positions within these new organizational units. It is not an uncommon phenomenon for armies in the newly emerging countries to play an important part in the life of civil society. However, in few countries has the army become an integral part of civil society. The military tradition in the Soviet Union has kept the armed forces largely segregated from civilian life. During the 1950's, the Chinese Communists pursued a similar policy. However, ever since the Great Leap Forward, the Chinese Communists have been narrowing the gap between army and society, and moving gradually toward the institutionalization of this trinity of state.

One of the main problems with which this emerging trinity is designed to cope is the role of young cadres in the new society. Youth constitutes a major leadership element in any society, but its leadership functions are normally activated only in a military context. In civil society, they are forced to pursue long career lines until they can attain positions of authority and responsibility. Young Red cadres led the Chinese Communists to victory, and Mao is clearly determined that they shall continue to play a major leadership role in Chinese society. Government, as almost everywhere, is staffed largely by older men. The Chinese Communist party is rapidly becoming middle-aged, largely due to a low attrition rate. The army, on the other hand, governed by a high turnover rate, remains young.

Having now listed the areas of concern discussed in this book, I would like to say a few words about the methodology of this study. It was not possible to start with an *a priori* framework of analysis. There was almost no secondary literature to be used as a guide, in the sense that such literature often points out major problems, introduces concepts, and does the spadework by organizing a confused mass of material. Knowledge of Soviet organization was necessary, in view of the heavy borrowings made by the Chinese Communists. But the Soviet model could not be mechanically tested on China. The only initial approach, then, as it seemed to me, was to put one's fingers on the major problem areas and immerse oneself in the documentary and human material.

Intuition is a major part of the rational process, for one has to sense the relevance of problems before one can use the ordering capacities of the mind to construct patterns. Yet much had to be done before confidence in intuition was strong enough. Hundreds of articles had to be read in the original Chinese, with precision and at the same time extensively. It was imperative to interview people who had significant organizational experiences, and this required a fluent knowledge of Chinese as it is spoken in China today. Translations and interpreters proved to be inadequate for the task. They can transmit "information," but obstruct intuition. It was necessary to listen to radio broadcasts from the mainland to sense the tone of agitation and propaganda. Intuition was necessary to gain a feeling of assurance that I was moving in the right direction.

On the other hand, intuition alone could lead to a dead end, where one sensed what was right but could not explain it. Recourse had constantly to be taken to the theoretical and comparative literature. How could such and such an organizational function be explained in general theoretical terms? How did such and such an approach to the Chinese Communists compare with the Soviet? If intuition gave a sense of assurance, readings in theoretical and comparative literature made it possible to identify crucial issues and find the conceptual language to express them.

What made it difficult to separate one approach from the other in neat systematic fashion was the factor of change. Despite the fact that Communist China has been in existence only a few years, it already has passed through three major phases of development—phases in which profound changes took place in the structure and function of organization. The Chinese Communists entered the cities not knowing how they would govern, beyond the conviction that it had to be through total organization. Their initial effort was to introduce the apparatus of Soviet-type organization into China. But while doing so, they faced immense difficulties. In the mid-1950's, they veered from the Soviet model, and began to develop their own approaches. The Great Leap Forward constitutes an alternative to the Soviet approach. Since the early 1960's, they have entered a new phase, for which no official designation exists. Ideology and organization, politics and economics are not as closely linked as they were in the earlier phases. It is under conditions of change that one gets an idea of what the real problems are.

Organizations arise as mechanisms to attain goals and cope with change. A study of organization must trace it through the battles it has waged under fluctuating conditions, much as the history of an army would have to be traced through a war. Sociological writing on traditional China has treated Chinese society as "system," more or less abstracted from time. Social systems, in fact, can be formulated in no other way. But it would have served no useful purpose to do an abstract structural or functional analysis of organization in Communist China. Structurally, all that would have emerged would have been arid organization charts, which, in any case, would have had relevance for only one short period of time. Functionally, the same would apply, because the roles and relationships of the actors have changed constantly. The functional situation that prevailed under one-man management was far different from what prevailed under Party leadership later. It is for this reason that I have chosen to follow most of the problem areas in their changing and developing contexts. As a whole, the narrative does not go beyond the 1950's, and tends to concentrate on the first half of the 1950's. The trends and problems that characterize the later periods were already visible at that time.

Sociologists, it is said, are concerned with patterns, whereas historians are concerned with continuity and change. In this sense, I have written this book both as sociologist and historian. While organization and action seem constantly to be changing in Communist China, they are also governed by basic patterns that do not change or do so slowly. The Chinese Communists speak of the "law of the unity of opposites." They mean by this, in effect, that opposites change and new opposites arise, but the laws that govern their interrelationships remain constant.[18] As a sociologist, I have tried to sketch out these "laws"; as a historian, I have tried to record the "opposites."

The alternating use of the empirical and intuitional approach on the one hand, and of the theoretical and comparative approach on the other, has given this book a dual appearance. Using the first approach, I have tried to sketch out the patterns inherent in the material itself. Since the Chinese Communists are systematic in their thinking and writing, one can find patterns in the way they discuss problems, particularly if they introduce their discussions, as they often do, with a general review of what came before. Thus, for example, in our discussion of industrial management, we sketch out empirical patterns which the Chinese Communist documents themselves reveal. However, since the categories and language of the ideology take time to learn, one has to read the documents carefully until intuition indicates that the major patterns have been correctly perceived.

The sketching out of other patterns, however, required the use of the second approach. Sometimes, organizational theory pointed to patterns which were not immediately apparent in the literature. At other times, comparison with the Soviet Union suggested patterns. At yet other times, it was clear that some problems, seemingly peculiar to the Chinese Communists, were but variants of general organizational problems, for which general theory suggested patterns. Thus, for example, our three-tiered conception of organization and our discussion in terms of the staff-line concept (see pp. 68-73) were suggested by general theory, but made sense when the relevant material was studied.

At the end of our Prologue, we asked the question: Where is China in all these processes? Since much of what we understand by "China" was bound up with the traditional social system, that question has been partly answered by our discussion of the Chinese Revolution in the Prologue and by our discussion of social system and organization in this Introduction. However, the full answer has not been given. We begin the body of this book with a discussion of ideology, a new phenomenon in China; we continue with organizations that are also new to China. But we end with cities and, in particular, villages, where it becomes clear that the links with the past were not entirely broken in 1949.

---

18 As a Czech joke puts it, socialism has two stages: first, the difficulties of development, and second, the development of difficulties.

CHAPTER I

IDEOLOGY

In 1949 the victorious Chinese Communists began the tough struggle of pulling the broken parts of China into unity and transforming a backward society into a modern nation. To achieve that unity and to bring about that transformation, the Chinese Communist party, a political body of a type never before known in Chinese history, made use of the same tools with which it won the Chinese Revolution—ideology and organization. This book describes the methods and processes whereby the Chinese Communist party, through a consistent yet changing ideology, created a web of organization which covers all Chinese society and penetrates deep into its fabric.

But while ideology and organization have brought about unity and transformation, they have also created contradictions which have made that web of organization into a polylithic structure where power, once concentrated at the apex, has begun to spread to other parts. Through this book goes the thread that contradictions have been essential to the methods and inherent in the processes of the struggle for unity and transformation.

DEFINITIONS

Ideology is generally defined as "the manner of thinking characteristic of a class or an individual." [1] In this book, we regard ideology as a manner of thinking characteristic of an organization. If organization is "a rational instrument engineered to do a job," [2] then the human beings who create and use it must do so on the basis of a set of ideas. However abstract these may be, they must have action consequences, for the purpose of organization is action. The more systematic organization becomes, the greater is the need for a systematic set of ideas to govern it.

Discussions of class or individual ideologies, such as those of Karl Mannheim, assume that ideologies are sets of ideas which have their unity not in the ideas themselves, but in the collective or individual unconscious.[3] Thus, a class or an individual may express a range of ideas which phenomenally appear to be diverse, yet noumenally have a unity in an underlying spiritual matrix. To say that ideas are systematic means consciously to make them into a coherent, integrated whole. The mentioned conception of class and individual ideologies implies that their sets of ideas need not be consciously systematic.

Organizations are different from classes and individuals in that they are the products of conscious creation. Thus, ideologies which serve to create organization require a conscious conception of unity; they cannot rely on an underlying spiritual matrix to give unity to their ideas. Such ideologies achieve unity through systematization of their ideas. In fact, since real organization can rarely be fully systematized, it is often only in the realm of ideology that systematization is achieved.

We therefore suggest that there are ideologies of organization in addition to those of classes and individuals, and define an organizational ideology as *a systematic set of ideas with action consequences serving the purpose of creating and using organization.*[4]

---

1 *The Oxford Universal Dictionary* (London, 1955), p. 952.

2 Philip Selznick, *Leadership in Administration* (Evanston, Ill., and White Plains, New York, 1957), p. 5.

3 Karl Mannheim, *Ideology and Utopia* (New York, 1949), p. 5 ff.

4 Reinhard Bendix, in discussing various definitions of the word ideology, states: "in this [one] sense, ideology is a type of goal-orientation, a special aspect of the teleology that is characteristic of all human action"; "The Age of Ideology: Persistent and Changing," in *Ideology and Discontent* (David E. Apter, ed.), (New York, 1964), p. 297. For us, what distinguishes organization from a social system is the goal-orientation of the former as contrasted to the value-orientation of the latter. Therefore,

The ideology of the Chinese Communist party is one of the great organizational ideologies of the modern world. Having taken its basic elements from Marxism, Leninism, and ideas developed in the Soviet Union, the Chinese Communist party, over the four decades of its history, has made its ideology into a systematic set of ideas which it has used to create its own organization and to achieve its goals.

If Chinese Communist ideology is a systematic set of ideas, one would expect to find a systematic presentation of those ideas in some major document, somewhat in the manner of a constitution. Such a major document exists in the form of the Party Rules. Each Party congress ends with the formal adoption of a new set of rules which state the major ideas that govern Party policy, organization, and action. The Party Rules can be said to contain the formal ideas basic to the ideology. In the chapter on the Party, we shall analyze those rules to indicate the self-conception of the Chinese Communist party.

However, analysis of these formal ideas does not in itself reveal the manner of thinking characteristic of the Chinese Communist party. Ideas are formulated thoughts expressed in a particular language. The ideas set forth in the Party rules are formulated in the language of Marxism-Leninism. They are like the differently shaped parts of a machine. Each idea is different, but is shaped by a uniform language. Together, these ideas constitute the structure of the ideology. Some students of the Chinese Communists often speak of their "ideology" as being the cause of a particular policy. In such a case, they implicitly regard ideology as a whole machine, seen only from the outside, and performing some task. How the machine works in the inside is not taken into consideration. Other students of the Chinese Communists go deeper, focus on the formal ideas, and describe their shapes; they look at the parts of the machine. Such an approach may be described as exegesis, and, indeed, is the approach we have followed in our discussion of the Party's self-conception. Yet, neither of these approaches tells us how the different parts function with each other, how they move within the ideology to produce a particular effect. In short, these approaches do not reveal the manner of thinking to which the ideology gives rise.

---

organization must have a body of ideas that is explicitly goal-oriented or teleological. Bendix states that "the term [ideology] is not properly applicable in Western civilization prior to the seventeenth and eighteenth centuries" (p. 295). I would suggest that the same is true of the term organization, except, perhaps, as it applied in the military field. The development of ideology and organization oriented toward the attainment of social goals strikes me as one of the unique products of the modern world.

It is this manner of thinking which we shall attempt to describe in the present chapter. Only men, not classes or organizations, think. Therefore, we want to describe the way a Chinese Communist individual, thoroughly imbued with the ideology, uses its ideas. The Party rules, and other ideological documents, present abstract formal ideas; as such, these ideas have no immediate relevance for action. A man can recite them by rote, but one will not know whether he really thinks with them. Only by seeing how these abstract ideas are transformed into concrete action can one begin to perceive the manner of thinking. In a machine, a few parts have central significance. So in ideology: there are ideas which give a certain energy to all the other ideas with which they come in contact. In this chapter, we shall try to single out the central ideas of Chinese Communist ideology by determining which have the greatest importance for organization.

To find out these central ideas, we have drawn from a broad range of published material. Since the Chinese Communist party, as a modern rational organization, requires conscious efforts to maintain itself and achieve its goals, it demands a high level of consciousness from its members. Consciousness is achieved by making its members speak, write, and publish. Meetings are marked by intensive discussion; members must continuously write reports; Party material is published all the time, particularly in the form of ephemera, such as newspaper articles and pamphlets. Since publication is carefully controlled, only such material which accords with the central ideas of the ideology is made public. The massive outpouring of written material that has emerged from Communist China thus may be said to constitute concrete expression of the ideology. In this chapter, we have drawn broadly from this material, on the assumption that it expresses the central ideas, even if these change from time to time.

The material we have used consists of writings by men who play a crucial role in organization, either at the top or at some lower levels. In these writings, they use ideas to analyze concrete problems and recommend action. The moving threads that go through all these writings can be said to constitute the central ideas of the ideology.

This chapter ends with a section called "The Dialectical Conception of Chinese Society." In this section, we explicitly attempt to describe the manner of ideological thinking most characteristic of the Chinese Communists, that is to say how formal ideas are combined with central ideas to produce an analysis of concrete reality with action consequences. This section must be last, because we cannot formulate the manner of thinking until we have dismantled the structure of the ideology and located its central parts.

The structure of the ideology consists of its sets of ideas. Although every published document can be regarded as a reflection of the ideology, some documents are regarded as doctrinal; these contain the conscious systematization to which the ideology aspires. The Party rules, of course, are such a document. More important are the four volumes of *The Selected Works of Mao Tse-tung*. In addition, there are doctrinal articles written by Mao Tse-tung, Liu Shao-ch'i, and other major leaders. Though their systematic character is apparent, it is not easy to dismantle the sets of ideas presented into a few major component parts. Therefore, we shall suggest a different approach whereby the total structure of the ideology can be broken apart into two major components.

Let us recall one phrase in our initial definition of ideologies of organization, that is "a systematic set of ideas with action consequences." Though such ideas ultimately give rise to action, the link between idea and action may be direct or indirect. Thus, the leaders of organization may propound an idea, for example a policy, which they expect their followers to implement. Such an idea may be said to have "one-to-one" action consequences. However, these same leaders may propound an idea which aims mainly at shaping the thinking of people, rather than producing immediate action. The former type of idea we may regard as "practical," and the latter type of idea we may regard as "pure."

Let us now see how the Chinese Communists have labeled their ideology. In the Party Rules adopted at the Seventh Party Congress (April-June, 1945), the preamble states: "The Chinese Communist party takes the theories of Marxism-Leninism and the unified thought of the practice of the Chinese Revolution, the thought of Mao Tse-tung, as the guideline for all of its actions." In contrast, the preamble of the Party Rules adopted at the Eighth Party Congress (September, 1956) states: "The Chinese Communist party takes Marxism-Leninism as the guideline for all of its actions." Despite the linking of the two, the Chinese Communists, during the mid-1950's, made a distinction between "Marxism" and "Leninism." "Marxism" was regarded as the *Weltanschauung*, the "world view" (*shihchieh-kuan*). "Leninism" was regarded as the principles of revolution and organization. Since the latter part of the 1950's, the dualism originally stated in the 1945 Party Rules has been revived, but in stronger form: "Marxism-Leninism and the thought of Mao Tse-tung." As we shall see in our subsequent discussion, the ideological role assigned "Leninism" in the mid-1950's has now been unreservedly assigned to "the thought of Mao Tse-tung." However, for the present discussion it is significant that the Chinese

Communists, in their official labeling of doctrine, have always regarded the total structure of their ideology as consisting of two major components.

A world-view may give the individual a certain outlook, but it does not indicate to him how he should act. But principles of revolution and organization have action consequences. We shall therefore suggest that the two major components of Chinese Communist ideology are analogous to the pure and practical ideas described above; one component of the ideology is pure, the other is practical. We shall speak of them as pure ideology and practical ideology.

Since this distinction also applies to ideologies of organization other than that of the Chinese Communists, we shall offer a general definition. Pure ideology is a set of ideas designed to give the individual a unified and conscious world view; practical ideology is a set of ideas designed to give the individual rational instruments for action. Let us illustrate this distinction by the example of an organization governed by Marxist ideology. The members of that organization will accept the view that all political and social conflict is basically class struggle. This view gives them a certain outlook through which they can put the complex phenomena of history and actuality into perspective; it does not, however, indicate to them how they should act. If that organization now adds the Leninist principle of the vanguard party to its ideology, it has acquired an instrument for organizational action.

In this book, we are concerned with the ideology of the Chinese Communist party, and not with the ideology of the world Communist movement, and, except for a few comparative remarks, not with the ideology of any other Communist party. For us, every organization has its own ideology. Since there is no such thing as an organized world-wide Communist party, there is no such thing as a "Communist ideology." However, as we shall indicate subsequently, there is a body of theory (pure ideology) which many—if not all—Communist parties share. But since, in varying degrees, they no longer fully share principles and methods of practice (practical ideology), one cannot equate a sharing of theory with an over-all sharing of ideology. Thus, though the Chinese Communists, historically and actually, share their pure ideology with other Communist parties, fundamentally it is an inherent part of their own total ideology. When we put "Marxism" and "Leninism" in quotation marks, it was meant to indicate that these are not the works of Marx and Lenin, or the ideological forms they have achieved in the Soviet Union, but to indicate the forms they have been given in the ideology of the Chinese Communists. Mao Tse-tung and Liu Shao-ch'i have spoken of the "Sinification of Marxism." By this they mean the incorporation of the Marxist world-view into Chinese Communist ideology. It is this incorporation that has transformed a general body of theory into pure ideology.

The total structure of Chinese Communist ideology therefore consists of a pure ideology essentially derived from Marxism and Leninism, and a practical ideology, whose derivation will be discussed in the following sections. The changing natures of and relationships between the pure and practical ideologies and the way both have served to create and use organization will be one of the main subjects of this chapter.

Before we discuss concretely Chinese Communist ideology, let us make a few remarks on the general significance of the distinction between pure and practical ideology. Pure and practical ideology, though different, are closely linked. Without pure ideology, the ideas of practical ideology have no legitimation. But without practical ideology an organization cannot transform its *Weltanschauung* into consistent action. Though all revolutionary movements must have an ideology, not all of them have evolved practical ideologies through which effective organization can be created. For example, nationalistic movements tend to generate only pure ideology; although they give their members a sense of identity in the world, they do not furnish them with rational instruments for action. Nationalistic movements, therefore, tend to be eclectic or old-fashioned in their organizational methods. Though these organizational methods often suffice to create and use organization, they are not constituted into a body of practical ideology, such as is the case with Communist movements. This, in many instances, has led to serious organizational weakness and political instability in nationalistic movements.

Lenin created a practical ideology for the revolutionary movements leading to the creation of the world's Communist parties by propounding principles of organization derived from the application of Marxist theory to the problems of contemporary reality. The Chinese Communists have gone further by developing a practical ideology based on Leninism but enriched by their long experiences in revolutionary struggle.

For our conceptual terms of pure and practical ideology, the Chinese Communists use the words "theory" and "thought" respectively. Theory is pure ideology, and thought is practical ideology.

To obviate possible confusion, let us repeat a few basic observations. At the present time, the total ideology of the Chinese Communist party is officially described as "Marxism-Leninism and the thought of

Mao Tse-tung." Of these two elements, the Chinese Communists re-gard Marxism-Leninism as theory (pure ideology) and "the thought of Mao Tse-tung" obviously as "thought" (practical ideology). Since the total ideology is "Chinese," so is, in effect, what the Chinese Communists call "Marxism-Leninism." In his works, Mao expounds the theories of Marxism-Leninism, but only those that he considers relevant for the Chinese Communist ideology, in particular the *Weltanschauung*. However, Mao never says that the *Weltanschauung* is his or that of the Chinese Communist party. Thus, while the Chinese Communists claim credit for having created a practical ideology (the thought of Mao Tse-tung), they regard the theories they have selected (Marxism-Leninism) as derivative from a universal doctrine which is binding on all Communist parties.

We must also remember that there is as yet no codified body of published doctrine labeled the thought of Mao Tse-tung. Though the Chinese Communists have published four volumes of his *Selected Works*, these do not constitute a fixed body of doctrine, for writings of Mao's not included in the *Selected Works* are periodically singled out as of major ideological importance. If one were asked what is the thought of Mao Tse-tung, one would have to say that it is not a set of doctrines, but a manner of thinking revealed in systematic sets of ideas. These ever-changing and ever-expanding ideas, which derive from a fixed body of theory, Marxism-Leninism, constitute the thought of Mao Tse-tung.

THE CHANGING POSITION OF IDEOLOGY

Time	Pure ideology	Practical ideology
Seventh Party Congress (1945)	Marxism-Leninism	The Thought of Mao Tse-tung
Eighth Party Congress (1956)	Marxism	Leninism
Since 1960	Marxism-Leninism	The Thought of Mao Tse-tung

PURE AND PRACTICAL IDEOLOGY

Theory and Thought

The words theory (*lilun*) and thought (*szuhsiang*) play an important part in Chinese Communist ideology. As we have said, they designate the pure and practical components of the total ideology. However, it took the Chinese Communists some time to transform the conventional meaning of these words into their ideological significance. Let us first consider "theory," and then move on to "thought."

The development of the ideological significance of the word theory is revealed by the way that word is treated in two versions of a statement of Mao Tse-tung, originally written in 1942 and emended in 1953.[5] In a speech before the Yenan Party School in 1942, Mao Tse-tung said:

> Marxism-Leninism is the theory that Marx, Engels, Lenin, and Stalin created on the basis of actual fact, and it consists of general conclusions derived from historical and revolutionary experience. If we have only read this theory and have not used it as a basis for research in historical and revolutionary actuality, *have not created a theory in accordance with China's real necessities, a theory that is our own and of a specific nature,* then it would be irresponsible to call ourselves Marxist theoreticians.[6]

The emended version, published in Volume III of his *Selected Works*, dropped the italicized phrases. In the 1942 version, Mao spoke of the need to create "a theory that is our own and of a specific nature." Obviously that phrase was considered "incorrect" in 1953. Thus, in the meantime, the word theory had acquired an ideological significance that required its dropping from the later version.

The Chinese term rendered as "specific nature" in this quotation is *t'eshu-hsing*, the same as in Mao's formulation of the two types of contradictions in his essay *On Contradiction*: universality of contradiction (*maotun-ti p'upien-hsing*) and particularity of contradiction (*maotun-*

---

[5] The continuous editing and reediting of Mao's works is well known, but the reasons behind this have not been fully explained. See, for example, Dennis J. Doolin and Peter J. Golas, "*On Contradiction* in the Light of Mao Tse-tung's Essay on 'Dialectical Materialism'," *The China Quarterly*, 19 (July-September 1964), 38-46. For an exegesis of Mao's works, see Arthur A. Cohen, *The Communism of Mao Tse-tung* (Chicago and London, 1964). One explanation for this editing and reediting becomes apparent in this chapter. Since the thought of Mao Tse-tung is practical rather than pure ideology, it constitutes an ever-changing and ever-expanding set of particular ideas (see pp. 24, 104). If the thought of Mao Tse-tung, on the other hand, were doctrine, then its ideas would become universal truths. This would mean that his works would be treated by the Chinese Communists in the same doctrinal fashion as those of Marx, Engels, Lenin, and Stalin; excerpts might be made, but no words in the original texts could be changed. Interestingly, the works of Khrushchev are now treated by the Chinese Communists in doctrinal fashion, that is, as illustrations of false doctrine (see p. 33).

[6] See Stuart R. Schram, *The Political Thought of Mao Tse-tung* (New York, 1963), pp. 115-116, note. The original version can be found in *Chiehfang jihpao*, April 27, 1942 and also in *Chengfeng wenhsien* (Hong Kong, 1949), p. 10. The emended version can be found in Vol. III of Mao's *Selected Works* (Chinese edition), published in February 1953.

ti t'eshu-hsing). By particularity of contradiction, Mao meant that the concrete form in which contradictions are manifest and the manner in which they are to be resolved will differ according to time and place. Such concrete manifestations of contradiction thus cannot be universal. Therefore, when Mao called for "a theory of a specific nature," he implied that theory could be nonuniversal. The dropping of this phrase in the emended version indicates that there can be none other than universal theory. Only "the universal truths of Marxism-Leninism" qualify as theory.

If the nonuniversality of theory was rejected by 1953, it had not yet been in 1945, when Liu Shao-ch'i gave the official commentary to the Party Rules adopted at the Seventh Party Congress. In that commentary, subsequently entitled "On the Party," Liu Shao-ch'i spoke of the thought of Mao Tse-tung as "the only correct theory (*lilun*) and policy (*chengts'e*) by which the proletariat and all the toiling people of China can liberate itself." In the section of the commentary called "On the Problem of the Guiding Thoughts of the Party," Liu not only credited Mao with having created the theory and policy of "Chinese communism and Chinese Marxism," but stated that he "critically took the best and useful [of Marxism] and rejected the wrong and useless." He unequivocally declared that the works of Mao Tse-tung were to be the basic teaching material of the Party.

In the present campaign to train a new revolutionary generation, the young revolutionists are told that they must be armed with the theory of Marxism-Leninism and the thought of Mao Tse-tung. Despite the resurrection of the thought of Mao Tse-tung, Liu Shao-ch'i's description of it as a specific Chinese theory has not yet been reinvoked; theory, being universal, is attributed only to Marxism-Leninism. The following passage from a *Jenmin jihpao* editorial, published on August 3, 1964, may be regarded as a doctrinal formulation of Marxism-Leninism and the thought of Mao Tse-tung:

The spirit of Marxism-Leninism in its philosophical-ideological aspects is dialectical materialism, especially the law of the unity of opposites. In its political-ideological aspects, it is the theory of class struggle, especially the theory of proletarian revolution and proletarian dictatorship. Real Marxist-Leninists must use the law of the unity of opposites to resolve problems, must always uphold the proletarian revolution and the proletarian dictatorship. . . . The thought of Mao Tse-tung is one which, in an era moving toward the collapse of imperialism and the victory of socialism, in the great revolutionary struggle of the Chinese people, united the universal truths of Marxism-Leninism with the practice of revolution and construction in China and creatively developed Marxism-Leninism. Our proletarian revolutionary successors must be real Marxist-Leninists and thus must firmly and unflaggingly study the works of Mao Tse-tung, actively learn and actively use the thought of Mao Tse-tung.

Thus, as we have indicated earlier, the Chinese Communists now regard their total ideology as consisting of two major components: Marxism-Leninism and the thought of Mao Tse-tung. The passage cites the law of the unity of opposites and the theory of class struggle as the essence of Marxism-Leninism. The distinction between "law" and "theory" relates to our discussion on the action consequences of ideas. The passage states explicitly that the law of the unity of opposites must be used to resolve problems. Indeed, as we shall see, the theory of contradictions, derived from Marxism, serves as the central idea linking pure and practical ideology. The theory of class struggle constitutes the essence of the Chinese Communist world outlook. Though the Chinese Communists have often departed radically from classic Marxist definitions of class, they have consistently regarded all conflict, whether internal or external to China, as of class nature. Whether a "struggle" between poor and rich peasants in a village, or one between socialism and imperialism, any "struggle" is consistently defined as a class conflict. Thus, for example, the Chinese Communists regard their struggle with the bourgeois-feudal forces of Chiang Kai-shek (in Communist class conceptions, an alliance between the modern urban bourgeoisie and the traditional rural gentry) as in the same category as their struggle with the "bourgeois-capitalist" United States and its "feudal-reactionary" allies in the backward countries. The essence of their theory or *Weltanschauung* is that, at all times, a manifest or latent polarization exists between progressive and reactionary social forces in the world.

The Chinese Communist notion of class polarization is, of course, orthodox Marxist. However, their faithful adherence to this belief takes on special significance in view of the fact that, first, reformist ideas have become prominent in the Communist world (e.g., the idea of "structural reform," originally propounded by the Italian Communists), and, second, the Chinese Communists have particularly stressed the development of practical ideologies to transform universal theory into specific action.

Despite the distinction made in the quoted passage between law and theory, the word "theory" is generally used by the Chinese Communists to designate their pure ideology. In his works, Mao Tse-tung consistently refers to Marxism-Leninism as theory; that this word has special

ideological significance has been mentioned in the introductory remarks to this section.

Granting, as the passage from the *Jenmin jihpao* editorial indicates,
that theory must consist of universal truths, we may well ask why Mao
Tse-tung has not, to this day, again been credited—as he was by Liu
Shao-ch'i in 1945—with having created new theory.[7] The passage implies clearly that universal truths derive only from Marxism-Leninism;
the thought of Mao Tse-tung, therefore, is something other than universal truths. Let us review the subject of the derivation and creation
of theory.

In 1953, when the volume of the *Selected Works* containing the
emended version of Mao's 1942 Yenan speech was published, the dele-
tion of the phrase "a theory that is our own and of a specific nature"
indicated that Mao was not to be regarded as the creator of new theory.
However, given the importance of the word "thought" in the Chinese
Communist ideological vocabulary, it is significant that, during the
mid-1950's, in contrast to the mid-1940's, he was not regarded as the
creator of new thought. Since, as we have pointed out, references to
the thought of Mao Tse-tung in the 1945 Party Rules were omitted in
the 1956 Party Rules, we may conclude that Mao underwent a demotion on the ideological ladder between those two periods of time. In the
mid-1950's, Mao's contributions were generally described as the appli-

---

[7] When this book was in proof, Marshal Lin Piao, early in September 1956, gave
a speech which is one of the most important theoretical documents to have emerged
from Communist China in recent years. The tone and substance of that speech are
reminiscent of Liu Shao-ch'i's speech "On the Party" given in 1945 during the Seventh
Party Congress. Lin Piao stated: "The whole series of theories and policies of Comrade Mao Tse-tung concerning people's war have creatively enriched and developed
Marxism-Leninism." Since there are several references to Mao's "theories and policies" (as there were in Liu Shao-ch'i's 1945 speech), Lin Piao's speech may be regarded
as an initial attempt to proclaim Mao as the creator of doctrine as well as of practice.
Since doctrine has universal relevance, it is important that Lin Piao devoted a long
section to "the international significance of Comrade Mao Tse-tung's theories on
people's war."

As far as *Weltanschauung* is concerned, Lin Piao stated that the pattern of world
revolution will follow that of the Chinese Revolution, namely that revolution in "the
world's villages" (Asia, Africa, and Latin America) will encircle "the world's cities"
(North America and western Europe). Thus the Chinese Revolution was given universal significance comparable to the Russian Revolution for its own time. As far as
practice is concerned, Lin Piao argued for a nationalistic, united-front approach to
fight "American imperialism," comparable to that pursued by the Chinese Communists when preparing to resist Japanese invasion in the mid-1930's. He stated: "Only
after completion of the national (*mintsu*) democratic revolution, can one speak of
the socialist revolution."

cation of the truths of Marxism-Leninism to the Chinese Revolution. The fact that at present he is again credited with having evolved "thought" indicates a move up on the ideological ladder. Nevertheless, he has not yet reached the top, like Stalin, to propound a *Weltanschauung*. Since theory now can only be universal, to attribute the creation of theory to Mao would have far-reaching international implications. At present, what the Chinese Communists designate as "theory" still derives entirely from Marxism-Leninism.

In 1953, when the mentioned volume of the *Selected Works* appeared, Stalin had just died. Stalin, as a living member of the Marxist pantheon (Marx, Engels, Lenin, Stalin), had the legitimate right to create new theory which became binding on all Communist parties, including the Chinese Communist party. Since Stalin's death, no one has succeeded to the pantheon, either in the Soviet Union, or in China. If Mao's picture were ever to be ranged alongside the sacred quadrumvirate, symbolically this would mean that Mao would have become the creator of new theory, binding on all Marxist-Leninist parties.

Why the Chinese Communists have not done so cannot be explained in detail at this point, because this is a matter relating to the nature of the world Communist movement. Since our concern is the ideology and organization of the Chinese Communist party, suffice it to say that, to this day, the pure ideology of the Chinese Communist party is Marxism-Leninism—a set of doctrines from which theories and laws can be derived, but to which no new ones can yet be added.

Because the quoted passage from the *Jenmin jihpao* editorial may be regarded as a doctrinal formulation of Marxism-Leninism and the thought of Mao Tse-tung, it deserves comment. The passage describes the thought of Mao Tse-tung as "one which united the universal truths of Marxism-Leninism with the practice of revolution and construction in China." This phrase may be said to describe a basic process of creating ideology. It implies that first there were the universal truths, second there was concrete practice which may not have had any relationship to the universal truths, and third there was the active mind of Mao Tse-tung linking the two together to produce thought. Thus ideology arises, not by applying truths to real problems, but by uniting universal theory (which may or may not have relevance for real problems) and concrete practice (which may or may not be determined by the truths). Thus, according to Mao's epistemology, ideology (or knowledge) is the product of action, and not the reverse.

Mao's creation of thought is a continuing process without any foreseeable conclusion. Unification of theory and practice continues, adding to thought. The new revolutionary generation is instructed to do more than read the thought of Mao Tse-tung. It is urged to use it as a model for combining theory and practice, and so develop an outlook in which ideology becomes a central part of everyday living and working.

THE PROCESS OF CREATING IDEOLOGY

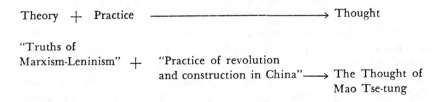

From all this we can conclude that, although Mao has not created pure ideology, he has again been credited with having created a practical ideology; this is his main contribution to the world. Moreover, in view of the freezing of the pantheon through the death of Stalin, no new theory can now be created. This means that the further ideological development of the Chinese Communist party, and, in the Chinese Communist view, of other Communist parties as well, can only take place in the realm of practical ideology. In the light of the following discussion, it is significant that the formulation of the practical ideology took place in the mind of an individual, namely Mao Tse-tung.

After this discussion of the ideological significance of the word theory, we now come to consider the ideological significance of the word thought (*szuhsiang*). This word, in the ideological vocabulary of the Chinese Communists, has been widely used since the Yenan period in connection with "thought reform and indoctrination," and consistently in the sense of the socially conditioned thinking of the individual.[8] The "rectification" documents of the Yenan period speak of the "correct" and "incorrect" thoughts of individuals, but never use *szuhsiang* to designate the sets of ideas characteristic of an age. Though the manifest meaning of *szuhsiang* is "thought," in translation it is often also rendered as "ideology." In the beginning of this chapter, we sug-

---

[8] On *szuhsiang*, see John Wilson Lewis, *Leadership in Community China* (Ithaca, New York, 1963), pp. 51-53. Lewis, discussing the development of "correct" thoughts in cadres, stresses the perceived contradiction between theory and practice as the psychological matrix of action. These contradictions, as they are perceived, lead to total awareness and moral choice. The cadre takes a position (*lich'ang*), and thus is ready to act. See pp. 45-46.

gested that ideology can be defined as the manner of thinking characteristic of a class, an individual, or an organization. Clearly, *szuhsiang* does not mean a manner of thinking characteristic of a class. The Chinese language once used a word, *chuyi,* as an independent noun to designate an ideology of a class. At the present time, it is generally used only as a suffix to be appended to other nouns, in the manner of the English "-ism."

There is an analogy to the differences between *szuhsiang* and *chuyi* (in its old autonomous sense) in Karl Mannheim's distinction between "particular" and "total" conceptions of ideology: particular conceptions of ideology regard sets of ideas as having achieved integration within single human beings; total conceptions see the integration within a class, society, or age, that is to say, at a level above that of the individual. Mannheim states: "It was Marxist theory which first achieved a fusion of the particular and total conceptions of ideology. . . . Marxism was able to go beyond the mere psychological level of analysis and posit the problem in a more comprehensive, philosophical setting." [9] Mannheim's particular conception of ideology thus would correspond to *szuhsiang,* his total conception to the old *chuyi.* But Mannheim also credits Marxist theory with having achieved a fusion of the two. The total ideology of the Chinese Communists—Marxism-Leninism and the thought of Mao Tse-tung—has also achieved this. Theory (corresponding to the old *chuyi*) and thought constitute a single whole. That whole is the ideology of organization.

Officially, the Chinese Communists regard Marxism-Leninism as a class ideology, namely that of the proletariat. However, not only is it not the product of the Chinese proletariat, but the latter has not even contributed to it. The historical class ingredients of Marxism-Leninism derive from proletariats foreign to China, among which the Russian proletariat plays a singularly important role. Thus the pure ideology of the Chinese Communists is a universal class ideology with no particular roots in China. But their practical ideology has its roots in the experiences of particular individuals, not of classes. Although *szuhsiang* may be socially conditioned, it is the end, not the beginning, of consciousness. Thus, even an individual of nonproletarian class origins could combine "correct" theory and "correct practice" and come up with "correct" thought. None of the major leaders of Communist China, one might note, is of proletarian origin.

The Chinese Communists, then, regard their total ideology, which we place in the category of ideologies of organization, as arising from

---

[9] Mannheim, *op. cit.,* pp. 49-52, especially p. 52, and also p. 66.

the fusion of a universal class ideology with particular individual ideologies. The social basis of their ideology of organization, being universal, thus does not lie in the Chinese proletariat. Rather it is their ideology of organization which is used to create a proletarian social basis, through the transformation of the entire Chinese people into a society of modern workers.

Given the importance of *szuhsiang* in Chinese Communist ideology, it is clear that the Chinese Communists have paid particular attention to the thinking of individuals. This is obvious in the practice of thought reform in Communist China. In accordance with orthodox Marxist theory, the Chinese Communists regard the thought of individuals as arising from a class-determined social matrix. If a man is a bourgeois, his thought will be bourgeois. The Chinese have put this belief into concrete practice by giving each individual a legal class status. However, it is possible for an individual to change that status after having undergone thought reform and produced "correct thought." Thus, a bourgeois, before thought reform, will "naturally" have bourgeois thought. But, by combining "correct theory and practice," he can transform himself, as one can see in the common Chinese Communist word *fanshen*, which may be freely rendered as "transformation of identity." The Chinese Communists thus believe that the arena of class struggle cannot take place abstractly within the class as a whole, but must be fought out within each individual human being.

One can illustrate this with the example of the revolutionary terror during the late 1940's. It was not enough physically to eliminate the landlord class, but each individual peasant had to be raised to a level of consciousness so that he would personally step forward and denounce his landlord. Each landlord, moreover, had to confess his sins as an individual before punishment was meted out; this was the famous "lowering of the head" (*tit'ou*). The Chinese Communists, by individual rather than collective denunciation, thereby aimed at rooting out the very idea of the landlord class. For this it was crucial to make the landlord express his true thoughts, and to give the peasants consciousness to "speak out their bitterness" in full. When the individual peasant pointed the finger of accusation against the landlord, he finally had vanquished his traditional awe before the embodied authority of the old ruling class.

The implication of the Chinese Communist conception of thought is: it can change. In principle, every individual can hope to arrive at "correct" thought. However, change also means that it never ends. The thought of Mao Tse-tung continually evolves. Similarly, no man can say that his "standpoint" (*lich'ang*) has arrived at a point of perfection. The Chinese Communists tell their people always to use the thought of Mao Tse-tung, that is, to engage in the basic ideological process of combining theory and practice. However, since Mao's thought too changes, no end to the process is in sight.

The implication of the Chinese Communist conception of theory, however, is that, as universal truth, it cannot be changed. Symbolically, one can see this in what has happened to the word *chuyi*. It is now only used as a suffix, as in feudalism, capitalism, socialism, and, recently, Khrushchevism. *The word Maoism does not exist in the Chinese Communist vocabulary.* When the Chinese Communists use the suffix *-chuyi*, they mean a set of ideas characteristic of a class, society, age, or group. The currently used phrase "Khrushchevism without Khrushchev" thus can be seen as an attack on a whole group of people in the Soviet Union and elsewhere. Moreover, labeling a set of ideas as *-chuyi* also implies that they constitute a world view, albeit a false one. To show that Khrushchevism is false doctrine, the Chinese Communists have started the publication of the complete works of Nikita Sergeievich Khrushchev.

We can now say that the Chinese Communists have produced their ideology of organization through a continuing combination of unchanging universal theory with changing individual ideology. The changing individual ideology of greatest importance has been the thought of Mao Tse-tung. The fact that the Chinese Communists regard theory or pure ideology as unchanging means that it alone is not capable of leading to action; theory without thought is meaningless. The Chinese Communists disdain the traditional propensity of many Chinese intellectuals to think out grand schemes of history and change. Implicitly, that attitude is directed even against the highly intellectual founders of the Chinese Communist party, Ch'en Tu-hsiu and Li Ta-chao. What counts in thinking, in the Chinese Communist view, is the use of theory to create thought, and thought can only come about within the individual human being.

Though this book is concerned with the ideology and organization of the Chinese Communist party, it shares significant elements of its ideology with other Communist parties, particularly the Soviet Communist party. However, it is now also apparent that it has serious ideological differences with these other parties. Therefore, before we continue our discussion of Chinese Communist ideology, we would like to identify some differences between the Chinese Communist and Soviet approaches to theory and thought, and follow with a brief discussion of some of the world-wide implications of these differences.

The Chinese Communist view of theory differs from the classical Marxist view. Marxism, as Mannheim puts it, regards theory as a function of the process of becoming and thus as a function of reality: a theory leads to a certain kind of action; the action, if successful, changes reality, or, if unsuccessful, forces a revision of the theory.[10] The classical Marxist view is that theory itself changes in the process of becoming. Official Soviet philosophy accepts this view, denounces "dogmatism and spiritual ossification" of Marxism, and constantly speaks of the "development of dialectical and historical materialism." When the Soviets speak about the creative development of Marxist-Leninist theory, this is precisely what they mean. Stalin, of course, "creatively developed" theory. The absence of a new theoretical successor to Stalin in the Soviet Union has not done away with the Soviet belief that theory can and should be changed, although Khrushchev, when propounding his ideas of peaceful coexistence, for example, always was careful to ground them in Lenin.

The Chinese Communists, as we have seen in the quoted passage from the *Jenmin jihpao* editorial, also speak of the creative development of Marxism-Leninism. However, they mean something different from what the Russians mean: for the Chinese it is the development of new thought on the basis of unchanging theoretical doctrine; the Russians argue that theory itself must be developed. They accuse the Chinese of dogmatism, and the Chinese accuse the Russians of violating theory. Both, of course, are right.

There is no equivalent of thought (*szuhsiang*) in the Soviet ideological arsenal. The confessions of leading Bolsheviks during the great purge trials of the 1930's are somewhat similar to confessions which came from prominent men in China during the early 1950's. However, the Russians have never developed systematic methods of thought reform, such as the Chinese have. The Russians, particularly under Stalin, appear never to have understood the need for a basic transformation of the spiritual identities of individuals in organization. Or, if they did, they could not devise methods for bringing about such transformation. In fact, the Russians have shown impatience with what they call "psychology," which may be understood as the equivalent of the Chinese *szuhsiang*. An official Soviet primer on philosophy states:

The social ideology of a class does not arise out of the generalization of the psychology of that class nor from the simple systematization of whatever is

---

10 Mannheim, *op. cit.*, pp. 112-113.

going on in the heads of the members of that class. . . . Ideology assumes the understanding [osmyslivanie] of real social relationships, of social processes, of class war.[11]

For the Chinese Communists, "the systematization of whatever is going on in the heads of the members of that class" has been of greatest importance. Through such systematization the Chinese Communists have created and used their ideology of organization.

There are indications that the Russians, perhaps under Chinese influence, have sought to remedy this gap in their ideological arsenal. Khrushchev put great emphasis, for example, on the need to create a "new Soviet man." Since the death of Stalin, the need for moral training of the people has been stressed. The educational implications of the Soviet campaign for obshchestvennost', which may be freely rendered as "social will," are similar to those of the Chinese Communist "mass line." Interestingly, there are reports now of greater use of mental hospitals to deal with political deviationists. All this would indicate greater Soviet awareness of the importance of "psychology."

Nevertheless, the Soviets have never had a practical ideology demanding the psychological transformation of individuals comparable to that of the Chinese Communists. Under Stalin, practical ideology consisted, in effect, of whatever norms were laid down by Stalin, legitimated by the theories of Marx, Engels, Lenin, and Stalin himself. When Khrushchev attacked Stalin, he appealed to Leninist doctrine to justify his new ideological norms. As a result of Khrushchev's ouster, whatever norms he proposed have been nullified, as can be seen in the intensive campaign waged against him. As a result of de-Stalinization and de-Khrushchevization, the Soviets are left without a unified practical ideology, while loudly proclaiming their continued devotion to the pure ideology of Marxism-Leninism. The Soviet Union is today caught in a conflict between one group which advocates a practical ideology of technical rationality and another group which seeks to create a new practical ideology derived from Marxism-Leninism. However, regardless of the outcome of this ideological conflict, the Soviets will hardly ever develop an ideology similar to the "thought" of the Chinese Communists.

The differences between the Russians and the Chinese in pure and practical ideology have had serious consequences for the organization of the international Communist movement. As we have indicated, Stalin earlier had preempted the field of new theory. We suggest that there was a link between this fact and Moscow's power to enforce ideological and organizational uniformity on the world's Communist parties. The-

---

[11] Osnovy marksistskoi filosofii (Moscow, 1958), pp. 326 ff., 589-590.

ory was alive and changing in Stalin's day, but only Stalin had the legitimate authority to change it. As we shall argue in the section of this chapter on the function of ideology in organization, theory constitutes the keystone in all Communist organization, despite its only indirect relevance for action. Thus we can say that the theories of Marxism-Leninism have decisive organizational significance for the Chinese Communist party, as they have had and continue to have for other Communist parties. The fact that Stalin had sole control over theory gave him a powerful weapon for the manipulation of every Communist party. This helps explain the disorientation that arose within the Yugoslav Communist party at the time of the split with Moscow in 1948.

If theory now has become universal and unchanging, no new Stalin can arise. Without active power over theory, the Soviets no longer have any authority to impose their organizational norms on the international movement.

The Chinese Communists, at the present time, argue that each movement must develop its own norms adapted to the particular context in which it acts. This means that the Chinese Communists reject the old Comintern approach to international communism, where Moscow laid down the norms. The proper role of the Soviet Union, as the Chinese see it, is the maintenance of the sanctity of theory; the various Communist parties generate their own practical ideologies.

The Chinese Communists do not believe, however, that the range of possible practical ideologies is infinite. Since, in their view, there are laws of development valid for all societies, the "correct" combination of theory and practice in societies at similar stages of development must result in "correct ideology"—in other words, ideology (and action) similar to that evolved by Mao Tse-tung. As Vsevolod Holubnychy puts it, "to Mao these laws [of development] are an utter *force majeure*." [12]

It follows from the Chinese position that successful national liberation movements will emerge with an ideology similar to that of Mao Tse-tung. The question then arises: what can they learn from the thought of Mao Tse-tung? They cannot simply accept Chinese Communist ideology, as they could the theories of Lenin and Stalin, for it is the unique product of the particular circumstances of the Chinese Revolution. However, they can learn the methodological model for the creation of a practical ideology. They can begin by finding out the contradictions (class conflict, balance of forces, organizational opposites, and so on) within a given real situation, and on the basis of such an

---

[12] Vsevold Holubnychy, "Mao Tse-tung's Materialistic Dialectics," *The China Quarterly*, 19 (July-September 1964), 27.

analysis make a "principled" choice of action. In arriving at this, they can read at length exactly how this was done in the Chinese Revolution.

The Chinese Communists, at the present time, speak of the world-wide revolutionary forces as national liberation movements. In our chapter on the Party, we shall see how the Chinese Communist party, as well as the Soviet Communist party, conceives of itself in national terms. This self-conception has implications for the creation and use of practical ideology. Since the practical ideology of the Chinese Communists, what is now called the thought of Mao Tse-tung, arose within China, it can be directly used there. However, since the particular national contexts of other countries in which national liberation movements are under way are different from those of China, the thought of Mao Tse-tung can only serve as a model, not as a body of doctrine.

This approach to ideology helps explain the curious behavior of the Chinese Communists on the international scene. Though they support pro-Chinese movements, they do not organize them, as the Comintern organized Communist parties in the 1920's (the Chinese Communist party itself was organized on Comintern initiative). They usually work behind the scenes, give advice, and finance movements and publications. They work for the development of national parties which accept Peking's pure ideology of "true Marxism-Leninism," but evolve their own practical ideologies.

However, Peking's conception of pure ideology creates a dilemma. As we shall see in our discussion on *Weltanschauung*, the Chinese Communist conception of Marxism-Leninism assigns a key role to the Soviet Union as the first socialist country in the world. Thus, even during the bitterest moments of anti-Soviet tirades in China, they have come forth with a "defense of the Soviet Union," similar to that heard from Trotskyites in the 1930's. They accuse the "Khrushchevites" of having betrayed Marxism-Leninism to their own Soviet people, and have taken up the struggle to defend Marxism-Leninism and the role of Stalin in the development of the Soviet Union.[13] The dilemma arises from the fact that this conception of Marxism-Leninism, with a central role assigned to the Soviet Union, is basic to the ideology of organization of the Chinese Communists.[14] Thus, while fighting the Soviets at

---

[13] *Hungch'i*, 18 (1963), 1-12.

[14] The *Weltanschauung* of Marxism-Leninism is also essential to the writings of Mao Tse-tung. With the exception of his few writings on philosophy and war, the remainder deal with particular and practical problems. However, as long as there is Marxism-Leninism, Mao's writings are seen as particular instances of universal truth. Otherwise they would merely be the expression of one man. Without Marxism-Leninism, Mao becomes simply a successful practitioner of nationalism. Mao has

almost every turn, they ostensibly do so to force the Soviet Union to return to its proper role as the guardian of sacred theory. Thus, the Soviet Union should furnish the doctrines of pure ideology, whereas Communist China should furnish the model of practical ideology.

Our discussion of the world-wide implications of the Sino-Soviet ideological differences suggests two observations which have relevance for our further discussion of Chinese Communist ideology. The first, that the thought of Mao Tse-tung is not a body of doctrine to be offered revolutionary movements, but rather a manner of thinking to be learned. The second, that the Soviet Union still plays a major part in the *Weltanschauung* of the Chinese Communists. Let us also recall our earlier formulation of the basic Chinese Communist process of creating ideology, namely the combination of universal truths, particularly the law of the unity of opposites, with concrete practice. These three statements together will help explain the structure of the discussion in the remainder of the chapter.

The following section deals with the Chinese Communist *Weltanschauung*, stressing the role of the Soviet Union. We will then proceed to a discussion of ideology and behavior, that is, the way in which thought is produced in the individual. That will bring us to the central idea in the thought of Mao Tse-tung, the theory of contradictions. In the section "Ideology in Action," we will shift our concern to organization. In the last section, "The Dialectical Conception of Chinese Society," we will attempt to indicate the manner of thinking characteristic of the thought of Mao Tse-tung.

Weltanschauung

Since pure and practical ideology together constitute the ideology of organization, they should be tools for the creation and use of organization. However, they function in different ways. The ideas of pure ideology state values: moral and ethical conceptions about right and wrong. The ideas of practical ideology state norms: rules which prescribe behavior and thus are expected to have direct action conse-

---

been the subject of criticism within China, judging from sentiment in the wake of the Great Leap Forward; see *Kungtso t'unghsün* (documents released by the U.S. State Department), January 1, 1961, I, 13-14. Without theory, his mistakes would be just mistakes. With theory, they are part of the dialectical process of history.

For a different treatment of the thought of Mao Tse-tung, from the viewpoint of its Chinese and Western components, see Stuart R. Schram, "Chinese and Leninist Components in the Personality of Mao Tse-tung," *Asian Survey*, III:6 (June 1963), 259-273.

quences.[15] The values and norms of the total ideology are tools through which two important organizational functions are accomplished. First, they serve to motivate individuals to give full commitment to the organization. Second, they give individuals a set of rational ideas with which to carry out the actions demanded by the organization. The ideal organization man thus is an individual fully committed to the organization's cause, but also knowing how to act "correctly" on the basis of his commitment. The central value of the pure ideology of the Chinese Communists is the notion of struggle.[16] From this value has emerged the central idea of the thought of Mao Tse-tung, which we shall subsequently discuss in terms of the theory of contradictions. The notion of struggle, however, has its roots in the basic *Weltanschauung* of the pure ideology. The *Weltanschauung* has a decisive organizational function, particularly for the proper motivation of individuals.

The core of the Chinese Communist *Weltanschauung* is formed by the theories of Marxism-Leninism, as the Chinese Communists under-

---

[15] There is great imprecision in the sociologists' treatment of values and norms, but there is at least agreement that values are related to ideas of what is desirable and norms to what behavior ought to be. Values have action consequences only in conjunction with an intervening element such as a norm. A man may value honesty, but the value is only actualized behaviorally if he can translate his conception of honesty into behavioral rules, such as telling the truth, never betraying a friend, and honoring one's obligations. Sociologists have generally tended to assume that values and norms are closely related. The important distinction is that the proclamation of norms (let us say with enforcing sanctions) is done with the expectation of behavioral compliance. The expression of values, on the other hand, suggests a general direction which behavior ought to take, but gives no prescription about the form it should take. See: Henry W. Riecken and George C. Homans, "Psychological Aspects of Social Structure" in *Handbook of Social Psychology* (Reading, Mass., and London, 1954), II, 786. Elsewhere, Homans speaks of values that "men bring to a group from the larger society"; George C. Homans, *The Human Group* (New York, 1950), p. 127. Parsons speaks of values as elements "of a shared symbolic system which serves as a criterion or standard for selection among the alternatives of orientation which are intrinsically open in a situation"; *The Social System* (Glencoe, Ill., 1951), p. 12. Elsewhere, Parsons speaks of norms as "verbal descriptions of the concrete course of action thus regarded as desirable, combined with an injunction to make certain future actions conform to this course"; Talcott Parsons, *The Structure of Social Action* (Glencoe, Ill., 1949), p. 75. The concepts "value" and "norm" are widely used, though not usually clearly differentiated. The predominant attitude appears to be, as Riecken and Homans put it, that "the line between norms and values is obviously not sharp."

[16] Arthur F. Wright, "Struggle vs. Harmony: Symbols of Competing Values in Modern China," *World Politics* VI:1 (October 1953), 31-44.

stand them. These theories expound a doctrine of the inexorable forces of world history.

The Chinese Communist *Weltanschauung* is, in effect, the orthodox Marxist conception of the materialist forces of world history. The driving force both of world and national history is class conflict; the inevitable resolutions of class conflict propel history in a unilinear direction. The proletariat, according to this view, will eventually emerge as the dominant class of all societies. Concretely, this means that the proletariats of the developed nations will ultimately destroy capitalism, and the nonproletarian poor of the underdeveloped nations will ultimately be transformed into proletariats. The Chinese Communist party sees itself as a national revolutionary instrument to industrialize and modernize China, and so make its peasantry into a class of workers; and as an international revolutionary instrument to aid similar processes elsewhere in the world. Given the unilinear development of history, the process of world-wide proletarianization is inevitable. However, this same view of history assigns a particular role to the Soviet Union, as the first socialist country—the country in which the proletariat first seized power. Moreover, having seized power, the Russian proletariat, through Lenin and Stalin, furnished a vital body of theoretical doctrine to all other revolutionary movements.

Before 1949, despite serious differences with Stalin, the Chinese Communists remained consistently loyal to the Soviet Union. After 1949 they tried to create a second soviet union on Chinese soil. They translated thousands of Soviet writings on every conceivable subject. They modeled their entire institutional structure on that of the Soviet Union. They adopted an economic strategy directly copied from the Soviet Union; permitted the Russians to draft their First Five-Year Plan; and made Russian the first foreign language of the country. Though such far-reaching Soviet influence can in part be explained by Russian presence in Manchuria and by Chinese dependence on the Soviet Union in the face of unremitting hostility from the United States, one cannot deny the effect of ideological belief.

The utopian element in Chinese Communist ideology can hardly be doubted. The Chinese Communists have the vision of "final communism," as much as all other Communist parties. But final communism has always been regarded as far away; except for a brief period in 1958, it has not played an active part in the pure ideology of the Chinese Communists. More important has been their image of the Soviet Union.

China always had a tradition of belief in a golden age. This has never been a mythical paradise, but rather a lost age in the past—real, but far away. The Soviet Union in many ways has served as the modern version of that golden age. The Chinese Communists, even now, regard the Soviet Union as the fatherland of socialism. In the early 1950's, they believed that they could proletarianize China through direct emulation of the Soviet Union. Though they have increasingly expunged Soviet ideas from their practical ideology, they have not changed their final goal: the proletarianization of China.

The philosophical basis for the certainty of the Chinese Communists that they can accomplish this proletarianization is the *Weltanschauung* of Marxism-Leninism, in which the Russian Revolution holds a decisive place. If they ever proclaim that revisionism has led to a capitalist restoration in the Soviet Union, as they have already indicated has happened in Yugoslavia, this would mean that the Marxist-Leninist theory of unilinear historical development was false. This would be a crushing blow to the pure ideology of the Chinese Communists.

As we have stated, the central value of Chinese Communist ideology is the notion of struggle. However, since values imply ultimate goals, one must ask: struggle for what? In its simplest form, this question can be answered by saying that the ultimate goal of the Chinese Communists is the proletarianization of the Chinese people. In other words, the model to which all Chinese should aspire is the modern industrial worker. One can see the strength of this value in the often proclaimed goal of communization (see pp. 467 ff.): the transformation of the village into a factory, and of the peasant into a worker.

There is no historical or cultural basis for this value in Chinese society. Though the conviction that social mobility was open to all was deeply rooted in Chinese society, the ultimate ideal of mobility has never been the urban worker. A peasant in recent times might have aspired to become a worker, but he hoped that his children would rise to something higher, notably to become educated men. We can therefore say that a new *Weltanschauung,* carried by an ideology, was necessary to implant this value in Chinese society. That *Weltanschauung* has been Marxism-Leninism, with its central doctrine that history inexorably will lead to the proletarianization of the entire world.

We can therefore see that the proclamation of a capitalist restoration in the Soviet Union would take away the historical-philosophical pillars on which the Chinese Communist values and ideals of proletarianization rest.

If this book had been written ten years ago, the discussion of the role of the Soviet Union in Chinese Communist ideology would not have caused major problems. However, the Sino-Soviet ideological conflict has created serious dilemmas for the Chinese Communists; these seriously affect their image of the Soviet Union.

Before we consider these dilemmas, let us look at the Chinese Communist view of the world today. The present stage of history, according to them, is marked by the struggle of socialism against imperialism. The modern manifestation of the class struggle is the fight of the emerging nations against the imperialists. The Chinese Communists see the arena of struggle not among the established proletariats of the developed nations but among the emerging proletariats of the underdeveloped nations. Just as they achieved victory within their own country by a revolution fought out in the hinterland and ended by capture of the cities, the Chinese Communists now feel that world revolution must first be organized in the poor countries and from there proceed to victory over the rich countries. One might, for example, cite their great interest in Latin America, which they regard as the testing ground of their view of contemporary world history. They believe that the growing wave of revolution in the poor nations will inevitably lead to continuing international crises, for imperialism cannot peacefully accept its own demise.

The Chinese Communists believe not only that coexistence is impossible in the long run between capitalist and socialist nations, but also that conflict will break out among the capitalist nations themselves. Their predictions are similar to those which Stalin made in the spring of 1929, when the world seemed at peace.[17]

Given such a view of the world, one can see why the Chinese Communists assign themselves a major role in these world revolutionary forces. As the greatest of the world's underdeveloped countries and the first to have undergone total social revolution, they see themselves as carrying the burden for world proletarianization, in contrast to the Soviet Union which, as a nation of an established proletariat of a developed country, has refused to shoulder it fully. Such a view of the world also makes it clear why they regard their practical ideology as of major significance for revolutionary movements in the underdeveloped nations.

The Chinese Communists, in taking a hostile attitude toward the Soviet Union, not only fight the Soviets abroad, but within China; in contrast to what prevailed during the early 1950's, they are trying to expunge every trace of Soviet influence. The Russian language has been dethroned and replaced by English; Soviet methods have been at-

---

[17] Stalin, *Problems of Leninism* (Moscow, 1954), p. 299.

tacked and ridiculed; revisionism, by which word the Chinese designate both the external and internal practices of the Soviet Union, has
been declared to be the mortal foe of the thought of Mao Tse-tung. The
violent attacks once directed against Yugoslavia have now, in essence,
been replaced by direct attacks on the Soviet Union, with the exception
of the accusation of a capitalist restoration. In effect, the Soviet Union
is regarded by the Chinese Communists in much the same terms as
the Trotskyites regarded it in the 1930's, namely as a "degenerate
workers' state."

The major ideological dilemma faced by the Chinese Communists
can be stated through the following question: How can they continue
to proclaim the Soviet Union as the first socialist state, and yet attack
it with such bitterness? The simplest answer is that they believe the
eventual struggle between capitalism and socialism will sooner or later
force the Soviet Union to reassume its historical role as leader of the
world-wide revolutionary movement. Thus, they would say that their
ideological conception of the Soviet Union shows its "correct" historical
reality, but their attacks on it expose its "incorrect" contemporary
actuality. By their actions, they hope to bring reality and actuality back
into line.

However, their attacks on the incorrect actuality of the world's first
workers' state cannot but do harm to their own values of proletarianization. In the early 1950's, they preached that whatever was Soviet was
proletarian, and whatever was proletarian was good. They no longer
preach the former, and, in fact, no longer so loudly preach the latter.
Despite continued adherence to the ultimate value of proletarianization, they have shifted away from immediate stress on proletarian
values. This change in attitudes perhaps is tied in with their present-
day greater orientation to agriculture and light industry. Proletarianization of the peasantry has become a distant goal which must await
a technological transformation of rural China that can only come
about after decades.

There has been a noticeable slackening of emphasis on proletarian
values, but Chinese Communist belief in the unilinear development
of history has grown stronger. This belief lies at the basis of their indications that a final struggle between socialism and capitalism is
inevitable, that peaceful coexistence cannot be made into an ideological principle, as implied in the Italian Communist idea of structural
reform (a belief that socialism will evolve gradually under conditions
of continuing peace). Although the Chinese Communists have put the
weight of emphasis on their practical ideology, it is tightly linked to
their pure ideology of Marxism-Leninism. Thus one can say that their

conception of the role of the Soviet Union still holds a key position in their pure ideology.

In discussing their *Weltanschauung*, we must also mention their view of the United States. Though their attacks on the United States and the Soviet Union sometimes appear to be similar, there has so far been a basic difference: the United States is the enemy. They regard it as the leading capitalist and imperialist nation, irrevocably committed to halting the world revolutionary movement. Since the focus of that movement, in their view, has shifted from the developed to the underdeveloped nations, counter-revolutionary actions led by the United States are mainly directed toward that part of the world. Given China's revolutionary status and role in the world, the Chinese Communists regard the enmity between the United States and China as fundamental. This does not mean that they believe a major war between these two countries is necessarily in the offing. Following their own experiences which gave them victory only after decades of struggle, they see this enmity lasting for years and decades. Periods of peace and even collaboration between the two countries are conceivable, comparable to their united front with the Kuomintang between 1936 and 1946. But peace and collaboration cannot change the fundamental nature of the relationship.

The Chinese Communists' conception of the United States is intimately related to their idea of the Soviet Union. If the former is the "enemy," then Russia should be the "friend" who, in China's present state of material weakness, protects it against any threat.

Since the central value of the Chinese Communists' ideology is struggle, they believe that nothing can be accomplished without struggle. Thus, for example, in thought reform, struggle between the individual and the group will be carried to a point of polarization, at which point contradictions are resolved and the processes of unity set in once again. In many ways, they have adopted similar tactics in their dealings with the Soviet Union, in the face of recent Soviet reluctance to grapple any further with the Chinese. But, they deeply believe that all struggle springs from objective sources. In thought reform, struggle is not created; rather, latent and unconscious struggle is made manifest and conscious. Thus they see their struggle with the Soviet Union arising from the objective fact of world-wide conflict. Every intensification of that conflict confirms their beliefs that the struggle is real and not artificial. In their view, the more imperialism resorts to force, the more it confirms the Chinese Communist *Weltanschauung*.

In conclusion, we can say that, despite the Chinese Communists' stress on the thought of Mao Tse-tung, their *Weltanschauung* of

Marxism-Leninism remains the core of their pure ideology, and thus the core of their ideology of organization. Their present ideological conflict with the Soviet Union forces them to seek confirmation of the historical truths of Marxism-Leninism in the events of the actual world scene. Every intensification of the struggle between socialist and capitalist nations further confirms their beliefs.[18]

Ideology and Behavior

If pure ideology is the core of the total ideology of organization, practical ideology is its instrument for action. But the individual cannot use practical ideology until he has worked out "correct thought." By correct thought, the Chinese Communists do not mean simply a certain manner of thinking, but a manner of behaving. One can only know that an individual has attained correct thought through seeing his actual behavior. Correct behavior is manifested through correct speaking and correct acting. This the Chinese Communists call "taking a standpoint" (lich'ang).[19]

Thus, simply reading the classics of Marxism-Leninism and of the thought of Mao Tse-tung is not enough to produce correct thought. According to the basic process of creating ideology stated above (p. 29), correct thought can only come about through the unification of universal truth and concrete practice. Mao Tse-tung evolved his practical ideology through such unification. Each individual member of organization must repeat what Mao did, thus emerging with a manner of thinking similar to that of Mao. But since that manner of thinking is practical, it will be manifest through correct behavior.

Early in the preceding section, we stated that the values and norms of the total ideology are tools with which individuals are motivated to commitment and are given rational ideas for action. The values of the ideology are designed to bring about a moral and psychological trans-

---

[18] Our discussion of the *Weltanschauung* of the Chinese Communists is largely based on statements made by them in the recent Sino-Soviet ideological exchanges. Since the material available in English on these exchanges is voluminous, we shall only refer to a few relevant sources. See *Diversity in International Communism, A Documentary Record, 1961-1963* (Alexander Dallin, ed.) (New York and London, 1963), Document 106, pp. 726-727; William E. Griffith, *The Sino-Soviet Rift* (Cambridge, Mass., 1964), pp. 112-114, also Documents 1 (pp. 241-258), and 2 (pp. 259-288). For recent Chinese statements on the historical role of the Soviet Union, see Lo Jui-ch'ing, "In Remembering the Victorious War against German Fascism, Let Us Carry to the End the Struggle against American Imperialism," *Jenmin jihpao,* May 11, 1965; and an editorial entitled "The Historical Experiences of the Fight against Fascism," *Jenmin jihpao,* May 9, 1965.

[19] Lewis, *op. cit.,* pp. 53-56; see also note 8, above.

formation of the individual. By acquiring a pure ideology and internalizing its values, the individual develops commitment to the organization. The norms of the ideology give him practical ideas (principles and methods) for concrete action. By acquiring a practical ideology and learning its norms, the individual becomes an effective actor in the organization. When an organization consists of individuals with the same commitments and the same action ideas, it has a basis for solidarity.[20]

We have pointed out the differences between the pure and practical ideology of the Chinese Communists, but we have also stressed the link between them, notably through the theory of contradictions. We shall here suggest a more abstract way of describing that link. Karl Mannheim's conceptions of substantial and functional rationality have relevance for our analysis. The former he describes as "intelligent insight into the inter-relations of events in a given situation"; the latter he describes as an individual's means of acting "in such a way that it leads him to a previously defined goal." [21] The ideas of pure ideology are substantial rationality; the ideas of practical ideology are functional rationality. What we suggest is that the fundamental philosophical assumption underlying the total ideology of the Chinese Communists is a rational conception of world and man. The Marxist-Leninist view of the world may not be correct, but it is rational, not emotional. Similarly, as should become apparent in the subsequent sections on ideology as a communications system, the Chinese Communists regard practical ideology as taking concrete expressive form through systematic sets of categories and language. The Chinese Communists are not unaware of the emotional aspects of ideological indoctrination; Mao

---

[20] Apter makes a distinction between the identity and solidarity aspects of ideology. He states that ideology "helps to perform two main functions: one directly social, binding the community together, and the other individual, organizing the role personalities of the maturing individual." David E. Apter, "Ideology and Discontent" in *Ideology and Discontent*, pp. 18-21. Apter's two functions, we suggest, are comparable to the conceptions of class and individual ideologies discussed earlier. Our conception of ideologies of organization indicates that ideology also has a political function, namely the creation of organizational solidarity.

We regard ideologies of organization as instruments of change. By creating practical ideologies fitted to concrete conditions but derived from pure ideologies, often of foreign origin, they are able to effectuate change in the face of conservative ideologies that are deeply rooted in local tradition and culture. What makes it possible for them to effectuate change is their ability to generate new organization.

[21] Karl Mannheim, *Man and Society in an Age of Reconstruction* (New York, 1954), pp. 52-53.

Tse-tung, for example, speaks of the "emotional stage in cognition." [22] They have often, in the past and now, made use of traditional and nationalist appeals to gain support from people; all these appeals were aimed at commonly held feelings. However, when it comes to organizational processes of ideological indoctrination, such as thought reform, the approach is fundamentally rationalistic. It is thinking, not feeling, which the Chinese Communists stress. Thus we may say that the Chinese Communists have created an ideology of organization that gives individuals both substantial and functional rationality. The commitment and the action of individuals that ensue from such an ideology rest on a common foundation of rationality.

The subject of ideology and behavior takes us into the realm of psychology which neither our knowledge nor available studies permit us to discuss adequately. In the following paragraphs we shall therefore only make some observations which are relevant to the general subject of ideology and behavior.

One of the most important questions of concern to us is whether "thought reform" (szuhsiang kaitsao) can produce "correct" behavior in the individual. Thought reform is, in effect, the method by which ideology is created within the individual. Since it is intensive and time-consuming, it is usually only the cadres who fully undergo it. Other means, such as mass movements and propaganda, are used to bring ideology to the masses. Every individual who aspires to become a member of the Party must go through the process of thought reform. First, the Party collects as complete a dossier (tangan) as possible on his background. If he measures up, he becomes a candidate member. Then, in Party small group sessions, he must recite, day after day, every detail of his personal life, both public and private. His statements are checked against the dossier. As the recital goes on, the group begins to criticize him intensely. This or that deed of his life, or fact of his background, is analyzed in great detail and criticized with vehement hostility. All the while, the individual is forced to use the categories and language of the ideology to analyze himself. Criticisms from the group are stated in similar ways. When he has completed his recital, he has made public every shred of what was earlier private. Moreover, he faces a hostile group that attacks every fault of his. This is the point of juxtaposition of opposites, when the contradictions have become most acute. At this time, the attitude of the group changes, and they begin to "help" him develop a correct standpoint. All this, one must add, does

---

[22] "On Practice," in Selected Works (Chinese edition), I, 274.

not only take place in Party small group sessions. The candidate member must go forth and prove himself through correct actions. If he
finally arrives at the point of correct behavior, the group will then recommend that he be formally taken into the Party.

Though thought reform has been used with varying intensity, and
sometimes may be little more than play-acting, it is the basic method of
ideological indoctrination of the Chinese Communists. A fair amount
of Western literature on the workings of thought reform now exists. The
general conclusion of this literature appears to be that thought reform
has a deep psychological impact on those who undergo it, although the
literature is not in agreement on the nature and durability of its effects.[23] Similarities between thought reform and "group therapy" practiced in the United States indicates that there are valid psychological
foundations to thought reform.

Since we have little direct evidence to indicate what the actual
effects of thought reform on the Chinese Communist cadres are, let
us make a few observations which would suggest possible effects. In this
respect, let us indicate two impressions gained from years of inter-
viewing refugees from Communist China in Hong Kong. First, these
refugees, both intellectual and nonintellectual, are articulate; and
second, they have the habit of analyzing (fenhsi) everything. Even
peasants, dirty and clad in rags, will talk with eloquence about their
experiences. The sociologist finds it rewarding to talk with refugee
intellectuals, for they usually understand exactly what he wants. The
Communists have always had a policy of forcing individuals to speak
out (fayen), not just in group sessions, but in almost all collective
settings. There has been a great campaign to make people literate and
get them to participate in public processes through the expression of
opinions. In addition, the Chinese Communists have a habit of analyzing everything that happens in everyday life. If a minor industrial accident occurs, meetings will be held in which every human and material
factor in the accident is discussed. Individuals may resent this, but no
one can avoid participating when he is there.

If articulation and analysis are characteristics of everyday life, this
applies even more so to "Party life." Party life is mostly talk, discussion, group interaction, criticism and self-criticism. Every individual

---

23 For example, Robert J. Lifton, *Thought Reform and the Psychology of Totalism*
(New York, 1961), "Thought Reform of Chinese Intellectuals, A Psychiatric Evaluation," *The Journal of Asian Studies*, XVI:1 (November 1956), 75-88, " 'Thought Reform' of Western Civilians in Chinese Communist Prisons," *Psychiatry*, XIX:2 (May
1956), 173-195; Edgar H. Schein, "The Chinese Indoctrination Program for Prisoners
of War," *Psychiatry*, XIX:2 (May 1956), 149-172.

Party member must participate actively in these processes of articulation and analysis.

Anticipating our subsequent discussion of ideology as a communications system, the least we can say is that the individual, through thought reform and similar processes, acquires the categories and language of the ideology. He learns to speak like a Communist. Moreover, since speaking must be accompanied by acting, he also learns to act like a Communist. In sum, on the surface at least, he develops "correct behavior."

In this respect, one can say that thought reform gives the individual norms, that is, rational tools for action. It is thus not uncommon to find, in Hong Kong, anti-Communist refugees whose way of thinking and acting is still essentially the same as it was on the Mainland. Such refugees have changed their pure ideology, but have carried the practical ideology with them out of China.

If it is not difficult to conceive of ideology inculcating special categories and language, it is more difficult to conceive of a fundamental moral and psychological transformation of the individual. The values of Chinese Communist ideology diverge sharply from traditional Chinese values. Thus, struggle differs from harmony, the stress on public life differs from the earlier Chinese love of privacy, collectivism differs from earlier beliefs in individuality, and proletarianization, as we said, has no historical basis in Chinese traditional values. If the ideology of the Chinese Communists is an instrument of value transformation, it is not easy to see how such a transformation could be successful in the face of such a traditional cultural heritage.

Our earlier observation on the habits of articulation and analysis among refugees suggests that the values of rationality have spread widely through China. Both the substantial rationality of the pure ideology and the functional rationality of the practical ideology can be said to have contributed to this phenomenon. Although China has a long history of civilization, it does not have a tradition of analysis. Chinese intellectual writing of the last few centuries, by comparison with that of Europe, has tended to be superficial and unsystematic. Most likely, it was under the guerrilla conditions of Yenan, where the collection of intelligence was so important a military-political function, that the Chinese Communists acquired their habit of analysis. This habit of analyzing everything, including all individuals with whom one comes into contact, cannot but produce some fundamental change in an individual.

Though the psychological transformation of the individual may come about through the rationality imparted by the ideology, his moral transformation can only come about if the ideology also imparts moral force. Chinese Communist ideology has such moral force—because it can often only be sensed, it remains elusive. The Chinese Communists speak of the forces of world history which are universal and cosmic. Though this belief clashes with traditional Confucian beliefs of *tao* (something akin to "natural law"), it bears certain similarities to the Taoist belief in Heaven as a real force. That Taoist belief, which had become widespread in China, regarded Heaven as having an independent will.[24] It is significant, in this respect, that Chinese rebellions in past centuries have often had religious ideologies, notably Taoist and Buddhist.

We have already indicated that the practical ideology of the Chinese Communists evolved under the concrete conditions of the Chinese Revolution. However, despite the fact that its pure ideology of Marxism-Leninism has its origins outside of China, there may be elements in it which link up with deeper Chinese cultural traditions. We suggest that the rationality of the ideology has come from Europe, but that its morality has its origins in the Chinese past, specifically in the earlier religious ideas of Heaven, so closely associated with rebellion.

If the emotional appeals of Chinese communism (chiefly expressed through nationalism) are added to those of its rationality and morality, a combination of elements results which must have a profound impact on those exposed to them. Thought reform is a method of identity transformation which is designed to indoctrinate the individual with an essentially rational pure and practical ideology. However, along with it come moral and emotional appeals which undoubtedly are major factors in the transformation.[25]

In sum, we suggest that thought reform has a range of instruments to produce motivation for commitment in individuals, and that, in all likelihood, it has been widely successful in bringing about identity transformations in individuals.

One further observation must be made about ideology and behavior. Since the ultimate aim of ideological indoctrination is to produce organizational solidarity, the individual can only create and maintain his commitment within the organization, or, more specifically, within

---

[24] C. K. Yang, *Religion in Chinese Society* (Berkeley and Los Angeles, 1961), pp. 247-253.

[25] Barnard, long ago, called attention to the functional importance of morality in executive roles; Chester Barnard, *The Functions of the Executive* (Cambridge, Mass., 1938), pp. 258 ff., and especially pp. 274 ff. The cadre, in effect, is trained to be an executive.

a group. If the organization is the Party, that group will be an elite group. The individual's reward for commitment and action is elite status. However, once in the group, the individual will constantly be exposed to group pressures that reinforce his rational, moral, and emotional commitments. Thought reform continues all the time. It is probably these factors that help explain the remarkably low rate of cadre defection from Communist China. Since the psychological ties of the cadre are so closely linked to a group (though its real membership may constantly change), leaving it for exile could have deep psychological consequences. The role of the group in creating and maintaining correct thought in the individual thus is crucial.

The purpose of the processes of ideological indoctrination, notably thought reform, is to create a political elite of cadres. Armed with pure and practical ideology, the cadres are members of an elite organization and leaders in society. However, as we state various times in this book, two new elites appear to be developing in Communist China: the educated professionals and the red cadres, symbolized by the oft-heard slogan "red and expert." [26] The bifurcation of elites suggests that another set of values may be operating which are not the same as those described above.

The educated professionals have periodically been attacked because of "individualism," and one can presume that this charge is justified. Education in Communist China operates on individual competitive principles, as it does elsewhere. As a result, the professional acquires through education a unique personal identity (as an "expert") which cannot be taken from him, though sometimes he is not permitted to exercise his expertise.

The value of expertise in China stems from the introduction of Western technology. That value has been further reinforced by the Chinese Communist ideological goal of the ultimate industrialization of China. During the early 1950's, as we shall see in our chapter on management, they elevated the value of expertise to a point which almost seemed to be higher than the value of "red." During the Great Leap Forward, they reversed the position of the two values. One can see the relationship between the two values in the question of proletarianization and industrialization. Proletarianization is essentially a human goal; it calls for the transformation of human beings. Indus-

---

[26] These two elites may be regarded as elites of prestige and power, respectively. There is no new elite of wealth in China, since the basis of sustained wealth, namely private property, in effect no longer exists. On the matter of status and wealth in the Soviet Union, see Alex A. Inkeles and Raymond A. Bauer, *The Soviet Citizen* (Cambridge, Mass., 1959), p. 152.

trialization, however, is a technical goal; it calls for the transformation of things. These two goals can also be conceived in terms of our discussion of the human and technical order (see pp. 231 ff.). In the early 1950's, the Chinese, in effect, argued that industrialization would lead to proletarianization. During the Great Leap Forward, they argued the reverse.

The value of expertise is essentially a technical goal, in the sense that the educated individual aspires to acquire specialized skills and knowledge. The value of "red" is essentially a human goal, in that it requires the total transformation of an individual, a "resocialization," as the sociologists say. However, the human consequence of expertise appears precisely to be "individualism." And individualism is in its essence anti-organizational. These consequences of expertise are what the Chinese Communists have in mind when they attack the professional intellectuals. However, on theoretical and empirical grounds it can be argued that the indoctrinated red cadre develops capacities for organizational commitment and solidarity, but at the cost of not becoming a technical expert himself. The Chinese Communist ideal of uniting the values of red and expert within the same individual has not worked, according to their own admission.

The present-day educational system of Communist China has its origins, not in schools copied from the Soviet Union, but in Western-type schools introduced into China three-quarters of a century ago. As in contemporary Hong Kong, these schools were attended mostly by children of the growing urban bourgeoisie of the coastal cities. Their values derive from Western doctrines of "liberalism," which stressed competition, individualism, and technical proficiency. Soviet educational influence of the early 1950's contributed to strengthening these values.

The types of ideological indoctrination we have described relate to cadre-training, not to formal education. They serve essentially political and organizational purposes. Since bourgeois influence is still strong in China's higher schools, it is significant that the Chinese Communists have, with the exception of the early 1950's, continuously stressed that the bulk of their cadres must come from the worker and peasant population. At the present time, when Peking is calling for the training of a new revolutionary generation, that stress has become even greater than before.[27]

---

[27] In the past, strong Chinese emperors, acutely concerned with maintaining the stability of the political system, often reached down deep into society to find recruits. For example, Ping-ti Ho says about the first Ming emperor: "The extremely wide

Thus we may say that the bifurcation of elites has its roots in the competing values of red and expert. The Chinese Communist ideology of organization strives to create "correct" behavior in individuals, but chiefly in the political elite of cadres. A competing set of values (sometimes attacked under the label of "modern revisionism") has given rise to a different kind of behavior in the social elite of professionals.

The Theory of Contradictions

We now come to the central idea of the thought of Mao Tse-tung, the theory of contradictions. The two major philosophical writings of Mao Tse-tung are a pair of essays called *On Contradiction* and *On Practice*. The fact that the two essays are usually referred to together not only indicates the centrality of the notion of contradictions in Chinese Communist ideology, but also that contradictions are regarded as having practical functions. This notion, formally called "the law of the unity of opposites," is the most important specific theory which the practical ideology has taken from the general body of theory of the pure ideology. It is the core of "the thought of Mao Tse-tung"—the practical ideology of the Chinese Communists. Its practical functions are indicated by a statement in *Jenmin jihpao*: "True Marxist-Leninists Must Use the Law of the Unity of Opposites to Resolve Problems." [28]

There are two types of contradictions, according to Mao Tse-tung in his speech "On the Question of Correctly Resolving Contradictions among the People": contradictions "between the enemy and ourselves," which are "antagonistic," and contradictions "among the people," which are "nonantagonistic." The law of unity of opposites does not apply to the former—sooner or later the enemy is to be destroyed and unity to be created by "ourselves." But it does apply to the latter—nonantagonistic contradictions can be resolved by peaceful means.

The theory of contradictions has been put to three practical uses. First, it has been used for analysis, as described in our discussion of the dialectical conception of Chinese society in the last part of this chapter. Second, it serves as a basis for behavioral norms, particularly in group settings such as thought reform—the juxtaposition of individual and

---

range of social statuses from which his officials and generals originated would seem to suggest that the amount and degree of social mobility represented among them were unprecedented since the founding of the Han Dynasty in 206 B.C." (*The Ladder of Success in Imperial China* [New York and London, 1962], p. 216.) Despite mythology to the contrary, the Yüan Mongols relied heavily on a traditional bureaucratic elite to rule the country. Many of these bureaucrats remained loyal to the Yüan after 1368.

[28] *Jenmin jihpao*, August 8, 1964.

group through struggle which sharpens contradictions to a point of polarization leading to a dialectical resolution. Third, the theory of contradictions has been used as an approach to create and use organization. This use we shall discuss here.

One of the most revealing documents on the use of contradiction in the organizational thinking of the Chinese Communists is a little-known speech from the early 1940's of Liu Shao-ch'i, never made public in China, but available in a clandestine publication put out by the Malayan Communist party. In this speech, Liu stated: "Democracy and centralism—these are two contradictory concepts." Liu had taken the familiar Leninist concept *democratic centralism*, where "democratic" was merely an adjective modifying "centralism," and had split it into two nominal entities. The Chinese Communists understand "democracy" essentially as impulses coming from below, in contrast to "centralism," which means impulses coming from above (see p. 86). Therefore, Liu, in effect, maintained that there is a necessary contradiction between these two types of impulses. Why this is so, Liu made clear in the beginning of his speech, when he stated that the juxtaposition of leaders and followers always gives rise to contradictions.[29]

Liu's speech was replete with discussions on contradictions, indicating that the notion of contradictions is inherent in Chinese Communist ideological thinking. However, Liu made a startling assertion which indicated that the Chinese Communists also regard contradictions as inherent in organizational function. Liu began his speech with the statement that the Party is a "contradictory structure." Such an idea would appear to be at variance with the commonly held notion that every Communist party must have monolithic unity. Subsequently, however, Liu made it clear that the Party must be based on absolute unity as to principle. Concretely this means that, once a decision has been made, "the minority follows the majority." However, Liu indicated that this does not mean that the minority should therefore give up its original opinions; he stated clearly that "one must in principle hold on to one's own opinions." [30] Unfortunately, without going into detail, he cited the

---

29 Liu Shao-ch'i, *Tsuchih-shang ho chilü-shang ti hsiuyang*, Hoover Library Chinese Collection 4292.52 7294.2. This speech was given by Liu Shao-ch'i before the Central China Party School sometime in the early 1940's. It is in the same category as his other writings on training and organization written approximately at the same time. The publication is dated April 5, 1952. A postscript states that it was published without having been "personally emended" by Liu Shao-ch'i. For a biography of Liu Shao-ch'i, see Howard L. Boorman, "Liu Shao-ch'i: A Political Profile," *The China Quarterly* 10 (April-June 1962), 1-22.

30 *Ibid.*, p. 12. "Opinion" (*ichien*) is a commonly used word in the Chinese Communist vocabulary. Everyone must have "opinions," for it is only thus that "discus-

Sian incident of 1936, when the fate of the captured Chiang Kai-shek was being decided by the Communists, as an instance where the minority ultimately turned out to be right.

If we put Mao's notion of nonantagonistic contradictions together with Liu's notion of the Party as a contradictory structure, we can say that nonantagonistic contradictions are a basic aspect of Party organization, and thus of organization in general. The Party must, of course, have unity based on absolute agreement as to principle; but such unity comes about through the workings of the law of unity of opposites.

Liu's argument implies that contradictions within the Party take two forms. First, they take the form of contradictions between those at the top and those at the bottom. In our subsequent discussion on decentralization, we shall find that the Chinese Communists indeed felt that there was a contradiction between concentrated power in Peking and dispersed power at the provincial level (see pp. 89-90). Second, they take the form of cleavages of opinions within Party committees, notably within the Politburo.

The application of the notion of contradictions to the Politburo suggests that there may be definite patterns in the way discussion is carried out in that body. Discussion (*t'aolun*) is the basic form of "Party life," whether at the bottom or at the top. As we have indicated, discussion is carried out according to certain principles and methods; it is not merely individuals getting together to exchange opinions and come to a decision. Discussion requires that, at a certain point, a juxtaposition or polarization of opinions develop. When that point is reached, a decision can be made. Then the minority must follow the majority.

If the Politburo does indeed function according to these principles of discussion, then one would expect that, as the discussion over particular issues sharpens, two opposed sets of opinions will emerge. Only one set of opinions can ultimately be adopted. This does not mean, however, that the contradiction will have irrevocably been resolved. Instead, as Liu Shao-ch'i indicated, the minority opinions must be preserved against the possibility that they may eventually prove correct.

Since only individuals can hold opinions, such a minority set of opinions implies the existence of an opinion group. This would appear to indicate that the Chinese Communists accede to the necessity for factions within the Party. However, there is a difference between an opinion group and a faction. Whereas a faction may be regarded as an opin-

---

sion" and "struggle" can take place. Moreover, at the inception of discussion, opinions must be divergent, then gradually fall into two opposite directions, and finally be resolved.

ion group with organized force behind it, an opinion group is simply an aggregate of individuals.

Although the Chinese Communists have combated factionalism as vigorously as any Communist party, indirect evidence concerning basic policy struggles within the Politburo indicates that the Chinese allow opinion groups. And although an organized opinion group is a faction and must be destroyed, groups constituted solely on the basis of a likeness of individual opinions are necessary to the process of the dialogue. There is a built-in safety factor in all this, for an opinion group without organization cannot act. The Politburo functions as a committee, and its members participate as individuals. This makes it possible for them to form an opinion group and precludes the development of factions with organized force behind them.[31]

If the law of the unity of opposites works in practice, it creates the possibility of dynamic politics within a framework of general agreement on ultimate ends and values. In discussion, for example, it makes possible debate through a sharp juxtaposition of views. In the process, all relevant facts and opinions come to the surface. As long as "the

---

[31] A classic case of a faction in the Soviet Politburo was that of Beria. Whether others in the Politburo were allied with him was less important than the fact that he commanded the organized branch-type force of the Secret Police. There has been factionalism in the history of the Chinese Communist party; the most important instance of factionalism after 1949 was that of Kao Kang and Jao Shu-shih, Party chiefs respectively in Manchuria and East China until 1955 (see pp. 333-334). It is possible that Marshal P'eng Te-huai and his close associate Huang K'o-ch'eng, respectively Minister and Deputy Minister of National Defense until 1959, also formed factions within the Party. As advocates of the professional approach, they favored the branch principle in military organization and had organized military force at their disposal, conditions generally making for factionalism. In contrast, others at the top level have at times disagreed with major policy but have apparently not formed factions. For example: Ch'en Yün opposed the new line emerging in 1957; Teng Tzu-hui disagreed with Mao Tse-tung on agricultural policy; Li Hsien-nien seems to have had serious reservations about the Great Leap Forward. We would say that these individuals formed opinion groups, but not factions. Chou En-lai seems to be preeminently the "man of opinions." He has no organized force at his command, but has voiced opinions on an extraordinary array of subjects, both domestic and foreign.

An organization structured along branch lines commands organizational power; it has soldiers, so to speak, to carry out its orders. But a committee has no organizational power at its command, though it includes men who may head branch-type organizations. A committee can talk, but it cannot move easily. The use of committees may be seen as a way of countering the danger of factionalism. In this respect, opinion groups perform some of the more useful functions of factionalism, namely expressing different interests and demands, without incurring the ultimate dangers of factionalism.

minority follows the majority," the basic unity of the group remains intact. The Chinese Communists would argue that, indeed, it becomes stronger, for final agreement reached through a process of discussion is more effective than agreement reached through unquestioning assent.

The theory of contradictions has organizational significance beyond the Party as well. In their fear of seeing one particular organizational sector concentrate too much power, the Chinese Communists have been in the habit of creating countervailing forces. The practice of dual rule, which we will discuss in the chapter on government, is a practice of using offsetting forces. The extensive use of committees and other coordinative agencies was often justified by the need to counterbalance the accumulating power of branch-type agencies, such as ministries. In provincial government, it has long been their habit to have an "insider" (that is, a local man) as governor and an "outsider" as Party secretary.

Aside from the organizational approaches based on the theory of contradictions, the Chinese Communists sometimes appear committed to preserving contradictions even when it is not necessary. After the complete nationalization of private business in 1956, one could have expected a proclamation to the effect that a bourgeoisie no longer exists, inasmuch as there is no bourgeoisie in the Soviet Union. However, despite severe attacks on the national bourgeoisie, it remains one of the official classes of Chinese society. One of the most significant manifestations of this commitment to the preservation of contradictions may be the practice of not liquidating opponents. Those accused of "rightism" in 1957 and 1958 suffered badly, yet were subsequently rehabilitated. At the highest political levels, those who opposed Mao's grand vision of continuing social mobilization receded into oblivion, but later came back into prominence when their services were needed.

The three practical uses of the theory of contradictions are closely linked together. Organization is marked by contradictory elements. Despite the fact that they may be nonantagonistic, this cannot be known until they are brought to a level of consciousness. Analysis, using the theory of contradictions, reveals what and where the contradictions are. But analysis must be followed by behavior. Thus it is imperative that analysis lead to discussion (t'aolun), in which the contradictions can be revealed and resolved. Given the Chinese Communist conception of thought (szuhsiang), it is only within the individual and among individuals in a group that contradictions become real and can be resolved.

The theory of contradictions is a thread that starts in the pure ideology of Marxism-Leninism, goes through the practical ideology of the thought of Mao Tse-tung, emerges in discussion, and finally finds its way into the structure of organization.

IDEOLOGY IN ACTION

A System of Communications

One of the most important expressions of ideology in action is as a communications system in organization. Organizations cannot function without a constant flow of information. If the organization is systematically structured, then the flow of information must likewise be systematic. Ideology, as a systematic set of ideas, provides the basic elements of the communications system.

Practical ideology as a system of communications reveals itself in verbal expression. A communications system requires common categories of thought and a common language. Once a communications system develops categories and language, it becomes closed, because outsiders cannot understand the communications. Everyday language, in a sense, is a closed communications system, because "foreigners" cannot understand it. Its categories are those provided by the common culture, for which the language acts as a vehicle of expression. In addition to everyday language, all societies have communications systems of smaller dimensions. For example, every professionalized science may be viewed as a communications system—closed because special training is necessary before new recruits can understand and use it.

The practical ideology of the Chinese Communists is a closed communications system because it has a complex operational vocabulary which requires effort and perseverance to understand. People who know the Chinese language well are often misled into believing that they "understand" what the Chinese Communists are saying. Such false understanding comes from the fact that the Chinese Communists often use seemingly conventional words with special significance which only someone who has studied the ideology can understand. The words "discussion" and "opinion," mentioned above, are conventional words with special communicative significance.

It is not difficult to demonstrate the need of the Chinese Communists for good communications. Since China is a vast country, the leaders have need of a continuing flow of information on actual conditions. At the same time, they must transmit their policy commands to every corner of the country. This cannot be done unless there are standardized categories and language. If local cadres, for example, reported on political, social, and economic conditions in conventional terms, the leaders would have no basis for comparison and generalization. Standardization of economic language poses no problem in principle, for the Chinese Communists have accepted the idea that economic information must be relayed in the language of standard statistical series. However, the leaders need more than economic information. They also need precise political and social information, such as people's attitudes, capabilities, relationships. It is particularly for the transmission of this type of political and social information that practical ideology has evolved special categories and language.

The Chinese Communist concern with communications goes back to their long military history. As General Griffith has stated, "intelligence is the decisive factor in planning guerrilla operations." [32] The scattered guerrilla forces of the Yenan period had to report back to headquarters in systematic ways; otherwise, unified operations could not be planned. Given the importance attached by the Chinese Communists to political and organizational as well as military problems, communication from the guerrilla bands was required to report on much more than simple military questions. Thus the systematization of ideological categories and language was accomplished before the Chinese Communists came to power in 1949.

The fact that the communications system of the Chinese Communists is closed can partly be explained by the historical connection between intelligence and communications. The basic aim of military intelligence is to communicate to the insider in such a way that the outsider does not understand. Much of the obsession with secrecy, which the Chinese Communists share with the Soviet Communists, can be explained in this way. However, this explanation is not sufficient, for the communications system which we shall describe is public; it is manifest in the mass media which all can read. The Chinese Communists have their "internal communications" (neipu t'ungpao) which are not public. However, they rely heavily (if not mainly) on their public mass media for the transmission of important information. Intelligence communication requires that the insiders know the meanings of messages. This requires definitions. Thus, one would assume that, for purposes of public communication, the basic categories and language should be clearly defined, particularly when conventional terms have special significance. In fact, the Chinese Communists, despite great precision in the use of categories and language, show a consistent reluctance to define them. Thus, while editorial offices are carefully controlled to make certain that the right terms are always used, those same terms are rarely defined with similar precision.

---

[32] Samuel B. Griffith, Mao Tse-tung on Guerrilla Warfare (New York, 1961), p. 22.

One must therefore ask: how can the readers of the mass media know the meanings of key terms if they are not defined? This is a problem of particular concern to the student of Communist China. He sees a set of key terms used with precision and consistency, but does not know what they mean. Before we suggest an answer to the question, let us look at the problem of "meaning." A word may be said to be the expression of a formulated thought. When someone generates the same formulated thought as the person who first stated it in words, we can say that meaning was transmitted. This may be likened to the encoding and decoding of messages. As long as the categories and language of communication are systematic, the receivers of communication will decode the messages in the way they were coded, thus assuring congruence between the intent of a message and its interpretation.

The answer to our question about the meanings of key terms can be provided by considering the context in which the decoding of communication takes place. Mass media are not only to be read when a man is reclining in a comfortable chair, but mainly in "study" sessions. By "study," the Chinese Communists mean the organized reading and discussion of key ideological documents. A cadre will, for example, read and explain a key editorial in the *Jenmin jihpao*. Thus, it is through such oral transmission that the key terms are given meaning. One must remember that "study," like "discussion," goes on constantly. Therefore, over time, people learn the real meanings of these terms. In effect, only someone who has gone through an extended experience of "study" can fully understand the meanings of the categories and language. It is thus easy to see why the outsider finds it difficult to understand the language of the ideology. What he sees openly in the mass media, for example, are the coded messages. What he cannot see is the encoding and decoding of these messages, which take place within the organization.

Another characteristic of the categories and language of the ideology must be mentioned. Since a great amount of information flows down and up, categories and language must be precise enough to be applied practically, but also general enough to cover a wide range of different conditions. Policy orders are put in general terms, but they must be carried out under particular conditions. The local cadres must understand the intent of the central policy decision. If all key terms were exactly defined, it would make them too precise and so tie down the policy makers. On the other hand, the precision with which these key terms are used prevents them from being so vague and abstract that no one can apply them. It is the combination of precision of use — despite no definition — with reliance on oral transmission of meaning in "study" and "discussion" sessions, that assures the leadership of always

being able to communicate the intent of its decisions throughout the
length and breadth of organization.

Some writers have regarded the language of the ideology as a set of
signals.[33] Thus, when the official press, notably the *Jenmin jihpao,* uses
new terms for discussing major problems, the readers, who are sensi-
tized to terminology and its changes, interpret them as signals indicating a major policy change or decision. To cite an example: A student
at Tsinghua University in Peking who participated in the free discussions of late May 1957 said that discussion broke off suddenly when an
authoritative editorial appeared in the *Jenmin jihpao* on June 8 denouncing rightists.[34] The appearance of the word rightist and the general tone of the editorial were immediately interpreted as a policy signal
from the Politburo; thereupon the anti-rightist movement commenced.

Though we accept the notion of signals, the categories and language
of the ideology are more than that. The Chinese Communists have
developed a rich vocabulary which has in many ways changed the
Chinese language. Ideas and terms have come into popular usage
which never existed before. In fact, without these, the processes of
analysis and articulation mentioned above could not take place. One
of the major contributions of the practical ideology of the Chinese

---

[33] The notion of signals is a major point in Allen Whiting's study of the background to the Korean War. According to Whiting, the Chinese Communists sent
out signals about their intentions as early as August 1950, two months before
intervening in Korea. Looking at it strictly in terms of the arguments we are making,
the Chinese Communists could not expect people who are not a part of the communications system to interpret (i.e., give meaning to) those signals in a correct way.
 The first and major universe of communications is China, that is, all of China
within the Communist network. Here mechanisms have been laboriously created
to make certain that signals are always translated into meaning and action. Second,
there is a broader universe which may loosely be called "the Communist world."
Here the Chinese do not control the mechanisms of signal interpretation, but the
common language of Marxism-Leninism is preserved. Thus the Sino-Soviet dispute
has been carried on largely in terms of "principles." Beyond that, is there a
broader communications universe other than that of common human language and
diplomatic language? If the Chinese Communists wished their signals to be interpreted by the United States, would they have used language which is explicitly
intended for their own internal universe? I do not argue against Whiting's point
that internal Chinese signals were disregarded or misinterpreted by American observers. But I do argue that the Chinese think in terms of different universes of
communication. They do not talk to Western businessmen in the same way as they
do to visiting Communist leaders. Communication, like struggle, must always have
an "object" *(tuihsiang).* See Allen S. Whiting, *China Crosses the Yalu* (New York,
1960), pp. 53 ff., 168 ff.

[34] From a personal interview conducted in August 1958 in Hong Kong.

Communists has been the generation of these many new and useful categories and language. It has also given the Chinese a new manner of thinking.

The Mass Media

It is often difficult for Westerners, accustomed to the idea that Communist China is wrapped in secrecy behind a bamboo curtain, to realize how much open, rather than secret, communications are stressed in China. Given their deep concern with communications, the Chinese Communists, from the moment of victory, began to set up networks of mass media throughout the country. Today every part of the country has newspapers and radio stations which, each day, pour forth volumes of information. The few documents of "internal communication" that have come to the West, such as the *Work Bulletins* (*Kungtso t'unghsün*) of "the People's Liberation Army," indicate no fundamental difference between the type of communication that goes through internal channels and public communications. The quantity of printed material from Mainland China in Western libraries has already reached staggering proportions; English translations of this material are so numerous that it would take years to read them all. Far from being stereotyped propaganda, this material is often rich and diverse, giving detailed insight into real conditions.

Despite this volume of available material, the impression is still widespread in the West that little is known about Communist China. Though the reason usually given for this impression is false, the fact of the impression is true. Communist documents cannot be read as if they were written in conventional language. In a Hong Kong newspaper one can translate almost any item and have it come out in perfectly intelligible English; but a translated Communist newspaper article will come out in jargon, which many readers will dismiss as "propaganda." We have, in the preceding section, tried to indicate the reasons for this. The translated but unexplained products of a closed communications system will always appear jargonistic; just as, for example, a French article on economics translated into English will not be *prima facie* intelligible to the ordinary English reader.

To show how the ideology functions as a communications system, we shall, in this section, examine the mass media of Communist China, specifically the newspaper. Since, as we have indicated, newspaper articles constitute key documentation (*wenchien*) for "study" and "discussion" sessions, we shall categorize the types of articles that appear in the newspapers in order to show the kinds of communication that are transmitted.

Lenin, in his earliest major work on organization, *What Is to Be Done*, devoted a long section to a discussion of the need for an all-Russian newspaper and stated: *"There is no other way of training strong political organization except through the medium of an all-Russian newspaper."* [35] The newspaper appears every day, and so can communicate changes in policy and conditions as they occur. The *Jenmin jihpao*, official organ of Party and government, is read throughout China on the day of publication—it is printed in six simultaneous editions, aside from the Peking edition (Shanghai, Canton, Sian, Mukden, Chungking, and Urumchi). Radio stations relay its editorials and important articles. Every meeting, regardless how small, must start off with documentation; if major problems are under discussion, then the documentation must include the relevant articles in the *Jenmin jihpao*.[36] The mass media present the language to be used; discussion is the process of transforming language into meaning and action.

We have classified the articles that appear in the newspapers into six major types. Each type of article has functional significance.

A first type may be called articles on policy decisions. All mass media, particularly newspapers, devote a considerable amount of space to the publication of major policy speeches, policy directives, and explanatory articles relating to policy decisions. Dissemination of policy decisions ranges from those which are made at a national level to those made at a local level. As we shall indicate in our chapter on management (see pp. 238 ff.), all organizations require the setting of policy, that is, the goals of organizational action. Since Communist China is an organizational society *par excellence*, policy statements of all varieties and implications are handed down all the time.

Major policy statements of the broadest significance are, of course, published in the leading national newspapers. However, the habit of publishing policy statements also exists at the lowest levels of organization. For example, an enterprise will announce a policy decision in much the same way as the national newspapers: by printing speeches on the new policy by the factory manager and the Party secretary, setting forth the general directives, and adding explanatory comments. Such enterprise policy statements usually include the following elements: goals and targets, reasons for the decision, a review of what went on be-

35 Lenin, *Selected Works* (Moscow, 1952), p. 576.

36 On mass media in China, see Fredrick T. C. Yu, *Mass Persuasion in Communist China* (New York and London, 1964); and Franklin Houn, *To Change a Nation, Propaganda and Indoctrination in Communist China* (Glencoe, Ill., 1961). The latter book is a rather mechanical emulation of Alex Inkeles' study *Public Opinion in Soviet Russia* (Cambridge, Mass., 1950).

fore, an indication of the sectors affected, and the means to be used to implement the decision.

A second type of article in the newspapers discusses concrete experiences in policy implementation. Almost every issue of any newspaper contains reports of experiences of some particular organizational unit. For example, a copy of the *Jenmin jihpao* selected at random (January 8, 1962), on its front page, reported on the experiences of (1) the winter production movement in Shanghai suburban villages, (2) a large production brigade in a Szechwan commune, (3) several communes in Kiangsi, and (4) wheat planting in one district of Kiangsu. Much of this reporting deals with production successes, but the purpose is not just to make propaganda. Attention is given to the means employed to achieve such successes.

The interminable recountings of these concrete experiences make the *Jenmin jihpao* one of the dullest newspapers in the world. Nevertheless, they have an important function. Concrete experiences are stressed because the Chinese Communists believe that policies are best understood in practice. The editors of *Jenmin jihpao* select the concrete experiences they wish to publicize, and cadres in similar lines of endeavor quickly get the point. To make these diverse experiences generalizable, the language used must be standardized so that individuals in different contexts will be able to apply the experiences. The categories and language of the ideology serve the important function of standardization.

Though only select experiences are published, all types of experiences are constantly reported upward, sometimes through public and at other times through internal channels. Concrete experiences provide the top leadership with vital information for decision-making. Economic plans, for example, are designed through a back-and-forth shuttling of information between ministries, regional agencies, and enterprises. The Chinese Communist habit of trying things out "experimentally" demands that the leaders have detailed and comparable information on concrete experiences before they can decide whether to transform experiment into policy.

A third type of article consists of discussions of general principles. In the *Jenmin jihpao*, such articles always appear on a special inside page. They are often extraordinarily long. These discussions of general principles, though seemingly unrelated to policy and reality, are intended to reveal the thought processes of the leaders concerning major questions. If such a discussion appears in the *Jenmin jihpao*, one can be sure that it reflects a dominant strain of thinking among the highest leaders, since the *Jenmin jihpao* is the highest official organ in the country. However, discussions of general principles also appear in less official newspapers, such as the *Takung-pao* and the *Wenhui-pao*. In the latter case, they may reflect a dominant strain of thinking which is not yet ready to be transformed into policy, or a nondominant strain of thinking which the leaders consider appropriate to have expressed; in other cases, discussions of general principles in these latter two newspapers may take the form of feelers. At any rate, they are not binding on the leaders.

One understands the necessity for these discussions of general principles by looking at the speeches of Communist leaders. Not only in China, but in other Communist countries, leaders give extraordinarily long speeches. Every speech, even those relating to minor policy decisions, starts out with a review of the over-all situation before it finally comes to the important message. The length of these speeches serves to communicate the manner of thinking of the leaders. The articles which discuss general principles can be regarded as comparable to the initial overviews of the speeches; but they are not followed by a policy announcement.

Discussions of general principles are a way of gauging the thinking of the leadership at a time when decisions have not yet been formally announced. Such discussions need not necessarily be followed by policy decisions. Circumstances may change, and the leaders will decide to pursue a new policy direction. However, if a decision actually follows, these articles, read in retrospect, provide valuable clues about the thinking that went into the decision. Often it is only as the result of a decision that one can find out what was really meant by the discussion of general principles.

Such discussions are published before decisions are made because they prepare the country, in particular the cadres, for the decision to come. Implementation of decisions is impossible under conditions of ignorance. The Communists call this pre-decision situation "distillation" (*yünniang*). Post-decision ideological discussions communicate the strain of thinking that won out. Here too, words are chosen with great care. A vocabulary is being built up for cadres to use when the time for implementation has come.

A fourth type of articles may be called criticisms. They discuss failures, errors, deviations, crimes, and shortcomings. Much criticism, of course, never appears in public print. However, if a particular kind of criticism serves as an example, just as a particular kind of concrete experience can serve as an example, then it will be published. Such criti-

cisms must never be general, for general criticism is the sole prerogative of the leadership, although lower level repetition of official general
criticism is allowed. Most prominent are criticisms directed against individuals. These are published all the way from *Jenmin jihpao* down
to the wall newspapers, *tatzupao*, of particular institutions. Criticisms
of situations, such as production failures, are also published. The newspaper column entitled *Party Life* (like its Soviet counterpart *Partiinaia
zhizn'*) is an important vehicle for the expression of criticism. "Why
Is There Still Commandism among Party Cadres in Our Factory" is
the title of a typical letter to the Party Life column. Every newspaper
has a special department to process letters from readers; these are all
answered, even though only a few are printed. Criticisms are published
more frequently in local newspapers, because these are closer to concrete reality. This is one reason why local newspapers are such important sources for the researcher.

These first four types of articles can be further classified according
to one of the favorite organizational principles of the Chinese Communists: "From Top down and from Bottom up" (*tzu-shang erh hsia,
tzu-hsia erh shang*) (see p. 86). Of the four types of articles mentioned,
the first and third are instances of communications going down. This
is information of a general character as it relates to policy and principle. The second and fourth are instances of communication going
up. This is information of a particular character—it is "concrete."

These first four types of articles also are in the category of what the
Soviets call *agitatsiia*, agitation. *Agitatsiia*, as Alex Inkeles puts it,
is "broadly directed toward the broad masses and seeks to acquaint
them with the party's slogans and decisions, to explain the policy of
party and government, and to mobilize all the workers for active and
conscious participation in the building of the new social order."
Agitatsiia is contrasted with *propaganda* which "is strictly defined as
the intensive elucidation of the teachings of Marx, Engels, Lenin, and
Stalin, and of the history of the Bolshevik party and its tasks." [37] The
distinction between agitation and propaganda, if we may use the English terms in their Russian sense, can be applied to the publications of
the mass media in China.

Agitation is specifically action-oriented, propaganda is not. If the
article serves to "arouse and educate the masses," it is agitation. But
if it serves the general "raising of consciousness," as the Chinese say,
then it is propaganda. Although it is often difficult to say whether an
article is agitation or propaganda, the criterion for judging is whether

---

[37] Inkeles, *op. cit.* (in n. 36), p. 41.

it directly or indirectly serves policy purposes. Thus, since the first four types of articles, in one way or another, relate to policy, they can be considered in the category of agitation.

A fifth type of article can be considered in the category of propaganda. This type consists of a wide variety of material: general ideological discussions, technical argumentation, foreign news, didactic literary tales, commentaries on theory and principles, and others. Propaganda articles appear in the latter part of the newspaper. Since they sometimes appear on the same page as the general discussions of principles, it is often not easy to judge whether the article on that page is propaganda or agitation.

Foreign-news articles are usually in the propaganda category. They are so slanted as to illustrate general theoretical conceptions, such as the evils of imperialism or the successes of socialism. The extensive reporting of Latin American events, for example, serves to illustrate the concrete manifestations of the Chinese Communist *Weltanschauung*.

The didactic literary tales illustrate basic principles of social behavior: loyalty and heroism of Party members, the need for discipline, the importance of discussion and criticism, the honor of work, the significance of study and investigation, and so on. The reader generally realizes that there is no immediate policy implication to these articles. They have much the same function as dramatic plays which are highly favored as methods of indoctrination. They set forth the positive and negative models toward which the people are to orient themselves.

A sixth type of article serves neither propaganda nor agitation functions, but "public information." Publications of technical journals, for example, fit into this category. News of natural disasters is regarded as public information and has a technical character until human beings are involved, when it becomes political. One of the most important categories of public information consists of advertisements, which are now prominently featured on the back pages of Chinese newspapers, including the *Jenmin jihpao*. With greater stress given direct exchange between production units, advertising is taking on ever-increasing importance. Publication announcements are also important items of public information. Interestingly, since China now has greater contact with the outside world, international airline schedules have also been published.

The bulk of articles published in national as well as local newspapers consists of the first four types, indicating the importance of the newspaper as an instrument of communication. Moreover, since these four types are written in ideological language, they are the most difficult for the outsider to understand. In these articles, we see how the communications system, albeit public, is in fact closed. Only through learning the categories and language of the ideology can the student understand what is meant.

The Function of Ideology in Organization

We have now discussed one aspect of ideology in action, namely ideology as a communications system. We shall now consider another aspect, namely ideology as a tool in the hands of leaders for using organization. Whereas in the preceding section we regarded practical ideology as a rich and varied body of categories and language, in this section we shall again treat pure and practical ideology as whole bodies of ideas, and see how they are used to activate organization.

So far we have spoken of organization in general terms, without specifying its parts. When we discuss concrete forms of organization in the body of this book, such as Party, government, enterprise, and so on, it will be clear that we do not regard either organization in particular or organization in general as an undifferentiated whole. As ideology, we can also liken organization to a machine with different parts that mesh to produce action. In ideology, we have suggested two major components into which it could be divided. Now, in organization, we shall suggest three major components. Through such an analysis, we shall indicate how pure and practical ideology serve to activate the various components of organization.

As a working conception, organization in general may be seen as a three-tiered structure. Since organizations are goal-oriented and thus require leadership and policy, we may regard the top tier of organization as consisting of those individuals and bodies of individuals who direct the organization. Once policy is set, it must be implemented. This requires that policy be translated into operational commands for each separate component of the organization. Implementation also requires men to give the orders and direct other men in carrying out the work called for. The former function is normally performed by staff men, who are the technicians of an organization. The latter function is performed by line men, who are its supervisors. We may thus regard the middle tier of organization as consisting of staff and line men. Since action ultimately must be carried out by workers, we may regard the bottom tier of organization as consisting of workers, understanding the word worker to mean anyone who does basic mental or physical labor in an organization.

The Chinese Communists tend to see organization as essentially consisting of three levels, a view similar to, though not exactly the same as, our working conception. For example, in industry the normal pattern of internal plant organization has become one of plant, shop, and production team. In the communes, the "three-level system of ownership" has officially become predominant: commune, production brigade, and production team (see pp. 484 ff.). Party and administrative organization are also largely seen in three levels: center, region, and basic-level. Within units of production, Party organization tends to fall into three levels: committee, branch, and team. This does not mean that all organization necessarily is divided into three levels, but rather that this is a common Chinese Communist conception of organization in general.

Let us now compare our working conception and the Chinese Communist conception of organization, taking as an example a factory. The factory is governed by a Party committee or a management council; the two may be the same or distinct, depending on time and circumstance. This is the top tier of organization. The factory will consist of a number of shops concerned with different operations; each shop is headed by a number of supervisors. These supervisors are the line men, for they are concerned with implementing and directing operations. However, attached both to the Party committee or the management council, and the shop supervisors, are a group of technicians whose task is to work out concrete operational details. Thus, what we call the middle tier of organization is not the same as the shop level of a factory, but comprises both technicians and supervisors. Since technicians have their main contact with management, and supervisors have their main contact with workers, this suggests that the middle tier of organization has a special function, namely linkage between top and bottom. The lowest unit of factory organization is the production team; its main task is physical or mental labor; it coincides well with our conception of the bottom tier of organization.

In our concern about how pure and practical ideology activate the various components of organization, the middle tier of organization has special importance. Since the middle tier of organization, in general, consists of staff and line men, it is interesting to note that Western organization theorists, whose empirical focus relates entirely to American and Western society, have written widely about the "staff-line conflict." As Robert Sampson says, "the problem of working out harmonious working relationships between the staff man and the line is still unresolved." [38] Staff men in American industry are generally educated professionals who do research and advisory work; line men tend to

---

[38] Robert Sampson, *The Staff Role in Management* (New York, 1955), pp. 24-25.

be men who have risen up the ladder from the bottom. Conflicts spring from their different backgrounds and temperaments, the relative importance of their jobs, the differential status they enjoy. As we shall see in our chapter on management, Communist China also has staff-line conflicts, and for reasons similar to those of the West. Technical staff men in Chinese factories tend to be the products of higher education, although a fair percentage are trained in the factory itself. On the other hand, the Chinese Communists, from 1949 on, have pursued a policy of promoting workers to managerial and line supervisory positions.[39] The staff-line conflict in Chinese factories has taken the form of conflict between the "intellectual" staff men and the proletarian line men. The conflict is further exacerbated by the fact that Party organization in factories tends to be largely of working class composition.

In addition to the staff-line conflict that characterizes the middle tier of organization, another type of conflict involving the middle tier has relevance to our concern with the function of ideology in organization. Writers on organization, such as Peter Drucker, have indicated that the proper functions of middle-level management pose great problems in contemporary American industry.[40] By middle-level management, Drucker means both staff and line men. The conflict, in essence, arises from the different perspectives of an industry's leaders at the top, and its staff and line men in the middle. The former are concerned with the broad goals of the industry; the latter with everyday operations. These different perspectives often make it difficult to promote middle-level managers to top management positions, and also make it difficult for top managers fully to understand the problems of the former; these and other problems give rise to conflicts.

The different perspectives of top and middle-level management in American industry are similar to those between top policy makers and administrators in the government of Communist·China. As we shall indicate in our discussions of government and management, the Party leaders in Peking, concerned with the broad goals of economic development, often were extremely impatient with lower-level planners, administrators, and managers, whom they accused of "conservatism" and excessive concern with "balancing." In other words, the Party leaders, like some American big-business executives, wanted to expand rapidly, but ran against the resistance of their "middle-level managers." Max Weber made a point which helps explain the conflict between

---

39 This is the policy of *t'ipa kungjen*, which was widely discussed in the literature of the early 1950's. See p. 168.

40 Peter Drucker, *The New Society* (New York, 1950), pp. 191 ff., 213 ff., 305-307.

leaders and administrators in Communist China, namely that professional bureaucracies can exercise control over their superiors because of the power of their technical knowledge.[41]

Our organizational analysis suggests three conclusions: first, the middle tier serves as a linkage between top and bottom; second, the middle tier is characterized by fundamental conflict of the staff-line variety; and third, the middle tier tends to be conservative, technically minded, and concerned with everyday operational problems. Having thus suggested the different components of organization, let us now see how pure and practical ideology can be used to activate them.

To approach this problem, let us use as a concrete example three phenomena of the Great Leap Forward, to which we shall refer again in different contexts in various other parts of this book. First, during the Great Leap Forward, professionals, who constituted middle administration in the national bureaucracy and middle management in industry, were ruthlessly attacked; large numbers were dismissed from their positions. Moreover, whole administrative and managerial structures were dismantled. Second, cadres, who may be regarded as line men, were told to leave their offices and directly lead the masses, as in the production teams. Third, the three years of the Great Leap Forward were marked by intensive propagation of ideology, particularly pure ideology; one need only recall the widespread utopian preaching of the imminent advent of pure communism heard in the summer and fall of 1958. Organizationally, the Great Leap Forward can be seen as an attempt to eliminate the middle and to join top and bottom directly; leaders and masses were to be in intimate relationship, bypassing the professionals who earlier stood between them.

From this example, and from others which could be cited, the conviction of the leaders emerges that through the intensive invocation of pure ideology, they could arouse the masses to action. Within organization, this took the form of Party cadres going into the industrial and agricultural production teams and preaching *Weltanschauung* to the workers and the peasants. Most characteristic of this preaching was its utopianism, the promise of a bright future just in the offing, "three years of suffering leading to a thousand years of happiness."

The positive function of utopian ideologies for inspiring the popular masses in revolutionary movements is well known. The use of utopian ideology by the Chinese Communists during the communization of 1958 can be explained by the fact (as we shall show in our chapter on

[41] Max Weber, *The Theory of Social and Economic Organization* (Glencoe, Ill., 1947), p. 338.

villages) that the Chinese Communists regarded communization—in which the peasant was finally to be liberated from his past—as another phase in China's continuing revolutionary process.

Utopianism has a negative side. As Karl Mannheim has indicated, utopianism also gives rise to hostility against an existing order. In the late 1940's, utopian hostility against the existing order took the form of terror directed against the gentry. One may therefore ask whether the utopianism of 1958 also generated mass hostility. Aside from the general belligerence against internal and external enemies of the new order, the year 1958 was marked by deep hostility against intellectuals and professionals, namely a class of people who occupied positions in the middle tier of organization. Thus, we might say that pure ideology was used by the leaders to appeal to the masses over the heads of the professionals, who were exercising constraints of the type described by Max Weber on the ambitious policies of the leadership.[42]

We suggest that those in the middle tiers of organization, such as administrators, are generally insensitive to the appeals of pure ideology. They are basically practical men, who have learned to distrust the continuing proclamation of ideas by their leaders. If they are susceptible to any ideology, it will be to practical ideology.

If there is a fundamental conflict between the staff men and the line men who constitute the middle tier of organization, then one would expect different values to appeal to them. In Communist China, the middle tier of organization, in the broadest sense, consists of expert professionals and red cadres. As we have indicated in our discussion of ideology and behavior, different values do indeed appeal to them. The former hold to values of expertise; the latter hold to values of "red." Modern professional bureaucracies, as described by Max Weber, are oriented toward expertise. Contemporary Chinese professionals may not accept the values of legal rationality of which Weber speaks, but their values of technical rationality come close to Weber's conceptions of expertise. These are not the values of the practical ideology of the Chinese Communists. That practical ideology, as we have indicated, is a set of ideas basically aimed at creating and using organization, whose core is constituted by its cadres. Thus we may say that the practical ideology has greatest appeal for the political cadres who form the great body of line men in the middle tier of organization.

---

42 The absence of pure ideology, that is doctrines of values and goals, makes it difficult for policy makers in democratic organization to reach down to the bottom and bypass the middle. Communication tends to be technical, which gives great powers to the middle levels of bureaucratic organization.

Our discussion has suggested two ways in which pure and practical ideology can be used to activate different components of organization. Pure ideology can serve as a tool to activate the bottom tier of organization. Practical ideology can serve as a tool to activate the line component of the middle tier of organization. In addition to these two ways of using ideology to activate organization, our discussion suggests a third, albeit nonideological way, of activating a component of organization. Since the values of expertise appeal to the staff component, that is the professionals, the leaders can always invoke those values if they are in great need of the services of the professionals. However, the values of expertise have anti-organizational and individualistic consequences. When early in 1961 Peking appealed directly to the professionals to help rescue the country from economic crisis, it also allowed liberalization to set in. Similarly, when it began to restrict the "small freedoms" once again in the summer of 1962, it loudly proclaimed the thought of Mao Tse-tung and sought to strengthen its cadres, who had been hurt by the rectification movements of the winter of 1960-1961.

Our analysis suggests that the different components of ideology and of organization give the leaders a tool for great leverage. Clearly there are contradictory elements in both ideology and organization. Though they create conflict, they also provide the leaders with multiple possibilities for action.

THE THREE-TIERED CONCEPTION OF ORGANIZATION

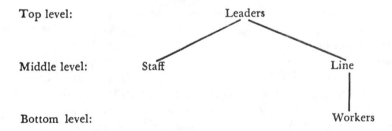

Top level: Leaders

Middle level: Staff   Line

Bottom level: Workers

THE DIALECTICAL CONCEPTION OF CHINESE SOCIETY

The thought of Mao Tse-tung, as we have indicated earlier, is not a body of doctrine, but a manner of thinking which, as practical ideology, is meant for use. Having dismantled the structure of the ideology and identified the theory of contradictions as its central idea, we are now ready to examine that manner of thinking directly. However, since the thought of Mao Tse-tung arose through "the unification of theory and practice," we cannot describe it abstractly, but only in connection with real problems.

In 1958 the leaders of Communist China launched an ambitious program of economic, political, and social development, known as the Great Leap Forward, which was designed, in a few short years, to lift China out of its backwardness and make it into a modern industrial nation. The Great Leap Forward was the product of a vision rather than of a plan. A plan is a carefully worked-out blueprint of action based on a matching of goals with capabilities. A vision is a total insight into the essential interrelationships of a situation. During 1956 and 1957 the Chinese Communists drafted a second five-year plan which was to guide them through the period of 1958 to 1962. Late in 1957, that plan was abandoned and a program initiated which was based on Mao Tse-tung's vision of Chinese society. Since the core of that vision was the insight that Chinese society was marked by essential economic, political, and social contradictions, and that rapid development could take place by resolving those contradictions, we shall call it the dialectical conception of Chinese society. Whereas the plan was essentially economic, Mao's vision of society encompassed all factors of societal dynamics: political, social, as well as economic.

Mao Tse-tung's vision of Chinese society arose from his manner of thinking. Applied to the reality of contemporary world history, this manner of thinking gave rise to Mao's vision of the struggle between imperialism and national revolutionary movements, which we have mentioned above. Applied to the reality of China, it gave rise to the dialectical conception of Chinese society. Since the Great Leap Forward was based on that conception, it must be regarded as the most momentous instance of ideology in action in the brief history of Communist China.

In the following pages, we shall try to reconstruct that vision. It is a reconstruction, for nowhere in the literature can one find a comprehensive presentation of such an analysis. Our reconstruction derives primarily from two of Mao's speeches and secondarily from the reflections of Mao's thinking in the writings and actions of men who prepared and carried out the program of the Great Leap Forward. The two speeches are: "The Ten Great Relationships," delivered in April 1956, and "On the Question of Correctly Resolving Contradictions among the People," delivered on February 27, 1957.[43] The first was never published but its

---

43 The speech was originally recorded on tape and widely distributed throughout the country for discussion. A copy of the tape has reportedly reached the outside

general content is known from references made to it; the second was published but in a highly condensed and edited version. Since the Chinese Communists lay such stress on action, we can make use of the action consequences of Mao's vision in order to reconstruct some of the details of that vision, even though they are not fully spelled out in his known speeches. Some of our secondary material thus derives from policies which were implemented during the Great Leap Forward; other material derives from statements made by various writers during the mid-1950's when the state and future of Chinese society were under serious discussion.

The two key elements in Mao's vision are the recognition of contradictions and the resolution of contradictions. Let us illustrate the recognition of contradictions by quoting a passage from the opening section of his February 1957 speech (which we shall hereafter refer to as the introduction):

Under present conditions, the so-called contradictions among the people include contradictions within the working class, within the peasant class, within the intellectuals; contradictions between the working and peasant classes; contradictions of workers and peasants with the intellectuals; contradictions of the working class and other toiling people with the national bourgeois class; contradictions within the national bourgeois class, and so on. Our government truly is a government that represents the interests of the people; it is a government that serves the people. But there are certain contradictions between it and the popular masses. These contradictions include contradictions of state interest and collective interest with individual interest, the contradiction of democracy and centralism, the contradiction of leader and led, the contradiction of bureaucratism of some workers in state agencies with the masses. This is also a contradiction among the people. In general, contradictions among the people are contradictions on a foundation of basic harmony of the people's interests.[44]

Let us now illustrate the resolution of contradictions by describing briefly an actual policy implemented during the Great Leap Forward, one called the "three-unification movement." This movement was aimed at uniting cadres, technicians, and workers into single work teams. Cadres are leaders; technicians are intellectuals; and workers are the masses. Judging from the quotation from Mao's speech, each must be seen as in a contradictory relationship to the others. The three-unification movement launched by the Party was aimed at resolving these con-

---

world. In June, the Chinese Communists published an official and emended version of the speech. It has remained a basic document in the ideological arsenal of the Chinese Communists until the present time.

44 *Jenmin shouts'e 1958*, p. 10.

tradtions and thereby creating a unity of opposites. Resolution was
not just the product of putting the three together. Rather, each was expected in effect to become the other: workers becoming technicians,
technicians becoming workers, and both sharing leadership with the
cadres. Thus the three-unification movement was an instance of attempted resolution of the political and social contradictions implied in
the above-cited quotation.

The dialectical conception of Chinese society was not universally
shared by all leaders. This is indicated by Mao's statement, in the February 1957 speech, that there are "contradictions between some individuals who correctly reflect objective laws and other individuals who
incorrectly reflect objective laws." Foremost among the latter undoubtedly was Ch'en Yün, then one of the most powerful members of the
Politburo, whose views can be seen in his concluding recommendations
to the Eighth Party Congress: "We must be prudent and practical, go
forward slowly, gather experiences, push ahead gradually." [45] It was
such thinking that was at the basis of the second five-year draft plan
which was replaced by the Great Leap Forward. It was also such thinking which led to Ch'en Yün's fall from power in 1958.

The dialectical conception of Chinese society became the developmental model of the Great Leap Forward. The new model saw development in political and social, as well as economic terms, in contrast
to the First Five-Year Plan which was conceived in purely economic
terms. Moreover, the economic elements of development were seen in a
different way. Whereas in the First Five-Year Plan the Chinese economy
was analyzed in standard technical terms, the developmental model of
the Great Leap Forward included an ideological analysis of the Chinese
economy. This meant seeing the elements of the economy in dialectical
as well as in technical terms. Every element in the economy was regarded as being in a contradictory relationship to another element.
Thus the manner of thinking which Mao had already applied to political and social analysis of Chinese society was now also applied to the
economy.

Since the basic aim of the Great Leap Forward was rapid economic
development, we shall begin our discussion of the dialectical conception
of Chinese society with an analysis of its economic elements, and then
continue with the political and social elements.

The Dialectic of the Economy

The key economic slogan of the Great Leap Forward was "Simultaneous Development." By contrast, the First Five-Year Plan was seen

---

[45] *Ibid. 1957*, p. 88.

as a period of select development, characterized mainly by the emphasis on the building up of a modern heavy industrial sector. The dialectic conception of Chinese society saw the First Five-Year Plan as a part of a necessary process, in which one element in various sets of dualities underwent preferential development. During the Great Leap Forward, all these elements would be developed even further (as indicated by the phrase "Under Conditions of Preferential Development of Heavy Industry" which was added to the main slogan "Simultaneous Development of Industry and Agriculture"). However, those elements of the economy which were not emphasized during the First Five-Year Plan period, notably light industry and agriculture, would now also be rapidly developed. Earlier it was felt that heavy industry could only develop rapidly at the expense of the other sectors. That fact was now seen as a contradiction capable of resolution to produce simultaneous development.

Although Mao speaks only briefly about economic development in the last section of his February 1957 speech, the outlines of his dialectical conception of the economy are revealed in his speech "The Ten Great Relationships," which we know mainly through a summary given by Liu Shao-ch'i in May 1958, at the second session of the Eighth Party Congress. At that time, the dialectical conception of the economy had won out. The following quotation contains the core of Liu's summary of the ten relationships:

(1) The relationship of industry and agriculture, of heavy and light industry; (2) the relationship of coastal industry and inland industry; (3) the relationship of economic construction and defense construction; (4) the relationship of state, cooperative, and individual; (5) the relationship of center and region; (6) the relationship of Han and minority peoples; (7) the relationship of Party and non-Party; (8) the relationship of revolution and counter-revolution; (9) the relationships of right and wrong within and without the Party; (10) international relationships.

In this report, Comrade Mao Tse-tung laid down a series of important policies for the realization of the general line of much, fast, good, and economical socialist construction. Of these, numbers one and five suggested the principle of simultaneous development of industry and agriculture under conditions of preferential development of heavy industry, as well as the principle of unifying the concentrated authority of the center and the divided authority of the regions. Numbers two and three suggest that one must make sufficient use of industrial base areas on the coast, sufficiently concentrate capital in the area of economic construction. Number four suggests that one must correctly resolve the relationships of individual and collectivity, of part and whole, of consumption and accumulation. The other items mainly concern an outlook on correctly resolving contradictions among the people which was subsequently further developed. The general spirit of this report was that all positive factors must be mobilized, all usable forces mobilized, in the struggle to make of our country a modernized, rich, and powerful socialist country as rapidly as possible.[46]

Although Mao's formulations and Liu's summary give little concrete detail, the manner of thinking is clear. The first five relationships concern the economy. In the terminology of his 1957 speech, these relationships can be regarded as nonantagonistic contradictions. The economic dualities mentioned are the basic elements of the dialectical conception of the economy. Let us now see what the leaders of Communist China meant concretely by these dualities.

One can find a persistent train of thought in Chinese Communist economic writing that can be called "the idea of sectoral contradiction." Mao Tse-tung speaks of the "relationships" of industry to agriculture, of heavy to light industry, of coastal to inland industry, of center to region. Liu Shao-ch'i, in his political report to the Eighth Party Congress in 1956 (which he later claimed was based on Mao's thinking), speaks of the need "to coordinate coast and inland, large-scale industry with medium- and small-scale industry, central state-owned industry with regional state-owned industry." [47] In rough terms, one can regard these as contradictions between the modern and the traditional sectors, although it is difficult to define modern and traditional in any rigorous way.[48] The Chinese Communists inherited an industrial establishment which was concentrated in two major geographical regions: Manchuria and East China (centered on Shanghai). Despite some attempts made during the First Five-Year Plan period to move industries inland, the emphasis in regional economic development during the years 1953-1958

---

[46] *Jenmin shouts'e 1959*, p. 21. In the following discussion, we use the words "relationship," "duality," and "contradiction." "Relationship" is the word used by Mao to designate an interacting linkage between a pair of elements, e. g., industry and agriculture. "Duality" is my own word to indicate such a pair of elements. "Contradiction" implies that the elements of the duality are in a state of struggle with each other. The Chinese Communists have been careful not to label all dualities contradictions, for this would have policy consequences.

[47] *Jenmin shouts'e 1957*, p. 15.

[48] T. C. Liu and K. C. Yeh state: "The factor that distinguishes the Chinese economy from the more industrially advanced economies is that in the manufacturing, transportation and communications, and trade, the modern enterprise can be separated from the traditional." They warn, however, against taking the differentiation too literally. See *The Economy of the Chinese Mainland: National Income and Economic Development, 1933-1959* (Santa Monica, Calif., 1963), I, 27. See also Chi-ming Hou, "Economic Dualism: The Case of China 1840-1937," *The Journal of Economic History*, XXIII:3 (September 1963), 277-297.

remained on Manchuria and East China.[49] The Communists were in a difficult position. On the one hand, they had to build on existing industrial areas, which, as Liu Shao-ch'i stated, contained more than 70 percent of all Chinese industry in 1949; as a result, during the First Five-Year Plan, great successes were scored in the industrial development of the Liaoning, Tientsin, and Shanghai regions. On the other hand, ideological and strategical considerations made the leadership wish to extend the industrial complex to other regions. Liu Shao-ch'i stated: "During the Second Five-Year Plan [Great Leap Forward], aside from sufficiently making use of the Manchurian and East China industrial base areas, we must rationally expand the role of the Hopei, Shantung, and South Chinese regions in regard to industrial development." [50]

Manchuria and East China constituted China's modern sector.[51] The rapid development of Manchuria under Japanese control and the World War I industrial revolution in Shanghai were major factors in China's industrial progress. The Japanese, during their Greater East Asia Co-prosperity Sphere days, envisaged an industrial complex comprising Manchuria, Korea, and Japan. The rest of the Far East would consume the industrial products of this northern tier and provide it with needed raw materials. If the world is concerned today over the growing north-south gap between industrialized and nonindustrialized countries, the Japanese, in forthright imperialist fashion, saw this as the basis of their domination of the entire Far East. What was a north-south developmental division for the Japanese became an east-west division (or gap) for the Chinese Communists. In contrast to the Japanese, who viewed the gap as essential, the Chinese Communists were concerned about it. They had to build on what they found, else the ambitious goals of their First Five-Year Plan could not be reached. On the other hand, they were worried that the gap between a rapidly developing modern coastal sector and a less rapidly developing traditional inland sector would grow.

The concern about the gap was partly ideological: the radical wing

---

49 Yuan-li Wu, "The Pattern of Industrial Location and Its Relation to Railway Transportation"; unpublished paper for the first research conference of the Social Science Research Council Committee on the Economy of China, Berkeley, California, January 31, February 1, 2, 1963, p. 12.

50 *Jenmin shouts'e 1957,* pp. 15-16.

51 A new major region of modernization appears to be developing in South China around Canton. If Hong Kong is added to the Canton region, the South China complex may one day rival the Shanghai region as an important center of industrial development.

of the Chinese Communist leadership was inland-born and consistently regarded change and development of the inland as a basic revolutionary goal; and partly practical: rapid development in the modern coastal areas could not continue at the same pace without economic revolution of the inland regions. The inland regions had undergone thorough social revolution through the land reform and had experienced collectivization in 1955-56; but there still was no great visible payoff in increased economic performance.

Thus one can isolate three economic contradictions in the minds of the leadership: the contradiction of industry and agriculture, of modern and traditional sectors, and of the coastal East and the inland West. Despite the qualms of the leadership, the most rapid development during the First Five-Year Plan period occurred in industry, the modern sector, and the coastal areas.

In "The Ten Great Relationships," Mao Tse-tung speaks of the relationship of heavy to light industry. Both Mao and Liu have repeatedly stressed the need to adjust this relationship as well as that between large-scale industry and medium- and small-scale industry. Before looking at the substance of the heavy-versus-light-industry relationship or contradiction, it would be well to see what the Chinese mean by heavy and light industry. In contrast to the Russians, the Chinese have defined heavy industry as a "general term for all industrial production which has a decisive function for realizing industrialization and modernization and which supplies all branches of the national economy with modernized material and technical equipment." Light industry is defined as a "general term for all industrial production that, in the process of industrialization and modernization, only supplies all branches of the national economy with general producer and consumer goods." [52] It is important to note that the distinction is not economic (that is, between producer and consumer goods industries), but political. What the Chinese call heavy industry consists of industries strategically important for the developmental goals of the regime; whatever remains falls into the category of light industry. The concrete consequence of this distinction was the investment preference received by any industry classified as heavy.

Related to the heavy-light distinction is that between large-scale industry and medium- and small-scale industry. During the Great Leap Forward, more was heard of the latter than the former distinction. The

---

[52] Wang Hu-sheng, "Kuan yü chung-kungyeh ho ch'ing-kungyeh huafen ti chiko went'i," *Chingchi yenchiu* (April 1963), p. 19. See also P. J. D. Wiles, *The Political Economy of Communism* (Cambridge, Mass., 1962), pp. 281–282.

reason is that, at a time when the leaders of China were calling for "the simultaneous development of both large- and medium- and small-scale industry," the term light industry still had a pejorative connotation. In fact, light industry meant more or less the same as medium- and small-scale industry. During the First Five-Year Plan period, the Chinese Communists "laid utmost emphasis upon large-scale enterprises." [53] During the Great Leap Forward, medium- and small-scale enterprises were redefined as equally important to industrialization.

Another relationship or contradiction Mao mentions, center and region, is closely related to that of heavy and light industry. During the earliest years of Communist rule, the new regime nationalized a broad range of industry. All industries regarded as necessary for the industrialization program were put under direct central ministerial rule. These comprised not only heavy industrial plants, but much industry falling into the light industrial category. The remainder were put under provincial or city administration. Central state-owned industries enjoyed investment preference over regional state-owned industries, which had to fight hard for the remaining capital resources. Most regional state-owned industries were medium- or small-scale light industrial enterprises.

In his report to the Eighth Party Congress, Liu Shao-ch'i indicated the thinking of the leadership which led them to see heavy and light industry in contradiction and suggested ways through which the contradiction could be resolved:

> But there also are some comrades who one-sidedly stress the idea of developing heavy industry; they want to cut down on the rate of development of light industry and other economic sectors. This kind of thinking also is wrong. They do not understand that: (1) since the people's need for consumer goods is constantly growing, if we do not properly develop light industry, conditions of commodity scarcity can appear, which will [adversely] influence the stability of prices and the market. This is especially so in the villages. If industrial commodities in sufficient quantity are not available to be exchanged at stable and rational prices for farm goods, then this will obstruct consolidation of the workers-peasants alliance, and also will [adversely] influence the development of agricultural production. (2) Capital investment needed by light industry is relatively small; the duration of enterprise construction is relatively short; capital circulation is relatively quick; therefore capital accumulation is also relatively quick. Capital accumulated by light industry can be used to aid the development of heavy industry. From this it is evident that, within the framework given by capital, materials, and market, proper

---

[53] Shigeru Ishikawa, "Choice of Techniques in Mainland China," *The Developing Economies* (Tokyo: September-December 1962), p. 34.

stress on the development of light industry is not only not harmful for the construction of heavy industry, but is useful.[54]

Liu Shao-ch'i cited two aspects of the contradiction between heavy and light industry. The first was in effect a "scissors crisis," so familiar to the students of Soviet history: insufficient development of consumer-goods industries presented the peasant with unfavorable terms of trade, inducing hoarding and the curtailment of farm output. The second aspect related to the fact that light industry was a major source of government savings. If the development of light industry failed to keep pace with the development of heavy strategic industry, the whole accumulation program of the state was threatened—a fact evident from the statistical data of 1956-57.

The fourth relationship mentioned by Mao differs from the others: it contains three rather than two elements: State, cooperative, and individual. Liu Shao-ch'i explains this relationship, as one "between the individual and the collectivity, the part and the whole, consumption and accumulation." Thus he takes a triangle of relationships and breaks it into a series of dualities. Thinking in terms of a triangle of relationships is another manifestation of dialectical thinking on the economy. Let us illustrate this with a triangle which has remained basic to Chinese economic thinking: agriculture, light industry, and heavy industry.

Since the early 1960's, the Chinese Communists have stated their developmental priorities in terms of these three economic sectors.[55] However, already in the mid-1950's, the Chinese Communist leaders envisaged a triangular relationship between the three. As Mao Tse-tung indicated in his 1957 speech on contradictions, an integrated national economy could be achieved by properly adjusting the relationships between heavy industry, light industry, and agriculture, or, in somewhat different terms, between production, accumulation, and consumption. The solution seemed simple: push the rapid development of agriculture and light industry, and the country will be sufficiently supplied with consumer goods. In turn, agriculture will supply light industry

---

[54] *Jenmin shouts'e 1957*, p. 15.

[55] Note the following recent comment: "A [priority] sequence of agriculture, light industry, heavy industry means that the unified state economic plan must proceed from the agricultural plan. Starting out from the development of agriculture, one can proceed toward the development of our country's socialist construction. Moreover, on the basis of the capacities and needs of agriculture, one can arrange the developmental plans of light and heavy industry (including scale, speed, and composition), achieve comprehensive balance, thereby assuring maximally rapid proportionate development of the national economy." From "Shanghai chingchi hsüeh-hui 1962-nien nienhui t'aolun ti chuyao went'i tsungshu," *Chingchi yenchiu* (April 1963), p. 63.

with an increased volume of raw materials, and light industry will generate additional savings for investment in heavy industry. Heavy industry will provide products for the strategic goals of the state but also will have "agriculture as a major market."

Thus, by adjusting the relationships (or contradictions) between heavy industry, light industry, and agriculture, the contradictions between production, accumulation, and consumption could be resolved. The non-dialectical economic conception held that what was gained for accumulation, for example, would be lost for consumption. In other words, under conditions of scarcity, the country could not accumulate and consume at the same rate simultaneously. Indeed, during the period of the First Five-Year Plan, the consumption goods industry lagged behind economic development as a whole, as Po I-po pointed out in August 1957.[56] However, by May 1958, Liu Shao-ch'i was able to proclaim the new view of simultaneous development; he severely attacked those who drew the "negative conclusion that because of our great population, the more we consume, the less we can accumulate." This triangular conception of the economy was tied in with the fact that light industry bore the major burden of the accumulation program, as the economist Sun Yeh-fang pointed out in 1957. Thus, as Mao implied in his 1957 speech, the raising of agricultural output and the development of light industry would make it possible to resolve the contradictions between production, accumulation, and consumption.

Two other major economic contradictions, not indicated in the speeches of Mao and Liu, but evident from the literature of 1957 and 1958, may be singled out. One is the contradiction between capital-intensive and labor-intensive modes of operation. Economic critics during 1956-57 pointed out that insufficient use was being made of China's vast human resources. The idea of maximal utilization of labor became one of the leading policy themes of the Great Leap Forward. Rather than being concerned about the country's huge population, the new theme stressed that population was an asset, not a liability. Let's start off from the fact that we have six hundred million people, cried Yang Ying-chieh, a member of the State Planning Commission.[57] What created a contradiction, however, was the fact that the developmental strategy followed until 1958 acted against maximal use of labor. As critics pointed out, one of the shortcomings of the strategy of the First Five-Year Plan was that the stress on big modern industries led to capital-

---

56 T. J. Hughes and D. E. T. Luard, *The Economic Development of Communist China 1949-1958* (Oxford, 1959), p. 66.

57 "Lun ts'ung liu-i jenk'ou ch'ufa," *Chingchi yenchiu* (June 1958), pp. 39 ff.

rather than labor-intensive modes of operation. Modern enterprises wanted to build up their fixed-capital assets, while keeping their labor force down. They hungered for modern equipment and scarce materials, while showing reluctance to bring in new numbers of unskilled workers. The adoption of labor-intensive modes of operation during the Great Leap Forward was designed to resolve this contradiction.

The other economic contradiction may be regarded as one of long-term versus short-term goals. Chang Hsing-fu, a member of the State Planning Commission, contrasted two paths to ultimate industrialization: one which aims only at "long-term interests" and disregards "short-term interests" (the strategy of the First Five-Year Plan); another which takes into consideration both long- and short-term interests (the strategy of the Great Leap Forward). Concretely this meant that during the First Five-Year Plan a strategy was followed which, by the creation of a heavy industrial base, served the long-term, but not necessarily the short-term interests of the Chinese economy. The Great Leap Forward, by stressing the development of agriculture and light industry, and at the same time continuing to stress the development of heavy industry, tried thereby simultaneously to serve both the short-term and the long-term interests of the Chinese economy. The new strategy brought about radical changes in the planning system.[58] Already in 1956, long-term and short-term planning had been institutionally separated, as in the USSR. During the Great Leap Forward, planners were told to concern themselves with programs which would bring about a quick payoff for the Chinese economy.

One could list other economic contradictions, but those given should suffice for making the desired point: a manner of thinking had arisen which saw the Chinese economy as a dialectical structure marked by contradictions. Since systematic presentation of the contradictions is not available in the literature, I have appended to the end of this chapter an analytical chart of the contradictions. For the economy, I have classified the contradictions into five types: (1) sectors, (2) goals, (3) scale, (4) functions, and (5) operations. Under each heading, one or more pairs of specific contradictions are listed. For each of the specific contradictions, one of the elements had priority during the First Five-Year Plan period. Together, they may be said to constitute the Soviet model of development which the Chinese followed at that time.

The dialectical analysis of the economy had suggested to the Chinese that the Soviet model formed one half of the whole picture. The time

---

[58] Chang Hsin-fu, "Wo-kuo kungyeh-hua ti taolu ho fangfa," *Jenmin shouts'e 1958*, pp. 446-448.

had come in 1958 to create a true unity of opposites by pushing the other elements of the duality. Thus a truly integrated national economy could be created. The literature of this period repeatedly refers to "one-sided development." Juxtaposed to "one-sided development" was the idea of "simultaneous development." The criticism of the First Five-Year Plan (and implicitly of the Soviet model) which became increasingly frequent during the mid-1950's pointed out that the road of development hitherto traveled would not lead to an integrated national economy, or to a general integration of society. To achieve this new greater harmony, all elements in the various dualities that had remained disadvantaged during the First Five-Year Plan would now be pushed. Heavy industry would not be sacrificed, but light industry (read: "medium- and small-scale industry," as they were termed during the Great Leap Forward) would be developed to a par with the former so that each would contribute to the national economy. And so with the other dualities: the stress would henceforth be on inland industries, agriculture, light industry, medium- and small-scale industries, accumulation, consumption, labor-intensive modes of operation, short-term planning, regional state-owned industries, and so on.

The Dialectic of the State

The dialectical conception of the economy is not spelled out in Mao's 1957 speech on contradictions, but the dialectical conceptions of state and of society are. In the passage from the introduction quoted above, Mao states the major social and political contradictions in Chinese society. In February, when the speech was delivered, the concrete implications of his conception of social and political contradictions were not yet manifest. By the fall of 1957, these implications became manifest in two great movements: the anti-rightist campaign and decentralization. In the next section (pp. 90-101) we shall discuss the social contradictions as they became clear during the anti-rightist movement. In the present section, we shall discuss the political contradictions which were of importance for decentralization. As will be indicated in the chapter on government, by "state" the Chinese Communists mean the structure of formal rule, notably administration. Therefore, we shall focus our discussion of political contradictions on the state administration.

In his 1957 speech on contradictions, Mao speaks of the contradiction between democracy and centralism. In "The Ten Great Relationships," Mao speaks of the relationship between center and region. Not only are these two conceptions related, but both were at the basis of the thinking that led to the decentralization decisions implemented late in 1957. During the Eighth Party Congress of September 1956, there was general agreement that greater emphasis must be given to "democracy." So far as state administration was concerned, this meant arousing the "initiative and creativity" of administrative units below the central level. This could only be done by modifying the centralized systems of policy, planning, and control that had arisen during the First Five-Year Plan. As we shall point out in our discussion of decentralization in the chapter on government, there was disagreement as to how centralism should be modified. One opinion group, headed by Ch'en Yün, then Minister of Commerce, argued for expanding "democracy" at the production unit level, which ultimately would have led the country in the direction of a Yugoslav-type economy.[59] Another opinion group, headed by Mao Tse-tung and Liu Shao-ch'i, argued for a different kind of decentralization, namely expanding the decision-making powers of regional administrative units, notably at the provincial level. The kind of decentralization finally adopted followed the Mao-Liu approach. Thus the resolution of the contradiction between centralism and democracy, and between center and region, took the form of a "downward transfer of authority" to the regional level.

To understand the thinking that underlay the decentralization decisions of late 1957, one must look at the Chinese Communist conceptions of centralism and democracy. As we have pointed out, the Chinese Communists have broken the old Leninist term "democratic centralism" into two component nominal units, democracy *and* centralism, and in their dialectical fashion, have juxtaposed the two. Their conception of democracy and centralism may be said essentially to relate to the direction from which impulses come, as is evident from another related duality that was expressed in a slogan widely used during the Great Leap Forward: "From Top down and from Bottom up." Impulses are related to policy, since every policy can be said to be based on an impulse leading to a decision. The Chinese Communists distinguish between various kinds of policy, ranging from the general to the specific.[60] Cen-

---

[59] During this period, Yugoslavia had not yet become the pariah in Chinese eyes that it became later when the Great Leap Forward gathered momentum. For example, articles appeared describing the Yugoslav workers-council system.

[60] The Chinese Communists have three words for what in English is called policy: *luhsien, fangchen,* and *chengts'e.* The term *luhsien* is normally translated as "line," as in "mass line." Despite the denotation of direction in the word, it essentially relates to methods of operation; always consulting with the workers, for example, is an instance of the mass line in practice. *Fangchen* may be rendered as "line" or "policy" in English, but relates to direction, goals, rather than to working methods. It means policy in its most general sense. *Chengts'e* refers to a particular policy at

tralism implies a system where both general and specific policy impulses originate from the center. Democracy, on the other hand, implies a system where policy impulses originate from a level below the center. The Chinese Communists have never advocated instituting democracy at the full expense of centralism, but rather a system which combined the two in a unity of true opposites. During the Great Leap Forward, this took the form of centralization of general policy impulses and decentralization of specific policy impulses. There were many slogans which expressed this approach, for example, "Centralized Policy and Divided Management." In other words, Peking laid down the general policy guidelines, but the regions were allowed to develop specific policies to make sure to "do the best according to local conditions" (yinti chihyi).

Two implications in the conception of democracy are relevant for decentralization and the Great Leap Forward that followed. One is the notion of diversity and the other is the notion of freedom. Insofar as the conceptions of democracy and of region are related, a certain plural connotation is attached to the former. Region is in itself a plural conception, for it implies different areas of the country with different conditions and problems. During the First Five-Year Plan, the Chinese Communists tried to create a centralized administrative system in which regional differences would have been submerged in a larger unity. By the mid-1950's, the leaders began to recognize that this was not possible. Regionalism remained a powerful force in Chinese society which could not be overcome by the kind of Gleichschaltung attempted in the early 1950's. What made the idea of region contradictory to center was the inherent tendency for the regions to develop vested interests (localism) which acted against the goals of the center. If Gleichschaltung did not succeed, then, the leaders felt, regionalism should be accepted, but made to work for the interests of the center. To paraphrase a traditional Chinese expression: regionalism would be used to fight regionalism. Thus the recognition of regional diversity became a basic element of the decentralization decisions and of the Great Leap Forward.

In a sentence from his February 1957 speech on contradictions, Mao Tse-tung related the ideas of freedom and democracy: "The unity of this kind of democracy and centralism, the unity of freedom and discipline—this is our system of democratic centralism." Clearly impressed

---

a particular time; see T. A. Hsia, The Commune in Retreat as Evidenced in Terminology and Semantics (Berkeley, California: Center for Chinese Studies, University of California, 1964), pp. 47-53. The words fangchen chengts'e are often seen together, always in that order. In this combination, the term can be rendered as general and specific policy. Luhsien, therefore, sets the general operational framework. Fangchen specifies the broadest goals. Chengts'e specifies the immediate goals.

by the Hungarian revolt, which he mentioned explicitly in his speech, Mao appeared to be advocating more democracy and freedom within the Communist world. That some people in China took Mao's words about freedom and democracy at face value is indicated by the few short weeks of free expression that burst forth among the students of China's higher schools in May 1957.

However, the idea of further developing "freedom" did not disappear with the initiation of the anti-rightist movement in June of that year. Though the freedom exercised in May was denounced as petit bourgeois and counter-revolutionary, a new freedom theme was intoned: the creativity and initiative of the masses. This freedom theme was in fact what Mao Tse-tung meant by freedom. Freedom for him was a kind of populist upsurge of the masses, similar to the spontaneity (*stikhiinost'*) which the Russians, ever since Lenin's time, have consistently denounced. This notion of freedom also underlies the slogan of "liberation" (*chiehfang*) constantly used in Communist China. Mao has consistently taught that if restraints were lifted from the masses, particularly the poor peasants, there would ensue a great outflow of energy. In other words, impulses would come forth from the masses. Centralism would be used to channel and direct those impulses, thus realizing a unity of freedom and discipline. During the Great Leap Forward, Peking went far in loosening administrative controls over the population, leaving it to the Party to lead the masses. Whether the energy that welled up during 1958 was spontaneous or induced may never be fully known. What is known is that for one year the entire population of China was caught in a frenzy of activity which was not halted until serious dislocations had been brought about in the fabric of the society.

If decentralization was intended to strengthen "democracy" to a level equal with "centralism," this meant giving greater scope for creativity and initiative to the regions. In the chapter on government, we shall point out that, by 1957, the Party as an organization had become the dominant force at the regional and local levels. Since the Party, in contrast to the state administration, was regarded as the direct expression of the masses, unleashing the creativity and initiative of the masses in its most direct sense meant giving the Party at the regional level greater "freedom." However, to do this certain contradictions within the state administration had to be resolved first.

One of the most important contradictions within the state administration was that between vertical rule and dual rule (see pp. 188 ff.). Since these administrative principles will be discussed in detail later, suffice it here to say that they are mutually exclusive principles, one implying single command and the other implying multiple command. During the First Five-Year Plan period, Peking tried to create a straight-line chain of command for every branch of government with general and specific command originating from central government agencies. A "contradictory" situation arose as Party committees in the center and the regions tried to exercise command over these vertically ruled branches and to create a *de facto* dual rule. Decentralization to the regional level could only be accomplished by implementing dual rule. Specifically, this meant giving greater power to the Party, which was the champion of "democracy and freedom," and taking power from government agencies, who were the champions of "centralism and discipline." Dual rule meant the introduction of an element of radicalism to counteract the element of conservatism inherent in vertical rule.

The contradiction between vertical and dual rule also implied contradictions between different types of administrative structure and function. The system of administration which the Chinese took from the Soviets in the early 1950's was based on the branch principle (*otrasl'* in Russian, *pumen* in Chinese). According to this principle, all administration was divided into parallel branches, each of which administered a sector performing certain common functions. Command came down vertically from the center. Counterposed to the branch principle of administration was another which we may call the committee principle. According to this principle, administration is dominated by committees made up of members from different branches, and therefore cuts across branch lines. Administratively, committees were regarded as having the function of coordination. If at a regional level, administrative powers are vested in a committee which includes representatives from branch agencies of the central government, then command may be said to flow horizontally. If a regional agency is subject to dual rule, coming vertically from the center and horizontally from the regional Party or government committee, then a contradiction may be said to exist: The more the agency is controlled by the committee, the more reduced its branch-type functions; the reverse also holds true. One may thus envisage a structural contradiction between the branch and committee principles of government, and a functional contradiction between straight-line chain of command and lateral coordination.

The decentralization decisions of late 1957 were aimed at increasing the power of coordinative committees at all levels of the state administration. This was also the intent of the Soviet economic reforms of 1957 which led to the establishment of the district-level (*oblast'*) regional economic councils (*sovnarkhozy*); however, these Soviet coordinative committees were unable to break the powerful lines of branch-type administration which had been effectively institutionalized during the years of Stalinist rule. In China, regional coordination became the dominant policy of the Great Leap Forward, as is evident in the discussion on "regional economic cooperation" from late 1957 onwards. That a real contradiction existed is indicated by the fact that the growth of regional coordinative committees in China led to a far-reaching weakening of the system of branch administration. Commands from the center often became unenforceable against the more powerful commands coming from the regional committees. The consequences of decentralization were thus different in the Soviet Union and in China.

As with the economic contradictions, I have grouped the political contradictions in a chart at the end of this chapter and divided them into two major categories: contradictions of conception and contradictions of administration.

The Dialectic of Society

If the decentralization decisions revealed the concrete implications of the political contradictions in Mao's dialectical conception of Chinese society, the anti-rightist movement revealed the concrete implications of his conception of social contradictions.

The anti-rightist movement started as a Party counterattack against critical intellectuals who had expressed themselves freely during May 1957. But it spread in scope and took the form of a large-scale movement directed against all intellectuals. Although the intellectuals (*chih-shih fentzu*) cannot be called a class in strictly Marxist terms, they in fact constitute one of the three great social groupings of Chinese society. It will be recalled that in the passage from the introduction of his 1957 speech, Mao begins by speaking of contradictions among the working class, the peasant class, and the intellectuals. In the popular mind, the intellectuals constitute a distinct social stratum. They are the educated professionals, conscious of their membership in a restricted social elite.

The fact that Mao's writings in general are preoccupied with only two of the three great social groupings, peasants and intellectuals, indicates that these two, and not the working class, generated the major contradictions in Chinese society. This is clearly revealed in the anti-rightist movement. From its inception in June 1957, it was directed against the intellectuals; from August 1957 onward, it was directed against the peasantry in the form of a "socialist education movement."

Aside from isolated individuals, the working class was not a target of the anti-rightist campaign.

Though the anti-rightist movement started as a campaign directed against the critical intellectuals of May 1957, it soon turned into a campaign against the entire professional intelligentsia. Their great sin was not simply deviation but conservatism. Thus, as the year 1957 rolled on, the anti-rightist campaign turned into a movement to "oppose conservatism." Administrators, managers, and technicians were attacked, not only for critical expression during the Hundred Flowers period, but for lack of enthusiasm toward the mass line. The punishment that befell many of them was *hsiafang*, that is, being "sent down" to the front line of production, to peasant villages or to the factory work floor. The professional intellectuals were denounced for their technological fetishism, for their arrogant conviction that modern scientific and technical learning was only accessible to the educated. The "mass line" rapidly took on concrete content as simple peasants and workers were enrolled in "worker-peasant universities" and told that they too could participate in administration, accounting, designing, and scientific experimentation. Reducing the gap between mental and physical labor, an old Marxist dream, was taken seriously during the Great Leap Forward. The professionals were told to work with their hands and spend less time in classrooms and offices. The masses were told that the "mystique of technology" was a myth; technology was not the exclusive domain of the social elite. By the time the anti-rightist movement was declared to be at an end in May 1958, all segments of the intelligentsia had suffered through denunciation or *hsiafang*: academic critics, professionals, administrators, and managers.

In our initial remarks on the dialectical conception of Chinese society, we noted that Mao Tse-tung's vision of Chinese society saw it as marked by essential economic, political, and social contradictions. When these contradictions were sketched out in "The Ten Great Relationships" and in "On the Question of Correctly Resolving Contradictions among the People," the analysis did not yet show concrete action consequences. But in late 1957, the anti-rightist campaign, decentralization, and the economic program of the Great Leap Forward revealed the concrete action consequences of Mao's vision. The anti-rightist campaign, with its attack on the intellectuals, can be considered the first implementation of Mao's conception of social contradictions. However, later in 1957 and throughout 1958, other social contradictions became manifest and were worked into the over-all program of the Great Leap Forward. Since the text repeatedly cited during this period was Mao's

1957 speech on contradictions, let us look at the social contradictions sketched out in that speech and supplement them with secondary evidence from this same period.

Mao, in the introduction of the 1957 speech, in effect had stated that Chinese society was composed of three great social groupings—workers, peasants, and intellectuals—with the national bourgeoisie constituting a fourth, though limited one. He then had listed contradictions within and among these groupings: within the working class, within the peasant class, within the intellectuals; between the working and peasant classes; between workers-peasants and intellectuals; between workers and the national bourgeoisie; and within the national bourgeoisie.

In the eleven sections of the body of the speech, Mao did not explicitly discuss all the contradictions he had outlined in the introduction. None of the sections is devoted specifically to contradictions involving the workers—undoubtedly because they posed no great problems as a social group; they were, after all, a favored class under the First Five-Year Plan and became even more favored under the 1956 wage reform. Mao did discuss a group not included among the three (or four) classes of the introduction, the minorities, but we shall not comment on them because they are of minor importance to Chinese society as a whole. This leaves the specific contradictions among the peasants, the intellectuals, and the national bourgeoisie.

Though Mao stated the two basic contradictions affecting the *peasantry* in economic terms, he implied social contradictions. The two basic contradictions were: one between accumulation and consumption, and the other between the state and the cooperatives over the allocation of savings. The two contradictions were reflected in Mao's phrase: "The state must accumulate, and the cooperative must accumulate; but neither must do so excessively." Since Chinese industrialization, like that of the Soviet Union, was realized by savings accumulated in agriculture, the first contradiction arose from the fact that the peasants sacrificed consumption so that industry could accumulate for development. The second contradiction arose from the fact that the state and the cooperative competed for savings coming from the peasants' surplus. Whereas the state needed savings for industrialization, the cooperative needed savings to reinvest in its own production program.

The social contradictions arising from these two economic contradictions are implied in Mao's admission that more than 70 percent of the country's peasants were still in the poorest categories, that is, "poor and middle peasants." Though low agricultural productivity was the basic cause of the peasants' poverty, a contributing factor was the heavy extraction of savings by the state and the cooperative. Without stating them openly, Mao, in effect, indicated three social contradictions: between the state and the peasant, between the state and the cooperative, and between the cooperative and the peasant. In the absence of increased agricultural output, what the one gained the other necessarily lost.

Mao devoted a long section to the *intellectuals*. The major contradiction among them was that between red and expert. Despite the fact that the regime had trained thousands of new intellectuals in modern learning, the greater their expertise, apparently the more resistant they became to political indoctrination. Mao noted: "Change in world view is a basic transformation; we still cannot say that the majority of intellectuals have completed this transformation." And further: "In the eyes of some of these [intellectuals], there is no need to be concerned about politics, about the future of the fatherland, about the ideals of humanity." Mao said, in effect, that the majority of intellectuals had not yet undergone an ideological transformation which would have made them truly "red and expert." As we have indicated earlier, the values of red and expert were not entirely compatible.

Mao's concern about the intellectuals must be seen against the fact that in 1956, of China's total population of well over six hundred millions, only 3,840,000 were classified as intellectuals. The Chinese Communists have never defined exactly who an "intellectual" is. Since, theoretically, social classes are defined according to relationships to the means of production, the Chinese Communists do not speak of an intellectual class; they commonly speak of "intellectual elements" (*chihshih fentzu*), a term which is widely used in the everyday language of China. Moreover, Party membership accepts the category of intellectual element. If asked to define an intellectual, almost any refugee from Mainland China will respond: an intellectual is anyone with a higher education; more specifically, higher middle school and up.

Mao's concern did not arise from the small numbers of educated people in the country, but from the fact that the intellectuals constitute a social elite. Traditionally, schools in China have been the forging ground of life-long friendships, of social attitudes, and, in the most basic sense, of public identity. This is not true of lower middle and primary schools, for "everybody" can attend, but of the higher schools which are still, now as earlier, restricted to a small select number. As a social elite, the intellectuals are a cohesive group sharing basic social values, exercising authority in society. Mao was concerned that these social values did not fully encompass the political values of Chinese Communist ideology, thus producing the contradiction of red and expert. That Mao's concern was justified can be seen by the few weeks of free criticism that erupted only three months after his February speech —criticism much of which came from the country's leading young technical intellectuals.

An even deeper concern on Mao's part must have been the fear that the contradiction of red and expert would further increase that bifurcation of elites which we have discussed earlier. This bifurcation could lead to a juxtaposition of a Party made up largely of workers and peasants and an intelligentsia made up of the most educated people in the country. The Party might be the master of ideology, but the intelligentsia would be the master of technology.

What was the main problem concerning the *national bourgeoisie,* of a sort that Mao would conceive of it as a contradiction? The contradiction may be seen as one between socialist relationships of production and capitalist class mentality. In simple terms, despite the fact that all Chinese business had been nationalized by 1956, not only did a capitalist class continue to exist, but a capitalist mentality remained deeply imbedded in the business community. The reasons for the continued official toleration of the capitalist class can be seen in Mao's admission that the capitalist elements still constituted the managers of the joint state-and-private-owned enterprises.

The regime had reluctant need of the scarce managerial talent provided by the national bourgeoisie. Chinese business and industry, as we shall point out in the chapter on management, were exceedingly complex, with far-flung supply, production, and sales networks. The administrative rationalization introduced by the Communists proved to be no adequate substitute for the cumulative experience of the capitalists. They have been repeatedly attacked in China, but have always bounced back. After the eruption of the great economic crisis of 1960-1961, the leadership acknowledged their importance, extended their "fixed interest" payments, and let them improve their relatively high levels of living; they were given a major role in pulling the country out of the crisis. Like the intellectuals, the national bourgeoisie remains a socially necessary class (though in a more limited way) governed by thought (*szuhsiang*) which clashes with the official ideology. If the contradiction between the "red" thought of the Party and the "expert" thought of the intelligentsia was basically seen by Mao as a nonantagonistic contradiction, the contradiction between the "red" thought of the Party and the capitalist class mentality of the national bourgeoisie must, *in ultima res,* have been seen by him as an antagonistic contradiction; for, if socialism is to be built in China, capitalism must finally be destroyed. Indeed, the production relationships had been socialized, but the capitalist mentality remained. Since *szuhsiang* is so important to the Chinese Communists, the transformation of capitalism into socialism cannot be completed until the capitalist mentality has been completely eliminated.

The contradictions affecting the peasants, the intellectuals, and the national bourgeoisie were explicitly discussed by Mao Tse-tung in the body of his speech. However, as indicated, Mao, in the introduction to his speech, sketched out a much broader range of contradictions. Though he did not explicitly discuss all these (at least not in the official version), he must have thought of real, concrete contradictions. In the following discussion, we shall try to indicate what he possibly had in mind, drawing on secondary material from the periods before and after 1957.

Mao, in the introduction, spoke of contradictions between workers and peasantry. He apparently meant more than the social consequences of a policy that favored industry and disfavored agriculture. We suggest that one of the contradictions he had in mind was that between skilled and unskilled workers, a topic frequently discussed in the literature of the period.

The Great Leap Forward policy of maximizing labor use confronted the managers and the skilled workers with an influx of new, unskilled workers. The bulk of the new employees were peasants, either directly from the villages or more remotely after some sojourn in the cities. During the First Five-Year Plan period, the conflict was not yet too serious in view of the prevalent policy of holding down employment and building up a skilled labor force. However, since factory managers operated with a fixed wage fund, the sudden influx of new workers threatened the economic position of the old established workers. As we shall see in our discussion of urban communization, the economic problem of keeping wage payments within the limits of the wage fund was partly resolved by paying old and new workers according to entirely different wage scales. Since this meant, in effect, that the new workers were being paid less for the same labor than the old workers, this created conflicts, hence contradictions.

Reference group theory in sociology teaches that those lower on a status scale often model themselves on those above them. There are indications that the skilled workers in Communist China, though resentful of the educated technicians, took on that same elite mentality toward the new unskilled workers, as the technicians showed toward the workers. The phenomenon is not unknown in other industrial societies.

The next contradiction Mao listed in his introduction was that between worker-peasants and intellectuals. To see what he might have had in mind, let us take factory organization as an example. The Chinese Communists make a fundamental distinction between two basic types of industrial employees, analogous to the white-collar and blue-collar distinction current in other industrial countries. All employees who do managerial and administrative work are called *chihyüan*, which may be rendered as functionary (the word is also used in a narrower sense to designate clerical employees); all employees who do basic physical labor are called *kungjen*, workers. *Chihyüan* and *kungjen* are normally paid according to different wage scales. Before 1949, functionaries and workers were usually physically separated; company offices and plant sites were often situated in different areas. After 1949, however, they were brought together, thus putting functionaries and workers into close contact. The most important group of functionaries are the technicians, who, as we have indicated, are mainly individuals of higher education; accordingly, they are colloquially called "intellectuals" by the workers. Thus, the contradiction between worker-peasants and intellectuals, mentioned by Mao, may have had one of its concrete manifestations in this conflict between white-collar and blue-collar workers.

The issues in the contradiction between intellectuals and peasants were more obscure. In 1956, there were only 500,000 "technicians" in the country from an official intellectual population of 3,840,000; there were only 100,000 "higher intellectuals."

Though these 600,000 highly trained intellectuals plus a large number of "ordinary intellectuals" lived in the cities, there must have been a sizable number of intellectuals living in the rural areas. The most prominent rural intellectual undoubtedly is the schoolteacher. In the past, most rural areas had their poverty-stricken *laoshih* who taught the peasants and formed a link between the villages and the outside world. If traditional attitudes carried over, as they undoubtedly did to some extent, the rural intellectuals were not inclined to put their fingers to the soil and actively aid the peasants to carry through their economic revolution.

The contradiction between the national bourgeoisie and the workers, which Mao mentioned in the introduction to his speech, was a management-labor problem. The national bourgeoisie, as mentioned, mostly worked in formerly private companies which gradually were transformed into joint state-private ownership. Though, in 1949, the ownership relationships were not immediately changed, all private companies were subjected to "democratic reform." In contrast to the state-owned enterprises, where tight managerial controls were enforced, in the private (and later joint state-private) companies the factories were in effect run by the powerful workers' unions and controlled by the Party. The fact that management positions were formally held by the capitalists but that management functions were in actuality carried out by the unions and the Party undoubtedly created conflicts, that is, contradictions.

In his 1957 speech on contradictions, Mao did not call for a renewed onslaught against the capitalists, but urged them to "study" and "reform" so that they could better cooperate with their workers. In fact, a course of study lasting only a few weeks would suffice, Mao indicated.

All social contradictions so far discussed in the dialectical conception of Chinese society may be regarded as contradictions of *social* stratification. But there are also social contradictions arising from *political* stratification, that is, between those who have power and those who do not. These latter contradictions take on particular importance in view of the role traditionally played by officials in Chinese society. The idea of official is so ingrained in the Chinese mind that a common word for God is "celestial bureaucrat." In the introduction of his speech on contradictions, Mao spoke of "certain contradictions" between the government and the masses, by which he meant conflicts between bureaucrats and the people. The Chinese Communists have a long tradition of hostility to "bureaucratism." Antibureaucratism was a major theme in the 1955 *Sufan* movement, in the 1957 anti-rightist movement, and throughout the Great Leap Forward. Party handbooks have always taken great care to point out that a cadre is not an official, and that the Party is different from a bureaucratic apparatus.

As regards contradictions arising from political stratification, Mao indicated that the main contradiction was between bureaucrats and masses. Even though this contradiction is nonantagonistic, in Mao's terms, the assertion that it existed implied a contradiction between the state and the people. In strictly theoretical terms, this could not be admitted, for the state is regarded as the instrument of the ruling class, namely the proletariat. However, as we shall point out several times in the course of this study, the Chinese Communists appear to have a "populist" hostility to formal state administration, which makes it possible for them to envisage a contradiction between state and people in practice, if not in theory.

Liu Shao-ch'i, in his May 1958 report to the second session of the Eighth Party Congress, made the contradiction between bureaucrats and masses more explicit. He juxtaposed "administrative personnel and mental workers" on the one hand with the masses on the other. That speech came after months of attack on bureaucratic and managerial conservatism. Liu's speech revealed another train of thought relevant to our discussion of social contradictions arising from social and political stratification. By coupling administrative personnel and mental workers, he implied that the offices of state administration and management were filled with intellectuals, in other words, that the social stratum of bureaucrats and the social stratum of intellectuals had become increasingly similar. We know, for example, that planning agencies recruited largely from higher school graduates who studied the nontechnical sciences. In fact, the normal career line of a young graduate who did not become a technician was to go into the state administration.

A second contradiction, not explicitly mentioned in the literature, but clearly in the minds of the Chinese Communist leaders, was that between bureaucrats and cadres. One of the policies implemented during the Great Leap Forward was the replacement of administrators by dedicated Party cadres. When Mao made his speech on contradictions, Peking still pursued a policy of collaboration between administrators and managers on the one hand, and Party cadres on the other. However, by the following year, collaboration had turned into contradiction. Therefore, we can speak of an implicit contradiction between bureaucrats and cadres.

A third contradiction, only dimly hinted at, was implied by Mao's reference to contradictions between leader and led. It will be recalled that Liu Shao-ch'i used this same term in discussing contradictions within the Party. Mao probably had in mind a contradiction between Party cadres and masses. If the contradiction between state and people could not—in theoretical terms—be admitted, it was even more necessary to avoid any implication of a contradiction between Party and people—because the Party considers itself the organizational expression of the true will of the people. For Mao and Liu to envisage a contradiction between Party and masses would have been akin to the Hegelian negation of the self.

Mao Tse-tung and Liu Shao-ch'i must have been disturbed that the whole sociopolitical policy of the First Five-Year Plan period, in emulation of the USSR, was leading to the formation of a single unified elite, a "new class" in Milovan Djilas' sense. If the First Five-Year Plan was a period of selective development in the economy, the same was true in the sociopolitical field. Until 1955, when a great mass recruitment campaign began, the main efforts of the leadership went in the direction of building up the Party at the top and middle rather than the bottom level. "Higher intellectuals" were favored over lower, intellectuals in general over masses, workers over peasants, skilled workers over unskilled. Perhaps most important, the leadership felt that it could develop a new elite that was both red and expert, by professionalizing its Party cadres and intensively indoctrinating the professionals it needed so badly to run the country. The 1956 wage reform, with its open favoritism shown to the "higher" elements of society, indicated that, at that time, the leadership was still committed to a "new class" policy. One of the most important implications of Mao's speech on contradictions was that stratification along social and political lines was again emerging in China. However, as the real policies of the Great Leap Forward showed, Peking was to veer away from its earlier attempt to bring about a "new class" through the merging of the social and political elites.

Social contradictions in Chinese society included yet more than those arising from social and political stratification. In the chart appended to the end of this chapter, we speak of contradictions of *value*, of *social cohesion*, of *role*, and of *motivation and incentive*.

The contradiction of value (red and expert) needs little elaboration, since it has been discussed and will be repeatedly touched on in this book. As a conflict between political and professional orientations, it was to have far-reaching ramifications during the Great Leap Forward. The social contradictions to be discussed were regarded as directly deriving from the contradiction of red and expert.

The contradiction of social cohesion was seen in the general context of a need to integrate society. Since the mid-1950's, the Chinese Communists began to call for more collectivity in the social field and more coordination in the political field. The attacks on the intellectuals, for example, singled out the opposites to the social ideals of collectivity: "individualism," "egoism," "self-interest." Similarly, the attacks on the bureaucrats singled out the opposites to the political ideas of coordination, notably "localism" (literally: "vested-interest-ism"), "partiality," "lack of cooperation," and so on. ("Vested-interest-ism," *penwei chuyi* in Chinese, is too awkward a word to be used in our further discussion, and will be rendered as "localism"; it is one of the more serious wrongdoings in Communist China and means identification with one's organizational unit rather than with Party or state as a whole. The word is analagous to the Russian *méstnichestvo* or *védomstvennost'*.)

Implicitly, the Chinese Communists attacked the kind of social cohesion produced by the policies of individual responsibility, individual incentives, and division of labor which prevailed during the First Five-Year Plan period. This produced a social cohesion which Durkheim would have described as "organic" solidarity, rather than the "mechanical" solidarity toward which the Great Leap Forward aspired.[61]

The contradiction of social cohesion was closely related to the contradiction of role. The Chinese Communists argued that, during the First Five-Year Plan period, there was too much emphasis on training specialists rather than generalists. During the Great Leap Forward, a new ideal worker appeared on the scene: He was the generalist or jack-of-all-trades, *tomienshou*, who could do a little of everything, in contrast to the specialist or master-of-one-technique, *ichi-chih-chang,* who had only one narrowly defined skill.[62] The idea was that a few months of training could turn a peasant into a jack-of-all-trades, whereas years of learning and experience were necessary to produce a. master-of-one-technique.

The link between social cohesion and role can be seen in the fact that the Chinese Communists felt that the jack-of-all-trades could more easily be integrated into a work team on an egalitarian basis than the old specialized master-of-one-technique. During the First Five-Year Plan period, each worker had his specified skills, tasks, and responsibilities, which were pegged to differential wage grades. Moreover, he had his specified "work post"—a place and a set of tools for which each worker was individually responsible. The work team was thus seen as an aggregate of individuals, each doing different things and rewarded differently, but held together by the division of labor. During the Great Leap Forward, however, the Chinese Communists revived the old Chinese work-gang principle, except that instead of being led by a gang boss, *pat'ou,* the teams were now led by dedicated Party cadres. To produce "mechanical" rather than "organic" types of social cohesion, the Chinese Communists felt that the basic roles of the team workers had to be changed from those of specialists to those of generalists.

Since the work teams of the Great Leap Forward consisted of different types of workers than those of the First Five-Year Plan period, different kinds of motivation and incentives were necessary. The contradiction of motivation and incentives, in a sense, may be regarded as the most important of all during this period, inasmuch as it related directly to the argument between the proponents of social mobilization and the proponents of material incentives (see pp. 196 ff.). Mao Tse-tung believed

---

[61] The Chinese Communists use the concept "organic solidarity" in the Durkheimian sense.

[62] After the great shift in economic policy in 1961, articles appeared arguing in favor of the "master-of-one-technique." See *Jenmin jihpao,* November 20, 1961. For a Great Leap Forward advocacy of the "jack-of-all-trades," see *Hungch'i* 5 (August 1958), 16-18.

that, human nature being malleable, social mobilization (making use of organization) could motivate men to work far better than material incentives could. During the First Five-Year Plan period, the Chinese Communist conception of motivation and incentive gave rise to a wage policy based on the principle of individual material rewards. During the Great Leap Forward, the Chinese Communists adopted a new conception of motivation and incentive. Individual rewards were replaced by collective rewards. Piece-rate systems were replaced by time wages. In 1958, wages as a whole were seen as out of date, and workers were paid by "distribution," especially in the construction industry and the new commune industries, where large numbers of unskilled workers (that is, peasants) were employed. Distribution meant that each worker was supplied with a sum of money and goods which he needed to live and maintain his family, with cash wages reduced to the function of pocket money.[63]

The conviction that social mobilization could motivate men through organization arose from the belief that men in a truly solidary group can work better than in a team which is only an aggregate of individuals. That belief is similar to what American sociologists call "group dynamics." Moreover, since Chinese Communists believe that group participation is essential to processes of political indoctrination, it should follow that a work group functioning by "mechanical" principles of social cohesion will be susceptible to ideological appeals. Lin Piao's famous statement that men are more important than weapons has its counterpart in the Great Leap Forward policy on motivation and incentive; men must be appealed to, not through material rewards or techniques, but through the spiritual values transmitted by ideology.

The Resolution of Contradictions

The following chart summarizes the contradictions discussed in the preceding pages. As we stated earlier (p. 78, footnote 46), the Chinese Communists have been careful not to label all dualities contradictions; some dualities are still considered relationships. When the elements of a duality are stated to be in contradiction, resolution must follow; this means policy consequences. Thus, while many of the dualities listed below were still regarded as relationships during the mid-1950's, by 1957 and 1958, when Mao Tse-tung's vision of Chinese society began to unfold, relationships turned into contradictions. When the elements of a duality are in relationship, each is regarded as having an auton-

---

[63] Charles Hoffman, "Work Incentives in Communist China," *Industrial Relations,* III:3 (February 1964), 81-97.

omous existence and operating according to particular principles, such as the so-called planned and nonplanned sectors during the First Five-Year Plan period. However, when a relationship turns into a contradiction, struggle between the two elements of the duality begins. Struggle demands resolution so that a "unity of opposites" can be produced, as indicated in the prevalent slogan of the Great Leap Forward: Solidarity—Struggle—Solidarity. Mao Tse-tung's vision of Chinese society saw all major contradictions in it capable of resolution with a single grand program—the Great Leap Forward. The Great Leap Forward thus became a total program of action carried out simultaneously in the economic, political, and social realms. Its driving force was ideology.

The following overview of the dialectical conception of Chinese society which arose from the thought of Mao Tse-tung, lists the major contradictions which gave rise to the Great Leap Forward:

(A)	(B)

I. ECONOMIC CONTRADICTIONS (THE DIALECTIC OF THE ECONOMY)
Contradictions of Sectors

modern	traditional
coast	inland
industry	agriculture
heavy industry	light industry

Contradictions of Goals

select development	simultaneous development
long-term	short-term

Contradictions of Scale

large-scale industry	medium- and small-scale industry

Contradictions of Function

production	consumption
production	accumulation
accumulation	consumption

Contradictions of Operation

capital-intensive	labor-intensive

II. POLITICAL CONTRADICTIONS (THE DIALECTIC OF THE STATE)
Contradictions of Conception

centralism	democracy
"from the top down"	"from the bottom up"

Contradictions of Administration

center	region
centralization	decentralization
vertical rule	dual rule
branch principle (vertical)	committee principle (horizontal)

III. Social Contradictions (The Dialectic of Society)

Contradictions of Social Stratification

workers	peasants
intellectuals	worker-peasant toilers

Contradictions of Political Stratification

bureaucrats	masses
bureaucrats	cadres
cadres	masses

Contradictions of Value

expert	red

Contradictions of Social Cohesion

individual	collectivity
"organic" solidarity	"mechanical" solidarity

Contradictions of Role

specialists	generalists

Contradictions of Motivation

material incentives	ideology
individual rewards	collective rewards
wages	distribution

We have labeled the contradictions in the chart as (A) and (B). All (A) elements were stressed during the First Five-Year Plan period; the Chinese Communists, in 1958, referred to this period as one of "one-sided development." Contradictions arose when the (B) elements were no longer seen as in relationship to the (A) elements, but as in contradiction. Resolution, and hence a new solidarity, would be achieved by (A) + (B); that was what the Chinese Communists meant by the simultaneous development envisaged by the Great Leap Forward.

At the beginning of this section, we stated that the manner of thinking characteristic of the thought of Mao Tse-tung could not be described abstractly, but only in connection with real problems; this we have tried to do by interpreting Mao's general statements on contradictions in the light of those economic, political, and social problems of Chinese society which were of importance for the formulation and implementation of the Great Leap Forward. We have, through this interpretation, reconstructed Mao's vision, or his dialectical conception of Chinese society. Through that vision goes the theme that contradictions are essential to the struggle for unity and transformation. The program of the Great Leap Forward, to which Mao's vision gave rise, was an attempt, within a few short years, to complete the unification of Chinese society and transform China into a modern nation.

Extraordinary about this manner of thinking is its simplicity. Having accepted a few basic philosophical premises from Marxism-Leninism, it then proceeds to combine ideas into a never-ending series of dualities. The main criterion for subjecting an idea to ideological thinking is that it has a clear-cut connection with practical reality; if so, then ideological thinking will eventually ferret out its real dialectical opposite. If the duality turns out to be a contradiction, then ideological thinking will proceed further to envisage the way in which resolution is possible.

Thus, whereas the pure ideology of the Chinese Communists consists of a fixed set of universal ideas, their practical ideology consists of an ever-changing and ever-expanding set of particular ideas, derived from the dialectical combination of ideological thinking with concrete problems. That some combinations may have been wrong or useless makes little difference, since the products of such thinking will always be particular, and not universal, ideas. The manner of thinking, and not necessarily its particular products, will always be universal and true.

That such a consistent yet changing ideology has served to create a web of organization which goes throughout Chinese society is its most remarkable accomplishment. But that web is itself marked by inherent contradictions, as we shall see in the body of this book. Thus, the Chinese Communist ideology of organization shares the same qualities as the organization it has served to create and use.

CHAPTER II

PARTY

SOVIET AND CHINESE CONCEPTIONS

The Party as Organization

In our study of ideology and organization in Communist China the Chinese Communist party occupies a central place. All Communist parties arise in situations of actual or potential revolution. The ultimate aim of all Communist parties, regardless of internal disputes over the means, is the seizure of state power. But what role does it play in society after that aim has been achieved? Where Communist parties seize power, they set up complex structures of organization. Could these structures continue to function without the Communist party—is the Communist party the keystone to the whole structure, so that its disappearance would mean the collapse of the structure? The weight of evidence, in my opinion, is that this is so: given Communist-type organization of state power, a Communist party would have to be created if it did not exist.

This may sound paradoxical, but Cuba provides a case in point. Cuba had an old-line Communist party which was not directly involved in the revolution. On the contrary, Communist-dominated sections of the organized working class appear to have collaborated with Batista to some extent. When Castro came to power, two revolutionary organizations existed: the Castroites, who emerged from the Sierra Maestre as an organized revolutionary force led by urban intellectuals and supported by sections of the peasantry; and the old-line Communist party, deriving its strength mostly from the urban working class. The existence of two revolutionary organizations prevented the formation of a unified organizational instrument. Nevertheless, Castro created a political system increasingly similar to that of the Communist countries. Since such a political system demanded a true Communist-type party, Castro proceeded gradually toward the formation of a single unified party, the United Party of the Cuban Socialist Revolution. The UPCSR has now begun to play a role in Cuban society comparable to the role of the Chinese Communist party.[1] In Cuba, organizationally speaking, it was the revolution which created the party, and not the party that created the revolution.

This was obviously not so in China, yet there are some similarities between China and Cuba. The Chinese Communist party directed the revolution and war that led to the seizure of state power in 1949. After that, the new regime created military and bureaucratic structures. These developed so rapidly that for a time they began to obscure the role of the Party. Victory had brought the Party into an environment, the cities, in which it lacked strength. But the Party quickly started to build up organization in breadth and depth until it was able to take over active leadership and coordination at all levels of the system. This was called the process of Party construction (*chien-tang*), and was similar to the building up of the UPCSR in Cuba.

People from Communist countries speak of "the Party" as if it had a life of its own, transcending the individuals in it. In many interviews with refugees from Mainland China, I asked them to specify whom they meant when they talked abstractly of the "Party." Most of them vigorously defended the abstract reality of the Party by pointing out that when problems arise in an organizational context, you "call the Party" and not a specific individual. Different individuals may appear on call, not as persons but as representatives of the Party. The Party has such clearly perceived functions that the differences of individual personality are submerged, just as with priests administering sacraments.

In some highly routinized organizations the human relationships provide the dynamics the organization needs to function; such organizations often continue to function precisely because of the particular

---

[1] New York *Times*, July 7, 1964.

individuals in it who play the leading roles—if they are transferred, it usually has significant consequences for the functioning of the organization; men are more important than the roles they are required to perform.

Yet there are other organizations where the dynamism flows from the organization itself, where the prescribed roles can be effectively assumed by men of different personality and temperament. In these organizations, values and norms are powerful enough to make men act in strict compliance.

Every Communist party relies heavily on ideology. In parties, such as the Chinese, where the revolutionary tradition has remained alive, ideological indoctrination has a distinct function. Party members are subjected to intensive indoctrination to keep their beliefs effective. In the more bureaucratized Communist parties, ideological indoctrination is less important. Nevertheless, even in such parties, ideology remains a latent instrument which can be reactivated if the leaders, and the external situation, call for it. Khrushchev's attempt to make the Soviet Communist party into a more active organizational instrument was accompanied by a renewed stress on ideology. All organizations tend toward routinization; Communist parties are no exception. Ideology gives the Party's leaders an instrument for combating such tendencies.

The Party has no specific concrete task, such as, let us say, a ministry has. It is an organization in which the leaders are gathered in a context which strengthens their capacity to lead; it is a unique training ground for moral-political leadership, actualized in some other organizational role, not in the Party itself. Party members go forth from Party meetings armed with new policy instructions from the leadership and activated by new ideological and political indoctrination. Routinization of such an organization would simply make the Party into an elite club in which the political leaders meet to renew their solidarity. Routinization would make men more important than their roles; it would make the Party a pluralistic entity held together by interpersonal relationships, somewhat like the Partido Revolucionario Institucionalista in Mexico; it would do away with the unity which gives the Party its unique leadership role in a Communist society, namely that at any time all its members act in a unified fashion throughout the society to carry out policy determined by the top leadership.

In an organization characterized by powerful values and norms, the factor of consciousness becomes important. Values can only be held consciously, and norms can only be acted on if people understand them. All Communist parties have a revolutionary history, even though power itself may have been seized in "old-fashioned" political and military ways. The Party member must be conscious of the values and norms of the system.

Another object of consciousness is the nature and role of the Party. Chinese Communist teachings on "thought" compel the individual to be conscious of the external world, but also to be conscious of himself. In a broader sense, this is true of the Party as well. Periodically its ide-ologists try to see the Party within the larger context. Such self-reflec-tion can be dangerous, for it has often led to crystallization of different views and factionalism. Self-reflection was extremely dangerous during the Stalin period, in view of the chasm between theory and practice. Yet there always has been this will to explain the nature of the Party, state its position, formulate rationally its role in society. Such self-definitions have usually been tortured and evasive, but they have been necessary. Party self-definition can be seen as an inevitable consequence of com-mitment to the importance of ideology.

In a traditional, routinized organization, periodic self-definition means little, because what counts is not so much the values and norms governing the organization but the men in key positions. But, as we have said, Communist parties have always resisted routinization, some-times by purges, more often by renewed outbursts of ideological ac-tivity. If the Communist party plays the role of unified leadership and coordination in society, then it is only the ideology, ultimately, which provides the cement for such unity. The Party is an organization that fulfills executive roles in society. It must provide leadership in a con-text that not only does change but is supposed to change. Any execu-tive decision maker in a rapidly changing organization must be able to justify his impulses leading to certain decisions on the basis of general values and norms. In routinized organizations, it is the advisory and supervisory personnel—"the staff and line of bureaucracy"—that insures continued operation. In a dynamic organization the leader may have a sudden insight of what to do; but the legitimacy for transforming that insight into decision depends on his ability to link it to the broad values and norms that everyone more or less accepts. The more unified such decision-making is supposed to be, the greater number of discrete organizational units it involves, the more important are values and norms. The maintenance of ideology is therefore crucial to executive function and to the continued role of a Communist party. But men do not just manipulate ideology to justify their impulses toward decision. The ideology gradually takes on more concrete form as a body of teach-ing and policy, and begins to have a reverse forcing effect on the deci-sion makers. Cynical playing with ideology has often had disastrous results for those who saw it simply as a useful tool. Despite the manipulation of ideology during the Stalinist period, the Communist party in the Soviet Union has continued to feel the need for meaningful ideology, not just as a façade but as an indispensable part of the whole process of organizational operation. In this sense, it is important to see what sort of self-definition the Party has evolved. If the Party remains the keystone of organization in a Communist society, the way it defines itself throws sharp light on its function.

Party and State

A brief look at the self-definition of the Soviet Communist party should add perspective to that of the Chinese Communist party. In the ideological literature of the Soviet Union, the Party is not construed as an element of the apparatus of state, but as the organized expression of the will of the dominant class of society, namely the proletariat. But it is the Party which leads and controls the state. The 1958 edition of the official primer of Soviet philosophy, published at the height of the anti-Stalin campaign, states the function of the Communist party in the following words:

All these state and public organizations can only function successfully under the leadership of the Communist party, which works out the correct political line, and determines the direction of their practical activity . . . Only the Party, expressing the interests of the entire nation, embodying its collective understanding, uniting in its ranks the finest individuals of the nation, is qualified and called to control the work of all organizations and organs of power. . . . The Party realizes the leadership of all state and public organizations through its members who work in these organizations and who enter into their governing organs.[2]

State and Party are therefore linked but not identical. The distinctions between state and Party seem to be scholastic, but an examination of the organizational history of the Soviet Union and Communist China shows that this is not so. All Communist countries accept the fact that under "socialism" a distinction remains between state and Party. To define the state has been a thorny problem in Marxist polemics since the days of Marx. Nevertheless, Soviet and Chinese Communist literature makes it clear that "state" (gosudarstvo or kuochia) means the formal organization which dominates society. The state is a conscious contrivance. It is the most important element of the superstruc-

---

[2] Osnovy marksistskoi filosofii (Moscow, 1958), pp. 549-550; hereafter referred to as Osnovy.

ture of society, the instrument of its ruling class; in the dictatorship of the proletariat, it is the instrument of the proletariat. As an instrument it has "structure"—a word commonly used in Communist lexicons in association with the concept of state. The state is bureaucracy, army, law; the body of organized formal instruments from which command flows.

The Party, on the other hand, is the organized expression of the will of society. For the Soviets, it is the expression "of the interests of the entire nation"; for the Chinese it represents "the interests of the people." [3] The Party actualizes the control of society over the state. But the Party, theoretically, does not command, for formal command must flow from some instrument of the state. The Communist party may propound policy, but technically it cannot issue orders. These must come from an organ of the state. As long as this fine distinction is maintained, the Party cannot be regarded as an instrument of the structure of state power.

This distinction is not so scholastic as to be meaningless. Any organization must try to maintain a separation between executive functions on the one hand and staff-and-line functions on the other. The task of staff and line is to translate the policy directives of the executive into concrete commands. In the Soviet Union and China, the actual commands come from some organ of state, although they may follow long after the policy has already been announced and wheels have begun to turn at lower levels without waiting for formal communication from the government. Even during the Great Leap Forward, when the Chinese Communists believed that policy could be directly translated into

---

[3] It is significant that the ambiguity of the Russian word *narod* is absent in the Chinese. The official ideological literature of the Chinese Communists states explicitly that the Party is the organized expression of "the interests of the people" (*jenmin*). In other words, the Party is clearly the expression of the will of society, and not of a political entity, the nation. In the Soviet Union, the will of the people and the will of the nation are theoretically identical because all exploiting classes have been eliminated. The Chinese do have a concept of nation, expressed in the word *kuomin*, but the Chinese Communists do not make use of it, because *kuomin* includes exploiting classes which have not yet been fully eliminated from Chinese society. Therefore, the Communist party cannot yet be the expression of the will of the nation, but only of the people, *jenmin*. These remarks, too, may appear to be scholastic, but they illustrate something which I feel to be an important aspect of the Chinese Communist self-conception, namely, that they are still involved in a process of nation-building. This means, concretely, that the Chinese Communist leadership regards the revolution as still in progress. In the Soviet Union, the revolution was concluded with the consummation of the October Revolution.

action and deprecated the technical command functions of the state administration, formal commands, such as they were, still came from the state organs, though many directives did come from the Central Committee.

There are powerful ideological reasons for maintaining the principle that the Party is not a state organ, but there are also practical reasons. The more an organization turns into a command-issuing body, the more it has to grapple with the concrete technicalities of command. This inevitably begins to limit the freedom needed for a wide range of innovative and creative decisions. The Chinese Communists in particular have sharply fought any tendencies toward bureaucratization of the Party, and so have had a strong material interest in maintaining the ideological principle that the Party is not part of the apparatus of state. In the Soviet Union under Stalin where extreme centralization of policy-making functions prevailed, the major concern was that the ministries adequately performed their staff-and-line functions of issuing effective commands. Stalin encouraged far-reaching bureaucratization of the Party (apparatization, so to speak), but theory held that it was still qualitatively different from an organ of state.

State and Society

Soviet and Chinese Communist theorists agree that the Party is the expression of the will of the proletariat, and in a broader sense expresses the will of the nation or the people. The Party may lead the state, but it has its roots in society. The intimate involvement with society, so characteristic of the Chinese Communist party, may be seen as a consequence of this belief. The core of society, for the Chinese Communists, is the masses. In China, the mass line has been a continuing feature of Communist organizational philosophy since Yenan times. The mass line demands that the Party be physically close to the masses. In the Soviet Union, something in the nature of a mass line has been emerging in recent years in the policy of "social will" (*obshchéstvennost'*), which has already had concrete expression in the popular militia, the comrades courts, Party control commissions, and the like. As the Chinese see it, the Party must be close to the masses, for the state has an inherent tendency to become alienated from the masses. One might cite a passage from Friedrich Engels' *Origin of the Family, Private Property, and the State*, which the Chinese have often quoted during their antibureaucratic periods:

The state is therefore by no means a power imposed on society from without; just as little is it "the reality of the moral idea," "the image and the reality of reason," as Hegel maintains. Rather, it is a product of society at a particular stage of development; it is the admission that this society has involved itself in insoluble self-contradiction and is cleft into irreconcilable antagonisms which it is powerless to exorcise. But in order that these antagonisms, classes with conflicting economic interests, shall not consume themselves and society in fruitless struggle, a power, apparently standing above society, has become necessary to moderate the conflict and keep it within the bounds of "order"; and this power, arisen out of society, but placing itself above it and increasingly alienating itself from it, is the state.[4]

The last sentence conveys a feeling that runs through Mao's 1957 speech on internal contradictions within the people. Bureaucracy (an arm of the state) inevitably leads to alienation from the masses, unless a corrective is applied. Mao proclaimed, to the chagrin of the Soviets, that contradictions continue to exist within socialism. One of these is the contradiction between bureaucracy and masses or, more broadly speaking, between state and society. Mao's solution was simple: *the Party is the instrument that forges the resolution of the contradiction between state and society in socialism.*

Since the Marxists regard the state as an instrument of oppression, Soviet theorists have found it difficult to establish the positive role of the state under socialism, especially with the immense growth of formal state power in the Soviet Union. The Chinese Communists have accepted standard Soviet formulations of the role of the state under socialism, but appear to be much less bothered about this question than the Soviets. Both the Soviet and Chinese Communists periodically attack bureaucratism, but the type of attack differs. For the Soviets bureaucratism means the immoral use of state power. For the Chinese Communists, bureaucracy seems inherently evil. This is an expression of the populist strain in the Chinese Communists and also has roots in Chinese revolutionary history. The most terrifying slogan of the Taiping rebels was the cry *ta-kuan*, "Smash the Officials." Hostility to bureaucracy crops up again and again in Chinese Communist history and reached its high point during the Great Leap Forward when the leadership appeared convinced that the economic revolution could more or less dispense with the instruments of formal administration.

The state under capitalism "disposes over the instruments of power: army, police, gendarmerie, court organs, prisons, etc., for the preservation of the economic dominance of the governing class and for the subjugation of contradictions between different classes," but under socialism its role changes.[5] Under socialism, "the army, punitive organs,

---

[4] Fredrick Engels, *Origin of the Family, Private Property, and the State* (New York, 1942); quoted in *Hsienfa went'i ts'ank'ao wenchien* (Peking, 1954), pp. 14-15.

[5] *Osnovy*, p. 477.

intelligence are turned against external enemies. It is economic-organizational and culture-educational work which occupies the main place in the activity of the socialist state." [6] But once communism has definitively triumphed, "in place of administration by people there will come, as Engels has said, administration by things and leadership by productive processes. Then the leadership of the economic and cultural life of society will not have political character, but will be realized without the state." [7] Yet, "under socialism, this leadership still has political character." One might illustrate this Soviet conception of the difference between socialism and communism by the nature of economic planning. When economic planning has become perfect, the command component of planning will vanish and perfect information alone will govern men's decisions. This is the "administration by things and leadership by productive processes" of communism. But under socialism, the command (or political) component in planning is still necessary. Hence there is objective need for state power. State power under socialism, however, means "administration by persons," and, by implication, rule through arbitrary will.

If the Soviet theorists accept "administration by persons" as a necessary evil under socialism, the Chinese Communists in practice have shown far greater reluctance to accept it for socialism in China. One of the cardinal sins of leadership behavior in Communist China is "commandism," a theme which usually arises when the bureaucracy is under attack or when bureaucratic tendencies within the Party are being criticized. But Party leadership, as the Chinese Communists see it, does not mean what the Soviets see as the only alternative to administration by persons, namely leadership through impersonal objective processes. The Marxist distinction between leadership by persons and by things is somewhat similar to the distinction made by some sociologists between personal and institutional leadership. If the state can only rule through personal or institutional leadership, society has other choices for governing itself. The Party, by reaching down into society can tap these instrumentalities of rule, and in so doing needs not make maximal use of formal state power for achieving the development of society. If Soviet theorists are concerned with explaining the role of the state under socialism, the Chinese Communists stress the role of the masses under socialism.

Many contemporary sociologists see society as an integral entity in which the political "subsystem" is a functionally necessary sector. There

---

[6] *Ibid.,* p. 543.
[7] *Ibid.,* p. 544.

is no way in which a theory of "the withering away of the state" can be derived from such a conception. But both Soviet and Chinese theorists distinguish between state and society, accepting the Marxist distinction between substructure and superstructure. In effect, they accept Engels' statement that the state is "that force which arises from society but stands above it and daily becomes more distant from society." In class societies, the alienation of the state from society leads to tyranny. Under socialism, the alienation of the state from society leads to its redundancy, climaxed by its withering away. The withering away of the state is not brought about by its becoming closer to society and thus turning into a functionally integral element of society, but—to the contrary—by the constant diminishing of its functional importance in the operations of society.[8] Soviet theorists do not say much about the distinctions between state and society, at least not for socialist societies. They usually revert to the substructure and superstructure conceptions of classical Marxism: "The substructure of society includes the totality of economic relationships between people that are formed in the process of material production and reproduction of their life." [9] But society is more than a network of economic relationships. The Soviet theorists state:

Economic relationships in real life are tightly interwoven with political, legal, customary, familistic, national, religious, moral and other relationships. Let us take as an example the nation or the family. Characteristic of the nation is the commonness of language, of economic life, of territory, of psychic mentality, of culture. Nations in bourgeois society consist of antagonistic classes—the bourgeoisie and the proletariat. In the family we find elements of economic, customary, work, legal, moral and other relationships between their members. It would be imperative to have a vast force of scientific abstraction so that in all the complex networks of social relationships one could sort out productive, economic relationships as the primary and basic ones, and establish that ideological relationships are dependent on them.[10]

One may not have "a vast force of scientific abstraction" available, but one can deduce from the statement that the "nation," whether in bourgeois or socialist society, does include the state. The "nation" is an organic conception that implies some essential unity between all elements that make it up. Indeed, in this sense it is like the family.

---

[8] Soviet theory, following some of Stalin's latter-day contributions on the subject, nevertheless maintains that "the state is vitally necessary in the first phase of communism" (*ibid.*).

[9] *Ibid.*, p. 441.

[10] *Ibid.*

Nation

We have already alluded to differences in Soviet and Chinese views of the "nation." When Soviet theorists speak of the *sovietskii narod*, they mean the essential unity of all elements that make up the Soviet Union. The Chinese theorists speak not of nation but of people. Such a conception denies the idea of an essential national unity, for the concept "people," *jenmin*, excludes the exploiting classes which still exist in China. China, theoretically speaking, is not yet fully an integral national entity. Mao Tse-tung's theory of the new democracy accepted the existence of basic contradictions within Chinese society—contradictions which were not wholly overcome with the revolution. Mao Tse-tung's speech on internal contradictions among the people changed that conception somewhat, not by asserting that contradictions had been overcome, but by implying the qualitative distinction between "antagonistic" contradictions within the nation and nonantagonistic contradictions within the people. This may be regarded as a step forward in a theoretical conception of the essential unity of the Chinese nation, but it is not the full final step. Stalin denied the existence of human contradictions in Soviet society, though he admitted technological contradictions between the advanced nature of the system and the backward state of the productive forces. Thus, for the Chinese, the existence of the state in a society still marked by contradictions was easier to explain than it was for the Soviets. It also made it easier to conceive of the state as an essentially oppressive instrument, even when used in the interests of the dictatorship of the proletariat.

The dualist distinction between state and society, characteristic of Marxism, was not made by Hegel. Hegel distinguished three elements in human society: family, civil society, and the state. Hegel's conception of civil society greatly influenced Marx's thinking on the nature of society. However, whereas for Marx civil society was the realm of economic relationships, for Hegel it was the realm of human freedom.

Hegel's organic conception of the family seems to be the harbinger of later nineteenth-century thinking on the nature of the nation. If one substitutes the word "nation" for the word "family" in the following passage from Hegel, a statement about the core beliefs of nationalism results: "It is its unity that it feels, the love for its purpose that constitutes the immediate substantiality of spirit for the family. . . . Love in general means consciousness of my unity with another, such that I am not isolated, but gain my self-consciousness only through surrender of my being-for-self, and through knowing myself as in unity with the other and the other with me." [11]

From the mid-nineteenth century, organic conceptions of the nation, often influenced by Hegel, spread outward from western Europe, giving rise to that political phenomenon now known as nationalism. These conceptions struck responsive chords in diverse peoples, even before the abstract teachings, such as those of Hegel, were understood. They led to ideas of "national organism" (*kokutai*) in Meiji Japan; in China, they underlay the ideology of the Kuomintang; in Russia, they shaped the thinking of tsarist intellectuals. Though submerged by Marxism, nationalism re-emerged during the rule of Stalin. For our discussion of state and nation, it is significant that the organic conception of the nation includes the state as an integral element of the national body. Nationalism appeals to the desire of being a part of a larger organic national body; it has turned out to be a powerful ideological instrument for mobilizing popular support to accept revolutionary and authoritarian political systems. In contrast to nationalism, Marxism regards the state as alien to society, despite the fact that it has roots in society. Soviet theorists have in vain attempted to demonstrate the contrary. For Marxism, the state's ultimate fate is disappearance; its task is to aid the forces of history to produce its own disappearance.

Hegel felt that only in civil society is individual freedom realized, even though freedom arises from the existence of the state and the internalization by the individual of the universals of the state. Freedom, according to Hegel, may presuppose the state, but it cannot be attained within the state. Hegel saw the development of freedom as the great achievement of modern Western society, as contrasted with other societies.[12]

Nationalism is unconcerned with the development of civil society. So is Leninism, which saw as its immediate aim the creation and development of the dictatorship of the proletariat. Marxism has retained the ideal of ultimate human freedom for all Communist countries, but postponed it to the future; communism, in its final sense, means the constitution of a truly free and materially effective civil society.

For the new countries of the modern world governed both by nationalist and Communist ideologies, national unity has taken priority over the development of civil society. The ideal of the nation replaced the Hegelian and Marxian conceptions of freedom. Whereas Hegel

---

11 Georg Wilhelm Friedrich Hegel, *Sämtliche Werke*, VII: *Grundlinien der Philosophie des Rechts* (Stuttgart, 1952), pp. 237-238.

12 *Ibid.*, pp. 339-342.

saw civil society as a link between state and family, nationalistic ideologies (including the ideologies of many Communist parties) regard the nation as a link between state and society.

The idea of nation implies the existence of other nations. A nation may be characterized by organic unity, as modern nationalism would have it, but nothing binds one nation to another in any essential fashion. On the other hand, the concept of a proletariat, in Marxist terms, transcends national boundaries. Marx did not perceive bourgeois society in national terms, because the economic relations of capitalism transcended national boundaries. To the extent that capitalism is universal, the proletariat is too. National differences between the working classes of different countries are less important than the common class interests that unite them. Inasmuch as the Communist party expresses the will of the entire nation, it is a national party, and as such has nothing in common with any other national political party. But since it remains a party of the proletariat, it has an essential unity with all other proletarian parties. It would be hard to deny that the whole history of the Communist party of the Soviet Union has seen increasing emphasis on the national, as against the proletarian, conception of the Communist party. In many ways, the stress on the national character of the Communist party is even clearer in the lands of people's democracy. As *Osnovy* puts it: "In the countries of people's democracy, the major role is played by organizations of the national (or people's) front." [13]

Nationalism has developed as a revolutionary ideology aiming at the seizure of state power in a national context. But as the ideology of a triumphant movement, it has also shown an extraordinary predilection toward the conventional instruments of state power: bureaucracies, regular armies, police networks, political parties of an *apparat* type. No nationalist movement has enunciated any doctrine on the eventual withering away of the state. If a doctrine of pure nationalism had superseded Marxism in the U.S.S.R., talk about the withering away of the state would itself have withered away. As it is, official Soviet doctrine now proclaims that state power will continue to exist even in the early stages of communism. In the countries of people's democracy, the nationalist strain is even more apparent because the dominant parties are often united-front parties rather than Communist parties in the classical sense.

In China, the situation appears to be somewhat different. There is a continuing united-front policy, but there is no united party, as, for example, in East Germany and Poland. There is a strong nationalist

---

13 *Osnovy*, p. 537.

strain in China—a phenomenon that few would deny. Nevertheless, the organic conception is that of the "people" rather than that of the "nation." The whole Chinese Communist conception of "the people" implies a continuing revolution, at home as well as abroad. One of Sun Yat-sen's most famous statements was that the revolution had not yet been completed. There is no doubt that this same phrase reflects the thinking of Mao Tse-tung. Though the Chinese conception of the people is different from the classical Marxist conception of the proletariat,[14] it is still closer to it than to the Soviet conception of nation. For the Soviets, the revolution has been completed in theory and in practice. For the Chinese it still continues.

THE PARTY RULES

The document spelling out the Chinese conception of the Communist party is the Party Rules. In China, as in the Soviet Union, each Party congress establishes new Party rules. Although the rules change, the Marxist and Leninist substance has never been seriously modified. The Party rules in force in China at the present time are those adopted at the Eighth Party Congress in September 1956. This congress came at a time of stock-taking in China. The intensive drives in industry and agriculture launched in the fall of 1955 had been slowed down. Though there was discussion about the road China should follow during its Second Five-Year Plan, no decisions had yet been made. The Eighth Party Congress thus can be seen as a time of self-reflection.

We shall analyze the Chinese Communist conception of the Communist party by looking at the general outline of the Party Rules of that congress.

The General Outline of the Party Rules

The introductory sentences give the classic ideological explanation of the nature of the Communist party: "The Chinese Communist party is the vanguard of the Chinese working class. It is the highest form of class organization of the Chinese working class. Its goals are to realize socialism and communism in China."

These sentences and other official commentaries make it clear that the Chinese Communist party sees itself as the party of the industrial

---

[14] Mao Tse-tung has frequently alluded to the fact that in any country 90 per cent of the population is for the revolution and 10 per cent is against it. One of his latest percentile statements in this regard was on the civil-rights movement in the United States.

proletariat of China. Nevertheless, China is still officially regarded as a country made up of different classes. China today is officially described as being in the stage of the "people's democratic dictatorship." The "people" consists of four classes: workers, peasants, urban petite bourgeoisie, and national bourgeoisie.[15] As we have stated earlier, the concept "people," *jenmin*, does not coincide with the concept "nation," *kuomin*, as in the Soviet Union. Reactionary elements remain in Chinese society, inside and outside China. Taiwan is theoretically a part of the Chinese People's Republic, but is ruled by a "reactionary clique." This would presumably mean that China cannot consummate a full transition to socialism until unification has taken place. When the people's democratic dictatorship was proclaimed in 1949, China was construed as being in a "transitional period" leading toward the stage of socialism.[16] In 1955, Mao Tse-tung proclaimed: "At present, our country is in the high tide of the great socialist revolution. . . . In about two or three years, the socialist revolution will have been basically completed within the entire country." [17]

Though there have been a number of references to China being in a socialist stage, there never has been an official proclamation signaling the final transition to the stage of socialism (as in Czechoslovakia, for example). Thus China presumably remains somewhere between "new democracy" and full socialism, though the term new democracy is not used nowadays. Theoretically, it would seem that China could not enter full socialism until the bourgeoisie and other reactionary classes have disappeared. As long as Taiwan is not united to the Chinese People's Republic, a bourgeois and reactionary class remains a part of the Chinese nation. But even if Taiwan were united to the Mainland, the question would remain whether full socialism could be reached as long as even a benevolent bourgeoisie existed which constitutes a segment of "the people." If one looks at the official conception of the nature of the Party and the official class analysis of Chinese society, one must conclude that the Chinese Communist party sees itself as a party engaged in a continuing revolutionary struggle, inside and outside the country. Indeed, as Sun Yat-sen stated, the revolution has not yet been completed.

Mao Tse-tung stated: "The basis of the people's democratic dictatorship is the alliance between the working class, the peasant class, and the

---

15 Mao Tse-tung, "On the People's Democratic Dictatorship," in *Selected Works* (Chinese edition, Peking, 1960), IV, 1480.

16 See the preamble to the 1954 Constitution.

17 See Li Ta, *Chunghua jenmin kunghokuo hsienfa chianghua* (Peking, 1956), p. 47.

urban petit bourgeois class, but mainly between the workers and the peasants." [18] The existence of a bourgeois class is not only admitted, but a segment of it is regarded as a part of the people. Moreover, the bourgeoisie is officially represented by the minority parties, whose existence is sanctioned by adherence to the united-front policy. There are no references in the Party Rules to the fact that the Chinese Communist party expresses the will of the nation or of the people, although Teng Hsiao-p'ing, First Secretary of the Party, in his report on the Party Rules notes that "the Party reflects the interests and the will of the popular masses." [19] Such a conception is theoretically impossible because both "nation" and "people" include elements of the bourgeoisie. A Communist party cannot express the interests of the bourgeoisie. Again, one might argue that such distinctions are scholastic, but the recent ideological history of the Soviet Union and China suggests that this is not so. The Chinese Communist party is not a "united workers party," as are many of the parties of Eastern Europe. The official formulation is that the Chinese Communist party is the party of the proletariat.[20] Nevertheless, whatever it is in name is not exactly what it is in fact.

Strange as it may seem, the Party Rules list no class criteria for membership in the Party: "Any Chinese citizen who works, who does not exploit the labor of others, who recognizes the Party program and rules, who participates in a Party organization and works in it, who carries out the Party's resolutions, and pays Party dues according to regulations, may become a member of this party." Nevertheless, Party documents categorize members as workers, peasants, intellectuals, and "others." Workers and peasants are two of the four classes that make up "the people." But who are the intellectuals? They are not the equivalent of the urban petite bourgeoisie, for many are neither urban nor petit bourgeois. Althought the intellectuals, as we have indicated, constitute a clearly recognizable social stratum, they cannot, according to Marxist theory, be considered a class. The Chinese Communists are extremely careful in their phrasing of written documents, but also operate in highly flexible fashion within whatever interstices are left open within the formal wording. The orthodox Chinese Communist approach in formulating the nature of the Chinese Communist party, compared to that of the Soviets, indicates a persisting radical strain, even though in

---

[18] "On the People's Democratic Dictatorship," p. 1483.

[19] Section 2 of Teng Hsiao-p'ing's report, 1956.

[20] Although this is the formulation in the Party Rules, Teng Hsiao-p'ing in his comments adds: "The Communist party is the collective body of the advanced elements of the proletariat and the toiling people."

their practical recruitment policies, as the quoted statement shows, they have allowed for considerable flexibility.

The Party Rules say nothing about the class origins and class composition of the Party; and they say nothing about the organic relationship between the Party and the people, aside from references to leadership of the masses in the struggle for building socialism. One of the provincial Party primers, however, does make some statements on this problem:

> The Chinese Communist party represents the interests of all races [*mintsu*] of China and of the Chinese people [*jenmin*]. Because the Chinese working class and all the toiling people are the substance of the Chinese race, the interests of the Chinese working class and the Chinese people are identical at all times. It is only when the working class has liberated all the people that it can liberate itself. Therefore, the Chinese Communist party must stand for the interests of all the people, and not just for the immediate interests of its own class. It must organize and solidarize all races in the country and the people of the country, and not just organize and solidarize its own class to carry on the struggle. It is only thus that its leadership of the revolutionary task can succeed.[21]

This is a curious statement which goes beyond the formulations of the Party Rules and Teng Hsiao-p'ing's comments on them. It could hardly have been thought out very carefully, for the term "Chinese race" was deliberately excluded from the 1956 Party Rules, as we know by comparing them with the 1945 Party Rules. Since the format and even the words of the two sets of Party Rules are identical except where deliberate changes have been made, it is significant that the following phrase of the 1945 Party Rules was omitted in the 1956 Party Rules: "The Chinese Communist party represents the interests of the Chinese race and the Chinese people." The crude formulations in the primer therefore reflect a real contradiction in the Party's self-conception. The Communist party is the party of its own class, namely the proletariat, and as such has a revolutionary mission to liberate itself through the liberation of all the people. At the same time its interests are identical with those of the Chinese people (a conception which includes minority nationalities) and also with the Chinese race (a conception which excludes non-Chinese).[22] Although the Party is the party of the proletariat, it recruits "any Chinese citizen" who meets its qualifications. It is both

---

21 *Chungkuo kungch'antang changch'eng chiaots'ai* (Canton, 1957), p. 7.

22 The word *mintsu*, here rendered as race, is also used by the Chinese Communists in the sense of nation, viz., *mintsu-chuyi*, "nationalism." In contrast to the word *kuomin*, which connotes a politically unified national entity, *mintsu* connotes an ethnically unified national entity, in the manner of the German *Volk*.

a "Chinese" and a "Communist" party. Moreover, it is "Chinese" in two senses, in the broad sense of including all races within China's national borders and in a narrower sense of comprising individuals of Chinese race. The Chinese Communist party lives with the same contradiction between its class and its national character as the Soviet Communist party. The difference is, as we have pointed out, that, short of final unification and full socialism, the people and the nation are not yet identical in China.

The second paragraph of the Party Rules proclaims the official ideology of the Chinese Communist party: Marxism-Leninism. The provincial Party primer cited above, which was based on the 1956 Party Rules, describes Marxism this way: "Marxist philosophy (dialectical materialism and historical materialism), the theory of political economy, and the theory of socialism." The primer does not define Leninism, but describes it by two quotes from Lenin: "Without a revolutionary theory, there can be no revolutionary movement"; and: "Only if there is a party guided by advanced theory can one realize the functions of advanced fighters." Thus, the primer implies that Marxism is the pure ideology, and Leninism the practical ideology. Though neither Liu Shao-ch'i nor Teng Hsiao-p'ing, in their reports to the Eighth Party Congress, makes any sharp distinction between Marxism and Leninism (except for Teng's explicit references to the Leninist organizational principle of democratic centralism), Liu's repeated statements about the "standpoint, outlook, and methods of Marxism-Leninism" imply that Marxism-Leninism covers both pure and practical ideology.

In contrast to the 1945 Party Rules, the 1956 Party Rules make no reference to "the thought of Mao Tse-tung." An indirect reference to the contributions of Mao Tse-tung to revolutionary theory and action is contained in the following sentences from the General Outline:

> Marxism-Leninism is not a dogma, but a guide for movement; it demands that people, in the struggle to realize socialism and communism, proceed from reality, actively and creatively use its principles to solve all kinds of problems in the actual struggle; moreover, that they make its theory constantly develop. Therefore, the Party in its actions firmly holds to the principle of tightly unifying the universal truths of Marxism-Leninism with the concrete realities of the Chinese revolutionary struggle, and to oppose any tendencies toward dogmatism or empiricism.

Before the Sino-Soviet dispute, the official view of Mao Tse-tung's contributions, as we have indicated in the chapter on ideology, was that he had successfully applied the truths of Marxism-Leninism to the concrete problems of the Chinese Revolution. This view prevailed during most of the 1950's, despite the fact that in 1945 the thought of Mao

Tse-tung, as the "unified thought of the practice of the Chinese Revolution," had been written into the Party Rules. Mao's demotion on the ideological ladder between 1945 and 1956 undoubtedly is the result of Sino-Soviet ideological relations. In 1945, Liu Shao-ch'i suggested that the experiences of the Chinese Revolution were applicable to other revolutionary situations, thus implying an international ideological role for the thought of Mao Tse-tung.[23] Though the exact nature of the relationships between Moscow and Yenan from 1935 to 1949 still remains to be studied, enough is known to indicate considerable friction and conflict. However, Mao's visit to Moscow in 1949 initiated a period of close collaboration between the Soviet Union and China. Mao's ideological demotion, as further indicated by the treatment of the word "theory" in his *Selected Works* (see pp. 25-26), was perhaps a major ideological concession on the part of the Chinese to the Soviets. At the present time, the generally accepted rubric for the total ideology has again become "Marxism-Leninism and the thought of Mao Tse-tung," and the Chinese again say that the experiences of the Chinese Revolution are applicable to other revolutionary situations. If a Ninth Party Congress were to be held in the near future, such a formulation for the total ideology undoubtedly would be written into the Party Rules.

The third paragraph of the Party Rules recounts the historical de-

---

[23] In his "On the Party," Liu Shao-ch'i stated: "The thought of Mao Tse-tung has led and is leading the Chinese people to achieve final liberation; it also represents an important and valuable contribution to the liberation of all peoples, in particular the liberation of the peoples of the Far East." *Lun-tang* (Peking, 1950), p. 35. However, in his "On Internationalism and Nationalism," written in November 1948, Liu Shao-ch'i was more careful in discussing the applicability of the thought of Mao Tse-tung to national liberation movements. In contrast to the stridently nationalistic tone of "On the Party," the latter speech stresses the fact that "we Chinese Communists are absolute proletarian internationalists"; *Lun kuochi-chuyi yü mintsu-chuyi* (Hong Kong, n. d.), p. 6. If the thought of Mao Tse-tung were directly applicable to other national liberation movements, one would expect to find detailed concrete analyses in official Chinese publications of revolutionary processes in countries other than China, comparable to the voluminous Comintern literature on world revolutionary movements. I have seen few such analyses. In a way, Chinese Communist ideology prevents them from officially presenting such analyses. If practical ideology is the result of the combination of pure ideology with concrete actions, it can only be created and used by someone who is from the country in question. No Chinese could presume to have the requisite knowledge. It is therefore up to the revolutionary forces themselves in each country to produce the kind of analysis that Mao developed for the Chinese Revolution. The Chinese may advise them, but they cannot hand them such an analysis from Peking.

velopment of the Chinese Revolution and the Chinese Communist party. The victory of the Chinese revolution in 1949 over "imperialism, feudalism, and bureaucratic capitalism" resulted in the establishment of the Chinese People's Republic, which "is led by the working class, is based on the alliance of workers and peasants, and is a people's democratic dictatorship." In the transition period from the establishment of the Chinese People's Republic to the building of socialism, "the main tasks of the Party are gradually to complete socialist reform vis-à-vis agriculture, handicraft industry, capitalistic industry and business, and gradually to realize the industrialization of the country."

The fourth paragraph explains these goals in more concrete form. Socialist reform has already been completed, it states. However, there still are remnants of capitalist and individual property, as well as "capitalistic factors." The transition to socialism cannot take place until these have been removed. As is clear, the Chinese Communist party, in 1956, still saw itself in a struggle for the completion of tasks necessary for entrance into complete socialism. By 1956, private industry and business had been nationalized, agriculture had been collectivized, and the handicraft industry cooperativized. In 1958, many cadres thought China was ready to pass into communism, but that dream soon vanished. By 1960, the official literature admitted that China had a long way to go before it ever could enter the stage of full socialism.[24]

---

[24] Since property relations are criteria for determining the nature of social systems, according to Marxism, the stages of socialism are often discussed in these terms. The USSR is officially in full socialism with a dual property system: state and collective property. Private property exists but is not construed as part of the socialist system. Though the Soviets distinguish between collective and cooperative property, the legal and theoretical differences are unimportant (*Iuridicheskii Slovar'* [Moscow, 1956], II, 193-194).

Since the USSR still remains the model of socialism, let us see what the Chinese have said on the subject of socialist property. The following statement was made in 1960 at a time of retreat in the agricultural sector: "From a consideration of the overall process of development, one must distinguish the two stages of socialism and communism. In the socialist stage, one must further distinguish the two stages of socialist collective property and socialist all-people's property. In the stage of collective property, one must further distinguish the stages of basic ownership by the production brigades and basic ownership by the communes. . . . At the present time, the people's communes are in the stage of basic ownership by the production brigades within the stage of socialist collective property. It will still be necessary to go through a long period of effort to create the necessary conditions in order to pass from this to the next stage" (*Jenmin jihpao*, December 20, 1960).

Just as the Chinese Communists distinguished between lower- and higher-stage agricultural producers cooperatives, they now appear to distinguish between lower

The fifth paragraph further develops the theme of the Party's tasks. The Party is to take the lead in providing China with a "great modernized industry, a modernized agriculture, a modernized communications and transportation system, and a modernized system of national defense." The Party must also lead in developing science, culture, and technology; and it must seek to improve the people's welfare and standard of living. The sixth paragraph reaffirms the need for solidarity with China's national minorities. The seventh paragraph calls for further emphasis on the united front. The eighth paragraph announces the external goals of the Communist party: peace, solidarity with fraternal socialist countries, opposition to imperialism, and so on.

Having stated the immediate internal and external goals of the Communist party, the ninth paragraph of the General Outline returns to the question of the Party's role in Chinese society. It states, in strong terms, that Party policy can only be carried out by Party organizations that are deeply imbedded within the masses. The basic method of the mass line is stated in the slogan: "From within the Masses—Back into the Masses." It reiterates:

The Chinese Communist party and its members must establish broad and tight relationships with workers, peasants, intellectuals, and other patriotic people. . . . Every Party member must . . . discuss with the masses, listen to the opinions of the masses, concern himself with the sufferings of the masses. . . . One must make the greatest effort in every Party organization, in every state organ and economic organization to struggle against alienation from the masses, alienation from real life, and against bureaucratic phenomena.

These phrases sound almost scriptural and seem to have little more than hortatory meaning. This is not so. The Eighth Party Congress made explicit that henceforth the Party would concentrate its attentions on the masses and that the Party was to become the link between state and society. And it is here that the great role of the Chinese Communist party was defined for the coming years. The concern of the Chinese Communist leadership over the alienation of state and society was to take concrete ideological form in Mao Tse-tung's famous speech of February 1957 on internal contradictions among the people. The ninth paragraph implies, in effect, that only the Party, not the state, can penetrate into the masses and provide the cement for linking state and society together.

---

and higher stages of socialism. The Soviet Union may be in the state of socialism, but the Chinese are in the process of building socialism. There is a dynamic quality to the latter which is lacking in the former conception.

The tenth paragraph deals with the question of Party organization. It restates that democracy and centralism are the basic organizational principles of the Party. But the weight of emphasis is put on the need to strengthen "democracy":

> The Party must take all efficacious measures to develop internal Party democracy, to encourage the positivism and creativity of all Party members, basic-level Party organizations, and local organizations. . . . Only in this way can the relationships between Party and people be broadened and strengthened . . . and can the Party actively respond to all kinds of concrete conditions and local peculiarities, can Party life become spirited. . . . All Party members and all Party organizations must undergo supervision from the top down and from the bottom up.

Here again we see strong emphasis on the basic-level functions of the Party. The emphasis on "democracy" means emphasis on mass action, and it is thus in line with the new policy of strengthening the basic-level organization of the Party.

The last three paragraphs of the General Outline reaffirm the basic principles of Party organization and action. Having stressed the need to broaden internal Party democracy, the General Outline, in dialectical fashion, once again emphasizes the need for centralism as an instrument for maintaining Party solidarity: "It is the sacred duty of each Party member to be concerned constantly with maintaining the Party's solidarity . . . one must not allow any actions which break up the Party, create factionalism, demand independence from the Party, and place individual interests above those of the Party."

This is followed by a call for continued criticism and self-criticism. As a whole, methods of persuasion are to be used, as indicated by the slogan: "Cure the Disease and Save the Man." However, those who "resolutely refuse to rectify their errors" are to be "struggled against" and even expelled from the Party. The general outline ends with a call to every Party member to subordinate his personal interests to the grand ideal of making China into "a great, powerful, and advanced socialist state," and thereby prepare the road for the attainment of full communism.

So much for the ringing statements of the General Outline. It is the heart and soul of the Party's self-conception. It introduces the line that the Party is to follow in subsequent years. The theme that runs through the General Outline as well as through the whole Eighth Party Congress is the mass line. The Party must get closer to the masses, imbed itself in them. This was proclaimed explicitly as the Party's policy line for the years to come. Beneath the actual words, there is an *implicit* self-conception. It is not easy for the foreigner who has not lived in the

Sturm and Drang of the system to sense this, and, if he does sense it, to put it into words. Let us make the attempt.

The Chinese Communist party conceives of itself as engaged in a continuing revolutionary struggle. The 1956 Party Rules are rather mild on the question of struggle, reflecting the atmosphere prevailing in 1956. Two years later, the tone becomes sharper and more militant. Nevertheless, even in 1956, the sense of an uncompleted revolution is still there. So long as Taiwan is not reunited with the Mainland, China is incomplete as a nation. So long as the stage of full socialism has not been reached, the domestic revolution must go on. By contrast, this sense of struggle is absent in recent Soviet theorization on the nature and role of the Party. As *Osnovy* states: "Under the conditions of Soviet socialist society, where there are no antagonistic classes and where the social-political and ideological unity of the nation has been affirmed, there is no ground for the existence of parties other than the Communist." [25] The Soviet Union has not only completed its revolution, but is well on the road toward the construction of communism.

One also senses in the Chinese Party Rules the fear that state and Party could become alienated from the masses; and a hostility to formal state administration, which comes out much clearer in Teng Hsiao-p'ing's harsh attacks on bureaucratism. In recent years, the Soviets too have been stressing the need for public (*obshchéstvennyi*) control of the bureaucracy, but not with that sense of hostility expressed in the Chinese writings. In the mid-1950's, both Soviets and Chinese moved in the direction of decentralization. Yet the Soviets never undertook such an onslaught against the state administrative system as the Chinese Communists in 1958. Officials have remained internal enemies for the Chinese Communists, just as they were in the revolutionary period. The belief in continuing revolution and the hostility to formal state power go hand in hand. The Chinese word *kuan* traditionally had a broad range of connotations: state, government, administration, and also official. *Kuan* was the enemy of the Taipings, as it was for the Communists during their long struggle for power. If *kuan* is necessarily evil, there is strength in the masses. The Party will wither if it becomes an appendage of the state. It remains strong as long as its *élan vital* comes from the masses. Where the Chinese Communists stress the link of the Party to the masses, the Soviets stress the fact that the Party includes "the advanced, most conscious segment" of the Soviet people. The Soviet Party is an elite, albeit of a popular nature. It is the vanguard in

---

[25] See the 1962 edition of the *Osnovy*. This statement is not found in the 1959 edition, and can be construed as a criticism of the Chinese.

the process of creating an affluent society. The Chinese conception of the Party member is close to that of a guerrilla fighter, sharing the sufferings of the people in an almost never-ending struggle.

Whereas the Soviet Communist party is the elite of a triumphant nation, the Chinese Communist party is the vanguard of a people still engaged in the struggle to build a nation. China, in a sense, has not yet completed its own struggle for national liberation. One might say that Mao's great task in life was not only building a new China on the foundations of a revolution, but completing the revolution itself. This he has not yet accomplished. Socialism is still a long way off, and national unification may be equally far away. At the present time, the Chinese leaders are instilling into the younger generation their own ideology of struggle, in anticipation that they may not be around much longer. Their actions in the economic and international fields are generally flexible and practical but the ideological drums beat again and again: "Learn from the People's Liberation Army." The message to the younger generation is that the revolution has not been completed and that the hope of the new China lies in the masses.

THE DEVELOPMENT OF THE PARTY

The Communist party of China developed from a small conspiratorial organization with little more than fifty members in 1921 into one with a membership of more than 17,000,000 in 1961. This makes it the largest Communist party in the world.[26] Data on Party membership and recruitment are closely guarded secrets, and available figures are usually very general. Yet even the crude figures tell something about the stages in the Party's organizational history. The change in Party recruitment policy which began shortly after 1949 is reflected in the slow growth of Party membership in the next few years. The sharp rise in membership between 1954 and 1956 reflects the new policy of building up a nation-wide Party network which would penetrate the entire country in breadth and depth.

The growing leadership role of the Party is indicated by a continuing rise in membership during the period of the Great Leap Forward. We have no figures on Party membership since 1961, but we know that the scope of the Party's leadership role was reduced after the radical change in economic policy launched early in 1961. One would assume

---

[26] For a similar discussion, see John Wilson Lewis, *Leadership in Communist China* (Ithaca, N. Y., 1963), pp. 108-120.

that this would be shown in a smaller total membership figure and that therefore the leadership has been unwilling to publish Party membership figures. On the other hand, this tendency may already have been reversed. Since the summer and fall of 1962 the Party's leadership role has been consistently stressed, though it is not clear what this means in concrete terms.

The growth of the Party since its founding is shown in the following figures:[27]

YEAR	MEMBERS	YEAR	MEMBERS
1921	57[a]	1948 (mid-year)	3,000,000[t]
1922 (July)	123[b]	1948 (year end)	3,065,533[u]
1923 (June)	432[c]	1949 (October)	4,488,080[v]
1925 (early)	950[d]	1949 (year end)	4,500,000[w]
1927 (April)	57,967[e]	1950 (mid-year)	5,000,000[x]
1927 (later)	10,000[f]	1950 (year end)	5,821,604[y]
1928	40,000[g]	1951 (mid-year)	5,800,000[z]
1930	122,318[h]	1951 (year end)	5,762,293[aa]
1933	300,000[i]	1952 (year end)	6,001,698[bb]
1934	300,000[j]	1953 (mid-year)	6,000,000[cc]
1937	40,000[k]	1953 (year end)	6,612,254[dd]
1940	800,000[l]	1954 (early part)	6,500,000[ee]
1941	763,447[m]	1954 (year end)	7,859,473[ff]
1942	736,151[n]	1955 (year end)	9,393,394[gg]
1944	853,420[o]	1956 (mid-year)	10,734,384[hh]
1945 (April)	1,211,128[p]	1957 (mid-year)	12,720,000[ii]
1946	1,348,320[q]	1959 (mid-year)	13,960,000[jj]
1947 (January)	2,200,000[r]	1961 (mid-year)	17,000,000[kk]
1947 (year end)	2,759,456[s]		

[a] The figure 57 is given by Ho Kan-chih, *Chungkuo hsientai koming-shih*, p. 37. Hu Ch'iao-mu, on p. 7 of his *Chungkuo kungch'antang ti sanshih-nien*, cites the figure 50. *Shihshih shouts'e* (hereafter referred to as *SSST*) 1956, no. 18, pp. 26-27 gives

[27] There seems to be some indication, at least since the "Liberation," that Party membership figures are aggregated twice annually, once at mid-year and again at the end of a year. Figures published late in the summer or the fall, I have assumed to be based on mid-year computations.

an official listing of Party membership figures from 1921 to 1956. Unless otherwise indicated, they are year-end figures. A table based on these figures can be found in Lewis, *op. cit.*, p. 100.

ᵇ Ho Kan-chih, *op. cit.*, p. 40. *SSST* (1956) gives the round figure 100.

ᶜ *Ibid.*, p. 48. *SSST* (1956) gives the round figure of 300 at the time of the Third Party Congress.

ᵈ Hu Ch'iao-mu, *op. cit.*, p. 15. *SSST* (1956) gives the round figure of 1000 at the time of the Fourth Party Congress.

ᵉ Ho Kan-chih, *op. cit.*, p. 106. The rapid increase was spurred by recruitment following the May 30, 1925, incident.

ᶠ *SSST* (1951), no. 16, June 5, 1951; also *Jenmin jihpao*, July 1, 1953.

ᵍ *SSST* (1956). These are figures given at the Sixth Party Congress held in Moscow.

ʰ *SSST* (1956).

ⁱ *SSST* (1956).

ʲ *SSST* (1951). There are grounds for questioning the accuracy of this figure. Nationalist sources claim membership did not exceed 10,000; see *Kungfei chits'eng tsuchih chih yenchiu*, p. 130; hereinafter cited as *Kungfei*.

ᵏ *SSST* (1956).

ˡ *SSST* (1956).

ᵐ *SSST* (1956).

ⁿ *SSST* (1956).

ᵒ *SSST* (1956).

ᵖ *SSST* (1956).

ۊ *SSST* (1956).

ʳ *Kungfei*.

ˢ *SSST* (1956).

ᵗ *Kungfei*.

ᵘ *SSST* (1956).

ᵛ *SSST* (1956).

ʷ *SSST* (1951).

ˣ *Kungfei*.

ʸ *SSST* (1956).

ᶻ *SSST* (1951).

ᵃᵃ *SSST* (1956).

ᵇᵇ *SSST* (1956).

ᶜᶜ *Jenmin jihpao*, August 1, 1953.

ᵈᵈ *SSST* (1956).

ᵉᵉ *Jenmin jihpao*, February 18, 1954.

ᶠᶠ *SSST* (1956).

ᵍᵍ *SSST* (1956).

ʰʰ *SSST* (1956). These are the figures released at the Eighth Party Congress. It was reported that total Party membership comprised 1.75 percent of the total population of China. This means that as of September 1956, the regime reckoned with a population of about 616,700,000.

ⁱⁱ *Hsinhua panyüeh-k'an*, 22 (1958).

ʲʲ *Jenmin jihpao*, September 28, 1959.

ᵏᵏ *Jenmin jihpao*, July 1, 1961, and November 17, 1961.

The periods of rapid recruitment are of considerable interest. The Party grew fast after the great workers strike on May 30, 1925, but declined after the April 1927 break with the Kuomintang. Party strength during the Kiangsi Soviet period is a controversial problem because of the conflict with the Central Committee in Shanghai and the indiscriminate recruitment policy in the red areas. Whatever its strength then, it did not matter in the long run, for the Party was decimated by the loss of the soviet regions. Recruitment started to climb rapidly again as soon as the Communists were established in the Shensi borderlands, but strangely enough membership remained around the 800,000 mark from 1940 until 1945. We know that after 1949 the Party discontinued its policy of rapid recruitment, expelled many members taken in during the civil war, and began to concentrate on building up an urban proletarian base. The impression prevailed in 1952 that, as *Jenmin jihpao* reported on October 23, 1952, "there was a fixed quota for Party membership; when at the 5,000,000 mark, recruitment would end." The adoption of the eight criteria for Party membership late in 1952 even further stressed the Party's policy of qualitative rather than quantitative development.

Reflecting this policy, Party membership between 1950 and early 1954 rose at a slow rate—only 1,500,000 above the 1950 figure of 5,000,000. The jump of almost 1,500,000 in 1954 must be related to the new policies adopted at the Fourth Plenum of February 1954. By mid-1955, Party recruitment intensified once again. Between the summers of 1955 and 1956, membership rose by 3,000,000. New membership was above all the result of the Party's policy to extend its organization over the entire rural area of China. Recruitment slowed down again somewhat during the years of relaxation in 1956 and 1957, but picked up fast during the Great Leap Forward. In general, when the Party felt the need for basic-level work, particularly in the rural regions, the pace of recruitment accelerated. In 1955 the Party announced its program of agricultural collectivization, a policy which could only be carried through with the instrument of Party organizations deeply imbedded in the rural villages. In March 1955, "the first national conference on the work of village basic-level organizations of the Chinese Communist party" was held in Peking. The conference called for an intensification of organizational work in the rural sector. At that time it was announced that of the 220,000 *hsiang* throughout China, basic-level Party organizations had already been established in more than 170,000; and it was reported that there already were 4,000,000 Party members in the rural regions.[28] The conference was held just at the time when the cul-

---

[28] *Jenmin shouts'e 1956*, p. 268.

mination of the struggle with the Kao-Jao clique was announced. Clearly, the leadership was making preparations for a major step forward on the rural scene. To this end, the network of Party organization in the rural areas had to be strengthened. The next large jump in Party membership came in the aftermath of the Great Leap Forward: during 1959 and 1960, Party membership increased by more than 3,000,000. As at the end of the civil war, the failure of the Great Leap Forward found the regime with a Party apparatus that was too big for the new tasks.

If the figures on national Party membership are general, those on the social origins of the membership are even more general. Although figures have been released from time to time, it is difficult to make much of them. The most detailed figures on social composition of membership are those for 1956 and 1957:[29]

SOCIAL COMPOSITION OF PARTY MEMBERSHIP

	1956	1957	Percent increase
Workers	1,502,815	1,740,000	15.7
Peasants	7,417,459	8,500,000	14.5
Intellectuals	1,255,923	1,880,000	49.6
Others	558,188	600,000	7.5
TOTAL	10,734,385	12,720,000	18.5

The categories "worker" and "peasant" are standard class categories, but "intellectual" has always posed difficulties, since an "intellectual" cannot easily be defined by standard Marxist class criteria. Nevertheless, Party membership cards in most Communist parties use the status classification "intellectual." Chou En-lai, in his lengthy report on the intellectuals in January 1956, says nothing on the classification criteria, although he distinguishes between "top-level intellectuals" and "general intellectuals." [30] Presumably, both education and occupation (i.e., mental as against physical labor) enter into consideration. The category "others" is not spelled out, but may refer to the military.[31] The rapid

---

29 Both sets of figures were made public by Teng Hsiao-p'ing, the first during the Eighth Party Congress (*Jenmin jihpao*, September 14, 1956), and the second during the Third Plenum of the Central Committee a year later, in September 1957 (*Jenmin shouts'e 1958*, p. 39).

30 Chou En-lai, *Kuan-yü chihshih-fentzu went'i paokao* (Peking, 1956), p. 12.

31 A Nationalist source gives a breakdown of Party membership by occupation which is apparently based on that given in *Shihshih shouts'e*, XVIII (1956), 27. The figures coincide except that, for some unaccountable reason, the categories "organs"

rise in the recruitment of intellectuals came in the wake of a new attitude toward intellectuals which was outlined in Chou En-lai's speech of January 1956 and which took tangible form in the Hundred Flowers movement which started in the spring of that year.

More detailed breakdowns are not easy to find. The 1956 figures published in the *Shihshih shouts'e* give a breakdown of the aggregate figure for peasant Party membership. The aggregate figure, for the end of June 1956, is 7,417,459. Of these, 5,360,000 are described as poor peasants, and 2,050,000 as middle peasants, with the comment added that most are former poor peasants. These are the only round figures in an otherwise apparently precise listing of membership figures. The implication is that the definition of poor and middle peasant posed practical problems. This same source gives a breakdown by occupation:

OCCUPATIONAL COMPOSITION OF PARTY MEMBERSHIP

	Number	Percent
Industry	1,121,283	10.45
Communication and Transportation	233,631	2.18
Agriculture	6,212,703	57.88
Finance and Trade	532,462	4.96
Culture and Education	416,196	3.87
Organs	1,039,419	9.68
Others	1,178,690	10.98

The figures actually add up to the total, 10,734,384 Party members, and to 100 percent. The category "organs" seems to refer to Party members employed full-time in the Party bureaucracy. "Others" must mean the military and related occupational sectors (e.g., the police). We do not have data by occupation for other years to make possible an estimate of changes. In 1961, it was stated that 80 percent of all Party members had been recruited since 1949, 70 percent since 1953, and 40 percent since the Eighth Party Congress. This would mean that almost 12,000,000 new members were added since the beginning of 1954, and almost 7,000,000 since September 1956. John Lewis has computed that the general rate of attrition is less than 5 percent annually, indicating a low purge rate.[32]

In 1956, Teng Hsiao-p'ing announced that there were more than

---

and "others" have been lumped together into one category, and have been interpreted as Party members in the military. See *Kungfei chits'eng tsuchih chih yenchiu* (Taipei, 1957), p. 132.

[32] Lewis, *op. cit.*, pp. 111-113.

538,000 Party branches in the country; in principle, all *hsiang* throughout the country by that time had Party basic-level organizations. In 1959, Liu Lan-t'ao announced that there were 1,060,000 basic-level Party organizations in contrast to 250,000 in 1949.[33] However, the same figure, 250,000, was also given by Liu Shao-ch'i as the number of basic-level units in the country in July 1951. If these figures are essentially correct it would mean that the development of basic-level organization slowed down in the years immediately following victory—a fact which would accord with the known policy of limiting recruitment and raising the quality of Party members. If we interpret Teng Hsiao-p'ing's references to "Party branches" as meaning basic-level Party organizations, then the following might be noted:

NUMBER OF BASIC-LEVEL PARTY ORGANIZATIONS

1949	250,000
1951	250,000
1956	538,000
1959	1,060,000

If these figures are meaningful, they would indicate a gradual expansion in the size of basic-level units into the early 1950's, followed by a reversal of the trend. This would be expressed in the following calculations:

AVERAGE MEMBERSHIP OF BASIC-LEVEL PARTY ORGANIZATIONS

1949	18
1951	23
1956	19
1959	13

In the early 1950's, the Party concentrated on quality and skills of Party membership, and allowed the basic-level organizational units to expand in size. The low average membership figure for 1959 indicates a policy of small tight basic-level groups spread as widely as possible over the country.

One of the most vexing problems in the data is the Party membership of the military. Party members in the armed forces are included in the

---

[33] *Jenmin jihpao*, September 28, 1959. See Lewis, *op. cit.*, pp. 115-117.

general totals of Party membership. In 1951, Liu Shao-ch'i announced that there were 2,700,000 Party members, out of a total of 5,800,000, in "the military, state organs, factories, mines, and schools." This listing presumably reflects the order of magnitude of Party membership in each branch. In 1953 it was revealed that there were 1,200,000 Party members in the armed forces.[34] Such membership presumably remained high during the Korean War, and declined only with the large-scale demobilization in 1955.[35] If there were indeed as many as 1,200,000 Party members in the armed forces in 1953, this would have left only 4,800,000 civilian Party members.[36] This would make the build-up to 10,000,000 civilian Party members in 1956 even more remarkable. Many demobilized Party cadres probably went back to their villages in 1955 and became core cadres in the collectivization movement. The demobilized veterans formed a nucleus for Party build-up in many villages where Party organizations had not yet been established.

During July-August 1956, several articles appeared in *Jenmin jihpao* giving figures on Party membership in various provinces. Information is not given for all provinces.[37] (See next page.)

Despite the incompleteness of the figures, a few tentative conclusions may be drawn. Teng Hsiao-p'ing, in his report to the Eighth Party Congress, gave the ratio of Party membership to total population as 1.74 percent. The regions that approach or surpass the national ratio are Inner Mongolia, Kansu, Shantung, and Shanghai. All are regions of major industrial and urban development. During the middle of 1959, Party membership in Inner Mongolia had risen to 224,000. This would make for 2.1 percent of an estimated population of 10,264,000. Party membership in Inner Mongolia thus increased at a faster rate than the

---

[34] *Jenmin jihpao*, July 1, 1953.

[35] See Peter Tang, *Communist China Today* (2nd edition, Washington, D. C., 1961), p. 403.

[36] *Jenmin jihpao*, July 1, 1953, lists the combined membership (civilian) of North China, South China, and Manchuria as 3,400,000.

[37] The figures for provincial Party membership are printed in the following issues of the *Jenmin jihpao*, 1956: July 3, 4, 12, 13, 20, 25, 27, 28, 29; August 4, 8, 16, 19. On August 31, a new figure of 167,000 was stated for Party membership in Inner Mongolia. The figures for Kweichow published on July 3 also noted that there were 104,000 Party members in villages, and 4,598 in enterprises. Figures for Kiangsu and Kwangsi are taken from Union Research Institute files. The figure for Hunan is given in Lewis, *op. cit.*, pp. 114-115, where a similar table can be found. The population figures are based on the census figures which relate to mid-1953 and to figures given in *Chūgoku nenkan 1961* (p. 400) which purport to give the 1957 year-end population. Calculations for the mid-1956 population are based on the assumption of an even rate of increase or decrease between these two points in time.

population in general. Party membership for the country as a whole also increased at a faster rate than population. According to John Lewis' calculations, there was one Party member for 94.8 individuals in 1950 and for 39.4 in 1961.[38] This would still make only for a 2.5 percent ratio, compared to 4.2 percent (or less) in the U.S.S.R., not to mention the very high ratio of 11.6 percent in Czechoslovakia.[39]

PARTY MEMBERSHIP IN THE PROVINCES (MID-1956)

Region	Party membership	Population	Percent
North China:			
Inner Mongolia	151,756	8,164,000	1.87
Northeast China:			
Kirin	195,720	12,130,000	1.6
Liaoning	400,000	23,891,000	1.6
Northwest China:			
Kansu	216,000	12,852,000	1.7
Shensi	200,000	17,381,000	1.15
Sinkiang	68,000	5,384,000	1.3
East China:			
Kiangsu	600,000	43,904,000	1.36
Shantung	1,120,000	51,042,000	2.19
Shanghai	150,000	6,669,000	2.25
Chekiang	190,000	24,462,000	0.7
South-central China:			
Hunan	282,000	35,222,000	0.8
Honan	509,540	47,195,000	1.08
Kiangsi	250,000	17,997,000	1.3
Kwangsi	108,598	19,447,000	0.5
Southwest China:			
Kweichow	139,000	16,273,000	0.88
Yunnan	182,000	18,553,000	1.0

Whatever the true population figures were for 1953, the Party to population ratio could have been little more than 1 percent. However, the figures available suggest important regional differences in the ratio.

---

38 Lewis, *op. cit.*, p. 116.

39 See *China News Analysis*, No. 309. The U.S. Department of State publication *World Strength of Communist Party Organizations* for January 1962 gives Soviet Party strength as 7 per cent of the adult population, and that of Czechoslovakia as 11.6 per cent of the total population. It gives the figure 2.4 per cent for Communist China.

A few other fragmentary figures may be cited to illustrate this. In September 1959 it was reported that Canton City had 60,000 Party members organized into 3,000 basic-level units. They constituted 3 percent of the total city population.[40] In March 1959 Party membership in Kwangtung Province came to 710,000, which included 230,000 new members recruited since the beginning of 1958. If one assumes a population of around 38,000,000 for Kwangtung in March 1959, this means 1.8 percent of the total population.[41] In July 1959, it was reported that Shanghai had a total of 240,000 Party members organized into 15,000 basic-level organizations. This represents a significant increase over the 150,000 reported for the middle of 1956. This means that Party membership comprised 3 percent of the city population, assuming that the population of Shanghai had surpassed the 7,000,000 mark. The same report also mentioned that 60,000 workers had joined the Party during the preceding year, thus making it apparent that the bulk of new recruitment had taken place in 1958.[42]

The Canton and Shanghai instances suggest that a ratio of 3 percent may be standard in the cities. Around mid-1959, the total urban population evidently was around 98,000,000.[43] Party membership for that period was just under 14,000,000. The corresponding figures for mid-1957 would be approximately 91,800,000 and 12,720,000. Three percent of the population totals in each case would amount to 2,940,000 and 2,754,000 respectively. The total number of worker and intellectual Party members for mid-1957 came to around 3,600,000. Since the bulk of the workers live in cities, one can conclude that the difference is accounted for by intellectuals in rural areas. If the reports about stepped-up worker recruitment into the Party during 1958 are generally true, this might indicate a considerable transfer of intellectuals from urban to rural areas. This was the period of *hsiafang*, the transfer of intellectuals and professionals to farms and factories to do manual labor.

At no time has the Party to population ratio exceeded 2.5 percent. The ratio in China is the lowest of that for any country in the Soviet bloc, as can be seen from the table on the next page.[44]

The three countries with the highest ratios, Czechoslovakia, East Germany, and North Korea, are also the most industralized countries in

---

[40] *Kuangchou jihpao*, September 27, 1959.

[41] Hong Kong, *Takung-pao*, July 2, 1959.

[42] Shanghai, *Wenhui-pao*, July 1, 1959.

[43] Based on Leo A. Orleans, *Professional Manpower and Education in Communist China* (Washington, 1960), p. 155.

[44] Based on *World Strength of Communist Party Organizations*, January 1962.

the bloc. In China, many reports indicate that Party membership in factories may constitute as much as 20 percent of the labor force. The ratio of urban Party membership to total urban population seems to be consistently higher than that in rural areas. It could be that a high Party-versus-population ratio is compatible only with a high level of industrialization and modernization. One major reason for this might be education. Since the Party is such an important instrument of communication, Party members must have enough education to fulfill their information-gathering and policy-interpreting functions adequately.

RATIO OF PARTY MEMBERSHIP TO POPULATION (1961)

Country	Estimated Population in 1961[a]	Party membership[b]	Ratio (percent)
Albania	1,660,000	53,659	3.2
Bulgaria	7,943,000	500,000+[d]	6.3
Cuba	6,933,000	27,000[c]	3.9
Czechoslovakia	13,776,000	1,600,000[d]	11.6
Eastern Germany	16,061,000	1,600,000	9.9
Hungary	10,028,000	478,000[d]	4.8
Mongolia	968,000	43,902[d]	4.5
North Korea	8,430,000	1,311,563	15.5
North Vietnam	16,690,000	600,000	3.6
Poland	29,956,000	1,300,000[d]	4.3
Romania	18,567,000	869,759	4.7
USSR	218,000,000	9,176,005[d]	4.2
Yugoslavia	18,607,000	1,000,000+	5.4

[a] United Nations Statistical Yearbook, 1962.
[b] Official claim in 1961.
[c] No date of official claim given.
[d] Including candidate members.

Membership standards in most Communist countries are high and invariably require a certain level of education. In China, there have been two periods of great transfer of intellectuals from urban to rural areas, once during *hsiafang* in 1957-1958 and more recently in 1963 and 1964. There have been similar campaigns in the Soviet Union to get educated city youth out onto the farms. The implication of these moves is that educated people are needed in the rural areas. Judging from the figures, there was reluctance to raise Party to population ratios in rural areas to the urban level. We suggest that one of the main reasons for the low Party to population ratio in rural areas may be the educational qualifications required by Party membership. However, another reason may be the greater need for a small core cadre group in the rural areas.

THE STRUCTURE OF THE PARTY

The formal structure of the Chinese Communist party is essentially like that of the Soviet Communist party. It is hierarchically organized, which means that the whole structure resembles a pyramid. It has a far-flung base ramifying throughout the society and culminating in an apex where supreme power resides. The Party stands in alter-ego fashion alongside every organized unit of state and society. Wherever there is a factory, bureau, school, production brigade, military company, there also is a unit of the Communist party. This parallelism makes it possible for the Party to exercise direct leadership over every unit of organization to which it is linked. Linkage is created by the fact that leaders of the organizational unit are members of the Party and thus subject to Party discipline.

There are four levels, or echelons, of Party organization, following exactly the structuring of state and society. They are (1) the central organizations of the Party, (2) the organizations of the Party in the provinces, autonomous regions, directly attached cities, and autonomous *chou*, (3) the organizations of the Party in the *hsien*, autonomous *hsien*, and cities, and (4) the basic-level Party organizations.[45] The

---

[45] The administrative divisions of China were fixed by Article 53 of the Constitution. Although boundary lines have been redrawn from time to time, the basic system has remained unchanged. The main divisions are: (a) provinces, (b) autonomous regions, and (c) directly attached cities. As of 1960, there were the following provinces (in official order): Hopei, Shansi, Liaoning, Kirin, Heilungkiang, Shensi, Kansu, Chinghai, Shantung, Kiangsu, Anhwei, Chekiang, Fukien, Honan, Hupei, Hunan, Kiangsi, Kwangtung, Szechwan, Kweichow, Yunnan. There were five autonomous regions: Inner Mongolian Autonomous Region, Ninghsia Hui Autonomous Region, Sinkiang Uighur Autonomous Region, Kwangsi Chuang Autonomous Region, and the Tibetan Autonomous Region. There were 14 directly attached cities (i.e., under direct administration of Peking) in 1953, but by 1960 only Peking and Shanghai remained under direct central administration (Tientsin was returned to the administrative jurisdiction of Hopei province in February 1958); see Union Research Institute, *Chungkung shihnien* (Hong Kong, 1960), p. 18; *Chūgoku nenkan 1961* (Tokyo, 1961). Provinces and autonomous regions are further divided into autonomous *chou*, *hsien*, autonomous *hsien*, and cities. *Hsien* and autonomous *hsien* are further divided into *hsiang*, nationality *hsiang*, and towns (*chen*). Directly attached cities and the majority of regular cities are divided into districts (*ch'ü*). Autonomous *chou* are divided into *hsien*, autonomous *hsien*, and cities. See Chou Fang, *Wokuo kuochia chikou* (Peking, 1957), p. 104.

first three levels are parallel to the state administration; the basic-level Party organizations are for the most part parallel to units of production or to small-scale units of territory.

The Central Organizations of the Party

The National Party Congress theoretically represents the source of authority and the agent of legitimation of the operative central organizations of the Party. Under the 1945 Party Rules, national congresses were to have been held once every three years; under the 1956 Party Rules, they are to be held every five years. There have been eight Party congresses in the history of the Chinese Communist party: 1921 Shanghai, 1922 Shanghai, 1923 Canton, 1925 Canton, 1927 Wuhan, 1928 Moscow, 1945 Yenan, September 1956 and May 1958 Peking (two sessions).[46]

The Party congresses have the important function of adopting long-term policy lines for coming periods. The long intervals between Party congresses usually reflect the inability of the Party to emerge with an over-all Party line. Indeed, the setting of "line and policy" is explicitly stated in the Party Rules as one of the major functions of the Party congresses. The Party congresses also ratify changes in the membership of the Central Committee, thus revealing something about the constellation of power at the supreme level. The adoption of new policy decisions is always preceded by long reports from the leadership which sum up the existing situation in various sectors of national life and point the way toward the future. Thus, far from being a ritual, the Party congresses mark decisive periods in the political development of Communist leadership.

The National Party Congress legitimates the appointments to the Central Committee of the Party. The Central Committee includes all top leaders of the Party. It meets in plenary session only on special occasions, which are marked by the announcement of new policy decisions worked out in the Politburo or the Standing Committee. Plenary sessions are attended not only by full and alternate members, but as the occasion demands by others, such as provincial Party cadres. Since 1949 the following plenary meetings of the Central Committee have been held:

The Second Plenum of the Seventh Central Committee (March 1949): preparations for convening a political consultative conference

---

[46] This is the only instance where a second session of a Party Congress was held. The second session of the Eighth Party Congress adopted Mao Tse-tung's ambitious plan for the development of Chinese agriculture, and thus paved the way for the establishment of the communes.

and a government of democratic union; discussion of the eight-point proposal for negotiations with the Nanking government.

The Third Plenum of the Seventh Central Committee (June 1950): discussion of measures to improve the economy, on land reform, on foreign relations, on the united front, on financial and economic measures, and on military questions.

The Fourth Plenum of the Seventh Central Committee (February 1954): initiation of the struggle against Kao Kang; discussion on convening a National People's Congress.

The Fifth Plenum of the Seventh Central Committee (April 1955): affirmation of the Kao-Jao purge announced in the March National Party Delegates Meeting; appointment of Lin Piao and Teng Hsiao-p'ing to the Politburo; establishment of Party control commissions at all levels.

The Sixth (enlarged) Plenum of the Seventh Central Committee (October 1955): implementation of agricultural collectivization; discussion of a plan to convene a National Party Congress.

The Seventh Plenum of the Seventh Central Committee (August-September 1956): discussion of the impending Party Congress.

The First Plenum of the Eighth Central Committee (September 1956): election to leadership positions in the Central Committee.

The Second Plenum of the Eighth Central Committtee (November 1956): discussion of the Hungarian uprising, of economic and financial plans for 1957, and of the food situation.

The Third (enlarged) Plenum of the Eighth Central Committee (September-October 1957): discussion on the rectification movement; discussion of plans for decentralization of economic administration, and of a new wages and welfare policy; unexpected ratification of Mao Tse-tung's plan for the development of agriculture.

The Fourth Plenum of the Eighth Central Committee (May 1958): implementation of Mao's plan for the development of agriculture and the general line of socialist construction.

The Fifth Plenum of the Eighth Central Committee (May 1958): ratification of new appointments to the Central Committee and to positions within the Central Committee.

The Sixth Plenum of the Eighth Central Committee (November-December 1958): discussion of the reorganization of the communes; of 1959 production targets; of Mao Tse-tung's retirement from the position of chairman of the Republic.

The Seventh Plenum of the Eighth Central Committee (April 1959): discussion of the 1959 economic plan; of commune reorganization; ratification of appointments to government positions.

The Eighth Plenum of the Eighth Central Committee (August 1959): discussion of revised figures for 1958 production; of a decision to launch a movement against rightist tendencies.

The Ninth Plenum of the Eighth Central Committee (January 1961): discussion of a new economic policy; of the Moscow meeting of Communist parties; of a rectification movement within the Party.

The Tenth Plenum of the Eighth Central Committee (September 1962): discussion of the new economic policy stressing primacy of agriculture; strengthening the role of Party, military, and police.[47]

In addition to plenary meetings, the Central Committee has from time to time held extraordinary meetings which convene some or all members of the Central Committee, as well as select personnel outside the Central Committee. Such meetings are held presumably because the full Central Committee, for one reason or another, cannot or should not meet in plenary session. Thus the National Party Delegates Meeting (enlarged) which met in March 1955 was informed of the purge of Kao Kang and Jao Shu-shih. The Central Committee most likely could not meet in plenary session in view of the purges. But a plenary meeting was held immediately thereafter in April, which ratified a reorganization of the Central Committee. There have been other meetings of the Central Committee or parts of it, which have not been officially announced. Such meetings often become known some time after the event in the form of casual references. Thus, in November 1951, the Central Committee held a meeting which discussed basic decisions on the mutual-aid-team movement, on economizing, and on the *Sanfan* and *Wufan* movements (see p. 318). That such a meeting had been held was made known by a reference late in 1953. Again, the Central Committee met in December 1953 to discuss collectivization; nothing became known about it until 1955. There have been large meetings of Party cadres from all over the country, such as that convened in July 1955 to discuss the implementation of collectivization. Why this was not labeled an enlarged meeting of the Central Committee is not clear. There were several important meetings of Party leaders in late 1957 and early 1958 which discussed the Great Leap Forward: the Hangchow meeting of December 1957, the Nanking meeting of January 1958 (both of which discussed amalgamation of collectives), and the Chengtu meeting of March 1958 (which presumably paved the way for the implementation of Mao Tse-tung's plan for the development of agriculture).[48] Although little is known about the nature of these meetings,

47 *Chungkung shihnien*, pp. 8-11; *Jenmin jihpao*, September 29, 1962.
48 *Chungkung shihnien*, pp. 8-11.

they are apparently different from meetings of the Politburo or the Standing Committee. Yet, enlarged meetings of the Politburo also take place. We know from Liu Shao-ch'i's speech to the second session of the Eighth Party Congress in May 1958 that there was an enlarged meeting of the Politburo in April 1956.[49] From later indications, it seems that at this meeting Mao's twelve-year plan for the development of agriculture was rejected.

The form that these various meetings take clearly is an indication of top-level power politics. The fact that some of these meetings were not announced and that no communiques were issued indicates that no hard and fast policy line was adopted. But one thing is certain: If a plenum of the Central Committee is announced, this means that a policy decision has been made. Such plenums thus take on the form of meetings that discuss policy in operational terms. Invited to those meetings are all those directly responsible for implementation, such as local Party secretaries. One would presume that the ideal pattern of decision-making is that the Politburo makes the policy decision and the Central Committee discusses modifications and operational measures. But it may not always be so. Judging from the length of many of these meetings, vigorous discussion goes on. Long reports are read, and participants break up into small group sessions to discuss them. The intriguing question is whether these enlarged sessions ever lead to a reversal or decisive modification of a decision made by the Politburo.

We do not know much about the internal dynamics of Central Committee meetings, and only a little more about its internal structure. The Party Rules are not very informative on the subject. They state simply (Article 37 of the 1956 Party Rules) that the full Central Committee elects the Politburo; it further elects one chairman, several deputy chairmen, and one secretary. The Politburo and its standing committee "exercise the authority of the Central Committee" when the full Central Committee is not in session; the Central Secretariat "resolves routine business of the Central Committee." The chairman and deputy chairmen of the Central Committee are simultaneously chairman and deputy chairmen of the Politburo. An honorary chairman may be selected by the Central Committee. As of November 1960, there were ninety-six full members and ninety-four alternate members of the Central Committee. Mao Tse-tung was chairman, and Teng Hsiao-p'ing general secretary. There were five deputy chairmen: Liu Shao-ch'i, Chou En-lai, Chu Teh, Ch'en Yün, and Lin Piao. The Politburo consisted of nineteen full members and six alternate members. The Standing Committee consisted of seven members: the chairman, the general secretary, and the

---

[49] *Jenmin shouts'e 1959*, p. 21.

five deputy chairmen. The Secretariat consisted of eight full members and three alternate members. One of the significant aspects of the top leadership is that loss of power by one or more members of the establishment is not always reflected in loss of position. It seems fairly clear by now that Ch'en Yün advocated an economic strategy during 1956 and 1957 that was opposed to Mao Tse-tung's comprehensive plan for the development of the national economy. Though he has not often appeared in public in recent times, he continues to function in name as a member of the Politburo. The same is true of P'eng Te-huai who continues in name as a member of the Politburo, despite his removal from the post of minister of national defense in September 1959. In general terms, this appears understandable because of the reluctance of the Chinese (in contrast to the Russians) to tamper with formal structure, preferring to change content.

In the previous chapter we pointed out that the theory of contradictions, applied to the Politburo, leads to the juxtaposition of different opinion groups. Since the men representing these opinions are not removed from the Politburo, it cannot easily act as a body at times. As a result, other organizations of the Central Committee have risen in importance, notably the Secretariat.

For the most part, the Secretariat appears to be staffed by men loyal to the Mao-Liu mode of thinking. Some Japanese observers have suggested that the Secretariat serves as an important channel of direct command and communication between the *de facto* top leadership and the local Party apparatus. There is also a Military Affairs Committee, of which very little is known. Presumably it is a kind of Supreme Council of National Defense. The 1956 Party Rules called for the establishment of a General Political Department, *tsung-chengchih-pu*. This organization was assigned the task of carrying out ideological and organizational work in the army "under the leadership of the Central Committee." Of late, this organization has achieved greater prominence with the establishment of political departments, *chengchih-pu*, in branches and units of economic administration and management. This campaign has been tied in directly with a movement "to learn from the People's Liberation Army." One wonders why the various operational bureaus of the Central Committee were not entrusted with the new administrative tasks. There may be a clue in the fact that the chiefs of these operational bureaus are all second-stringers. Only one, Lu Ting-yi, Chairman of the Propaganda Bureau, is an alternate member of the Politburo. We know that Li Hsien-nien is the chief of the General Political Department for Finance and Trade, yet the chief of the Finance and Trade Bureau of the Central Committee is a minor figure, Ma Ming-fang. The Chinese operate with a fairly clear distinction between policy and operational functions. The work bureaus of the Central Committee appear clearly to be of the operational type. The growing importance of the general political departments would thus appear to indicate that greater attention is being given to policy functions in the economic field. China had its period of economic laissez-faire during 1961 and 1962, and benefited from it by a remarkable recovery. Since then Peking has been planning a new program of positive economic development, namely its Third Five-Year Plan. These general political departments undoubtedly will play a major role in working out economic policy.

The Party Control Committee, headed by Tung Pi-wu, is concerned with maintaining internal Party unity. Its role grows whenever an internal discipline problem faces the Party. The Control Committee was active in 1955, undoubtedly during the internal Party rectification movement of the winter and spring of 1957 and 1958, again in the fall of 1959 when the movement against rightist tendencies started, and again in the winter of 1960 and 1961. It does not make major policy decisions.[50]

Little is known about the functions of the different departments and committees of the Central Committee. The Party Rules (Article 34) state only that "the Central Committee, through Party fractions in central state organs and in national people's bodies, directs the work of these organizations." All members of the Central Committee who hold high governmental position are members of the so-called Party fractions (see pp. 159-162). Departments and committees of the Central Committee presumably are in constant contact with these fractions and serve as coordinating bodies. Basic administrative decisions are made by the Party fraction. Almost nothing is known about decision-making and discussion within the Central Committee itself. Political analysis of the workings of the Central Committee or of the Politburo is usually based on knowledge of the organizational functions, opinions, and personal history of the members (so far as they are known), and known changes in the composition of the Central Committee or the Politburo. The Eighth Party Congress introduced some changes in the structuring of the Central Committee, namely the establishment of a Standing Committee. As Teng Hsiao-p'ing states in his official report on the new Party Rules: "The Standing Committee of the Politburo will continue to exercise the tasks of the Central Secretariat which many years of Party experience have proved to be necessary and proper; . . . the Central

---

[50] See *Biographic Directory* (U.S. Department of State, Bureau of Intelligence and Research, July 20, 1960), Vol. I.

Secretariat will undertake the resolution of the routine business of the Central Committee, under the leadership of the Politburo and the Standing Committee of the Politburo."

The decision to establish a Standing Committee reflected fears that a strong Secretariat could assume independent power, as during Stalin's and Khrushchev's rise to power. Kao Kang, boss of Manchuria and leading opponent of Mao Tse-tung during the early 1950's, may have used the Secretariat to advance his power position. If one applies the distinction between policy and operations, discussed in the management chapter, to the Standing Committee and the Secretariat, one can conclude that the changes announced at the Eighth Party Congress gave policy-making power to the former and operational functions to the latter. The members of the Standing Committee were, in late 1956, the old stalwarts of Yenan: Mao Tse-tung, Liu Shao-ch'i, Chou En-lai, Chu Teh, Ch'en Yün, and Teng Hsiao-p'ing (Lin Piao was added in May 1958). However, in view of Ch'en Yün's apparent opposition to Mao's economic programs, Chu Teh's inactivity in politics, and Lin Piao's reported illness, it is questionable whether the Standing Committee as constituted in 1956 now represents the full top-level leadership core.

The Politburo is the supreme decision-making body within the Central Committee. Given its membership of nineteen full and six alternate members (as of November 1960), it indeed represents a "small group," of a size that allows for free and effective discussion. Here again little is known of the actual nature of the internal decision-making and problem-discussion process, and inferences can only be made from knowledge of the personalities and views of the members. Meetings of the Politburo are rarely announced, and it is only in retrospect that one knows that a meeting has been held.

Thus, for example, the communiqué of the Fourth Plenum of the Seventh Central Committee revealed that the Politburo had met in October 1953 to discuss "the general line during the transition period," and again in December 1953 to discuss "the draft·proposal on the strengthening of internal Party solidarity" which was to be presented to the Fourth Plenum;[51] likewise it was revealed that there was an enlarged meeting of the Politburo in August 1958 in the resort town of Peitaiho which decided on the formation of the people's communes and the intensification of action in the Taiwan Straits;[52] again, we know that there was an enlarged meeting of the Politburo in February 1959 in Chengchow which discussed reorganization of the people's communes.[53]

[51] *Jenmin jihpao*, February 18, 1954.
[52] *Ibid.*, September 1, 1958.
[53] *Chungkung shihnien*, p. 11.

Undoubtedly every plenary or nonplenary meeting of the Central Committee is preceded by a full or enlarged meeting of the Politburo. The "enlarged" (*k'uota*) meetings of the Politburo or the Central Committee include outside individuals expected to be of use in formulating the final decisions.

The scholar K. C. Chao has stated: "The present large size of the Central Committee combined with the relative infrequency of its meetings has made it more and more difficult for that body to play a major role in the day-to-day decisions of the party." [54] It is doubtful, however, whether the full Central Committee has, in recent times, ever concerned itself with "the day-to-day decisions of the Party." Decision-making, where it occurs collectively, requires a small, manageable group. The larger the group, the more formalized the situation, and the less the possibility for effective discussion, let alone making of decisions. After 1945, the Central Committee became a large body, consisting of upwards of forty full members, and almost as many alternate members. The Eighth Party Congress increased the size of the Central Committee, which probably reflected the growing role of the Party. Major decisions made in the Politburo, and by the Standing Committee of the Politburo, are not necessarily followed by meetings of the Central Committee. The Peitaiho "enlarged" meeting of the Politburo in August 1958, which made the decision to launch the people's communes, was not followed by a meeting of the Central Committee. There are indications that the decision was made in a hurry, thus permitting neither time for detailed plans nor for the convocation of a full Central Committee meeting. The Sixth Plenum, which met toward the end of November 1958, was concerned with a different kind of decision: modifying extremism in the commune program.

In discussing the structure of the central organizations of the Party, mention must be made of the "central bureaus" and "central branch bureaus." After victory in 1949, six central bureaus were established: Northeast China (Mukden), North China (Peking), East China (Shanghai), South-central China (Wuhan), Southwest China (Chungking), and Northwest China (Sian). In addition, there were four central branch bureaus: Inner Mongolia, Shantung, South China, and Sinkiang. The six central bureaus were abolished in the summers of 1954 and 1955, when the struggle for unification had been won against "independent kingdom" tendencies in the Northeast (Manchuria) and in East China (Shanghai). At the same time, two of the four central branch bureaus were also abolished: Shantung and South China. How-

---

[54] Chao Kuo-chün, "Leadership in the Chinese Communist Party," *The Annals of the American Academy of Political and Social Science*, 321 (1959), 42.

ever, around this time a Shanghai branch bureau was established which remained in existence till 1958.[55] In September 1955, the Sinkiang central branch bureau was abolished with the formation of the Sinkiang-Uighur Autonomous Region. Shortly thereafter the Inner Mongolia central branch bureau was abolished with the formation of the Inner Mongolian Autonomous Region. Aside from the Shanghai bureau, no other bureaus of the Central Committee seem to have been in existence until 1961. In January 1961, the communiqué of the Ninth Plenum announced the establishment of six central bureaus of the Central Committee for the same six regions for which central bureaus were established in 1949. Since then little has been reported on the operations of these new central bureaus.[56]

The 1945 Party Rules provided for the establishment both of "central bureaus" and "central branch bureaus." However, the 1956 Party Rules speak only of "central bureaus." Clearly there must have been a difference between these two before 1956. Each of the four regions for which central branch bureaus had been set up after 1949 (Inner Mongolia, Shantung, South China, and Sinkiang) posed special problems for Peking. Inner Mongolia and Sinkiang are minority areas: in Sinkiang minority resistance against Peking is known to have continued into the early 1950's. South China (mainly Kwangtung) and Shantung posed a different set of problems, most likely connected with difficulties encountered in land reform. The word "branch" suggests that these central branch bureaus were direct arms of the Central Committee set up in order to exert central leadership over these problem regions. By contrast, the pre-1956 central bureaus may not have been so tightly bound to the Central Committee. Since the Large Administrative Regions, particularly Manchuria, enjoyed a degree of autonomy, it is equally possible that the central bureaus attached to these regions enjoyed similar autonomy. Since Party unity had been brought about by 1956, notably through the elimination of the Kao Kang and Jao Shu-shih factions, the distinction between central branch bureaus and central bureaus was no longer needed.

Though a distinction is no longer made between central bureaus and central branch bureaus, it is apparent that what are now called central bureaus correspond to the central branch bureaus of the pre-1956 period: direct arms of the Central Committee. As "representative or-

---

[55] *Chungkung shihnien*, p. 18.
[56] For a lengthy description, see Tang, *op. cit.*, pp. 133-136; also *Chungkung shihnien*, pp. 17-19.

gans" of the Central Committee, the central bureaus after 1956 are not only in direct communication with the Central Committee, but in view of the fact that leading members of the Central Committee probably head them, they can bypass the provincial committees. In this way, the leaders in Peking can bring their power directly to bear on a local region. (See charts on next pages.)

The Organization of the Party in the Provinces

Below the central level, Party organization parallels the administrative divisions of the country. There are twenty-one provinces, five autonomous regions, and two directly attached cities. The autonomous regions are for all practical purposes provinces, but the designation "autonomous region" recognizes the national minority character of the region: Mongol, Hui, Uighur, Chuang, and Tibetan. Less important national minorities are recognized through smaller administrative units, the autonomous *chou, hsien,* or *hsiang.* With the exception of Tibet and Sinkiang, Han peoples by now form the majority in all autonomous regions. The general structure of Party organization at these levels closely follows that of the central level. Party congresses, which, according to the 1956 Party Rules, are supposed to meet once every year, are theoretically the source of legitimation for all Party organizations in the administrative area. Real power and authority, however, rests in the Party committees. In November 1960, the first secretaries of the Party committees of all provinces, autonomous regions, and directly attached cities, with three exceptions, were either full or alternate members of the Eighth Central Committee.[57] The first secretaries of Peking, Shanghai, Hopei, Heilungkiang, Inner Mongolia, Sinkiang, Anhwei, Shantung, Honan, Kwangtung, and Szechwan were full members of the Central Committee; the remainder were alternate members. Of the five regions for which central branch bureaus of the Seventh Central Committee existed in the early 1950's, four are represented in the Central Committee through full membership: Ulanfu (Inner Mongolia), Shu T'ung (Shantung), Wang En-mao (Sinkiang), and T'ao Chu (Kwangtung). Tibet apparently does not yet have a fully stabilized Party or-

---

[57] The exceptions are Kao Feng, first secretary of the Chinghai Provincial Committee, Chou Lin, first secretary of the Kweichow Provincial Committee, and Yang Shang-k'uei, first secretary of the Kiangsi Provincial Committee. Kao and Chou have been Party first secretaries in their respective provinces at least since 1956. Yang has been secretary since 1953. See *Gendai Chugoku Jimmei Jiten*, pp. 247, 179, 477. Why they have been left out is not clear.

ORGANIZATION OF THE CENTRAL COMMITTEE I: BASIC ORGANS

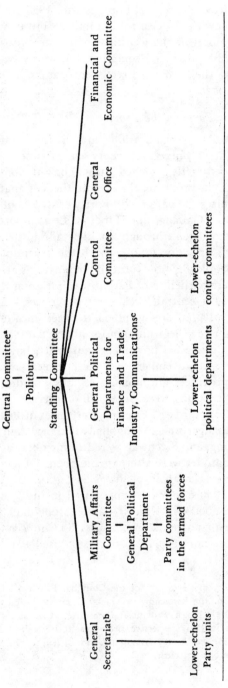

[a] The communiqué of the Ninth Plenum (January 1961) announced that six branch bureaus of the Central Committee had been established in China's six major regions. Aside from these, there undoubtedly are other Party committees in regional areas and in government agencies directly subordinate to the Standing Committee, and, unlike the regular lower-echelon Party unit, are not subordinate to the General Secretariat. It can be presumed that the six branch bureaus also were not subordinate to the General Secretariat.

[b] Lower-echelon Party units, such as Party committees in national and regional state agencies, appear to be directly subordinate to the General Secretariat.

[c] General Political Departments for Finance and Trade, Industry, and Communications were established in 1964. *See Current Scene* III: 3 (September 15, 1964), 4. Though they were set up in imitation of the General Political Department of the Military, it is not certain whether there is any linkage between them; see *Jenmin jihpao,* April 4, 1964.

SOURCE: Based on information in *Communist China 1949-1959* (Hong Kong, 1961), I, 24; and in *Biography Directory: Directory of Party and Government Officials of Communist China* (Washington, 1960), I, 5-8; modifications and interpretations are my own.

ORGANIZATION OF THE CENTRAL COMMITTEE II: AGENCIES

Central Committee

Politburo

Standing Committee

(Basic Departments)	(Basic Work Departments)	(Special Work Departments)	(Research Offices)
Organization department	Finance and trade work department	Higher Party school	Policy research office
Propaganda department	Industrial work department	Party newspapers committee	Political research office
	Communications work department	Editorial bureau of *Red Flag*	[Financial and economic research office]
	Rural work department	Bureau for translating the works of Marx, Engels, Lenin, and Stalin	[Culture and education research office]
	International liaison department	Women's work committee	
	United Front work department	Worker's movements committee	
	[Administrative and legal work department]a	Youth work committee	
	[Social work department]b		
	[Education and health department]		

a Agencies whose existence is uncertain are shown in square brackets.

b The Social Work Department was reputed in the early 1950's to be the most powerful disciplinary body in the Central Committee. It has not been mentioned, however, since that time. One can presume that it no longer exists, and that its functions have been taken over by other agencies.

SOURCE: Based on information in *Communist China 1949-1959* (Hong Kong, 1961), I, 24; and in *Biography Directory: Directory of Party and Government Officials of Communist China* (Washington, 1960), I, 5-8; modifications and interpretations are my own.

ganization, and Party affairs are handled by a "working committee."[58] A direct linkage therefore exists between the Central Committee and the overwhelming majority of regional Party committees.[59]

The internal structuring of the regional Party committees probably closely corresponds to that of the Central Committee.[60] Little is also known of their size and composition, but they are probably much smaller than the Central Committee. Most likely, they are in the nature of a "small group," and therefore capable of meeting frequently for discussion and decision-making. As in the Central Committee, the regional committees elect a standing committee and a secretariat, which are supposed to be concerned with "routine business." The specification that the Party secretaries must have served at least five years in the Party presumably is to assure against individuals of doubtful loyalty acquiring top positions in local organization.

The 1956 Party Rules state that the regional committees "are to direct the work of Party fractions in local state organs and in people's bodies." This implies that the regional Party committees do not have

---

[58] The word "working" (kungtso) prefixed to an organizational term often has the connotation of something ad hoc, as in "working committee" or "working squad" (kungtso-tui), operations squads which were instrumental in organizing land reform in the early days after the "Liberation." The Tibet Party Working Committee was established in November 1951, shortly after the Chinese occupation of the region (Chungkung shihnien, p. 17).Chang Ching-wu, secretary of the Tibet Working Committee, is an alternate member of the Central Committee.

[59] Aside from the administrative divisions mentioned in the Party Rules, there are others for which corresponding types of Party organization exist. There are, for example, so-called "special districts" (chuanch'ü) intermediate between provinces and counties (hsien). There are the special administrative districts which arise from particular ethnic conditions in some areas, such as Inner Mongolia and Chinghai. There are also special offices, administrative bureaus, and so on, set up to cope with particular problems. Each of these administrative units has a corresponding Party organization; in areas of military control there may be some question about whether the Party organization is tied to the military or to civilian organizations.

The autonomous chou are national minority regions set up in areas of mixed population. Though technically under provincial jurisdiction, Party organization appears to have some independence from provincial control. Minorities have always constituted a special problem, and therefore it may be presumed that Party organizations in the autonomous chou in many instances may be under direct central control. Article 44 of the Party Rules indicates that Party members of autonomous chou do not participate in the election of delegates to provincial Party congresses.

[60] Article 40 of the 1956 Party Rules states: "[The regional committees] are to establish all kinds of Party organs and direct their work, to administer and assign Party cadres in accordance with the system laid down by the Central Committee."

direct control over Party fractions in regional branches of the state administration which are subject solely to central control. As we shall point out in our discussion of decentralization in the next chapter, the provincial Party committees greatly increased their powers after late 1957. In view of the reduction in the powers of the central ministries, it can be presumed that the provincial Party committees then were in a position to issue commands to the regional branches of the central state administration.[61]

The Organization of the Party in the Hsien and Cities

The next-to-lowest level of Party organization is parallel to the subprovincial units of administration: hsien and cities. Again, as at the higher levels, local Party congresses are theoretically the source of legitimacy of the local Party organizations. The internal structuring of these organizations is essentially the same as for Party organizations at higher echelons. Their functions are defined as essentially the same as those for provincial Party organizations.

In cities with more than 500,000 population or in heavy industrial centers, Party organizations must be confirmed by the Central Committee. Party secretaries must have a minimum of five years' experience, in contrast to the usual two years for hsien-level secretaries. The 1956 Party Rules standardized Party organization by doing away with many ad hoc Party committees that were directly responsible to the Central Committee. Teng Hsiao-p'ing, in his report to the Eighth Party Congress, announced that many of these committees were either abolished or put under provincial jurisdiction.[62]

Party activity at regional levels has always been of great importance in carrying out policy. Lower-echelon Party organizations are not just manipulated from the center. In particular, since the Yenan period the

---

[61] Decentralization put great power into the hands of the local Party committees, but the leadership acted to make certain that men loyal to them and not to the local region exercised that power. See the discussion of "regionalization of the Party" by Chiang Hua, first secretary of the Chekiang Party Committee, in December 1957, published in Jenmin shouts'e 1958, pp. 68-69.

[62] Ad hoc commissions have traditionally been a favorite Chinese device to cut through clogged channels at lower bureaucratic echelons and bring the power of the center to bear on a particular local region. Such ad hoc commissions were used with particular frequency, for example, during the Sung Dynasty when excessive stability often led to stagnation at lower bureaucratic levels. Special commissioners of this type were also used in other periods. However, the use of this control device was possible only where the central government was strong and could impose its will.

Communists stressed the "creativity and autonomy" of lower-echelon Party units. The importance of the provincial and local party organizations can often be seen in the accounts of meetings of Party organizations at these levels. Such meetings are rarely stereotyped affairs in which Party secretaries simply inform Party cadres of the decisions made at the center. They are instead marked by vigorous discussion, in which Party cadres report on conditions in their own areas and suggest ways by which general policy can be translated into concrete action. Party meetings, like other meetings in Communist China, tend to follow a certain pattern. The meetings start with a general report by the highest-ranking Party cadre present and are then followed by particular reports from local Party cadres. These are interspersed with small-group discussions in which concrete problems are hammered out and solutions decided on which can be incorporated into the final resolutions.[63]

The concrete reports convey an idea of the problems which face local Party cadres. Implementation of Party policy is far from mechanical, and provincial and local cadres have considerable scope for decision-making. Since 1955 the power of regional Party organizations has been growing steadily.[64]

---

[63] As an illustration one might cite one meeting of district committee secretaries of Kwangtung Province that took place between November 13-23, 1955, and was reported in considerable detail in *Nanfang jihpao*, November 14-25. The general policy problem was the need to spur collectivization in the recalcitrant Kwangtung Province and to strengthen Party organization in the rural areas. The meeting began on November 13 with the reading of a general policy report by T'ao Chu, first secretary of the Kwangtung Province Party Committee and member of the Central Committee. This was followed by three days (November 14-16) of vigorous small-group discussion in which concrete problems were voiced. This was followed by three days of concrete discussion in plenary session, marked by reports of various district committee secretaries. This was again followed by three days of small-group discussion. The meeting ended with a summary report by T'ao Chu on November 23. The following day several follow-up sessions were held with the top Kwangtung Party cadres and 85 local Party cadres.

[64] The power of the provincial and local cadres at the present time is difficult to judge. The lower-level Party rectification movement launched in the winter of 1960-1961 reduced the role of the regional cadres, but we do not know how much. The Tenth Plenum of September 1962 appears to mark a turning point in the decline which began in the winter of 1960-1961. Since then, the regime has launched a strenuous ideological campaign to rebuild the image of the Party. But so heavily ideological has been the campaign that it is not clear how much of a power component goes along with all this. In 1958 the slogan "The Party Takes Command" was meant literally. There is no indication that there has been anything comparable to a return to the Great Leap Forward policy.

Basic-Level Party Organization

Basic-level Party units constitute the lowest echelon of Party organization, although not its smallest units. The concept of basic-level unit is important in both the Soviet Union and Communist China. It is at the basic level that state meets society. The Chinese divide society into units of production and units of territory; the former are based on a production system, the latter are geographical units. There also are basic-level units of the state administration.[65] The nature and size of the basic-level organization of the Party is thus determined by the unit of production, territory, or administration to which it is attached. Article 47 of the 1956 Party Rules indicates what the basic-level units of production, territory, and administration are, and hence the nature of the corresponding basic-level units of Party organization: "In each factory, mine, or other enterprise, in each *hsiang* or nationality *hsiang*, in each town, in each agricultural producers' cooperative, in each organ of the state administration, school, or street, in each company within the People's Liberation Army, and in other basic-level units, whenever there are more than three regular Party members, one must establish a basic-level organization of the Party." The basic-level units thus are: factory, mine, other enterprise, *hsiang*, town, cooperative, state organ, school, street, military company. When the communes were formed, they became basic-level units.

During the early years of communism's history, the basic-level units of the Party were just what their name implies: small groups of Party members. However, as Party organization was fitted to the structure of state and society, the basic-level units of the Party grew in size. In fact, in China the basic-level units are so large that within them a complex structure of formal organization exists, often with three or four echelons. It is not a simple task for the leader of a basic-level unit, let us say a commune or an enterprise, to get close to the nuclear units, namely the teams and the small groups.

Internal structuring within the basic-level Party organizations follows the same hierarchical principle which obtains in Party organization as a whole. The top leadership is placed in the Party committee,

---

[65] According to official theory, basic-level units of production are supposed to enjoy a degree of autonomy, in contrast to units of administration. Both the Chinese and the Soviets distinguish between economic units operating on a budgetary basis and economic units operating according to principles of "economic accounting." If a unit of production is granted the privilege of "economic accounting," this means that it has some range of decision-making autonomy, in contrast to the state agency whose actions are entirely determined by higher echelons.

in size generally a small group. Further structuring depends on the size of the unit and the number of Party members. Large basic-level units with more than a hundred Party members are structured hierarchically into Party committees, general branches, branches, and small groups. Smaller basic-level units have simpler forms of corresponding Party organization. The basic-level unit is supposed to function exactly like the Party at the national level; it has Party-delegates or Party-members meetings which theoretically are the empowering bodies for the unit. Again, though their decision-making powers are limited, the meetings represent forums for discussion. They probably function more or less as does the Central Committee. The Party committees are headed by a party secretary and from one to four deputy secretaries. Standing committees may be chosen.

The biggest basic-level units of Party organization are the communes. During the high point of communization, one could find references to communes as "little nations." Indeed, some larger communes had populations approaching that of some members of the United Nations. The chart of Party organization in a commune, as indicated on the next page, shows its structure.

The Party Committee technically was distinct from the commune administrative committee. However, at least in 1958, the difference between the two was only formal. Party organization in the communes was complex because the Party had gone far beyond its earlier linkage functions. It had assumed the reins of leadership. At every level of the commune, the Party Committee, branch, or team directed the work of the commune members. This is what "Politics Takes Command" meant concretely.

By 1958, most positions of organizational leadership were held by Party members. They therefore functioned in a dual capacity: they were cadres in some working unit and they were also Party cadres. Nevertheless, the Chinese Communists have never formally merged the two roles.

Other Party Organizations

Party organization as thus far described is hierarchical. However, some Party organizations do not fit into the hierarchical pattern. The central bureaus of the Central Committee discussed earlier are non-hierarchical in the sense that they bypass lower-echelon organizations, and represent direct off shoots of the Central Committee. Two other forms of Party organization are not within the hierarchical system: the Party control organs and the Party fractions.

Control organs and Party fractions have existed in the Chinese Com-

PARTY ORGANIZATION IN A PEOPLE'S COMMUNE (1958)

Administration

Commune Administration Committee ——————— Commune Party Committee —— Party

Standing Committee ——————— Standing Committee

(Special work committees)

Party school
Women's work
Youth League work
Militia work

(Basic work committees)

Political and legal
Financial and economic
Cultural and educational
Industrial
Agricultural, forestry, etc.
Political and ideological

Production brigades ——————— Party branches

Production teams ——————— Party teams

• Lines of administrative command.
—— Lines of Party command.

SOURCE: Based on *Communist China 1949-1959* (Hong Kong, 1961), I, 30.

munist party since its earliest days, and likewise exist in the Soviet Communist party. Each Party committee from the Central Committee downward is empowered to appoint control committees. However, control committees below the center must be certified by higher-echelon Party committees, thus ensuring that control functions never fall entirely into the hands of provincial and local Party committees. The functions of the control committees are supervisory and investigative, as spelled out in the Party Rules (Article 53): "The tasks of control committees of the center and the regions are: constantly to investigate and resolve cases of violations of the Party Rules by Party members, of Party discipline, of Communist morality, and of state laws and directives, to fix or cancel punishment of Party members, and to receive complaints and petitions from Party members."

Control committees are technically under the jurisdiction of corresponding Party committees. Nevertheless, as the Party Rules state, higher-echelon control committees "have the authority to investigate the work of lower-echelon control committees." Lower-echelon control committees, moreover, must constantly report on their work to higher echelons. "Dual rule" thus exists over the control committees. Undoubtedly, the higher-echelon control committee holds the decisive power over the lower ones. Thus in a sense the system of control committees constitutes a separate hierarchical structure, somewhat parallel to the Party itself.

The routine system of Party control functions at all major levels, concerning itself with disciplinary problems vis-à-vis individual Party members. The control committees represent a kind of "ecclesiastical court" which tries matters relating to intra-Party affairs. During rectification periods, the control committees take on special importance. Before 1955, control and investigative functions were exercised by so-called "disciplinary investigative committees" and more importantly by the mysterious "Social Department" of the Central Committee. However, at the time of the Kao-Jao purge, the Central Committee announced the establishment of control committees at both central and regional levels. These committees were given far-reaching power to investigate unreliable Party members, in particular partisans of the discredited Kao-Jao group.[66] The Control Committee of the Central Committee has been headed, since April 1955, by Tung Pi-wu, an important member of the Politburo. What has happened to the Social Department, which in the early 1950's may have been headed by Lo Jui-ch'ing, is unclear. Some of the functions of this department were pre-

---

[66] *Jenmin jihpao*, April 5, 1955.

sumably transferred to the Control Committee and others to the Ministry of Public Security.[67] In sum, therefore, the control committees at various levels represent Party courts which, of course, are subject only to Party policy and rules.

Aside from the control committees, the only other major form of Party organization is the Party fraction, *tangtsu*. Party fractions are for all practical purposes cells within one or another state agency, commonly called "Organs." The institution of Party fractions goes back to the earliest days of the Soviet Union, and arose with the need to assure control over the bureaucracy. An organ, in Communist parlance, is a state administrative agency which "carries out executive decision-making activity." [68] These decisions are supposed to be technical, deriving from a higher-echelon policy directive. The bureaucrat in charge of the state organ must make a complex decision, supposed to be a technical version of the more general policy directive under which he has to operate. However, technical decisions cannot be made easily, and require a degree of decision-making autonomy. It is usually for this reason that Party Rules contain strictures warning members of Party fractions against "directing the work of state organs." Otherwise, the fraction would be interfering with the delicate decision-making processes for which the decision maker needs some autonomy. But what difference should this make if all top people in a ministry, let us say, are in the Party fraction anyway? By 1958, it surely could not have mattered in China whether ministerial decisions were made by the Party fraction or by the minister sitting in his office.

The Party Rules adopted in 1956 still reflect a standard Soviet line on the functions of Party fractions.

As article 51 states:

Basic-level Party organizations in organs, because of the special circumstances of organ work, *cannot direct and supervise* the work of organs. However, they must carry out supervision over the ideological and political conditions of every Party member within the organs (including those charged with administrative responsibility).

In contrast, the same article states earlier:

Basic-level Party organizations in enterprises, villages, schools, and [military] units *must direct and supervise* the administrative structures and mass organi-

---

[67] Lo Jui-ch'ing has been in charge of security work in the military, as well as general security work for the country as a whole. Security and Party discipline are different matters. Therefore, the establishment of the control committees may have marked a clear differentiation of these functions.

[68] *Iuridicheskii slovar'*, II, 54.

zations of the units in question in positively realizing the resolutions of higher-echelon Party organizations and higher-echelon organs of state, and in constantly improving the work of the units in question.

From these quotations, it is clear that the Party fraction, in contrast to the Party committee, does not have decision-making powers. Its tasks are to watch and report on the agency to which it is attached.

A Kwangtung Party handbook points out another prerogative of the fractions: "Party fractions, in cases where it is necessary to carry out their tasks, may direct the work of the basic-level Party organizations in the unit concerned, and may mobilize all Party members in the unit concerned to assist them in their work." [69] This I can only interpret in one way. If the top leadership, for example, orders a campaign against bureaucratism, the Party fractions can take the lead in mobilizing all Party members within the organization to carry out criticism. In this way, the Party fraction can apply the mass line to the bureaucracy.

As we shall point out in the chapter on control, the Chinese Communists have shown a distaste for the Soviet practice of separating decision-making and control. According to the Chinese, control should be exercised positively by involving people in decision-making and decision-executing processes. Participation can be used as a form of control, and has been so used by the Chinese.[70] In this sense, one might say that the notion of Party fractions arose under particular Soviet circumstances, and though dutifully carried in the Chinese Party Rules, clashed with Chinese Communist political practices. The control instrument that should be used in all agencies organized along branch lines is a Party committee. According to general Chinese Communist practice, state agencies should have Party committees like all other organizational units; these committees should have powers both of decision and control.

There is evidence that the Chinese were dissatisfied with the role of the fractions. Early in May 1956, the *Jenmin jihpao* published a long editorial on the dilemmas faced by Party fraction workers:

Why do Party organizations in state organs [henceforth translated as Party fractions] take such a negative attitude toward supervising the work of Party members? The main reason is that these Party fractions are not very clear in their awareness of their own functions. . . . For example, there are some who think that, since Party fractions cannot exercise authority to supervise admin-

---

[69] *Chungkuo kungch'antang changch'eng chiaots'ai*, p. 112.

[70] James Townsend, "Mass Political Participation in Communist China" (unpublished doctoral dissertation, University of California, Department of Political Science, Berkeley, Calif., 1964).

istrative work the same way as Party organizations in enterprises, therefore they cannot do so over Party members in these organs. . . . They say: "We can only supervise the thoughts of Party members, but not their lives!" Or: "We can supervise ordinary Party members, but not Party members who are in charge of work!" . . . Under such ideological conditions, many Party fractions simply do routine work. . . . This not only reduces the requisite functions of the Party fractions, but lets them fall into the abyss of routinism.

The editorial prescribes that Party fractions must carry out evaluation of the work of Party members in state organs. However, "in this evaluation, it must be stated clearly, because of the special character of state organs, Party fractions cannot carry out supervision over the work of state organs. Nevertheless, they should and must carry out supervision over Party members in state organs, including Party members who are in charge of work." [71]

As can easily be imagined, the dividing line between supervising the work of the organ as such and supervising Party members is thin. The Party member is wholly responsible to his Party fraction for all his activities. As for cadres in state organs, these activities include his every day administrative and decision-making work. In fact, most discussions in Party fraction meetings concern the work of the organ. Therefore, what is the significance of saying that the fraction may not supervise the work of the organ, but must supervise Party members who are in charge of that work? Probably because it was considered imperative to keep the different channels of command and information clearly separated. A cadre who works in a bureau, for example, gets a constant stream of orders from the ministry. If the Party fraction supervised the work of the organ, he would be getting a second stream of orders from the Party channels. The possibilities for confusion can be imagined. It is still possible, however, to exert ideological control over the man. He can be criticized; his attitudes can be examined; his performance can be judged. In this way, pressure can be put on the man ideologically without interfering with the technical details of his work.

Since one can imagine the confusion resulting from a double source of command, it is easier to envisage what happened during the Great Leap Forward. As a result of the gradual extension of dual rule over

---

[71] The *Jenmin jihpao* article adds that Party fractions may "inform" cadres in the agency about deficiencies, but they may not "report." The distinction between "inform" (*t'ungchih*) and "report" (*paokao*) is important, for in the former case the action is advisory, and in the latter it is official. "Report" is a required intra-organizational function in which those who are technically subordinate report to their collective body or to higher echelons.

the ministries, a double source of command existed—and great confusion resulted. In 1956, when the cited editorial of the *Jenmin jihpao* and the Party Rules were written, it was still considered important to keep the channels of Party and administration absolutely separate.

THE PARTY CADRE

The Cadre Concept and its Development

Before we continue the discussion of the organizational development of the Chinese Communist party, something must be said about the cadres. The word "cadre" has by now become so common in the Western literature on Communist China that it is usually taken for granted. Yet the real significance of the cadre concept is not always fully understood.[72]

Strictly speaking, a cadre (or *kanpu* in Chinese) is someone who holds a formal leadership position in an organization. A Party secretary is a Party cadre; a military officer is a military cadre; an official is a government cadre; and so on. However, the cadre concept is so fundamental to Chinese Communist organizational thinking that it has acquired connotations far beyond its basic meaning. Colloquially, the word cadre generally refers to Party members who exercise leadership roles. It is also used to designate a leadership style. A cadre is a leader who is supposed to lead in a certain way. The ideal cadre is supposed to act as a combat leader, in intimate relationship with his followers, yet always responsive to higher policy.

Every cadre in Communist China has a specific rank. Tables of cadre rank (*pienchih*) exist for every unit of organization. These tables are essentially similar to the *nomenklatura* in the Soviet Union.[73] They are the basis for salary payments and promotions. When cadres are transferred from one unit to another, the basis for promotion and

---

72 For the best analysis of the cadre concept in Communist China, see Lewis, *op. cit.* For a discussion of cadres based on Soviet conceptions, see Philip Selznick, *The Organizational Weapon, A Study of Bolshevik Strategy and Tactics* (New York, Toronto, London, 1952), pp. 18-20. Selznick uses the term "deployable personnel" to characterize the Soviet conception of the cadre. As is evident from our discussion, this collectivist conception is different from the individualist conception of the Chinese Communists.

73 The *nomenklatura* is kept highly secret in the Soviet Union. Thanks to the Smolensk documents, we have some idea of how the *nomenklatura* operates in the Soviet Union; see Merle Fainsod, *Smolensk under Soviet Rule* (Cambridge, Mass., 1958), pp. 64-65. We have no comparable documents for Communist China.

transfer is the table of cadre-ranking.[74] In the strictly formal sense, the Chinese Communist cadre is similar to his Soviet counterpart. However, there are important differences in leadership style.[75] The following pages will briefly discuss the evolution of the cadre concept in Communist China.

Lenin ended his *What Is to Be Done* with a prediction that "the real vanguard of the most revolutionary class" would now émerge and lead the revolution. From the beginning, the Chinese Communist party never doubted that it was the vanguard of the Chinese revolution. During the first fifteen years of the history of Chinese communism, the vanguard emerged, but there were struggles as to who was the true vanguard. A new approach began during the Yenan period. It was now thought that the vanguard must not simply "emerge," but must be created, trained, and "cultivated." As a result, the Chinese Communists developed a continuing concern, in theory and practice, with the problem of leadership. The central concept in this new approach was that of the cadre.

During the Yenan period the Chinese Communists began to think systematically about cadres. The word was widely used in Chinese Communist literature before that time, but without discussion of what was meant by it. Even in some of Mao's writings during the early years of the Yenan period, discussions of the cadre concept and cadre policy are still phrased in generalities.[76] By the late 1930's, however, discussion of the cadre concept becomes more precise. Liu Shao-ch'i, in particular, began to write widely on the subject. Mao Tse-tung, in his "Position of the Chinese Communist Party in the National Struggle," dated October 1938, devotes a whole section to "cadre policy." [77] Mao starts off by saying that "without many leadership cadres possessing both

---

[74] The difficulty in obtaining information on the Chinese Communist *nomenklatura* is indicated by the fact that even Taiwan intelligence publications have little to report on the subject. The most complete treatment I have yet seen is *Kungfei jenshih ts'oshih chih yenchiu* (Taipei, 1957), particularly pp. 190 ff.

[75] The Russians use the word cadre to designate the men of the vanguard, but mostly in its collective sense. The Russian use is true to its etymology and the way it is understood in the West. The Japanese introduced the word into the Far East, and it soon found its way into the Chinese language. At first, the Chinese Communists understood the word *kanpu* in its collective sense, but in time it changed from a collective to an individual connotation—the Chinese Communist *kanpu* became an individual leader.

[76] See, for example, Mao Tse-tung, "Fight for the Participation of the Masses in the Unified Struggle against Japan," *Selected Works* (Chinese edition), I, 267-268; the report is dated May 7, 1937.

[77] *Ibid.*, II, 514-516.

ability and virtue, our Party cannot fulfill its historical tasks." The phrase "ability and virtue" is simply an earlier version of the later "red and expert"; the idea, at least in form, may have been borrowed from one of Stalin's speeches.[78] Mao continues that, though many cadres have arisen, more are needed; the systematic training of large numbers of cadres is the major task of the Party. In his call for more recruitment of non-Party cadres, Mao says that use must be made of "the great amount of [leadership] talent that exists outside of the Party."

Mao then proceeds to state his criteria for a good cadre: "[He is one who can] resolutely carry out the Party line, submit to Party discipline, be in close contact with the masses, have the ability to work independently, be willing to act 'positively,' and who does not seek private advantage." Mao ascribed to his enemy Chang Kuo-t'ao a wrong cadre policy: he "recruited his private party, organized factions, and finally rebelled against the Party."

If cadres had to have the right attitudes toward the masses, the top leaders also had to have proper attitudes to the cadres. Mao listed three requisites for the attitudes of top leaders toward their cadres: understanding them as persons; using them; and protecting them. To do this requires giving them directives, as well as allowing them to assume responsibility and develop their own "creativity." Their level of consciousness must be raised through education. And they must be constantly investigated in their work, "their successes praised and their errors corrected." Merely to investigate after an infraction has been committed is wrong. If they have committed errors, the correct method to be used is "persuasion." But against those who have committed serious errors, and "who do not accept guidance," the methods of "struggle" are to be employed. Patience and not hastiness in using "struggle" is required. Lastly, the top leaders must take into consideration the difficulties that the cadres face: sickness, poor living conditions, and family problems.

Mao described the ideal cadre, in effect, as a combat leader fighting in a context of guerrilla war. The distinction that Mao still made between cadres and leaders disappeared later, and the term came to be used to describe leaders in general. Top leaders were later simply called "leadership cadres," *lingtao kanpu.* The conception of the cadre as a combat leader was not ideally suited to the tasks of civil administration that faced the Chinese Communists after 1949. What was needed then was men to take over the administrative and managerial positions in civil society. Since these were labeled cadre positions, the term cadre,

---

[78] See Stalin's speech to graduates of the Red Army academies delivered on May 4, 1935 (*Problems of Leninism* [Moscow, 1954], pp. 657-662).

from 1949 on, began to acquire another connotation, namely that of institutional leadership. Yet at the same time, organizational leaders were expected to behave in the manner of combat leaders. Here was a new kind of "official" that was quite unfamiliar to the Chinese. The perplexity of the ordinary Chinese was reflected in a confused definition of the word cadre given in a New Phrases Dictionary published in Shanghai in 1951. Although all publishing houses were put under state control, the new ideology had obviously not yet completely penetrated the minds of the editors. In 1951, the dictionary gave the following definition of the word: "Cadres are all kinds of leadership core cadres in revolutionary brigades. . . . The cadre is not an ordinary person, *laopaihsing*, nor is he a so-called worker in a government bureau. He is different from the usual employees in bureaus, as well as fighters in [military] units. [Cadre] means one who has a certain degree of political awareness and is responsible for certain political tasks." [79]

Needless to say, the "definition" is not only confused, but meaningless. However, by 1954, a revised edition of the same dictionary came up with a more precise definition: "Cadre: generally speaking, it means a worker in a state institution. Persons who work in state institutions or a department of production, capable of unifying and leading the masses to carry out Party and government policies and directives, to implement duties and programs promptly under the leadership of the Party and higher-level government institutions are cadres."

Yet, at the same time, the cadre "must possess revolutionary character and revolutionary working manner, be capable of cementing ties with the masses and taking the lead actively. In other words, he must be capable of being the tutor of the masses and in turn being the pupil of the masses."

These two parts of the definition give the essential meaning of the word cadre, as stated at the beginning of this section. On the one hand, the cadre is someone who holds formal position of leadership in an organizational unit. On the other hand, he is to have the leadership style of a combat leader. He is to be both expert and red.

Sociologists distinguish between institutional and personal leadership, with the implication that they are mutually exclusive.[80] Leader-

---

[79] *Hsin mingtz'u tz'utien* (Shanghai, 1951), p. 5079b.

[80] Though the sociological terminology is not standard, the basic ideas run along similar lines. Institutional leadership derives from the formal position held—from the position invested with authority. Personal leadership derives from the voluntary acceptance of command on the basis of personal characteristics. Reinhard Bendix, in this sense, distinguishes between leadership and authority. For a summary of some current views on leadership, see Amitai Etzioni, *A Comparative Analysis of Complex Organizations* (Glencoe, Ill., 1961), pp. 115-116.

ship based on "expertise," in the Chinese Communist sense, means leadership exercised through some organizational office or role; in this sense, it may be spoken of as institutional. By contrast, the Chinese Communists regard cadre leadership as basically personal, in the sense of a combat leader directing his troops in battle. The Chinese Communists, by now, regard red and expert as at least somewhat contradictory. To put it in concrete terms, it is difficult for a person to act like a cadre in organizational office. Like everything else in Communist China, the cadre concept appears to have a basic contradiction built into it. This aspect of the cadre concept has made for the different connotations of the word at various times. During the early 1950's, when the Chinese Communists were emulating the Soviets, the "expert" aspect was most prominent. However, toward the latter part of the 1950's, the "red" aspect came to the fore. During the early 1950's, the institutional aspects of leadership were stressed, but during the later 1950's, the personal-leadership aspects.

A cadre is thus a leader. In the chapter on management, we shall discuss some other leadership styles that may be seen as alternatives to that of the cadre. There we distinguish four different styles: traditional bureaucrats, modern bureaucrats, managers, and cadres. Here we shall merely state some of these differences to make clear the nature of the particular leadership style.

Cadres and managers differ from both kinds of bureaucrats in their basic orientation to the world. Bureaucrats strive for routinization, for the creation of stable predictable environments. Cadres and managers live in a changing world and accept change as the norm. Traditional bureaucrats differ from their modern counterparts in the selection of means to achieve institutional routinization. Traditional bureaucrats try to achieve this through the creation of networks of mutual involvement, by human solidarity as expressed in webs of personal relationships. The Weberian modern bureaucrat, however, tries to create and maintain a system of rational and legal rules—he sees things in technical rather than human terms; he prefers the solidarity of formal rational organization—"organic" solidarity, as Durkheim would say. The traditional bureaucrat sees only "mechanical" solidarity as reliable; bonds of personal friendship and trust hold institutions together. The traditional bureaucrat, given his orientation to human beings, sees the need for values, for an ethos, for religion. The modern bureaucrat is concerned with norms, rules which compel certain modes of behavior.

Cadres differ from managers in similar ways. Though they both see themselves as living in a world of change, challenge, and insecurity, they differ as to the means through which organizational goals and solidarity can be achieved. The manager thinks in terms of techniques, both technological and organizational; he prefers rational organization, for he has the confidence that he can manipulate it and use it to achieve his own ends; he likes rules because he knows he can bend them to his will, to enforce compliance from his workers. The cadre, however, is a leader who thinks in terms of human solidarity. He knows how to "solidarize" men so that goals can be achieved; he can manipulate their thoughts and sentiments; he operates not with ethos but with ideology; he strives for a different kind of mechanical solidarity, namely that of the combat team.

During the past decade and a half in China, the "reds" and the "experts" have competed for leadership over economic affairs. Whereas the "experts" have advocated managerial styles of leadership, the "reds" have advocated cadre leadership. However, during the Yenan period, the cadre's opponent was not the manager but the traditional bureaucrat. During the revolutionary terror of the civil-war period, local officials were attacked as severely as the landed gentry. The traditional bureaucrat who wanted harmony and sought to maintain the status quo was regarded as the opposite of the red cadre who saw struggle as the means to change the status quo and create a new society. Yet, despite the great differences that separate the two, they both think primarily in terms of human rather than technical solidarity. This similarity accounts for the endemic Chinese Communist fear that the cadre, particularly when he reaches middle age and acquires status, may degenerate into a traditional bureaucrat.

Sources of Recruitment

During the first years after 1949, it seemed for a time that the Chinese Communists were deviating from the policy, developed during the Yenan period, of recruiting combat cadres. The need for men of skill forced them to recruit from sections of the population that did not promise to furnish large numbers of revolutionary cadres. As we have pointed out in the introduction, successful revolutionary movements often recruit from existing elites in order to find organizational leaders. The Kuomintang did this when it seized power in the middle 1920's. Although there was little left of China's traditional elites in 1949, one group existed from which men could be recruited: the intellectuals.

Late in 1952, An Tzu-wen, chief of the Orgburo of the Central Committee, reported on "cadre work" in the Chinese People's Republic over the preceding three years.[81] Given his dual involvement in organizational problems both of Party and Government, An Tzu-wen was directly concerned with basic policy-making on organizational questions. He began by listing the quantitative successes scored in cadre-recruitment policy. On October 1, 1949, exclusive of military cadres, there were 720,000 cadres in the country. By September 20, 1952, the number had risen to 2,750,000. Most new cadres were "recruited from below," and comprised three elements: worker and peasant "positive elements" (that is, activists) who had emerged "from the various movements and struggles"; students graduating from higher schools and middle-level specialized schools, who were assigned tasks in national construction; and a number of "old intelligentsia" recruited "from society" and trained as cadres.

Significantly, An Tzu-wen did not mention the Party as a source of cadre recruitment. In mid-1951, there were 2,700,000 Party members in the army, state agencies, factories, mines, and schools. In mid-1953, there were 1,200,000 Party members in the army.[82] Assuming that Party membership in the army in mid-1951 was around the one million mark, this means that there were only around 1,700,000 Party members in the nonrural civil sector. Many of these were probably ordinary people without leadership positions in organization. It is clear that the new rulers in Peking were looking far beyond the Party to find men to staff the new positions. An Tzu-wen cited three important sources of recruitment. First, the "positivists" who gushed up from the movements; most of these were working-class people with more "virtue" than "ability"; we know that many workers were rapidly promoted to supervisory positions in factories, but probably only a few of them were given complex administrative positions. Second, the students, undoubtedly a much more promising source of recruitment; most of them had been sympathetic to the Communists, even though they were usually not involved in the illegal Party organizations of the cities; these were the "new intellectuals." Third, the "old intelligentsia": the new regime preferred young to old intellectuals, but, as An Tzu-wen indicated, the older ones were needed as well.

The Communists were in a dilemma at this point. The Party was overwhelmingly composed of peasants on the day of the "Liberation." The

---

[81] An Tzu-wen, *Chunghua jenmin kunghokuo san-nien-lai ti kanpu kungtso* (Peking, 1952). An Tzu-wen is a Hunanese with training in the Soviet Union. He once was Mao Tse-tung's private secretary. He has been involved in personnel and control work in both Party and government since 1949. As of late 1960, he was the chief of the Orgburo of the Central Committee.

[82] *Jenmin jihpao*, July 1, 1951, and July 1, 1953.

new policy called for a halt in indiscriminate recruitment, a raising of standards, a lengthened probationary period, and expulsion of unusable peasant elements. Moreover, workers were the main target of recruitment, since their class position was "correct." Too many intellectuals were of bourgeois origin. This meant that a corps of non-Party cadres of workers began to join the Party rapidly.

At the same time, non-Party intellectuals began to move into administrative and managerial positions. If the Chinese Communists had simply changed their recruitment policy and allowed all the new intellectual cadres to come into the Party, the Party would probably have soon turned into an elite club, resembling the Soviet Communist party under Stalin, or into a new version of the Kuomintang. But Mao and Liu had not built up the Party so laboriously during the Yenan period to see it swamped by intellectuals, no matter how sympathetic to the new order.

The solution, for the moment, was to recruit and train intellectuals. More cadres had to be trained, for China faced urgent economic tasks. The only way to do it was to intensify the program of higher education. An Tzu-wen stated flatly that the chief training ground for cadres was the "regular schools." During the preceding three years, 66,000 students had been graduated from universities and assigned government jobs. Most of them went into the field of economic construction. In the summer of 1951, of 15,749 graduates, 15,643 had been assigned jobs by the government. In the summer of 1952, of 27,000 graduates, 16,000 had been assigned to the economic sector, and of these 12,000 directly to production units. In addition to the regular schools, national and provincial ministries set up special training classes. But An Tzu-wen also spoke as a Party man when he pointed out that "people's revolutionary universities" had been set up to train political cadres. The system of "people's universities" began to emerge as a parallel of the regular educational system. Peking has its People's University and it has Peking University. All China has this parallelism in the educational system. The Party schools are supposed to give the political cadres some liberal education. They learn a little of everything from science to literature, all within the context of heavy political indoctrination. Most students are from worker and peasant families. The difficulty in this early period was that the Party schools had just recently been set up, whereas the older schools had a solid tradition.

The leadership was unhappy about having to rely so heavily on the intelligentsia. An Tzu-wen complained that many cadres, particularly those recruited from the old intelligentsia, still suffered from "employee viewpoints, pure-technique viewpoints, and tendencies not to be concerned with politics." They have no confidence, he said, in the positive elements that have "gushed forth" from the movements; they dislike the young "superior" cadres, they insist on "qualification and seniority" as criteria for promotion, develop vested interests, obstruct the promotion of new cadres, insist on vertical rule, stress "culture and technique," disregard the merits of the man, and, lastly, have no interest in cadre-training programs. All this, he felt, impedes the promotion of deserving cadres, particularly those of worker and peasant origin.

These "wrong attitudes" were exactly those that later were attributed to bureaucrats in the *Sufan* and other movements. But here these attitudes were implicitly attributed to the intellectuals. The traditional bureaucracy was recruited from the country's literati, and it was not surprising that even under the Communists the educated moved back into the bureaucracy. Unless stern measures were taken, An Tzu-wen said, the intellectual non-Party cadres would sooner or later turn back into traditional bureaucrats; they must either be transformed into true cadres or be replaced.

GRADUATES FROM HIGHER SCHOOLS
(in thousands)

Year	Universities and higher technical schools	Middle and technical schools
1949	21	72
1950	18	75
1951	19	57
1952	32	68
1953	48	118
1954	47	169
1955	55	235
1956	63	174
1957	56	146
1958	72	191
1959	70	n.a.
1960	135	n.a.
1961	162	n.a.

SOURCE: *Weita ti shih-nien* (Peking, 1959), p. 172; and *Shin-Chūgoku Nenkan* (Tokyo, 1965), p. 382.

The recruitment problems discussed by An Tzu-wen were to remain during the subsequent years. He identified the two major sources of recruitment for cadre positions: the masses, that is, workers and peasants; and the intellectuals. This is a concrete social example of the red and expert problem. On the one hand, the regime needed trained men to fill positions of institutional leadership; the only possible source for such individuals was the body of intellectuals trained in the country's higher schools. On the other hand, the regime needed political men to lead the masses in the great drives for its social and economic development. The only possible source for the red cadres was the working masses themselves. The regime needed the professionals to fill the staff positions in industry, administration, and schools; and at the same time, it needed the red cadres to fill the important positions of line leadership.

NUMBER OF ENGINEERS AND TECHNICIANS
(in thousands)

Year	Number
1952	164
1953	210
1954	262
1955	344
1956	449
1957	496
1958	618

SOURCE: *Weita ti shih-nien* (Peking, 1959), p. 163.

As a result of this red and expert contradiction, and the recruitment policies that derived from it, a bifurcation of elites occurred in the country. The political elite consists of the red cadres, the social elite of the intellectuals. The former derive their status from political power based on ideology, the latter from social prestige, based on education. So far, there is no evidence of a single "new class," in Milovan Djilas' sense. The attempt to combine the two elites during the Great Leap Forward did not succeed. Mao's complaint, in his 1957 speech on contradictions, that the intellectuals had not yet fully accepted socialism, still appears to hold true today. This does not mean that the intellectuals are disloyal, but rather that, like all professionals, they are more motivated by self-interest than by commitment to collectivity. On the other hand, the attempt to raise the red cadres to the same intellectual level as the "good students" from bourgeois families has not fully succeeded. One girl I interviewed in Hong Kong explained why so many of China's brightest students still came from bourgeois families: education begins in the family, long before the child enters primary school. The environment in worker and peasant families clearly is not so conducive to preparing the child intellectually as that of urban bourgeois families.

From a sociological point of view, the red and expert contradiction is the most important in China today. It reflects not only the bifurcation of elites, but the gulf between a modern coastal sector and a backward inland sector. It also reflects the contradiction inherent in the cadre concept. We have argued that the cadre is supposed to be both an institutional and a personal leader. The former demands expertise, the latter ideology. One can imagine the tension this must produce in individual cadres. Worker-peasant cadres are constantly worried about their level of education, whereas intellectual cadres are worried about their ideological stance. Reinhard Bendix has argued that contradictory expectations can produce rational behavior in individuals. This indeed may be one of the positive results of the contradictory nature of the cadre concept.

CHAPTER III

GOVERNMENT

GENERAL TRENDS IN ADMINISTRATION

ONE OF THE most important yet least known areas of organization in China is that of state administration, or government. The Chinese Communists have created the most powerful government in Chinese history, but extreme secrecy about its operation makes it impossible for us to study it in detail. Nevertheless, as is the case with other areas of organization in Communist China, one can gain an idea of how the state administration at top and middle levels operates by seeing how it operates at the bottom level. Since documentary and oral information is available on state administration in cities and counties, a number of leading political scientists and sociologists have lately begun to study state administration from this point of view, thus promising to throw light on a hitherto obscure area of organization in Communist China.

Though we know the general structure of government, it is often difficult to say how structure and function are related. What an agency is formally empowered to do may not be what it actually does. Nevertheless, by making inferences from scattered evidence and by comparison with Soviet government, on which the state administration of Communist China is modeled, one can gain a general idea of the workings of government and of the main administrative trends.

Although there has been a general trend from concentration to distribution of administrative powers from 1949 to the present, the process has been marked by periodic swings from one to the other. Because this trend has been bound up with the issues of centralization and decentralization, we shall make these issues the focus of our discussion.

A few preliminary points must be made. First, the Chinese Communists, in contrast to the Soviets, combine structural conservatism with functional flexibility. That is to say that the Chinese have carried out no wholesale changes of the system of state administration, such as Khrushchev did in May 1957, when he abolished almost all of the Soviet Union's economic ministries and turned them into offices of the State Planning Commission.[1] The formal administrative changes in China have been, on the surface, less radical than those of the Soviets. However, if one goes beneath the surface one finds that the administrative changes in Communist China are in fact much more radical than those in the Soviet Union. This is particularly apparent when the Soviet and Chinese decentralizations of 1957 are compared. On the surface, the former appeared more radical, but in practice, the Chinese decentralization decisions led to a wholly new approach to economic administration and management.

Second, the Party, as an organization, plays a far more important role in China than in the Soviet Union under Stalin. Though Party membership was universal among Soviet leaders of the Stalin period, there was no administration by Party committees, such as has been the case in Communist China. The purges which Stalin carried out in the mid-1930's greatly weakened the Soviet Communist party, particularly at the regional level. It was Khrushchev who rebuilt the Party into a more effective organizational instrument. The Party, in fact, turned out to be one of his major supports in the struggle against the Stalinists, whose power was still based on the great ministries that had arisen under Stalin's rule.[2]

Third, regional government has a unique importance in Communist China. In the discussion of the dialectical conception of Chinese society in our chapter on ideology, we pointed out that the Chinese Communists see the duality of "center" and "region" as a contradiction. Though there have been few separatist tendencies in China, most of

---

[1] Harry Schwartz, *The Soviet Economy since Stalin* (Philadelphia and New York, 1965), pp. 88-91.

[2] *Ibid.*

the provinces have a distinctive character, the product of long historical development. Before 1949 much of the warlordism was based on provinces. There are thus historical reasons for the operational autonomy of provincial government in Communist China.

State administration during the First Five-Year Plan and the Great Leap Forward was characterized by different tendencies. During the former period, the Chinese Communists, emulating the Soviets, stressed branch-type administration and centralization. During the latter period, they stressed administration by interbranch coordinative agencies and decentralization. The branch principle of organization means that administrative units are linked hierarchically according to functional principles. That is to say that all units concerned with similar operations, such as, for example, administration of the machine-building industry, form a single branch. The most characteristic form of branch organization is a ministry which, from a central point in the national capital, operates a hierarchy of regional bureaus and enterprises. In economic administration, this principle of organization has also been called the production principle.[3]

In both the Soviet Union and Communist China, the application of the branch principle of organization has generally meant centralization of command and administration. By contrast, interbranch coordinative agencies cut across branch lines. As a whole, they take the form of "committees." At the central level, the most important coordinative agencies are the state planning and economic committees. Even more important is the fact that the top policy-making agencies of the Party take the form of "committees." Again, both in the Soviet Union and in Communist China, emphasis on coordinative agencies has gone together with certain kinds of decentralization, as will be indicated below.

Decentralization means that decision-making powers are transferred downward from some central point. It can take two forms. Either decision-making power is transferred all the way down to the production units themselves, or it is only transferred down to some lower level of regional administration. Scholars have generally regarded only the former as true decentralization. The Yugoslavs carried out such decentralization during the early 1950's. At the present time, it is this type of decentralization that is being advocated by liberal economists, such as Evsei Liberman in the Soviet Union and Ota Šik in Czechoslovakia. However, I would regard both as "real" though different types of decentralization, and shall call them respectively decentralization I and

---

[3] P. J. D. Wiles, *The Political Economy of Communism* (Cambridge, Mass., 1962), pp. 43-46.

decentralization II. In the mid-1950's, when the Soviets established their regional economic councils (sovnarkhozy), they carried out decentralization II. This Soviet decentralization was ineffective, because the regional economic agencies were not able to exercise real decision-making power in the face of entrenched interests of the central agencies.[4] Although decentralization I was considered in Communist China during the mid-1950's, the form of decentralization adopted late in 1957 was of the second type. Decision-making powers were put into the hands of provincial government, not into the hands of the production units.

However, provincial government in China is not simply an offshoot of central government, as so often in the Soviet Union. It has a considerable range of operational autonomy, made possible by the great strength of the Party at the provincial level.

Though the Party, at all levels, has its branch agencies, its most characteristic organizational form is the committee. In contrast to the ministries, whose branch agencies are under central jurisdiction, the Party's branch agencies are under the jurisdiction of the Party committee of the same level, though there are exceptions such as the control committees and the recently formed political departments (see pp. 156-159, 303-307) which bypass regional Party committees.

Since committees tend to have interbranch coordinative functions, a regional Party committee has the power to pull together a broad range of discrete activities. At the central level, the power of coordinating committees is often frustrated by the branch agencies of the government, notably the big ministries. However, at the provincial level, branch organization is much weaker. Local governments are dominated by the all-powerful people's committees, and these in turn are dominated by the provincial Party committees. Therefore, decentralizing decision-making powers to these bodies meant that the powers of the central branch agencies were weakened. Once a provincial people's committee had gained control of an industrial sector, it was difficult for the industrial ministry to maintain whatever jurisdiction it still had over that sector. To get what it wanted, it usually had to go through Party channels. Decentralization II thus greatly increased the power of provincial Party committees and correspondingly reduced that of the central ministries.

---

4 For example, Gregory Grossman, "The Structure and Organization of the Soviet Economy," Slavic Review, XXI:2 (June 1962), 217-218; Oleg Hoeffding, "The Soviet Industrial Reorganization of 1957," American Economic Review, XLIX:2 (May 1959), 65-77.

From the mid-1950's on, government in Communist China was increasingly characterized by decentralization II, by the growth of inter-branch coordinative agencies, and by the development of Party-dominated regional government. These tendencies were clearly at variance with administrative practices in the Soviet Union under Stalin. Soviet administration then was highly centralized, and was characterized by an extreme application of the branch principle. This resulted in a complex structure of parallel bureaucracies; that is to say, administratively separate but functionally similar administrative organizations. Thus, for example, economic control was exercised by a number of different agencies: Ministry of State Control, Secret Police, banks, courts, and the various economic ministries themselves. By contrast, in Communist China, economic control tended to become concentrated in the hands of a single body, the Party. This development will be discussed in our chapter on control.

The Great Leap Forward marked a high point of government by committee. Branch agencies, notably the central ministries, found their operations greatly obstructed by their inability to deal with the power of local Party committees. Since 1961, Peking has once again stressed branch administration, though there is no sign of a return to the situation of the early 1950's. The Ministries of Finance and Commerce, as well as the People's Bank, have been strengthened, and given greater control over the economy. On the other hand, the formation of the so-called political departments for Finance and Trade, Industry, and Communications, which are directly attached to the Central Committee, indicates a reluctance to try straight ministerial rule again. Coordinating committees continue to play an important role in Chinese administration, both at the center and in the regions.

In early 1961, the Chinese Communists started to apply decentralization I, namely granting broad decision-making autonomy to the production units themselves, that is, industrial enterprises and agricultural production teams and brigades. This meant lessening the power of provincial government; it was a reversal of the practice during the Great Leap Forward, when provincial government and Party committees had reigned supreme and the individual production units had very little autonomy. However, since 1962, provincial government appears to have regained some of the powers it lost early in 1961 when the Great Leap Forward was suddenly terminated.

The situation in China today is obscure. One may say that it is characterized by conflicting tendencies: some toward centralization, others toward decentralization of one or the other type. This three-fold situation is symbolized, for example, by practices prevailing in supply and prices. There are three categories of supplies: those centrally controlled, regionally controlled, and uncontrolled (that is, freely procurable according to supply-demand conditions by the production units). A similar three-fold categorization prevails in prices: some are fixed centrally, others regionally, and the remainder are determined by market relationships, subject only to state regulatory controls.

It is clear that such functional tendencies as described cannot be inferred from the structure of administration. Moreover, since centralization, decentralization I, and decentralization II are in contradiction to each other, no completely rationalized administrative structure can be set up in which structure and function would be directly interrelated. Since China appears today to operate administratively only through an interplay of these conflicting tendencies, the leaders of the country undoubtedly think it wiser to leave the structure of government essentially as it is, and to work through nonformal modes of operation.

COMMAND RELATIONSHIPS OF ADMINISTRATIVE AGENCIES

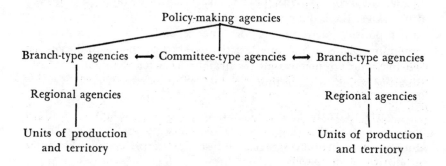

CENTRAL GOVERNMENT

In September 1949, the Chinese People's Political Consultative Conference met in plenary session in Peking and proclaimed the establishment of the Chinese People's Republic. The CPPCC was construed as "carrying out the authority of the National People's Congress," which, however, was not convened until September 1954. The National

People's Congress is today the supreme source of governmental authority in the Chinese People's Republic. In 1949, however, in the absence of national elections, the legitimation of the new republic came from the CPPCC which the Communists had formally established in the same year, as a successor to the old Political Affairs Conference.[5] The CPPCC was composed of "representatives of the Chinese Communist party, the various democratic parties, the various people's bodies, the various regions, the People's Liberation Army, the various minorities, Overseas Chinese, and other patriotic, democratic elements."[6] The Chinese People's Republic was thus legitimated "by the people."

The formation of a National People's Congress theoretically inaugurated a period in which legitimation came from a body directly elected by the people. It is typical of the persistence of vestiges, characteristic of so many governmental structures in Communist China, that the CPPCC did not cease its existence in 1954, but has continued as a body to the present time. After going through a period of inactivity during the years of supreme Party power, the CPPCC was reconvened at the time of the economic crises of 1960-61, in order to reaffirm a national solidarity threatened by the crisis.[7]

The first meeting of the CPPCC in 1949 passed basic organizational laws for the central government and for the CPPCC, and adopted a "general program" for the CPPCC. It set up a central committee for the

---

[5] Chinese Communist concern for proper legitimation is interesting. The old Political Affairs Conference was originally set up in January 1946 to work out a coalition government. It met in Chungking and included representatives from the KMT, the Communists, the Democratic League, the Chinese Youth Party, and nonparty representatives. It was reconvened in August 1948 by the Communists, and met in Harbin. Its purpose was discussion for convening a National People's Congress and setting up a "democratic coalition government." When it met again in Peking in September 1949 under the changed name of the CPPCC, it formally proclaimed the establishment of the republic.

[6] Chou Fang, *Wokuo kuochia chikou* (Peking, 1957), p. 36. The original edition appeared in December 1955. A revised edition came out in December 1957. A Russian translation is based on the 1957 edition. Revised versions of standard books in Communist countries always provide an opportunity of seeing where the Party line has changed. A thorough comparison of these two editions would disclose where the changes have been made. My citations refer to the 1957 edition.

[7] The CPPCC met in plenary session about a month before the convocation of the 1962 National People's Congress in April. Members of the CPPCC had been instructed to travel through the country to study concrete conditions, and then discuss basic problems at the sessions. This was a part of the United Front policy then once again stressed.

government consisting of sixty-three members, headed by Mao Tse-
tung and six vice chairmen. It also elected a national committee of the
CPPCC with Mao as chairman. With the formal actions of the CPPCC,
the new political system received its legitimation. On October 1, 1949,
the Chinese People's Republic was formally proclaimed.

In this chapter, we are primarily concerned with "government," that
is, with the state administrative system. However, the entire structure
of the state is officially regarded as consisting of three great branches:
government, army, and judiciary. These three branches are headed by
the State Council, the National Defense Council, and the Supreme People's Procuracy and Supreme Court. Before 1954, the same three-fold
division existed except that the bodies were called the Government Affairs Council, the People's Revolutionary Military Council, and the
Procuracy and Supreme Court. As we have explained earlier, official
Marxist theory regards the state as the formal instrument of class power.
Thus one can say that officially bureaucracy, military, and judiciary
are regarded as the three great branches of state power.

In the Introduction, we noted that one could speak of a trinity of
state power in China today, made up of government, army, and party.
By this we meant not only that these three are the great branches of
state power, but that they play interlocking roles in the direction of the
country. That trinity has become apparent in recent years, as the Party
has in effect supplanted the judiciary as the instrument of law, and as
the army has begun to play an increasingly vital role in the civil life
of the nation.

The State Council

The predecessor of the State Council was the Government Administrative Council. Of the three major administrative bodies created by
the CPPCC in 1949, the Government Administrative Council was the
most complex and unwieldy. The great number and the character of its
subordinate agencies were indications of the speed with which the new
regime was reaching out to control broad areas of the life of the
country. This was especially true of economic affairs. The structure
became more complex between 1949 and 1954—in particular because
of the addition of new economic agencies.

The creation of the State Council in 1954 brought further structural
complexity. More specialized agencies were set up. The State Council
became so large that it was difficult to hold plenary meetings of all
agency heads. In size, the State Council came to resemble the Central
Committee of the Party. As a practical result, it was the Standing Com-

mittee of the Council (consisting of the premier, the vice-premiers, and the chief secretary) which met most frequently.[8] Thus, both Council and Party came to be directed by a small—and largely identical—leadership core.

Other factors contributed to the complexity of the State Council. To the many branch-type agencies (ministries, departments, offices) were added numerous committees, some permanent, others temporary. Having acquired the habit of committee government from their Yenan period, the Chinese Communists, after 1949, continued this practice. The 1949 Government Administrative Council had eight permanent committees for continuing policy problems. The 1954 State Council reduced these to five: Planning, Construction, Physical Education, Minority Affairs, and Overseas Chinese Affairs. Additions took place in 1956, and, by 1959, there were again eight permanent committees: Capital Construction, State Planning, State Economics, Science and Technology, Physical Education, Minority Affairs, Overseas Chinese Affairs, and Foreign Cultural Liaison.[9]

Of these eight permanent committees, the most important are the first four; it is significant that they all relate to economic affairs. It should be borne in mind that neither military nor political affairs come under the control of the State Council. Even though military and economic affairs interlock, as, for example, in the operations of the Ministry of National Defense and of some other ministries (notably of industry and transportation), it is probably the Military Affairs Committee which exercises supreme direction over military affairs. As far as political affairs are concerned, they are in the exclusive domain of the executive organs of the Party's Central Committee.

The State Planning Commission was established in 1952 as an economic high command, comparable to the *Gosplan* of the Soviet Union during Stalin's time. It was in charge of both long-range and short-range planning. When the State Economic Commission was established in May 1956, the tasks of the State Planning Commission were confined to long-range planning; the State Economic Commission was given the task of compiling short-range plans and co-ordinating current economic activity. The State Construction Commission was set up in 1954 but was abolished in 1958, being succeeded by a State Capital Construction Commission, which in January 1961 was incorporated into the State

---

8 Chou Fang, *op. cit.*, p. 97.
9 Union Research Institute, *Chungkung shihnien* (Hong Kong, 1960), pp. 42-47.

Planning Commission; it was re-established in 1965. The State Commission for Science and Technology was established in 1958, and is mainly responsible for basic research and development.[10]

Aside from the permanent committees, there have been varying numbers of temporary committees. In the 1949-1954 Government Administration Council, there were six temporary committees: Marriage Law, Flood Control, Illiteracy, Employment, Economizing, and one called "Resolving Production by Central Agencies" (possibly a mediation and arbitration board). In 1956, the State Council set up a committee on wages. In 1957, a committee on disaster relief was created.[11] Some committees which originally seemed to have been temporary have become permanent, such as the Committee to Propagate the National Language (created in February 1956), the Scientific Planning Commission (created in March 1956), and the State Technological Commission (May 1956), the latter two combining in November 1958 into the State Commission for Science and Technology.[12]

Most of these temporary committees seem to be primarily oriented toward social and cultural problems. This may indicate a conviction on the part of the leaders that, whereas economic affairs are recurrent and require permanent committees, social and cultural affairs change, requiring the more flexible device of temporary or *ad hoc* committees. This may be illustrated by the fact that the marriage law, which was a major problem in the early 1950's, has disappeared entirely from public concern in Communist China.

From even the brief discussion presented, the conclusion appears to be warranted that the fundamental administrative work of the State Council relates to the economy.

Although there were periodic changes in the structure of the State Council between 1954 and 1958, the most significant reorganization took place during 1958, coming in the wake of the decentralization decisions of late 1957 and the *hsiafang* campaign which emptied bureaus of administrative personnel. The changes were described as "structural simplification." The main result was the amalgamation of ministries, bureaus, and other agencies of the State Council with similar functions into unitary bodies. The Ministry of Commerce (whose powers were greatly reduced in February 1958 by being split into two ministries) and the Ministry of Urban Services, in September 1958, were combined into a single Ministry of Commerce. The first and second Machine Tool Industry ministries were combined into one. The Ministry of Electric

---

[10] *Ibid.; Gendai Chūgoku jiten* (Tokyo, 1959), pp. 189-190.
[11] *Chungkung shihnien,* p. 46.
[12] *Ibid.*, pp. 45-46.

Power and the Ministry of Water Works were combined into a single ministry. And so on. In April 1959, Peking announced the abolition of the Ministries of Justice and of Control. By 1959 the structure of the State Council looked simpler than in 1954: There were six as compared to nine offices, and fourteen as compared to twenty "directly attached agencies." Though the number of ministries was about the same (thirty-one compared to thirty), it was far fewer than the forty-one in 1956. On the other hand, the rise in the number of committees (eight as compared to five), indicates the importance attached to the function of co-ordinating committees.

The bureaucratic changes of 1958 were a direct reflection of decentralization and *hsiafang*. With greater powers transferred to provincial government, there was less for the central ministries to do. The amalgamation of ministries and the enlarged powers of the coordinating offices indicate the stress placed on cutting across branch lines, and setting up mechanisms for more comprehensive integration at top policy-making levels. This was the great period of "dual rule."

ORGANIZATION OF THE STATE COUNCIL

PREMIER

VICE PREMIERS   SECRETARIAT

OFFICES:

Political:	Internal affairs[1]
International:	Foreign affairs
Economic:	Finance and trade
	Industry and communications
	Agriculture and forestry
Social:	Culture and Education

SPECIAL AGENCIES:

Economic:	State Statistical Bureau
	General Bureau for State Surveying and Cartography
	People's Bank of China
	Agricultural Bank of China[2]
	Central Meteorological Bureau
	General Bureau for Chinese Civil Aviation
	State Maritime Bureau

Administrative Bureau for China Travel and
Tourism[3]
Central General Administrative Bureau for the
Handicraft Industry
Central Administrative Bureau for Industry and
Business[4]
National Price Commission[5]
General Administrative Bureau for State Materials[6]
Administrative Bureau for State Buildings and Land

Sociopolitical: New China News Agency
Bureau of Broadcasting Affairs
Bureau for Foreign Languages Publication and
Distribution Affairs
Committee for Reforming the Chinese Language
Bureau of Religious Affairs

Administrative: Bureau of State Archives
Bureau for Scientific and Technological Cadres in the
State Council
Bureau for Foreign Experts
State Personnel Organization Commission[7]
Administrative Bureau for [Government] Agency
Affairs
Counselor's Office
Staff Office of the Premier

MAJOR MINISTRIES AND PERMANENT COMMITTEES:

Political: Ministry of the Interior

International: Ministry of Foreign Affairs

Military: Ministry of National Defense
Ministry of Public Security[8]

Economic: State Planning Commission
State Economic Commission
Science and Technology Commission
State Capital Construction Commission

MINISTRIES:

Economic: Finance
Food
Commerce

Foreign Trade
Aquatic Products
Metallurgical Industry
Chemical Industry
First Machine Building
Second Machine Building
Third Machine Building
Fourth Machine Building
Fifth Machine Building
Sixth Machine Building
Agricultural Machinery
Coal Industry
Petroleum Industry
Geology
Building and Engineering
Textile Industry
Light Industry
Railroads
Communications
Post and Telecommunication
Agriculture
Farms and Reclamation
Forestry
Water Conservancy and Electric Power

Social: Labor
Culture
Higher Education[9]
Education
Public Health

SPECIAL COMMITTEES:

Social: Physical Culture and Sports
Nationalities Affairs

International: Overseas Chinese Affairs
Foreign Economic Liaison[10]
Foreign Cultural Liaison

NOTES: The listing of agencies of the State Council in the annual handbook *Jenmin shouts'e* implies, I believe, a rank order of importance. Since the ranking has periodically changed, the changing importance of the various agencies can be determined by comparing different issues of this handbook. In categorizing the types of agencies, it was not necessary to make any changes in the rank order given. Our categories (political, economic, and so on are based on the functions of the agencies. The division into five major groups (offices, special agencies, major ministries and permanent committees, ministries, and special committees) is implicit in the way the agencies are grouped in the *Jenmin shouts'e*. Agencies can be divided into branch and committee types. The former include ministries, bureaus, and banks; the latter include offices, commissions, and committees.

A few words may be said on the different kinds of bureaus. As a branch-type agency, a bureau commands an organizational network with lower-echelon units. A general bureau is simply a higher-ranking bureau; a central bureau implies comparable bureaus at the regional level; an administrative bureau may have a network, but does not necessarily manage it (in contrast to a ministry); this is evident from administrative bureaus for industry and commerce at city levels.

In general, the ranking of agencies indicates a greater role for the special agencies and a lesser role for the ministries than in previous years.

1 In previous years, this office was called the Political and Legal Affairs Office. The change in name may reflect the growing importance of the Ministry of the Interior which ranks first among the major ministries and permanent committees.

2 An agricultural bank existed from 1955 to 1957; the present one was established late in 1963 for carrying out a rural credit program. See *Current Scene*, "Rural Finance in China," II:29 (March 1, 1964), 6.

3 The listing of the Tourism Bureau with other economic agencies indicates the growing importance the Chinese attach to income from tourists; this bureau was only recently established.

4 The Central Administrative Bureau for Industry and Business administers the affairs of the joint state-private-owned enterprises, that is, formerly private enterprises which were seminationalized, and which in large part are still managed by the national bourgeoisie.

5 The National Price Commission was established in 1963, reflecting the growing stress Peking places on financial mechanisms.

6 This bureau was also established in 1963. In May 1956, a General Bureau for Materials and Supply was established, but in 1958 it was absorbed by the State Economic Commission.. The establishment of the 1956 General Bureau undoubtedly was aimed at eliminating the allocation conflicts between the various ministries by bringing about coordination of materials and supply allocation. The same purpose is undoubtedly served by the present agency.

7 The task of this commission is promotion and transfer of cadres working in the government. The term here rendered as "organization" is *pienchih*, which is the Chinese equivalent of the Russian *nomenklatura*.

8 Since the Ministry of Public Security is listed directly after the Ministry of National Defense and in view of the consistent functional ranking of agencies, we have placed it into the military category.

9 This ministry is also a recent establishment, indicating a renewed commitment to "expertise" on the part of the government.

10 This committee was established in 1960 for the purpose of economic liaison with non-Communist countries in the wake of greatly increased trade.

SOURCE: Based on *Jenmin shouts'e 1964*, pp. 273-275.

The Military Branch

The subject of the military in the organizational system of China is an important one that should be dealt with in detail. More is needed than a study of a defense force, for the army has become a vital part of civil organization. Within society as a whole, it has become closely associated with economic and industrial organizaton. Young men trained by the army are assuming important positions in economic administration and management. The military has also played a role in high politics, as is evident in the controversy over P'eng Te-huai. Here we can only make some brief remarks on the relationship of the military to government.

Two governing bodies have played major roles in the direction of the military in China. One is the National Defense Council, and the other is the Ministry of National Defense. The first is a committee, headed by the Chairman of the Chinese People's Republic; it includes a broad representation from all areas of government and military. As Chou Fang states, it has "command of the country's armed forces." The second, in Chou Fang's words, "is a part of the state administrative system, is responsible for assuring the build-up of the country's armed forces, and strengthening national defense." [13] In other words, the National Defense Council is a coordinating committee, whereas the Ministry of National Defense is a branch agency. As a branch agency, the Ministry of National Defense operates on principles of straight-line command. Originally it was in full charge of the country's armed forces. Orders emanating from the Ministry went directly to all armed forces along straight vertical channels. The National Defense Council, on the other hand, was a body which exercised supreme authority, but not direct command. As in all state committees, its policy decisions had to be transformed into commands through some branch agency.

In addition to these two bodies, there also is the General Staff of the People's Liberation Army. It is not clear whether direct commands to the army before 1958 were issued by the General Staff or by the Ministry of National Defense; in other words, there has been vagueness about the exact relationship of the General Staff to the Ministry of National Defense. However, since both the General Staff and the Ministry of National Defense were until the late 1950's headed by "professionals," one can assume that single unified command did exist.[14] Toward the latter

---

13 Chou Fang, *op. cit.*, p. 100.

14 On this difficult question, see Alice Hsieh, *Communist China's Strategy in the Nuclear Era* (New York, 1962), pp. 21-23.

part of the 1950's, the National Defense Council appears to have acquired greater influence over the country's armed forces by placement of the General Staff directly under the council's jurisdiction. The change was symbolized by the dismissal of Su Yü as chief of the General Staff in October 1958, and his replacement by the politically reliable General Lo Jui-ch'ing.[15] These changes reflect the internal struggles at the highest levels of the leadership at the time, but organizationally they may be seen as part of the general shift from branch to committee government which was so characteristic of this period.

The Judicial Branch

China has its system of formal law and justice, modeled essentially on Soviet institutions. Its apex is the People's Supreme Court and the People's Supreme Procuracy. As students of Chinese law have noted, formal law plays a much smaller role in Chinese life than it does in the Soviet Union. In 1957, nonjudicial institutions were given broad powers to impose sanctions on individuals, including corrective labor for long periods of time. Courts became less of a force in the exercise of justice, as the Party began to assume the tasks of meting out sanctions. Party justice was swift, informal, and often harsh. In the spring of 1959, the Ministry of Justice was formally abolished. Law has not disappeared from China, even though work on the compilation of a law code has been halted. It continues to function in the economic realm, particularly in the area of contracts. Undoubtedly, criminal courts continue to act in a wide variety of cases, notably counter-revolutionary crimes. Nevertheless, as control began to assume political forms, the instrument of control, and so of justice, became the Party. In this way, one can argue that the Party, in effect, has displaced the system of law as the third arm of the state.[16]

VERTICAL RULE AND DUAL RULE

The general functional principles on the allocation of authority to government agencies are those of vertical rule and dual rule. As has been pointed out in the chapter on ideology, the concepts of vertical and dual rule were taken by the Chinese Communists from the Soviet conceptions of vertical and dual subordination; these ideas were origi-

---

[15] *Ibid.*, p. 175.

[16] See Gene Hsiao, "Legal Institutions in Communist China," *Problems of Communism* (March-April, 1965); Jerome A. Cohen, "The Criminal Process in China," unpublished paper, Harvard Law School, February 1965.

nally expounded by Lenin during the early days of the Soviet regime. Vertical rule means that an agency has full policy and operational control over all units of organization within its jurisdiction. Commands flow directly down; information comes directly up. Dual rule, as indicated by the term, means multiple rather than single channels of command and information. A lower-echelon agency receives commands from two or more higher-echelon agencies, and likewise has to submit reports to two or more agencies. Dual rule, in practice, means that an agency is partly under the jurisdiction of another body on the same administrative level. Dual rule may be seen as a combination of vertical and horizontal control, that is, one channel of command and information going up, and the other going sideways. This characteristic of dual rule makes it important in the problem of allocation of authority between central and regional government.

The most clear-cut examples of vertical rule are the ministries and other branch-type agencies (such as the People's Bank). Such agencies are called *pumen* in Chinese, which corresponds to the Russian *otrasl'*. When the term *pumen* is used to designate agencies at the central level, it almost always means ministries and comparable agencies. The ministries run a hierarchy of branch offices spread throughout the country, similar to the old Soviet *glavki*. The latter, in turn, direct the units of production under their jurisdiction. These branch offices and production units are responsible only to the ministries. Although liaison may take place with local government agencies, the span of control is direct and vertical. Through the operation of the principle of vertical rule some ministries created far-flung empires. Most notable, for the period before the Great Leap Forward, were the Ministry of National Defense, the Ministry of Commerce, some of the ministries for the machine-building industry, the Finance Ministry, and the People's Bank of China.

The most clear-cut examples of dual rule are those where a branch agency is subordinate both to a higher-echelon agency and to a coordinating committee. We have already pointed out that committees differ from branch agencies in that they cut across branch lines. A committee will comprise representatives from several different organizational sectors. Therefore a committee usually does not have the apparatus that the branch agencies have. The scope of its activities is primarily horizontal. This can be seen in the planning system. The State Economic Commission, which is in charge of short-term planning, collects its information from other agencies, both central and regional. It does not maintain an organizational empire spread throughout the country in the form of branch offices. The same is true of the State Planning Commission, which does long-term planning. There are regional planning agencies, but they are primarily responsible to regional government, rather than to the central State Planning Commission. The absence of a branch-type planning system has been one of the major factors impeding the work of central planning in China. Dual rule is exercised both at central and regional levels, but its greatest importance has been at the regional level.

It is impossible to lay out charts of organization which would indicate precisely which agencies are subject to vertical, and which to dual rule, because all depends on the swing of the pendulum of organizational policy. The main policy factor is whether centralization or decentralization is emphasized at any given period. In general, one can say that stress on vertical rule means centralization, and stress on dual rule means decentralization II. Dual rule, in fact, may be seen as a way of implementing decentralization II.

Vertical rule reached a high point around 1954. Not only the major economic, but other ministries as well, had created nation-wide networks of organization. The People's Bank, for example, had rapidly set up a banking empire which was instrumental in bringing China's inflation under control and assuring that the flow of money and credit was subject to central command and regulation. The Ministry of Commerce, through its specialized trading corporations, its purchase and procurement stations, and its retail outlets had acquired centralized control over the country's supply and sales system. In the chapter on control, we shall describe how the Ministry of Control was in the process of becoming a powerful agency for checking on the country's far-flung production system. Judging from the attacks made during the Eighth Party Congress by Lo Jui-ch'ing, then (and still) chief of the public security forces, against the excesses of vertical rule in the Ministry of Public Security, one might conclude that the latter ministry too had begun to create its own branch empire. The decentralization measures of late 1957 give an indication of the ministries, which, up to that point, had engaged in vertical rule, and henceforth were to share authority with agencies of provincial and local government. However, already by 1956, Peking had committed itself to a policy of implementing dual rule at all levels.

Chou Fang, the author of a text on government in China, writing in 1957, discusses the question of dual rule and vertical rule in the following terms:

Vertical rule in operational branches is a necessary precondition for assuring the implementation of operations. In the period of socialist construction, the division of operations becomes ever more specialized and complex. Without vertical rule specialized assignments cannot be made; problems cannot be resolved simply with broad general leadership. However, unified regional leadership also has its importance. If, within the framework of a single administrative region, work is not unifiedly assigned, confusion will be created. In regard to all questions having a regional aspect, if the opinions of the people's committees in that area are not respected, if the regional peculiarities of that area are not considered, then deviations will develop in the execution of tasks. Therefore, the proper way to resolve this is to carry through dual rule.[17]

Unfortunately Chou Fang does not go into greater detail on the actual problems arising from the simultaneous operation of both kinds of rule. However, from his remarks on the command relationships between the offices of *hsien* government and lower-echelon agencies at the *hsiang* and town levels, we get a clue about the nature of the problems. Under vertical rule, the offices issued commands directly to corresponding offices in *hsiang* and town government, thus acting in the same way as the ministries of the central government toward lower-echelon agencies. This in miniature reflects vertical rule at the national level. However, dual rule acts against such direct lines of command. If each office in *hsiang* or town government receives its instructions largely from a higher-echelon office, then this clearly disrupts the "unified leadership" of the *hsiang* and town people's committees. Thus dual rule means in effect that all commands must be routed through the *hsien* committee and then transmitted directly to the *hsiang* or town committee. Yet, as Chou Fang admits, some form of vertical rule is still to be considered as "permissible." This situation must have created great confusion within the state administrative apparatus. Are instructions to be accepted from a higher-level office or from the people's committee? Whose leadership is primary? Furthermore, what does the specification "primary" and "secondary" leadership mean in concrete terms?

In the light of the organizational history of Communist China, we can say that policy favoring vertical rule strengthened the ministries and branch agencies, but policy favoring dual rule ultimately increased the authority of the Party committees. The main purpose of dual rule was coordination, and nobody could better coordinate across branch and agency lines than the Party committees. The Party alone was not bedeviled by the cross-currents of multiple jurisdiction. Every Party committee was responsible to one and only one higher echelon in the Party apparatus. But every local Party committee had key Party cadres in every one of the agencies of local government. It was in the Party meeting that everyone came together. Agency loyalty took second place to Party loyalty in these meetings. What better situation could there be

---

[17] Chou Fang, *op. cit.*, p. 132.

for coordinating disparate activities, not to mention that the Party always knew exactly what real policy was.

Party committees achieved their greatest power at the regional level, particularly by taking control of regional government agencies. In this respect, the nature of the relationship of regional government agencies to regional agencies of the national ministries takes on particular importance. Both types of agencies are a part of the administrative system. However, regional government agencies came increasingly under Party control, whereas regional agencies of national ministries were originally exempt from control by regional Party organizations. Through the device of dual rule, however, the regional agencies of the national ministries came under the jurisdiction of regional government agencies, and so under control of the regional Party organization.

In one of his unfortunately brief discussions of the relationship between national and regional government, Chou Fang comments on the role of regional government agencies versus regional agencies of the national ministries.

> Carrying out the principle of regional supervision means that one can guard against an agency stationed away [from the center] engaging in violations of law or infractions of discipline because of the fact that they are separated from their own leadership. This principle of regional supervision, if further developed, can turn into a kind of dual rule, whereby the leadership of the center or higher echelon government is primary and that of the regional areas is secondary.[18]

Thus we see that in 1956, the regime already admitted the need for some sort of regional control even over central agencies which originally enjoyed regional immunity. Significantly Chou Fang uses the word supervision, *chientu*, which is much stronger than the word control, *chiench'a*. *Chientu* means the right to check on work in progress, and so gives the checker influence in determining later stages of the operation. *Chiench'a* is inspection of work done. *Chientu* thus means the right to participate in decision-making processes. In a sense the whole notion of dual rule moved from control to supervision and finally to coordinated interagency decision-making. The final stage was reached when the regional Party committees were powerful enough to assume the coordinative and decision-making role.

As in the Soviet Union, the Party in China is territorially organized. It is therefore to be presumed that the Party committees, even in units

---

18 *Ibid.*, p. 133.

of production under the jurisdiction of central rather than regional ministries, were subject to regional Party committees. Thus no matter how explicit vertical rule, regional Party interests were able to make themselves felt even in organizations under central-government jurisdiction. The more powerful the Party became, the greater the intrusion of horizontal power. During the Eighth Party Congress in 1956 one senses a growing hostility against vertical rule. Lo Jui-ch'ing comments on this problem as it relates to the public-security agencies, but his remarks can be taken as indicative of Party thinking on the relationship of the Party to the bureaucracy as a whole:

We must thoroughly emphasize the leadership function of the Party vis-à-vis the public-security agencies. . . . During the [Kiangsi Soviet period], we erroneously emphasized vertical rule in the security agencies, with the result that, at all levels, the security agencies were not subject to leadership and supervision by Party committees. . . . After the Tsunyi Conference of 1935, the Party rectified this error and . . . put the public-security agencies at all levels under the real leadership of the Central Committee and [lower] level Party committees; the public-security agencies in the army were placed under the leadership and supervision of army Party committees and political agencies. . . . At present, in public-security agencies at all levels, we [now] carry out a system of collective leadership by the Party fraction and individual responsibility by the chiefs. In this way we have avoided the errors of the past.[19]

Lo Jui-ch'ing thus makes the real intent of dual rule clear, namely to increase the power of the Party over the branch agencies. The constant references to "all levels" or "all echelons" means that at every tier of the branch structure, Party committees or Party factions are to have a voice in the decision-making process. This turned out to be most significant at the middle tiers of organization, notably at the level of provincial and local government.

In this book, I have been hesitant to advance propositions, for the task has been mainly theoretical and descriptive. However, the evidence from China, as well as from other Communist countries, would suggest that the realm of government where the Party, as an organization,

---

[19] *Jenmin shouts'e 1957*, p. 84. It was probably at the Tsunyi Conference in 1935 that the conflict between Mao Tse-tung and Chang Kuo-t'ao arose. Ho Kan-chih, the official historian, accuses Chang Kuo-t'ao of using "unprincipled methods to solidarize the cadres, creating a personalized system, carrying out a system of intimidation within the Red Army such as existed in warlord armies." (*Chungkuo hsientai komingshih* [Hong Kong, 1958], p. 177.) It may have been at this time that Mao realized that the only way to hold the whole structure together was to maintain tight Party control over all organized units, military and civilian.

achieves its greatest power is the regional level. At the center, the Party competes with an army of trained professionals who are in charge of the complex operations of branch agencies. At the bottom, it must reckon with the demands of the masses. However, at this middle level of government, there are fewer professionals to compete with than at the center, and the masses are not represented as in the production units.

VERTICAL AND DUAL RULE
(Command Relationships)

VERTICAL RULE:

Central government:	Branch-type agency
Regional government:	Regional branch-type agency
Unit of production:	Enterprise

DUAL RULE:

Central
government: Committee-type ——— Branch-type ——— Other
agency   agency   branch-type
                                          agency

Regional
government: People's committee ——— Regional branch-type
                                    agency

Unit of
production: Enterprise

I would further suggest that the coordinative role of the Party fits in well with the nature of regional government. In the economic field, for example, regional governments administer a complex array of small enterprises which cannot be governed according to strict production principles. Indirect controls and coordination are far more important administrative needs than direct vertical management. This would further suggest that decentralization II, as it operates in Communist countries, must take the form of a Party-led decentralization. The fact that the Chinese were able to realize decentralization II in 1958 and the Russians were not, undoubtedly mirrors the different organizational strength of the two parties.

DECENTRALIZATION

The Eighth Party Congress of 1956 called for a strengthening of dual rule in all agencies of government. This put an end to the development toward centralized vertical rule of the early 1950's. But it also paved the way for decentralization in 1957, on the eve of the Great Leap Forward. The Eighth Party Congress initiated a discussion of decentralization that mainly found expression in academic, particularly economic, journals. The discussion intensified greatly in 1957, partly because of legitimation by the great economic reorganization carried through by the Soviets in May 1957. Decentralization was one of the major topics discussed in the meeting of the Third Plenum of the Central Committee which lasted from September 20 to October 9, 1957. The length of the meeting indicates that basic changes in policy were discussed. There can be no doubt that some crucial policies leading to the Great Leap Forward were decided during this meeting.

The Third Plenum was an "enlarged" meeting, which means that Party first secretaries from the entire country attended. Such "enlarged" meetings are normally held whenever new policy is announced which requires implementation down to the basic levels of organization.

Teng Hsiao-p'ing reported on the rectification (that is, the anti-rightist) movement. This constituted the major political report of the Third Plenum; it was published in full by *Jenmin jihpao* on October 19. Teng reviewed the first and second phases of the anti-rightist movement, and called upon the Party to prepare for the third and fourth phases. His references to the problems of "serious rightist tendencies" and "regionalization of cadres" in the Party foreshadowed attacks on conservative professionals and Party localism which were to take place in November and December.

Ch'en Yün reported on proposed changes in the system of economic administration and on the problem of raising agricultural output. This constituted the major economic report of the Third Plenum. It is apparent (though his speech was not published) that Ch'en Yün discussed the draft proposals on administrative decentralization which were ratified by the Third Plenum. The linkage between decentralization and agriculture will be made clear in the following discussion.

Chou En-lai reported on wages and welfare. This constituted the major social report of the Third Plenum—it was, also, not published.

The fact that only Teng's report was published indicates clearly that

the "opinions" represented by Teng were the ones which finally predominated; Teng was the leading spokesman of the Mao-Liu group.

The brief communiqué of the Plenum ends with the following statement:

The meeting basically passed the 1956-1967 [twelve-year] program for the
nation-wide development of agriculture (revised draft). This revised draft is
to be circulated among the country's villages for discussion. Thereafter it is to
be submitted to a National Party Congress for ratification, and subsequently
brought up before the National People's Congress for discussion and ratification.

The meeting also basically passed regulations for improving the system of
industrial management (draft), regulations for improving the system of commercial management (draft), regulations for improving the system of financial
management and on division of authority over financial management between
center and regions (draft), as well as (draft) regulations on the question of
employee wages and welfare. These draft documents will be submitted to the
State Council for discussion and affirmation, or will be submitted to the Standing Committee of the National People's Congress for consideration. Comrade
Mao Tse-tung gave the concluding speech of the meeting.[20]

The decentralization policy adopted late in 1957 is one of the most
widely discussed questions among students of Communist China. The
Third Plenum ratified the decisions, made by the Politburo in September 1957, for a far-reaching decentralization of the economic system.
Decentralization had been discussed for more than a year, and general
agreement was reached to move in that direction. The draft regulations
approved by the Third Plenum indicate that the administration of industry, commerce, and finance was to be decentralized. However, as we
pointed out, decentralization can take two different paths: either decision-making powers are put into the hands of the producing units
themselves (decentralization I) or they are put into the hands of lower-
echelon administrative units (decentralization II). The type of decentralization implemented has a profound influence on the way government functions. We have pointed out, in the chapter on ideology, that
there were sharp cleavages of opinion among members of the Politburo
as to what "correct" economic strategy should be. One group, headed
by Mao Tse-tung, advocated a policy of *social mobilization* in order to
achieve rapid economic growth. Another group, headed by Ch'en Yün,
advocated a policy of *material incentives* in order to achieve a more
balanced, though slower, economic growth. These divergent opinions

---

[20] *Jenmin shouts'e 1958*, p. 182.

had different consequences for the centralization-decentralization problem.

Hsüeh Mu-ch'iao, head of the State Statistical Bureau, published an article in September 1957, on the problem of decentralization. Hsüeh is generally considered one of the more cautious economists in the country, and thus may be regarded as advocating the Ch'en Yün approach. The fact that his article was published in September would indicate that the ideas of that group still prevailed at that time. Hsüeh, in effect, called for a revision of economic administration which would give greater decision-making powers to the ministries, provincial government, and enterprises. The body whose powers were to be reduced was the State Council, or more specifically the supreme policy-making economic agencies in Peking.

In substance, Hsüeh was calling for a policy of simultaneous centralization, decentralization I, and decentralization II. This can be illustrated, for example, by Hsüeh's proposed changes in the production planning system. The central economic agencies would retain planning controls only over a small number of vital products. The central ministries and provincial governments would be allowed to impose planning controls over a range of products not covered by central economic controls, but considered important for the production programs of these administrative agencies. Production planning for all other products would be determined by the enterprises according to supply and demand, that is, the market. The Ministry of Commerce would exercise regulatory control through the medium of interenterprise contracts. Thus, the central branch agencies, provincial government, and individual enterprises would each acquire greater decision-making powers. This "contradictory" combination of centralization, decentralization I, and decentralization II is indeed the kind of economic administration that prevails today in China.[21]

The discussion below indicates that this was not the kind of decentralization decided on at the Third Plenum, or the one which formed the basis of the Great Leap Forward. What came out of the Third Plenum was a clear-cut decision for decentralization II. Economics in a Communist country means political economics, hence administration. If we can understand the elements that went into the decisions of the Third Plenum, we shall have gained an insight into governmental function in Communist China.

---

21 Hsüeh Mu-ch'iao, "Tui hsienhsing chihua kuanli chihtu ti ch'upu ichien," *Chihua chingchi,* 9 (September 1957), 20-24.

To understand that decision, we must look at agriculture. At the core of the dispute was the problem of increasing agricultural output. Both the divergent approaches of social mobilization and material incentives aimed at resolving this problem; both also demanded decentralization. But the material-incentives approach, advocated by Ch'en Yün, called for some degree of decentralization I. Putting decision-making powers into the hands of producing units also meant creating external conditions for the autonomous exercise of such powers, namely some form of market conditions. It is apparent from Ch'en Yün's speech to the Eighth Party Congress, where he called for an expansion of the free market, that implementing his program of changes in economic administration would have meant greater reliance on the market.

It has been an assumption of Chinese Communist economic theorists that where production units are not subject to directive and regulatory controls, they will produce for self-gain; they will increase output only if they can gain something in return. In other words, if the autonomy of production units, notably agricultural cooperatives and industrial enterprises, is to be expanded, material rewards must be given them as incentives. This means greater output of consumer goods, for example, which can only be produced by light industry.

Since light industry was to a large extent under the control of regional government (and would be even more so under whatever kind of decentralization was implemented), the introduction of some degree of decentralization I with its consequent stress on consumer-goods production would have had a direct effect on regional administration. Regional government would have had to direct its attention toward consumer-goods production to satisfy the growing material demands of the peasants. Moreover, the growth of free-market tendencies would have reduced the powers of regional administration to direct the economy in the area of their jurisdiction.

Since the Ch'en Yün program also advocated an increase of the powers of the ministries, this would have meant a strengthening of the main competitors of regional government in the economic realm. Therefore, the net effect of the Ch'en Yün program (with its combination of centralization and the two kinds of decentralization) would have resulted in a squeeze on regional administration. The fact that regional administration was Party-dominated meant that Ch'en Yün's ostensibly economic program had direct political and administrative consequences.

A further factor relevant to the controversy between the social-mobilization and the material-incentives approaches was the fact that the Agricultural Producers Cooperatives in 1957 were apparently again coming under the control of what was euphemistically called "prosperous middle peasants." Tolerance toward "prosperous" peasants in Communist China has generally gone together with economic relaxation and permissiveness toward the market. Since the "prosperous" peasants were less amenable to Party control, greater freedom for them inevitably meant less control by Party-dominated regional government over the peasantry. Social mobilization, of course, was intended to have the opposite effect. Thus both the *economic* consequences of decentralization I and the *social* consequences of cooperatives dominated by "prosperous" peasants would have had significant *political* consequences.

Since the evidence indicates that, sometime during the Third Plenum, a basic decision was made for decentralization II, let us attempt an analysis of the factors that entered into this decision, particularly those concerning agriculture.

First we might note that of the four draft regulations mentioned in the second paragraph of the above-quoted part of the communiqué, only the first three were implemented (in the regulations promulgated in the State Council and published on November 18, 1957); there was no implementation of the fourth draft regulation, dealing with wages and welfare.[22]

Failure to promulgate a regulation on wages and welfare indicates disagreement among the leadership—undoubtedly concerning low-wage versus high-wage policy. Late in 1957, the Chinese Communists began to move in the direction of a "rational low-wage policy," [23] tied in with the new approach to work, namely stressing social mobilization rather than material incentives. This new policy was diametrically opposed to the spirit of the great wage reform of early 1956, which emphasized material incentives and provided even greater rewards than before for skill and productivity. It is not impossible that Chou En-lai's report on wages and welfare either reflected the material incentive approach to wages or constituted a compromise between the incentive approach and the mobilizational approach. If so, it had to be scrapped in view of the radical policy shift that emerged after the Third Plenum.

The first paragraph of the above-quoted part of the communique announced that the draft program for the development of agriculture

---

[22] A general statement on improvement in working conditions, and temporary regulations concerning the employment of seasonal workers from villages, were published in November and December, respectively. Neither of these constituted a new wage policy. *Jenmin shouts'e 1958*, p. 595.

[23] See Charles Hoffmann, "The Basis of Communist China's Incentive Policy," *Asian Survey*, III:5 (May 1963), 252.

had been "basically passed." One cannot overstress the symbolic importance of this statement. It related to something far transcending agriculture, affecting the basic strategy of the Great Leap Forward. The revival of the draft program decided the conflict over decentralization, namely whether to move in the direction of decentralization I or decentralization II. Symbolically, the reappearance in 'the communique of the phrase "the 1956-1967 program for the nation-wide development of agriculture," so closely associated with the collectivization drive of 1955-1956, meant that social mobilization and not material incentives was to be the dominant agricultural policy. This excluded decentralization I and cleared the road for decentralization II. Because of the great importance of the draft program for the development of agriculture, it undoubtedly was the main subject of Mao's concluding address to the Plenum.[24]

On September 14, six days before convocation of the Third Plenum, three Central Committee directives on agriculture were announced. These were probably decided on in an earlier Politburo meeting (perhaps an enlarged meeting). The directives contained conservative statements on the cooperatives and on agricultural policy in general.[25] Though Ch'en Yün's speech on agriculture at the Third Plenum was never published, "a part" of the report on agriculture by Teng Tzu-hui, who was director of the Rural Work Department of the Central Committee, was subsequently published. Teng Tzu-hui evinced the same

---

[24] It was originally published under Mao Tse-tung's name in *Jenmin jihpao*, January 26, 1956. At that time it was announced with great fanfare at a "supreme meeting of state." Subsequently, reference to it disappears. It was not mentioned in Teng Tzu-hui's report to the Eighth Party Congress, nor was it reprinted in the *Jenmin shouts'e* for 1956. In his report to the Third Plenum, Teng Hsiao-p'ing discusses "the forty article draft plan for the development of agricultural production decided on in January 1956." He discusses it in a rather cautious way; *Jenmin shouts'e 1958*, p. 37. The September 14 communique of the Politburo also refers to it, as "the draft plan for the national development of agriculture"; *ibid.*, p. 518. The first reappearance of its original full name: "the draft plan for the national development of agriculture from 1956 to 1967," was in the communique of the Third Plenum. The revised version was published shortly thereafter by the *Jenmin jihpao*, on October 25, 1957. An introductory comment noted that "it was brought forth by the Central Committee in January 1956." It was widely discussed in April and May 1958, but was not officially ratified by the National People's Congress until April 1960. The term "twelve years" or "from 1956 to 1967" symbolically signified continuing social mobilization. The official adoption of the term, and the publication of the draft program indicate clearly that a general policy decision on social mobilization had been made during the Third Plenum.

[25] *Jenmin shouts'e 1958*, pp. 517-520.

BURNING OF THE LAND DEEDS DURING THE LAND REFORM IN 1951

NEW CONSTRUCTIONS IN A PEKING SUBURB

STRUGGLE BEFORE THE OVEN

POSTER READS: "PROTECT THE OVEN, REDUCE REPAIRS, SAVE MATERIALS, AND CUT COSTS."

EIGHTH PLENUM OF THE CENTRAL COMMITTEE OF THE CHINESE COMMUNIST
PARTY, 1959

LEFT TO RIGHT: LIN PIAO, CH'EN YÜN, CHOU EN-LAI, MAO TSE-TUNG, LIU SHAO-
CH'I, CHU TEH, TENG HSIAO-P'ING

K'O CH'ING-SHIH (LEFT) AND CH'EN YÜN (NEXT TO HIM) AT THE TENTH ANNIVERSARY OF THE FOUNDING OF THE PEOPLE'S REPUBLIC, 1959

JOINED FIELDS, THE RESULT OF COLLECTIVIZATION

THE PEOPLE'S MILITIA

NOTE: The first six illustrations are from *Shanghai* (Shanghai: The People's Art Publishing Company, n.d.); the last from *Peking* (Peking: The Peking Picture Book Editorial Committee, 1959).

conservative tone as that in the mentioned three directives. He made no reference to the draft program for the development of agriculture, surprising in view of the fact that the communiqué stated that it had been "basically passed." [26] Both Ch'en Yün and Teng Tzu-hui have been generally identified with more conservative policies toward the rural economy. Conservative policy toward agriculture, in 1957, meant confining the size of the Agricultural Producers Cooperatives to the "natural village," promising the peasants that there would be no new changes in the organization of the cooperatives, and enlarging the sphere of their economy (see pp. 456-457).

Despite the disagreement between the radicals and the conservatives over future economic policy, there was agreement that whatever the policy adopted, it would have to deal with the core problem: raising agricultural output. Thus both sides apparently agreed to launch a big campaign to improve irrigation and water works (though the social-mobilization approach meant that methods different from the material-incentives approach would be used to carry it out).

A statement issued by the government at the time of Mao Tse-tung's visit to Moscow in November 1957 indicates some of the general thinking of the leadership on the state of the economy:

Because of the good harvests of 1952 and 1955, the development of the national economy was quite rapid in 1953 and 1956. The gross output value of industry (including handicraft industry) rose respectively by 30 percent and 28.2 percent. Because the 1954 and 1956 harvests were bad, the development of the national economy was rather slow in 1955 and 1957. The gross output value of industry rose respectively only by about 5.6 percent and 4 percent (the [1957] plan will be overfulfilled). The reason is that about 80 percent of the materials needed by our country's light industry depend on agriculture, and light industry constitutes about 50 percent of the relative weight of all our industry.[27]

This statement revealed a simple but important principle of economic doctrine in the minds of China's leaders: the quality of industrial performance in a given year depends on the quality of agricultural output during the preceding year. The implication of this principle was that 1958 would be a bad industrial year if 1957 were a poor agricultural year. Subsequently, it became known that agricultural output for 1957 was not much better than in 1956.[28]

26 *Ibid.*, pp. 520-525.

27 *Ibid.*, p. 445.

28 See Choh-ming Li, *Economic Development of Communist China* (Berkeley and Los Angeles, 1959), p. 220.

Given the disagreement between Mao Tse-tung and Ch'en Yün over agricultural policy (social mobilization versus material incentives), the revival of the twelve-year program for the development of agriculture took on particular importance. Mao Tse-tung is the presumed author of that program, first published in January 1956 and widely discussed for a short period after that. That program called for continuing collectivization with stress on mobilization rather than incentives.

On October 27, 1957, the *Jenmin jihpao* published an editorial on the revised program for the development of agriculture in 1956-1967—the first public reference to it since its disappearance from view in the spring of 1956. In the Plenary meeting of the Central Committee, which lasted three weeks, apparently no reference to the twelve-year plan was made by the two men, Ch'en Yün and Teng Tzu-hui, who reported on agriculture. The only discussion was by Teng Hsiao-p'ing in his report on rectification, and there in a cautious way. Suddenly, during the very last days of the Plenum, the program was publicly resurrected. An editorial in the *Jenmin jihpao* may not have manifest significance to the outsider, but to the insider will immediately be apparent as a signal indicating policy change. The resurrection of the twelve-year program undoubtedly announced that a policy decision had been made once again to turn in the direction of social mobilization. In political terms, this meant a victory of the Mao group over the Ch'en group.

In view of the close relationship between agriculture and light industry, as is apparent by the fact that light industry obtained 80 percent of its raw materials from agriculture, let us look at the different approaches of the radicals and the conservatives toward this relationship, and the implications of these approaches for decentralization.

There was general consensus that administrative centralization such as prevailed up to 1957 would have to be modified, particularly in the administration of light industry. The term "light industry," as explained in the chapter on ideology, means not just consumer-goods industries, but medium- and small-scale industries that manufacture both producer and consumer goods. Light industry constitutes a link between agriculture and heavy industry in the Chinese economy. Light industry derives most of its raw materials from agriculture, and is one of the major sources of savings for investment in heavy industry.

Both the decentralization decisions and the social-mobilization policy toward agriculture have to be understood in terms of the crucial importance assigned to the light industrial sector of the national economy.

The decentralization decisions called for a rapid build-up of regional industry, which was almost entirely of the light type. The industries transferred from central to provincial control were also almost entirely in the light category. The great construction programs launched in 1958 took the form of building large numbers of medium- and small-scale enterprises. If light industry was to be rapidly developed, then a leap forward in agricultural output was necessary. Moreover, if Peking envisaged increased trade with the Soviet Union (as happened in 1958 and 1959), an even greater spurt in farm output was needed. With the projected rapid development of light industry and increased trade with the Soviet Union, one can imagine the burden placed on agriculture. Agricultural output statistics for each current year are known by November. Therefore, when the statement on the state of the economy mentioned above was issued, China's economic leaders must have known that, unless something radical was done, the disappointing results of the 1957 crop would be followed by a poor industrial year in 1958, particularly for light industry.

The conservatives agreed on the need to develop light industry and agriculture. This is apparent from Ch'en Yün's speech to the Eighth Party Congress, in which he recommended greater reliance on the market for China. Ch'en Yün was at the time chief of the first Ministry of Commerce. The commercial network was a powerful administrative structure handling procurement and distribution for much of the economy. Clearly Ch'en Yün was vitally interested in more farm output and in improved procurement conditions for light industry.

Teng Tzu-hui, in the published part of his speech at the Third Plenum, outlined a seven-point program for "self-reliance" (*tzuli kengsheng*) in agriculture.[29] Essentially, the program called for an intensification of rural construction, particularly in water works, increased fertilizer resources, and a stepped-up program of capital accumulation in the Agricultural Producers' Cooperatives. In particular, Teng Tzu-hui called for more investment in industrial crop acreage. Clearly, if light industry was to be stressed in the coming period, more industrial crops had to be made available. There is no hint in Teng Tzu-hui's speech that anything more than a stepped-up program of capital and labor investment should be followed. Teng Tzu-hui, in fact, urged that sufficient consideration be given to individual labor,

---

[29] The term *tzuli kengsheng* appears to have come up sometime in the summer of 1957. It was used during the Great Leap Forward, but largely in terms of regional autarky. It became a prominent slogan in 1962, in the wake of the breakdown in Sino-Soviet commercial relations.

in marked contrast to the slogans of 1958.[30] Teng did call for more cadres to "go down" (hsiafang) to the front line of production, but that was in accord with the campaign which was beginning to develop and which greatly accelerated in the next two months. There is no indication in Teng Tzu-hui's speech that major restructuring was being contemplated in agriculture.[31]

Both the Mao Tse-tung and the Ch'en Yün groups agreed that agriculture and light industry had to be developed during the Second Five-Year Plan. However, they disagreed on method: was development to be fast but risky, or slow but safe? The choice for fast development meant a greater need of heavy industry for capital goods. One must remember that Mao Tse-tung had called not just for simultaneous development of industry and agriculture, but had added: "on a basis of preferentially developing heavy industry." Ch'en Yün's approach was far more in line with complete self-reliance, for it was based on a slower rate of growth for heavy industry.

Trade between the Soviet Union and China increased greatly in 1958 and 1959. China was able to import most capital goods needed for its program of heavy industrial development. Although the details were worked out among the technical experts, there must have been some preliminary agreement at the highest levels for trade to be increased to such a magnitude. I would like to suggest that it was Mao's political influence with Khrushchev, late in 1957, which secured for China a Soviet promise for stepped-up trade. If Ch'en Yün envisaged an economic strategy of self-reliance, with balanced relationships be-

---

[30] On December 21, 1957, the State Council issued a directive that indicated a hardened attitude toward "individual peasant households." By contrast, section 4.5 of Teng's speech states: "In the past many APC cadres misunderstood collective labor. There were serious wastages of labor resulting from the use of methods such as 'banging the gong and all get together to go down to the fields,' 'let's work like a hive of bees,' 'squad, brigade attack'; these have to be overcome."

[31] This does not imply that a decision was made to set up the communes. To the contrary, evidence indicates that the commune idea, as distinct from the amalgamated Agricultural Producers' Cooperatives, arose in the summer of 1958, in connection with the militarization of the peasantry (see pp. 472 ff.). The move to combine the Agricultural Producers' Cooperatives (pingshe) started in April 1958, and by May detailed accounts appeared in book form describing the process. In retrospect, these enlarged Agricultural Producers' Cooperatives were early versions of the communes. But as late as May 1958, they were still regarded as experimental. The Jenmin shouts'e for 1957 was only published in May 1958 and contained Teng's expurgated speech. The implication is that full agreement on agricultural policy had not yet been reached.

tween heavy industry, light industry, and agriculture, the strategy advocated by Mao Tse-tung required heavy dependence on the Soviet Union. That could only come through aid or trade. In fact, it was realized in 1958 and 1959 through a greatly enlarged trade.

The sudden and unexpected adoption of the twelve-year program for the development of agriculture during the latter days of the Third Plenum early in October 1957 indicates a triumph of the radical view over the conservative, specifically of Mao's approach over that of Ch'en Yün. On October 4, 1957, Sputnik soared into the air, creating worldwide reverberations—and the implication that the power balance had shifted from the United States to the Soviet Union. The events of October 1957 in the Soviet Union presumably convinced Mao that the balance of forces in the world had decisively changed, and that he could rely on the Soviet Union for major material support. Besides, in October 1957 Khrushchev completed his struggle for unchallenged power in the Soviet Union through the ouster of Marshal Zhukov. Earlier in June, he had triumphed over the "anti-Party clique" of Molotov, Kaganovich, and others (there are indications that, at the time of this conflict in Moscow during May and June, the Chinese leaders were extremely unsettled). Thus, in October 1957, the Soviet Union appeared to have made the decisive breakthrough in the weaponry field and faced the world with a now firmly established leadership. It is likely that, in the discussions of the Central Committee, Mao invoked the changed international situation to dispute Ch'en Yün's program. The fact that Mao shortly thereafter went to Moscow, from where he returned with a nuclear sharing agreement and presumably Khrushchev's promises for a greatly increased trade, lends weight to the argument that Mao invoked the assurance of Soviet support to gain acceptance of his radical policies.

Let us return to the decentralization decisions. The program of self-reliance was not to apply to heavy industry (because of need for Soviet capital goods), but it was to apply to light industry. Since there was little modern capital equipment to invest in light industry and agriculture, these two sectors had to rely on greater use of labor and the development of new, notably local, capital resources which had not been hitherto tapped. The decentralization decisions, as finally adopted, led to the downward transfer of almost all of China's light industry. Where formerly light industry was mostly under the control of central ministries, now it passed into the hands of provincial government. In accordance with self-reliance, this also meant that these industries could no longer look to the central government for the supply of major investment resources. Resources now were to be supplied locally, which meant a greater burden on agriculture.[32]

At this time, consensus existed on the economic policies to be followed in the light industrial and agricultural sectors. This was symbolized by the following slogans: (1) *yinti chihyi*: Get the Best out of Each Area; (2) *tzuli kengsheng*: Self-reliance; and (3) *ch'üanli hsiafang*: Downward Transfer of Authority. But, as we have indicated, the dispute was: should a policy of social mobilization or of material incentives prevail? If Ch'en Yün's policy of material incentives had prevailed, a more permissive attitude toward the Agricultural Producers Cooperatives (as indeed was indicated by the September directives) would have followed. Such an attitude would have favored the wealthy peasants who, as had happened in 1954 and 1955, were once again acquiring influence in the cooperatives. The more influence the wealthy peasants had, the weaker the control of the Party over the cooperatives. The same was the case with enterprise managers: a policy of material incentives would give them greater powers and inevitably put limits on the powers of the enterprise Party committees. We know that by 1957 the Party was in firm control of regional government. Its instrument in the cooperatives and the enterprises was the Party committee.

A policy of decentralization I, with its stress on material incentives and production-unit autonomy, would have meant at best a sharing of power between Party and production units, or at worst a situation where the latter could exert considerable economic pressure on the former. In the chapter on management, we shall discuss the phase of sharing of power between Party and managers in the enterprises in 1956 and 1957. However, the decision to adopt a policy of social mobilization, that is decentralization II, put all power into the hands of the Party. This was symbolized by the slogan of the Great Leap Forward: *chengchih kuashuai*: Politics Takes Command. This meant a transfer of all power to Party committees in the production units, and thus the establishment of an uninterrupted span of control from provincial Party committee to production-unit Party committee. Under decentralization II, there was to be no sharing of power.

On November 18, 1957, the State Council announced three regulations on changes in the system of industrial, commercial, and financial

---

[32] Dwight H. Perkins, "Centralization and Decentralization in Mainland China's Agriculture 1949-1962," *The Quarterly Journal of Economics*, LXXVII (May 1964), 208-237; "Centralization and Decentralization in Mainland China and the Soviet Union," *Annals of the American Academy of Political and Social Science*, 349 (September 1963), 70-80.

administration. In contrast to what had been advocated by Hsüeh Mu-ch'iao in September, no mention was made of increasing the decision-making powers of central branch agencies. The preamble to the regulation on changes in industrial management makes it clear that "the downward transfer of authority" was to increase the decision-making powers of regional government and of enterprise managers. Thus, apparently, a combination of decentralization II and decentralization I was advocated. Strictly speaking, such changes would still be in accord with what was advocated by the Ch'en Yün group. Again, however, structural changes do not tell the full story. As a result of the third phase of the anti-rightist movement, which had already started in November, enterprise managers were attacked and power passed into the hands of enterprise Party committees. These committees, however, were under the control of the provincial Party apparatus. Therefore, decentralization I never was realized. The acquisition of complete managerial control over the economy by the Party meant that decentralization II was to triumph.

Let us outline in brief detail the major administrative changes enacted by the three regulations on industrial, commercial, and financial administration. First, on industry. The most important change was the transfer to provincial governments of a broad range of industries. This included: almost all light industry, nonstrategic heavy industrial enterprises, the timber industry, ports, some enterprises under the jurisdiction of the Ministry of Communications, and many construction enterprises. The principle of dual rule was to be universally implemented in industry. Enterprises still subject to central jurisdiction were henceforth to be linked to regional authorities through dual rule. Regional authorities acquired greater powers over allocation of materials. They now got a greater share of above-target production, as well as a share of enterprise profits. Regional authorities also acquired greater control over personnel, including those working in central state-owned enterprises.[33] The planning system was greatly simplified, with greater leeway given factory managers to practice flexibility. A system of profit-sharing made it possible for enterprises to derive some of their investment funds directly from enterprise profit.

Second, on commerce. As in industry, a broad range of commercial agencies and enterprises were placed under provincial control. The big "specialized commercial corporations," which earlier had acquired needed goods for central government agencies, were abolished. Whole-

---

[33] Control of personnel was one of the major aims of Party organizations in economic units.

sale trading stations, formerly entirely under central control, now came partly under provincial control. The planning system was greatly simplified. A profit-sharing system was introduced, and provincial authorities were given greater control over enterprise profits (this to be done "gradually" and "experimentally"). Provincial authorities were given the right to set some prices in their areas of jurisdiction, although here too the regulations indicated that great care had to be exercised, and all efforts made to achieve coordination in price-setting between the center and the provinces. Again, as in industry, the principle of dual rule was universally introduced into the commercial network.

Third, on finance. Unlike in the other two sectors, no structural rearrangements were indicated, and no mention was made of dual rule. The regulations on finance laid down general lines of revenue division between the center and the regions, with the latter given a greatly increased share of budgetary revenue.

It is quite clear, then, that the heavy losers were the ministries. Perhaps the greatest loser was the Ministry of Commerce, until that time headed by Ch'en Yün. It had controlled the greater part of the country's supply system. Under Ch'en Yün's plan, as outlined by Hsüeh Mu-ch'iao, a major part of the supply system would have been made subject to the market with the Ministry of Commerce exercising regulatory control. Under the regulations as actually promulgated, controls over allocation of supplies and fixing of prices passed into the hands of provincial government; the specialized trading corporations, which had been the main instruments of the Ministry of Commerce for controlling the supply system, were abolished.

What the central branch agencies lost, the provincial governments gained. In addition to the powers gained in industry, commerce, and finance, provincial government also acquired important control over the transportation system. This can be illustrated by a brief review of the history of the railroad network.

The Ministry of Railroads constituted a branch-type agency par excellence, and until 1957 administrative policy was one of rigorous centralization. Centralization of the railroad system had been one of the most urgent tasks of the new regime after the "Liberation." But centralization was not easy to achieve, because the Central Manchurian Railway was under Soviet control until late 1952. When returned to China, first-echelon administrative control over the Manchurian railroad system remained in Mukden. But Peking had its bureaucratic weapons as well, and set up a powerful Ministry of Railroads which gradually spread its administrative branches throughout the country. In time, the Ministry of Railroads established a nation-wide network of fifteen centrally controlled "railroad administration bureaus" and forty-four "branch bureaus." The network kept a tightly centralized hold over every aspect of the transportation system. Late in 1957, the regime decided to abolish the branch bureaus and to cut down the size of the administration bureaus. Though centralization had served its purpose in 1953, by 1957 the power of the Ministry had grown so great that unified transportation policies at regional levels became impossible. Moreover, "difficulties were further increased in regard to the unified leadership of Party committees over enterprise and the carrying out of democratic management." Transportation was crucial to any development program. If the regional Party committees were to have a commanding voice in development, they had to have firm control over transportation in their areas.[34] It was undoubtedly this aspect of decentralization that contributed materially to the subsequent chaos in the transportation system.

The regulation on financial administration indicates no major structural changes, in contrast to the regulations on industrial and commercial administration. This conservatism undoubtedly reflected the great sensitivity which the Chinese Communists have always shown for financial matters, and the fear that decentralization of monetary and credit controls might have adverse consequences, such as inflationary pressures. However, "Politics Takes Command" did not halt at the gates of the Ministry of Finance, and the events of 1958 indicate that Party-controlled provincial governments had indeed acquired broad control over the country's financial institutions and resources.

The regulation on the decentralization of industrial administration consisted of two parts. One was called "suitably enlarging the authority of provinces, autonomous regions, and directly attached cities over the management of industry"; the other was called "suitably enlarging the managerial authority of personnel in charge of enterprises over the internal [affairs] of the enterprise." The first clearly constituted decentralization II; the latter, at least, constituted a degree of decentralization I. If both had been carried out in spirit and in letter, a kind of checks-and-balances condition would have been created, marked by the juxtaposed authorities of provincial cadres and enterprise managers. This would have impeded centralization of power at the regional level. However, since actually decentralization II took place, a rapid process of province-level centralization set in. Once the provincial cadres acquired power, they began to act in a manner similar to that

---

34 *Jenmin shouts'e 1958*, pp. 546-565.

of the central government during the early 1950's. An example of local centralizing tendencies was provided by the communes formed in the summer of 1958. Far from allowing the actual producing units, namely brigades and teams, to enjoy the fruits of decentralization, commune headquarters tried to manage them centrally, much as earlier the ministries had managed the agencies and enterprises under their jurisdiction. What happened in the communes was repeated at the level of the provinces.

There also was a new element in economic thinking which favored increase of provincial power. This new thinking, revealed in the strategy of the Great Leap Forward, called for the development of economic cooperation regions. There was much discussion as to what geographical expanse should constitute an economic cooperation region, but there was general agreement that self-sufficiency demanded some degree of autarky at regional levels. Some articles spoke of dividing China into seven large economic zones. Others urged the development of autarkic complexes at subprovincial levels. At one time, the communes were proclaimed as self-sufficient units that could supply the peasant population with their basic needs. Nevertheless, insofar as the range of political authority was a determining factor in economic decisions, economic cooperation tended to develop at the provincial level.[35] It was the provinces, and not the larger economic cooperation regions or the smaller communes, which began to develop as autarkic entities. The result was that, particularly in 1958, many provinces began to act like underdeveloped nations, desiring to create integrated complexes of industry, agriculture, commerce, and education within their borders.

The implementation of decentralization II had a profound effect on the function of government in Communist China. Provincial government emerged as a powerful level of administration with great control over the economic system, specifically over supply, production, and sales. Without such changes in the function of government, the Great Leap Forward could have never taken the form it did.

REGIONAL GOVERNMENT

In the preceding two sections, we discussed the power acquired by regional government through dual rule and decentralization II. Here we shall briefly discuss regional government itself. Strictly speaking,

---

[35] Franz Schurmann, "China's 'New Economic Policy'—Transition or Beginning," *The China Quarterly*, 17 (January-March 1964), 73-80.

the term "regional government" comprises all levels of administration, from the provincial on down. However, the Chinese Communists use the same word, *tifang*, to mean both regional and local; it is applied broadly to all administration below the central level: provincial government, city government, *hsien* government, and *hsiang* government. The practice of using a single word, rather than several, to designate these levels of administration undoubtedly derives from the three-tier conception of organization so common in Communist China. Just as there normally are three levels of organization in an enterprise (factory, shop, and team), so the entire structure of the state is seen as consisting essentially of three levels: center, region, production unit. The idea of regional government assumes that there must be some intermediate level between the state at the highest levels and the producing units at the lowest. As has been pointed out, it was not always certain where that level should be. In the early 1950's, the so-called Large Administrative Regions were the intermediate levels. In 1958, on the other hand, the establishment of subprovincial units as intermediate levels was under consideration. However, it is by now clear that the real intermediate level is that of the provinces or their equivalent administrative regions.

The structure of provincial government more or less follows the pattern of administration at the central level. As could be expected, there are fewer bureaus and departments. In general, provincial government bureaus are small-scale versions of central government ministries. Such a structure of provincial administration was purposely set up in the early 1950's to permit vertical rule. Thus, a central government ministry was able to have immediate contact with its counterpart in provincial government. However, as Chou Fang pointed out in 1957, the operation of dual rule put these provincial bureaus under the close jurisdiction of all-powerful people's committees: "All the working branches of the people's committees in the provinces and directly attached cities receive unified leadership from the people's committees, but also leadership from the corresponding branch in the State Council. Thus, the civil administration office in the provinces receives leadership from the provincial committee, but also from the Ministry of the Interior of the Chinese People's Republic." [36]

In this instance, dual rule may be said to have acted against the straight-line chain of command from the central Ministry of the Interior. However, dual rule need not operate in exactly the same way

---

[36] Chou Fang, *op. cit.*, p. 132. The 1957 version is slightly different from that of 1955.

at subprovincial levels. A civil administration bureau in *hsien* government, for example, is formally under the jurisdiction both of the civil administration office in the provincial government and of the *hsien* people's committee. If the latter is under the complete domination of provincial government, vertical rule prevails in effect, hence provincial centralization.

Hsien government again largely follows the pattern of provincial government but with fewer sections. According to the general rules on *hsien* government promulgated in January 1950, the typical *hsien* government was to have the following kinds of bureaus: *hsien* office, civil administration, public security, finance, food, taxation, industry and commerce, agriculture and forestry, communications, culture and education, and hygiene. With the exception of the directly attached cities, which have province-type government, city government is much the same as *hsien* government, with adaptation to urban problems.

At the *hsiang* level, the administrative structure changes. One might remember that traditionally formal government did not go below the *hsien* level. Instead of bureaus and departments, one finds the ubiquitous committees. The prevalence of committee-type government at the *hsiang* level undoubtedly reflects the need for greater flexibility and coordination, but also the realization that formal bureaucratic administration still cannot function at this low level. When the communes were formed, *hsiang* government for the most part merged with the commune administration. This made the commune not only a large-scale unit of production, but also the lowest rung of the state administrative structure. Nevertheless, given the qualitative difference between *hsien* and *hsiang* government, it still is not clear how tightly the commune administration is linked in to the state apparatus.[37]

The urban counterpart of the *hsiang* is the *ch'ü* or district. Significantly, *ch'ü* government relies more on bureaus and departments rather than on committees—undoubtedly because cities are easier to rule bureaucratically than rural areas.

At every level of the administrative system, executive committees cut across branch lines and are supposed to coordinate agency activities. In this respect, the Chinese people's committees follow Soviet precedent with its *ispolkoms*. The *ispolkom* is regarded as a "collegial organ" in contrast to the agencies which are characterized by "branch

---

[37] The commune remains a basic-level organization, but it is no longer the unit of production. The production brigades and teams are now regarded as the units of production, with the brigades more or less the equivalent of a village. The teams are the accounting units. Judging from Liao Lu-yen's figure of "more than 70,000 communes," it would appear that *hsiang* and commune administration are identical.

administration," *otraslevoe upravlenie*.[38] The Russians do not seem to have made a principle of the juxtaposition of these two forms of administration, but the Chinese have. This has made it possible for the Chinese to stress one or the other function, depending on policy at the time. Thus, in October 1954, at a time when centralization had reached its highest point, the *Jenmin jihpao* said: "Regional agencies of the state at all levels are agencies in which the masses themselves govern state affairs, but also they are inseparable parts of the state structure of our country." [39] In customary Communist practice, the statement that follows a "but also" is always what counts. Four years later, the component parts of the statement would be reversed, with the stress on regional leadership. We have already discussed "dual rule," and the growing role of the Party committees. The formal provisions for coordinating committees created the opening wedge for the Party committees to move in.

The problem of center versus region has bedeviled Chinese governments for centuries. In the early 1950's, the Chinese Communists thought that Soviet-type administration could resolve this problem by a straight-line span of control from top to bottom. By the mid-1950's, it was clear that this would not work. The Chinese Communists tried administrative centralization in order to bring about political unity in a country that had been disunited for fifty years. Administrative centralization achieved its aims, for it permitted the establishment of a uniform governmental system throughout China. However, administrative centralization created rigidities at the middle and lower levels of the system, which required a loosening up. This meant once again the acceptance of a difference between center and region. It may be of interest to quote the just-cited editorial of the *Jenmin jihpao* to see how it described this problem for the pre-1949 period:

The local political system under the rule of the KMT reactionary forces and other reactionary forces was oppressive of the people. The reactionary rulers made use of a bureaucratic system from top to bottom, but they also relied on small and big landlords, rotten gentry, and warlords to create a hierarchical system of control weighing on the heads of the masses. The further one got down to the basic level, the more they directly enslaved and trampled on the people. But because the reactionaries who controlled the so-called central power quarreled over self-interest with reactionary cliques who controlled the regional power, they regarded the center and the regions as mutually juxtaposed. The consequence could only be the unity of despotic rule or the divisiveness of regional feudalism.

---

[38] *Iuridicheskii slovar'* (Moscow, 1956), I, 404*b*.
[39] *Jenmin jihpao*, October 8, 1954.

The ruler in the national capital before 1949 was faced with the dilemma that the more bureaucratic rule he imposed from the center, the more regional coordination broke down. This presented the ruler with the choice of using despotic approaches or arriving at some compromise with regional interests. Earlier dynasties had tried alternative solutions. During the Sung period, "special imperial commissioners" were periodically sent to the provinces to enforce policy orders and shake up the web of mutual involvement at the regional level. This they did without destroying these networks, which formed once again as soon as the commissioners left. The Mongols further expanded the procedures by setting up "mobile bureaus." But no dynasty was ever able to create a continuing nation-wide organization under the effective control of the center which was *outside* both of the formal bureaucracy and of regional power groups. The use of special commissioners, even when permanently appointed, was still an *ad hoc* device designed either to counteract bureaucratic rigidity or congeries of local power interests.

Despite the power of the new administrative system, the Chinese Communists still faced problems of center versus region, similar to the pre-1949 period. Power groups continued to develop in regional government, with regional loyalties stronger than their commitment to Peking. The following statements of Chiang Hua, first secretary of the Chekiang Party Committee, clearly indicate the problem:

Many individuals who have serious capitalistic and individualistic thoughts at the same time often also have factionalistic and regionalistic thoughts. They make use of these tendencies to satisfy their personal ambition and carry out anti-Party activities. The way they carry out factionalistic or regionalistic activities is by looking at problems from the point of view of personal or factional interests. If something is in their favor, they are for it; if it is not, they are against it. Usually, they develop personal prestige, manipulate old comrades, old followers, make use of contacts with regional cadres, pulling and drawing them together. They attack the Party in small group activities, looking for cronies and support, and make trouble for the Party. Regionalism is a form of factionalism, and its harm to the Party is just as serious. In the past, the Party advanced the slogan of "regionalization of cadres." The spirit of this was that we wanted the cadres to develop close ties with the local [*tangti*] masses. Local cadres already had the advantage of having close ties to the local masses. But the cadres coming in from without, after some time, also developed close ties with the masses, and became regionalized. We must not allow that the slogan "regionalization of cadres" be used to further regionalism. We must not allow individuals with other ideas to use this slogan to alienate outside cadres from local cadres, and carry out factional activities. Some people take pride in being called "local cadre representatives." Some people demand that Party secretaries at all levels be local people. This is wrong. As Comrade

Teng Hsiao-p'ing pointed out: "Regionalization of cadres is by no means a supreme principle of Party cadre policy. Our supreme cadre principle is commitment to communism. Regardless of whether they come from without or from the local area, cadres must all first and foremost be committed to communism. Regionalism is incompatible with communism." [40]

Chiang Hua spoke in 1957, but the problem he alluded to is not confined to that date. On the one hand, Peking needed regional cadres with sufficiently deep roots in the local situation to permit them to operate effectively. Yet it also demanded that the regional cadres be primarily loyal to Peking rather than to the regional area. Policy on this problem differed from time to time, as Chiang Hua noted. For example, in the early 1950's, Peking felt the need to recruit regional people into provincial government in order to avoid the appearance of an occupation from the outside. However, by the mid-1950's, regional power blocs began to develop, as they had earlier in Chinese history. Peking was faced with a dilemma. Having decided on decentralization, it nevertheless faced the danger that power would pass into hands more committed to regional rather than to national interests. The only solution was a Party rectification movement that would purge cadres guilty of "regionalism" and replace them with others completely loyal to Peking. Decentralization could be risked only if the problem of "regionalism" could be resolved.

Starting in December 1957, the anti-rightist movement struck at the regional Party apparatus. The first major purges reported, interestingly enough, were from Chekiang, Chiang Hua's province. Most leading officials of the Chekiang provincial government were expelled from the Party and replaced by individuals more committed to Peking, like Chiang Hua. During the early months of 1958, the purge spread to Anhwei, Kirin, Chinghai, and Szechwan. In May 1958, when the second session of the Eighth Party Congress was held (designed to rectify the moderate line of the September 1956 session and clearly establish the supremacy of the radical group), the purge spread to several other provinces: Kansu, Hopei, Honan, Shantung, Kwangsi, Kwangtung, Sinkiang, and Yunnan. It continued through the summer, reaching its climax in October when a great purge changed the whole leadership of Liaoning Province. Most significant, probably, were the events in Honan and Liaoning, two major centers of communization. In Honan, for example, the old Party leader P'an Fu-sheng, an alternate member of the Central Committte, was replaced by Wu Chih-p'u, provincial

[40] *Jenmin shouts'e 1958*, p. 68.

Party first secretary as well as already being provincial governor. Wu Chih-p'u was one of the leading organizers of communes in the summer of 1958.[41]

We have said earlier that decentralization II meant Party control over provincial government. However, from the present discussion it is clear that it was a Party "rectified" of regionalism. Those purged were guilty of "localism," or vested interests. The new Party men who came to power at the provincial level were obviously committed to the radical line that had triumphed in the Politburo. How does such a conclusion square with the far-reaching provincial autonomy which prevailed during the Great Leap Forward? Here one must remember the Chinese Communist distinction between policy and operations. The new Party leaders were regarded as completely loyal on policy and ideological questions. However, precisely because they were so, Peking felt it could grant them a broad range of operational autonomy to carry out policy in terms of the slogan "Do the Best According to Local Conditions." The powers given provincial government by decentralization II were to go only to men who could be trusted politically and ideologically. In this way, the leaders in Peking believed they could find a way out of the dilemma of all rulers of China before 1949—the dilemma, as the *Jenmin jihpao* put it in the editorial we have quoted, that the only choice was "despotic rule" or "local feudalism."

The results of the Great Leap Forward indicate that decentralization was not a way out after all. Since then, Peking has gone back to a checks-and-balances approach. In a large number of provinces, one can note a common pattern: Party secretaries come from outside the province, and provincial governors come from inside. The balance is thus between the "outsider" and the "insider," a pattern found in other areas of organization.

POWER AT THE PROVINCIAL LEVELS

The most important consequence of decentralization II had been to make the regional Party committees supreme decision-making bodies for all regional economic activities. Since the scope of regional economic activity had greatly expanded, this meant great economic power. Under the Great Leap Forward program called "simultaneously developing central and regional industry," regional Party committees began to launch ambitious construction, production, and welfare projects.

---

[41] *Chungkung shihnien*, pp. 28-32.

However, in order to do so, they had to have capital and labor. We shall briefly discuss the kinds of powers they acquired, which made it possible for them to mobilize capital and labor.

As for capital, the decentralization decisions gave provincial government control over a broad range of industries formerly under central jurisdiction. However, in addition to that, provincial governments acquired the right to place orders with enterprises still under central jurisdiction. This meant that the latter became a part of the regional planning system. As an article prepared by the Industry and Communications Office of the Kansu Party Committee put it:

> On the one hand, we meet the demands of central industry on regional industry by setting up a number of satellite factories. But on the other hand, we assign concrete tasks to central industries to help and support regional industries. This way we achieve mutual aid, mutual development, mutual encouragement, mutual development of central and regional industries.[42]

In short, the planning powers of regional government were increased by giving them control over the output of a wide range of industries.

The provincial governments also received a much greater share of control over the supply system. The regulation on commercial administration promulgated in November 1957 in effect created a two-category supply system. Commodities regarded by the central government as strategic, comprising basic industrial and agricultural products, remained under central control and were procured by so-called first-class purchase and distribution stations. All other commodities came under regional control and were acquired by so-called second-class purchase and distribution stations. No reference was made to a third category of commodities, to be freely acquired by the production units according to the market, such as was suggested by Hsüeh Mu-ch'iao. Such a three-category supply system was proclaimed by the State Council in April 1959, at a time when it was beginning to tighten controls in the wake of the excesses of 1958.[43] However, the third category did not yet exist in 1958. But provincial government also acquired power to re-allocate scarce capital equipment assigned to regional areas, as long as they observed the state plan. Enterprises, and by implication ministries, were explicitly told that they had to accept such re-allocation. Provincial government thus obtained far-reaching powers to procure and distribute the output, not only of regional industries, but even of central industries.

---

42 *Hsinhua panyüeh-k'an*, 18 (1958), 114.

43 *Takung-pao* (Peking), April 4, 1959.

On the financial side, provincial governments were given a greater share of state budgetary revenue.[44] According to the regulation on financial decentralization, deficits would be made up by subsidies from the central budget, and from the retained profits of enterprises. In other words, even the increased profit share which enterprises were allowed to keep under the terms of the decentralization was made accessible to tapping by provincial government. As regards prices, the provincial governments were given the power to set prices for all "secondary markets and secondary commodities"—those not defined as being under the control of the center. The latter presumably consisted of the thirty-eight items kept under state control according to the mentioned April 1959 regulations. The regional governments thus did obtain broad price-fixing powers.

As for labor, the decentralization decisions explicitly granted provincial governments power to shift labor in all industries in the province, including those that remained under central jurisdiction. The only exceptions were highly skilled individuals who could only be moved with the permission of the State Council. Since labor mobilization was the key device of the Great Leap Forward, it is clear that provincial governments, through the Party apparatus, had a great labor force at their disposal for the projects in which they were investing.

The Great Leap Forward was thus made possible by the full implementation of decentralization II. What the provincial governments gained, the ministries at the top and the enterprises and other production units at the bottom lost.

In December 1958, Peking made an attempt to halt the extremes of decentralization II by propounding a policy under the slogan, "All the Country Is a Single Chessboard." That policy was not too successful, for in the fall of 1959 a second attempt was made to propel the Great Leap Forward again, though this time with a greater emphasis on the basic level than on regional government. The decisive reversal of economic policy did not come until January 1961, in the midst of the great economic crisis. That reversal was marked by a new Party rectification movement, which struck at Party cadres at provincial and local levels. This could not but weaken the powers that had been granted the Party at the regional and local levels. Peking thus had to try recentralization, and at the same time decentralization I. Those parts of the decentralization decisions that gave greater powers to industrial managers were put into effect for the first time. Managers, professionals, and intellectuals, who had been attacked only a short time before, were

---

[44] *Chūkyō no zaisei (1950-1960)*, (Tokyo, 1961), pp. 143-151.

called back to run the economy. Hand in hand with the new "independent operational autonomy" granted the enterprises was the expansion of the "little freedoms" of the agricultural production teams and individual farm producers.[45]

At the same time, some recentralization along branch lines has occurred, particularly in the financial sector. For example, in the spring of 1962 reports began to appear about a tightening up of the banking system. *Red Flag* published an article on the banking system, pointing out: "In a socialist society, a national bank which is large in scale and spread over cities and villages, but concentrated and unified, is the country's one and only center of credit, center of accounting, and center for the issuance of currency. All credit activities, settling of accounts, disbursements of cash throughout the country are concentrated in the national bank." [46] Recentralization has also taken place in the transportation system, made necessary by the structural bottlenecks that developed during the economic crisis. Otherwise, the patterns of ministerial recentralization are still unclear.

At the present time, all three levels of the organizational system—center, region, and producing unit—have some degree of decision-making power. In Peking, some ministries have once again become powerful, notably in finance and trade. Recent reemphasis on the need for central planning indicates that the state economic agencies are playing more of a role than they did during the Great Leap Forward. Regional governments still remain important factors in government, as can be seen in the role they play in smoothing out allocational problems. The practice of "materials exchange conferences" (*wutzu chiaoliu-hui*), whereby buyers and sellers come together under regional government auspices and agree on supply contracts, has become institutionalized. Provincial Party committees have apparently recovered some of the power they lost in 1961. Judging from the prevalence of the contract system, enterprises still enjoy "independent operational autonomy." The free market also still operates in China.

It is clear that government in China cannot be characterized in simple terms. Functionally, it tried extreme centralization in the early 1950's, and extreme decentralization II during the Great Leap Forward. It obviously cannot try extreme decentralization I, because that would be Yugoslav revisionism, particularly as it was tried in the early 1950's. Since everything else in China operates in terms of "threes," perhaps this three-fold system will continue and may eventually become institutionalized.

---

45 Schurmann, *op. cit.* (in n. 35), pp. 80-91.
46 *Hungch'i*, 6 (1962), 12.

CHAPTER IV

MANAGEMENT

BUREAUCRACY AND MANAGEMENT

Distinctions

When the Chinese Communists came to power in 1949, they found themselves with new roles to perform. As rulers of a vast country, they had to find bureaucrats to run the new administrative systems; and as owners of a widespread network of nationalized enterprises, they had to find managers to run the factories. There was little in their background that had given them much training for either of these roles.

The administrative systems in the old "liberated" areas had been relatively simple affairs, and the only factories they had owned earlier had posed few serious managerial problems. In many countries, "revolutions" simply sweep away the executive pinnacle of government, leaving the professional bureaucracy intact. Max Weber pointed out that in all modern countries, bureaucracies tend toward professionalization, with the implication that whatever happens at the top, the administrators remain. China has one of the longest and most impressive traditions of bureaucracy among civilized countries. Though not professional in the Weberian sense, the bureaucrats came from a well-entrenched status group that had continued to furnish officials to whatever dynasty was in power. The 1911 revolution did not change China's bureaucratic character, though it did lead to an erosion of the social basis of the bureaucracy. As the governmental system of the new republic became modern after 1911, China faced the necessity of moving from a bureaucracy of status to a bureaucracy of expertise. Its inability to accomplish this transition was a major reason for the failure of government to create an effective state administration before 1949. Although expert administrators were rare in China in 1949, the Chinese Communists kept few of them in their positions, except at the lower levels of the administrative system. For the Communists, the officials constituted a class enemy that had to be destroyed in the same way as the landed gentry.

The owners and managers of business were not in the same category as the officials. Mao Tse-tung had promised private business a positive role in the New China. Many businessmen stayed on in the hope that the Communists would keep their word, in the recognition that without private business they could not get the economy moving again. In the cities, the Communists were willing, initially, to make a distinction: the old bureaucrats had to go, but managers who were willing to declare loyalty to the new regime could stay. It was not just the ideology of the "new democracy" that made for this distinction, but the appalling shortage of administrative and managerial talent that faced the Communists on the morrow of victory.

Managing a factory and administering an office are different undertakings. In a material sense, a factory is concerned with the production of goods and an administrative office with the production of services. In a human sense, both organizations are concerned with decision-making and with compliance with those decisions.[1] In advanced Western organization, the differences between factories and offices have become increasingly obscured. Modern companies, as sociologists have pointed out, are concerned with more than creating products for the market. They have become "institutions" in which the human element is as important as that of material output.[2] Conversely, administrative bureaucracies have taken on operational and managerial functions. In some countries, this has come about through nationalization of enterprises; in others through the growth of government-directed activities. For

---

[1] Amitai Etzioni, *A Comparative Analysis of Complex Organizations* (Glencoe, Ill., 1961), pp. 3 ff.

[2] Philip Selznick, *Leadership in Administration* (Evanston, Ill., and White Plains, N. Y., 1957), pp. 5 ff.; Alvin J. Gouldner, "Organizational Analysis," in *Sociology Today* (New York, 1959), p. 406.

Weber, bureaucratization in the political and economic realms appeared as the same phenomenon, and so he made few distinctions between administration and management. Nevertheless, it is still widely felt that whatever the convergence between administration and management, there still is a difference.[3] Conservative ideology in the United States still sees the bureaucrat as the enemy of the honest businessman. The distinction between administration and management is institutionalized in the Soviet Union. The Soviets draw a line between what they call "budgetary organs" and "economic accounting organs," the former fulfilling "administrative-political functions" and the latter "economic-operational functions."[4] Soviet state agencies operate with funds earmarked for specified purposes. Enterprises are given a lump sum by the state which they may use as they see fit in order to achieve the goals set for them. The conflict between the bureaucratic-minded *glavks* and the management-minded enterprises is a major theme in Soviet organizational history. The *glavks* attempted to impose bureaucratic controls on the enterprises, and the enterprises resisted them. Joseph Berliner has well described the tortuous means devised by Soviet managers to circumvent the hold of the bureaucracy on economic activity.[5]

Business and Industry, Management and Bureaucracy

In the West, administration has been historically associated with government, and management with business. Whatever the informal ties that link government and business, the two remain formally separate. In China, the historical legacy has been different. Government and business were closely intertwined ever since the beginning of modern civil enterprise at the end of the nineteenth century.[6] Initially government involvement in enterprise was seen as the only way to get the industrialization process started. But as time went on "bureaucratic capital" was increasingly attacked by liberal and radical economists as

---

[3] John M. Pfiffner and Frank P. Sherwood in their text on organization note: "While Weber has had substantial influence on social scientists, it is noteworthy that he has had relatively little impact on the more vocational management literature" (*Administrative Organization* [New York, 1960], p. 58).

[4] *Iuridicheskii slovar'* (Moscow, 1956), II, 633b.

[5] Joseph S. Berliner, *Factory and Manager in the USSR* (Cambridge, Mass., 1957).

[6] The slogan *kuantu shangpan,* "Government Supervises and Merchants Operate," appeared to imply a functional separation. In actuality, it started a process of meshing of government and business (Albert Feuerwerker, *China's Early Industrialization* [Cambridge, Mass., 1958]).

one of the main obstacles to economic development.[7] Whereas the late Ch'ing system of government supervision and merchant operation was seen as serving national goals, its subsequent version, "bureaucratic capitalism," was attacked as a system using political power to serve private interests. The mechanics of the government-business alliance, however, remained the same. In both cases, political power was a source of capital for private enterprise, and business leaders acquired position and influence in government. It was difficult to say where the dividing line between big business and government was, or, as the Communists put it sarcastically, public and private were not differentiated. Given the political conditions before 1949, it could hardly be expected that major economic enterprises be either strictly public or strictly private. This does not mean that Chinese businessmen were unable to mount true private enterprise. Where the political system has called for separation of public and private, such as in British-ruled Hong Kong, Chinese businessmen have carried out an industrial revolution entirely based on private enterprise. The alliance between government and business in China before 1949 was not so surprising if seen in the light of early industrialization in France, Germany, and Japan. What distinguished bureaucratic capitalism in China from its counterparts in these countries was its lack of success in launching basic industrial development.

The Dichotomy between Policy and Operations

Though the lines between government and business before 1949 were unclear, the Chinese recognized a distinction between policy and operations. The typical large Chinese business firm was a complex affair, consisting of many layers of holdings spread out over considerable territory. The businessman himself was usually not interested in managing his factories and stores, and usually lacked the knowledge to do so. Management was commonly turned over to someone trusted by the board of directors who was given autonomy to do what he wanted, so long as he abided by the policy decisions of the board and turned over his profit to the company.[8] The board decided policy questions, whereas

---

[7] The attack on bureaucratic capital was launched by the liberal economist Ma Yin-ch'u, and then taken up by the left wing (Hsü Ti-hsin, *Kuanliao tzupen p'ip'an* [Nanking, 1958]).

[8] Ubukata Naokichi describes the practice for a semimodern type of Chinese business organization: "As far as the management of the *hoku* (a Chinese version of the joint-stock company) was concerned, it was carried out dictatorially by a director who was originally selected by the stockholders and to whom management was entrusted. The director was someone who knew the enterprise very well (ten or more years of experience). Aside from major matters such as stoppage, dissolution, and large-scale

the manager took charge of operations, namely production and sales. This distinction between policy-making and policy-executing functions is known in the Western literature as the "policy-administration dichotomy." To avoid confusion with our use of the word administration, we shall refer to this phenomenon as the policy-operations dichotomy.[9] Organizational literature uses administration generally in the sense of implementation of policy; we prefer to use administration in the more general sense of bureaucracy in action. (When we talk about implementation of policy, we use the word "operation.")

The Chinese Communists are aware of the policy-operations dichotomy. The Great Leap Forward was predicated on the idea that policy should only set general guidelines for action, whereas operations should be worked out in specific contexts.

The policy-operations dichotomy also was a problem at the enterprise level, as will become clear later in this chapter. In the early 1950's, the Chinese felt that policy and operations had to be closely linked; this was made possible by the practice known as one-man management. In the mid-1950's, the Chinese began to make a functional separation.

---

debts, he had complete responsibility for enterprise management, hiring and firing of personnel, without consulting the stockholders. The effectiveness of his actions was the deciding factor in the management of the enterprise. The selection of a director was the most important matter to be decided by the stockholders when the company was set up. It was crucial that, as well as knowing the enterprise and having experience, he be a socially trustworthy individual" ("Chū-shi no gōko ni kansuru sho-mondai," *Mantetsu chōsa geppō*, 23 [1943], 94).

[9] "... it is often said that policy is the formulation of goals and administration involves their *execution*" (Pfiffner and Sherwood, *op. cit.*, p. 82). The terms "administration" and "management" are used in the literature with considerable divergence of meaning. For example, Pfiffner and Sherwood understand administration to mean execution of policy. But elsewhere we read that "administration: this is concerned primarily with the management function and consists of decision and policy making" (Evan D. Scheele, William L. Westerman, and Robert J. Wimmert, *Principles and Design of Production Control Systems* [New York, 1960], p. 29). Peter Blau and W. R. Scott have singled out four management models, of which the first two are of interest to us. One sees management as executive leadership; the other emphasizes the hierarchy of bureaucratic authority in the organization (*Formal Organizations* [San Francisco, 1962], pp. 165-167). We shall use the term "administration" in the second ("Weberian") sense. Administration is the functional side of bureaucracy. Administration involves both policy-making and policy execution, but essentially for purposes of what Etzioni calls "compliance . . . a relation in which an actor behaves in accordance with a directive supported by another actor's power, and the orientation of the subordinated actor to the power applied" (*op. cit.*, p. 3). On the other hand, we shall use the term "management" to mean leadership concerned with operational ends and means. Management is the functional side of executive position.

Party committees set policy, and managers worked out operational measures. By 1958, the Chinese felt that policy could be directly translated into action without going through the laborious process of translation into operational commands.

The policy-operations dichotomy implies a separation of ends and means. The policy makers decide what they want to do and then hand their decisions over to the staff-and-line men for execution. There has been criticism of this notion in the West, particularly from the theoretically oriented social scientists. A few words on these Western theoretical critiques of the policy-operations dichotomy will help to show what the problem is in the Chinese context.

Max Weber, in effect, criticized the dichotomy by arguing that the expertise of administrators increasingly exercises a forcing effect on the actions of policy makers. Philip Selznick has attacked the dichotomy from another direction by arguing that means cannot be separated from ends even in the purely operational spheres of organization.[10] Weber saw a growing separation of man from his role in organization, thus doing away with the element of arbitrary human action. Selznick sees man as constantly growing into his role, humanizing it. Both Weber and Selznick see organizations as moving in the direction of integration, but in terms of opposite crucial factors. For Weber, it is "policy" that gives way to "administration," producing a comprehensive unity of expertise. For Selznick, it is the opposite: policy concerns diffuse throughout the organization gradually involving its members consciously and with commitment into the system. But both Weber and Selznick assume something which is not necessarily so, namely the unity of ends and means. In pre-1949 China, the policy-operations dichotomy existed because business could not link ends and means together into a single framework of action. Since businessmen did not understand the problems of technical management, they turned them over to management experts, who quite often were foreign experts. If such a policy-operations dichotomy exists, this can pose dangers to organizational unity. Other means have to be found to tie together the members of the organization.

Organizational Unity

Every executive wishes the members of his organization to be imbued with his own values and goals. If they are, he need only worry about the mistakes his employees make, not their basic intent. Such unity would constitute the basis for true integration within the organi-

---

[10] *Op. cit.*, pp. 56-61.

zation and would make unnecessary a gap between policy and operations. Max Weber and Philip Selznick have suggested two roads organizational integration can take. Modern organizations are highly articulated structures characterized by complex division of labor and rationality of action. We may speak of this as the network of technical organization. But within organization there is another network that links men together, not in terms of their formal roles, but as individual human beings. This we may call the network of human organization. Weber, in effect, saw organizational integration as arising from the perfection of the network of technical organization by the comprehensive diffusion of rationality throughout it. But, for Weber, the consequence of the rationalization of administration was depersonalization. Selznick, in contrast, sees the perfection of the network of human organization as the road to integration. When this occurs, "organization" gradually turns into "institution." These two antithetical approaches to organizational integration can be found elsewhere in the theoretical literature. Frederick W. Taylor saw the way to integration in "scientific management." Several decades after Taylor wrote, the "human relations" approach to industrial management made its appearance on the scene.[11] Integration through legal rationality—scientific division of labor—constitutes a new and modern approach to an age-old problem. The remarkable developments of science and technology made it possible to break down human behavior in organizations into highly defined patterns. The world has had many examples of highly developed traditional bureaucracies, but none has been able to elevate expertise to an end in itself. Integration in purely human terms is a more traditional approach. It assumes that depersonalization of roles can never go far enough to give organization that unity which human commitment can give it. It suggests recourse to patterns of solidarity that have worked in the past and can be made workable again under modern conditions.

These antithetical approaches to organizational unity pose the same alternatives of choice as are implied in the "red and expert" dichotomy of the Chinese Communists. The "red" approach asserts that organizational unity can only be produced by perfecting the network of human organization. The "expert" approach asserts the contrary, namely that organizational unity can only be produced by a rational division of labor supported by modern technology. However, even before 1949, something comparable to the "red and expert" dichotomy existed in Chinese business. As we have said, pre-1949 Chinese business

---

11 Blau and Scott, op. cit., pp. 87 ff.

recognized the policy-operations dichotomy. But business integration was to be achieved, not by operational unification based on technology and rationality, but by webs of human organization that linked the key members of the organization together.

Chinese business executives before 1949 wanted organizational unity within their companies as much as any executive, but the nature of business organization forced them to see policy and operations as two different functions. Company offices were often situated in places distant from the factories. They usually had to be located in the commercial districts of the big coastal cities, where they were in close contact with financial and commercial agencies. Companies were dependent on short-term loans, which had to be negotiated with the banks.

The main concerns of company headquarters were thus financial and commercial, not operational. On the other hand, the production and sales units were managed independently by experienced professionals who were given a wide range of authority. If company headquarters had little technical control over the enterprises, it made sure that the managers were trustworthy. Few attempts were made by the company to alter operational patterns in the enterprises. It was this lack of operational concern on the part of the company directors and the consequent deterioration of conditions in the enterprises that gave rise to the severe criticism of Chinese business and industry in the 1930's.[12] This led to a gap between the financial and production functions of the company. The board of directors, mostly money-minded businessmen, kept a tight grip on all monetary flows. Matters of money were considered policy questions *par excellence*. Since the company directors were not very knowledgeable about the technicalities of production, they were incapable of suggesting improvements that would raise productivity and efficiency. On the other hand, the main task of the manager was to generate the profit quota expected of him, regardless of how he carried out operations. It was clearly not a Weberian type of legal rational system that held the company together. The typical Chinese company was a sprawling organization that frequently added and dropped units. New plants were acquired, old ones sold off. Mergers and combinations went on much of the time. What held the whole thing together was personal relationships. These reached upward into government and outward into foreign business concerns, and also downward and inward into the factories and stores. The managers were not simply overseers; they were the representatives of the board of

---

[12] In particular, the criticisms of the economist H. D. Fong which appeared in the *Nankai Social and Economics Quarterly*, published in Tientsin in the mid-1930's.

directors and usually had considerable financial interests themselves in the company.

Personal Relationships in Chinese Management

Chinese businessmen, starting around the time of World War I, developed a successful light-industry complex in Shanghai. Businessmen who fled from Shanghai to Hong Kong after 1949 have been mainly responsible for the industrial revolution in that British colony. Much of the industrial development in Southeast Asia has been the work of Chinese businessmen, and under conditions that were less than optimal. A major factor accounting for the success of Chinese business has been the web of personal relationships that goes through the Chinese community. Entrepreneurs in Hong Kong have found it possible to acquire capital, not just because of cold calculation as to their prospects for payoff, but because of some element of "trust" which they enjoy. Loans are made to them with the assurance that the personal bond is strong enough for the beginning entrepreneur to know that to violate it would mean permanent ruin.[13] It was this web of personal relationships which left-wing economists had attacked. Whatever the evils of bureaucratic capitalism were, it cannot be argued *a priori* that it impeded economic development. Economic development and personal corruption often go hand in hand, however distasteful this may appear. The fact is that modern business demands complex organization, and personal relationships can provide durable cement to hold organization together.

Before 1949, personal ties linked the director and the managers, the managers and the staff, and in many instances employers and employees. Personal relationships did not imply "harmony." Working conditions were extremely poor in Chinese industry, salaries and wages were low. Within companies and between companies, conflict and competition were rife. Under the mantle of personal relationships, all kinds of economic and technological irrationalities flourished, so that they impeded the rational development of Chinese industry. These were the "feudal" vestiges so bitterly criticized by the Chinese Communists. In the West, the industrial evils of the nineteenth century have often been blamed on conditions of inhuman impersonality which dominated the factories. In pre-1949 China, these same evils existed, but within a very different

---

13 Marion J. Levy Jr. and Shih Kuo-heng, *The Rise of the Modern Chinese Business Class* (New York, 1949), pp. 13, 55, 40. For an analogous situation, see Davis Landes, *Bankers and Pashas* (Cambridge, Mass., 1958).

context of close personal relationships between different working groups of the factories.

If a policy-operations dichotomy existed in the structure of technical business organization before 1949, it did not exist within the framework of human organization. Chinese society has traditionally had an extraordinary capacity to link human groups by intermediary devices. Gang foremen acted as intermediaries between managers and workers; managers functioned as the link between company and plant; compradores linked foreign and domestic businesses; prestigious families linked government and business. Whatever the evils arising from such a situation, it nevertheless provided channels through which the policy makers at the top of organization could make their intent felt throughout organization. Much of the insufficient economic development during the Republican period (1911-1949) was not caused by the system, but by the failure of those in control of policy to make full use of the organizational opportunities. During the early 1920's, the Chinese business class responded positively to the rising Nationalist movement, contributing to the thought then current in the Comintern that bourgeois-democratic revolutions in colonial and semicolonial countries could serve to undermine Western capitalism and imperialism.[14] The Kuomintang allied itself with the business class but, like so many regimes in modern times, was obsessed by the problem of political control, with insufficient appreciation of the importance of basic economic development. Governmental commitment to economic development could have made use of the business class to provide economic leadership. The fact that the Chinese bourgeoisie in contemporary Hong Kong and Southeast Asia has developed entrepreneurial qualities shows that the potential was there. Yet business classes everywhere tend to be conservative and are not inclined to take great risks. Clearly some outside support, either from government or from a favorable market, is necessary to make them take the risks of entrepreneurship.

Before 1949, however, the Chinese bourgeoisie needed decisive leadership to take the risks of creating new industries. Japan provides an example of industrial leadership and business conservatism working together to create a modern nation. In Japan, technology-minded samurai allied themselves with money-minded merchants to lay the basis for modern industry. Industry and business are not the same thing. Industry, particularly in its formative stages, requires a radical, innovative

---

14 Joseph T. Chen, "The Shanghai May Fourth Movement" (unpublished doctoral dissertation, University of California, Department of History, Berkeley, Calif., 1964).

mentality. Industry requires capital, which in turn depends on the careful management of money. The conservative mentality of Japanese merchants fitted in well with the radical ventures of the samurai, creating conditions for stability and continuity after the industrial and technological leaders had struck out in new directions. Industry was something new; business had been around for a long time. Both industry and business were necessary components in the modernization process.

In China, there was no equivalent of samurai leadership to impress businessmen with the need for technological innovation and development. Industry did develop in China, despite the absence of positive leadership. But since it was the conservative business group that had to take the initiative, they built up their organizations on the basis of the only principles they knew, namely the networks of personal linkage. The result was that technological integration failed to match integration deriving from human organization. The attacks on bureaucratic capitalism claimed that the two were incompatible, that only when these networks were eliminated could Chinese industry develop in Western fashion. But the Japanese example indicates that this is not so. Japanese industry and business during the early Meiji was an amalgam of the modern and the ancient. Technical organization was modern, but human organization remained "feudal." Despite their vocal radicalism, the Meiji entrepreneurs were willing to separate the technical from the human, while giving both their due importance.

While the network of human organization developed in Chinese business and industry, that rationally defined form of organization so necessary to modernization and industrialization failed to develop. The policy-operations gap was glaringly present in the whole sphere of technical organization. Businessmen made decisions on money and rarely on operations. Government, officially or unofficially, provided capital but was ignorant of its use. Managers worked through gang bosses but knew little of how production was going on. Staff workers came from the educated elite; they rarely went down into the plant to observe production. The level of technological integration was very low in pre-1949 Chinese industry. Policy decisions, at whatever level, were usually made in ignorance of the means that would be used to carry them out.

The traditional Chinese approach to organizational integration thus was to find linkages between those at the top who ruled and those at the bottom who worked. In pre-1949 China, it was the growing urban bourgeoisie which provided the linkage between government and business. In the rural areas, it was the gentry which performed a similar linkage role. They were for the most part solidly rooted in some particularistic local situation. At the same time, they furnished recruits for the state bureaucracy. The local and the bureaucratic gentry were not held together functionally, but by class and social ties. No gentry existed in the new commercial cities of China. A new business class was growing up. The stronger it became, the more it began to play the same linkage role as the gentry. The higher bourgeoisie went into government, formally or informally. The lower bourgeoisie went on with its private small-scale business.[15] Aside from the distinctions made by the Communists, there was no line dividing the two, except relative status criteria. The big bourgeoisie had wealth, power, and prestige, but the road of social mobility was open to all.

If linkage groups are available, it is an old practice of Chinese statecraft to make use of them. When the Kuomintang assumed power in China in the mid-1920's, they followed this age-old pattern. In the rural areas, they once again employed the local gentry. In the cities, they made use of the bourgeoisie. But China during the 1920's and 1930's needed leadership more than administration, management more than bureaucracy. Because of the close association with an already highly bureaucratized government, both the rural gentry and the urban bourgeoisie became so bureaucratized that they were unable to provide the operational leadership that a country as backward as China needed. Personal relations made for solidarity, but also made it impossible to fill positions with managerially- and entrepreneurially-minded individuals. In the cities, the result was that industries were increasingly taken over or started by entrepreneurially-minded foreigners, notably British, American, and Japanese. In the rural areas, the Chinese Communists countered the impotence of the gentry with their own type of dynamic leadership.

Technical and Human Organization in Industrial Management

We have suggested that all organization consists of two different networks of organization, one technical and the other human. Both can be used or manipulated to achieve the ends desired by the leaders

---

[15] The Chinese bourgeoisie always created theoretical and policy headaches for the Chinese Communists. Mao finally solved the problem by dividing the bourgeoisie into a higher and a lower stratum. The former was the bureaucratic capitalists, to be expunged from society. The latter became the national bourgeoisie, who still had a useful role to play. See Mao's December 1947 piece "The Present Situation and Our Tasks," *Selected Works* (Chinese edition), IV, 1253-1255.

of organization. If an organization lacks sufficient technological means, it cannot use technology alone to achieve its ends. On the other hand, if the basis for operative human organization is lacking, it has no choice but to use technology. The Chinese Communists recognize the difference between technical and human organization. One might say that it is one of their fundamental insights into the structure and function of organization.[16] This distinction is also widely recognized in the Western literature, as, for example, in the contrasting "scientific management" and "human relations" approaches to industrial management.[17] In a modern factory workers must be placed into the system because their skills will fit into the division of labor. On the other hand, skill does not automatically mean performance. A work situation in which good human relations prevail may elicit more concrete performance from workers with lesser skills than one in which skilled men function under poor human-relational conditions. The Chinese Communists tried two different approaches to the problem of organizational integration. Sensitive to China's backwardness and impressed by the Soviet model, they introduced, in the early 1950's, a highly technical system of organization into industry. Men were placed in work positions because of their skills. Work processes were subjected to a highly specifistic division of labor and responsibility. In time, the Chinese Communists reacted against the extremes of these Soviet-type systems and began increasingly to emphasize the importance of human solidarity. It was believed that the Party could bring about the factory-wide human solidarity which technical management alone was unable to do. The Great Leap Forward was a period when "men were more important than weapons." When the Chinese Communists imposed systems of

---

16 This distinction is rarely made as explicitly as this, although it underlies all polemics about red and expert. I have found it most clearly stated in a series of lectures on the principles of industrial management. One lecture deals with the principles of formal organization in an enterprise. It divides formal organization into two spheres: administrative management and technical management. The first is described as "reflecting the production relationships and management order within the enterprise." The second is described as "reflecting the objective laws of the production process." The first are various structural and functional principles of human organization. The second are specifications of work processes in terms of physical criteria ("Ch'iyeh kuanli chich'u chihshih chianghua," *Chungkuo Ch'ing-Kungyeh*, 22 [1959], 23).

17 The idea that this constitutes alternatives of approaches to management is indicated in Robert C. Sampson's distinction between executives who are "thing-minded" and those who are "people-minded" (*The Staff Role in Management* [New York, 1955], p. 78).

technical management, they did it with the concentrated power of a totalitarian system. When they decided to try the other, they turned with a vengeance on those who had earlier been proponents of techno- logical rationality, namely the factory managers. Earlier, the Chinese Communists had honestly believed that stress on technical organization would not imperil human solidarity. They later equally honestly be- lieved that Party-led solidarity would not imperil technical develop- ment. We can overlook the question whether that solidarity was real or not. The point is that during the Great Leap Forward, people worked very hard. But their work was technically barren. Agriculture failed and structural bottlenecks hampered the economic system.

Emphasis on technical organization implies defined division of labor, and therefore specificity of role and function. Emphasis on human or- ganization, on the other hand, leads to impreciseness in the definition of role and function. The Chinese Communists have taken different attitudes to the question of role and function. During the early 1950's, when they were emulating the Soviet Union, they demanded preciseness in the division of labor and exact specification of work tasks. However, during the Great Leap Forward, the ideal worker was supposed to be a "jack-of-all-trades," *tomienshou*. After the economic crisis, 1960-61, their attitude changed again, and the "master of one technique" was now hailed as the ideal worker.[18]

In terms of role and function, a Party cadre has no specific role to per- form. Today he does this and tomorrow something else. The key to the changing attitudes of the Chinese Communists on the question of speci- ficity or diffuseness of roles is their belief that diffuse roles create hu- man solidarity whereas specific roles break it down. Thus, during the Great Leap Forward, when they proclaimed the primacy of human or- ganization over technical organization, they attacked, with great vehe- mence, the notion that each man should have a defined expertise. This preference for diffuse rather than specific roles the cadre shares with the traditional bureaucrat, though clearly not with a modern indus- trial manager.

Few regimes in the world have shown as much hostility to bureau- cratic behavior as that of Communist China. Even during the high point of the attack on "conservative managers," the venom was reserved for bureaucrats. One of the reasons for this hostility is the suspicion that the bureaucrat creates networks of human solidarity that only in-

---

18 *Jenmin jihpao*, November 20, 1961.

clude a small restricted circle, whereas true solidarity should encompass all the people. The cadre is the Chinese Communist answer to the official. The official commands from his office. The cadre goes out and leads personally. Still, both have one thing in common: they see solidarity in human rather than in technical terms. Neither has much sympathy or understanding for the manager. The modes of solidarity are different, but both fail to understand the importance of clear-cut expertise. The Chinese official in the Republican period preferred to see a fluid line between administration and management. The Chinese Communist cadre takes the same view. Policy, operations, and work can be united into a single whole; "Cadres, Technicians, and Workers Amalgamate," as a Great Leap slogan put it. The Great Leap Forward appears to have seen a return to that "human" approach to organization that was so marked in pre-1949 China. The Great Leap Forward, however, demonstrated that modern organization must rest on a solid technological basis. The Chinese Communists, since the beginning of 1961, have finally realized this.

The contrast between technical and human organization is similar to that made by Philip Selznick in regard to his concepts "organization" and "institution." He states: "The term 'organization' thus suggests a certain bareness, a lean, no-nonsense system of consciously co-ordinated activities. It refers to an *expendable tool*, a rational instrument engineered to do a job. An 'institution,' on the other hand, is more nearly a natural product of social needs and pressures—a responsive, adaptive organism." [19]

Nothing could have been further from traditional Chinese conceptions of human relationships than "organization" in Selznick's sense. The traditional Chinese preferred to regard all organization as essentially "institution," as a "responsive, adaptive organism." This approach to modern organization failed because it was unable to accept an environment marked by never-ending challenges and changes. The search for organizational integration in terms of networks of human relationships led to inertia. The Chinese Communists, however, have always been clearly committed to "organization." They agree with Selznick that organizations are to be marked by "bareness, a lean, no-nonsense system of consciously co-ordinated activities." Enormous production challenges had to be met in the face of extreme scarcity and difficulty. Yet ideology proclaimed that, under the new order, organizations were communities, that socialism made true human solidarity

---

[19] *Op. cit.*, p. 5.

possible. But even more than that, the whole cadre tradition of the Chinese Communists led them to stress human over technical solidarity. They wanted human solidarity that would produce action rather than inertia. They wanted something that would *function* like "organization," but *be* like "institution." The lessons of the Great Leap Forward indicate that this still is an irresolvable contradiction.

Leadership Alternatives for Management

One of the basic differences between "organization" and "institution," in Selznick's sense, relates to the definition of the environment. "Organization" sees the environment essentially one of change and challenge; "institution" sees it as one of continuity and stability. These different perceptions of the environment also characterize the modern manager and the traditional bureaucrat. The traditional bureaucrat saw change as a passing challenge to stability. The modern manager, like the military commander, sees danger around every corner; for him change and not harmony is the natural order of things. In a basically harmonious world, man need not rely solely on the instruments of rationality. He can use all factors that enter into human relationships. But in a world defined as hostile, the insights and tools deriving from a rational approach to the world may be the only mechanisms of survival a man has. The turn from "institution" to "organization" demands a radical redefinition of the environment.

In discussing the Party cadre, we have suggested (pp. 166-167) four different leadership types: traditional bureaucrat, modern bureaucrat, manager, and cadre. Each of these can be compared and contrasted in terms of their attitudes toward (1) change and stability, and (2) human or technical organization. In regard to change and stability, the manager and the cadre agree in defining their environment as one of constant change and challenge. Neither can accept stasis as the natural condition of life. They both face competition, challenge, and danger. They must act innovatively and creatively in order to survive personally and keep the organization moving ahead. Both types of bureaucrats, on the other hand, are primarily oriented to routine, maintenance, and stability. These they regard as the natural conditions of life. The pattern changes when their attitudes toward human and technical organizations is considered. As we have argued in the discussion on the Party cadre, the modern bureaucrat and the manager agree that techniques and expertise are the basic means for organizational integration. In contrast, the traditional bureaucrat and the cadre regard human organization as most significant for achieving this goal.

ORIENTATIONS OF LEADERSHIP TYPES

Change	Stability
Manager	Traditional bureaucrat
Cadre	Modern bureaucrat

Human organization	Technical organization
Traditional bureaucrat	Modern bureaucrat
Cadre	Manager

In both Russia and China, the revolution brought about a radical change in the definition of the environment. As Arthur Wright has pointed out, for China[20] struggle and not harmony was now seen as the natural condition of life. Both Russia and China agreed on their basic goals: the complete industrialization and modernization of their countries. But they differed about the human instruments chosen to direct these programs of development.

The Soviets wanted a solid phalanx of managers to direct industry. No Weberian-type bureaucracy was contemplated, because the legal rational basis for an efficient modern bureaucracy was lacking in Russia. Russia was threatened with the seepage back into Russian administrative life of the traditional *chinovniki*. Stalin's answer to this threat was to push for the most strenuous development of professional expertise. What Stalin meant by a "workers' intelligentsia" was a corps of managers. To make sure that the new young managers triumphed over bureaucracy, during the mid-1930's, Stalin undertook great purges which struck at the growing bureaucratic apparatuses in the Soviet Union. Stalin wanted a society resting on technical and not on human organization. He suspected networks of human organization as potentially subversive. This led to that kind of atomization of society that Barrington Moore Jr. attributes generally to totalitarianism.[21] Since Stalin's death, Soviet leaders have been paying greater attention to the importance of human organization.

The Chinese Communists started to take the same approach as the Russians during the early 1950's. Clearly, they felt, industrialization required managers and not bureaucrats. Our discussion, in this chapter, of the responsibility system and one-man management indicates how

---

[20] Arthur F. Wright, "Struggle vs. Harmony—Symbols of Competing Values in Modern China," *World Politics*, VI (October 1953), 31-44.

[21] *Political Power and Social Theory* (Cambridge, Mass., 1958), p. 26.

assiduously they copied the Russian model of complex technical organization. However, when, from the mid-1950's on, they began to change their approach, they believed that they could achieve with their army of political cadres what they could not achieve with their small corps of professionals: rapid economic development. In its cadres, China had a resource the Russians did not have. The long guerrilla struggle of the Chinese Communists produced the politically committed combat leaders who, the Chinese felt, could take command of developmental programs throughout China. In some ways, the Chinese red cadre was similar to the Japanese samurai of the early Meiji period. Both had the capacity to lead men, were committed to higher ideals, and regarded the development of industry and technology as basic goals for themselves and for their country.

The military aspect still remains inherent in the cadre concept, as it does in the image of the Japanese samurai. The qualities of the cadre which the Chinese Communists felt were essential in the struggle for economic development are similar to those that Morris Janowitz attributes to the combat soldier. His description of the combat soldier is remarkably similar to many statements about cadres made during the Great Leap Forward. He says:

> The combat soldier, regardless of military arm, when committed to battle, is hardly the model of Max Weber's ideal bureaucrat following rigid rules and regulations. In certain aspects he is the antithesis. The combat fighter is not routinized and self-contained. Rather, his role is one of constant improvisation, regardless of his service or weapon. Improvisation is the keynote of the individual fighter or combat group. The impact of battle destroys men, equipment, and organization that need constantly to be brought back into some form of unity through on-the-spot improvisation. In battle, the planned division of labor breaks down.[22]

What Janowitz says on "manipulation" is also similar to the Chinese Communist approach to the problem of human and technical organization: "Manipulation involves influencing an individual's behavior less by giving explicit instructions and more by indirect techniques of group persuasion and by an emphasis on group goals."

The Chinese Communists, during the Great Leap Forward, saw the problem of economic development in military terms. The production brigade was the combat team. It received general-policy commands from the Party committee, but then proceeded on its own, improvising as it went along. The cadre in charge of the team used rarely crude com-

---

[22] Morris Janowitz, "Hierarchy and Authority in the Military Establishment," in Amitai Etzioni, ed., *Complex Organizations* (New York, 1961), pp. 210–211.

mand to move his workers, but all the devices of psychological manipulation associated with the practice of thought reform.

Policy and Bureaucratism

If an organization regards its environment as constantly changing, yet wishes to react to it in systematic fashion, it must evolve policy. Policy is a statement of goals with prescribed direction and means of action (see page 86, note 60). A good manager can develop successful policies for his enterprise. But in Communist countries, it is not the manager who make policies, but the government. Few words in the Chinese Communist vocabulary are used with greater frequency than those that mean policy. In industry, as in all organizations, managers are faced with a constant stream of policy documents from above. Sometimes these documents are precise, sometimes vague and general. The manager is expected to know what higher echelons want from him. One of the purposes of ideological indoctrination is to make organizational leaders sensitive to the intent of the top leadership. The functions of ideology and policy are thus closely linked.

Given the nature of organization in a Communist country, what kind of industrial leader is most sensitive to policy? The Russians and the Chinese agree that bureaucrats tend to thwart the policy intentions of those at the top. One of the most serious organizational problems in both countries is what the Russians call *méstnichestvo* and the Chinese *penwei chuyi*, "vested-interestism," but which we have rendered as "localism." The lack of a comparable term in English does not mean that the problem does not exist with us, but rather that it has not yet been widely accepted as a disease of bureaucracy. Localism means primary commitment to the interests of one's own organizational unit rather than to the intent of higher echelons. Since these are often in conflict, this means the presence of tendencies which block and even sabotage policy commands from above. Later in this chapter (see p. 295), we shall point out that the planning agencies in Communist China exercised conservatizing restraints on the policy commands of the leadership.[23] In the eyes of the Chinese Communists, this was seen as bureaucratic restraint on those who made policy, and was attacked as a manifestation of localism. In Russia too, it is bureaucracy that is most often accused of *méstnichestvo*.

In Russia and China, bureaucrats were purged wholesale when the regime felt that its policy commands were not being heeded. The great

---

[23] See also chap. i, pp. 88, 91, and chap. iii, pp. 216 ff.

Soviet purges of the mid-1930's cleared out the whole middle level of bureaucracy. Late in 1957, the Chinese Communists undertook a similar attack on bureaucracy, though *hsiafang* was less brutal than the methods practiced by Stalin. Large-scale purges of this sort have been rare in both countries. Nevertheless, a continuous drum fire goes on against "bureaucratism." Max Weber pointed out that the consequence of bureaucratization is routinization and stabilization. For Weber, this was a desirable phenomenon. In Communist countries, it is constantly feared because bureaucratization impedes the implementation of policy; commands become enmeshed in the intricacies of the bureaucratic apparatus at its middle levels and are not transformed into action at the bottom. In a more fundamental sense, they see bureaucratization leading to an erosion of ideology, for ideology and policy are intimately linked.

Policy is not only a response to change, but a way of producing change. Every policy command demands that something new be done, and, in this sense, is the opposite of routine. The word policy is sometimes loosely used in the West to mean any course of action. In Communist China, policy, whether meant in a general or specific sense, always refers to the objectives to be attained. Russia and China have made different use of managers and cadres as leaders for the implementation of policy, but both regard bureaucracy as an impediment to policy. In 1958 the Chinese Communists came close to destroying bureaucracy altogether; bureaucrats were ordered out of their offices to the front line of production. But the Chinese Communists soon realized that no organization can function without bureaucracy. No matter how innovative and changing an organization, it needs consolidation when change has taken place and continuity when some new leap forward has been taken. But the deep commitment to change on the part of Communist countries creates an endemic suspicion that bureaucracy, if uncontrolled, can deprive the society of its élan.

THE SOVIET MODEL OF MANAGEMENT

Rebuilding Management

Industrial reconstruction began before the civil war was over, although officially it spans the years 1949 to 1952. Though the Soviets despoiled Manchurian industry during their brief occupation, that same industry was restored with Soviet help. The first official agreement was a one-year trade agreement concluded in July 1949 between the

Soviet Union and the People's Government of the Northeast (Manchuria). The treaty was signed in Moscow by Kao Kang.[24] In February 1950, the Sino-Soviet Treaty of Friendship, Alliance, and Mutual Aid was signed in Moscow, following a visit by Mao Tse-tung to the Soviet capital. In March of the same year an aviation agreement and an agreement to set up jointly owned companies in Sinkiang were signed. In April, a trade agreement and an agreement to establish the Chinese Central Manchurian Railroad Corporation were also signed.

Sino-Soviet economic cooperation began with a commitment by the Soviet Union to help China launch a program of basic industrialization. One feature of Soviet aid to China was the furnishing of complete industrial units. The 1950 treaty of friendship provided for fifty basic industrial units to be supplied to the Chinese. A September 1953 agreement mentioned 141 units, which apparently included the 50 supplied in 1950. Agreements concluded in 1954 and 1956 called for 15 and 55 new units to be furnished. Speculation over exactly what was involved became a numbers game and need not concern us here.[25] It does concern us, though, that the Russians agreed to set up these plants down to the smallest operational details. Moreover, because the industrial units were key elements in the Chinese First Five-Year Plan, this meant that the Chinese had decided to follow closely the Soviet model in launching their program of basic industrialization. Since the First Five-Year Plan stressed heavy industry as the model for the whole industrialization program to follow, the new plants became showpieces for the country. Soviet methods could here be seen in operation.

Whole industrial units cannot be imported without the introduction of large corps of advisers. The September 1953 agreement provided for a broad range of technical assistance to China. Soviet specialists were to train the Chinese in advanced methods of work and production organization. They were to help the Chinese develop latent forces in their industrial enterprises and supervise the installation of the new equipment.[26] These specialists not only were to show the Chinese how to introduce new methods, but to work alongside the Chinese giving specific directions. The joint Sino-Soviet companies were largely run by the Soviets, as was the Central Manchurian Railroad Corporation. The industrial units delivered to the Chinese, at least in the initial years, were probably managed operationally by Soviet technicians.

24 *Chungkung shihnien*, p. 234.

25 Kusano Fumio, *Chūkyō keizai kenkyū* (Tokyo, 1962), pp. 371 ff.

26 *Ibid.*, p. 374.

Looking at it from a purely organizational point of view, the function of the Soviet technicians was management and supervision of operations. In this respect their role was not much different from that of earlier Western technicians. However, very early the Chinese drew up duplicate plans and designs for plants brought in from the Soviet Union, to prepare for the possibility of a Soviet withdrawal. When the Soviets helped the Chinese set up their major oil-refining plant in Lanchow in 1956, the Chinese began to make preparations to produce spare parts to be independent in the event of a cut-off of supply from the Soviet Union.[27] Nevertheless, whatever suspicions the Chinese may have had of the Soviets, organization and methods introduced were and had to be Soviet. The Soviets provided precisely that managerial know-how that the Chinese lacked. The Soviets were well-paid, which was often resented by the Chinese. Stories about the extravagant behavior of the Soviet specialists were similar to the "Ugly American" stories. Nevertheless, the attitude of the Chinese toward the Soviets was different from the earlier Chinese attitude toward foreign advisers. When Western technicians had been hired to operate Chinese enterprises before 1949, Chinese businessmen rarely had bothered to see how the experts functioned. Now the policy was to learn "advanced methods" from the Soviet Union. Soviet methods of industrial technology and management were widely discussed, and Russian texts were translated and circulated, with some being reprinted many times over. The proposals made by the Soviet specialists were usually accepted, but every proposal was discussed in factory meetings. In more generalized form, they were published in local and sometimes national newspapers. This was the first time the Chinese Communists faced the problem of industrial management, for the small crude plants they had formerly operated in the hinterland had hardly posed serious managerial problems. The Chinese were not only learning technology from the Soviets, but also how to become managers.

During the early 1950's, the Chinese were aware of their technological backwardness. Whatever their suspicions about the Soviets, they realized that there was much to learn. However, within a short time, the Chinese began to realize that management was not just a question of technology and division of labor. The Soviets were imposing a system on China that had evolved under Soviet conditions and could not be applied blindly to China. Hundreds of articles began to appear in the national and local press, suggesting improvements or cautiously explor-

---

27 Personal information from informant in Hong Kong.

ing alternative ways of doing things. By the time of the Eighth Party Congress, the Chinese Communists had decided that they could enunciate a new line on industrial management. The Soviet Twentieth Party Congress had broken the ice by attacking Stalin and hence the infallibility of the Soviet model. The Soviet model was criticized in a backhanded way during the Chinese congress. The Chinese felt strong enough to embark on their own organizational path. What had earlier been a technological approach to management now turned into a political approach. The Soviet planning system was criticized for its rigidity and wastefulness, and loosening up was called for. Flexibility was needed, particularly in view of China's size and backwardness. Flexibility could not be provided by a technological approach, with its orientation toward bigness and precision. Management had a political side to it as well. From 1956 on, the political approach in management dominated until the collapse of the Great Leap Forward. Since late 1960, the Chinese Communists have returned to a more technological approach to industrial operation.

The Responsibility System

Manchuria had been "liberated" earlier than the remainder of China, and production was resumed there even before the civil war ended. Therefore, methods of management became an issue for the Chinese Communists in Manchuria in the late 1940's. The introduction of Soviet methods of industrial organization was not just a matter of emulation. The Soviets controlled the Central Manchurian Railroad, and ran plants and shops connected with the railroad. They also operated enterprises in the Dairen and Port Arthur areas. Moreover, the Manchurian government was under the control of Kao Kang, who presumably was already closely linked to the Soviets. Considering the importance of the railroad system in regard to the Soviet presence in Manchuria, it is not surprising that the railroads were selected as the first branch of industry to introduce Soviet methods.

Soviet methods of management have by now been widely studied in the West, and detailed reference to them need not be made here.[28] Their essence is a highly technical organization of production, based on product specialization. Central planning gives the manager a complex set of targets to achieve; and one-man management gives him power to mobilize resources to achieve his targets. Soviet managers and workers

---

[28] Berliner, *op. cit.*; David Granick, *The Red Executive* (Garden City, N. Y., 1961).

are held individually responsible for work performance. Thus technical management and individual responsibility may be regarded as key characteristics of Soviet industrial management.

In 1949, official publications began to call for the introduction of "responsibility systems" into Manchurian work organization. This meant that individual workers were made personally responsible for their work site and work performance—a new idea in Manchuria, for the Japanese had followed Chinese forms of work organization, such as reliance on work gangs headed by gang bosses (pat'ou). The "responsibility system" was in effect a means of enforcing labor discipline, badly needed in the face of the great disorganization which then reigned. The Tungpei Jenmin jihpao, late in 1948, called for the comprehensive introduction of the responsibility system into Manchurian industry:

> The "responsibility system" is not just something that concerns the operation of railroads, but a matter of general principle in industrial construction. It is a reform of paramount importance in industrial management. What is the "responsibility system"? It is a system that demands that each worker assume a defined responsibility for production in a defined work post, that he develop to a high degree his creativity and positivism, thereby doing away with the disorderly phenomenon of nonindividual responsibility, and that he thus raise work productivity. This system will greatly raise the initiative, organizational spirit, and discipline of the working masses. It will prevent slackness on the job by minority elements. It represents one of the most·important ways for assuring the leadership of the proletariat in industry.[29]

Thus a principle of individuation of work was introduced which was new for a Chinese setting, where collectivistic traditions were strong. A work post was a place with a set of tools for which each worker was responsible. If something broke down, it was the duty of the worker to get things fixed again, otherwise he would be punished. The Russians have been so disturbed by the lack of individual concern for equipment that they have a special word for it, obezlichka, to wit, the depersonalization of a situation: something breaks down and no one cares. Stakanovism created material incentives to spur on individual performance, and the responsibility system provided the punitive counterpart for it. In both cases, what counted was the individual worker. Chinese concern with labor discipline was certainly justified by reality. On the other hand, to some extent the Chinese were reflecting the endemic Soviet concern about this problem. They could have gone back to the

---

[29] Tungpei Jenmin jihpao, November 2, 1948.

work-gang system, as they would later, but "advanced Soviet methods" suggested that work gangs were feudal remnants.

To show the legitimacy of the concern over lack of personal responsibility, the *Tungpei Jenmin jihpao* article quotes Stalin in 1931:

> The phenomenon of lack of individual responsibility is not assuming any responsibility for the work with which one is entrusted, for one's machines, apparatus, and tools. When lack of individual responsibility flourishes, there is naturally no way one can really speak of raising labor productivity, improving the quality of products, loving one's machines, loving one's apparatus.

The article ended by noting that the responsibility system had been in effect for twenty years in the Soviet Union and had created "a new kind of socialist production-management system."

The responsibility system was first introduced into the railroad network, a branch of the economy which closely linked the Chinese with the Russians. Complaints about work practices in the railroads centered on the fact that locomotives were operated by rotating crews without any one crew having specific responsibility for a particular locomotive. The result was that maintenance was poor and accidents occurred. Once an axle burned out, which "lost billions in state property." To remedy this, a responsibility system had to be introduced. Every locomotive was assigned to two or three two-man crews. If anything went wrong, one of the crews was held entirely responsible. Though not yet a completely individuated system of work organization, it set up a much tighter link between man and machine. The workers were happy, saying "the locomotive is our good friend, and we must take loving care of her."

There were objections to the responsibility system, particularly from the locomotive engineers. They claimed that this new nonrotating system would be wasteful of manpower, and first should be tried out. Besides, the rotating system was being used in all countries of the world, although, to be sure, not in the Soviet Union. The Party replied that it was precisely the Soviet model that ought to be followed, that capitalist methods are not suitable for a socialist country, that in the long run the new system would save manpower, and that by relying on the twenty years of experience of the U.S.S.R., costly mistakes could be avoided. By adopting this system, the railroads would provide a model for industry as a whole. In concluding, the editorial in the *Tungpei Jenmin jihpao* warns: "Our comrades in industrial work must overcome habits acquired during long years of work in the villages, and at the same time they must avoid getting involved in backward and antiquated tendencies toward capitalistic industrial management."

Disdainful remarks about rural work habits were common at that time and were reflected in the switch in Party recruitment policy. "Let's Be Modern and Soviet " was the slogan of the time.

The talk about the need for responsibility systems that had begun in Manchuria soon spread to other parts of China. Articles appeared suggesting that responsibility systems be introduced into Shanghai industry.

An article in the *Chiehfang jihpao* admitted that, although Shanghai industry had done well in the face of enemy blockade, there still were shortcomings that had to be corrected.[30] The author, Huang I-feng, picked out what he saw as serious obstacles to rational management: first, unwillingness to make individual decisions and to assume individual responsibility; second, the old habit of "talking things over" and letting decisions happen in some collegial fashion. Thus, either decisions are not made or a lot of time is wasted while things are incessantly talked over. The demands of rational management were in conflict with traditional Chinese work habits. Personal authority has always been resented in China, particularly among higher social groups. If things had to be done, they were done in a group where individual responsibility could be submerged and where no one clearly dominated. "Talking things over" meant explaining circumstances and thoughts, even though everyone knew what the decision would be.

After citing Stalin to show that the model society once also faced these problems, Huang I-feng proceeded to describe the consequences of lack of individual responsibility:

> Much important work goes around in circles through meetings and official documents. We still have no really good work plans which even approach practicality, nor a work system with a rational division of labor and a clear specification of authority. In many factories and mines public property has been ruined because of the lack of individual responsibility. We always cry about how we lack tools and materials, but everywhere tools and materials are thrown about at will and wasted at will.

Huang I-feng stated five reasons for lack of individual responsibility. First, the informal work habits deriving from village days and experiences with small-scale handicraft industry: everyone did everything by himself, without relying on organization; there was much talk, but few decisions made, and if there were decisions, there was little checking on execution; there was neither concentration of effort, nor planning, nor organized work methods.

---

[30] *Chiehfang jihpao*, January 13, 1950.

Second, the factor of "serious bureaucratic work methods": many cadres entered the cities with the attitude of victors; once they got charge of industries, their ideas began to change, and they became arrogant and distrustful of the workers and the masses; they assumed that work could be done simply by issuing orders; yet they did not concretely assign work, nor did they check up to see if it was being carried out.

Third, the new responsibility system needed adequate preparation, in particular ideological preparation of workers and managers. "The old personnel does not dare assume responsibility, whereas the new positive elements have not yet been trained." They take the attitude that they would rather "stand in the castle tower and watch the scenery," and "even if Heaven were to crash down, it's no concern of mine."

Fourth, "immediately after the liberation, the feelings of the masses soared and swelled," and as a result work discipline relaxed. Many persons busied themselves with meetings, and with cultural and recreational work. As a result few were willing to do practical work. But the old administrative personnel "did not dare to assume responsibility."

Fifth, because "we had no experience in managing large-scale industry, we had never established a real one-man management system; division of labor was vague, and authority unclear." And "we were not yet able rapidly and honestly to study the advanced country, the Soviet Union."

The five bad conditions that Huang I-feng singled out were a good empirical sociological analysis. What he said undoubtedly existed, though it remains a question of how bad the situation actually was. When the Chinese introduce a new policy, they often exaggerate the shortcomings of the situation in order to justify the change. Who were the people guilty of village habits? They could hardly have been the Shanghainese managers and workers, but rather the cadres who took charge after 1949. Most cadres did not know how to run a modern factory. They had the authority to make policy decisions, so to speak, but the real power lay with those who had managerial and operational knowledge. The gap between policy and operations which was endemic to Chinese industry got worse when country cadres assumed control. Presumably to compensate for their lack of knowledge, many cadres resorted to "commandism," issuing orders backed up by force rather than information. The reference to "positive elements" (mentioned in the third of Huang's five reasons) points to a favorite device of the Communists: selecting promising individuals from within the organization, training them, and putting them into leadership positions. Becoming a "positivist" was a way of getting ahead, and hence most came from the lower strata of the population. In the meantime, the old personnel, which normally should have been in charge of operations, were unwilling to take any responsibility, caught between the cadres at the top and the rising positivists at the bottom. The talk about meetings and the soaring feelings of the masses reflects the euphoria of the postrevolutionary situation. Everyone wanted the euphoria to continue, but meanwhile little work was being done. Industrial management was a cold, grim task, so it was felt at the time. One had to learn from the Soviet Union, which by that time was beginning to send its own cold, grim specialists to help the Chinese.

Huang I-feng's article had a textbook ring. It was similar to many articles in the thirties when similar conditions were being assailed by Western-trained Chinese economists. Here were actual conditions, Huang argued, and there was the model one should follow. Huang himself had probably never seen a modern Soviet factory in operation, and undoubtedly quoted from something he had read. Articles of this type hardly led to much modification of procedure in factory activity. To make the system workable, production control had to break down operations into technical components. No one was able or willing to do that at the time, certainly not in the well-established Shanghai industries. The net effect of articles such as the one by Huang was ideological and indoctrinational.

The introduction of the responsibility system required more than making individuals accountable for their work and equipment: it meant the introduction of a rational work order, based on "the scientific system of industrial management in the Soviet Union." An article in the *Tungpei Jenmin jihpao* described the process of introducing Soviet work methods in a farm-machinery factory.[31] The factory had been wrecked during the civil war, but the workers had managed to rescue tools, machinery, and equipment. Though the factory resumed production, work was confused, unplanned, and wasteful, production costs rose, and work discipline was slack. After "democratic discussion," the workers decided "to study the scientific system of industrial management of the Soviet Union" and to introduce the responsibility system. On the basis of "the spirit of specified accountability" a new work order was established. The engineering section was divided into two main work groups, one for production and manufacturing, the other for planning and study. Within the production and manufacturing group, three shops and two sections were set up. Each shop was further divided into teams on the basis of specific production tasks. Each work team was led by a "democratically elected" team chief. Within the team

---

[31] December 11, 1949.

specific work tasks were assigned each worker. Thus a rational division of labor was established.

Monthly production plans were drawn up, said the *Tungpei Jen-min jihpao*, specifying the tasks of each work team. Each work team discussed the section of the draft plan which applied to it. The production and manufacturing group then called a meeting of all work-team chiefs, and agreement was reached on the final plan. The plan was then posted for all to see, and for all to understand their own individual role in the plan. The technical sections drew up plans for their own work, such as supply plans. The role of the labor unions was emphasized to assure maintenance of worker discipline, safety, and workers' welfare. Taking over "advanced scientific Soviet methods of management," daily production logs (*paopiao*) were introduced, in which production records of each work team and each individual worker were to be recorded. Work and time expended for each item of work were recorded in detail. Norms and quotas were established, "laying the groundwork for a system of rewards for overfulfillment of quotas and a piece-work wage system."

The daily reports assured a continuing upward flow of communication from the production floor, according to the article, but more steps had to be taken to tighten the span of control. It was decided that every day all team chiefs should meet a half hour before work time in the manager's office to iron out immediately any difficulties that had arisen. There was to be no more gap between policy and operations. The two were to be linked tightly together by a smooth flow of command and information.

Although work was supposed to be discussed each day in terms of past performance and future expectations, the responsibility system could not operate without control and inspection. At the end of each month, the factory manager, the engineers, all section chiefs, the union chairman, and the inspector formed a control team. All products were checked in detail, and only after this collective control did the inspectors formally sign the monthly production report. An independent accounting system was established. The chief accountant had "the authority to stop payment in any case where the budget was being exceeded." Even the factory manager could make no disbursements of funds without his permission.

Labor discipline was strictly enforced. If a worker reported for work five minutes late he was subjected to "criticism." The new system had reduced lateness and absenteeism. But, as in other factories, this did not always meet with the full enthusiasm and approval of the workers, "it had not struck deep roots among the masses." Here the

Party was to play the crucial role in raising the workers' positivism. The article said:

Each Party and Youth League member must act as the core for a mass movement to introduce the system of specified responsibility in production. Each Party member must gather around himself at least three positivists. Once you create the proper fermentation, you can then start a movement for new production records throughout the factory. Point out the rewards that can be obtained for overfulfilling production quotas, and the bonuses to be got for improving skills.

The humorous aspect of the matter was that this highly scientific apparatus of work organization was being introduced in a factory employing only sixty workers and producing only sixty tons of goods each month.

Many newspaper articles at the time were of a similar kind. Far fewer articles gave details on the larger plants, probably because of their strategic importance and because the Russians were running the show. But like that in the *Tungpei Jenmin jihpao,* articles had their educational value and made clear that Soviet methods were not just to be used in elite enterprises. The whole country was encouraged to strive to introduce Soviet methods.

Several important innovations were introduced which have since become standard features of Chinese industry. One was the shop system, known as *tsekh* in Russian and *ch'echien* in Chinese. Each shop constituted a more or less unified production area defined according to technological criteria. Setting up shops was the first step toward technological integration of the production process. Another was the production-team system. What distinguished the team from the old work gang was the specificity of its work tasks.

An essential part of Chinese factory life are the daily production logs. They are the basis for complex individual wage payments and also the basic source material for the physical output data so vital to the planning system. The habit of drafting production plans among the workers and then sending them up to management appears to be a Chinese innovation. It was initially regarded as a way of democratically involving the workers in the system, but later was seen as the key to rapid economic breakthrough. Wild production plans made within the team later contributed to the economic dislocation of the Great Leap Forward. Of great importance was the insistence on continuing personal contact between management and workers. The periodic visits by managers to the production floor became the origin of the great campaign to get managers to do physical labor alongside the workers. The role of the unions in managing the welfare of workers emerged at that time. The core cadre function of the Party was here singled out for emphasis. The independent authority of the chief accountant to veto expenditures was a Soviet practice.[32]

On July 10, 1953, the Ministry of Heavy Industry issued a directive on "implementing the responsibility system and raising the quality of work in basic construction." The directive specified the rational work order that was to be introduced in industry, and clearly indicated a trend toward the introduction of one-man management.[33]

The directive noted that, despite some successes in the movement against waste and for responsibility launched in April 1953, the "development of the central work of the movement was still very uneven." These facts demonstrated that the full implementation of responsibility was not easy and would require "considerable ideological education, political, and organizational work." Though the idea of planning was universally accepted, the thought that all work should be specified to the minutest detail and execution should take place strictly according to plan apparently was not yet completely accepted. The directive said: "All work must be carried out strictly in accordance with technical designs and operational plans. In order that the workers correctly grasp the technical standards demanded by the plan, before operations blueprints must be carefully studied, and the work standards to be achieved learned."

Simply instructing workers to operate in a planned, rational fashion was not enough. To assure a high-level performance, men of skill were to be put in charge of the work teams. Taking an experienced worker and turning him into a foreman with authority over his fellow workers caused trouble in many industries. The new foremen found themselves resented from below and from above. But the professional ideology of

---

[32] Before 1949, accountants in China were closely involved with company administration. When the Chinese Communists assumed power in 1949, they began to use financial mechanisms to exercise regulatory control over enterprise operations. This could only be done by detaching the accountant from the manager, associating him closely with the bank through which all the enterprise's accounts went, and giving him special veto power over the enterprise's financial dealings. During the Great Leap Forward, however, accountants lost their independent authority and became the tools of the enterprise Party committee. Thus a situation returned which was similar to that which prevailed before 1949. The breakdown in the authority of the accountants was one of the main reasons for the financial chaos which ensued from the Great Leap Forward. In 1961, the government undertook a major effort to reinstitute financial soundness. As a result, the powers of the accountants were explicitly reconfirmed by government directive, and subsequently strengthened even further by new regulations.

[33] *Jenmin jihpao*, July 23 and August 27, 1953.

the time regarded skill as the basic source of authority in a socialist society.

The directive made the following prescriptions:

I. *The system of sole responsibility by management.*—This involves two basic aspects. (1) A system of unit production areas, ranging hierarchically from the entire factory to the work section. Each production unit is to be headed by a single individual leader. (2) At the factory-wide level, an adequate system of staff sections must be established, with defined tasks and responsibilities. These involve sections for planning, production, technology, machine power, materials, finance and accounting, labor and wages, personnel, technological control, safety technology, sales promotion, and welfare. At the shop level, as needed, various staff sections are likewise to be set up such as planning, production, technology, statistics, and safety. "The individuals responsible for every task, for every item of work, must be clearly designated, so that hereafter all management work has a defined organization and designated individuals who assume responsibility."

II. *The system of technological responsibility.*—This involves the following three aspects. (1) Every factory manager must designate one chief engineer (or one general engineer), and every shop supervisor must designate one chief technician. These individuals, under the direct leadership of the factory manager or the shop supervisor, are responsible for guiding the work of production technology. (2) Every single item of technological work must be directed by a specifically and individually responsible engineer or technician, thereby "to counter the phenomenon of lack of individual responsibility for technological work." (3) A sound and independent structure of technological control must be established. Under the direct leadership of the factory manager, supplies are to be checked to see if they accord with technological requirements, and the production process is to be controlled to make sure that the technical work order is being observed. Furthermore, quality controls are to be carried out on semi-finished products to make sure that they come up to standards.

III. *The system of responsibility for production order.*—This involves three major aspects. (1) A sound system of work planning must be laid out. Where work planning is inadequate or wrong, constant revisions are to be made by the production planning staff. (2) An efficient production order can only be maintained if there is daily checking to see if work plans have been carried out. There must be constant supervision over all shops (or mine shafts), work sections, and all supporting departments, as well as the materials-transportation departments, to make sure that coordination takes place. (3) Responsibility for production order must be well-grounded at the shop level, which involves, among other things, a sound system of shift rotation.

IV. *The system of responsibility for maintenance and repair.*—This too involves three major aspects. (1) There must be a single individual responsible for the maintenance of each item of major equipment. Use and handling of all major equipment must be accompanied by a defined responsibility and by concrete *modi operandi*. (2) Repairs must take place at definite periods, and are to be done by the machine-power section. (3) An adequate supply system for repair and maintenance must be set up.

V. *The system of responsibility for safety technology.*—This involves (1) the establishment of safety technology teams, with one person in charge (although factory managers and shop supervisors still retain responsibility for safety), (2) the formulation of and constant improvement on a regular safety-technology system, (3) the carrying out of safety education, and (4) the rigorous implementation of "a system of reward and punishment for safety."

VI. *The system of responsibility for supplies.*—This involves (1) planning of the supply system under the direction of the materials department, (2) improving supply management, and extending responsibility to all supply operations, such as purchase, inspection, storage, care, billing, receiving, and returning, and (3) setting up supply reserve quotas and depreciation quotas for each item of material.

VII. *The system of responsibility for production costs and finances.*—Probably because the financial side of industrial operations was so complicated, no further elaboration in general terms was made on this point.

The details of the responsibility system as outlined by the directive are so similar to Soviet methods that there can be little doubt that the directive was drafted on the advice of Soviet experts. This is implied by an article in the Peking *Kungjen jihpao,* July 3, 1953:

The state-owned Harbin Measuring and Cutting Tools Plant has already begun to put through the responsibility system proposed by Soviet experts, thus making the proposals of the Soviet experts much more effective in the process of building up the plant. . . . Since the responsibility system proposed by the Soviet experts was implemented, the Soviet experts have had much more time to go deep into the plant, to discover and study problems; in one month, they made more than two hundred valuable proposals.

The responsibility system made it easier for the Soviet experts to function. Soviet experts had been in the habit of giving commands on the spot without going through formal channels. With individual authority clearly defined, they knew precisely whom to contact in order to implement a command. Since the Chinese lacked technical personnel to implement such complex systems, *de facto* managerial control by the Soviets was often the case.

The responsibility system was introduced in its most rigorous form in the joint Sino-Soviet companies. Thus a 1950 article[34] notes that in the Dairen joint Sino-Soviet plants, "the system of sole individual responsibility in all sections of production has been most rigorously carried through," whereas in the purely Chinese state-owned plants, "the

---

[34] *Ibid.,* May 23, 1950.

lack of individual responsibility in production is still a very serious phenomenon."

However, though the Sino-Soviet plants had already instituted Soviet management methods, some of the most important Chinese industries still had not. Thus the Anshan Iron and Steel Plant did not introduce them until 1951, and then only put them into full operation in 1953.[35] In 1956, when one-man management was officially revoked,[36] it became clear that many factories had never put the Soviet methods into operation. These factories were mostly light industries and industries distant from North China. It became clear that the new methods radiated out first from the Sino-Soviet industries, then were used in the industrial enterprises established or improved with Soviet aid, and finally reached Chinese industry as a whole. The degree of implementation thus appeared to depend directly on the strength of Soviet influence. Where the Soviet experts had operational control, the new methods were employed. Where their control was partial or absent, less serious efforts were made to introduce them.

One-man Management

The early articles on the responsibility system tended to be hortatory. As time went on, the real purposes of the responsibility system became clear: a system that could fit into central planning. A plan in a Soviet-type country may be thought of as having two essential components: it transmits information on the basis of which economic action is to take place; and it has force behind it to compel compliance. Functionally, the force component tries to make up for the imperfection of the information component. This means that a system of central planning needs: an organizational structure that permits maximal and optimal flows of information upward and downward; and effective channels of command. Thus, as one moves into the 1950's, reports on managerial policies increasingly emphasize coordinated technical organization of production so as to permit information flow of output data, and the need for clearly defined and smoothly flowing channels of command. The new systems to assure this were borrowed from the Soviets. They were called the "production-territorial system of organization," and "one-man management." [37]

---

35 *Ibid.*, February 23, 1954.

36 See p. 285.

37 The term "production-territorial system" is a literal translation from the Russian *proizvodstvenno-territorial'naia sistema*. It was officially adopted in the Soviet Union in 1934 (Gregory Bienstock, Salomon Schwartz, and Aaron Yugow, *Manage-*

On December 31, 1953, the Tientsin *Takungpao* published a schematic outline of basic principles of industrial management, derived from the experiences of a Taiyüan cement factory. Still called the "responsibility system," it was nevertheless clear that the concept had undergone considerable enlargement since 1950. Responsibility was now seen as consisting of three aspects: (1) management according to production areas, (2) sole responsibility by management, and (3) work post and technical responsibility. Of these three, only the last was a carry-over from the early conception of responsibility. It meant that every worker was personally responsible for his work post and his tools. The first two were new conceptions, well known in the Soviet Union but hitherto not generally applied in China. As becomes apparent later, the Chinese never became enthusiastic about one-man management. That may be why so many articles on these systems were published in the "neutral" papers like the *Takungpao* rather than in the *Jenmin jihpao*, where every article has policy force. These new managerial procedures were introduced because China was in the first year of its Five-Year Plan and central planning was the order of the day; production-territorial units of work and one-man management were regarded in the Soviet Union as building blocks of the planning system.

The *Takungpao* article first discusses the implementation of the production-territorial principle. The factory is to be organized into areas, each of which is characterized by a certain product specialization. All operations concerned with the manufacture of the given product are to be concentrated in one single area. Thus, for example, the rail transportation system in a steel factory constitutes a single unified production area. It is defined territorially, because all operations are concentrated in one place; it is defined in terms of production because all of its operations are aimed at the output of a single product, in this case transportation services. The article admits, however, that no general operational rules can be laid down since industries differ so much technologically.

---

ment in Russian Industry and Agriculture [London, New York, Toronto, 1944], pp. 14-15). It is a basic principle of industrial organization that applies to the economy as a whole, as well as to the organization of individual plants (see Peter Wiles, The Political Economy of Communism [Cambridge, Mass., 1962], pp. 43-46; also chap. ii, p. 175). From the vocational literature on plant organization in the West it becomes clear that no dogmatic principles on how to organize a plant technologically can be laid down in a priori fashion. The intra-enterprise production-territorial system must therefore be regarded as important for the command structure rather than for the technical organization of production. It is an adjunct to one-man management, and serves as a device for tightening managerial control over the enterprise.

The article then goes on to the command structure. Once the production units are delineated, the system of management is to follow them; for every production unit, there is a corresponding management structure; one man is in charge of the whole enterprise; he has under his sole control various staff sections: planning, transportation, labor and wages, machinery, work force; every shop is similarly headed by one shop supervisor who is in sole charge. The staff sections are to assist the shop supervisor in his work, but can give no orders; below the shops, there are work sections, each headed by a section chief. The chain of command goes vertically from plant manager through shop supervisor, section chief, and finally to the production-team heads. Command flows from individual to individual.

The *Takungpao* article calls this "the system of sole responsibility by management," and points out that this is the same as the Soviet system of one-man management, namely a basic principle of socialist industrial management. The Chinese apparently had some trouble translating the Soviet word *edinonachalie*. They called it, quite honestly, the one-boss system, *ichang-chih*.

The article then tries to answer the question why a one-boss system is necessary:

It is [necessary] because the scale of modern industry is great, its equipment complex. Work processes must be rigorously coordinated, and industry must be operated with a clearly defined plan. Under these circumstances, unless there is one unified command to direct all operations, there is no way of getting economic efficiency. Lenin once said: "Any large-scale industry—which is the material source and foundation of production in socialism—unconditionally must have a rigorous unified will to direct the collective work of hundreds, thousands, and even millions of men. But how can the rigorous unity of wills be assured? Only by the wills of the thousands and millions submitting to the will of a single individual." [38]

Such a frank statement about bending millions of wills to one will must have been disquieting to Chinese ears. So the article hastily adds:

But here one point must be emphasized when considering the system of sole responsibility by management so far as it concerns the leaders. They must rely on the working masses. The system must be tied in with managerial democracy. The system of sole responsibility by management is not one of an individual "arbitrarily deciding and arbitrarily acting." To carry out good management, there must be reliance on the working masses. The working masses must be drawn in to discuss important work problems, collective discussion must be carried out. Though one man is responsible, he must open-mindedly listen to

---

[38] Lenin, *Selected Works* (Moscow, 1952), II, 398.

the opinions of the masses. This not only will arouse the creativity and positivism of the masses and aid management, but will increase the respect of the
masses for management leaders and help strengthen the system of sole responsibility by management.

The article spends more time discussing one-man management than
the details of the production-territorial system, undoubtedly because it
was hard to lay down general principles on how a plant should be organized technologically and because the real importance of the system
lay in the management command structure.

The article thus presents one-man management in classic Soviet form.
Every production unit is in charge of one and only one man. Staff sections assist him but are precluded from issuing commands that bypass
the vertical chain of command. In 1934, the Soviets established one-man
management replacing something they called *funktsionalka* and the
Chinese *tot'ou lingtao* (multiheaded leadership). What the Russians
and the Chinese actually meant when they talked of the "functional
system" was old-fashioned bureaucracy. In the early 1950's, one could
find critiques of the functional system that supposedly prevailed in Chinese industry. If the chain of command was not made crystal clear, commands coming down from above would be watered down somewhere
within the organizational structure. The solution was strict one-man
management at all levels of the system. In the critiques of *funktsionalka*,
we find stress on the need to pass from bureaucratic to managerial direction of enterprises. Both the Soviets and the Chinese, at their respective
stages of development, were concerned over the tendency for management to turn once again into bureaucratic administration. The answer to this tendency toward bureaucratism was one-man management.

In the early 1950's the Chinese, emulating the Soviet experiences,
sought to place great power in the hands of the managers. The Party's
role was to be limited to that of moral leadership. The commands that
counted came from higher echelons in the administrative system. Management commanded and the worker had to obey. Everyone was responsible individually for the fulfillment of his production tasks and the
maintenance of his work post. One-man management was predicated on
the assumption that stakhanovism would be universally introduced at
the production level. Time wages and forms of collective payments
would be replaced by piece rates. The factory, under one-man management, was conceived of as a coldly rational arrangement of individual
workers commanded by an authoritarian manager.

One of the most comprehensive discussions of the production-territorial system and one-man management was published by a writer, Liu

Che, who earlier had written other articles on the subject.[39] He stated flatly that modern state-owned industry was the key to China's industrial development and the model for other industries to follow, and that the basic managerial principle in state-owned industry was the production-territorial and one-man management systems. Liu Che stressed that the complexity of modern large-scale industry demanded coordination and centralization, and these could only be achieved with concentrated management: "Modern large-scale industry and dispersed management are incompatible." [40]

Liu Che then went on to state what one-man responsibility at the managerial level really meant. First, you cannot hold a manager responsible for performance unless you give him a concomitant authority over operations and a certain degree of freedom to make innovative decisions. Liu Che admitted that maximizing the authority of managers created problems for management-Party relations. But he answered that the managers must still "submit to the unified *ideological* leadership of the Party," and quoted Stalin to the effect that the political and the economic cannot be separated. Second, he said, managers must remain close to the masses; "this is one of the differences between one-man management in socialist industry and capitalistic autocracy." Third, it was the duty of Party leaders to study management economics and production technology so they could understand what management was doing.

This was precisely the difficulty, however. Most of the top Party cadres in industry were political men, either sent down from Peking or promoted up from the ranks. Few had any hope of understanding the intricacies of management, in particular the fact that the manager had

---

[39] Tientsin *Takungpao*, May 13, 1954.

[40] This assertion is exactly the opposite of the organizational line enunciated at the Eighth Party Congress. Li Fu-ch'un, announcing changes in the planning system, stressed the need for "unified planning but divided management." During the Great Leap Forward, the line was "unified policy but divided management." Liu Che was saying that modern industry cannot allow for a policy-operations dichotomy, and therefore there must be concentrated management. Li Fu-ch'un, on the other hand, intimated that one must allow for the policy-operations dichotomy in the interests of basic level flexibility. Under these circumstances, management, inasmuch as it is understood as functions relating to execution of policy, can be dispersed. The dispersion of management went so far during the Great Leap Forward that major operational decisions were being made on the production floor. The history of large industrial corporations in the West by no means supports Liu Che's assertion that modern large-scale industry needs concentrated management. The story of General Motors would indicate the opposite. See Alfred P. Sloan, Jr., *My Years with General Motors* (Garden City, N. Y., 1964); Peter F. Drucker, *The New Society* (New York, 1962).

to make decisions that were not outlined in the often vague commands he got from the ministries.

In describing the decision-making authority of the ideal one-man manager Liu Che said: "The plant manager has the authority, within the framework of presently constituted law, to decide on all matters of resources, equipment, and money in the plant, to protect socialist property against destruction by enemies, and against damage and thievery. Furthermore, the plant manager has the responsibility for unearthing all latent forces, and fully utilizing national resources for fulfilling and over-fulfilling state plans."

In effect, Liu Che said, the ideal plant manager has three kinds of power: he makes the final decision on use of labor, materials, and money; he has the right to take punitive action against anyone tampering with state property; and he can take independent action to guarantee plan fulfillment. In other words, he has the right to resort at times to actions that might be technically illegal in order to achieve his one supreme goal: fulfillment of the plan.

Such power undoubtedly made the Party committee nervous. Besides, the manager had the right to select and train personnel as he saw fit, and had full powers of reward and punishment. Here one-man management touched a very sensitive area, namely that of personnel. One of the big fights between managers and cadres in factories was over hiring and firing, rewarding and punishing of personnel. The manager saw personnel problems largely in technical terms. What counted was skill and performance, because plan fulfillment was the overriding goal of factory activity. The Party, on the other hand, felt that personnel was a "human" as well as a "technical" matter. For example, the Party felt that a good line supervisor must be able to lead men, and leadership was construed as a function of political involvement and action. In this case, the Party should have the main say as to who would be appointed to such supervisory positions. In the West, struggle over personnel control has often seen management and union pitted against each other. In Chinese industry, management and the Party stood juxtaposed.

Liu Che said: "In short, the plant manager is the fully authorized representative of the state, who assumes full and complete responsibility for all work in the plant. The plant manager acts as a model for the observance of state laws."

By "state," as is clear from other contexts, Liu Che meant the ministries, from which the economic directives came. Liu Che earlier had stressed that the proper role of the party was to exercise *ideological* leadership over management. This clearly excluded any kind of policy or operational leadership. Policy decisions came from the ministries, and only from there.

Liu Che's systematic outline of one-man management is the strongest case put forth that I have seen for full implementation of Soviet-type management. If it had been fully implemented, it would not only have greatly increased the powers of the ministries, but that of the State Planning Commission, a group at that time dominated by pro-Soviet professionals.

Liu Che then discussed proper staff functions under one-man management. The chief of every staff section, he said, was in full charge of the work in his section. But, more interestingly, Liu Che felt it necessary to stress that "the staff chiefs are the assistants to the plant manager. The relationship between the plant manager and the deputy plant managers is that of leader and follower. The deputy plant managers do their work in accordance with the orders and instructions of the plant manager."

Liu Che had to state this point so strongly because in many Chinese business firms, the director is either a figurehead or an intermediary. In Southeast Asia today, it is common for many Chinese firms to hire locals as directors in order to avoid the charge of being purely Chinese businesses. While the ostensible director has little power, his assistants run the firm. Still, this does not mean that the director is simply a dummy; he may play an important role as intermediary with the government. In purely Chinese contexts, directors often also played roles of intermediaries with outside groups. This practice, curiously enough, has been followed in Communist China. It is not uncommon to have enterprises where the director remains mostly in Peking and acts as the representative of the enterprise with the ministries. Real power is in the hands of the deputy directors and deputy managers. The more the intermediary role of the director is stressed, the less operational power and influence he usually has in the enterprise itself.

Liu Che's insistence on maximizing the power of the top manager was meant to close any gap that might have existed between ministry and enterprise. As long as the manager was in complete charge, the chain of command could function smoothly from ministry down to the lowest unit of the plant. In later years, the gap between ministry and enterprises began to widen. Not only did the deputy plant managers gain increasing power, but most of them were powerful Party cadres whose linkages went first and foremost to local Party organization. The decentralization decisions of late 1957 which gave local Party committees a powerful voice in the direction of *all* enterprises, including central state-owned enterprises, within their territory, formalized this tendency.

Continuing, Liu Che described the scope of the shop supervisors' authority and functions:

The shop supervisor is the fully authorized leader of all production and other economic activities in the shop. He assumes full responsibility for all work in the shop. He accepts orders only from the factory manager or the deputy manager in charge of production technology. The other deputy managers have no authority to issue orders to him. Furthermore the staff sections have no authority to issue orders to him. The tasks of the shop supervisor are: (1) to direct the formulation of the shop plan, (2) to take all measures to assure fulfillment of the shop plan, (3) to assure quality, standards, and types of products, (4) to hire personnel, (5) to reward and punish personnel, (6) to direct personnel, (7) to assure the uninterrupted raising of labor productivity, (8) to organize repair of equipment, (9) to organize supply, (10) to assure economy, (11) to assure the observance of technical safety rules and work protection rules, and (12) to assure the "spreading of advanced experiences."

Liu Che recommends that in the larger plants shops be broken down into two smaller levels of organization: work sections and production teams. However, other descriptions of factory organization indicate that the three-tier form of organization has been most common in Chinese industry: plant, shop, and team. The production team in industry is usually attached to a specific work area, according to the principles of the production-territorial system. Each production team may consist of several shifts, depending on whether the plant operates around the clock or not. In this case, three eight-hour shifts are normal.

Membership in the production teams remains constant, but shift membership varies, usually because of holidays and time off. Team members generally rotate from shift to shift, depending on how days off are staggered among the workers. The authority wielded by the team chief has always been a major concern for the Chinese Communists. The team is in effect the basic unit of production. How it performs determines ultimately the performance of the whole enterprise. Before 1949 the team foreman was a man of considerable power. The *pat'ou* ran the work gang. He was the intermediary with management. Wage payments went through his hands, usually in the form of a lump sum of which he kept a part and distributed the rest to the workers. When the Communists came to power they denounced the *pat'ou* system as feudal and autocratic, and demanded its replacement by more democratic forms of worker leadership. The old work gang, however, was different from the production team. The ties that held workers together were usually "human" rather than "technical." This gave the foreman great leverage with management, for he was usually the only one who could get maximal performance from the workers. If his treatment of workers was sometimes autocratic, it also was paternalistic. The worker could often rely on him to get favors from management. The Communist production team was different. It was devised as a function of the over-all technological organization of the plant. Workers were assigned to teams not on the basis of personal but of technical criteria (skills, job requirements, and the like). As a result, the team foreman had to be someone who had more qualifications than simple leadership ability. He had to know about the job. Later, the Chinese Communists once again stressed the leadership ability of the foreman and naturally felt that the ideal leader was the cadre. But during the early 1950's, the emphasis was still on skill and experience.

Liu Che stressed the need for technical qualifications for the ideal team chief. He also pointed out that the team chief was the lowest-echelon one-man manager. Like the warrant officer, the position of foreman in many industrial countries is a mixed one; he has attachments to management, but also to the workers. For Liu Che, there was no ambivalence; the production team chief was the lowest arm of management:

The work chief is the lowest echelon manager in the plant or mine. It is he who determines the destiny of production. Fulfillment and over-fulfillment of plans depend on the performance of each work area. Therefore, the work chief is the direct and concrete leader of each single work area. Hence he holds an extremely important position in factory and mine production. To implement one-man management effectively, one must strengthen the authority of the work chief at this level.

Liu Che specified the role of work chief as follows:

(1) He is the fully authorized leader in the work section, (2) he is under the direct leadership of the shop supervisor, (3) he transmits all managerial and production orders, (4) he must not assume any tasks outside of his own specified work, (5) with the permission of the shop supervisor, he has the authority to punish workers who violate labor discipline, (6) he has the authority to hire and fire, (7) he has the authority to determine wage rates of workers, and (8) he has the authority to "check in detail" on output quotas and piecework wage rates.

The work chief or foreman thus was not only the executor of management's orders, but he had an extremely broad range of personal authority. Not since the early days of capitalism had the power to hire and fire workers been given to the foreman. Furthermore, the foreman had the full, sole, and individual authority to determine at what wage rate a worker should be paid. And lastly, he had the power to "suggest" raising or lowering of output quotas, as well as changes in piecework rates. Though factory planning called for exact setting of norms and wages, nevertheless a considerable degree of "adjustment" was allowed. The foreman had the right to make adjustments. Of course, the foreman was supposed to respond to suggestions made within his team by Party members, positivists, and union people. Nevertheless, Liu Che made it clear that in the final reckoning his personal decision counted. One-man management must operate from the top right down to the bottom.

Liu Che ended by pointing out that one of the main purposes of one-man management was to do away with "multiheaded leadership." One-man management made leadership "concrete and efficient." Earlier all kinds of staff people had issued orders to the production floor. Now only the properly designated line executive was to do so. Staff sections henceforth were to play a purely advisory and supportive role. Multi-headed leadership invariably led to "routinization," another way of saying bureaucratism. Industry needed managers, not administrators. One-man management would produce "unity of command."

All these standard terms of Western organizational literature are used by the Chinese in the standard international sense. Liu Che may not have been acquainted with the voluminous Western literature criticizing standard staff-and-line type of organization, but he understood well that one-man management was not going to have an easy time in Chinese industry: "In implementing organizational construction, one must also implement ideological construction. Because the introduction of one-man management is encountering all kinds of ideological obstacles, one must first eliminate these obstacles. Then we can start to work effectively." These "ideological obstacles" ultimately turned out to be too great to overcome.

We have discussed Liu Che's detailed account of one-man management at length, not just to indicate what was meant by one-man management, but to show how strong the stress on the authority aspects of the system had become. The July 10, 1953, directive from the Ministry of Heavy Industry on introducing the responsibility system, discussed above, stressed the purely technical aspects of organization. By contrast, Liu Che, writing in May 1954, stressed the command aspect of the system, almost to the exclusion of the technical. It is not difficult to see why this created "ideological obstacles."

THE ATTACK ON ONE-MAN MANAGEMENT

Criticisms

It is rare in Communist China to find instances of new policy encountering such an overt lack of enthusiasm. If the *Jenmin jihpao* had hailed one-man management as the newest step forward in socialist management, unanimous enthusiasm would undoubtedly have been reported from the entire country. As it was, the most positive responses to one-man management came from Manchuria and Eastern China. The Shanghai *Chiehfang jihpao* made some interesting comments in reporting implementation of one-man management in Eastern China:

> Earlier in factories and mines of Eastern China, we adopted the system of plant manager responsibility under the collective leadership of the Party. The reasons for this were that, in the period just after Liberation, the Party had to concentrate on carrying out land reform. Moreover, [Party] cadres knew very little about industrial management. Democratic reform had not yet been completed in most enterprises. Conditions were not yet ripe for introducing systems of plant manager responsibility and one-man management. Given the conditions of the time, it was correct and necessary that at that time we made use of the system of plant manager responsibility under the collective leadership of the Party. And we had considerable success in implementing it.[41]

Now, however, continued the newspaper, the time had come to introduce the more advanced system of one-man management. If the writer had only known that two years later the Eighth Party Congress would proclaim the system of plant-manager responsibility under the collective leadership of the Party as the managerial system henceforth to be followed by all industry in the country, he might have thought twice about writing as he did. The article continued that the main trouble that came with collective leadership by the Party was that Party cadres wanted to do everything (*ilantzu*). In the process, cadres were becoming bureaucratized and neglected political-ideological work. What the Party committees must do now was to get to exercising political and ideological leadership. Management too had to get away from bureaucratic habits, and had to try to develop concentrated and unified management. The article noted that many Party cadres resisted the introduction of one-man management. They thought that this system led to a diminution in the functions of the Party committee. Such thinking was false, the article stated. By wanting to do everything, Party commit-

---

[41] May 16, 1954.

tees not only were unable to exercise effective political and ideological leadership, but were unable to develop proper control functions. The task of the Party was to watch over the actions of management. One-man management would not only develop a spirit of independent responsibility on the part of management, but would contribute to strengthen the Party's political and ideological leadership. The article made it clear that Party committees were to stop running factories, and leave that to management.

Thus even the relatively few articles that spoke positively about one-man management generally pointed out that Party cadres were not always in favor of the new system. Of course, no open attacks on one-man management were published. The general tenor of reaction was to point out the difficulties in introducing one-man management, and to suggest gradualism.

An article in the *Kwangsi jihpao* of July 10, 1954, illustrates the cautious opposition to one-man management. The article, discussing the new system as introduced at the Wuchou Hydroelectric Plant near Nanning in Kwangsi Province, pointed out that management cadres were reluctant to issue orders and "did not venture to direct production." After "study," their "courage to command" was raised. Then there were many cadres and workers who took the position that once the system was put through, "it will only be the factory manager whose word counts," "all we'll have now is centralism, and no democracy." And then there were the division chiefs who felt that now that their responsibility had diminished, it didn't matter whether they performed or not; if there was a problem and a decision needed the factory manager was available. Henceforth political work was immaterial. All that counted was raising production. "For raising production one will have to rely completely on the factory manager. The staff sections, the Party, the union, the youth-league—all are simply his helpers."

The article uttered some pious statements about wanting to implement one-man management, but made no concrete suggestions, except to say there must be better division of labor and specification of tasks. Everyone was confused. What were the deputy managers in charge of technology supposed to do? What was the connection between staff work on costs and staff work on wages? Conferences between factory managers and shop supervisors did not work very well. Commands from the manager were usually vague. Staff sections just did not know how to control the execution of commands. The only answer to all these problems was more general, half-hearted exhortations. A month after the publication of the *Kwangsi jihpao* article, similar plaints were heard from the same Wuchou area:

When the one-man management was instituted in industry, some people thought "henceforth there will be no more democracy." They said that the factory manager, the shop supervisors, the work chiefs issuing orders and directing production were simply "the same old bureaucracy." Some said: "the leaders ducked low during the *Sanfan* movement, but now that one-man management is being put through they're strutting about again." Some go so far as to say that the shop supervisor and the work chiefs have become bosses. What was once the boss, is today "the work-section chief." [42]

Again, no real answers, aside from some general remarks, were given to these complaints.

Kwangsi is in the hinterland, far from East China and Manchuria. The article indicates how strong Party resentment against the new system was. The words "boss" and "bureaucrat" are among the worst epithets in the Chinese Communist political vocabulary. To think that "henceforth there will be no more democracy" meant in the first instance that the Party would have a small role to play under one-man management.

But aside from the political implications of one-man management, some objective factors had to be considered. One-man management required managers; there had to be technologically capable men all along the line and in top staff positions. If technical personnel was in short supply in East China and Manchuria, the situation was even worse inland. Moreover, factories were smaller, and procedures had always been more informal than in the more advanced areas of the country. In the inland regions the Party had taken a more active part in factory management than in East China and Manchuria. The managers left there from the era before 1949 were far less impressive figures than the Manchurian experts and the Shanghai businessmen; they were mostly local people whose main talents were financial and administrative rather than managerial. Perhaps they had indeed "ducked low during the *Sanfan* movement," and were now "strutting about" again.

Despite the sporadic appearance of complaints about the new system in local newspapers (indicating that the press in Communist China is by no means one undifferentiated whole), the *Jenmin jihpao* continued to publish articles about the implementation of one-man management in Manchuria. Although these articles tended to preach the need for improvement of the system, they rarely failed to point out the difficulties that one-man management created. One article (May 22, 1954) described in detail the introduction of work-chief system in the

---

[42] *Wuchou kungjen jihpao,* August 14, 1954.

Anshan Iron and Steel Corporation, and the difficulties it created. Multiheaded management had created many problems over the years, and *ad hoc* attempts to remedy the situation had not produced good results. Therefore it had been decided to introduce the Soviet work-chief system. But, the article pointed out, many engineers and technicians were "not pleased" after they had been appointed work chiefs. Some were "worried": "I came from Eastern China to Manchuria to work for Anshan Iron and Steel. I never thought that I would be made a work boss!" There were others who in the past complained that "they had tasks but no authority," but now misunderstood the new system to mean that they would simply have routine administrative tasks to do, which also displeased them. Among workers promoted to the position of work chief many were afraid that "their cultural level was low, their management ability doubtful," and "they really couldn't understand blueprints, and couldn't do the job." Then there was the other "obstacle," that because of the newness of the system, the new work chiefs were not always able to give proper and detailed work assignments to the workers in their charge. "This shook the faith [of the workers] in the work-chief system," the article said.

The article continued that mass meetings had been held from which it had become clear that several serious human-relations problems existed. For one, those work chiefs selected from among the technicians had to find some way of getting along with the workers. The new system "demanded the tight unity of work and technology." One had to "change the situation that the technicians did not care about the workers." One solution was to hold small "speak-out-one's-mind meetings" between technicians and workers, thus "eliminating alienation." The old antagonism between workers and technicians, between unskilled and skilled workers, so well known in industrial relations in the West, not only existed in China, but was exacerbated by a system which made the technician "boss."

On the other hand, the article further continued, the major problem regarding those work chiefs promoted from the ranks of workers was raising their level of skills so that they could adequately perform and gain the respect of their erstwhile fellow workers and now their subordinates. Special after-hours study classes were introduced for these new work chiefs. More advanced work chiefs were assigned to give lectures to the more backward. By October of 1953, the Rolling Mill Company claimed to have trained all its new work chiefs save six to read simple blueprints, and some to read more complex blueprints. Such were the problems encountered by Anshan Iron and Steel in its attempts to extend the one-man management down to the level of work chief and foreman.

All these oblique praises and veiled criticisms were aimed at the authority implications of one-man management. By contrast, little criticism was voiced against the responsibility system or the production-territorial system. Even in later years, when Party domination in industry was stressed, formal adherence to the responsibility system was kept up. When Party domination of industry was modified early in 1961, the official press called for a "reaffirmation of the responsibility system." Similarly, up to the present time there has been no serious objection to the production-territorial system, as long as it was seen as a matter of technical organization.

One-Man Management and Kao Kang

As is clear from the discussion so far, one-man management had developed furthest in Manchuria. Since Manchuria was the center of China's heavy industry, the area of greatest Soviet influence, and the power base of Kao Kang, head of the State Planning Commission and chief of China's First Five-Year Plan program, the idea of one-man management was closely associated with all of these elements. It was inevitable, therefore, that the larger political changes affecting Manchuria and Kao Kang would have a direct effect on one-man management.

In retrospect, it is evident that the struggle between Peking and Mukden took a new turn during the Politburo meeting of December 1953. Since the occurrence of this Politburo meeting was revealed during the Fourth Plenum in February 1954 (*Jenmin jihpao*, February 18, 1954), we can presume that the policy decisions taken in February were an outgrowth of the meeting of the previous December. When the suicide of Kao Kang and the expulsion from the Party of several leading figures (Jao Shu-shih and others, all of whom served in East China and Manchuria) was announced in March 1955, repeated reference was made to the decisions of the Fourth Plenum. It is this chain of evidence that points to December 1953 as a time of major political change.[43]

The decisions of the Fourth Plenum called for an immediate return to collective leadership by the Party. In the light of the events of 1955, this can now be interpreted as the first open signal for an attack against

---

[43] It might be pointed out that the Third Plenum was held back in 1950, only a few weeks before the outbreak of the Korean War.

Kao Kang and the "independent kingdom of Manchuria." The struggle between Peking and Mukden involved many issues: a personal struggle between Mao Tse-tung and Kao Kang (with possible relationships to the struggle between Khrushchev and Malenkov in the Soviet Union), disagreement over basic economic strategy, over methods of administration, over allocation of resources, over control of the Party apparatus. All these conflicts, however, in one way or another related to the command system. Since one-man management constituted a distinct approach to the command system, it was inevitable that the decisions of the Fourth Plenum would have a major effect on one-man management.

Kao Kang, as chairman of the State Planning Commission since 1952, had become identified with a program of rapid industrialization concentrated in Manchuria and relying heavily on Soviet aid. His organizational policy for Chinese industry was one-man management. Although the communiqué of the Fourth Plenum revealed no open disagreement between Peking and Mukden on the economic program in general or one-man management in particular, there was covert alarm about the policies pursued by Mukden. Since it was not yet possible to attack Kao Kang openly, it was also not possible to attack one-man management. One has to read between the lines of the series of articles, that appeared after the Plenum, discussing "increasing and strengthening Party solidarity." Thus, on February 16, 1954, a writer named Hsü Pang-i, not further identified, published an article in the *Jenmin jihpao* which, in effect, linked the political and economic themes of the Fourth Plenum, and so may be said to have begun the official, though as yet indirect, attack on one-man management. He said:

In maintaining the principle of unified Party leadership, we must resolutely oppose and resist dispersionism. Many facts show that dispersionism is one of the evils in the work of national construction. On all levels of organization there are some operational branches which often excessively emphasize vertical rule and the work of their own branch, just as if they were an independent government assigning tasks to lower echelons . . . they do not request directives from higher-echelon Party committees; self-righteously they decide and act independently, thus committing serious errors. . . . Those comrades who have committed the fault of dispersionism often have not correctly resolved the problem of the relationship of the individual and the Party, nor have they been able correctly to resolve the problem of the relationship of lower echelons to higher echelons, of parts to the whole. They erroneously put the individual and Party organization on the same plane, sometimes going so far as to transcend Party organization.

Asking for resolute struggle against these deviant tendencies, Hsü recalled that acceptance of the principle of collective leadership by the

Party meant unconditional submission to the leadership of the Central Committee: "The Central Committee of the Party is the brains and heart of the Party. It is the command section of the entire Party."

Hsü then proceeded to discuss the problem of developing the national economy, and in so doing alluded to a sensitive area:

The first five-year construction plan of our country has the development of heavy industry as its central focus. The 141 large-scale projects with which the Soviet Union is aiding our country form its nucleus. We must preserve this crucial sector which has such decisive significance, concentrate large numbers of superior cadres and large amounts of capital, and all varieties of resources to support the construction of these 141 projects. But if there are people who will not act according to the state plan, who noisily [work toward] dispersionism and localism, who one-sidedly emphasize the importance of their own branch work, who only demand that Party and state give them even more superior cadres, allocate them more capital, and who are against more and superior cadres being assigned to strengthen other even more important branches, then this will have bad consequences for the task of national construction, and slow up its progress.

To fight these tendencies toward "dispersionism" and "localism," Hsü called for a renewed observance of collective leadership and of Party democracy: "Therefore at all times, the Party must demand of its members that they respect the party's collective leadership, that they oppose the idealistic point of view of blindly worshipping individuals."

In Chinese Communist statements, the word "but," *tanshih*, has crucial significance. Everything that precedes the "but" constitutes a partial concession to an argument; what really counts is what follows the "but." Hsü Pang-i says of course the 141 projects furnished China by the Soviet Union are the key elements in the First Five-Year Plan, *but,* he implies, they must not make sole claim on China's limited resources; other branches and sectors of the economy had to develop also. Worse than that, Hsü hinted, particular interests were growing up which began to disregard the need for absolute submission to central Party leadership. They began to act like "independent governments." Moreover, these powerful branches of the economy, by inference heavy industry, were "blindly worshipping individuals." Dispersionism can be interpreted to mean that powerful individuals were in command of sensitive branches of organization. (The implicit reference to Kao Kang is unmistakable. Who else was meant is more obscure.)

Hsü suggested further that to promote Party democracy and collective leadership, the "Party committee system" be strengthened. "All important work plans, directives, and resolutions must first undergo collective discussion by the Party committee." "No individual or small group of individuals is allowed to decide crucial problems at will."

"In no matter what Party organization, regardless of how much ability or how deep the knowledge a leader has, he can never replace collective wisdom and experience." Collective discussion and, most important, collective decision-making must replace individual authority. Hsü continued to develop the theme of harmful individualism:

There are some Party committee secretaries who often put themselves above the Party committee. They do not accept Party supervision. They do not report on their work to the Party committee. They do not accept criticism. There are some Party members who do not care at all about the overall work of the Party organization. They just want individually "to do everything themselves." In regard to many important problems in their work, they do not present them for Party discussion but go ahead and decide on their own.

If there was to be a return to collective leadership by the Party, this could not be construed to mean that initiative and creativity were to be neglected. To take the position that "now that we put through collective leadership, the individual can loosen up a bit—if he makes a mistake, all will get the blame," was equally wrong. "We must strongly emphasize," Hsü says, "division of responsibility under the unified leadership of the Party."

Unified leadership in no way does away with proper division of labor and individual responsibility. Thus, for example, we are now implementing the system of factory manager responsibility in state owned industries and mines. This is required by the production processes of a socialist modern industry. But this one-man management has nothing in common with the tyrannical system of autocracy in capitalistic industries. One-man management also does not mean separation from Party supervision. There is no contradiction between one-man management and collective leadership by Party organizations in factories.

Hsü suggested renewed emphasis on ideological work, and vigilance against "the capitalist class which, with the weapons of individualism and liberalism, tries to corrupt unstable elements within our own Party." To climax the article, Hsü cited some remarks by Malenkov at the Soviet Nineteenth Party Congress on the importance of ideological work.

In retrospect, what Hsü was saying is quite clear. Like it or not, Peking saw one-man management being introduced into the modern industrial sector, notably Manchuria. Of course, there was a contradiction between one-man management and collective Party leadership. On linguistic grounds alone, the two concepts were mutually exclusive. There was no capitalist class in Manchuria; whatever capitalists there had been had left together with the Japanese. Clearly, there were elements in the Party who were not fully loyal to Peking. We know this from a look at the purges of second-stringers which followed the announcement of the Kao-Jao affair. All came from Manchuria and East China.

Hsü Pang-i was undoubtedly talking about the Kao-Jao group. These individualists were not just leading figures in administration and management in Manchuria, but also members of the Party. Theoretically, they were subject to Party discipline. But at that time Kao Kang was extremely powerful at the highest levels of the Party. After the Eighth Party Congress, a standing committee of the Politburo was set up which took over operational leadership of the Party. Presumably before that, Kao Kang had been able to use his position in the Party to put his own men into important positions.[44] Kao Kang also had been chairman of the People's Government of the Northeast, and later of the Administrative Committee for the Northeast. If one-man management created "unity of command," ergo centralization, the place of centralization was not Peking but Mukden, and even if the chain of command went to Peking, who but Kao Kang was in control of the economic apparatus?

One-man management thus can be regarded as a form of industrial management which was an essential part of branch-type administration. The one-man manager was solely responsible to higher-echelon branch agencies. Moreover, since one-man management was mostly implemented in the heavy industrial sector, it contributed to the power of the industrial ministries, over which Kao Kang, from his entrenched position in Manchuria and in the State Planning Commission, was able to exercise great power. Thus the way to fight Kao Kang, ministerial power, and one-man management was by stressing the collective leadership role of the Party. Peking's struggle to acquire control over the

---

[44] In his report to the Eighth Party Congress, Teng Hsiao-p'ing says the following about the Kao-Jao affair: "The basic characteristic of the Kao Kang Jao Shu-shih anti-Party alliance lay therein that they carried on widespread and unprincipled conspiratorial activities in order to seize supreme power in Party and state. This alliance took control of certain regions and operational branches and turned them into 'capital' for opposing the Central Committee and carrying on robbery actions, and for the same objective, in every region and within the People's Liberation Army carried out agitation against the Central Committee. Their conspiratorial activities completely went against the interests of Party and people, and only served the interests of the enemies of the Chinese people." The reference to "operational branches" undoubtedly means ministries concerned with the modern industrial sector. The reference to the People's Liberation Army implies that pro-Kao elements (and perhaps also pro-Soviet elements) were active there too.

system of economic administration thus can be said to have started in December 1953 and became open in February 1954 with the Fourth Plenum.

The Intensifying Critique

The Fourth Plenum had marked the beginning of the campaign to strengthen the authority of the Party at all levels of organization. The instruments of this campaign were the Party committees which existed in every unit or organization. Once Party solidarity had been reestablished after the purges of Kao, Jao, and the second-stringers, the campaign could begin in force. Decision-making power was to be returned unequivocally to the Party. But the struggle could not be won with one blow. One-man management was, after all, a viable method. It had worked in the Soviet Union and had helped it create the world's second-largest modern industrial establishment. One-man management had not made much headway in the smaller, more traditional industries of China, but it was the dominant method of management in the big modern industries. One could preach the principle of collective leadership by the Party committee, but what did this mean in practice? Managers have to make sudden decisions which do involve basic enterprise policy. A manager may have to clinch a deal on the spot for the supply of some material needed for production. Must all this be submitted now to the time-demanding processes of collective discussion? If it be granted that the Party committee has the power to make policy decisions, what then is the dividing line between "policy" and "technical" decisions? Could Party collegiality not end up the same way as bureaucratic collegiality in industry before 1949? These questions could not be answered by a decision of the Central Committee in Peking. Peking could only lay down the general policy and remove the organizational obstacles opposing it. But the concrete content of the new policy would have to be worked out slowly in individual enterprises.

In the course of 1954, fewer references were made to one-man management, and more to the need for collective leadership by the Party.[45]

An article published in *Ch'angchiang jihpao*, April 28, 1954, and written by a Wuhan City district Party secretary, denounced patriarchalism, individualism, arrogance, and complacency on the part of Party, government, and police cadres, and called for a return to collective leadership. The district Party secretary suggested: raise the quality

---

[45] See, for example, *Jenmin jihpao*, April 23, 1954. Interestingly, while *Takungpao* was publishing articles describing one-man management, *Jenmin jihpao* continued to sound the line of collective leadership.

of district committee meetings to allow for better decision-making; specify tasks but under unified over-all leadership; improve on planning by reducing the number of meetings, documents, directives, plans, and orders; and exercise more criticism and self-criticism, and rigorously check on work each four months.

Did individualism and arrogance in Wuhan Party, government, and police circles have any connection with one-man management? The following statements in the article suggest that they did:

> It is said about the leadership of the security police bureaus, "they do more work than other departments, and have had greater success"; "the cadres of that department are of higher quality and greater ability"; "they indulge and pamper the cadres of their own department." About the leadership of the industrial department of the district committee it is said that "factory work is the exclusive concern of the cadres of that department." They demand that the work of other departments submit to their own. They put their own department over all others, thus weakening Party solidarity and unity. The chief of the security police bureau [a member of the district committee] says, "I am an old Red Army cadre. In my personal history, I have never committed any errors." Therefore, he is arrogant about his bureau's successes, despises others, and always compares his own personal history, salary, and status with others.

We know that one-man management fostered independence on the part of industrial technocrats; it also created wedges between the Party and the ministries. If not the system of one-man management itself, the spirit of "individualism" and individual authority undoubtedly contributed to such tendencies. The criticism of the growing independence of the police is interesting. The suggestion that police work be more closely integrated into Party work indicates that here too no separate organizational entity was to be allowed to grow up.

More and more articles began to appear in national and local papers demanding a return to collective leadership and an abandonment of one-man decision-making. One article attacked the indifference of management cadres to Party-committee activities.

> Once in the [Shihchiachuang Textile Factory] Party committee, when we were studying the question of how to strengthen political and ideological work, the deputy factory manager in charge of technology (who was a member of the Party committee) didn't utter a word, and kept his head low reading some routine documents.[46]

The Chinese Communists have always been in the habit of singling out cases of offending individuals in order to prove a point. If one-

---

[46] *Hopei jihpao*, November 3, 1954.

man management was to be discredited, it was not difficult to find culpable one-man managers. There was, for example, the case of one Chao Han-ch'en, manager of the construction site where the new Hopei Province Labor Union Cadres School was being built. The case was published in detail on November 19, 1954, in *Hopei jihpao*. Chao was guilty of "violating the principle of collective leadership and causing grave damage." He had failed to realize that "any leader, no matter how much experience he has, who makes decisions individually, will always or almost always be wrong. Errors will develop in his work, which will cause grave damage to the affairs of the Party and the state."

The construction site had been started on July 1 of that year, but since the work plan had been only half completed, the training school had not been able to open in time. Because of his failures, other related construction projects were adversely affected. This came about "because the chief of the construction site, Chao Han-ch'en, violated the principle of collective leadership by the Party, arbitrarily made decisions, and would not accept control by Party organizations."

Chao Han-ch'en felt, the article continued, that the Party secretary and Party cadres knew nothing, that they were less capable than he, and that collective leadership was a waste of time; that management could get along without Party supervision. Why discuss anything with the Party committee? had been Chao's attitude. Make decisions yourself and carry them out. Even when things were going wrong, he had refused to accept suggestions from the Party committee, the article alleged. He had refused to report to the Party committee on his work. What reasons had he given for such behavior? "He was implementing one-man management. Others therefore have no authority to question his work. He failed to realize that this extremely serious tendency of alienation from control by the Party and the masses has nothing in common with implementing one-man management. Nor did he regularly participate in Party life. The head of his Party small group, Lu Ming-i, would always let him know when meetings were being held, but he never came." And furthermore, "he tried to create a little independent kingdom in the unit he managed . . . this is something that the Party cannot tolerate."

The term "independent kingdom" is significant: this was the chief accusation against Kao Kang. Chao Han-ch'en was a Party member, like most technocrats in Manchuria and elsewhere. He was accused of elevating his own managerial position above his responsibilities as a Party member. In fact, he had been doing no more than acting in accordance with the system of one-man management, which was still officially sanctioned. Despite the statement that Chao's actions had nothing in common with real one-man management, he was being attacked for one-man management.

On December 7, 1954, the *Jenmin jihpao* published an article by the deputy secretary of the Shihchiachuang City Party committee calling for a further strengthening of collective leadership by the Party. He made the by then common call for collective decision-making. Yet he pointed out that this had produced some adverse effects:

> There are some leading cadres and work departments who, in order to avoid the error of dispersionism, go to the opposite extreme. That is to say, regardless of whether the matter is big or small, regardless of whether the Party committee has or has not made a decision in principle on these matters, for every little thing they ask for an instruction, and make reports . . . Superficially they seem to be respecting leadership, but in reality they are simply shirking responsibility.

Here there was another problem. Administrations and managers, only a short time before urged to assume responsibility and authority, now got scared. The pendulum had begun to swing to the other extreme. To avoid trouble, every minor matter was submitted to the Party committee. The Chinese Communists wanted managers to assume responsibility without authority, but that was easier said than done. The Soviets had an answer: if a manager was to have responsibility under which he could be severely sanctioned, then he had to be given authority to try and do what he must. The Chinese had not yet worked out their own answer to this organizational dilemma.

During 1955, positive references to one-man management became still fewer. One article discussed ways of improving management in the paper-making industry, but failed to mention one-man management as one of the methods.[47] Other articles talked about strengthening responsibility, but usually in regard to production workers and industrial safety.

In January 1955, Ts'ao Ti-ch'iu, then First Secretary of the Chung-king Party Committee, published a report entitled "Raising the Level of Leadership of Cadres in State-owned Factories and Mines in the Management of Enterprises."[48] In contrast to the usual Communist reports, Ts'ao's was murky, indirect, cautious, and even conservative in tone. He began by pointing out that every factory and mine had "special conditions" which made it difficult to prescribe a definite system

---

[47] *Szechwan jihpao*, January 14, 1955.

[48] *Ibid.*, January 15, 1955. In February 1955, Ts'ao was transferred to Shanghai where he became deputy mayor of the city. From the latest information, he is still active there.

of management for each. He went on to point out how important co-ordination in a factory was, not only between individual sections of the enterprise, but between different enterprises: "If we are able to grasp the peculiarities and different arrangements obtaining in each factory and mine, if we understand their contradictory peculiarities, then it is not generally but concretely that we must proceed to resolve the problems of that factory or mine. This is beneficial for raising the management level of the enterprise."

Ts'ao then proceeded to make four general suggestions about how to raise the level of management: start from the actual conditions obtaining in the enterprise; study the advanced experiences of the Soviet Union, their experiences in industrial management, their advanced technology and science; study the advanced experiences of similar industries in China; and carry out directives from higher echelons.

Ts'ao made few further references to "the advanced experiences of the Soviet Union." He suggested that higher-echelon directives be rigorously obeyed, yet, "in carrying out the directives from higher echelons, we must adapt them to the real conditions in the factory or mine. That is to say we must carry out directives from higher echelons according to our own particular real conditions, and we must not regard these directives from higher echelons as dogma."

Then Ts'ao came to speak of one-man management:

In some factories the conditions for carrying out the one-man management system were not ripe, and the system was prematurely put through. On the other hand, in order to carry out the directive from higher echelons, we felt that many factories and mines were ready, but many did it too mechanically. Thus some factories, when carrying out instructions from higher echelons to put through the one-man management system, failed to solve many key problems which at that time obstructed production, threw aside all kinds of work plans which had already demonstrated their effectiveness, forgot about production, forgot about reality, just in order to put through the one-man management system. They erroneously thought that once the one-man management system was put through all problems could be solved. The result was that serious confusion resulted in production; tasks were not completed. This is the inevitable result of not observing objective reality.

Ts'ao then suggested that there were four aspects of management, all of which together constituted socialist management: plan management; technological management; the system of sole responsibility by management, namely one-man management; and cost-accounting management. He stated that all four aspects must be properly developed in order to have good management; yet it was difficult to develop them simultaneously. He bewailed the fact that few factories as yet had the requisite conditions for "fully implementing all four types of management." He noted that many industrial managers were still hold-overs from the prerevolutionary period, men who were not ideologically prepared to carry out a fully socialist system of management. Besides, there were many cadres from local areas and the army who "ideologically still have many ideas which are not beneficial for socialist industrial construction." Ts'ao offered as a recommendation only that economic and political work, economic and political decision-making, be tied closely together. The Party committee was to be consulted on all major questions.

As far as management in factories and mines is concerned, their most important task is to do economic work, to manage the enterprise well, constantly work to raise the level of management in the enterprise, and to raise technology. The major task of the Party committee is to do political work. *The object of political work is men, that is to say the men who manage the enterprise and who take part in production.*

Ts'ao's comments on the difficulties of implementing one-man management illustrate dilemmas faced by all developing economies. The history of industry in the West is not only one of technological development, but one of constant struggle to devise organizational forms to realize the fruits of that development. The industrial revolution brought with it the organizational revolution. In China, we see a similar struggle to find adequate organizational forms for implementing economic development. The struggle is complex because politics enters into everything. Every minor readjustment can be interpreted as a political action with grave consequences. Modern technology is complex, but organization, at least in its early stages, should be clean-lined and simple. The immense apparatus of reasoning which the Communists brought onto the Chinese scene would indicate that here they had an instrument for making things simple. Instead, as in the Soviet Union, endemic confusion resulted. Ts'ao's statement about every enterprise having its own peculiar circumstances makes good sense. Peking could have allowed different management procedures to fit concrete circumstances and then applied regulatory pressures from above. But this was not possible, for the command system demanded organizational uniformity. Orders came down through the channels of economic command insisting that one-man management be implemented. The professionals were in charge in Peking, and their commands were diffused outward throughout the country. Orders have to be obeyed. Yet at the same time, local Party people knew that a Party struggle was going on. The ministries sought to enforce one-man management, but the

Party committees told the manager to go easy. What should the manager do? He was caught in a cross-fire of command. He was, after all, responsible to the ministries for plan fulfillment, and on that hinged his future investment quotas, supply allocations, profit premiums, and so on. If the ministries were unhappy with him, they could be very hard on him. But then to obey the ministries meant making the local Party people unhappy. Ts'ao was an old Party man and told the enterprises to "observe objective reality." In effect, he was saying: do what you can to keep production going, and forget about one-man management. By January 1955, everyone knew how the wind was blowing.

A Chinese View of Soviet Methods

By the middle of 1955, one-man management as a system was clearly declining. Its demise was a consequence of the struggle of the Chinese Communists against the development of centers of power other than the Party. It was, in particular, the political consequences of one-man management which the Chinese Communists regarded as dangerous. But one-man management also was an economic method closely linked to the needs of a centrally planned economy. One may therefore ask whether the Chinese Communists realized that in rejecting one-man management they were also doing away with a key element in the administration of a Soviet-type economy. When Stalin introduced one-man management into the Soviet Union in the early 1930's, he saw it both as a political method for assuring centralized control and as an economic method for making central planning operative. Moreover, he saw it as a means of making technology dominant in the Soviet system. In 1931, Stalin said:

It is time we cast aside the old slogan, the obsolete slogan of noninterference in technique, and ourselves become specialists, experts, complete masters of our economy. It is frequently asked: Why have we not one-man management? We do not have it and will not have it until we have mastered technique. . . . Hence, the task is for us to master technique ourselves, to become masters of the business ourselves. This is the sole guarantee that our plans will be carried out in full, and that one-man management will be established. . . . It is time to adopt a new policy adapted to the present times—the policy of *interfering in everything*. If you are a factory manager, then interfere in all the affairs of the factory, look into everything, let nothing escape you, learn and learn again.[49]

A few months later at another conference of business executives, on June 23, 1931, Stalin made the new policy even more explicit:

---

[49] *Problems of Leninism* (Moscow, 1954), pp. 454-455, 457.

Further, our combines must substitute one-man management for collegium management. The position at present is that there are from ten to fifteen men on the board of a combine, all writing papers and carrying on discussions. We cannot go on managing in this way, comrades. We must put a stop to paper "management," and get down to genuine, businesslike, Bolshevik work. Let one president and several vice-presidents remain at the head of a combine. This will be quite enough to take care of its management. The remaining members of the board should be sent to the factories and mills. That will be far more useful, both for the businesses and for themselves.[50]

Stalin was passionately determined to create a mammoth heavy industry in the Soviet Union. He knew that it was impossible to build a modern industry with bureaucrats.

In the early part of this chapter, we noted that the Russians implemented industrialization with a corps of professionally trained managers whereas the Chinese Communists relied on their politically trained cadres. However, until the final struggle with Kao Kang, the Chinese Communists were committed to the Russian method; it was only at the Fourth Plenum that the Chinese Communists started a process that gradually shifted emphasis from managers to cadres, a process that reached its high point during the Great Leap Forward. There is enough evidence from the early 1950's to indicate that the Chinese Communists knew that their political cadres were incapable of managing modern factories. One may therefore ask: once the struggle with Manchuria had been won, why did the Chinese Communists not go back to a policy of rapidly developing a technological and managerial elite? A general answer to this question is provided by a theme that goes throughout this book—until the economic crisis of 1960-1961, the Chinese Communists felt that all decision-making powers must be concentrated in the hands of the Party, regardless of the economic consequences. In the mid-1950's, they believed that a division of labor between cadres and managers was possible; cadres would control policy, and managers would control operations. By 1958, they so extolled politics over economics that they came close to dismantling their planning system. They cut down management staffs to the bone, and reduced complex industrial designing to meaningless simplicities. Their attitude to the economic consequences of "Politics Takes Command" was expressed in the frequently heard phrase "the fetishism of technology"—*chishu shenpihua*. The extremes of this attitude were not reached until 1958, but the beginnings were in the period under discussion, the middle fifties.

---

[50] *Ibid.*, p. 481.

We have early in this section asked whether the Chinese Communists were aware of the economic consequences of doing away with one-man management. The same question can be put in a slightly different way —did they have a real understanding of the history of industrial management in the Soviet Union? During the early 1950's, much of the literature on the Soviet Union consisted of translations from the Russian and of hagiographic writings by the Chinese. The character of these writings makes it difficult to know whether the Chinese really understood the reality of Soviet history, and in particular the history of industrial management. However, in 1950, a Shanghai publisher (Commercial Press) "reprinted" a small volume on Soviet industrial management by a man named Wu Ch'ing-yu.[51] This small volume differs from most similar publications by its frank language and lack of jargon. Wu Ch'ing-yu gives the following remarkable account of the development of Soviet industrial management (pp. 22-26):

"In discussing the authority of the Soviet factory director, we must think of it in connection with the problem of the origin of the Soviet system of factory management and the training and selection of management personnel. Once the civil war was finished, the Soviet Union undertook the task of industrial reconstruction. At that time, the Soviet Union already carried out a policy of nationalization of industry. It had great need for new talent for industrial management. These new people, on the one hand, had to be absolutely reliable politically, and on the other hand they had to have special education and experience for managing industry.

"Therefore, there arose a particular kind of system adapted to the real conditions of the time. This system was: on the one hand putting economic commissars (equivalent to factory directors) in factory leadership positions (most of them were selected from Party members who were advanced working-class elements); on the other hand, appointing an assistant director who was called the technical supervisor (he had to be an engineer with considerable experience). Together the economic commissars and the technical supervisors constituted a two-layered system of management. (Sometimes the factory director was the expert and a Party committee man stood at his side as supervisor.) This, together with the subsequent union structure, constituted a triangular relationship among factory director, Party organization, and union. As the process of industrial reconstruction came to an end, at a time when further development and industrial planning were being implemented,

---

[51] *Sulien ti kungyeh kuanli* (Shanghai, 1950).

the Soviet government recognized the necessity of radically reforming its policy of selecting factory-management personnel.

"Therefore, in July 1928, a plenary meeting of the Soviet Central Committee decided to push for the training of new technical talent, mostly within the working class. Study time in engineering colleges and technical schools was shortened; specialized courses were stressed; it was decided that working-class elements should constitute at least 65 per cent of all new students in engineering colleges and technical schools. Also, special scholarships were set up, and other kinds of incentives. Each year, at least one thousand Party members were sent to school to study engineering. These were people who had to have had concrete experience in Party, government or union activities. Old factory members who were in the Party were given more technical training. Aside from their vacations, these factory managers were given six weeks to two months off each year to increase their knowledge and skills. At the same time, ways were devised to allow these managers to continue on the job while undergoing training. There were correspondence courses, private courses organized by the government, special courses, and other similar devices. After 1929, the Central Committee and the Central Control Commission again stressed setting up more short-term engineering colleges, and ruled that workers must constitute at least 70 per cent of all new students. Party members sent for special instruction would be increased to 2,000-3,000 annually. The Komsomol was instructed to prepare 5,000 students each year to go into engineering colleges. Moreover, ways were to be devised to raise the educational level of outstanding workers so they could be promoted to manager.

"The social significance of this cadre policy remained unchanged, but the actual educational methods vis-à-vis the new cadres were revised in 1932. In order to speed up the training of technical personnel, more engineering colleges and technical schools were set up which took in several hundred thousand students for extremely specialized education, with the result that standards for technical education declined. Thereupon, the Soviet government ordered an extension of the educational period, improved courses, and instituted more rigorous entrance requirements. As a result of this new cadre policy, the old technical intelligentsia lost its dominant function in the factories and began to be replaced by Party economic commissars who had undergone technical training. From that time on, Party specialists rose to top positions in ever increasing numbers. During the period from 1936 to 1938, widespread and far-reaching changes took place in Soviet industrial leadership personnel. As a result of the Party purges, leadership personnel that had occupied important positions in Soviet industrial enterprises and who were in opposition to the Soviet government were liquidated and replaced by new people. With new models, new backgrounds, experiences, and attitudes, they represented a new social stratum. The purge of old cadres in industry was very far-reaching; the scope of liquidation was not restricted to engineers but reached just about everyone in the factory. Those purged not only lost their political position, but suffered the most severe punishment.

"The new industrial leaders were youths just out of school. They had received a good education, one which stressed their specializations as well as political problems. Most of them tended toward authoritarian thoughts: Leninism and Stalinism. Therefore, they were completely loyal to Stalin. They recognized that only under the system represented by Stalin did they have the chance to get ahead. This kind of faith had already taken deep roots. Since these young Communists matured at a time when opposition groups within the Party collapsed and lost their honor and when positive faith in Stalin was growing, in their eyes Stalin was the root source of Russia's economic progress and international status. They understood that for industrialization and rearmament, you must pay a considerable price. Thus they were willing to suffer privation in order to construct industrial progress and a society the like of which capitalism did not have—a proletarian society, leading to wealth, power, harmony, and happiness."

Wu Ch'ing-yu, in effect, said that Stalin was the god of the new technical intelligentsia of the Soviet Union. The old technical intelligentsia, remaining from prerevolutionary days, was liquidated in the great purges. The new young technocrats hardly remembered prerevolutionary Russia. They were schooled under Stalin, and when opportunities were created by the purges, they stepped into the positions of those liquidated.

In many respects, the Chinese Communists followed the same policy. Recruitment of worker and peasant children for higher education was stressed. Special schools for technological training, along lines of Soviet *tekhnikums*, were set up all over China. Favoritism was consistently shown to students going into technical fields. As in Russia during the 1920's, a technical intelligentsia deriving from the period before 1949 continued to exist in China. These were largely individuals of bourgeois origin, coming from the great Westernized coastal cities of China. There are indications that the bourgeoisie even today continues to supply many of the students for China's institutions of advanced learning.

When the Chinese Communists, during the mid-1950's, began to reduce the power of the managers, they were intent on replacing an old technical intelligentsia with a new group of politically loyal cadres. In this respect, they tried to do more or less what Stalin did in the early 1930's (as Wu Ch'ing-yu correctly described it). However, whereas Stalin created a new technical intelligentsia loyal to himself, the Chinese Communists appeared to despair of bringing into being a corps of new industrial leaders with an education which "stressed their specializations as well as political problems," as Wu Ch'ing-yu put it. Earlier in this chapter, we have noted that in the early years after 1949, the Chinese Communists emphasized education and skill as criteria for Party membership. However, from the mid-1950's on, they increasingly stressed political loyalty and leadership ability for potential candidates. Despite the favoritism shown the children of workers and peasants in the fields of higher education (particularly scientific and technical), not enough "red and expert" cadres were produced to match the kind of technical intelligentsia that Stalin trained in the Soviet Union. Given the weakness of technical organization in China, the Communists had to rely mainly on the instruments of human organization to achieve their goals. For this, they had far greater resources at their command than the still small number of technically trained workers and peasants. It was thus that the Chinese Communist cadre with his roots in a combat tradition, from the mid-1950's on, began to emerge as the dominant figure in the country's economic affairs.

A full answer to the questions posed above, why the Chinese did not go back to a policy of developing a technological and managerial elite, can probably only be given by a comparative study of Soviet and Chinese educational capabilities at comparable periods of their development. Wu Ch'ing-yu describes what in effect was a crash program for the training of technical intellectuals launched in the Soviet Union in 1928. By the mid-1930's, when Stalin's purges liquidated the old technical intelligentsia, enough new technical intellectuals had been trained to take over the vacant positions. China in 1949 was far behind Russia in 1917 as to levels of education and literacy. The Chinese Communists did not have sufficient educational facilities for the rapid training of a new technical intelligentsia. Thus one might conclude that, even if the Chinese Communists had wanted to continue a one-man management policy, with young technically trained managers supplanting the old, they did not have the human resources to do so.[52]

One can also conclude that they were fully aware of the real history

---

[52] In 1955, only 5 percent of the top leaders and only 50 percent of the technical personnel of industrial enterprises were graduates of higher schools; see *Hsinhua panyüeh-k'an*, 2 (January 1957), 89.

of industrial management in the Soviet Union. They knew that in the mid-1930's Stalin wanted to put individuals in charge of industry who were both red and expert, and to a large extent succeeded in so doing. Like Stalin, they too wanted politically loyal men managing factories rather than men characterized only by technical and managerial skills. Since they were unable to combine red and expert effectively in the form of a new worker-peasant intelligentsia, they turned over greater power to the red cadres.

THE GROWTH OF PARTY AUTHORITY OVER MANAGEMENT

The Abolition of One-man Management

The decline of the one-man-management system occurred during a significant period of Chinese economic history. Though the First Five-Year Plan had theoretically been in operation for several years, it was only in the summer of 1955 that a great drive was launched to speed up plan fulfillment. It was also in the summer of 1955 that the program of agricultural collectivization was laid out, and made ready for implementation during the fall of that year. It was the political unity, finally achieved late in 1954, that made both these drives possible. In many ways, the latter half of 1955 was a prelude to the Great Leap Forward. The theme of "attacking production" began to appear at this time; Youth League cadres began to lead production teams. But early in 1956, the political atmosphere changed radically. Mao's plans to continue with uninterrupted collectivization and industrialization were abruptly checked, and China entered a period of consolidation. The regime ordered a slowdown both in industry and agriculture. The Hunderd Flowers policy (encouraging freedom of expression among intellectuals) which commenced in May 1956 became symbolic of the new relaxation. The wage reform improved living conditions in the cities. The peasants were in bad shape, but at least the collectivization drive had been slowed down. In September 1956, the Chinese Communists held their Eighth Party Congress, the first since the Seventh Party Congress in April 1945. The Eighth Congress took place in a spirit of unity and stock-taking, with the general policy lines for the future being set forth.

It was in this context of a new sense of unity, particularly of Party unity, that the official demise of one-man management was announced. The announcement was somewhat anticlimactic, for already on July 8, the *Jenmin jihpao* had published an article about the "experiences" of a factory in Mukden which had tried one-man management and had abandoned it in favor of collective leadership by Party committee. The fact that a factory in Manchuria had been singled out was significant, in view of the close association of one-man management and Manchuria. Clearly, by the summer of 1956, Party organizations had acquired control over the country's industrial system.

The new system of industrial management, henceforth to be the norm in all industry, was announced in a report to the Eighth Party Congress by Li Hsüeh-feng, Director of the Industrial Bureau of the Central Committee of the Party. The new system was officially called "factory-manager (director) responsibility under the leadership of the Party committee." In Li Hsüeh-feng's words, the new system combined Party collective leadership with individual responsibility. Thus, though the extensive authority conferred on the factory managers by one-man management was now withdrawn, full individual responsibility for performance was to remain with them. Li stated that there were still comrades who demanded the retention of one-man management. They "one-sidedly demand concentrated administration." "They mechanically say that since the manager has full responsibility, he should have full authority." Such attitudes are false, said Li, for they ignore the successful experiences the Party has had in the army with "the system of divided responsibility by [unit] chiefs under the collective leadership of the Party committee."

Li continued his criticism of bad practices in industry. There are still some comrades, he stated, who ignore the Party's call for a furtherance of the mass line, and instead develop bureaucratic tendencies. They one-sidedly demand administration from the top down. They emphasize the giving of orders, and disregard criticism and suggestions from the masses. They are a small minority who sit behind closed doors and make up plans. They do not thoroughly investigate and study what is going on in the plant. They are contemptuous of worker delegate meetings. They take the attitude that at such meetings the plant manager reports, the Party issues directives, the unions coin the slogans, and the masses carry them out. Many plant managers do not rely on persuasion, education, and administrative discipline in mobilizing the workers to fulfill their targets. Often they simply use punitive measures to maintain discipline. Nor is it the factory managers alone who are at fault. Quite often Party organizations and labor unions themselves use coercion to get workers to participate in after-hours activities. Furthermore, they often completely ignore the workers' problems, thus worsening relations between the Party and the masses.

This, said Li, is the phenomenon of bureaucratism and subjectivism. These adverse phenomena can only be countered through combining highly centralized administration with a high degree of democracy. Too many factory managers are only concerned about production tasks and machinery, and pay insufficient attention to the development of positivism and creativity of workers. The leadership methods of the mass line have been shown to be effective, Li argued. Practically, this can be done in the following way. Management must take the initiative in drawing up a draft plan. However, this plan must be presented to the mass organizations for discussion. After that, the actual plan can be drawn up. Though the factory plan must be based on targets given by the state plan, still it must take into account the real situation in the plant. It is only by allowing the targets of the state plan to be modified by the requirements of concrete conditions that the fulfillment of plan targets can be assured. Centralized planning alone may achieve temporary successes, yet in the long run it cannot guarantee constancy in plan fulfillment. Some may object that the complex technology of modern industry does not allow for such a system, said Li, but this is not so. By constantly urging the workers and technicians to study and make new rationalization proposals, the new system of plant management can be made effective. Factory managers must henceforth accept criticism from the workers, from below. The Party committees must also improve the quality of their work. Incompetent Party cadres are to be transferred. Criticism and self-criticism are to be furthered. At the present, Li added, between 10 and 20 per cent of all workers in industrial enterprises are Party members. Almost all factory leaders are now Party members. With such a powerful Party apparatus, closer links between leadership and the masses can be forged. Not only at the local plant level, but in higher-echelon bureau and Party organizations as well, a new attitude must be developed. Higher echelons must also adopt the policy of "the top following the bottom, of officers following their men."

Li ended by stating that if the new system of collective leadership was not adopted, "one cannot maintain constancy" in plan fulfillment, though he admitted that targets could still continue to be met.

Li's description of the new policy on industrial management must be seen in the over-all context of the Eighth Party Congress. The theme of the mass line foreshadowed two developments that were to be of great significance for the coming years: growing Party domination and moves toward decentralization. As we have indicated in the chapter on government, both of these developments ultimately led to a weakening of ministerial control, vertical rule, and branch-type administration. Since one-man management was designed to fit into such a system of economic administration, its replacement by collective leadership of

the Party committee was the beginning step in a far-reaching modification of that system. Moreover, since one-man management was also a
mechanism for implementing a centralized economy, its abandonment
meant a concrete step on the road to decentralization.

Management under Collective Leadership

The new system of collective leadership in some ways was a reversion to traditional management practices in Chinese industry. All
major decisions were to be made collectively at the top, but the manager still was responsible for operations. He operated with authority
delegated to him by a body which somewhat resembled the old board of
directors; but the Party cadres making up the Party committee were
usually workers promoted from the ranks, and thus were much closer
to the employees than the old bourgeois directors.

As a result, the traditional manager-worker gap was no longer tolerated. Collegiality now meant getting together with the Party committee
at the top and also with the workers at the bottom. All top Party committee members were expected to talk with workers, find out their
problems, ferret out bottlenecks. The new system facilitated decision-
making. If trouble arose, the manager went down into the plant, consulted with those involved, and made an *ad hoc* decision. Although
collective leadership deprived the managers of some powers, it also
gave them a new sphere of action. This was expressed in the distinction
made between policy decisions and technical decisions. If any matter
related to policy, the manager had to bring it before the Party committee for collective decision; if the problem was technical, he could
make the decision on the spot. To make sure that these decisions were
realistic, the manager had to make them on the production floor where
he could see what the concrete problems were. In practice, however, it
was difficult to differentiate policy from technical matters, as became
evident soon.

Under the management system that prevailed in the early 1950's,
the manager usually left technical decisions about operations to his
staff. Since Chinese factories have tended to be overstaffed (both before
and after 1949), there were enough staff assistants around to direct operations. The manager, on the other hand, was mainly concerned with
policy problems: production targets, negotiations with ministries, conclusion of contracts with other firms, outside contacts in general; aside
from his role as top executive, he was also an intermediary between the
factory and outside organizations. Now, in 1956, these functions were
taken over by the Party committee. The manager's main responsibility

was operational, to assure the achievement of policy goals within the factory. He became more of a technician and was thrown into increasingly close contact with the workers, although not yet to the extent that would be true at the time of the Great Leap Forward, when the Chinese Communists tried to erase distinctions between managers and workers by making managers work and workers manage.

The Eighth Party Congress was followed by campaigns to implement its decisions. Many articles appeared publicizing collective leadership. Thus, the Peking *Kungjen jihpao* of October 6, 1956, discussing the system in the Construction Work Company of Anshan Mine No. 2, wrote:

> Under the leadership of the Party committee, we regularly held team production meetings, section workers' delegates meetings, economic activities analysis meetings, staff operations analysis meetings. Thereby we developed and concentrated the wisdom of the masses, and changed the system of management in the enterprise. . . . The Party committee regularly organized cadres to go into the workers' quarters, to resolve difficulties in workers' living, to improve work done by workers' dependents, thus raising the awareness and production positivism of the workers.

Other articles began to point out the evils of one-man management. *Kwangsi jihpao* (September 25, 1956) stated that under one-man management the manager simply issued orders without bothering to consult the workers. The workers complained: "He never asked us anything, and just wanted us to work ourselves to death!" But now, stated the paper, the members of the Party committee talked over things with the workers, urging them to make proposals about the best ways to achieve targets.

The distinction between "policy" and "technical" decisions must be rigorous, asserted the paper, adding:

> The leadership system which combines collective leadership with the Party as core and individual responsibility means that all important problems in the factory must undergo collective discussion and decision by the Party committee. Everyday work within the factory, however, is to be directed by specialists in charge.

And the *Kiangsi jihpao* of November 2, 1956, commented that in some factories the new system was misunderstood to mean that management would henceforth be carried out by the Party. This was attacked as an erroneous view. In one factory, the paper said, the manager wanted to buy a rubber ball. He solemnly submitted the problem to the Party committee for policy decision. This action was wrong and a manifestation of failure to understand the principle that "everyday work was to be done by specialists in charge."

Collective leadership had actually been in effect in many factories, simply because one-man management had never been universally implemented. Articles now appeared extolling the traditions of collective leadership which such factories had built up. One was a state-owned cotton-spinning mill in Wuhan, where collective leadership had prevailed since August 1953. As an article in the *Jenmin jihpao* (December 16, 1956) put it: "Before every meeting of the Party committee in this factory, the top leaders took up the problems to be discussed and together created the necessary 'distillation.' "

The term "distillation," *yünniang*, is often used to describe processes of discussion and collective decision-making. The leaders of the meeting, of course, already have the ultimate decision in mind. But Chinese Communist procedures of decision-making require that the problems be precisely formulated so that the decision appears to flow naturally from this formulation. It is hoped that contrary opinions will be expressed, so that the dissenters can be convinced, *shuofu*, by the logic of the presentation. Decisions must never be forced.

The article described a concrete instance of how this new method operated:

This year when the Party committee was making up the plan for the entire year, some of the Party committee members felt that the method of speeding machine revolutions could be used to increase this year's production of cotton yarn by 1,000 pieces each. But the factory manager feared that this could adversely influence the quality of the yarn, and disagreed with their opinions. Despite the fact that these opinions had gone through a preliminary "distillation" and repeated discussion by the Party committee, unity was not achieved. After this, the Party secretary and the factory manager, who persisted in their disagreement, talked over the problem privately, and decided that both together should "penetrate the reality" and find out the truth. Thereafter, after a number of trials in the shop, it became clear that increasing yarn production by a thousand pieces would not result in a decline in quality. Both then achieved unanimity of opinion. And indeed in the light of current production, it has again been shown that the decision of the Party committee was correct.

The question of whether to speed up the machines or not required a policy decision. It meant not only that the workers would have to adjust to a new pace, but that the quality of the yarn might suffer. If quality fell, the factory manager would be held responsible. He naturally supported the more conservative course of leaving machine speeds as they had been. But through persistent discussion and talk, the factory manager was brought around "to agree." This, then, was a model case of the proper approach in collective decision-making.[53]

Though the collective leadership system called for a change in management practices, not all aspects of the one-man management system were to be changed. Some good things had been introduced into industry with the old system which were to be retained.

We must not confuse leadership in a factory with scientific management in the sphere of production and administration. . . . Many management systems which were established at that time, such as setting up regular production order, defining responsibilities, strengthening labor discipline, overcoming confusion, and so on—all of these have a definite function.[54]

In other words, those aspects of one-man management which contributed to rationalization and specificity in the division of labor were to be retained.

The same article emphasized that collective leadership did not mean a reduction in the importance of individual responsibility. It attacked the prevalent notion that collective leadership "denies the function of the individual." In some factories, managers were afraid of making independent decisions and constantly went to the Party committee with every problem, large or small. "This is an incorrect phenomenon," the article pointed out, and is "a perversion of the system of collective leadership by the Party." It continued:

Because of the peculiar characteristics of industrial production, we will demand that the system of work responsibility be strengthened. All important questions are to be discussed by the Party committee and jointly decided on, but everyday work must be directed individually by specialists. The Party organization must allow management leaders to have all the necessary authority. In every way the system of factory-manager responsibility must be strengthened, so that [the managers] decisively and resolutely can resolve problems relating to routine production and administration work.

Even when it was possible to separate "policy" from "technical" problems, other difficulties arose. The members of the Party committee, often the committee secretary himself, lacked the competence to decide on major policy questions, which included plan-drafting, finances, im-

---

53 For an account of how the Party increased production by speeding up the machines, see Stanley Karnow, "The G.I. Who Chose Communism," *Saturday Evening Post*, November 16, 1963.

54 *Nanfang jihpao*, December 18, 1956.

portant technological procedures, workers' wages and welfare problems, and the like. An article in a Manchurian paper noted these problems:

The members of the Party committees lack knowledge of production; they are not experienced in business. This has brought about considerable difficulties in correctly making decisions on important production problems. In order to strengthen the Party's core leadership function, cadres in planning, technology, finances, and so on should be recruited to supplement the Party's core leadership forces. This is very necessary. Naturally it is also very important that we strengthen study of production and business by leadership cadres who are presently members of the Party committees.[55]

Many of the technocrats were undoubtedly older men who had received their training before 1949. Though less amenable to Party indoctrination, they were now to be brought into the Party to undergo the full effect of training and indoctrination.

If the change represented a shift from individualism to collectivism, it also represented a swing from "centralism" to "democracy." "Democracy" meant not only that the cadres must now move into the front line of production, but that information from below was to flow up faster and better than before. "Democracy" meant more meetings, more talk, *shangliang*.[56] Many articles noted the dangerous tendency toward numerous and never-ending meetings, yet collective leadership could not function without such meetings. The Chinese penchant for *shangliang* so irritated the Soviet experts in earlier years that they pressed for one-man managers with authority to whom they could make their "proposals" with the expectation that fast action would be taken on them.

Collective leadership meant not only a lateral shift of authority (from managers to Party committee), but also a downward shift of decision-making powers. Under one-man management, the authority of technicians, staff section cadres, and others farther down the hierarchy had been limited. All orders had to come from the factory manager before they could be implemented. As one article put it, "it had been required that all personnel mechanically obey the orders of the factory manager as an individual."[57] Under the new system, lower-level cadres again acquired decision-making powers:

The Talien Steel Factory Party organization . . . changed the shortcoming that all business in the factory was concentrated in the hands of a small

[55] *Kirin jihpao*, December 19, 1956.
[56] *Tsingtao jihpao*, December 26, 1956.
[57] *Ibid.*, December 28, 1956.

minority of men. High-ranking cadres and factory managers who earlier acted in a free-wheeling manner now encouraged independent responsibility on the part of the deputy managers and staff section chiefs. It also changed the earlier habit of management cadres fearing to take responsibility, of always asking for instructions on every matter.

In the scores of articles which appeared in the months following the Eighth Party Congress, the new system of industrial management was not so much discussed in terms of specific policy lines laid down in Peking, as in terms of practical problems. One of the most difficult questions was a definition of what "important problems" required collective policy decisions. One article discussed this problem as it was faced in factories of the highly industrialized Liaoning Province. What was an "important problem for one factory was not for another." The article listed the following as generally "important problems": production planning, important economic and technological procedures for carrying out the state plan, workers' welfare, problems arising from directives from higher echelons, work assignments over a given time period, the appointment, transfer, rewarding, and punishing of cadres. The article called on Party committees to give management broad scope for making individual decisions, but also demanded that Party committees study economic problems, discover production bottlenecks, and carry on political and ideological work.[58]

Although Party and managers undoubtedly wrangled over spheres of authority, there were two decision-making areas where the Party demanded primacy, as the mentioned article pointed out: personnel matters and formulation of the state plan. All matters relating to employees (workers and cadres alike) had to be submitted to the Party committee, the article pointed out. Under one-man management, the manager decided on personnel problems. Now the issue was clearly decided in favor of the Party.

To have a voice in the setting of the state plan was extremely important. Draft plans which went up to the ministries were initiated by the enterprise on the basis of often vague control figures. These draft plans were important to the higher-echelon planners in designing their final plans. A voice of the Party committee in formulating the enterprise draft plan meant direct Party influence on the entire course of enterprise economic activity.

By this time, the technocrats had to concede this point. On the other hand, they wanted broad operational freedom to direct production. The Party was willing to concede such freedom in 1956. However,

---

[58] *Liaoning jihpao*, April 24, 1957.

later, when the Great Leap Forward came, the managers would find themselves accused of conservatism and, even worse, of "rightist tendencies" arising from their unwillingness to accept absolute Party leadership in operational matters.

INCREASE IN INDUSTRIAL EMPLOYEES

Year	Number of employees (in millions, rounded off)
1949	3.0
1952	4.9
1953	6.2
1954	6.4
1955	6.5
1956	8.7
1957	9.0
1958	25.7[a]

[a] Includes industrial employees in the people's communes.

SOURCE: *Weita ti shih-nien* (Peking, 1959), p. 162.

The Great Leap Forward Conception of Management

By 1958 the Chinese Communist conception of industrial management had come full circle from the early 1950's. Then, following the Soviet model, they gave full authority over policy and operations to the managers, warning the Party committees to restrict their activities to ideology and labor discipline. The abolition of one-man management and the adoption of collective leadership gave policy-making powers to the Party, but still left managers the right to operate the factories. In 1958 the Party assumed operational leadership as well. Party committees made policy decisions; production teams led by Party cadres carried them out.

The Great Leap Forward approach to management was characterized by Mao Tse-tung's slogan "Concentration of the Great Authority, and Dispersion of the Small Authority," or, as it was also put: "Concentrated Leadership and Divided Management." In essence, this approach held that once the major decisions were made at the top of an organizational unit, the authority to carry them out should be spread far afield and far down. Thus, once Peking made general decisions on economic goals, the provinces could fend for themselves in implementing them. Similarly, if the Party committee of an enterprise made decisions on basic production targets, the production units were to devise their own

operational means for carrying them out. There was to be little supervision and control, only a final accounting when the production period
had ended.

In many ways, this approach to management was a throwback to
pre-1949 practices. In the typical pre-1949 Chinese factory, operational
matters were left to the manager by the board of directors; the manager
in turn often left them up to the gang boss. The gang boss would make
an agreement with the manager to produce so and so much during a
given period, in return for a lump sum to be divided among the gang
members. This was earlier known as the *pao* system, and, indeed, the
word *pao* returned again during the Great Leap Forward. Production
teams both in industry and agriculture made *pao* contracts with managers and commune chiefs respectively, thus making it unnecessary for
the latter to bother with operational details.

Before 1949 the *pao* system predominated in small factories. These
undertakings relied heavily on labor, had little capital, and were technologically simple. The typical work area was characterized by a group
of people performing different kinds of tasks, where human relations
counted for more than technical division of labor. During the Great
Leap Forward, the Chinese Communists moved from the earlier extreme of building gigantic factories to the opposite extreme of building
large numbers of small- and medium-scale factories throughout the
country.[59] Since these factories often used·native techniques, they were
heralded as the models for all industry to follow. Obviously a steel
plant could not be operated with practices suited to a backyard steel
furnace, yet so great was the power of Party and ideology that even the
complex industries had to introduce the new methods.

The policy of concentrated leadership and divided management
brought about a break in the span of control which went beyond the
conventional policy-operations gap, where those on top set policy and
those on the bottom concerned themselves with operational details. It
was rather a situation in which operational details were disregarded.
There was an uninterrupted span of control in regard to all general
targets. If an order went down, it was promptly obeyed, usually with
even more zeal than was called for. Thus, in a political sense, authority
remained concentrated. But just as economic controls came close to
vanishing, so did technical and operational controls. The top was
usually uncertain what was happening on the production floor, except

---

[59] Shigeru Ishikawa, "Choice of Techniques in Mainland China," *The Developing
Economies* (Tokyo, September-December 1962), p. 34.

that it could rely on enthusiastic cadres. One area in which production suffered particularly was quality control. Shoddiness has always been a major problem in Soviet-type economies, but it reached disastrous proportions during the Great Leap Forward. Few at the top dared censure those below for turning out substandard products. As long as targets were fulfilled in some gross physical sense, the cadres had acquitted themselves adequately.

Much in this conception of management is similar to the guerrilla warfare waged by the men of Yenan. The production team was regarded somewhat like the guerrilla band. Policy-wise it followed orders strictly, but operationally it had considerable leeway to fend for itself. The Chinese Communists deliberately sought to model industrial management on guerrilla warfare; once Party cadres had taken control, they began to act like combat leaders. Moreover, decentralization had led to a growth of Party power in regional and local areas. The further down from Peking into the provinces, the less sophisticated were the cadres, and the closer to their worker and peasant backgrounds. These cadres, while denouncing the fetishism of technology, made a fetishism of production and construction. They sincerely believed that the wisdom and experiences of the masses could produce and construct much more than the complex designs of engineers. The press printed numerous stories of cadres who told draftsmen that a few lines would suffice for blueprints, or that planning and balance charts could be reduced from one hundred and fifty pages to a single page. It was enough that the Party committee ordered that a new textile factory, for example, be built, without going into great detail how it should be done. Tasks were handed out to the production teams, which often had the full responsibility of finding construction materials, making their own tools, and doing their own accounting. Since there was little left for managers and technicians to do, they were sent down to the production floor to labor alongside the workers.

Given the conception of economic development which dominated the Great Leap Forward, the tasks of administrators and managers became redundant. In May 1958, Liu Shao-ch'i propounded the new conception, asserting that economic balance was an illusion, that development occurred through waves of balance and imbalance. A leap forward necessarily created imbalance, a phenomenon that was to be welcomed and not to be combated. This conception had a disastrous effect on the planning system. Chinese planners, most of whom were trained in the country's higher schools, spent most of their time drawing up comprehensive balances. These balances required continuing work to reconcile supply and demand under conditions of extreme scarcity. The state made constant demands on the economic system, while the planners were supposed to find the economic capabilities for meeting these demands. Of necessity, this made the planners into a conservatizing force, since real economic capabilities rarely matched the ambitious goals of the state. The result was that the planners acted to pare down the goals of the state in the interests of a "balanced" economic development. In their own way, Chinese planners were as equilibrium-minded as many old-fashioned economists in the West. In the mid-1950's, a collaboration began to develop between the policy-makers and the planners, somewhat similar to the partnership of Japanese samurai and merchants during the early Meiji period which we have mentioned earlier. The policy-makers took the risks, and the planners tried to make sure that the risks succeeded while not leading to imbalance. Also during the mid-1950's, collaboration of a similar sort between Party committees and managers at the enterprise level began to operate. Though many managers, particularly in the big industries, tried to beat their output plans, others tried to carry out one of the main policy slogans advanced during the Eighth Party Congress: "constancy," *chingch'ang wenting*.

In the chapter on ideology, we pointed out that leaders make use of pure ideology with its utopianism to link up directly with the masses and cut through the middle tier of organization. As far as the economy was concerned, the utopianism of the Great Leap Forward projected the vision of a rich and powerful society to be attained within the space of three years. It saw the dynamic masses as the key to the breakthrough, and regarded the men of the middle as conservative obstacles. There was thus not only less of a role for planners and managers, but they were even regarded as a pernicious influence. Their fate inevitably was *hsiafang*.

This section on the Great Leap Forward conception of management is short, for the simple reason that there really was no conception of management. A Chinese journal, *Chungkuo ch'ing-kungyeh*, started to publish a series of articles on industrial management in 1959, but ceased halfway through the promised series. Even those that were published sounded formalistic, and the subjects on which nothing was published were those for which the greatest "dispersion of the small authority" was allowed. There indeed was "free enterprise" during the Great Leap Forward, but "free" must be understood in the sense in which we have discussed it in the section on the dialectical conception of Chinese society, namely spontaneity.

TOWARD A MORE FLEXIBLE CONCEPTION OF MANAGEMENT

The Great Leap Forward (1958-1960) had industrial drive, but practically no industrial management. Industrial management returned once again early in 1961 when Peking frantically called on the discredited managers to rescue the country from its economic crisis. Factory after factory closed down or cut production drastically. The discontinuance of Soviet aid made scarce capital equipment even scarcer, and crop failure reduced the supply of raw materials for industry. The drive had failed; what was now needed was knowledge and experience. Fortunately, *hsiafang* had not been a Stalin-type purge; the managers were still alive and came back to their offices.

In January 1961, as we indicated in the previous chapter, the Chinese Communists abandoned the extremes of decentralization II and went back to the system envisaged by Ch'en Yün and Hsüeh Mu-ch'iao in 1956-1957. This consisted of a combination of centralization, decentralization I, and decentralization II. The consequence of this approach was a much broader distribution of economic power throughout the society. The ministries reacquired much of their lost power; though reduced, Party-dominated provincial and district governments retained much economic power; and the basic-level production units (enterprises and rural production teams) for the first time obtained a degree of economic autonomy. In industry, this meant greater autonomy for factory managers.

Although little detailed information has been published by the Chinese Communists on their economy since the change in policy of January 1961, there is much evidence to suggest that a system of broadly distributed economic power is becoming institutionalized. If this institutionalization continues during the period of the Third Five-Year Plan, scheduled to begin in 1966, it will mean that a definite Chinese management system has finally evolved. From what we know, it is different from one-man management and also from Party management. It is marked by much greater flexibility for the ordinary manager, as is indicated in the phrase "independent operational authority," commonly used in 1962 and 1963 to describe the system. This greater flexibility is to a large extent due to the fact that enterprise profit has been made a major success criterion in Chinese industry. To a large extent, managers no longer are held responsible for coming up with specified output quotas, but rather must produce fixed profit quotas, with above-target profits constituting a basis for additional rewards. Economic liberalization has been widely discussed in Eastern Europe and the Soviet Union; in China, there too has been discussion, though always phrased in seemingly orthodox and often peculiarly Chinese Communist terms. Though there is no Chinese counterpart to the noted Soviet economist Evsei Liberman, who argued for the introduction of the profit principle, many obscure economists take that position. Despite extreme political orthodoxy, economic liberalization has taken place in China.[60]

In the following discussion, we should like to suggest that the kinds of managerial practices evolved by the General Motors Corporation have some relevance for an understanding of the practices which the Chinese Communists are using today. Though China and the United States are very different countries, the possible forms of industrial and business organization are limited. The comparison is of further interest in view of the fact that the managerial practices of General Motors are generally regarded as alternatives to those of the Ford Motor Company, which were so admired by the Soviets when they were setting up their own system of industrial management.

One of the important similarities between many Chinese industrial organizations and General Motors is the fact that both were built from the bottom up. General Motors, at the very beginning, was an amalgam of many different operating divisions. The same is true of many large Chinese corporations (which is largely the reason why the Chinese Communists continue to use the word corporation or company, *kungssu*). The largest Chinese corporation, the Anshan Iron and Steel Corporation, is an industrial kingdom with many different plants producing different kinds of products. General Motors, unlike Ford, from

---

[60] The importance of the profit principle today in Communist China is a matter of dispute; some scholars have taken exception to the growing importance of profit I have indicated in my article "Economic Policy and Political Power in Communist China," *Annals of the American Academy of Political and Social Science*, 349 (September 1963), 62-65. In this respect, note the following two statements. The first was made by two conservative economists, Yang Jun-jui and Li Hsün, in one of the few articles on the economic debates published in the *Jenmin jihpao* (July 19, 1962): "We can say that the major criteria for evaluating enterprise economic effectiveness are the cost and profit targets." The second was made by another conservative economist in a criticism of liberal positions on the profit question; Ho Kuei-lin, writing in *Chingchi yenchiu*, 1 (1965), 24–25 stated: "Basically no one denies the importance of enterprises' earning profit; . . . the question is only whether . . . it should be one or the only criterion for judging the enterprise's fulfillment of the state plan and the level of its operational management."

the beginning faced the problem of linking its divisions into a larger unity. The formula ultimately arrived at was more or less the same as the Chinese Communist idea of "coordinated policy and operational autonomy." General Motors' Executive Committee laid down general principles, but eschewed centralized management. Coordination was achieved by interdivision committees and by centralization of financial controls.[61] Disregarding the fact that pre-1949 Chinese factories had poor management, this system was more or less the method of control they used. It seems to be the predominant method of control now used by the Chinese Communists, though one can presume management methods have improved over the pre-1949 period.

Like General Motors, most Chinese industrial organizations are characterized by diversified rather than specialized operations. Product specialization has been traditionally emphasized by the Soviets, and was emphasized by the Chinese during the early 1950's. In 1964, articles appeared in the Chinese press urging greater product specialization, but the moderate tone of the articles indicated no forcible return to Soviet methods, and testified to the tendency of Chinese industrial organizations to diversify rather than specialize operations.

Chinese industrial organizations tend to have many secondary divisions which produce a broad range of products beyond the major products for which the enterprise is mainly responsible. For example, in the highly industrialized Heilungkiang province of Manchuria, 2,100 out of 2,900 enterprises have such secondary divisions, with an average of six production units per enterprise. This is not just true of the big enterprises, but also of many smaller ones. Diversified operations also prevail in construction, transportation, commerce, and food industries. A typical enterprise will often produce a broad range of goods: steel, nonferrous metal products, chemical products, cement, bricks, construction materials, factory equipment, tools, consumer goods, food products, and processed waste materials. Such secondary industrial output accounted for 5 percent of the total industrial output in Heilungkiang in 1959, and for 10 percent in 1960. The Anshan Iron and Steel Corporation has more than 180 secondary production units, some of which are quite large. The Harbin Linen Plant has 41 such units, which account for 12.8 percent of the total output. The Mutanchiang Paper Making Plant has 33 units, which allow it to be 40-80 percent self-sufficient in supplies and equipment. Other examples could be cited.[62]

---

[61] Sloan, *op. cit.*, pp. 100 ff., 116 ff.

[62] Fukushima Hiroshi, "Kigyō no takaku keiei to rengōka," *Ajiya Keizai Junpō*, 462 (March 1961), 1–2.

The trend toward the creation of large combines was particularly marked during the Great Leap Forward. Scattered references since 1960 seem to indicate that these combines are being maintained, even though unit and division autonomy has been expanded in accordance with the policy prevailing since early 1961.[63]

Before 1949 Chinese business history was one of continuing combination and recombination. However, since the orientation was toward business rather than toward industry, few companies tried to integrate their different plants along technological lines. As long as the units contributed to company profits, the board of directors was satisfied. When the Chinese Communists came to power in 1949, their orientation was to industry rather than to business; their models were the technologically integrated, big modern plants imported from the Soviet Union. Technological integration was no problem, because the Soviets built them from the top down, in Ford fashion. But with their love of "gigantism," the Chinese Communists also tried to merge businesses into big units, and integrate them along technological lines. This they tried to do by product specialization; each unit would produce a different product and so constitute a part of an entire manufacturing process. This was too difficult to accomplish, so in the mid-1950's they curtailed the practice of merging. During the Great Leap Forward, they once again went in for large-scale merging, setting up what they called "united enterprises" (*lienho ch'iyeh*). This time, they tried a different kind of integration. The united enterprise was seen as an industrial community that should strive for self-sufficiency. Thus many enterprises acquired farms and food-processing plants to meet the food needs of their employees. Many of these united enterprises have continued to exist since early 1961, but there is less concern for internal integration. Despite the fact that they are state-owned, many have come to resemble pre-1949 large-scale business organizations. With the present stress on profit maximization and cost minimization,[64] it would not be wrong to say that some of the old Chinese orientation toward business rather than industry has reappeared.

The mentioned factors have led to an increasing stress on financial rather than output controls. Obviously, control is still exercised over capital allocation, in particular fixed capital equipment in scarce supply. Nevertheless, in many areas that should be strictly controlled according to Soviet-type planning principles, such as supplies, the in-

---

[63] See, for example, *Jenmin jihpao*, March 7, 1962.

[64] *Ibid.*, July 19, 1962.

dividual production units have great leeway in procurement. Particularly in light industry, the trend appears to be toward greater financial and fewer production controls. Thus broad areas of Chinese industry are probably once again operating as they did before 1949, that is to say, production units are given operational autonomy, while the company keeps a tight grip on finances. This pattern applies even to the economy as a whole, where the state is now stressing financial controls. It is this phenomenon, among others, that suggests the similarity to General Motors type procedures. (Of course, exempted from these patterns are the strategic industries, over which, as far as we know, the government maintains the strictest controls.)

What we have discussed may be called structural factors in Chinese business and industrial organization which bear similarities to the organization of General Motors. Inevitably these structural factors must have an effect on the way management functions. One-man management with its classical straight-line span of control was suited to the big Soviet-type plants, but clearly not to the type of organization we have described. A united enterprise containing many different divisions making different products cannot be conducted according to the principles of one-man management. Soviet adoption of one-man management (and in general imitation of Ford practices) was due to features of Soviet industrial organization which were different from those of China. Russia never had a business history like China, though it had a head start in major industrial development. In the following discussion, we should like to suggest that there are also some similarities in the phases of management development between General Motors and Chinese enterprises.

General Motors went through several organizational phases, although always according to the principle of "decentralized operations and coordinated control." [65] In its early days, the Executive Committee was made up of the division chiefs, which allowed for coordination but also created a situation where the division chiefs used their membership on the Executive Committee to further their own interests.[66] However, with the reorganization of the early 1920's, the Executive Committee became purely a policy-making body clearly separated from operational interests, strongly oriented toward financial administration. The role of the division heads changed, not in respect to their autonomy, but in respect to their relationships with the corporation. Their functions be-

---

[65] Sloan, *op. cit.*, p. 55.

[66] *Ibid.*, pp. 45, 48-49.

came advisory to the corporation's Executive Committee, thus relieving the latter of direct pressure from the various divisions. Thus a clear-cut line was drawn between policy and operations.

In many ways, the collective-leadership conception of management of 1956-1957 was similar to that prevailing during the early days of General Motors. The Party committee was the place where the top political and economic executives could get together with the various plant managers, as well as representatives from shops and production teams. The Party committee contained representatives from the entire enterprise. Decisions could be made in full knowledge of concrete conditions obtaining almost everywhere in the enterprise.

During the Great Leap Forward, Chinese Communist management practices seemed to have moved in the same direction as General Motors practices in the early 1920's. The managers were no longer necessarily members of the top Party committee. In many factories in Manchuria, an enterprise had a Party committee made up of Party cadres and an operations committee made up of plant managers. The Party committee, like the General Motors Executive Committee, made basic policy decisions which it then transmitted to the factory managers. The operations committee then worked out operational details. Since directives still came down directly to the managers from the ministries, the managers were told that before they could act on them, they would first have to be presented to the Party committee, which would make the specific policy decisions based on these directives. Once these decisions were made, the operations committee was to work out concrete details on construction, plans (annual, quarterly, monthly), production, technology, finances, summaries of economic activity, and any other special problems. Once the operational plans had been drawn up, the Party committee had to be informed so that it could check on plan fulfillment.[67]

Though this Manchurian Party committee and the post-1920's General Motors Executive Committee seemed to be similar in form, in content they were not. The authority of the factory managers had been too seriously undermined by 1958. Thus, for example, it was stated explicitly that "factory managers do not directly decide on work entrusted to deputy factory managers, in order that the 'positive functions' of the deputy managers may be developed in practical work." [68] However

---

[67] *Shenyang jihpao*, October 12, 1959. This is a fairly detailed report on management in a rotating press plant in Mukden City which consisted of a number of production units, each headed by a factory manager.

[68] *Ibid.*

laudable the sentiment, the fact was that the deputy managers were often powerful Party cadres who were agents of the Party committee. We have pointed out that it was an old Chinese practice to consider the president of a company as a contact man with the outside world, with real administrative power in the hands of one or more deputies. This was more or less true during the Great Leap Forward, except that the manager's contact functions were drastically reduced by the Party committee, which handled outside contacts. After all, what mattered were contacts with outside Party cadres with influence in different branches. Obviously only the Party committee could have such contacts.

It was this fact that made possible both policy and operational control by the Party; the Party committee made policy, and its agents in the form of deputy managers controlled operations. This is definitely not what General Motors intended with its separation of policy and operational functions; a General Motors division manager has real executive power.

However, with the changes introduced since early 1961, the "independent operational authority" of Chinese plant managers has greatly increased. If there is now indeed a similarity to the General Motors situation, one would expect some kind of "executive committee" with centralized financial controls. Given the disastrous record of the Party committees in regard to finances, it was not likely that Peking, in the wake of the 1961 economic crisis, would give the Party committees control over the enterprise's money. However, recently, a new type of coordinative body has come into being which appears to have many of the functions of the General Motors Executive Committee. In the spring of 1964, Peking announced that "political departments" were to be set up in all branches of economic administration. The form and even the name was borrowed from the army; indeed, the slogan has been: "Learn from the People's Liberation Army." However, despite the military aura, their functions seem to be purely economic. Moreover, despite the call for such political departments to be set up in all economic branches, what little information we have so far indicates that they have been set up mainly in the finance, trade, and transportation branches.

On May 15, 1964, a long conference was held in Peking to set up political departments in state financial and trading agencies. It was convened by the finance-trade political department of the Central Committee and presided over by Li Hsien-nien. Leading cadres from the branch political departments in the Finance and Trade ministries, the People's Bank, the Agricultural Bank, the Central Office of the All-

China Supply and Marketing Cooperatives, the Central Tax Bureau, and provincial Party committees took part. The obvious purpose of the conference was to discuss the activities of the new political departments.

The report on the conference was, as usual, general and vague. Political departments are to be set up in all agencies and enterprises down to the basic-level enterprises. The political departments are Party organizations under the jurisdiction of a central political department attached to the Central Committee. The political departments are subject to "dual rule." They are responsible to higher-echelon political departments, but also to local Party committees, "with the leadership of the local Party committee being primary." Their stated purpose is "to relate the business activities or operational units of finance and trading enterprises to the central tasks of local Party committees, and to local production and the people's livelihood." There is to be closer coordination between political and economic work.

Despite references to capitalistic tendencies in the finance and trading branches, there are grounds for believing that one of the purposes of the political departments is to bring about greater central control over local financial and commercial activity. Earlier, local Party committees were administratively connected only with higher-echelon Party organizations. Now they are connected with a structure of organization directly concerned with finance and trade. Under decentralization, local Party committees were able to exert direct pressure on state economic agencies situated in their areas. But the reverse was not true. Now there is a new Party (i.e., nongovernmental) structure which is functionally concerned with finance and trade, with which the local Party committees must cooperate. Aside from ideological indoctrination, the main function of these political bureaus would appear to be the assurance of strict compliance with state economic policies. On the one hand, they are to watch basic-level stores, food stations, and supply sales cooperatives. Yet, on the other hand, they are to work closely with local Party committees, presumably to make sure that state economic policy is being strictly followed.[69]

In contrast to the Great Leap Forward period, a new administrative committee now exercises power over the enterprise. Since most of the references to the political departments concern finance and trade, this would imply control over the enterprise's money and supply matters. Under these circumstances, one may well wonder what has happened to the earlier policy-making powers of the Party committee. Since there

---

[69] *Jenmin jihpao,* June 7, 1964.

have been references to recruiting "political commissars" from the army, they are presumably outsiders, in contrast to the Party secretaries, who for the most part have risen up the local ladder. Yet, despite the political-military tone of these references, the new political commissars are expected to have professional competence, particularly in finance and trade. Though these new political departments obviously are in a position to exert pressure on the managers to conform to national interests, they are even more in a position to displace the local and enterprise Party committees as decision-making bodies. Even in the 1956-1957 period money and supplies were considered "important questions" to be collectively decided by the Party committee. If the political departments now make these decisions, then the local and enterprise Party committees do not. All in all, the political departments appear to constitute an attempt by the Party to recentralize the economy by reducing the power of regional and local interests, though not necessarily those of the managers. Although there is some resemblance to Khrushchev's organization of large regional economic councils (sovnarkhozy) in 1960, there are important differences. The political departments, so far, do not appear to have been set up in industrial branches; this implies that controls over production have not been re-instituted in a major way.

The creation of the political departments is not likely to mean a return to "Politics Takes Command," although their overtly political-military character could possibly be used by Peking to try something of this sort once again. All signs indicate that the coming Third Five-Year Plan will be a somewhat intensified continuation of present economic policy. If this remains so, managers will continue to enjoy operational autonomy. One of the purposes of the political departments appears to be to assure financial responsibility: preventing waste of money, keeping prices stable, holding down inflationary tendencies by adjusting supply and demand. Peking has been strongly stressing capital accumulation during the past few years. In an economy in which money plays an important role, financial responsibility is a key element. Since the regional and local Party committees were prime transgressors in this respect during the Great Leap Forward, the political departments, with their training in military discipline and national loyalty, now seem to have the task of assuring a steady capital accumulation.

For General Motors, policy centralization meant first and foremost concentrated financial controls. This was accomplished by the development of a uniform accounting system which made it possible to evaluate the performance of each division and thus to exert pressure on them to move in the policy directions decided by the Executive Committee.[70] Since the statistical breakdown during the Great Leap Forward, the Chinese Communists have taken great pains to improve and standardize their accounting practices. This is one of the few areas of economic administration in which Peking has made public statements in recent years. Peking obviously regards a uniform and effective accounting system linked to the state banks as an important basis for the development of financial leverage to direct and influence economic activity.

If the Chinese Communists continue to follow a "General Motors principle of management," then the field is secure for professionally competent managers. The producing units need expertise in order to operate effectively. Expertise can only be furnished by the graduates from the country's higher schools, that is to say the "intellectuals." The intellectuals were rehabilitated in 1961 and 1962, and so far there has been no indication of a reversal of this policy, despite the increasingly shrill talk about proper ideological attitudes. Recent attacks on pro-Soviet individuals, like Yang Hsien-chen, chairman of the Party school in Peking, do not appear to foreshadow a return to the antiprofessionalism of the Great Leap Forward. Not only did the May-June 1964 conference of the political departments stress the need for proper economic work, but articles appearing in economic journals indicate new efforts to set up a working system of comprehensive balances and enterprise-level planning.[71] The General Motors principle of management

---

[70] Sloan, *op. cit.*, pp. 122–123.

[71] See Yo Wei, "On Some Problems of Comprehensive Balance in the National Economy," and Ma Wen-kuei, "Concerning Special Aspects, Tasks, and Methods of Planning in Socialist Enterprises," *Chingchi yenchiu*, 7 (July 15, 1964), pp. 1-7, and 8-17. These are among the first articles to appear in a long time on the subjects of balances and planning. It may be significant that they were published after the May-June conference of the political departments. The tone is clearly cautious and conservative, and, at first sight, nothing new appears to have been said. Nevertheless, there are some interesting aspects. First, little is said about national planning. The enterprises are requested to draft reliable enterprise plans on the basis of "plan tasks" given them by the state. Clearly, without reliable enterprise plans, the work of making up national balance tables is impossible. Balancing is seen as continuing adjustment which takes place according to reliable reflections and projections of concrete economic activity as given in enterprise plans. The operational order would appear to be: the state hands down "plan tasks" (i.e., policy commands), the enterprises draft comprehensive concrete plans, and the plans move back up to the middle level, so to speak, where the administrative planners work out balances. The planning system is

assumes that crucial decision-making impulses come from below, that is, from the divisions. These, of course, are supposed to arise in the context of general policy and be subject to strict regulatory controls. My own estimation of the attitude of the leadership to the economy is that the economy can run only if considerable latitude is given to the "basic level" to initiate impulses. This conception was basic to the Great Leap Forward, except that only political impulses were thought to count. Not the conception changed, but the recognition that the impulses have to be essentially economic. Such a recognition assures a future to the professionals. In a way, this constitutes a reversion to Stalin's policy of encouraging professional expertise but pairing it with the demand for absolute political loyalty. There are parallels to the 1930's in the Soviet Union. The recent stress on the need for bringing up a new revolutionary generation bears similarity to Stalin's call for a workers' intelligentsia.[72] The new generation is to come from the working classes, but is to be technically as well as ideologically prepared. The leadership has finally recognized that China's drive toward great power status demands expertise. The managers are here to stay, and as in the Soviet Union will probably constitute a new elite. But the differences are as significant as the similarities between China today and the U.S.S.R. thirty years ago. An economy organized along General Motors principles may ultimately turn out to be something quite different from that of the Soviet Union which was influenced by "Fordism." [73]

---

based essentially on the availability of comprehensive information *coming from the bottom up*. Moreover, greater importance is attached to balances at the national level than to planning at the national level. If this is the case, then economic leaders at the bottom (e.g., enterprise managers) must furnish optimally precise information to the administrators. This is a task that can hardly be expected from the Party cadres whose chief qualifications are locally based political power. It can only come from professionally-minded managers. However, control has to be exerted on the managers to make sure that they undertake planning work. Going to the trouble of drafting detailed enterprise plans is not always directly related to business success. Therefore, there has to be an external force that exercises pressure on the managers to comply. This pressure is now probably to come from the political departments, staffed by men who are not only politically reliable, but are supposed to have professional expertise as well. Thus the new political departments can be seen as a further step toward bringing about tighter integration of the national economy, but one still based on the principle that major impulses must come from below.

[72] *Hungch'i*, 14 (July 1964), 34-39.

[73] Drucker, *op. cit.*, pp. 22-23.

DEVELOPMENT OF COMMAND RELATIONSHIPS
IN INDUSTRIAL MANAGEMENT

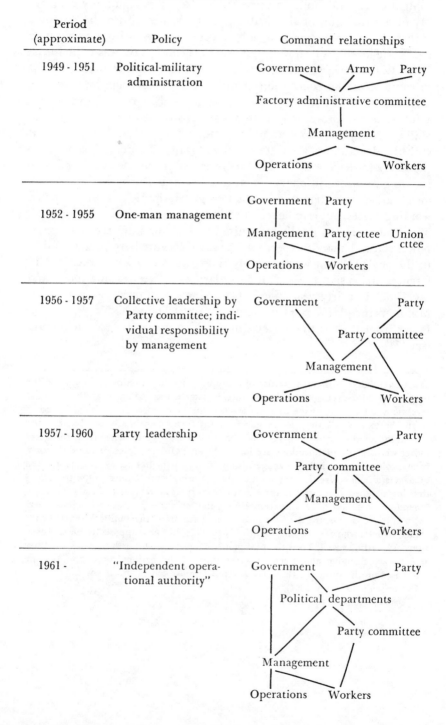

Period (approximate)	Policy	Command relationships
1949 - 1951	Political-military administration	
1952 - 1955	One-man management	
1956 - 1957	Collective leadership by Party committee; individual responsibility by management	
1957 - 1960	Party leadership	
1961 -	"Independent operational authority"	

CHAPTER V

CONTROL

CONCEPTS

EVERY ORGANIZATION must assure that its members are loyal and perform in the way expected of them. To this end, organizations use control. The word "control" has a range of meaning in English broader than that in other European languages. The first dictionary meaning given is usually "to check or verify," a denotation it shares with French and German, as in *contrôle des passeports*. But the English word control also means "to exercise restraint or direction upon the free action" of someone.[1] Although the latter meaning of the word control is the first that comes to mind in English, its former meaning of checking and verifying is of equal importance in discussing the question of organizational control.

A Soviet legal definition of *kontrol'* illustrates the checking and verifying meaning of the word control: "one of the leadership methods in the Soviet Union which involves checking on the fulfillment of laws, Party directives, government decrees, and instructions of higher-echelon agencies."[2] This definition implies checking the performance of

---

[1] *The Oxford Universal Dictionary*, 3d ed., p. 385.

[2] *Iuridicheskii Slovar'* (Moscow, 1956), I, 512*b*.

men by measuring it against some standard and making a judgment accordingly.

Exercising control by checking on the performance of an individual is only one way of assuring that the individual measures up to standards. Another way is to exercise "restraint or direction upon the free action" of an individual directly in order to elicit generally correct behavior and attitudes.

Modern organization theory has moved from an early concern with the arrangement of *things*, such as in Fredrick W. Taylor's time-and-motion studies, to a concern with the arrangement of *people*, as reflected in the human-relations school of industrial organization, which arose in the late 1930's. The problem of control has similarly taken on a "human" aspect, namely, a concern with the mechanisms which make for general compliance of organization members. This newer approach is reflected in Amitai Etzioni's study of organizational controls.[3] If at an earlier period business managers were essentially concerned with people as "things"—their skills, talents, and place in the division of labor—modern managers now are interested in personality and motivation of employees. Organizational control can be exercised either by judging the products of an individual's labor or by judging the individual himself. In the former instance, organization uses things to control the individual; in the latter instance it uses the individual to control things.

The English meaning of control, that is, "to exercise restraint," implies a direct means of assuring loyalty and compliance from individuals. The Chinese Communists have not dispensed with such direct means. The public security forces, the political-legal branches of the state administration, the people's militia, and the army itself together constitute a powerful body for maintaining law and order. While not underestimating their power and importance in Communist China, we regard these methods of control as conventional, and hence do not deal with them in this chapter. Modern organizations in the West and the Chinese Communists in the East have developed more sophisticated means of exercising control over men directly in order to assure their loyalty and compliance. In our chapter on ideology, we have spoken briefly of the use of ideology to elicit commitment. In this chapter, we shall discuss less personal and more organizational methods of control. These are essentially of two types: economic controls which check on the performance of men, and political controls which check the minds of men.

---

[3] Amitai Etzioni, *A Comparative Analysis of Complex Organizations* (Glencoe, Ill., 1961), pp. 233 ff.

Methods of Control in the Soviet Union and in Communist China

In the history of the Soviet Union the problem of control arose early. The Cheka, the first secret police, was created "on the second day of the Revolution," as Stalin put it.[4] It was the organized instrument of the revolutionary terror. But police terror is based on the assumption that the offending individual is already beyond the pale. He may not have gone so far as to justify his elimination from society or life altogether, but he is no longer usable within the organization. A different form of control is necessary to combat deviation within the organization and to put pressures on individuals to do what is expected of them. Thus, almost as soon as the Cheka was created, the new Soviet government established a Central Control Collegium on January 23, 1918, which in 1920 was transformed into the Commissariat of Workers and Peasants Inspection, *Rabkrin*. The main function of the *Rabkrin* was to exercise control over the personnel of the state bureaucracy. The *Rabkrin* evolved into the powerful Ministry of State Control. At the same time that this instrument was set up, a parallel instrument for intra-Party control was created, the Control Commission, directly attached to the Central Committee of the Party.

Stalin's leading role both in the *Rabkrin* and the Control Commission greatly aided his seizure of power in later years. Much of the tragic history of Stalinism arose from Stalin's obsession with problems of control. It will possibly never be determined how justified Stalin's fears were and how much flowed from a paranoiac personality. Each of the three control agencies, Cheka, Ministry of State Control, and Control Commission, expanded greatly in later years. The horrors of the Soviet secret police are notorious; the Ministry of State Control turned into a powerful watchdog over the Soviet economy; and the Party Control Commission, as it was known after the Seventeenth Party Congress in 1934, became the center of a nation-wide network of Party control commissions implanted in every unit of organization.[5] The three agencies hardly exhausted the apparatus of control available to the Soviet regime. The whole Soviet system was riddled with control devices, both over men and their performance. General suspicion aided the police in its control over men, and almost every economic agency carried out controls over their performance.[6]

---

4 Sidney Monas, "The Political Police: The Dream of a Beautiful Autocracy," in *The Transformation of Russian Society* (Cambridge, Mass., 1960), p. 181.

5 Merle Fainsod, *How Russia Is Ruled* (Cambridge, Mass., 1958), pp. 159-162, 170-171, 343-344, 347-350.

6 *Ibid.*, pp. 339-347.

So great was the terror during the Stalinist period that it is difficult for a Westerner to see how anything but paralysis could have resulted from such a system. Yet work went on, industry developed, people performed. The Stalinist terror in the Soviet Union has made many scholars assume that terror is a necessary element in any totalitarian system. But even in the Stalinist period of Soviet history some rational method, other than terror, was involved in the complex of controls. As far as Communist China is concerned, not since the early fifties has mass terror been used either as an instrument of control or of rule. Totalitarian systems of organization, therefore, are quite capable of evolving effective instruments of control without resorting to terror.

If terror has disappeared in the Soviet Union, the problem of control has not. As long as there is organization, there must be controls, in Russia or elsewhere. Since the time of Stalin, the patterns of control have changed. The Secret Police has lost much of its earlier power. In the wake of economic liberalization, managers are no longer constantly faced with punitive sanctions. With the reemergence of the Party as a major organizational instrument, the function of control by Party organizations has increased. The June 1959 plenary meeting of the Central Committee was mainly concerned with transforming lower-level Party organizations into more effective instruments of control.

Control in the Soviet Union has taken two basic forms: political and economic. It is not always easy to distinguish one from the other, and organizations exercising one have often exercised the other. Thus, for example, the Soviet Secret Police carried out both political and economic controls. Nevertheless, a formal distinction has always been maintained. Party control commissions, for example, are exclusively concerned with political controls, but agencies like the State Bank with economic controls. Political control is always directed against individuals, their actions, decisions, and behavior. Economic control aims at measurable performance, at the results of decisions. Political control pressures an individual to act "correctly" or punishes him if he acts "incorrectly"; economic control checks the tangible results of his actions against a standard imposed by the state. In the Soviet Union and Communist China control over the leaders of economic organizations usually meant the application of both forms of control. If a manager of a plant was thought to be disloyal, unreliable, or ineffective, a thorough economic accounting invariably followed. And conversely, if economic control brought up shortcomings, an investigation of the decision maker's political attitudes usually followed. Nevertheless, the fact that control had to be both political and economic demanded agencies of control capable of exercising both functions.

In the Soviet Union controls have also tended to be "external." That is to say the control agencies were never a part of the organizational unit they were to control, even though physically they may have had their representatives stationed in that unit. To use the words of the Chinese Communists, Soviet control agencies were "outsiders" rather than "insiders." [7]

The prevalence of external controls is directly related to the nature of Soviet state administration. Soviet stress on branch-type administration led to the development of what might be called "parallel bureaucracies." Every important administrative function had its branch-type structure, resulting in a large number of parallel bureaucratic hierarchies. Since control was an important administrative function and had its own bureaucracies, control agencies were therefore external.

One of the phenomena of Soviet administration which external controls were designed to combat was in Joseph Berliner's terminology, "the web of mutual involvement." [8] Political and economic leaders in different administrative branches often made alliances with each other in order to achieve the goals given them by the state. These alliances created lateral contacts between parallel bureaucracies. Though the attitude of the state always was ambivalent toward the formation of these webs of mutual involvement, recognition of the practical necessity for a degree of "informal practices" held back the state from uniformly sundering these alliances. Much of this restraint undoubtedly derived from the necessity for allowing adjustments. Not everything could be done "according to plan." Stalin's one-man management system was a recognition of the necessity of investing sufficient power in decision makers in the interest of unit-level flexibility. But the more the state had to tolerate informal practices, the greater became the need for control. Since the mutual involvement increased resistance to intra-unit controls (by chief accountants, Party secretaries, and so on), corollary forms of external controls had to be developed.

Thus we see the early development of external institutions of control such as the Secret Police, the Ministry of State Control, and the State Bank; the system of external controls experienced its greatest development during the Stalinist period.

Since Stalin's death, the Soviets have been experimenting with an alternative form of control which may be called "internal." Whereas

---

[7] Etzioni contrasts control mechanisms that are *built in*, i.e., mechanisms which have other functions but also act in some controlling fashion, with those that are *segregated* and explicitly serve control functions (*op. cit.*, p. 234).

[8] Joseph S. Berliner, *Factory and Manager in the USSR* (Cambridge, Mass., 1957), pp. 264 ff.

external controls mean supervision by a body not formally connected with the organization, internal controls mean supervision by individuals and bodies that are a part of the organization itself. This form of control, as we shall see, has played a major role in Communist China. An example of internal controls in the Soviet Union is the intra-enterprise Party control commissions.

The general structure of organization in Communist China having been modeled on that of the Soviet Union, one could expect to find similar approaches to control. Indeed during the first half-decade of Communist rule on the Chinese mainland, a structure of control began to develop like that of the Soviet Union. A secret police, known as the Public Security Forces, was created, reminiscent of the Soviet Cheka and its successors. A Ministry of State Control, before October 1950 known as the Central People's Control Committee (CPCC), developed with functions similar to those of its Soviet counterpart. Party control commissions in China were more or less the same as those in the Soviet Communist party. The People's Bank of China, established shortly after 1949, performed the same functions as the Soviet State Bank. The conditions which made it necessary for the Chinese to introduce such a control system were similar to those in the USSR. As in the USSR, the Chinese Communists, in the period immediately after 1949, were not sure of the loyalty of the population, particularly of men in key organizational positions. Hence the need for political controls. The adoption of central planning necessitated the imposition of complex economic controls. Moreover, since it took a while for the Party organizations to penetrate effectively into the production units, to become "insiders" rather than "outsiders," external controls were needed.

But in later years Soviet-type patterns of control were abandoned, and, indeed, reversed. Instead of the continued elaboration of bureaucratic systems of control, a process of gradual reduction in the power of these control organizations began. Bureaucratic control agencies had acquired their greatest power in 1954 and 1955; after that they declined. In 1959 the Ministry of State Control was formally abolished. Long before that, the ministry and its lower-echelon agencies had lost much of their power. This decline was part of a general shift from a system of parallel bureaucracies on the Soviet model toward a system of Party-dominated lateral integration.

In the chapter on management we pointed out that the Party, by the later 1950's, had assumed supreme leadership throughout organization. In the present chapter, we shall attempt to indicate how the Party assumed supreme control functions as well. A shift occurred from external to internal controls and from economic to political controls. Thus the Chinese Communists once again returned to a form of control more in keeping with their organizational philosophy, namely control of the man rather than of his performance.

THE CREATION OF A CONTROL SYSTEM

The Beginnings of Control Work

Since control poses different problems in war and in peace, the Chinese Communists had to find new instruments of control after 1949. Earlier, military government carried out administration in the occupied areas, and Party organizations exercised control functions. But a new phase began with the establishment of state power: rule by bureaucracy. As during the early years of the USSR, the new offices often had to be staffed with individuals carried over from the *ancien régime*. And, as in the USSR, the new rulers did not trust these indispensable but perhaps unreliable officials. The *Sanfan* and *Wufan* campaigns brought this distrust to the surface. The Chinese needed an independent control system to watch over the bureaucracy.

They decided to follow the Soviet example of a system of parallel bureaucracies (the "branch" principle of administration), and so necessarily had to set up a structure of external controls. The problem was to make it work.

In 1950 the CPCC published a report[9] on its first half year of operations in which it admitted difficulties encountered in the attempt to set up a control system: "There are not enough cadres, experience is lacking, hence the work of trial and error has taken a lot of time." During the period from January 1950 to May 1950, the CPCC received 142 formal complaints about officials. Complaints against top officials were directly handled by the CPCC; lesser complaints and those of a regional nature were left for the local control offices. The CPCC resorted to devices which strong Chinese governments had used for centuries. They sent down *ad hoc* "investigation teams" into critical areas.

Complaints listed in the CPCC report were largely of three types. Most of them concerned bureaucratic incompetence. Others were about economic waste, particularly of food supplies. And the third concerned the killing and wounding of "workers, peasants, soldiers, and cadres." The fact that criminal complaints were taken to the Control Commis-

---

[9] *Jenmin jihpao,* June 13, 1950.

sions indicates that in many areas the police was not functioning effectively. In listing its four main tasks, the CPCC report singled out first "the struggle against bureaucratism and commandism"; the Communists were anxious to get the administrative system on its feet again, but they also feared rebureaucratization along lines so familiar to the Chinese. The second task was the struggle against waste, a problem of checking on performance, of economic controls. The third task listed was to recruit "people's control correspondents" from among the population; in plainer language, this meant finding informers and spies. Lastly, ways had to be found to make the system of control over the bureaucracy workable.

The report made some concrete recommendations. More cadres were to be trained, particularly to be able to check on the financial activities of state agencies. Since comprehensive control was not possible, the control offices should make spot checks of agencies. More "correspondents" should be recruited both among the masses and in agencies. And, lastly, rules of control should be systematized, Soviet experiences studied, and a journal published to be called *People's Control*.[10]

When organization does not function well and the top leadership is alarmed that it no longer controls middle and lower levels, the temptation is great to have recourse to spies and informers. History has many examples of this. The crude administration of Tokugawa Japan was largely held together by the *metsuke*. The bureaucracies of Russia never seemed to work without a network of informants reporting to the top what was going on inside the apparatus. Thus it is not surprising that in the period just after 1949, the Chinese Communists resorted to these same crude though necessary methods. The fact that the Chinese Communists abandoned these methods later indicates that they managed to develop more sophisticated means of control.

Control Correspondents and Denunciation

In July 1951 the central government announced a set of tentative rules governing the operations of "people's control correspondents." Control committees at all levels of the state apparatus were to recruit control correspondents from among reliable workers in government bureaus. If there were more than three control correspondents in a bureau, they were to form a "small group" with a leader. Their duties were to be: to observe the operations of the offices and the behavior of the officials; to collect the "opinions of the masses" on policy, laws, and

---

10 *Hsinhua yüehpao*, September 1950.

operations; to propagandize the functions of control. If they discovered wrongdoing, the control correspondents were to inform the head of the organizational unit. If he resolved the problem on the spot, he was then to report to the control offices. The control correspondents were to have no power to make decisions on their own. They were to remain in close contact with the control committees. Without specific authorization from the control committees, they were not to reveal any information they collected. Successful correspondents were to be rewarded. If the correspondents were employees of the unit investigated, the unit was to provide them with special funds. If they came from outside, funds were to be provided by the control committee. Appointments, transfers, and resignations of correspondents were to be publicly announced in the units affected. Meetings of small-group leaders or control correspondents' delegates were to be held semiannually.[11]

The new regulations were called "experimental," reflecting the penchant of the Chinese Communists to try things out before systematizing and universalizing them. In 1953, the word "experimental" was dropped and the regulations were formally promulgated. Although these "people's control correspondents" were little more than informants, it is significant that they were known publicly. Spying was thus openly built into the system of organization.

The incentives offered to the control correspondents were attractive. Special funds were made available to them and rewards paid, presumably for denouncing offenders. Since they were employees of the organizational unit, they had considerable knowledge of what was going on.

The regime also encouraged direct control by the masses, particularly in the form of denunciations (k'ungsu) coming from below. Although many denunciations were anonymous, the regime also encouraged public denunciation, particularly through the mass media. By encouraging people to write to the newspapers about their complaints, the regime aimed at activating an important source of "public opinion." The comparative impersonality of a letter to a newspaper often made it possible to denounce an individual or report a situation without risking the kind of intra-organizational frictions arising from direct denunciation. From interviews with persons who worked in newspapers, it is clear that all letters are answered, though only a few are published. Halfway between the open mass media and the "internal communications" are the important "wall newspapers" (tatzupao), devices for publishing wrongdoings and criticizing specific persons. All in all, one can

---

[11] *Jenmin jihpao,* September 11, 1951.

say that the Chinese Communists have followed a line of making control operations public.

During this early period, when control methods were still crude, relying mainly on organizational informers and popular denunciations, the regime resorted to terror to enforce controls. This took the form of the Three-Anti (*Sanfan*) and Five-Anti (*Wufan*) movements. The *Sanfan* campaign, which started in the winter of 1951, was directed against "corruption, waste, and bureaucratism." "Struggle meetings" were held throughout China in which offending cadres were attacked, and by mass demand removed from office. In contrast to the *Sufan* movement of the latter part of 1955, *Sanfan* was not an attack against bureaucracy as such, but against offending individuals within the bureaucracy. In this sense it rather resembled the bureaucratic purges that Stalin carried out in the mid-1930's. Kao Kang played a major role in *Sanfan* and undoubtedly used the occasion to tighten his grip on the Manchurian bureaucracy. This was the first eruption of the endemic Chinese Communist fear that bureaucratization could mean a reversion to traditional bureaucracy. The *Wufan* movement began early in 1952 and was primarily directed against the bourgeoisie. The bourgeoisie was accused of bribery, tax evasion, fraud, theft of government property, and theft of state economic secrets. Here was an onslaught against a class as a whole but, in contrast to what happened to the gentry on the land, the bourgeoisie was not obliterated as a class. Hoarding has always been endemic in China, and the *Wufan* movement undoubtedly pried loose much frozen wealth. In scale, *Wufan* far surpassed *Sanfan,* and provided new recruits for the concentration camps in the interior.

According to the official Chinese Communist historian Ho Kan-chih, 4.5 percent of all state officials in China received some kind of punishment during the *Sanfan* movement.[12] As a result of the campaigns launched by the *Wufan* movement, more than 450,000 businesses were investigated in China's nine biggest cities. Normal control work clearly was ineffective, and therefore recourse was taken to terroristic methods. But if the purges struck fear into the hearts of the officials, they did not contribute to a consolidation of the state apparatus. The pressures of the Korean War undoubtedly were a factor in the *Sanfan* and *Wufan* movements. However, they only further confused the task of building regular instruments of control. The movements worked well for a few months, but could not be made into a permanent instrument of control. This was the last time that Peking used terroristic methods to exercise control.

---

[12] Ho Kan-chih, *Chungkuo hsientai koming-shih* (Hong Kong, 1958), pp. 366-367.

The Building Up of a Control Network

In April 1951 the First National Control Work Conference was held in Peking. During the previous year, people's control agencies had been established, according to *Jenmin jihpao* of April 29, 1951, "in five Large Administrative Regions, in one directly attached autonomous region, in twenty-eight provinces, in twelve cities directly attached to the central government or to the Large Administrative Regions, in eight administrative districts the equivalent of provinces, and in 345 counties, cities, and banners." Although considerable "experience" was available, the conference did not adopt firm regulations for the control agencies. (Such official regulations were not to appear until late in 1952 and even then were labeled "provisional.")

The speakers repeatedly stressed difficulties in work and the incompleteness of the control apparatus. They discussed three major problems: relationships between top and bottom echelons of the control system; relationships between control offices and the agencies to which they were attached; and cadre punishment. Organizational rules for control work varied in different Large Administrative Regions, but the conference merely "studied them." There was much talk about ferreting out counter-revolutionaries in state administration, and encouraging denunciation from below (through suggestion and opinion boxes). Control offices were urged to develop good working relationships with the agencies to which they were attached.

Although no real policy statement emerged from the conference, the three major problems discussed by the speakers revealed the main challenges facing the developing control system. The first, namely "relationships between top and bottom echelons of the control systems," arose because the structure of state administration was still not firmly established throughout the country and, more specifically, because of the autonomy of some of the Large Administrative Regions, notably Manchuria. The second problem, namely "relationships between control offices and the agencies to which they were attached," concerned the whole problem of external versus internal control, specifically the degree of independence control cadres were to have vis-à-vis the administrators and managers of the units under control. We shall deal with this problem in the following section. The third problem, "cadre punishment," related to bureaucratic corruption and incompetence.

Ostensibly, according to the speakers of the conference, the first problem arose because rules for control work differed among the Large Administrative Regions. In reality, the problem was one of lower-echelon control agencies being under uncertain jurisdiction, sometimes that of

Peking and sometimes that of the Large Administrative Regions. This problem is illustrated by a curious paragraph of a report issued in August 1951 by the Central People's Control Committee in Peking:

Control agencies are to set up in provinces and major cities following their lines of administrative organization. Moreover, before the year is past, control agencies also are to be set up in all "special offices." The personnel of these control agencies is to be included in the personnel rosters of the "special office" in question, and in the county and city personnel rosters connected with the "special office." In such counties and cities where control agencies have already been established, leadership is to be strengthened. However, where they have not yet been established, for the moment they are not to be set up. In areas where "special offices" have not been set up or where special circumstances or particular conditions prevail, this should be reported to the people's governments of the Large Administrative Regions (or to military government committees). *If permission is granted, then control agencies may be set up.*

The references are vague. The "special offices" are in the category of what the Chinese Communists call *p'aich'u chikuan,* that is, agencies which are local arms of some higher-echelon bureau. During these early days, they evidently were offices set up below the provincial level as a direct arm of the central government, to enforce policy in areas where regional government was ineffective or could not be relied on. Sending down special agencies from the center to unreliable regions is an old Chinese practice of statecraft. Where the Large Administrative Regions, such as Manchuria, were not entirely in harmony with Peking, such "special offices" often were set up to counteract regional government. Nevertheless, the fact that the report stipulated that permission had to be obtained from the Large Administrative Regions before control agencies could be set up indicates that Peking was not yet strong enough to impose a centrally directed control system on all parts of the country. Aside from Manchuria, there evidently were difficulties in the Shanghai region. Effective control agencies were not established in Shanghai until 1951.[13]

External controls will not function unless they can be centralized and unless command flows smoothly from top to bottom. As long as the Large Administrative Regions were in existence, particularly those that caused problems, such as Manchuria, it was difficult to create a unified control system.

Leaving aside for the moment the second problem mentioned above (to be discussed in the next section), let us illustrate the third problem, that of "cadre punishment." In June 1951, a control committee was

---

13 *Ch'angchiang jihpao,* August 8, 1951.

established in the Shanghai City municipal government under the chairmanship of Sheng P'i-hua. The need for a city-level control committee arose because of admitted "decay" in the administrative apparatus. Sheng P'i-hua stated, in his report, that from January 1951 to May 1951, "on the basis of very incomplete statistics among our workers" (that is, officials of the city administration), there were cases of bribery and corruption, extortion, blackmail, "loss of standpoint" (that is, ideological defection), harboring of landlords, hoodlumism, incompetence, and betrayal of state secrets. The rot apparently was not limited to the new recruits of the bureaucracy: "Even among old cadres, there are some who after coming into the cities, without caring a bit, lived merrily and corruptly, and began to manifest evil tendencies of arrogance and self-satisfaction." There was dark talk of officials being corrupted by "traitorous merchants." The main purpose of control was to root out such people.

The concern about control in Shanghai during this period is not surprising. Shanghai was still the most Western and "capitalistic" of China's cities, and many officials were of dubious reliability. Neither Party organization nor the apparatus of government were yet sufficiently strong to allow for internal controls. Yet even external controls were not sufficient. Thus, revolutionary terror, in the form of mass movements and mass denunciations, was still an instrument, as in the *Wufan* and *Sanfan* campaigns.[14]

Aside from the mentioned problems which impeded the creation of a control network, the August 1951 report of the Central People's Control Committee also pointed out that many control cadres themselves were not certain about "the nature, authority, and basic work methods" of the control agencies. Therefore it was difficult for them to operate effectively. Furthermore, cadres as a whole had misconceptions about the functions of the control agencies and regarded them as "administrative courts," "roving government inspectorates," "fly swatters," or "trouble-seeking" agencies.

NATIONAL CONTROL WORK CONFERENCES

First	April, 1951
Second	February, 1953
Third	April, 1954
Fourth	April, 1955
Fifth	January-February, 1956
Sixth	December, 1956
Seventh	February-March, 1958

---

14 *Chiehfang jihpao*, June 26, 1951.

ECONOMIC CONTROL

The Growing Concern with Economic Control

On December 27, 1952, the government issued temporary organizational rules for control offices in financial and economic agencies at province and major-city levels and "higher up," as well as for state-owned financial and economic enterprises; they were entitled "Temporary Rules of Organization and Principles of Recruitment." The rules were a recognition on the part of the government that the crude political controls hitherto used were not sufficient to resolve the most pressing control problems, which were increasingly economic.

The introductory paragraph of the rules made three stipulations. First, every administrative agency, from the central ministries down to province and city bureaus (including the Large Administrative Regions), as well as all state-owned enterprises, were to select a certain number of individuals to do full-time control work. Second, these control cadres were to be recruited from within the agency itself and from existing personnel rosters. Third, though political reliability was important, of equal importance was "understanding the business and technology" of the agency or enterprise in question. This last stipulation marked the beginning of a new policy to recruit individuals who had technical expertise and so could check on operations and performance.

The new rules consisted of fourteen articles which may be briefly summarized:

The control cadres were to make sure that the agencies and enterprises were carrying out the policies and commands of government. They were to check on basic construction, production, economizing, accounting, capital usage, safety, democratic management, finances, learning of advanced experiences (that is, Soviet), and rationalization proposals. They were to investigate all instances of deviation, whether political or economic. They were to receive and process denunciations and reports from all sources. Each control office was to have a single chief. The number of full-time control cadres was to depend on the needs of the unit. Each control office was to be subject to "dual rule" by the office or department head and by higher-echelon control offices. No one was to refuse investigation. Punitive action was to require the authorization of the department head. Rewards were to require the authorization of the personnel department of the unit in question.

Punitive action beyond the scope allowed the unit or counter-revolutionary incidents were to be reported to the People's Procurator's office, the people's courts, or the security bureaus. The control offices were to be entitled to send men to participate in unit meetings, and to collect all material necessary. They were entitled to name control correspondents, set up reception offices, and place opinion boxes as they saw fit. The control offices were to collaborate closely with the units in question. All important documents were to be countersigned by the unit head, though general instructions could be issued independently to lower-level control units. All work regulations of the control commissions were to be approved by the unit head.[15]

These temporary rules reveal a sense of "compromise." The lines of authority have still not been made entirely clear. *Dual rule in this instance meant veto power by the department heads.* The department heads' authority over control work deprived the controllers of just that independence from local authority that they needed to do their work. One of the reasons Lenin had argued for vertical rule in the Soviet procuracy was precisely to prevent local authorities from exerting pressure on the state procurators. The fact that all control reports had to be countersigned by department heads indicated that the control system was neither completely external nor completely independent. This was precisely the problem of "the relationship of control offices and the agencies to which they were attached" which we mentioned but did not discuss in the preceding section.

Still, these regulations indicated progress in the development of a control system. The need for economic controls was clearly spelled out. January 1953 marked the formal inauguration of the First Five-Year Plan; hence economic control had become much more necessary than before. The fact that Peking was determined to set up a formal control system throughout the country, even with concessions to local authorities, indicated that it was determined to get a foothold in all Large Administrative Regions. The development of economic controls was one of its weapons.

In February 1953, the Second National Conference on Control Work was held in Peking. The conference was attended by 135 cadres from all areas of China, and 32 observers. It was presided over by T'an P'ing-shan, then head of the Control Committee of the central government. By the end of 1952, people's control agencies had been established in six Large Administrative Regions, in one national autonomous region,

---

15 *Fukien jihpao,* January 7, 1953.

in 45 provinces and cities, in 170 special districts, and in 1,160 counties. Furthermore, control agencies had been established in 248 departments of governments from the provincial and city levels upward. There were now 26,611 people's control correspondents.

Still, T'an P'ing-shan stated in his report, there were defects. Aside from lack of experience, "some leading cadres in regional people's governments and some departments still did not think highly of control work, and hence neglected to set up control systems." Liu Ching-fan, deputy director of the Central Control Committee, made it clear that the major tasks of the control agencies during 1953 were supervision of economic work, in particular plan fulfillment. Liu emphasized that it was in the economic and financial sectors that the most rigorous controls must be carried out.

Considerable discussion took place on the draft rules for control work and workers—reference to "draft" rules and "discussion and study" indicates again that no definitive pattern had yet been evolved.[16]

Following the Second National Conference on Control Work, a two-day conference on control work was held in Tientsin. Tai Hsiao-tung, deputy director of the control committee of the North China Administrative Committee, read a long report. His report indicated that, without independent authority, the control cadres found it difficult to operate effectively. The managers of the enterprises being investigated were able to control the controllers! As is clear from his admissions about the poor quality of control workers, many were caught in the conflicting pressures coming from higher echelons and from within the organization. Since their authority was not clear-cut, they often did not know what to do.

The deputy mayor of Tientsin, Wu Te, also read a long report at this meeting. He declared that great importance must be attached to control work to prevent falsification in industrial enterprises: false reports, false claims of successes, falsification of production costs, substitution of inferior for superior goods, false reports of work norms, and so on. "If the leadership agencies have to judge conditions, determine policy, guide work, on the basis of their false reports, then this is most dangerous." These strong words reveal that the Chinese were becoming aware of a problem which faced the Soviets years before: how to insure reliable reporting of economic activity. Obviously, although corruption and "cheating to achieve personal status" (in Wu Te's words) were factors making for unreliability, other elements also entered the picture.

---

[16] *Jenmin jihpao*, March 11, 1953.

Even with politically reliable cadres, economic reporting could break down. Only an effective control system could counteract this, and such a control system required workable economic as well as political controls.

Lu Ta, deputy chairman of the Tientsin City Control Committee, reported on the importance of economic control. More than 50 percent of all incidents of corruption, waste, bureaucratism, violation of laws, and commandism concerned financial, economic, and industrial bureaus, he said. Henceforth, control offices would be established and strengthened in all domestic and foreign trading companies, in all construction and engineering offices, in short in all major offices and units of basic economic work in the city.[17]

On July 1, 1953, *Jenmin jihpao* reported in detail on the operations of the control office in the Shihchingshan Steel Works. The office had been set up in February. Because of support both from Party and management cadres, control work developed rapidly. The personnel had been increased from one part-time control cadre to five full-time control cadres. Control work proved particularly effective in protecting and saving state property. The office also concentrated on problems of work discipline, and by propagandizing one flagrant case of violation of work discipline "established respect among the masses." Henceforth, workers would go directly to the control office with complaints, rather than transmitting them to higher-level control committees or writing to the newspapers. At first most letters of complaint from workers had been about living and working conditions, but then gradually criticisms of management cadres and suggestions for improving work and economizing on materials had been voiced. The control office also had concerned itself with safety problems and had set up an "accidents-resolving team."

This was one of the first times that a fairly detailed account had appeared of the operations of a control office in a major industrial enterprise. It is significant that the office itself had not been established until the early part of 1953. That was still the period of one-man management, when the factory manager was powerful. The control office was directly attached to the manager's office. The factory manager was specifically mentioned as the key person in charge of control work. It is therefore not surprising that none of the control cadres were mentioned as having any particularly economic control functions. The tasks of the control cadres were still clearly political.

Thus it is apparent that factory managers were still in full charge of

---

17 *Tientsin jihpao*, March 30, 1953.

everything, which made the development of an independent system of control along Soviet lines difficult. Enterprises were subject to "economic accounting," but this was done by the enterprise itself and not by outsiders. The banks had the power to check on the financial affairs of the enterprise, but it is doubtful whether the enterprise accountants were more responsive to the banks than they were to their bosses in the factory. There was a real contradiction in policy, for while the control system was supposed to develop independent checks on management, control operations themselves were still subject to managerial veto power.

On July 31, 1953, the central government finally issued general rules for control correspondents at all levels of government. The earlier "temporary rules" were officially superseded by the new rules. The general rules were much like the previous temporary rules. Though they reaffirmed that the control correspondents were to remain in close contact with the masses, nothing was said about their exercising control over administrators in agencies or managers in industry.[18]

On September 26, 1953, *Jenmin jihpao* published a report on how the control offices were beginning to exercise economic controls. During the early part of the year, the report said, the Szechwan provincial government organized seventeen teams "to investigate storage of food, the use of funds for culture and education, and production conditions in construction and industrial departments of urban government." Furthermore, special district- and county-level leadership cadres also "organized their forces" to help investigate. (In total, 191 units were investigated.) There were many instances of "the leadership of certain units showing serious irresponsibility toward state property."

The report mentioned three main types of economic abuses:

In some units, budgets had not been made up, plans not been reported, or been put in operation without permission. For example, one middle school in Fuling County, without permission from higher authorities, built school dormitories with an enormous budget of 1.2 million yuan. This included an electricity generating shop. All this was done under the slogan "Complete Socialization." In Tachu County, the authorities were going to use a budget of 70,000 yuan to build a "culture district" in the city suburbs. The public security bureau in Ch'iunglai County built some dormitories with extraordinary waste of money. Tzukung City built a plumbing factory which even with maximal growth of the city's population could not use more than 50 percent of its capacity. All were instances of construction taking place accord-

---

18 *Jenmin jihpao*, August 1, 1953.

ing to plans and budgets which had not been cleared by higher authorities or had not been examined in detail.

In the expenditure of business funds, special funds had not been used for purposes indicated; there was false reporting and reckless usage; surplus funds were hidden and not returned to higher authorities; expenditures were made at will; waste was widespread. Three normal schools in Tachu County took 100,000 yuan meant for basic construction and used it for buying materials in Chungking. One cadre school in Fuling actually spent 1,200 yuan of its repair funds, but reported spending 18,400 yuan. Of their transportation funds they spent 100 yuan, but falsely reported more than 1,900. The remainder was "buried."

There had been extraordinary instances of molding and rotting of stored food supplies, particularly in areas where transportation was poor. Improper storage facilities and poor care of stored food were the main causes.

The report said that industrial enterprises had also been investigated. There were many instances of failure to fulfill plans. In one Chengtu machine shop, plan fulfillment was only 72.5 percent because of improper allocation and use of labor, deficiencies in equipment, the poor quality of the inspection system, absenteeism, and poor product quality. In 1952, total output was 580,000 yuan, but wastage amounted to more than 105,000 yuan. In addition, cases of corruption were uncovered. The director of the materials shop of a dyeing factory was discovered to have committed serious acts of corruption which had not been revealed during *Sanfan*.

Although the instances of economic laxness were serious, the report indicated that the basic method of dealing with the problem was still to convince the leadership of the unit to reform, "to set up systems and clear up their books." In one unit, a small exhibition was held. Elsewhere blackboard bulletins were used to criticize the offenders. With this investigative work, "some manifestations of misunderstanding between control workers and the units under investigation were removed, thus letting the control workers obtain the support of leadership and masses." [19]

The Introduction of the Harbin System

The preceding section makes it evident that the control problems facing the Chinese Communists became increasingly economic. Moreover, in contrast to economic problems during the period immediately

---

[19] *Ibid.,* September 26, 1953.

following victory, such as corruption and hoarding, the problems when the First Five-Year Plan went into effect were of a recurrent nature, such as waste, inefficiency, and nonfulfillment of plan targets. These could not be resolved with the crude methods of political control used to combat corruption and hoarding. They required a permanent structure of economic control, staffed by capable cadres. The Ministry of State Control, formally established in 1954, as a branch-type central ministry with a national network of control agencies, was designed as such a permanent structure of economic control. The model control method which it developed at that time was known as the Harbin system, so named because the Chief Accounting Office of the Central Manchurian Railroad was in Harbin. Since the introduction of the Harbin system was closely tied in with the struggle between Peking and Mukden, it is not simple to disassociate the general political from the specific economic aspects of the system.

The Harbin system of control work was the most ambitious method of exercising economic control devised by Peking. The method, in essence, consisted in setting up a network of accounting offices with far-reaching powers to investigate the activities of all state-owned enterprises. Such investigation meant not only a check on plan fulfillment, but on-the-spot checking of enterprises while production was in progress. To make sure that the accounting offices were independent of pressure from local sources, they were placed under the sole jurisdiction of the Central Control Commission in Peking. In short, the apparatus of the Central Control Commission (later in the year renamed the Ministry of State Control) was to become a powerful weapon in the hands of Peking for exercising control over the growing modern sector of the economy. Since Manchuria was the core of this sector, the Harbin system must be seen as Peking's weapon to wrest power from the Manchurian bureaucracy and those behind it. This is evident from the linkage between the decisions of the Fourth Plenum of February 1954 and the Third National Conference on Control Work, which met in Peking from April 5 to April 20, 1954, and decided on the adoption of the Harbin system. The Fourth Plenum, as indicated in the preceding chapter, marked the opening of the campaign to destroy "the independent kingdom" of Manchuria. The fact that the Harbin system was initially introduced in the railroad network indicated clearly that centralization of the railroad system was an important objective of Peking in realizing victory over Mukden.

Though the Harbin system was announced as official policy in April 1954, it apparently had been in effect "experimentally" well before that time. Late in 1953, Wang Han,[20] then chairman of the People's Control Committee for South China and later to become a major figure in the Ministry of State Control, mentioned the Harbin system in a speech delivered at a control work conference in Canton. Though he gave little detail, he indicated that the Harbin system had already been in operation for some time in the Central Manchurian Railroad, which, until late 1952, had been in Soviet hands. One of Wang Han's remarks at that conference characterized the real aims of the Harbin system:

> In order to supervise and investigate production and financial plans, one must carefully study operations; if one does not, then the "outsider" cannot get an idea of the "insider's" affairs, and he will not achieve good results in supervision and investigation.[21]

Wang Han was one of the leaders in the campaign to introduce the Harbin system into Manchuria. The fact that his work until early 1954 had been in South China meant that he was not associated with the Manchurian bureaucracy, which the Harbin system was designed to weaken. Indeed, he was one of the "outsiders" used by Peking to gain domination over the affairs of the "insiders" in Manchuria.

The long duration of the Third National Conference on Control Work indicated the seriousness of the subject matter and implied major disagreements. The substance of the conference, as announced, was the application of the decisions of the Fourth Plenum to control work. The conference was attended by 142 persons, all leading members of control commissions from province and major-city levels up. In other words, most of the country's important control officials were present. The major reports were given by Liu Ching-fan, Wang Han, and P'an Chen-ya, all vice chairmen of the Central Control Commission.

During the meeting, "important directives" from the central government were announced by Hsi Chung-hsün, chairman of the Secretariat of the Government Affairs Council. The experiences of the Harbin Ch'iulin Corporation were reported by Chang Mu-yao, then a member of the Central Control Commission. The experiences of the Harbin Railroad Accounting Office were reported by Yeh K'o-ming, then chief accountant of that office. The Tientsin *Takungpao* published a short

---

20 Wang Han was deputy chairman of the South-Central China control commission; later he became deputy chairman of the Ministry of Control. He was from Kiangsu. In the late 1930's and early 1940's, he had been chief of the political department of the New Fourth Army, then commanded by Li Hsien-nien. In the mid-1950's, he was a candidate member of the Party's control commission. See pp. 358ff.

21 Kwangtung *Nanfang jihpao*, February 17, 1954.

summary of the conference on April 24. However, it was not till May 8 that the *Jenmin jihpao* reported in detail on the conference and with official comment. On the same day, the *Jenmin jihpao* published an editorial announcing the new policy of introducing "the advanced experiences of the Harbin Railroad Accounting Office."

In view of the fact that the Harbin system was already in operation, judging from Wang Han's speech in Canton, the main purpose of the Third National Conference on Control Work must have been to discuss the results of its "experimental" introduction. In this sense, the summary published by the *Takungpao* four days after the conference ended takes on particular importance, since it appears to have reflected the general mood of the conference much more directly than the later *Jenmin jihpao* report. The *Takungpao* summary indicated clearly that the Harbin system could only be introduced gradually and experimentally, and that much preparation was necessary before its methods could be used.[22] The lack of agreement was indicated by the concluding sentence in the summary: "One must oppose conservative thoughts, but one also must oppose recklessness." The conflict was between advocates of external and advocates of internal control. As will be discussed in the following section, the parties to the conflict represented different political groups who were contending for power at the highest levels.

Disagreement led to ambivalence in the official reports on the decisions of the conference. On the one hand control work was criticized for not developing enough of an independent spirit toward the units they were supposed to investigate. Yet at the same time, control workers were criticized for disregarding the opinions of local Party and government organizations.

This ambivalence was also revealed in the editorial published on May 8 by the *Jenmin jihpao*. The first part of the editorial described the conditions that led to the introduction of the Harbin system. It began by noting that all kinds of harmful and illegal conditions still existed in the economic sector. One must "carry out a constant struggle" against these phenomena. The *Jenmin jihpao* editorial stated:

Among some workers and state agencies . . . extremely dangerous arrogance has developed. Because some success in their work has turned their heads, they have forgotten the attitudes of modesty and the spirit of criticism which all Party members must have. All they can take is praise, not criticism. . . . There are some who show manifestations of weakness, whose struggle against the above-mentioned evil phenomena is without force and who do not uphold principle. They worry about their personal fate, they are afraid of accusing individuals and suffering retaliation. Thus they cannot resolutely and promptly

---

22 Tientsin *Takungpao*, April 24, 1954.

expose all kinds of shortcomings and errors. In particular, they are afraid of exposing the errors and shortcomings of responsible cadres. These conditions seriously obstruct and prolong the resolution and overcoming of all kinds of evil phenomena.

This, the editorial said, had to be changed. Criticism and self-criticism had to be furthered, in particular criticism from below. The most crucial area for control work was the economic sector, particularly the state-owned enterprises:

This is because, on the one hand these sectors make massive use of state capital, but on the other hand must also accumulate capital in great quantity for purposes of socialist industrialization of the nation. The quality of their work directly influences the speed of socialist accumulation and the industrialization of the nation.

The editorial pointed out that the Harbin Railroad Accounting Office was directly under the leadership of the Ministry of Railroads of the Central Government. "This assures that control cadres do not come under the influence of any kind of regionalism or 'localism' and can carry out a resolute struggle against all errors, shortcomings, and evil tendencies of the enterprises or agencies under control."

But the second part of the editorial intoned an opposite note. The Harbin system had to be introduced resolutely, yet great care had to be taken. For one thing, competent cadres were still lacking. Where the Harbin system had not yet been introduced, it must first be studied carefully, and plans made to introduce it gradually. The editorial stressed that control cadres must always seek the support of Party committees and management in the offices and factories they are to investigate. It called upon them to be modest and careful, to avoid subjectivism, and not to make excessive use of their authority.[23]

First the *Jenmin jihpao* editorial called upon control cadres to be resolute in investigating "workers in state agencies," and then it called upon them to be the opposite of this, namely modest and careful.

Political and Economic Aspects of the Harbin System

In view of the manifest relationship between the April conference on control work and the politically important February Fourth Plenum, the implicit disagreements and the explicit ambivalences of that conference must have been bound up with the struggle between Peking and Mukden. Since that struggle involved political as well as economic elements, let us try to see how the two were related.

The conference was ostensibly concerned with the question of eco-

23 *Jenmin jihpao,* May 8, 1954.

nomic control. It was repeatedly stressed that control cadres must exercise "on-going" supervision over the activities of economic agencies and state-owned enterprises. The discussion of control work had come a long way since the first years after the "liberation," when intensive efforts were made to recruit organizational informers, the control correspondents. Now the concern was about the whole direction of economic development. The literature begins to make reference to the need for "supervision" as well as "control," for "before-the-fact" as well as "after-the-fact" investigation.

This is expressed by two words, *chienc'a* and *chientu*. *Chienc'a* meant essentially to check on performance after it was accomplished. *Chientu* meant to watch over performance in progress. If the latter supervision was to be allowed, control cadres could barge into offices at any time and demand to look at plans and accounts. Such supervision is one of the most extreme and disturbing forms of control. It means that the manager is constantly threatened with visits from control cadres, and when they show up he must produce all his documents for them. Since such forms of supervision were not without potential sanction, this meant that the manager had to be forever worried about punishment at a time when he should be putting all his efforts into achieving his plan targets.

The control cadres were understandably afraid of assuming the awesome responsibility of such "before-the-fact" supervision. Under one-man management, managers had acquired great powers, and were not easily to be intimidated by the "outsiders" coming inside the enterprise. But the managers were not alone. Most strategic state-owned enterprises, both old and new (i.e., the industrial units supplied by the USSR), were in Manchuria. Standing behind the managers of these state-owned enterprises was the powerful Mukden bureaucracy, under Kao Kang's control and perhaps even more under the influence, if not the actual power, of the Soviet experts. The Harbin Railroad Accounting Office had come under Peking's firm control with the centralization of the railroad administration. So when the *Jenmin jihpao* talked about control cadres being afraid to investigate economic bureaucrats and managers, it meant persons who were supposed to take their orders directly from Peking and move against bureaucrats and managers whose orders came largely from Mukden.

This brings us to another reference in the May 8 *Jenmin Jihpao* editorial. It castigates the state-owned industrial sector for using up huge quantities of capital but failing to do its part in the accumulation program. From the economic critiques which begin to be heard in 1956, it is clear that the main offenders here were the big state-owned enterprises. Under the policy of favoritism which they enjoyed during the First Five-Year Plan, these enterprises acquired almost unlimited capital and help from the central government, but "did not bear the burden of accumulation," as the economic critic Sun Yeh-fang put it in 1957 (see p. 83). As in the Soviet Union, the big enterprises were supposed to produce and not worry about accumulation; that would be taken care of by the remainder of the society. Since heavy industry was given top priority, these enterprises were allowed to engage in waste as long as they came up with the goods. Most of these strategic heavy industrial enterprises were in Manchuria. The remainder of China was paying for the industrialization of Manchuria, a region over which the central government had as yet only inconclusive control. Given these economic problems, Peking's interest in an independent structure of external economic controls is evident.

However, economics and politics, as we have pointed out, were closely related. This is apparent from the fact that China's economy at that time was directed by the State Planning Commission, a body which then had the nature of a political-economic high command. The State Planning Commission, set up late in 1952, was headed by Kao Kang. The membership of the Planning Commission included a surprising number of leading individuals who were later, at one time or another, eliminated from leadership: Ch'en Yün, who later receded into the shadows of political oblivion; P'eng Te-huai, purged in 1959; Jao Shu-shih, Kao Kang's comrade in the purge of 1955; Huang K'o-ch'eng, purged along with P'eng Te-huai; Ma Hung, purged at the time of the Kao-Jao affair. Of the remaining members of the Planning Commission, Teng Tzu-hui must be mentioned as an opponent of Mao Tse-tung's radical policies in agriculture; and Hsüeh Mu-ch'iao and Po I-po as professionals. Of the deputy chairmen of the Planning Commission, only Li Fu-ch'un played a major role in later years; Lin Piao, P'eng Chen, and Teng Hsiao-p'ing were on the commission, but only as regular members. We may never know what the real power constellations were at that time, but it is certain that the central political authorities could hardly have regarded the State Planning Commission as completely responsive to their wishes. If the Mukden bureaucracy controlled the Manchurian economic system, the composition of the Planning Commission made it unlikely that any effective counterforce would be launched from that direction.

Kao Kang and Jao Shu-shih came from the two industrial centers of China: Manchuria and Shanghai. Why Jao Shu-shih was linked up with Kao Kang in the anti-Party conspiracy has never been clear. Yet in the context of economic administration some linkage may be discernible. Not only were both on the State Planning Commission, but both undoubtedly had strong interests in economic development. Despite the hostility of the Yenan group to Shanghai, Shanghai remained a key center of light industry and contributed greatly to the program of national accumulation. A major share of national savings was being channeled toward Manchuria, and Shanghai must have made a considerable contribution to this program of resource allocation. After all, it was the State Planning Commission which made the major decisions on economic policy, both the determination of capital allocation (division of the national budget) and the setting up of developmental priorities. An alliance probably developed between Kao Kang and Jao Shu-shih, with the aim of acquiring a firm political grip on the economic system of the whole country. Shanghai and Manchuria were key areas in the country's economy. It is reasonable to presume that Stalin schemed to acquire organizational footholds in China, as he had in Eastern Europe. Perhaps he intended to do this by capturing the economy of China. Manchuria was rapidly being turned into the bastion of the Chinese economy, with a man in control who most likely was closely linked with the Soviets. The Chinese Communist party could not be captured, for the men of Yenan had built up the Party as their one great organizational instrument. But the system of economic administration could be infiltrated, and perhaps also the military.

The disagreements and ambivalences of the Third National Conference on Control Work become more understandable when seen in this larger political and economic context. The May 8 *Jenmin jihpao* editorial, on the one hand, stated that control cadres were to make a big push to carry out effective control over economic agencies and state enterprises. Yet at the same time they were told not to be too arrogant and to listen to the advice of local Party and government officials. The trouble in Manchuria was precisely that the officials and managers listened to the advice of pro-Mukden Party and government leaders.

Though the Party apparatus may have been under Kao Kang's control in Manchuria, the Party apparatus in Shanghai was probably much more responsive to the will of Peking. After all, Ch'en Yi and K'o Ch'ing-shih, later mayor of Shanghai, played major administrative roles in Kiangsu and Shanghai since the early 1950's. The disagreements and ambivalences would appear to imply that the conference advocated adopting the Harbin system and at the same time not adopting it! Our discussion suggests the conclusion that the May 8 *Jenmin jihpao* editorial in effect aimed a double blast, one at Manchuria and the other at Shanghai. For Manchuria, it ordered the implementation of the Harbin system in order to cut the links of economic administrators and managers with the Party and government bureaucracy in Mukden. For Shanghai, it ordered the control cadres to act as instruments of the Party, which was the one reliable arm of the central government. This meant the introduction of a Party-dominated Harbin system. As far as the remainder of the country was concerned, the system could be introduced "gradually and experimentally" and, by implication, not at all.

The Harbin System as an Independent Control Structure

Now that we have established the general political and economic background to the introduction of the Harbin system, let us see what kind of control structure it was. We have already pointed out that one of Peking's main weapons in its struggle with Mukden was centralization of the Manchurian railroad network. It was in the railroad network that the Harbin system was first introduced, as Wang Han pointed out in 1953.

On the same day that the May 8 *Jenmin jihpao* editorial and the report on the Third National Conference on Control Work appeared, the *Jenmin jihpao* reported in detail on "the control work experiences of the Harbin Railroad Accounting Office." This office was called *chiho-chü*, a term not encountered elsewhere—part of Manchuria's independence consisted in the right to coin its own special terminology. In the first sentence of the report, *Jenmin jihpao* had to point out that *chiho* meant *chiench'a*, control. *Jenmin jihpao* went into some detail on the history of the office. When the Sino-Soviet Changchun Railroad Company was established, a system of control over railroad operations was set up because of the "relative confusion then existing in the economic methods and management practices of the Chinese railroads," and because the political, economic, and operational knowledge of the cadres was low. Thus in May 1950, a control council (called *chienshih-hui*, again terminologically different from similar bureaus elsewhere in China) was set up. Its operational arm was the accounting office, which "combined the advanced experiences of control systems in the U.S.S.R. with concrete conditions on Chinese railroads." By the end of 1952, it had succeeded in getting rid of 6,248 excess employees, and saving an annual wage quota of more than 1.8 million yuan. Early in 1953 (according to *Jenmin jihpao*, but the transfer officially took place late in 1952), the USSR returned the Central Manchurian Railroad to China. The Ministry of Railroads of the Chinese government then set up the Harbin Railroad Accounting Office on the foundation of the original Control Office and Accounting Office. The *Jenmin jihpao* article pointed out explicitly that the Accounting Office received "direct leadership" from the Ministry of Railroads and had full powers of control over the

Harbin Railroad Administrative System, the Harbin Train Car Repair Shop, and the Dairen Train Car Manufacturing Factory. During 1953, the Harbin Railroad Accounting Office continued its practices of thorough economic accounting; it prevented the "illogical expenditure" of more than 1.5 million yuan and reduced excess personnel by 4,097, with a wage saving of 200,000 yuan. In the process, the Harbin Accounting Office became a model of good economic accounting and control work.

According to the *Jenmin jihpao* the Harbin Railroad Accounting Office was "an independent, vertical organizational structure" directly under the jurisdiction of the Ministry of Railroads. It was a model of a parallel bureaucracy. It set up its own "line accounting offices," *yen-hsien chiho-shih,* alongside every branch office of the railroad down to basic-level units. Accountants were placed all along the line to watch over the financial actions of the controlled units. By dispatching its own cadres to the units "it prevents control personnel from being restrained by the agencies under control, and removes them from the influences of localism." The *Jenmin jihpao* article noted that conditions in many units made for resistance against the uncovering of errors and shortcomings. The newspaper praised the advantages of such an "independent, vertical control organization" as they had been demonstrated for the past three years. It cited an example:

The section chief of the Anganghsi Work Section, without the permission of higher echelons or the agreement of the accountant stationed there, arbitrarily concluded an engineering agreement with a certain factory to make steam pipes for the work section, using workers intended for railway line repair and maintenance. Business funds for this purpose were not turned over to the accountant for booking, but were deposited with the union. The section chief wanted to cover this up before higher echelons, and make of his unit "a small family," thus seriously violating the state financial system.[24] The resident accountant repeatedly, verbally and in written form, proposed to the section chief that he mend his ways. Not only did the section chief not accept these proposals, but he used the funds to buy radios. Because the control worker firmly adhered to principles, this instance of behavior violating the state financial system was finally resolved. If the control worker had been a cadre of that unit, if he had been subject to the leadership of the unit, it would not have been easy for him to wage such a principled struggle against the man in charge of the unit.

Jenmin jihpao further pointed out that with the concentrated leadership of such a vertical independent system, 154 control workers were

---

[24] On the "web of mutual involvement" in the Soviet Union, see Berliner, *op. cit.,* pp. 264 ff.

able to exercise ongoing supervision over the more than 100,000 employees of the railroad and the two factories under its jurisdiction.

Jenmin jihpao described in some detail "the scientific methods of control" used by the Harbin Accounting Office.

The first was called "inspection of financial and production plans." All annual production and finance plans had to be submitted to the control office for "suggestions and proposals." The control office would suggest plan modifications by comparing the requirements of the railroad with the conditions of the national economy and the demands of the state vis-à-vis the railroad.

The second was called "everyday control." The management of the Harbin Railroad had 1,380 business units. The Harbin Control Office stationed control accountants in 340 of the largest of these to carry out everyday accounting control. They not only supervised all transactions in these offices, but no financial transactions could be carried out without their explicit consent. Control was not just done by the accounting offices. Part-time control workers (*pu-t'och'an chiho-yuan*, the equivalent of control correspondents, as the *Jenmin jihpao* explains) ranged through the unit to do on-the-spot checking.

The third was called "partial documentary investigation." This consisted of periodic key-point checking of all major economic documents in the unit.

The fourth was called "complete documentary investigation." This was one of the most complicated forms of control, for it required thorough checking of all books and papers of the unit. Such a task required the formation of special investigating teams, to which technical personnel from the unit itself was added. The Party committee was alerted to cooperate. Sudden, unannounced checks were carried out to prevent evidence from being covered up. The final full report was decisive and had to be prepared in detail. The control workers did not make any proposals themselves. The final report, however, had to be shown to the managers. They could add their own opinions to the report but could not change it in substance. A management meeting was then held to discuss the report, and minor reforms were carried out on the spot.

The fifth form of control was called "checking of annual and periodic business summaries." All units had to make annual and periodic (usually quarterly) summations of business operations, which constituted important material for planning and other financial-economic agencies. Control workers were to subject these reports to thorough checking.

Since so much of the Harbin system constituted financial control, it followed that one of the main tasks of the control cadres was to check on profits. The *Jenmin jihpao* said:

Enterprises as a whole come up with satisfactory earnings and profit figures. However, the control office, in investigating final accounting, can judge whether the sources of profit are proper or not. If a unit has earned too much profit, then this could indicate that its major production targets have not been met, or that in making high profits they have reduced product quality, or they have been wrongly saving on workers' health funds or technical safety funds, etc. This deserves criticism.

Linkages with the masses were not to be overlooked. Part-time control correspondents were to be recruited to pry out information from within the unit itself. The *Jenmin jihpao* report ended by praising the advantages of the Harbin system: Work was planned and there was a rigorous division of labor; all control work was coordinated; competitiveness among control workers was encouraged to create incentives for doing good control work; successful control groups and individuals were rewarded "spiritually and materially"; periodic work reports were made, couched in as simple a language as possible. The last comment noted that this was a control system first introduced by Soviet experts. It should be gradually extended to other enterprises, thus "allowing control work to develop its proper functions in the execution of the state's general goals, and in allowing control agencies, under the leadership of the Party, to become effective helpers in Party control over enterprises and for the execution of state policy and laws." [25]

The Harbin system was closely modeled on the type of external control that had been a major feature of Soviet economic administration, as the *Jenmin jihpao* report stated. Aside from its political importance as Peking's weapon to acquire control over the Manchurian economy, it had definite economic merit. For example, the Harbin system aided the state banks in exercising control over enterprise financial activities, one of the most important functions of the entire banking system. Though the state banks were powerful agents of financial control, their representatives were not able to go into the enterprises to check their books. Moreover, since enterprise accountants were all too often under the thumb of the manager, the banks were not always sure whether the presented accountings were correct. The control offices, which had the right of access to enterprise accounts, thus were important allies of the banks and the Finance Ministry in enforcing financial control. In contrast to the situation a few years earlier, when control cadres were

---

[25] *Jenmin jihpao*, May 8, 1954.

told to get along with managers, they were now given far-reaching authority over all officials and managers.

In 1954, the Harbin system was Peking's answer to Mukden's one-man management. If one-man management prevailed in industry, then a counterforce to check on management had to be found. Politically, this was a period of centralization, parallel bureaucracies, and vertical rule. In organization-theoretical terms, the only control system possible was external. The Harbin controllers had to be outsiders. Moreover, lacking political power, the only possible form of control they could exercise was over the performance of men, rather than over the men themselves. In short, external and economic controls went hand in hand. The Harbin system can be regarded as the most complex method of external economic controls developed in China.

In the following sections, it will become clear that the Harbin system was of short duration and was never even introduced in many parts of China. Though the main reasons were political, there were also economic factors. Before we continue our discussion of the return to political controls, a few of the economic factors may be cited there. One reason for the short duration of the Harbin system might have been the difficulty of recruiting enough technical personnel to do such complex control work. But since the Chinese have always been good at accounting, that difficulty alone would not constitute a reason for abandoning the system. A more important reason may have been the consequences of the system. The powers of the controllers and accountants were so great that in many instances they must have paralyzed the managers with fear of punishment. Chinese industry was not so well developed that it could run without lower-level flexibility and autonomy. The managers had such autonomy during the early 1950's, when even the Party was told not to interfere in production operations. The Harbin system, if pushed to an extreme, would have achieved its political goals of weakening the Manchurian bureaucracy, but could also have thrown a monkey wrench into industry at a time when the First Five-Year Plan was just starting.

POLITICAL CONTROL

The Shift Back to Political Controls

On June 13, 1955, *Jenmin jihpao* finally reported on the Fourth National Control Work Conference which had been held in Peking in April, 1955. Again, the reason for the delay in reporting the conference was not made clear. The reports on this conference by Minister of Control Ch'ien Ying—she was the first and only minister of state control in Communist China—and Deputy Minister Liu Ching-fan were not published until officially approved by the State Council on May 31, 1955. Both speeches had been given on April 7, 1955, thus indicating a delay of almost two months until the approval was given for publication. The delay was probably caused by disagreement over the nature of control work.

The *Jenmin jihpao* account of the conference does not mention the number of days the conference lasted, simply saying that the conference "was held in April," but one can surmise that it must have dragged on. There were 129 participants, representing top-level provincial and city control bureaus, and top cadres from control offices in all departments of the State Council. Liu Ching-fan reported on control work in 1954, and Ch'ien Ying outlined control work plans for 1955. Though "successes in control work" during 1954 were claimed, "considerable critical opinions were also expressed in regard to shortcomings in control work."

Successes in village control work were singled out for praise, particularly in the policy of "planned buying and selling." It was stated that in 1954, more than 500 industrial and construction units were investigated in regard to supply work, and more than 23,000 food-storage warehouses; that much wastage was prevented; that in 1954 the Harbin system was fully applied to the entire railroad network and introduced "experimentally" in twenty-four major industrial units. The results had been good, and had demonstrated the usefulness of the Harbin system in industry. Control offices, in collaboration with the units concerned, had continued to handle complaints from the people. But there had been serious shortcomings, particularly among control cadres, who often had failed to understand that their task was to help the units under control to rectify their errors and work for the execution of state policy. Apparently, there was serious friction between control cadres and unit administrators.

The tasks set for 1955 were outlined in general terms, but a new direction was proposed. The control cadres were to aid agencies to "reduce their staffs and simplify their structures." This was one of the earliest references to the "administrative simplification" policy that started early in 1956, upon completion of the *Sufan* movement. The conference called for "general study" of the Harbin system, and greater control over economic construction.

Ch'ien Ying's achievements had hitherto been entirely in the field of political control. Her connections in South China meant that she was clearly no participant in the political machinations of the Kao-Jao group. She had experience in political and organizational work, in contrast to the non-Party T'an P'ing-shan. Her long report on the direction and goals of control work is her first public pronouncement on the subject.

Ch'ien Ying stated that the three main tasks of control work in 1955 were: the completion of the third year of the First Five-Year Plan; the investigation of administrative and business bureaus at all levels "in order to tighten recruitment and simplify structure"; and the maintenance of state discipline. In sector terms, she said, this meant:

In industry and basic construction: investigating product mixes, quality, production costs, and labor productivity, fighting against plan falsification and false reporting of target achievements; in agriculture: investigating the carrying out of cooperativization; in transportation: investigating failures to fulfill transport plans and organizational weaknesses; in commerce: investigating excessive inventories, poor storage, and management failure.

Commenting further on the last of the three main tasks of control work envisaged for 1955, Ch'ien Ying said that in order to solidify work discipline in administrative units one must "maintain the concentrated and unified leadership of the state." In doing their work, control cadres "must respect the local Party organizations and submit to the leadership of the Party committee of the same echelon." The Party committee must be kept informed; control cadres must cooperate with the Party's control committees and with the People's Procuracy; stress must be placed on "key-point investigation," that is, on selection and investigation of crucial spots in the unit. For the first time, Ch'ien Ying outlined the way in which control tasks could be divided between different segments of the administration:

The Ministry of State Control and the state control agencies established in the financial and economic bureaus of the Central Government were to supervise state-owned industries under the jurisdiction of the Central Government.

Control offices in cities directly under central jurisdiction and in very large cities in general were to supervise local state-owned industries.

Control bureaus in the provinces and in special districts were to do political supervision over personnel in lower-echelon agencies, and to supervise the execution of state policy in agriculture. Special control agencies for agriculture were to be set up.

Since most major economic enterprises were, at that time, under central government jurisdiction (the so-called central state-owned enterprises), the allocation of tasks outlined by Ch'ien Ying indicated that the central government was to have sole authority and responsibility over the country's modern sector. Having just acquired control of the Manchurian economy, Peking was not yet willing to let it slip once again into provincial hands.

Ch'ien Ying, in effect, called both for more and less control work. First she stated that the methods of the Harbin system must be thoroughly learned and applied to economic-financial branches and state-owned industries. However, in discussing the application of the Harbin system, she mentioned only two branches of the economy: railroads and textiles. It is easy to read Manchuria and Shanghai for these two words, for the crux of the battle over the railroads lay in Manchuria, and the textile industry was still concentrated in Shanghai. Shanghai was, of course, the area of Jao Shu-shih's power. But Ch'ien Ying warned that one must be circumspect in generalizing the Harbin system, one must avoid "mechanical adoption," "wanting too much too fast." Second, she indicated that control work was becoming too far-flung. Control agencies, she said, have "an excessively scattered character." There must be greater stress on "key points" and on building up "core cadres." The number of control personnel should be reduced at *hsien* levels, but increased at province and major-city levels. In fact, it was enough to station control cadres in "key point counties." Financial and economic ministries should cut down on control personnel at the enterprise level and concentrate on setting up branch agencies in the big important enterprises and basic construction units. But one should proceed slowly, and not recklessly reassign cadres. Experience had shown, she said, that "the duties of state control agencies and the internal control agencies of the operational branches must be clearly delineated, leadership relationships changed, thereby making it easier for higher echelon state control agencies to unify command and concentrate the forces at their disposal."

This sentence expressed a serious organizational dilemma. Every ministry had its own control setup. In addition to this were the agencies of the Ministry of State Control. Here we see the struggle between the principles of internal and external control, in this case expressed structurally. At that time the regime was still wavering between the two. Ch'ien Ying pointed out that there were "two kinds of leadership relations" which the Ministry of State Control assumed toward the internal control agencies of the central ministries. ("Leadership relations," we may point out, means the command system.) (1) In control agencies whose organizational structure and work was relatively sound, vertical rule could be practiced. This meant that these agencies would take orders only from the Ministry of State Control. (2) Most control agencies were to continue to adhere to "dual rule." This meant that most ministries were not ready to accept control from "the outsider." Some control agencies stationed in ministries would be transformed into internal-control and investigative agencies of the ministry concerned, and "will be led by that ministry." Moreover, "the Ministry of State Control will only maintain liaison with them, and give them guidance in regard to control matters." This was an even greater concession to the ministries, giving them the right to take over some control agencies altogether. However, internal-control agencies within the ministries were empowered to carry out strict vertical rule in regard to control agencies and personnel stationed in enterprises under their jurisdiction. All central state-owned industrial and mining enterprises were not subject to leadership (read command) from local governments, but maintained liaison with the local control agencies. If needed, they could be coopted to help the enterprises in doing control work. Province and city control agencies were under the jurisdiction of province and city government, but maintained "guidance relationships" with control agencies of the central government.

One rarely gets a glimpse of the command structure within the state administration, and Ch'ien Ying had lifted the curtain a bit. Was the problem only one of internal versus external controls? Not entirely. None of the ministries was a bastion of vertical rule impervious to outside interference. Through a variety of devices the Party maintained a tight hold on the ministries: through the special coordinative offices set up directly below the State Council, through Party fractions which operated in every ministry and every department, and through the placing of Party people in key ministerial posts.

If the ministries were already subject to strict Party control, why should they object to supervision by the Ministry of State Control? Some hint may be given by Ch'ien Ying's statement that state control at the level of the central government should take essentially financial-economic forms, which could only mean auditing controls. But, considering the make-up of the Ministry of State Control, the right to examine books had political consequences, which meant in effect authority over personnel. Most top leaders in Communist China were well aware of the history of Stalin's rise to power, which, among other things, was greatly aided by his domination of the old *Rabkrin*. The *Rabkrin*, or workers-peasants inspectorate, that had been started by Lenin as a watchdog over the emergent Soviet bureaucracy, became an important weapon for behind-the-scenes control when it came into Stalin's hands. At lower levels, there were fights between management and Party over who should control hiring, firing, and promotion of employees. The managers took the position that this was a technical question, depending on the skills and performance of employees. The Party took the position that it was a "human," that is, political, problem. The Chinese Communists have always been opposed to the idea that anyone except the Party should have control over personnel questions. If the Ministry of State Control had been given significant rights of inspection over the financial and economic work of the ministries, a new powerful bureaucracy would have been created.

In the Soviet Union, the powers of the secret police and the Ministry of State Control had grown simultaneously. One had complemented the other. The police had the knowledge of who was who, and the Ministry of State Control was able to check on the performance of these individuals. There had been a division of labor between political and economic control. If the Ministry of State Control in China had been given greater powers, could this not have conjured up the possibility of a similar growth in police power? Clearly, the fear was there, for as Ho Kan-chih, the official Communist historian, says of the *Sufan* movement: "The first task of the movement was to strengthen the leadership of the Party over public security work, to put the public-security agencies under Party leadership."

From Ch'ien Ying's description of the command structure it was clear that, for most ministries, there was to be no interference from the control agencies outside the ministry. If there was going to be economic control, it would be from within.

There was another side to the picture. In September 1954, Kao Kang had been replaced by Li Fu-ch'un as chief of the State Planning Commission. What had been a powerful political-economic high command, directing the entire economy, had been changed into essentially a coordinative agency, concerned with compiling comprehensive balances (equilibrium tables), long-range planning, and doing its best to come up with adequate annual economic plans. One of the direct consequences of the loss of power by the State Planning Commission had been the gain of power by some of the big ministries. From the assault launched on the ministries late in 1957, one can conclude that their power had indeed become great. Thus, in addition to the fear that the Ministry of State Control might turn into a major bureaucratic weapon, there was also the determination of the big ministries to prevent outsiders from interfering in their own empires. Manchuria had been an "independent kingdom" based on territorial principles. Now new empires based on production principles were beginning to arise. None of them wanted to be faced with a Harbin system that would have meant inspectors watching over them.

But though Ch'ien Ying indicated that most ministries were to be allowed to control themselves, one ministry where the Ministry of State Control had the authority to exercise real external control was the Ministry of Railroads. The history of the railroad system brings us back into the murky politics of the time. On July 10, 1954, less than a month after the abolition of the Large Administrative Regions, the government had announced new regulations for the railroad administrative system. Explicit provision was made for external control to be exercised by control agencies of the central government. The railroad system in Communist China has always been closely tied in with the military. The Ministry of Railroads, since 1949, had been headed by T'eng Tai-yüan, a Hunanese who led peasant uprisings near Changsha in 1926 and since then had played important military roles in the Chinese Communist party. Judging from his long tenure in office, and the fact that most leading persons in the ministry held positions since the early years of the regime, one would not assume that the Ministry of Railroads had caused difficulties by demanding a bureaucratic autonomy for itself. As apparently in the Ministry of Public Security (also dominated by leading figures, such as Lo Jui-ch'ing, with long tenure in office), the difficulties were not in Peking but further down the system. Of the seventeen branch bureaus of the railroad administrative system, five were in Manchuria. The Ministry of Railroads had to cooperate closely with the army because troop movements depended heavily on the availability of railroad facilities. Just as some units of the Public Security Forces had apparently developed deviant tendencies, judging from Lo Jui-ch'ing's remarks at the Eighth Party Congress, likewise some of these lower-level bureaus of the railroad system may have been not completely responsive to the will of Peking. The implementation of the Harbin system (along with other political devices) was designed to rectify this situation. It is not only this larger context that must be taken into account in interpreting Ch'ien Ying's remarks on the Ministry of Railroads, but also the fact that preparations were under way for the *Sufan* movement, to begin in the summer of that same year.

Ch'ien Ying had started out by talking about economic control, and she ended up by once again stressing the importance of political controls. She criticized neglect of complaints from the people; and she criticized cadres who put all their emphasis on "supervision and investigation of production and finance problems." This, she said, was wrong. To overcome this attitude, outstanding cases should be thoroughly investigated and publicized "to educate the cadres and the broad masses." She warned cadres against developing traits of arrogance and self-satisfaction, and told them not to be discouraged by failures and shortcomings.[26]

The report is clearly ambivalent. It calls for more economic control, but at the same time tells control cadres not to go too far. It stresses a vertical control system, and yet most ministries are exempted. Throughout the report, there is a sense of distrust of bureaucracy, a suggestion of ultimate confidence in control "coming from below." A reassertion of the mass line was in the making.

The Shift to Internal Controls

Ch'ien Ying's report in April 1955 signaled a general shift from economic back to political, and from external to internal controls. This was a complex process, obstructed in many cases by the constellation of power relationships in the central government. However, later in 1955, these trends were becoming increasingly apparent, both in Peking and the provinces. The inauguration of the *Sufan* movement, the preparations for collectivization, and the general radicalization of the atmosphere furthered the process.

The shift back to political controls was obvious during the summer of 1955. All the lower-level control conferences held at that time stressed themes of political control. Thus, when the Wuhan City party congress laid down its general policy aims for the latter half of 1955, the control cadres met and decided that their main tasks should be the purging of counter-revolutionaries (*Sufan*) and economizing. It was made clear that their control work must take place in close collaboration with the local Party committees.[27]

Less obvious, though equally as important, was the shift from external to internal controls. Indications of this shift are given in the report of the Fifth Control Work Conference of Kiangsi province held from June 2 to June 30. The report of the chairman of the Kiangsi Province Control Department, Lung Piao-kuei, and the proceedings of the conference were not approved until August 4, and only published on August 13. Although the general policy outlines are the same as in Ch'ien Ying's report, Lung gives some details on the local situation. He still calls for continued study and application of the Harbin system. However, he makes some interesting and unusually specific remarks on

---

[26] *Ibid.*, May 13, 1954.

[27] *Ch'angchiang jihpao*, August 12, 1955.

the division of authority between central and provincial control agencies:

> In order to delineate the work responsibilities of the main administrative branch from the control branch and to make concentrated use of our control powers, the leadership (i.e., command) relationships between provincial control agencies and provincial financial-economic agencies are to take the following forms:
>
> 1) Vertical rule: the control offices in provincial departments of industry, agriculture, food, communications, and in the bureau of engineering construction are stationed there by the provincial department of control; therefore these control offices are under the command of the provincial department of control.
>
> 2) Control offices in other provincial financial-economic and business branches are subject to dual rule by the control agencies of higher echelons of the same branches (i.e., of the central ministries) and by the provincial department of control; leadership by the former is primary.
>
> 3) Control offices of agencies and enterprises directly attached to the central government in various areas of our province are already subject to dual rule by the control agencies of the [central] branch in question as well as by the leadership of that branch, or they may be subject only to vertical rule by higher-echelon [central] control agencies. In this case, our own provincial control agencies only maintain work liaison with them, and when necessary collaborate with them in work.
>
> In order to strengthen leadership and facilitate work, despite the described division of tasks, the heads of all provincial departments and bureaus must continue to emphasize leadership and direction of control work in the unit in question. They must give due attention to the work of their control cadres, aid and support them in supervision and investigation. This will help the branch to do its work well. But control workers, because of vertical rule relationships, must not disrespect the leadership of the heads of the units in question. They must open-mindedly accept guidance by the unit heads, obey unified instructions in their work, fit in with the central tasks of the unit, and thus develop their positive functions.[28]

Penetrating the jargon (alas, the never-ending trial of research on Communist China), a number of organizational facts are revealed.

Let us first look at point (3) of Lung Piao-kuei's report. It specifies that in agencies and enterprises which are subordinate to the central government ministries and situated in Kiangsi (at the time, these included all major economic agencies), the control machinery was not under the jurisdiction of the Kiangsi Provincial Control Department, or—by implication—the provincial authorities. This was in accordance

---

[28] *Kiangsi jihpao*, August 19, 1955.

with Ch'ien Ying's general policy outline. But exemption from provincial supervision did not mean that the control offices of all these central agencies and enterprises were under the sole jurisdiction of the Ministry of Control. Though Lung Piao-kuei mentions that some of these control offices were under dual rule and others under vertical rule from the central government, we can be sure, from Ch'ien Ying's remarks noted above, that most central ministries exercised direct jurisdiction over their own control offices.

Points (1) and (2) show that the provincial control department had relatively greater authority than the central Ministry of Control. It had sole jurisdiction in many departments of the provincial government, such as industry, agriculture, food, and communications. Even in departments where dual rule predominated—as mentioned in point (2)—it was specified that the provincial control department's role was primary. By contrast, we have noted that the direct vertical authority of the central Ministry of Control was limited to only a few ministries—notably the Ministry of Railroads.

The greater degree of horizontal authority on the part of the provincial control department indicates that branch-type administration and parallel bureaucracies were far less important at the provincial than at the central level. This point is important to remember in connection with our thesis, stated in the chapters on party and government, that lateral coordination, carried out by Party committees, was a significant phenomenon of regional government in Communist China.

From Lung Piao-kuei's report, the trend toward internal controls, both in central and provincial agencies, is apparent.

Though there still was some talk of implementing "vertical rule" and the Harbin system at regional and local levels, attempts to introduce them into the control system encountered considerable opposition. The *Ch'angchiang jihpao* (Yangtze Daily) published a detailed report by a control office on its experiences in using the Harbin system on a construction site for workers' dormitories of a textile factory. "Great success" was achieved, yet the report ended with several cautionings. The control cadres sent down to the construction site had been careful to remain on good terms with management and the Party branch. Furthermore, in carrying out the Harbin system of before-the-fact supervision, they had proceeded "from the easy to the difficult." That was to say, they began by inspecting the financial aspects of the operation and only gradually went over to inspection of production. They were careful not to demand that all doors be opened to their scrutiny at once. Though they were under the sole jurisdiction of the control office of the Wuhan

City Road Construction Company and hence "not subject to the influence of localism," still they were careful "not to arouse the anger and reactions of the unit under supervision." Furthermore, they were careful to explain their work procedures in much detail. Their authority was defined in terms of the concrete conditions they encountered. The report ended with a warning against applying these "advanced Soviet experiences" *in toto*. One was to take into consideration actual conditions as they existed.[29]

Despite the fact that vertical control was still to be exercised at provincial and local levels, the report showed the difficulties that such work encountered. Again it was the old story of "insider" versus "outsider," so often discussed in the Chinese Communist literature—*neihang* versus *waihang*. It became increasingly clear that only a Party committee that had its roots *within* the organization could provide the leadership and supervision the regime wanted.

What made organizational units so resistant to outside interference? I might offer the explanation that because of the necessary flexibility in day-to-day operations, any investigation, before-the-fact or after-the-fact, would come up with so many irregularities that, under strict interpretation of the laws, all management would march off to prison. Students of Soviet industry have noted the importance of illegal and informal activities in the management of Soviet enterprises. Without this *de facto* flexibility, industry would grind to a halt. The situation was worse in China, where the economy was not only more backward, but, because of the importance of the traditional sector, was also more complicated. Chinese business, as we noted in the previous chapter, always operated through webs of economic and human relationships that often covered great geographical areas. The Chinese Communists later called them "historical economic relationships." These relationships could not arbitrarily be translated into the formal Soviet-style system imposed by the Chinese Communists. Thus to get things done "illegality" had to be tolerated. The regime finally decided to use this flexibility rather than combat it, but to put the power to use it in the hands of the Party. Formal control work failed in China for the same reason that formal law failed. Business, in order to get done, required such an array of devious means and approaches that full application of control and law would have paralyzed it. During the Great Leap Forward, the regime tried direct political command. That did not work either. The introduction of N. E. P.-type policies since early 1961 was the final rec-

---

29 *Ch'angchiang jihpao,* August 17, 1955.

ognition that the Chinese economy had in-built complexities of its own that neither the Soviet system of the First Five-Year Plan nor the Chinese system of the Great Leap Forward was able to change.

The Consummation of the Process

At the Eighth Party Congress of 1956, the old methods of control were declared to be obsolete and new methods to be inaugurated. The mass line was henceforth to become the basic guideline for control work.

Ch'ien Ying delivered the report on control work activities. She began with a denunciation of "bureaucratism." After a brief listing of control-work successes in the preceding period, she added:

> First of all, Party committees at all levels must strengthen their leadership over government agencies and enterprises. At certain time periods they must make use of the methods of "rectification" to thoroughly expose and criticize bureaucratic tendencies. The Party committees concerned must constantly investigate the conditions of fulfillment of the Party's resolutions and policies in state agencies and enterprises.

Though the report manifestly dealt with Party control, it implicitly revealed a shift of emphasis from the formal control agencies to the intra-unit Party committees. Henceforth, basic controls would be exercised by the Party internally within the unit.

ECONOMIC AND POLITICAL CONTROLS OVER ENTERPRISES

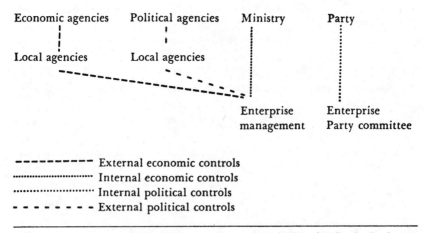

NOTE: Economic agencies designate agencies, such as the People's Bank, the former Ministry of State Control, the Finance Ministry, the Planning and Economic Com-

Ch'ien Ying announced that state bureaus were overstaffed and that there would have to be considerable "sending down"—*hsiafang*—that is, staff reduction. Excess personnel would be shifted to basic-level enterprises and villages. Then, Ch'ien Ying added: "If bureaucratism has not effectively been overcome, the state control agencies also bear a certain responsibility for this." This, she said, was due to serious deficiencies on the part of control cadres. To overcome this, "it is to be hoped that Party committees at all levels and Party organizations in all branches will strengthen their leadership vis-à-vis the state control agencies." Party fractions in state control agencies must constantly report to the Party committees. Furthermore, "close liaison must be established with the departments concerned, and all-sided coordination and support must be achieved."[30]

The report, in effect, announced the end of an independent system of control. Henceforth, political control would be under strict Party supervision and take place in close liaison with basic work in the unit. Economic control would presumably be carried out within the branches concerned and by external agencies such as the banks and the financial bureaus of the government. However, as far as the general approach to control was concerned, the shift from external to internal, and from essentially economic to essentially political controls had been consummated. Henceforth, men, rather than their performance, were to be the main object of control work. In this situation, the Party and not the Ministry of State Control had the decisive role to play.

In December 1956, the Sixth National Conference on Control Work was held in Peking (the Fifth National Conference had been held early in 1956, also in Peking). The theme of the conference followed that of the Eighth Party Congress: the struggle against bureaucratism. All control agencies in 1957 were reminded to emphasize investigation of the following problems: implementation of the policy of increasing production and economizing; implementation of the policy of reducing administrative structures; and working toward the implementation of control from below, that is, investigation of citizens' complaints, making personal visits, and using control correspondents.

---

missions, and, now, the General Political Departments, which check on but do not command the operations of the enterprise. Ministry designates the central or regional branch-type agency to which the enterprise is attached. Party designates the next-higher echelon of Party organization directly above the enterprise Party committee. Political agencies designate political and legal agencies, such as the Ministry of Public Security, the Ministry of Internal Affairs, the Political and Legal branches of central and regional government, and, formerly, also the Ministry of State Control.

[30] *Jenmin shouts'e, 1957*, pp. 132-133.

Collaboration with Party and government was emphasized, and control cadres were exhorted to coordinate their work as much as possible with the units being controlled. The conference was addressed by Chu Teh, Li Hsien-nien, Po I-po, and Liao Lu-yen.[31]

As usual after national conferences, regional meetings were held which repeated the themes. The stress, here too, was on the mass line, that is, control from below through criticisms, complaints, letters, and direct contacts with the people.[32]

An Exception to the Trend

The new policy enunciated in 1956 by Ch'ien Ying at the Eighth Party Congress meant a general shift from economic to political, and from external to internal controls. However there were some exceptions to the policy; in some areas and sectors of the country tight economic control still had to be exercised. Notable among them was Shanghai.

In March, 1957, a local control work conference was held in Shanghai. It was an important meeting, as indicated by the fact that it was attended by more than 800 cadres. The report on the conference spelled out in more detail than usual the concrete tasks of economic control. It is clear that the kinds of control problems described below could under no circumstances be resolved by political controls alone. The report stated:

> In industry, one must investigate waste in the use and storage of supplies, as well as the kind of "localism" where [enterprise] procurement plans demand too much or where [the enterprises] oppose reallocation of supplies they have hoarded. . . . In commerce, one must investigate loss and waste of property, investigate failure to calculate costs, shortcomings in economic accounting, as well as loss and waste resulting from spoilage of goods and poor manufacturing. . . . In basic construction, one must investigate projects to make sure they accord with immediate needs, to make sure that building costs and scale are not excessive, whether designs, manpower, building materials, tools, and equipment are available, whether earth-moving and tearing-down work can be completed in time. . . . As regards food, one must investigate how food storage is carried out, expose loss and waste of food due to poor arrangements. . . . One must also do key-point investigation (i.e., intensive spot-checking) of the branches concerned to see whether they are carrying out the directives of the city people's committees in regard to simplification of administrative structures, tightening up of organization, proposals for economizing in bureaus, opposing bigness in organization, extravagance and waste. One must investigate

---

31 *Jenmin jihpao*, January 14, 1957.
32 *Kweichow jihpao*, February 19, 1957.

and rigorously punish workers in agencies and enterprises guilty of corruption and stealing.[33]

This seems to be a sensible statement of the problems of economic control. The same problems are amply documented from other Soviet-type economies. Enterprises asking too much from the supply agencies and then refusing to surrender hoarded supplies are a common phenomenon. Localism was almost built into the system. Every enterprise became a kind of community—by design. The result was that almost all groups in the enterprise (with the possible exception of the Party) were in league with each other to maximize the enterprise's economic position. Under such conditions, it would have seemed senseless to insist that all economic and external controls be abolished. Technically competent control cadres still had an important role to play in areas such as Shanghai.

Shanghai posed control problems which were not typical of other areas and required continued economic controls. It was the country's center of light industry, and its commercial capital. It was a city known for its complex dealings and its many black marketeers (called "yellow oxen" in Chinese). The network of economic relations in Shanghai was so intricate that Peking had no alternative but to continue a policy of enforcing economic controls, despite the fact that this went against the general policy trend.

PURGES

Rightism in the Ministry of State Control

In June 1957, the anti-rightist movement broke out. Late in August, rightists in the Ministry of Control were attacked. They were identified by name, and long articles denouncing them appeared in the newspapers of the country. The leading figure attacked was P'eng Ta, deputy bureau chief of the Ministry. Attacks on him and others in his group continued for several weeks and then abated. This period constituted the first phase of the anti-rightist campaign in the Ministry of Control.

Early in December, the second phase of the campaign began with a severe attack on Wang Han, deputy chief in the Ministry. Wang Han, as we have mentioned earlier, was one of the leading figures in the history of state control in China and played an important part in the

---

[33] Shanghai *Chiehfang jihpao*, March 28, 1957.

introduction of the Harbin system. (The anti-rightist movement, as a whole, consisted of three stages. The first stage, which began in June 1957, was marked by attacks largely on non-Party intellectuals and political figures; intellectuals had been the leading critics during the few weeks of freedom in May. The second stage began around August and consisted largely of a "rectification" campaign in the rural areas, known as the "socialist education" movement. The third stage began late in the year and was marked by a purge of rightist elements in the Party and in the state bureaucracy.)

Neither P'eng Ta nor Wang Han could be considered major political figures. They were in the category of second-stringers. It has long been a Chinese Communist practice to attack second-stringers as a way of weakening the power and influence of individuals much higher up in the hierarchy of power. These higher individuals and organizations are never named. People in Peking generally know who is really the object of attack; students of Communist China abroad must try to decipher the clues given in the official criticisms. Evidence indicates that, starting in the summer of 1957, a severe struggle had broken out within the highest ranks of the leadership. In its broadest sense, this was a struggle between the reds and the experts, between those who advocated a radical policy of social mobilization and those who advocated continuing caution in domestic policy. In personal terms, it may be seen as a struggle between the views of Mao Tse-tung and those of Ch'en Yün. The attacks on P'eng Ta and Wang Han give us an insight into the power struggle; of these two, the purge of Wang Han is the more important.

The attack on P'eng Ta started in a special national meeting on control work held in Peking in July. However, it was not till August 20 that the *Jenmin jihpao* announced "exposure of the anti-Party words and deeds" of P'eng Ta. Along with P'eng Ta, a number of other minor functionaries were "exposed," indicating that a group and not just a person was being attacked. P'eng was accused of "paternalism" and of being a "capitalistic rightist element." He was accused of making "poisonous attacks" on the Party, of regarding members of the Party fraction as mere "yes men," and of ridiculing the proletarian dictatorship as bureaucratism. The July meeting set the stage for the denunciation. It was followed by an intense campaign of rectification meetings and posting of wall newspapers. The *Jenmin jihpao* article said that the campaign went along rather slowly until, on August 17, Ch'ien Ying, acting on instructions from the center (undoubtedly the Politburo), personally led a mass meeting of positivists. Several follow-up meetings were held "to clarify policy and dispel worries."

On the day that the *Jenmin jihpao* published the report on rightism in the Ministry of Control, it also published a long article entitled: "P'eng Ta—A Deviant Element Who Smuggled Himself into the Party." It dealt at length with P'eng's career and thus revealed some of the background to the anti-rightist movement. P'eng Ta, the article pointed out, had, in the course of the eight years of his activity with the Ministry of Control, constantly "plotted to usurp leadership authority in control work," and to use this authority to oppose the Party, the proletarian dictatorship, and socialism.

P'eng Ta had been a Party member for twenty years; he had risen to his high post in the second bureau of the Ministry; unfortunately, we know nothing of the functions of this bureau. The core of the accusation against P'eng Ta was that he was opposed to the Party fraction in the Ministry, which meant he was working against Ch'ien Ying, head of that fraction. The general description in the article was that of an individual who opposed the mass line, despised political control (e.g., ridiculing "letters from the people"), was against the control correspondents, and advocated technical, economic forms of control.

The *Jenmin jihpao* article revealed that in March 1956, P'eng had "publicly opposed" a directive from the central government making all control agencies subject to dual rule—which meant Party domination of the entire control system. The paper said, in Party fraction meetings P'eng, on the surface, had pretended agreement and even proposed some ideas as to how dual rule could be implemented. But once the meetings were over, he had carried out intrigues against the Party fraction and drawn others to his side (*lalung*, as the Chinese call it), thereby obstructing dual rule.

In passing, the *Jenmin jihpao* article mentioned that P'eng had been associated with the first Ministry of Machine Industry. This brief reference to P'eng's organizational background gave a clue to the possible real motives of the attack on him. We shall say more on this below. The article went into some detail on his attitudes and activities in the Ministry of Control. As early as 1953, he was alleged to have agitated against those of his colleagues who advocated Party leadership and political-ideological control. He was quoted as having said of one of the leading figures in the Party fraction: "He talks emptily of politics, but knows nothing of operations!" He was accused of insubordination, of refusing to carry out orders from above. But then he was described as being unhappy over the fact that he had never been promoted from the post of deputy bureau chief. He was said to have regarded the Party fraction as a paper tiger: "Pierce it and it will collapse." He had complained about the Party taking power and authority away from

officials such as himself in the Ministry. He was said to have thoroughly
hated the old cadres; he knew that they were "the core cadres of Party
leadership" and could easily see through his anti-Party activities. But
he apparently was also opposed to the managers in state-owned enterprises, the paper said. He had told the control cadres to disregard them,
but in return had demanded "special privileges," *t'ech'üan*, for his
men. As a proponent of vertical rule, he was in favor of tight bureaucratic control over economic activity.

The *Jenmin jihpao* article ended with a brief recapitulation of
P'eng's personal history: From 1936 to 1938, he was a "political trainee"
in the Suiyuan Province Anti-Communist Self-Defense League, a brigade leader, and chief of the political training section of the fourth
division of the Kuomintang Youth League. In August 1938 he "infiltrated" the Chinese Communist party. In 1941, he "confessed and reformed" to the enemy, which led to the destruction of the local Party
apparatus. He later came to Yenan, but kept quiet about his "history."

The struggle against P'eng Ta began in July 1957. Yet, the paper
stated, despite the great evidence of guilt, he remained stubborn; it
was now up to him to choose his own path into the future.

Clearly, the admonition to change himself was not so much directed
at P'eng Ta, as at those with whom he was associated. But who were his
associates and thus the real targets of the attack? As we have said, a
clue was given in the reference to the fact that P'eng Ta was associated
with the first Ministry of Machine Industry. The first Ministry of
Machine Industry had been set up in 1952 separate from the Ministry
of Heavy Industry. At the same time a second Ministry of Machine
Industry was also set up. The administrative jurisdictions of these
two ministries have always been clouded in secrecy, but guesses can
be made. The first Ministry was in charge of China's basic machine-
building industries, including those supplied and built by the Soviet
Union. The second Ministry, judging from the composition of its personnel, appears to have been in charge of machine industries directly
linked to national defense. The first Ministry, since its establishment in
1952, was headed by Huang Ching, more commonly known as David
Yui. Under the latter name, he played a leading part in the Chinese
student movement in the late 1930's, and later went to the Yenan
border areas.[34] The second Ministry, also since its establishment in
1952, was headed by Chao Erh-lu, formerly chief of staff of the Chinese

---

[34] See Nym Wales, *Notes on the Chinese Student Movement, 1935-1936* (Guidance
Notes prepared for the Nym Wales collection on the Far East in the Hoover Institute
of War, Peace, and Revolution).

Communist Fourth Field Army. For a time, in 1955, and then again from 1956 to 1958, there even was a third Ministry of Machine Industry, headed by Sun Jen-ch'iung, an old political-military figure. The conclusion might be drawn that there was considerable dispute about who should control strategic defense industries, since both the second and third ministries had a military character.

In his capacity as chief of the first Ministry of Machine Industry and as a member of the Sino-Soviet Friendship Society, Huang Chang must have had many dealings with the Russians. One might think that this would have tended to make him sympathetic to the Soviets. However, other evidence indicates that the opposite may have been true. Though he was not openly attacked as a rightist in 1957, he later disappeared form public view.

P'eng Ta's career was somewhat similar to that of Huang Ching; both were members of the Kuomintang youth movement during the late 1930's. Huang Ching had close connections with individuals in Taiwan; he was the nephew of Yü Ta-wei, former defense minister in Taipei. The first phase of the anti-rightist movement, it will be recalled, was primarily directed against non-Party intellectuals and politicians who were often accused of Kuomintang connections.[35]

---

[35] It is difficult to identify the political opinions of the Huang Ching group, if we may speak of them in these terms. Nevertheless, some other clues may be cited. When one individual is attacked, it is common to find attacks on other individuals with similar opinions. If the attack is mounted against a national figure, simultaneously attacks will be leveled against individuals prominent in provincial politics. On August 14, 1957, the *Anhwei jihpao* published a denunciation of a control cadre by the name of Keng Jen-yung. In essence, the wrongdoings imputed to him were of the same type as those imputed to P'eng Ta. However, some additional details were added. For one thing, he was accused of openly favoring the Kuomintang. Though a Party member, he was opposed, as was P'eng Ta, to political control over the bureaucracy. He was accused of aspiring to achieve great power at the provincial level, independent both of communism and imperialism. He was opposed neither to capitalism nor to socialism. Perhaps most interesting was the accusation that he regarded the Soviet Union as a new imperialism—a charge made openly by a number of leading critics in May 1957, notably by Lung Yün. Since the attacks on Keng Jen-yung were of the same order as those on P'eng Ta, one may conclude that P'eng Ta must have been regarded as part of an anti-Soviet faction, with links to political figures in the non-Communist parties still remaining in China. This brings us back to the opinions of Huang Ching. An indication of these opinions is contained in his report to the Eighth Party Congress. Speaking about the need to develop a machine industry adequate to China's needs, Huang Ching had stated: "For several years now, the machinery industry has been imitating the advanced products of fraternal countries and thereby has succeeded in greatly raising its manufacturing level. But [note the significant word "but"] the uninterrupted expansion of the national economy demands

Unfortunately, the revelations about P'eng Ta and his colleagues were too sketchy to allow firm conclusions about the real reasons for his downfall. Nevertheless, there can be no doubt that more was involved than just anti-rightist attitudes on P'eng's part or even just his wrong-doings within the Ministry of Control. P'eng Ta was attacked as a second-stringer, as part of a policy of discrediting others higher up in the hierarchy.

The Second Stage of the Attack

On December 5, 1957, *Jenmin jihpao* announced the exposure "as a rightist element" of Wang Han, one of the leading figures in the Ministry of Control. He was then deputy minister and deputy secretary of the Party fraction in the Ministry of Control and had been a member of the Party for twenty-five years. His exposure was announced as "a great victory" in the struggle against rightists. The substance of the accusation was that, for many years, he was "the head of an anti-Party clique," in collusion with P'eng Ta, Ch'en Ta-chih, and others.

The *Jenmin jihpao* article dealt mainly with his transgressions in the ministry. Wang Han was accused of trying to protect P'eng Ta when that phase of the anti-rightist movement started. Like P'eng Ta, he re-sisted Party discipline. The article also accused him of being pro-American in using the Dewey Decimal System for arranging the files in the

---

that imitation give way to the development of independent designing. Now already many problems have appeared which cannot be resolved by imitation alone. For many machine tools we must have designs which rely on our national resources, our natural peculiarities, and concrete conditions of utilization" (*Chungkuo Kungch'an-tang tipatz'u ch'üankuo taipiao tahui wenchien* [Peking, 1957], p. 539).

These statements would put Huang Ching in the same category as those who in 1957 advocated "self-reliance" (*tzuli kengsheng*). It meant, in the first instance, inde-pendence from the Soviet Union. The leading advocates of self-reliance were Ch'en Yün, Li Hsien-nien, Po I-po, and Li Fu-ch'un, that is to say, the economic profes-sionals. There is no indication of a link between P'eng Ta and that group, but there is one on the part of Wang Han, as will be indicated later. Wang Han, in the of-ficial literature, was directly linked to P'eng Ta. If there is a larger pattern in all this, it would appear that an anti-Soviet (i.e., pro-self-reliance) group (or groups) was purged by the Mao-Liu group, which favored collaboration with and reliance on the Soviet Union.

Such a pattern would help explain the significance of the first and third phases of the anti-rightist movement. During the first phase, individuals with contacts leading outside the Party (and perhaps as far as Taiwan) were purged. Such a group evi-dently advocated a break with the Soviet Union, and, possibly, reconciliation with Taiwan. During the third phase, the economic professionals were purged. They may not have agreed with the first group on future attitudes toward Taiwan, but they did agree that reliance on the Soviet Union had to be lessened.

Ministry of Control and in buying American-made powdered milk for his children. The general picture sketched by the article indicated a man who preferred intellectuals to the toiling masses and who tried to build up a power group within the Ministry made up of individuals like himself.

However, the most serious accusations leveled against Wang Han in the *Jenmin jihpao* were in the economic field; here a note was sounded which was different from those against P'eng Ta. Wang Han was accused of criticizing the state economic plan as "reckless retreat." He was said to have argued that "control agencies must constantly and comprehensively investigate the way state plans, decisions, and orders are being carried out." He was even said to have demanded that control agencies have a voice in the designing of state plans and in the making of basic economic decisions. Only in this way could one "grasp the great problems of primary significance, and get to the heart of matters." He was said to have firmly demanded that before-the-fact supervision be carried out, and that control agencies have "the authority to halt expenditures by financial and economic branches, and to fine them." He had been in favor of strict vertical rule and had demanded that the Ministry have command over all control cadres at all echelons of administration. He was said to have lauded P'eng Ta as "a specialist in industrial control work," and, in turn, had been praised by P'eng Ta as the only man of ability in the Party fraction. His anti-Party activities were said to have caused considerable confusion in the minds of control cadres, particularly in the industrial and transportation sectors.

From October 31 to November 6, and again from November 25 to 27, the Ministry of Control held sixteen mass meetings directed against Wang Han. Thousands of wall newspapers were put up criticizing him. The Ministries of Industry and Transportation sent deputations to attend these meetings, to make sure that the message was properly transmitted to those quarters. Wang Han confessed: "My crimes are terrible, my soul is evil; I am an-anti-Party, anti-people, anti-socialist rightist element!"

The attack on Wang Han, as a whole, took the same form as that against P'eng Ta. However, it went further, as indicated by the fact that additional articles discredited him for the work he did in the late 1930's. One of these articles was written by Cheng Shao-wen, then deputy minister of justice, who had worked with Wang Han in south-central China during the early 1950's. Cheng claimed that he had known Wang Han since 1938, when both were in the fifth division of the New Fourth Army.

According to Cheng, in 1939, when Wang Han was secretary of the

North Hupei Party Committee, "he let fall into the hands of Kuomintang agents" registers of Party members, and top-secret documents from the Central Committee. As a result, many Party comrades were imprisoned and killed; the North Hupei Party organization was destroyed. In 1940 he became deputy chairman of the Politburo of the fifth division of the New Fourth Army. While serving in that capacity for three and one half years, according to Cheng, he resisted outside control over his work, particularly from local Party committees. Though he was in charge of political work in the army, in fact he neglected it. This, as Cheng claimed, was an important factor in the later defeat of the fifth division. He was strongly prejudiced against cadres of worker-peasant origins and preferred intellectuals, said Cheng. He was against the 1942 rectification campaign; after 1949, when he was working in South-central China, he still violently opposed any control over his activities on the part of local Party and government organizations and would accept only control from the very top. Cheng ended his denunciation by stating that Wang's landlord origins and his disinterest in work among the masses left him alienated from the masses.[36]

The dredging up of Wang Han's past career as well as many of the opinions imputed to him indicate that the ultimate target of attack was someone other than Wang Han himself, possibly Li Hsien-nien. Li Hsien-nien was from Hupei. He had been commander of the 5th division of the New Fourth Army. After 1949 he was chairman of the South China Committee on Enforcement of the Marriage Law. He was the leading figure in the Politburo concerned with financial work. Why should Li Hsien-nien have been attacked at this time? As indicated in the chapter on government, in early October 1957 a radical group headed by Mao Tse-tung and Liu Shao-ch'i had finally succeeded in imposing their policy of social mobilization on the Politburo, in opposition to the more cautious advocates of gradual economic development. The great debate on the economic strategy of the Second Five-Year Plan had ended. The victorious group undertook a purge of its opponents.

Two key accusations of an economic nature were leveled against Wang Han. The first was his criticism of the state economic plan as "reckless retreat." This must have been a reference to the coming Great Leap Forward, which superseded the more cautious Second Five-Year Plan then in preparation (see p. 74). The second was his demand that control agencies retain the authority to halt expenditures by all financial and economic agencies. On the surface, Wang Han was merely de-

---

36 *Jenmin jihpao*, December 8, 1957.

fending the rights of accountants as laid down by state regulations. But late in 1957, the radicals wished no restraint on their ambitious programs by conservative financial men. Li Hsien-nien had become identified with programs of balanced budgets and inflation control. The only government agency in a position to exercise financial restraint was he Ministry of Finance. The Ministry of Control was weak. Accounting controls were supposed to be carried out by the Bank of China, but the fact that the bank was headed by a minor political figure, one Ts'ao Chü-ju, indicates that no great power was invested in the head of the bank. Wang Han's earlier association with Li Hsien-nien, so openly described in Cheng Shao-wen's article, indicated that Li Hsien-nien probably was the target. Li Hsien-nien must have been one of the moderate group that vigorously opposed the type of economic strategy of the Great Leap Forward. But opposition alone would not explain the need for a purge, since the Chinese Communists as a whole have been relatively tolerant of different opinion groups. So long as any structure of economic controls remained, there would be mechanisms for restraining the free-spending tendencies of the provincial Party cadres. The strategy of the Great Leap Forward envisaged immense wastage of resources but promised success so great that it would outweigh the waste. Economic controls were designed to prevent waste and had to be loosened so that "spontaneity and creativity" could burst forth throughout the country.

The End of State Control Work

The last talk about an independent control system was heard during the first half of 1958. All reports on the activities of control cadres and correspondents ceased. The country was in a "great leap forward," and the May speech of Liu Shao-ch'i at the second session of the Eighth Party Congress would lead to an even greater acceleration in the drive. As long as the anti-rightist movement was still in progress, the control agencies could carry out all kinds of political investigations. But the movement was officially terminated in the spring of 1958. Control work, like balancing in the field of planning, was conservative. The restraining functions of the middle tier of organization were to be eliminated. Controllers, like planners, had no role to play in the leap forward. What was needed now was active leadership, not restraint in the interest of "balanced development." In other words, even the residual political control functions left to the control agencies now became redundant.

The Seventh National Conference on Control Work was held in Peking from February 27 to March 20, 1958. The *Jenmin jihpao* reported the conference on April 8. The lengthy meeting reviewed the whole history of control work over the past eight years and set the tasks for 1958. Addresses were made by Chu Teh and P'eng Chen. They set forth "major directives," but also criticized shortcomings and errors in control work. They pointed out that the control departments were equal with all other government departments, and that control workers were not to get the idea that they had "special rights." A report was also read by Wang Ts'ung-wu, deputy secretary of the control committee of the Party's Central Committee. The concluding report was given by Ch'ien Ying.

After reviewing experiences of the past years and the exposure of the Wang Han clique, the conference went on publicly to repudiate the Harbin system. The main defect of the Harbin system had been its advocacy of an independent, vertical control structure. The conference agreed that henceforth all control work should take place under the leadership of *local* Party and government agencies. It was further agreed that: "If the decisions of higher echelon control agencies conflict with the decisions of local Party and administration leadership, then they must carry out the decisions of the local Party and administration leadership." The tasks outlined for 1958 were the usual ones mentioned in earlier national meetings. But under the new conditions of the Great Leap Forward, "control agencies in all areas must set their own tasks and determine the key points to be investigated *according to instructions from local Party and administration leadership and the concrete conditions of the area.*" The conference ended by suggesting some new work methods. Above all, control workers were to get out of their offices and personally ferret out problems. Cadres in offices and bureaus of the Ministry were to spend at least four months out of the year traveling about the country to investigate incidents. When problems arose, they were to be resolved rapidly and on the spot. Constant contact was to be kept with lower-echelon control agencies, and communications were to be answered promptly. All control agencies were to collaborate closely with local Party and government organizations.

For all practical purposes, the Ministry of Control had ceased to function. The Eighth Party Congress led to a process of decentralization which was implemented late in 1957 in the form of what we have earlier called decentralization II and reached a high point during the Great Leap Forward. The continuing *hsiafang*, the downward transfer of administrative cadres, brought new people into local administrative units. As the decision-making powers of the local committees and agencies grew, those of the vertical bureaucracies, notably the central ministries, diminished. Local power meant Party power. Technical personnel had some power in bureaucracy, for expertise always counts in bureaucracy. But when they were sent down to the local regions, they were under the thumb of strange local Party cadres, often contemptuous of the big-city intellectuals and hostile to expertise in any case. The local cadres understood "local conditions," and that was what counted. Earlier, dual rule created conflicts of command: Whose command was "primary"? But now, as was made absolutely clear, the primacy of command in every instance was from local Party organizations. Command could also come from local government, but local government at this time was solidly under Party domination. The summer of 1958 marked the end of verticalism and parallelism. Local coordination under Party leadership was now the ironclad rule.

On April 29, 1959, the Peking *Takung-pao* published a laconic report: "The first meeting of the Second National People's Congress [on April 28, 1959], on the basis of a proposal made by Premier Chou En-lai, decided: [1] to abolish the Ministry of Justice, and have work hitherto handled by the Ministry of Justice managed by the People's Supreme Court, [2] to abolish the Ministry of Control."

There was no need to indicate to which other ministries the work of the control ministry had been transferred. For by 1959, the Ministry of Control had little independent work left to do. The abolition of the Ministry of Control did not mean the abolition of control bureaus in other ministries. These continue to operate as far as I know. However, in view of the great loss of power which the central ministries sustained as a result of decentralization II, their own control cadres were probably unable to exert much control in the face of regional and local Party power. In the spring of 1959, Peking was making some attempts to bring the economy under control again. The slogan of the time was "All the Country Is a Single Chessboard." Efforts were made to reinstitute economic controls, particularly in the financial realm. Thus it is possible that the abolition of the Ministry of Control may have been designed to strengthen the position of intraministerial control agencies, by finally removing an unwelcome competitor. However, symbolically, the abolition must be seen as final recognition on Peking's part that it was unable to devise a system which could effectively bring the national economy under control. Without the Ministry of State Control, central planning could never have been enforced in the Soviet Union. This abolition may also be regarded as belated recognition of the impossibility of using Soviet-style central planning in China.

The Aftermath

Ch'ien Ying was appointed Minister of the Interior in 1959. In November 1960 she was relieved of her post and replaced by Tseng Shan. Tseng Shan was an old comrade of Mao's from the days of the

Kiangsi soviets. But, more significantly, he had long experience in financial and banking work during the early years of the Chinese People's Republic. He had been Ch'en Yün's predecessor as minister of commerce. November 1960 was a period of crisis. The disastrous harvest results were known, and the leaders were meeting to make the drastic decisions which would be announced at the Ninth Plenum in January 1961. This was a period when economic controls were being reinvoked, but there no longer was a Ministry of State Control. Tseng Shan's practical experience in financial-economic and commercial work was much more valuable than Ch'ien Ying's political acumen. Ch'ien Ying and some of her colleagues from the Ministry of State Control continued their work of political control on the Control Committee of the Party's Central Committee. Of the deputy ministers left in 1958, Li Ching-ying went with her to the Control Committee; Li Shih-chang and P'an Chen-ya went back to their provinces and political oblivion. Ch'eng T'an went to the Communication Works Department of the Central Committee, of which the director was Tseng Shan. Ch'eng appears later to have moved back to the Ministry of Interior. He was presumably a close collaborator of Tseng Shan and was able to help him out in his new task of enforcing economic controls. Since early 1961, Peking has made increasing use of the banking system for purposes of economic control. Moreover, one can assume that the newly formed political departments set up in various economic branches enjoy broad powers of economic control. Whether any centralized system of economic control, analogous to the Ministry of Control, will again arise is impossible to say.

CHAPTER VI

CITIES

PRE-COMMUNIST URBAN ORGANIZATION

Chinese Cities Before 1949

Although China is an overwhelmingly rural country, it has an urban population which now exceeds the entire population of industrialized and urbanized Japan. The total urban population of Mainland China in 1957 (the last time official figures were released) was over ninety million. Despite the reported return of more than twenty million people to the countryside in the wake of the 1960-1961 economic crisis, the urban population of Mainland China today most likely exceeds one hundred million.[1] If the world thinks of China as a peasant country, it overlooks its long urban history. In contrast to some peoples in Southeast Asia, for example, who do not like to live in cities, the Chinese have a strong affinity for urban life. Chinese migrating to other

---

[1] Judging from the table on p. 381, the average rate of urban population growth from 1950 to 1957 was about 7 percent; of this, natural increase accounted for more than 3 percent; see H. Yuan Tien, "Induced Abortion and Population Control in Mainland China," *Marriage and Family Living*, XXV:1 (February 1963), 36. (The Chinese Communists, in 1957, gave the lower figure of 2.5 percent for the rate of

countries have usually settled in cities and towns. In fact, many cities of Southeast Asia are essentially Chinese cities. Despite this propensity, Chinese emigrants have traditionally kept up strong ties with their "home villages." In earlier days, thousands of Chinese had their bones returned from cities outside China to graves in their rural homelands. This close relationship between home village and alien city is not only true of the Overseas Chinese. Within China itself, internal migration between country and city has been common for centuries. Chinese born and bred in an "alien city" still considered themselves "natives" of an ancestral rural area. This continuing link between country and city undoubtedly influenced the nature of the traditional Chinese city, which did not develop the urban character so typical of European and Japanese cities. A bourgeoisie, that is, a social class explicitly identified with the city, never arose in China—at least not until modern times. Indeed whereas the Chinese had to borrow a foreign word to designate the bourgeoisie, the Japanese long ago had their own word—*chōnin*. Even today, the urban-rural link remains. In the mid-1960's, the Communists launched a "back to the home village" campaign to drain off excess population from the cities. The former urbanites were expected to return to their native villages, and be reintegrated into a social structure which the Communists themselves had done much to weaken.

Today China has a stable urban population which is playing an increasingly important role in its national development. The process of urbanization which began with the coming of Western imperialism is continuing. Under Japanese influence, great new cities arose in Manchuria, making it China's most advanced and urbanized region. Western imperialism led to the formation of cities such as Shanghai, Hong Kong, Tientsin, and Hankow. Under Communist rule, new cities have

---

natural increase; see p. 381.) If the 7 percent increase had continued during the years 1957-1965, urban population should now be close to 140,000,000; the 3 percent natural increase alone would bring the figure well over 100,000,000. On April 11, 1960, the *Jenmin jihpao* reported that urban population was more than double the 40,000,000 figure given for the "pre-Liberation period." Though this statement appears to imply an urban population figure below 100,000,000, our own estimations are more likely to be true. Chou En-lai, when interviewed in Pakistan a few years ago, was reported to have said that twenty million people had returned to the countryside in the wake of the "return to the village" campaign. Even if this were so, it is hard to see how the total urban population today could be less than 100,000,000. The figures for urban population hinge on the definition of what a city is. The Chinese Communists have never made clear their exact criterion for defining a city; see p. 381, and also Ling Piao, "Chungkung yu-kuan ch'engshih chengts'e falü," *Tsukuo* [*China Monthly*] 6 (September 1964), 16.

arisen and old ones have been modernized. As a result, China is at the same time a great urban and a great rural nation.

When the Communists came to power, they faced the problem of controlling these cities and putting them to use for economic development. The task of establishing modern organization in the cities has been simpler, in some ways, than in the countryside: the urban population is more concentrated than the rural population and a higher level of education has made it easier to organize city dwellers. On the other hand, the cities have presented the Chinese Communists with problems which the villages do not have. Although population has tended to group itself around centers of production and trade, the "unity of living and working" which marks rural life is generally absent in the cities. Modern Chinese cities have become great residential slums, housing a vast labor force for the scattered enterprises of the city. Workers go to work in the concentrated business areas in the centers of cities or in factories on the outskirts. Systems of public transportation have been strained by the need to transport ever-increasing numbers of workers to distant work places. In many areas the Communists have built new housing projects alongside factories, thus making it possible to concentrate the workers on the confines of the factory. But the magnitude of the problem has never permitted realization of the ideal of "the unity of living and working." During the Great Leap Forward, the Communists, for a while, felt that the problem could be resolved by bringing production to the worker rather than the other way around. Residential blocks, they thought, could be transformed into production centers. This was the basic idea underlying the urban communes. But the program was utopian from the start. Few urban communes function now.

Cities in most parts of the world have grown up in confusion. Powerful governments have created planned cities from time to time, with monuments and buildings dominating the cityscape. However, it has not been the monuments that have attracted people to the city, but the diverse opportunities for a new life. Peking has its magnificent court structures, but alongside of the Forbidden City, there is the "Chinese City," a warren of narrow alleys earlier dominated by the merchant and artisan. The development of Chinese cities under the impact of foreign imperialism created new economic opportunities. As business in its diverse forms grew, so did the population. Cities thus became the permanent residences of millions of people. There was little planned development of Chinese cities in the nineteenth and early twentieth centuries. Urban government, whether exercised by foreigner or by Chinese, served essentially a facilitating and controlling function. Since urban government lacked positive goals, it was not able to do much more than try to keep things in check.

In traditional China, the hand of government on the cities was relatively light. As in the villages, the government ruled the cities indirectly, through all forms of internal urban organizations, guilds, native associations, occupational groupings, clan and family clubs. Like the village, the urban neighborhood was organized in one fashion or another. There were always neighborhood leaders with whom the magistrate maintained relationships. Occupational specialization of neighborhoods helped the problem of control. Artisans and merchants of similar occupation lived together in certain neighborhoods, and were grouped together in associations. Immigration into the city was largely determined by such associations. Immigrants regularly sought contact with city organizations which maintained links with their home villages, their family, or their occupational group. The functional equivalent of the "hotel," with its universalistic openness to all comers, was the association inn, accessible only to people with the same social ties.[2]

All this changed with the development of the new cities. Guild and native associations continued to operate, but played a lesser role in the life of the cities. New types of organization began to flourish. The secret societies, always strong in Chinese cities, became stronger. Political groupings began to sprout. The earlier amiable contact between social organization and political power disappeared. Where foreign influence predominated, administration took on Western forms. Formal city administrations were created, accompanied by powerful police forces to maintain order and control. The world of informal organization increasingly was filled by newer types of groupings, ranging from criminal to political. Though at times formal city administration collaborated with the complex world of subformal organization in the city, basically the two were juxtaposed. Neither was able to achieve complete hegemony in the city.

Paochia

After seizing power in the mid-1920's, the Kuomintang essentially took over the existing system of urban administration. Formal administration remained essentially of Western type, but organizations of

---

[2] See Niida Noboru, "The Industrial and Commercial Guilds of Peking and Religion and Fellow-countrymanship as Elements of their Coherence," *Folklore Studies* IX (1950), 179-206.

traditional Chinese type, such as the secret societies, continued to play a major role in the control of urban life. Thus, for example, a police force set up along Western lines often cooperated with traditional-type gangs to maintain public order. The Kuomintang, however, did extend the system of formal city administration further downward. Cities were divided into "districts," *ch'ü,* and district mayoralties, *ch'ü kungso,* were established.

Below the district level there was no formal administration, with the exception of the police. Police stations, *p'aich'uso,* were established in various sections of the city and were entrusted with the task of supervision of the populations in their areas. Police control proved to be the major form of state interference in the lives of the citizenry. Kuomintang administration was a combination of bureaucratic administration and police control.

The most important innovation in urban administration was the introduction of the *paochia* system.[3] It has a long history in China. Until it was introduced into the cities, it was mainly a form of village organization imposed by the state for population control. The rural history of the *paochia* system will be treated in the next chapter. Here we are concerned with *paochia* as a form of city organization. Though the Kuomintang revived the *paochia* system in the rural areas to counter Communist control of the villages, they never introduced it into the cities. It was the Japanese occupiers who first introduced *paochia* into the cities.

The idea was not so novel for the Japanese, because the "neighborhood association," *tonarigumi,* already served a similar function in Japan. Public security was the main problem facing the occupiers, and the *paochia* system seemed to be a device for the maintenance of order. In the summer of 1940, the *paochia* system was introduced into Tientsin and later spread gradually to other cities in occupied China. Territorially, the *paochia* system followed police lines, specifically areas under the jurisdiction of branch police bureaus and police stations. Each group of ten households was organized into a *p'ai;* each ten *p'ai* formed a *chia;* each ten *chia* formed a *pao.* The numerical specifications did not have to be rigorously followed but it was important that each unit contain all families in a neighborhood (although exceptions were made for public buildings, schools, and foreigners). Each unit had a designated leader who became the link between the local police authority and the population. The city police chief became the top official in

---

3 See also pp. 409 ff.

charge of all *paochia* organization in the city; at lower levels, leadership was exercised by local police officials, ranging down to the station chiefs.

So-called self-defense bodies were organized under the control of the *paochia* chiefs. These bodies were armed to some degree, although subject to strict police supervision. The *p'ai* chiefs, in contrast to *chia* and *pao* chiefs who had special offices, had their headquarters in their own homes. Their duties were defined as: carrying out the orders of the local police station and their *chia* superiors; checking on illegal activities in their *p'ai*; checking and reporting of "trouble-makers"; checking and reporting on "unusual activities" among the population; and doing anything else assigned by the *paochia*. All household heads were instructed to report to the police any suspicious people coming into the district; suspicions of robbery and theft, the comings and goings of the population, any changes in the population, and anyone suspected of being involved in crimes. All able-bodied males were to be recruited into the self-defense force, and given one month's military training each year. The regulations made clear that the *paochia* was primarily intended as a neighborhood extension of the police force. It is hardly likely that the *paochia* was welcomed with much enthusiasm by the population. Nevertheless, despite the openly repressive functions of the *paochia*, the *paochia* organizations are said to have played an important role during the latter years of the war in organizing food rationing and civil defense in the face of air raids.[4]

This attempt to get deeper into the urban population was in essence a form of expanded police control, and not a downward extension of civil administration.

The Kuomintang *paochia* in the rural areas essentially fulfilled the same control function as the *paochia* introduced by the Japanese. Despite the imprecations which the Kuomintang leveled at the Japanese-sponsored *paochia* ("poisoners of the people, helpers of the tiger"), they quickly saw the utility of the urban *paochia*. In postwar Shanghai, when the Kuomintang set up a Department of Civil Administration, they proclaimed a "reorganization" of the *paochia* and placed the *paochia* under the control of the Department of Civil Administration. Thus what only a few months earlier had been the "poisoner of the people" rapidly became a form of "autonomous administration." The Kuomintang divided Shanghai into thirty-one districts (*ch'ü*), and in twenty-nine of these established district mayoralties—*ch'ü kungso*. The

---

[4] *Hsienhsing paochia faling huipien*, August 13, 1940; notably articles 24, 25, and 38.

reorganized *paochia* system was put under the jurisdiction of the district mayoralties. Since the new system of "autonomous administration" was not yet fully understood, the Kuomintang city administration decided to institute a training program for 549 district mayoralty workers, 1,025 *pao* chiefs, and 23,311 *chia* leaders. One of the first tasks assigned the *paochia* organization was aiding city administration in the registration of the population.[5]

In theory, at least, the *paochia* system had been removed from police control and had been put under civilian administration. However, in fact the *paochia* remained an arm of the police. As Anderson Shih put it, it "could only assist the police and the government to register the population, press the people to pay taxes, to help draft conscription, and to handle miscellaneous errands required by the army or the government."[6]

The Kuomintang was never able to see more than control functions in the *paochia* system. It took the Communists to make the transition from organization for control purposes to organization for more positive goals.

URBAN ORGANIZATION DURING THE EARLY 1950'S

The Communist Takeover

When the Communists occupied the cities in 1949, chaos reigned. Thousands of Nationalist officials had fled. Urban services had broken down. Food shortages and inflation created great hardship for the population. The Communists immediately introduced military government and began to reestablish public order. Administrative functions exercised by the old bureaus of the Nanking government were transferred to the military government committees and finally, late in 1949 and in 1950, turned over to the newly formed people's governments. The Communists made a sharp break with the earlier administrative system. The whole structure of the Nationalist government was declared invalid, and a new structure was created from the bottom up. However, continuity seems to have been maintained in the police: The public security agencies which the Communists established in the cities, despite some terminological and functional changes, appear to have been largely the

---

[5] *Shanghai nienchien 1946* (Shanghai, 1946), pp. 36-37.

[6] Anderson Shih, *Urban People's Commune* (mimeographed), (Union Research Institute: Hong Kong, no date), p. 21.

same as those which operated under the Nationalists. Indeed, one Nationalist study of the Communist police states:

The formal establishment of [Communist] public security agencies and public security units really took place in 1950. Most were in effect police agencies at various levels left behind by our government, which were "reformed" and "expanded"; most of the public security units were composed of guard units of our local public order brigades and Communist military units. . . . The Communist people's police [in 1950] (i.e., police in public security departments in various areas), on the basis of incomplete statistics, was composed to about 60 percent of police personnel left behind by us. The public security agencies also for the most part still have the old addresses of our police departments, but the "branch departments" (in Canton called district departments) and the police stations [p'aich'uso] have been greatly expanded. Police personnel in many areas is double or more than before.[7]

It is difficult to say how correct this Nationalist estimate is but it is true that the general police system which the Communists set up on occupying the cities did not change fundamentally at the beginning. All Communist military units had "public security headquarters" attached to their "military district headquarters," and personnel from the former assumed control over the police system. The Communists probably had no choice but to retain the police system, for a sudden closing down of the police stations would have resulted in even greater social disorder.

The Communists rapidly abolished the *paochia* system. But until the urban residents committee system was introduced, there was no unified neighborhood organization to replace it. The main problem in 1949 and 1950 was once again to create a working civil administration. As at the level of central government, administration was largely carried out by committees. The people's committee became the supreme administrative organ for the city as a whole. Committee-type administration was extended down to the district level, but not below. Except for the greater flexibility allowed by committee-type administration, the structure of formal administration in the cities after 1949 was not greatly different from what had existed earlier.

However, the Communists realized from the beginning that they would have to press organization deeper into the urban population in order to control effectively. The one type of organization which already "penetrated deeply," to use a favorite Communist expression, was the police. The local police stations in fact began to take on civil administration functions. Each police station appointed from one to three

---

[7] *Kungfei kungan tsuchih yü jenmin chingch'a-chih* (Taipei, 1957), pp. 6-7.

"civil-administration functionaries" to deal with the special problems of civil administration, as contrasted with regular police functions.[8]

From these expanded police functions emerged a police figure who, according to the accounts of refugees, still plays an important role in neighborhood life, namely the so-called "household register policeman" (*huchi-ching*). He is generally not armed, is well acquainted with the people of the neighborhood, and has some of the qualities of a "local cop."

The process of organizing the urban population came from two directions. On the one hand, organization proceeded "from the top down" through the expanded civil-administration functions of the police. On the other hand, it also proceeded "from the bottom up" through what were called "organizations of a mass character." These were groups of residents, usually led by neighborhood Communists or activists, which were formed to help the new rulers of the country implement their policies. Such groups began to spring up everywhere in the cities. However, because of their *ad hoc* character, they created serious leadership and administrative problems.

An article written in 1952, when the first urban residents' committees were set up, gives some idea of these problems.[9] The article described conditions in a working-class quarter in Tientsin. Before the committee was established, there were more than twenty different residents' organizations in the quarter, the article said. There was no unified leadership among them. As a result, when it was necessary, for example, to launch large-scale mass movements, the leadership came either from the local police station or from "residents' representatives." A later editorial in another paper described a similar situation for the city of Tientsin as a whole; the editorial pointed out that organization below the district level was confused and sporadic; mass organizations of different kinds were set up on an *ad hoc* basis, but without unified leadership; this created heavy burdens for the "positive elements"; the setting up of residents' committees made it possible to amalgamate many of these mass organizations and "overcome multiheaded leadership and confusion."[10]

An editorial in the *Jenmin jihpao* on January 1, 1955 made a different point. Police stations, the editorial stated, did civil administration as well as police work. This made it impossible for them to "maintain

---

[8] *Kungfei chits'eng tsuchih chih yenchiu* (Taipei, 1957), p. 47.

[9] *Tientsin jihpao*, November 19, 1952.

[10] *Kuangming jihpao*, January 1, 1955.

social order." [11] Moreover, "given the nature of the tasks of the police stations," they were not able "to understand fully . . . policies of civil administration." The editorial made it clear that one could not depend on the police alone to assure the maintenance of social order.

Although it is hard to generalize, the outlines of the picture seem to be clear. The task of organizing the masses fell to the "positive elements," that is, activists being groomed for eventual Party membership. The Communists began to recruit sympathizers in every neighborhood, largely from among the poor and depressed parts of the population. Some were taken into the Party, others were simply registered in the dossiers as "positivists." The positivists assumed leadership of the many *ad hoc* mass organizations that began to spring up. *Ad hoc* organizations were set up for almost every task of a public nature: sanitation, population registration, neighborhood construction, discovery of counter-revolutionaries and "subversive elements," and so on. Although many of these committees were under the jurisdiction of the police stations, others were the creations of various departments' of district and city government. Whenever an administrative department wanted something done, the local positivists (who were duly noted in registers) were asked to establish an *ad hoc* committee. The result was a proliferation of committees, and general organizational confusion.

The Residents Committees

In 1951 the regime, cautiously, began to introduce a more uniform neighborhood organization into the cities, namely the residents committees. They were first reported from Tientsin and Shanghai, the cities in which the Japanese-sponsored urban *paochia* system had been most successful. One of the earliest reported urban residents committees was established in Hsüeht'ang Street in Tientsin in October 1951. As in so many other Communist experiments, the news was not divulged until some success could be reported. Hsüeht'ang Street was a working-class quarter, consisting of 114 households or 531 persons. Most were workers in state-owned factories. Sometime in 1951, the city government dispatched an "experimental work team for administrative construction" into the neighborhood to organize the residents. The 114 households were divided into fifteen residents groups. These groups, after suitable

---

[11] Significantly, Ho Kan-chih, official historian, writes that reassertion of Party control over the public security agencies was the foremost task of the *Sufan* movement which began during the latter half of 1955 (*Chungkuo hsientai koming-shih* [Hong Kong, 1958], p. 389). The retention of pre-1949 police officials probably created a serious loyalty problem.

education, elected 19 residents representatives, of which 16 were house-wives. In October 1951 a delegates meeting was held, and the urban residents committee was formally established.

One of the main tasks of the new urban residents committee, the report said, consisted in resolving problems and disputes affecting the residents. One of the earliest disputes settled was the installation of a clean women's restroom which the owners of one of the apartment houses in the neighborhood had long resisted. Another dispute ended by forcing a real-estate company which owned one of the big apartments in the block to rent rooms to needy families. Further, the residents committee adjudicated a dispute between shareholders in a neighborhood laundry.

The committee also organized literacy and sanitation work: inspections to check on hygiene within the home and the organization of garbage removal teams. The committee looked into the welfare problems of residents, for example into the case of a sick woman whose husband was away from home. The report noted that the organization of the residents committee greatly simplified the problem of "too much leadership," "too many things to do," "too many meetings." Above all it made it possible to relieve the burden on the positivists. Still there were shortcomings. It appeared that after the enthusiasm of the "patriotic sanitation movement " and the "literacy movement" had waned, meetings became less regular and work tended to slacken. Residents continued to make "suggestions," but no regularized work system developed to assure prompt execution of these suggestions, and resolution of the problems.[12]

Though the urban residents committees were still experimental, they were generally introduced into Tientsin City. In 1952, the city government issued two directives, one ordering the establishment of these committees throughout the city and the other the creation of street mayoralties, *chieh kungso*, later called street offices.[13] The former directive decreed that residents committees were to be established in industrial and commercial areas of the city, but not in areas with large numbers of office buildings or large-scale industrial and commercial enterprises. Urban residents committees were to include most residents, but "mainly families of workers, unorganized workers (including retired and unemployed workers), and other working people and their dependents." However, industrial and commercial workers, office workers, and school teachers who were already members of other organizations could join,

---

12 *Tientsin jihpao*, November 19, 1952.
13 *Kungfei chits'eng tsuchin chih yenchiu, op. cit.*, pp. 47-48.

"if they so wished." Offices, military, factories, enterprises, schools, hospitals were exempted. A residential unit was to consist of from 150 to 500 households, divided into residents groups of from ten to thirty families.

The tasks of the urban residents committees were defined as: (1) making residents aware of government policies, (2) carrying out public security, fire prevention, culture and recreation, public sanitation, public works, relief, arbitration of disputes, and (3) collecting and reflecting the opinions and demands of the residents. Administratively, the urban residents committees were under the jurisdiction of the street mayoralties. However, the public-security section within the residents committee was responsible to the local police station. No other organizations were allowed to make demands on the urban residents committees without the prior consent of the district government.[14]

Like the urban residents committees, the street mayoralties were set up only in essentially residential areas, and not in areas with heavy concentrations of offices, factories, schools, and other "units of production." Thus it becomes clear that the main purpose of the new policy was to organize the unorganized. Personnel in enterprises were already under the organizational control of the enterprises, but their dependents, who often lived in areas distant from the enterprise, were not; nor were workers in small establishments, housewives, "remnant bourgeois," and others. The fact that these first urban residents committees were established in Tientsin and Shanghai arouses the suspicion that they were but the old *paochia* in a different form. The experience in Tientsin and Shanghai with the *paochia* probably facilitated the organization of the residents committees. Some tasks of the residents committees clearly are reminiscent of those of the *paochia*, particularly such as safeguarding public security, preventing fires, and the like. One of the basic tasks of the residents committees was to keep an eye on the population under their jurisdiction and to report regularly to the local police station, more or less in the fashion known from *paochia* days.

However, many new elements differentiated the residents committees from the *paochia*. Whereas the old *paochia* were largely police control organizations, the new residents committees concerned themselves with the constructive tasks mentioned. The urban residents committee became a clearing house for complaints made by the residents and in fact turned into a kind of arbitration committee. In time, the residents committees acquired important new functions, such as the allocation of

---

14 *Tientsin jihpao*, October 28, 1952.

food rations and the granting of certifications to individuals who wished to move or even leave China.

Women played a decisive role in the residents committees. However, the caliber of female cadres was often low; illiteracy was widespread among them, a necessary consequence of the policy of recruiting from the proletariat. But the fact that the residents committees were subject to the district government through the street mayoralties indicates the essentially civil nature of the organization.

The development of the urban residents committees was a further step in the total organization of the population. By setting up street mayoralties, the formal city administration came closer to the mass level. The residents committees were never a part of formal city government, but neither were they just a unified mass organization; they were in between formal and informal government. As such they greatly aided government in spreading the network of organization over the population.

The city population was thus organized in two ways. The units of production organized those who worked in them, whereas the units of territory, on which the residents committees were based, organized those who did not work in units of production.

The residents committee system was not extended to all cities until the latter part of 1954, when a series of government directives were issued on basic-level administration in the cities. Technically, the residents committees, even in Tientsin and Shanghai, remained experimental until then. Why the system was not introduced more widely sooner is not explained by Mainland publications. However, refugees generally report on the unpopularity of the residents committees. They are said to interfere with private life and are often regarded as instruments of the police. Furthermore, strong female representation among the cadres of the residents committees must have made it difficult to operate in a society in which formal equality of men and women had only recently been proclaimed.

Three directives, approved by the standing committee of the National People's Congress on December 31, 1954, set forth the organizational framework of the police stations, the street offices, and the urban residents committees. There was nothing particularly new in the directives on the police stations, except that they were to maintain close liaison with the residents committees.

The police stations remained under the "vertical rule" of local departments of public security. In later years, with the growing influence of Party committees on the police system, "dual rule" began to make itself felt.

The specifications for the street offices were more precise. They were to be established as "branches" (*p'aich'u chikuan*) of city government in all major cities of China: they were mandatory in cities of more than 100,000 population; optional in cities between 50,000 and 100,000 population; and not required in cities of less than 50,000 population. Significantly, the area of jurisdiction of the street offices was exactly that of the police stations. Officials of the street office were appointed by the city government, and not selected from the residents. The street offices were directly responsible to the people's committees above them and were not to receive instructions from any bureau of city government.

The directive on the residents committees was the most detailed of the three. The directive specified nothing that was not already in existence in the Tientsin residents committees. Areas under the jurisdiction of the residents committees were to conform, for the most part, to "administrative divisions of public security and household registration sections," consisting of from 100 to 600 households, and divided into residents groups of from fifteen to forty households (with a limit of seventeen residents groups for each residents committee). The linkage of the residents committees with the civil police is significant. Police station, street office, and urban residents committee thus had jurisdiction over the same population group.[15]

Inevitably, editorials commented on these new directives. One of them listed two problems which faced the cities at the time: the massive increase in urban population (more than 40 percent between 1950 and 1953), and the continuing problem of subversive elements. In the face of these pressing problems, city administration in the large cities "did not have their own branch agencies in the streets, which made for difficulties in the carrying out of government policy, liaison with the masses, and supervision by the popular masses." The result, the editorial said, was not only that the police stations were increasingly carrying out tasks of civil administration, but some tasks of civil administration were being performed by enterprise management or union organizations. The street offices were to take over the tasks that had formerly been carried out by the police or by management and unions. The residents committees also were to assume certain routine tasks formerly carried out at higher levels, such as registration of marriage, issuance of notarized documents, and the like. The establishment of the residents committees

---

[15] *Jenmin jihpao,* January 1, 1955.

further simplified the problem of administration by doing away with multiheaded leadership, the editorial said; no longer could city departments make demands on citizens to carry out "urgent tasks." However, even if the residents committees were subject only to a single higher-echelon leadership (aside from the police), they were not considered a part of the formal system of administration.[16] Another editorial made clear that "since they are not an echelon of administrative organization, no government agency can issue orders to them." [17]

The extension of residents committees to all large cities by government decree does not seem to have been the result of a conviction that this institution was particularly successful; Minister of the Interior Hsieh Chüeh-tsai reported at the time that residents committees and street offices had been introduced into sixty different cities during the previous few years, but *Kuangming jihpao* said that street offices had been set up only in a few cities experimentally and in most areas not at all. There must have been considerable opposition to the move, not just from the population as a whole, but from bureaucratic quarters. In later years, little was reported in the newspapers on the activities of the residents committees, although most refugees from urban areas in China have much to say about them. When the urban people's communes were established in 1958, no mention was made of the residents committees, although an occasional reference could be found to the activities of the street offices. During meetings of the All-China Federation of Women, in 1958, some references were made to the work of women in the urban residents committees, but Teng Ying-ch'ao (Chou En-lai's wife) in her report to the Eighth Party Congress made no mention of them.

Why this lack of enthusiasm about such a basic form of organization? Certain inferences can be drawn from the testimony of refugees. The residents committees became increasingly linked with the police and the courts (as a result of their arbitration functions). This alone made them unpopular with the population. Furthermore, with the growth of other mass organizations, the residents committees, lacking any larger national affiliation, found it difficult to play a leading part in mass movements. Local Party committees, youth-league committees, and women's organizations became the foci of these new operations. Since enterprise workers were not under the jurisdiction of the ordinary residents committees, the conclusion appears warranted that the residents

---

[16] *Ibid.,* January 2, 1955.
[17] *Kuangming jihpao,* January 3, 1955.

committees exercised control only over such remnant parts of the population which were not involved in other segments of the organizational system, namely the least useful parts of the population.

As we have indicated, despite the similarity between the urban residents committees and the pre-1949 *paochia*, there clearly was an evolution from police-control to civil-administration functions. By taking over many mass-level tasks of civil administration, the urban residents committees greatly facilitated the task of city government. Their arbitration functions, for example, must have taken much pressure off the courts, the procuracies, and the police. The close relationships between the urban residents committees and the "household register policeman" (*huchi-ching*) must have been useful in maintaining social order and population control in the neighborhood. Above all, the urban residents committees created a uniform framework of organization for the neighborhood. It is therefore puzzling that they should not have become the nucleus from which the urban communes, to be described below, could grow. The answer might be that the urban residents committees tended to take on purely control functions, whereas the urban communes were based on a more activist principle of leadership. Moreover, one of the basic ideas behind the urban communes was that they would draw units of production (such as factories) into the web of organization. Under the regulations governing the urban residents committees, units of production were explicitly exempted from their jurisdiction.

URBAN ORGANIZATION DURING THE GREAT LEAP FORWARD

Conditions Leading to the Urban Communes

In the summer of 1958, the Chinese Communists introduced a new form of organization into the cities, called urban communes, in imitation of the rural communes in the countryside. In contrast to the residents committees, whose basic purpose was population control, that of the urban communes was population use. In order to understand the rationale behind the urban communes, one must look at the urban population patterns at the time of the Great Leap Forward.

During Communist rule in Mainland China the urban population grew enormously. The population of old urban centers increased, and new cities have grown at a fast pace, particularly in the northern and northwestern parts of the country. According to the official *People's Handbook* for 1958, in 1949 there were 157 "cities" in the country; by

1957, the number of "large, medium, and small" cities had increased to 177. In 1949, there were five cities with a population of over 1,000,000; in 1957, thirteen. The statements on the number of medium-size cities with population between 500,000 and 1,000,000 appear conflicting; at one point, it is said that there were "about thirty" such cities in 1949, but at another point that in 1957 "the number had risen to more than thirty." No definition of "city" is provided. The *Handbook* states that in 1949, China's urban population was 57,650,000; in 1956, it was 89,150,000. It goes on to say that, since the annual rate of natural increase is 2.5 percent, two-thirds of the population growth in the cities during the seven years from 1949 to 1956 has been the the result of migration from rural areas. The Chinese Communists have rarely published discussions on urban population, so that this report is of unusual interest, despite the ambiguities.[18]

POPULATION GROWTH IN CHINA

Year	Total population (millions)	Percentage increase	Urban population (millions)	Percentage increase	Rural population (millions)	Percentage increase
1949	541.670		57.650		484.200	
1950	551.960	1.90	61.690	7.00	490.270	1.29
1951	563.000	2.00	66.320	7.50	496.680	1.31
1952	574.820	2.10	71.630	8.00	503.190	1.31
1953	587.960	2.29	77.670	8.43	510.290	1.41
1954	601.720	2.34	81.550	4.99	520.170	1.94
1955	614.650	2.14	82.850	1.59	531.800	2.24
1956	627.800	2.14	89.150	7.60	538.650	1.29
1957	656.630	3.20	92.000	7.10	564.630	1.30

SOURCES: The figures from 1949 through 1956 are taken from John S. Aird, *The Size, Composition, and Growth of the Population of Mainland China* (Washington, D. C., 1961), p. 36. The 1957 figures are from *Jenmin jihpao*, November 14, 1957; the percentage calculations are our own. The 1964 *Jenmin shouts'e* gives slightly different total population figures for 1949 and 1953, namely 548.770 and 595.550 millions.

The report comments on the implications of such a large increase in urban population. It notes that the government had carried out a survey of population growth in fifteen cities. The "basic population" of these cities had increased by one million or 28 percent from 1953 to

---

[18] *Jenmin shouts'e 1958*, pp. 647, 649-650.

1956.[19] "Service population" had increased by only 5 percent. The "dependent population," however, had increased by almost two and a half million or 70 percent. The report notes that 60 percent of the total population of these cities consisted of dependents. Of these, 1,200,000 immigrated from the rural areas. This meant an immensely greater burden on housing, welfare, city engineering, and public services. The report ends by stating that every additional inhabitant required an outlay of from 558 yuan to 695 yuan for welfare construction and urban engineering.

The regime became alarmed at this massive population increase and in 1957 issued a directive ordering "prevention of blind emigration of peasants from the rural areas." [20] The directive ordered all government agencies, central and local, to pool their forces to halt the flow of urban immigration, particularly in the provinces Shantung, Kiangsu, Anhwei, Honan, and Hopei. The government was concerned not only about the inflow of the population, but about the permanence of the immigration. Peasants who brought their families with them had little intention of returning to their villages. In 1957 the regime was thinking in terms of a leap forward in agricultural production and did not wish the best rural labor force to leave the depressed rural areas to seek work in the cities. The great inflow of population and the presence of a large nonproductive population created new problems. The question was not simply how to maintain public order in the cities but how to use this vast population to further economic goals. A new form of organization had to be found. The old residents committees were useless for this purpose. The new form of organization was the urban people's commune.

Formation of the Urban Communes

Communization, as a movement, had started in the rural areas. As village communization had moved into high gear, the leaders of the country suggested that a similar commune system might be introduced into the cities. General Secretary of the Party Teng Hsiao-p'ing, traveling through Hopei early in September 1958, was quoted as saying:

People in our countryside have commune-ized. That leaves only the . . . people in the cities. Circumstances push men along; it is impossible not to communize. He [Teng] demanded that all areas draw up plans for organizing

---

[19] "Basic population" was defined as meaning people working in some political, economic, or cultural sector.

[20] *Jenmin shouts'e 1958*, p. 649. During the 1950's the government had issued repeated directives curbing rural immigration into the cities. See Ishikawa Shigeru, *Chūgoko ni okeru shihon chikuseki kikō* (Tokyo, 1960), p. 53. The 1957 directive, however, seems to have been the sharpest to date.

people's communes in the cities, positively try it in some experimental areas. He gave some principled instructions as to organizing people's communes.[21]

One might try, at this point, to visualize the situation in the summer of 1958. A wave of excitement was sweeping China, compounded of enthusiasm at the bountiful harvest and whipped up by mass movements led by excited Party cadres. The millennium truly seemed not far off. Both the country's leaders and mass-level Party cadres began to speak of an imminent transition to communism. China, it seemed, had reached the "break-through" point; the great harvest was only the beginning of the real agricultural revolution. In the industrial areas production figures were rising by leaps and bounds. Differences between modern city and backward village, between superior mental and inferior physical labor, would soon be overcome. The commune would become the form of social organization from which communism would develop. Total mobilization of the country's labor was to be the instrument by which the economic and technological revolution would be consummated. Liu Shao-ch'i exclaimed exultingly: "If everyone works, work hours can be shortened; all will have time to study, to rest. Half work, half study—half tilling, half study, thus education will be universalized and raised, and the difference between mental and physical labor will be overcome." [22]

Did the leadership have a precise idea of the vast movement? The inspection tours undertaken at the time probably reflected the fact that the leaders themselves were not aware of exactly what was going on and had to see with their own eyes. They too were swept along by the excitement, for Mao Tse-tung's words "Communes are good" launched the great movement that within a few months saw the almost total communization of the country. Judging from this, the leadership probably had no clearcut plan for the establishment of urban communes.

The fact that the high enthusiasm which led to the formation of the communes originated in the countryside and not in the cities may explain why the leaders were hesitant to launch a full-scale urban communization movement. Nevertheless, the commune movement did spread to the cities. The basic idea behind the urban communes, as with the rural communes, was to create a single integrated unit—combining industrial, agricultural, commercial, cultural, and military-police functions. Communes were easier to launch in areas which had a central production focus. Many communes, therefore, which were set up in

---

21 Shanghai *Wenhui-pao*, October 20, 1958.

22 *Hsinhua panyüeh-k'an*, 19 (1958), 35-36. See also D. E. T. Luard, "The Urban Communes," *The China Quarterly* 3 (July-September 1960), 74-79.

the autumn of 1958 centered on factories, mines, schools, and offices. In other areas, attempts were made to give a residential unit some common production focus, such as setting up a number of small handicraft shops.

In November 1958, *Red Flag* published an article written by the secretary of the Tientsin Party Committee describing the establishment of an urban residents commune. The concluding paragraph tends to confirm the impression that the "thundering communization movement" in the villages did not have its exact counterpart in the cities:

> At present our country's villages have already unfolded a thundering communization movement. The urban population should also organize people's communes and make of them the basic-level organizational form of the cities. However, conditions in the cities, especially the great cities, are different from those in the villages. People in the cities are just now considering and studying how to set up people's communes. In some areas, they are trying out several kinds of experiments, organizing street residents to participate in production, suitably collectivizing and socializing household work—these are all the bases on which people's communes can be organized in the cities.[23]

The note of caution, already apparent at that time, became even clearer in the communiqué of the Sixth Plenum of the Central Committee, in December 1958, which announced that, aside from some model cases, communization in the cities was to be halted. The prevalence of "bourgeois" thoughts among many urban residents was cited as a major reason for discontinuing urban communization.

After the Wuhan plenary meeting of the Central Committee in 1958, urban communization was more or less discontinued. Experimental communes were organized here and there, and those already established continued to function. But although the communization campaign as a whole was halted, Party cadres in the streets continued to press for the organization of small neighborhood factories known as street industries.

In 1959, "Commentator," author of an article in *Jenmin jihpao*, noted: "Some people seem to think that factories and servicing stations operated by urban residents is just 'play,' and has 'little economic value.'" Accordingly late in 1959 and during the early months of 1960 a new campaign to organize street industries was mounted. Curiously, the term "urban people's commune" was not widely used.[24] Yet, a number of government leaders referred to the new campaign as urban communization. Li Fu-ch'un, writing in the summer of 1960 in *Red Flag*, stated: "Urban communes are being widely set up throughout the country; as of June there are now 1,027 urban people's communes in the

---

[23] *Hungch'i*, 11 (November 1958), 30.

[24] See Anderson Shih, *op. cit.* (in n. 6), p. 57.

whole country, with 52,000,000 members." [25] In July, the figure was said to have risen to 1,064 communes with a membership of 55,500,000[26] or 79.3 percent of the total urban population. Thus, in July 1960, the average urban commune had a membership of about 52,100. Sometime in the summer of July and August, 1960, a Chinese official in Tientsin told a visiting Japanese delegation that the city had a total of forty-six communes, of which seventeen had more than 50,000 members, eighteen between 30,000 and 50,000, and only eleven between 10,000 and 30,000.[27] Up to April, when the National People's Congress met, newspapers avoided the use of the term urban people's communes. However, at the congress, the Party secretaries of five of China's great cities, Peking, Shanghai, Tientsin, Wuhan, and Canton, issued a joint declaration stating: "Now to begin with, we are operating people's communes with the street population as object; at the same time we are gradually getting under way people's communes centered on factories, mines, schools, and offices; this way we shall gradually realize communization of all the cities." [28] The mammoth size of these latter-day urban communes recalls some of the rural communes set up in the fall of 1958. Yet the urban communes which were established in 1958 rarely reached the size and proportions of those in 1960. One of the largest urban communes in 1958, in Mukden, had a membership of 18,000. Chiaotso City (Honan) had 11,000 members,[29] the model Chengchow textile factory commune 10,559.[30] A smaller, perhaps more typical urban commune was in Kweiyang City, with 1,920 members.[31]

NUMBER AND POPULATION OF URBAN PEOPLE'S COMMUNES

Period	Number of communes	Population in communes	Percentage of total urban population
November 1959	19,000	750,000	n. a.
April 1960	n. a.	20,000,000	n. a.
May 1960	1,000	42,000,000	60
June 1960	1,027	52,000,000	n. a.

SOURCE: *1960-nen no Chūkyō* [*Communist China in 1960*], (Tokyo, 1960), p. 365.

---

[25] *Hungch'i*, 16 (August, 1960), 3.

[26] *Chungkuo ch'ingnien*, 17 (1960).

[27] Fukushima Hiroshi, "Toshi jimmin kōsha," *Chūgoku kenkyū geppō*, 151 (November 15, 1960), 7.

[28] *Ibid.*, p. 8.

[29] *Liaoning jihpao*, October 9, 1958; Anderson Shih, *op. cit.*, p. 24.

[30] *Hsinhua panyüeh-k'an*, 21 (1958), 91.

[31] *Kweichow jihpao*, August 31, 1958.

Given the vagaries of the term urban commune, people must have wondered what exactly an urban commune was supposed to be. One idea was basic to the 1958 commune, namely that it represented an integrated unit of production, living, and administration. This becomes apparent from the Chengchow urban commune to be described in the following section. Judging from the mammoth size of these urban communes set up in 1960, it is difficult to see how they could have been thusly integrated.

By 1960 decentralization of the rural communes had already started. Hence it was unlikely that Peking would demand of the urban communes the type of centralization and internal integration that it had earlier demanded of the rural communes. The conclusion seems warranted that, by the spring of 1960, the term urban commune was used loosely to describe general urban areas with various kinds of street industries. Probably few of them were integrated units. The vagueness in the usage of the term probably came about because the leaders did not want to give the impression that urban communes of the type set up in the fall of 1958 were once again coming into being.

It is not known how many of the integrated urban communes set up in the fall of 1958 were still operating in 1960. Though the Chengchow commune, to be described below, still existed in 1960, the Tungheng Street commune in Mukden, so highly praised earlier as an example to other cities, was not mentioned in a report on street industries which appeared early in 1960.[32] The report speaks only of "amalgamation and reorganization" which had taken place during the preceding year. In 1960 the urban commune probably represented an administrative district which was supposed to coordinate the multitude of discrete production and other activities in the streets. The idea of integration had receded in regard to the urban commune, just as it had in regard to the rural commune. Thus, despite the revived use of the term urban commune in the spring of 1960, the real aim of the campaign was to spur the organization of small-scale street production. This, of course, had been one of the original ideas behind the formation of the communes, and in this sense one can speak of a continuity of policy. But in 1958 the regime wanted more than that: to make the urban commune an integrated living and working community, just as it had in the country. In 1960 the goals of the revived urban commune movement were purely economic. In 1958 the goals had been social as well. Officially, the leaders continued to use the term urban communes, because, after all, "the three-sided red banner," of which one was the people's commune, was

---

32 *Jenmin jihpao,* February 8, 1960.

still being upheld. Since the beginning of 1961, there has been no further mention of urban communes.

From this one can conclude that the real urban communes, that is,
those attempting to do in the cities what was done in the villages, were
tried out only for a brief period of a few months during the late summer
and fall of 1958. It was only during that time that the Chinese Communists had the utopian dream of transforming the nature of the city from
one where people just lived together to one where they would be members of a collective living and working community.

The Chengchow Urban Commune

To illustrate the nature of an urban commune we have chosen one
of the models emulated in 1958, the urban commune of Chengchow in
Honan province. It is significant that Honan was the source of this
new movement of social reorganization. Honan is the chief agricultural
area of North China, as well as the birthplace of Chinese civilization. It
lies in the heart of the great North China Plain. Chengchow, the capital
of the province and its largest city (766,000 population in 1957), is an
expanding industrial center. Unlike the cities of Manchuria, its industries are largely light and oriented to the predominant activity in
the province: agriculture. In June 1958, Chengchow became the site of
the Chengchow Textile Factory Urban People's Commune.[33]

This commune combined economy and politics, education and living, work and military service. The factory became the nucleus of the
new organization, but the entire surrounding residential population of
10,559 souls (service personnel, urban residents, peasants) was drawn
into the commune. New "satellite" factories were set up around the
nucleus. Commercial and service facilities around the factory, which
hitherto had been run by the city administration, were turned over to
the commune to manage. Two agricultural production brigades and one
sheep-milk station were turned over to the commune. Public mess halls,
kindergartens, nurseries, wet-nursing stations were set up. A red-and-
expert university was established with nine departments: technology,
Marxism-Leninism, industry, agriculture, finance and economics, medi-
cine, military exercises, cultural education, foreign languages. All kinds
of schools, including elementary and night schools, were set up. The
commune was "militarized" and transformed into an army unit. In the
factory each shop, in commerce each store, in agriculture each production brigade, organized regiment, battalion, company. Neighborhoods were militarily organized, and youths from sixteen to twenty-five

---

[33] See *Hsinhua panyüeh-k'an*, 21 (1958), 91-93.

bore arms. The factory director became the commune chairman. The factory Party committee became the commune Party committee. The youth-league factory committee became the youth-league commune committee. The factory deputy director in charge of management became the full-time deputy chairman of the commune.

Commune administration was divided into the following sections: industrial, agricultural, planning and finances, personnel and labor, commerce, civil administration and maintenance, welfare, culture and hygiene. These, except the industrial, agricultural, and commerce sections, were enlarged versions of the old staff sections of the factory. Thus the civil administration and maintenance section now no longer did simple economic maintenance work, but directed the arming of the populace and carried out tasks of civil administration. The industrial section managed the new satellite industries. Though accounting for factory and satellite enterprises remained separate, nevertheless the administration of factory and commune was combined.

The commune was to become as self-sufficient as possible. Some food needs could now be supplied by the adjacent farmlands that were drawn into the commune. Satellite factories could now process waste material from the big factory and turn it into products for factory or consumer use. Ten such satellite factories were created, three alone to process waste materials from the woodworking shop of the big factory. The latter turned the wood scraps into alcohol, fiber boards, and household implements. The fiber boards proved to be useful for replacing worn-out iron parts in the machinery of the big factory. Backyard steel furnaces, smelting shops, toy factories, shoe-repair stands, laundries, weaving and sewing shops sprouted up. The skills of commune members were surveyed. When it was discovered that one man knew "native methods" of paper-making, he was given the job of making new paper from the waste paper in the commune.

The satellite factories had two main functions: to do processing work for the big factory and to provide goods and services for commune members. Formerly, the big factory had to subcontract a lot of processing work to outside firms. Now it could be done within the commune.

All organizations within the boundaries of the commune came under commune control. All state- and city-owned stores were turned over to the commune. Adjacent farmlands became the agricultural sector of the commune economy. Workers went into the fields to work alongside the peasants engaged in flood control and harvesting. The commune made it possible to mobilize 1,500 unemployed dependents and put them to work. Of these, 570 went to work in the factory.

Collective life, it was said, replaced individual life. Families contributed their tools to the commune. Meals were taken in common in the public dining hall. With more people eating collectively, the commune was able to cut its coal costs by 50 percent. Collective shopping made it possible to cut down on the number of sales people. Children spent more time in nurseries and kindergartens. With the burden of household work reduced, more time was given over to cultural life in the family. Men and women became "truly equal."

But there were administrative problems, it was admitted. The factory was state-owned (that is, by the Honan provincial government), but the commune as a whole was not state-owned. All production materials taken over by the commune became state-owned property. The satellite factories, as appendages of a state-owned factory, now became state-owned. The agricultural production brigades also became state-owned. Administratively, state ownership meant that the enterprise in question was under the jurisdiction of a single higher-echelon agency of administration. The enterprise, satellite factories, and agricultural brigades presumably were all administered by the Industrial Department of the Honan provincial government. However, other units, such as stores, banks, post offices, though they were "transferred downward" and put under commune control, were still regarded as basic-level units of province and city government. They were thus subject to different higher-echelon agencies of administration.

Aside from the conflicting lines of administrative jurisdiction, the commune contained property which was not state-owned. Reports on the commune made clear that elements of collective property still remained. This gave rise to two different kinds of ownership—"all people's" (that is, state), and "collective" (that is, belonging to the organized community). Commune members were not all state employees; some joined voluntarily by payment of an entrance fee. As a result, dualism in the wage system arose. Workers in the big factory, in state-owned stores, and in state-owned service branches were still paid according to the old wage scale. But peasants, and workers in satellite factories, despite the fact that their units were now state-owned, were treated as if they were part of the collective property system. Thus, they were made subject to a "low-wage system."

The dualism was also apparent in the welfare field: "In principle all commune members are equal; however, under present conditions, there are still some distinctions in regard to public medical care; personnel in state-owned industry as heretofore continue to enjoy completely free medical care; half-free medical care for workers' families remains in effect as before; for peasants and other personnel, medical care that formerly had to be paid for has now been made half-free."

Between 1958 and 1960, the Chengchow Textile Factory Urban People's Commune grew considerably. In March 1960 it consisted of a complex of five branch communes, each of which was centered on state-owned enterprise. It had the following members:

Employees and workers 24,822
Dependents of employees and workers 13,923
Commune industries employees and workers 871
Consumer service personnel 1,337
Peasants 1,641

The commune had acquired a large network of satellite factories, stores, schools, hospitals, farm-production brigades, administrative offices, and warehouses.[34] If the over-all commune had grown to mammoth size, the original commune, now one of the five branch communes, had also grown. Membership stood at 13,249, consisting mostly of textile workers and their families.[35]

In 1958, the Chengchow urban commune became a model which other urban communes were exhorted to follow. The commune was in an area where most residents were workers in the textile plant. The area thus already had a certain unity based on common work rather than simply common residence. Most workers probably lived near the confines of the factory, which created favorable conditions for a community. The commune became an administrative unit which encompassed the factory and its satellite residential and production areas. The commune consisted of a solid bloc of territory. Since work was to be the common unifying factor in the new entity, the commune attempted to create an integrated production system which would link all component parts into a single unit.

How was this integration to be accomplished? In a similar commune, in Harbin, integration was said to have been accomplished by "developing the production of small-scale industries with the help of medium and large industries." [36] This is vague language, but the basic idea is clear. Small factories in Harbin, as well as in Chengchow, were to be established around the perimeter of the large factory. Although some help in the form of capital and equipment was to be forthcoming from the large factory, basically the satellite factories were set up through labor recruited from the nonproducing sections of the population. Integration would be further achieved by a coordination of activities within

---

[34] Fukushima, *op. cit.*, pp. 12 ff.
[35] *Ibid.*, pp. 12-16.
[36] *Ibid.*, p. 3.

the entire commune area, a coordination made possible by the presence of a single overarching administration which managed everything from complex problems of production to minute details of consumption. As during the entire Great Leap Forward, the predominant theme was minimization of capital outlay, maximization of labor input. Thus as increasing amounts of goods and services could be provided by new labor sources generated among the resident population, the enterprise's capital needs would diminish accordingly.

Under the new system, the factory administration, in Chengchow, as well as elsewhere, was replaced by a commune administration, in which the Party committee played the dominant role. This brought about a further decrease in the power and authority of the managers. The factory manager became the commune chairman, but real power was wielded by the Party secretary. Since the Party was close to regional Party organizations, this exerted a distinct "lateral" pull on the factory, forcing it to take seriously the new policy of local integration. The big factory would have to live up to its new local responsibilities, as well as to the expectations of the central ministerial leadership.

The Urban Commune as a Unit of Administration, Living, and Production

Late in 1958, the Chinese Communists felt that the urban communes gave them a way to introduce a wholly different form of administration into the cities. Instead of imposing a framework of bureaucratic administration onto the cities from the top, administration would now be built from the bottom up. The core of the new administration would be made up of units of production which at the same time would be basic-level units of administration. This began to pose the same problems as, on a larger scale, were created by the fact that central state-owned enterprises were situated on the territory of a province. What should now be done with the offices, agencies, and enterprises within the bounds of the commune? Should they be left under city administration, put under commune jurisdiction, or subject to some kind of dual rule? There was the further difficulty that communes centered on production units would not always coincide neatly with city administrative boundaries, and conversely that city districts could not always be transformed into units of production.

The Chengchow commune, for example, became a unit of city government, though it was never made clear whether the area covered by the commune coincided with a city district. Commercial departments and service operations within the commune area were transferred from city to commune administration. This meant essentially stores and perhaps various small shops which had been operated by the city. It was not clear whether branch banks and local police stations were also placed under commune control. They probably remained under some "vertical rule." There is no indication that the popular militia supplanted the police. On the other hand, the Chengchow commune did absorb certain local branch offices of administration, as did other communes. One of the mammoth communes of 1960 was said to include eight "administrative agencies."[37]

The example of the Chengchow commune, as well as of other communes, made clear that there were basic conflicts in the urban communes between the general policy of achieving complete integration and the specific fact that the units of the communes (factories, stores, banks, and so on) were under different administrative jurisdictions. Integration undoubtedly won by sweeping away the erstwhile residents committees. The status of the street offices, however, was less clear. Though the street offices lost much of their importance, since neighborhood administration was carried out by the "civil administration and maintenance sections" of the communes, formally they appear to have remained in existence.[38]

There were thus real contradictions between the statuses of the commune as a unit of administration, of living, and of production. As a unit of administration, it was a part of the city-wide administrative system. As a unit of production, it was a state-owned enterprise, thus subject, at that time, to provincial jurisdiction. At the same time, it was supposed to be a self-contained unit of living where all were members of a single community.

Aside from the different statuses of the members of the commune (resulting, for example, in different wage scales), other factors also made it difficult to transform the commune into a real unit of living. The ordinary citizen found himself in the grip of a new way of life. Private life was decried as old-fashioned, women were mobilized for labor, and collective life supplanted home life. The street, not the home, became the central focus of daily life. Benefits of all sorts were to accrue to the people through better education, culture, and recreation.

---

[37] *Ibid.*, pp. 12, 15.

[38] A description of the organization of street industries in one section of Chungking published in September 1958, in *Hsin kuanch'a*, 8 (1958), 16, still indicates an important administrative role for the street offices in providing authorization for the establishment of street factories and even materials for them. However, this was before the establishment of urban communes, and these functions presumably were transferred to the commune administration.

Undoubtedly, many of these benefits were provided. However, the intensity of work and constant pressure from Party cadres left little free time for the people. The accent was on production, not consumption; and on work, not on recreation. The militarized atmosphere diluted the civilian aspects of the new system. Mass movements became a substitute for private enjoyment. What could have been a noteworthy experiment in a new kind of urban living was thwarted by the fact that production was the main obsession of the cadres who organized the communes. The production fetishism of 1958 turned out to be one of the main human failings of the new experiment.[39]

Despite the ideal of making the commune into an integrated unit of administration, living, and production, it was the latter which was the basic aim of urban communization. The Chinese Communists wanted to take an underemployed population and put it to good use in production. Setting up communes of the Chengchow type was feasible because it was centered on a major factory nucleus. But the real challenge came in trying to impose a common production focus on purely residential areas. This was particularly difficult in many of the smaller, nonindustrial cities. There too large numbers of underemployed people existed. The cadres felt that labor was the energy, and organization was the magic key, that could make any residential area into a unit of production. Labor and organization would replace capital. All that was needed were waste materials, idle hands, and organization; thereupon street industries would come into being, which could then become producers of capital and ultimately a part of an expanding industrial network.

An example of this approach is the urban commune established in Kweiyang City in August 1958 to which we shall refer again below. As soon as the commune was established, the members wanted to start different kinds of production and welfare activities. But where was the

---

[39] In recent times, the Communists have begun cautiously to criticize the production fetishism of the Great Leap Forward. A recent article on a model village in Shensi makes this clear: "Within the Party branches of some large brigades, there were some comrades who thought: 'The people's commune is supposed to concern itself with production; if production goes well, then that's it!' Under the domination of such thoughts, they got wound up in everyday asks, tried too much to control production planning and the work pace, and did too little about policy and ideological-political work. Whenever ideological problems arose between Party cadres and commune members, either they glossed over them or evaded them, or they took an oversimplified view of them. It is quite clear that the spiritual conditions of people at that time [i.e., the Great Leap Forward] included some thought and behavior on the part of cadres that was not suitable for village conditions (*Jenmin jihpao*, April 20, 1964).

capital to come from? The commune had no natural economic base, so the commune committee decided to get production going by "self-reliance and with empty hands." All commune members were asked to contribute an amount from their wages which became the public accumulation fund. Of the fund, 70 percent was to be used for production and the remaining 30 percent for welfare. The slogan was: "If You Have Men, Give Men; If You Have Money, Give Money; If You Have Things, Give Things."[40]

For the next few years, street industries of various kinds were organized in the cities of China. Few amounted to more than small-scale undertakings operated with much labor, little capital, and often even less skill. *Jenmin jihpao* reported on street industries which had been set up in the streets of Peking. There were more than twenty different types in operation, producing five hundred kinds of items. The largest were shoe and hat factories, metal works, specialized handicraft industries, shops for making writing equipment, printing and paper-making. Many of them did manufacturing work for larger factories. One street in the Hsüanwu district of Peking had sixty-three different street industries, of which fifty-five did manufacturing for larger factories. They produced glass ware, insulation material, dyestuffs, glue, and many other articles.[41]

All varieties of tiny enterprises, some producing finished products, others producing goods for larger factories, can be seen today in the streets of the working class quarters of Hong Kong and Macao. In Mainland China street industries existed before the coming of the Communists and withered in the period of nationalization. In reviving these street industries, albeit in "socialist form," the Communists were making use of a predisposition which already existed in the Chinese city. What made them unattractive to the population was that they were not private. All gain went to the commune and ultimately to the state. Many of these industries turned out to be extremely wasteful in labor and capital. Much of China's consumer-goods production is accounted for by handicraft industries which are run by family or neighborhood groups. China has an old tradition of such industry, and communization sought to make use of this tradition.

How many street industries the Communists created in 1958, and then again in 1960 (when the second stage of urban communization was more explicitly oriented toward their creation) is difficult to say.

---

[40] *Kweichow jihpao,* August 31, 1958.

[41] *Jenmin jihpao,* February 8, 1960.

Despite the lack of enthusiasm for these collective ventures on the part of an individualistic population, quite a few of them probably turned out to be successful.

What has happened to these small enterprises during the present period of relaxation of controls? Some of the smallest have returned to private hands. Larger ones are probably being operated by the city administration.[42] Even though communization succeeded in creating many small street industries, they hardly contributed to over-all commune integration. Street industry consists mostly of tiny shops. They are dependent on contracts from larger firms or on market demand. They have little relationship with each other. As long as the communes were not able to contribute much in the way of capital, the street industries had little to contribute to the commune, except what the commune could extract in payments. Furthermore, the small entrepreneur needs a maximum of flexibility so that he can establish his contacts when and where the need arises. Just as in the rural communes, the centralization of activities in the urban communes restricted the freedom of these small entrepreneurs. During the 1960 phase of the urban communization campaign, the regime was more concerned with getting these small industries started than with creating integrated economic units within the city. Thus the larger the communes became, the less tightly controlled they were at the lowest level.

In 1958 and in 1960 the real aim of urban communization, as we have stated, was to tap unused resources of labor. But who were the idle people living in the cities? The bulk of the labor for the street industries came from women, although, as *Red Flag* indicated, "old people, weak and handicapped people" also were to be recruited.[43] However, in essence the urban people's commune became largely a woman's affair. Traditionally, the Chinese woman worked in the home and not outside. The development of modern industry and changes in social patterns brought about a substantial increase in the female labor

---

[42] A Reuters dispatch which appeared in the *Christian Science Monitor*, July 17, 1962, reported on the appearance once more in the streets of Peking of peddlers, barbers, repairmen. The dispatch notes: "Their reappearance apparently reflects changes in the scope of the urban people's communes, now seldom mentioned in the press. The communes, however, do still exist, and their small factories are still in operation. But shortages of raw materials and increased emphasis on agriculture rather than industry, the return to the countryside of many people who had come to live in the city in recent years, and the drive to provide more consumer goods have led to visible changes."

[43] *Hungch'i*, 11 (November 1958), 27-30.

force. The Communists from the beginning proclaimed equality between men and women and sought to draw women from private to
public life. While large numbers of younger women were employed in
public enterprises, many older women remained in the home. Articles
which appeared in the fall of 1958 pointed to the fact that until the
formation of the urban people's communes it had not been possible
to draw the bulk of urban women away from their household tasks.
Continuing immigration into the city—which the decrees of late 1957
surely did not stop entirely—brought in peasant women, even more
under the influence of traditional custom than urban women. But
peasant women were not the only ones reluctant to be drawn into
street collective life. In Tientsin, resistance came from other quarters:

> The dependents of some capitalist families and of some high-level intellec-
> tuals showed resistance to the idea. Some asked: "If we join the commune,
> is it all right if we don't work?" Others said: "If the commune accumulates
> profit, how much should an individual get?" "How much are we supposed to
> put out?" Others asked: "Is it all right if we hire someone else for money to
> work for us in the commune?" These people had many more worries about
> participating in collective labor than did the ordinary masses.[44]

But in contrast to "backward elements" which resisted the communes,
there were many other women who saw in the communes an opportunity for themselves. Women played an active role in the street Party
committees and in the leadership of mass organizations. They became
the cadres of the new organizations, just as women earlier dominated the
urban residents committees.

If the ideal urban commune was represented by the Chengchow
commune, the hope for the ultimate possibilities for the communes
was represented by the above-mentioned Kweiyang commune. The
description given by the *Kweichow jihpao* shows that this was originally a small residential neighborhood. It was an administrative unit
under the control of the local police station. There were 509 households and a total population of 1,920 individuals. Of these 867 were
working people. Of the remaining 1,057 individuals, 85 percent were
dependents, 10 percent were classed as privately employed, and 5 percent "belonged to other strata." When the Great Leap Forward began,
great emphasis was put on developing production work in the neighborhood. The Kweiyang commune set up five factories, five stores, one
savings station, kindergartens, public dining halls, libraries, clubrooms,
and so on. Women, who previously had not done public work, played

---

44 *Ibid.*, pp. 29-30.

a major role in these activities. "Some got so excited in working that they forgot to eat, forgot to sleep, forgot to return home. . . . Housewives who earlier simply took care of their own homes now cared about each other and helped each other." The core group consisted of ten people, each of whom was in charge of a working committee. They were aided by thirty "positivists," most of whom later became cadres.[45]

In essence, this brief description presents the problem and the challenge that faced the cadres late in 1958. There were about as many nonworking people in the Kweiyang Commune as working people. If a large number were children, there were also a large number of women who presumably did only household work. Collective life was supposed to make household work redundant, so their labor could be used for purposes of production. It would probably be wrong to disbelieve the enthusiasm of the women which the article mentions. The Great Leap Forward was a time of psychological liberation for many peasants; probably many women, one of China's suppressed populations, must have felt that the millenium was at hand, when they could freely enter the great public world on a par with men. The organizational methods used are typical of those used in the rural areas. A core leadership group of ten people, aided by thirty positivists, organized the almost 2,000 people in the area.

But the Kweiyang commune did not succeed in the long run. The reasons for the failure are apparent from the discussions above. Others may be mentioned. Most of the ablest men and women worked in factories outside the commune area. Commune labor depended on those left in the neighborhood. The workers were hardly pleased that their wives were so enthusiastic about their new tasks that "they forgot to return home." In earlier times, street enterprises were family affairs. The bonds of family ties kept these undertakings going even at times when economic difficulties endangered the operation. The commune industries were not held together by such ties. Low and uncertain wages made the workers even less enthusiastic. But if family income did increase because of commune industry employment, shortages of goods made money less attractive.

Aftermath of the Urban Communes

The communes, in one form or another, continue to exist in rural areas. But in the cities, they disappeared. Many street industries are still operating, but then they could just as well have developed

---

[45] *Kweichow jihpao,* August 31, 1958.

under free market conditions. Chinese factories had traditionally followed a practice of contracting with smaller shops to do various kinds of supplemental work. This is so in Hong Kong today.

Indeed, the whole economic pattern would have been much more rational had the market operated. So many small enterprises were started that when severe materials shortages occurred, they were unable to continue. At first, a labor-intensive approach made sense. What was lacking in capital could be made up in labor. However, as enthusiasm for commune work waned, as housewives retreated back into the home, the initial optimistic labor-capital ratio began to change. To maintain production, more capital was needed. But where would this capital come from? Commune earnings could supply some, at least in monetary form. Yet if shortages of materials and equipment became more severe, and money increasingly became just money, the capital needs of the communes could not be met. Production faltered, thus making outside help necessary. The state could hardly be expected to help when agriculture began to make heavier demands on the state and when the capital needs of industry remained as pressing as ever.

There was only one solution: to try to increase private incentives for workers. Only if the individual worker could envisage tangible self-gain in these enterprises, was there hope of bringing more labor to bear on street production. But this meant diminishing the collective aspects of the street industries, for the more the individual was submerged in the collectivity, the less chance he saw for self-gain. Thus decentralization of street enterprises meant encouragement of private enterprise. But permitting such private enterprise was equally futile unless the private entrepreneur could function in a market context: selling his products for money in the expectation of being able to acquire other products in exchange, either for consumption or for reinvestment in production. The restoration of private enterprise must mean the restoration of some market conditions.

This is what the regime has done since the beginning of 1961. The new policy has had tangible results. Small-scale private enterprise has begun to reappear in the cities of China. Cities have once again begun to take on a bustling appearance. It is amusing to read occasional accounts which reflect the "discovery" of a new way of doing things in the cities. One such account related one of these innovations. It said that the innovation arose from the discovery that retail stores function best when they are decentralized and widely distributed about a city. The case of a small shop in Shihchiachuang City was cited; it was the only store in an otherwise residential district, sold little, and was run by an old man. He sold odds and ends to the local residents—vegetables, stools, brooms, ribbons, any small item that the residents needed. The store was very simple, needed only a few hundred yuan of capital to operate, and could be managed by the one man.[46] The reporter who wrote the account stated that there were many such simple stores throughout the city. The larger retail stores had begun to distribute goods to these shops. This took pressure off the large stores and avoided the overcrowding of the main streets that had been so common before. Above all, it reduced the burdens on the public transportation system.

It is difficult to tell how far-reaching and permanent these concessions to private enterprise are. Since some measure of decentralization I now prevails (the "small freedoms"), Peking has presumably realized that not all human activity can be fitted into the framework of organization. Although ideologically no principle has been made of the "small freedoms," it is difficult to see how there could be a return to the conditions of 1958. The street industries started during the Great Leap Forward and those created through private initiative since 1961 are beginning to look much like those in Hong Kong.

THE CONTEMPORARY URBAN SITUATION

The Exodus from the Cities

The quiet abandonment of the urban communes signifies the end of the Communist attempt to change the nature of the city. Perhaps the regime never seriously thought that city life could be revolutionized. The Chinese city remains today what it has been for a century, an area of concentrated human residence. Residence, not production, remains the foundation of city life.

The problem of millions of nonproductive individuals, who made demands on the limited consumer supplies available, did not disappear with the abandonment of the urban communes. Recent population figures are not available, but it can be easily surmised that urban population has continued to grow. Whatever the attempts made by the regime to equalize conditions between city and country, the city remains an attractive area for the Chinese peasant during a period of adversity.

The continuing emigration out of Mainland China to Hong Kong must be viewed not only as flight from a depressed region, but as immigration into a prospering city. Hong Kong has absorbed more than a million refugees and new ones continue to enter, despite British attempts to stop the flow. But Hong Kong is not simply a strange place

---

46 *Jenmin jihpao,* May 8, 1962.

which indiscriminately absorbs the newcomers. It is a city with networks of social organizations, many of which tie up with Mainland China, through mechanisms which operated in traditional Chinese cities. There are the links of common kinship, common village or regional origin, common occupation, common religion, and common membership in certain types of associations. Only the most unfortunate of all immigrants is cast into a situation of anomie, and for him there are always the anti-Communist organizations, Chinese and foreign, ready to extend a welcoming hand. The typical immigrant can usually find a niche somewhere in a social relationship in which he is protected until he can find productive employment and repay the obligation incurred to the organization. On the Mainland, the traditional forms of organization have ceased to exist, at least on the surface. Yet regional quarters remain in Chinese cities, and most peasants have at least some relatives and friends in the city. The old city-country link has not been broken in Communist China.

During the April 1962 session of the National People's Congress, Premier Chou En-lai announced that the regime had launched a campaign to send excess population back from the cities to the rural areas. This campaign was known as the "return to the village"—*huihsiang*—policy. In contrast to the *hsiafang* of earlier years, when urban cadres were sent to villages with which they had no previous tie, the *huihsiang* campaign sought to get people to go back to their native villages. The newspapers carried accounts of how kinsmen were welcomed back by their relatives and reintegrated back into the production team (that is, the native village). The devices used to accomplish this reduction in urban population were unusual for the Chinese Communists. The mass movement, the wholesale organization of teams to march out into the countryside—these were conspicuously absent. Instead, the regime made use of more conventional methods to bring about the return to the village. Thousands of small factories were closed, which put large numbers of people out of work. Urban workers employed after 1958 were dismissed from their jobs and encouraged to return to their home villages. Indeed, there was little choice for many urban workers since work was impossible to find in the city. Furthermore, as a result of the freeze on new employment and the shortages of materials, industrial enterprises were told to concentrate on raising productivity. The economic philosophy of the Great Leap Forward was reversed: Emphasis on quantity gave way to emphasis on quality. Since capital remained in short supply, industry reorganized to stabilize production, raised technical skills, and emphasized orderly management to achieve a rise in productivity.

This massive return of urban workers to the villages was a major factor in the great flight of refugees to Hong Kong in April and May 1962. Not starvation pushed the refugees toward Hong Kong, but the fear of starvation. Indeed there were indications that the food situation in Kwangtung, although precarious, was somewhat better than it had been before. The descent of unemployed city people onto the villages produced a wave of panic which, combined with other factors, resulted in the outpouring of people to Hong Kong and Macao.

The refugees consisted of two kinds, urban people and peasants. Many of the former were workers who feared the return to the country-side; instead of returning to their villages, they headed for the one place where they still had hope of living in a city: the Hong Kong-Macao region. Many of the latter were panic-stricken peasants. Flight was made possible by the relaxation of Communist border controls, news of which spread through Kwangtung in April 1962. Border guards began looking the other way. Indeed, some even helped the emigrants escape to the other side. Moreover, the police began issuing exit permits in large numbers. Groups began to form in Canton and in the areas adjacent to Hong Kong. Some rushed to railroad stations to buy tickets to the Communist border station of Shumchun. Others made their way to the frontier region. Small groups coalesced into larger groups, in some cases forming small armies seeking a road across the frontier. There was little violence. The Communist border guards allowed the refugees to pass. There was more violence when the British tried to prevent the refugees from coming in, and particularly from Chinese Hong Kong residents, largely relatives or friends of the refugees, who were angered by the British interference. Then, the Communists unexplainedly re-imposed border controls. The exodus was more a mass panic than a revolt. As usual for collective fright, the panic quickly disappeared and the situation returned to normal.[47]

The flight of thousands of urban and rural people to Hong Kong and Macao was an illustration of the great pressures of rural emigration that the Chinese Communists have faced during all the years of their rule. However, the suddenness of the 1962 emigration seems to have been due to other than immediately economic causes. The rectification campaign against the rural cadres diminished the power and prestige of these

---

[47] The outside world understandably speculated whether the refugee exodus signified the beginning of a revolt and the breakdown of control. There were no signs of either. Relaxation of controls took place in an orderly manner, the Communists preserving discipline among their troops, police, and border guards. When the order was given to end the outflow, control was reimposed quickly, effectively, and with relatively little violence.

leaders of the Great Leap Forward in the eyes of the peasants. Concessions made to the peasants produced some improvement in the village situation, but also released new energies in them. The peasants began to assert themselves in more demanding ways. Leadership in the production teams reverted to the hands of the "old peasants." The "small freedoms" grew gradually larger. Private enterprise began to reappear. The state became increasingly cautious in the extraction of agricultural surplus. But the lessening of organizational pressure also produced a sense of anomie among the peasants. Traditional organization had disappeared, but now also the new organizational structures were shown to be incapable of meeting the needs and demands of the peasantry. Anomie went with growing self-assertiveness. Many again conceived the idea of migrating to Hong Kong, and indeed, the flow of small groups and individuals toward Hong Kong and Macao continued throughout 1962 and early 1963. Gradually pressure built up on the regime, posing the choice, either of clamping down decisively or of allowing the wave to spend itself.

The Dilemma of the Cities

The Chinese Communists have faced two dilemmas in the cities. First, they have not been able to create economic capabilities to match the rapid growth of urban population (through natural increase and immigration). Second, they have not been able to create effective forms of social organization to bring about a new sense of community to replace the anomie inherent in modern cities with their crowded tenements and mixed populations. The experiment of the urban communes was a grandiose attempt to make their huge urban pouulation economically useful and give it a sense of community at the same time.

The Chinese Communists share with other developing nations the problem of rapid economic development in the face of population pressures. The urban communes of 1958 lacked an adequate economic base. The Chinese Communists were aware of this and sought to use organizational methods to make up for material weakness, in short, to use human labor as a substitute for material capital. However, to make organization work, they felt it had to be turned into community. The experiment of the urban communes sought to create community. It failed because any attempt to create community by force is doomed. The more an external political group tries to impose communal organization, the greater will be the human resistance to it. A community must serve its own ends and not primarily those of an external power.

When they experimented with the urban communes, the Chinese Communists thought that by resolving the social problem of community first, they would obtain a means of then resolving the economic problem of population. Community would bring about greater individual effort through voluntary participation, and this would lead to economic plenty. The failure of the urban communes and the economic crisis of 1960-1961 left them with the same two dilemmas they had faced when they entered the Great Leap Forward. Since early 1961, Peking has shown that it regards the economic problem as primary; to resolve it, it has returned to a policy of offering material incentives. It has also accepted the fact that living standards had to be improved, though the cult of austerity still remains. The Chinese Communist leaders have realized that economic development in general, and resolution of their urban problem in particular, cannot be achieved by political-organizational means alone. They have realized that there must be some self-motivated participation by the producers. To this end, they have allowed the market to operate again at the lower levels of the economy. This has brought with it an expansion of the "small freedoms."

Since the end of 1960, no new attempt to change the nature of the city has been reported. One can presume that as organizational experiments have diminished, the control factor has become increasingly important. Bureaucratic administration, including the police, plays a much greater role than it did during the Great Leap Forward. Under these circumstances, basic-level administration may slowly be reassuming the forms of the early 1950's. All visitors speak of the cleanliness and order in Chinese cities, but the patterns of living and working may be much the same as they were before 1949.

In our introduction, we pointed out that long periods elapse before a new social system arises. Whether the present patterns of living and working are a recurrence of older pre-1949 patterns or represent something new is a subject to be studied. It is clear that the Chinese Communists have created effective political institutions for governing China's cities. They have yet to create effective economic institutions to resolve the dilemma of population, and effective social institutions to resolve the dilemma of community. Neither of these dilemmas will be resolved unless Peking allows true growth "from the bottom up," as well as growth "from the top down."

CHAPTER VII

VILLAGES

THE PROBLEMS of China's cities discussed in the preceding chapter are modern; those of its villages are traditional. In 1949 China's villages and the peasantry which inhabited them were little different from what they were centuries before. The Chinese Revolution destroyed the traditional rural elite, but it changed neither the villages nor the peasantry. The Chinese Communists have always realized that without a fundamental transformation of the traditional village and its peasantry they could not resolve China's most pressing problem: agriculture. In its simplest terms, China needed an economic revolution in agriculture to produce food for its growing population and provide savings for industrialization. But increased farm production could not be achieved by more intensive use of traditional methods because traditional farm technology had reached its limits. A new technological and economic foundation for the villages had to be created. Since little capital was available to invest in agriculture, the Chinese Communists decided to use organizational means to bring about a political and social transformation of rural society from which the needed economic revolution would develop. The theme of the present chapter is the organizational history of that political and social transformation. Since the roots of that history lie deep in the past, we must start our discussion with some of the problems of the villages and the peasantry in earlier periods.

PEASANTRY AND VILLAGE IN TRADITIONAL CHINA

State and Village

The relationship between state and village has been a central problem of Chinese history since the beginnings of Chinese civilization. Chinese civilization began in the second millenium B.C. through the establishment of a state power (the Shang dynasty), based on an urban foundation (the city of Anyang), which extended its dominion over great expanses of agricultural territory (the North China Plain). As dynasty succeeded dynasty, state power grew and its empire extended over ever greater domains. As a result, the state, and the cities on which it was based, needed increasing amounts of agricultural products which only the villages could supply. A bond thus developed between state and village.

But the material basis of this bond was not the irrigation system, as Karl A. Wittfogel has argued. In his view the state played a vital role in the material life of the villages by linking them, through irrigation systems in ecological networks. It is true that such systems have linked villages in many parts of China for centuries, and it is true that the state, for centuries, has carried out extensive projects of water works. Yet, there is enough evidence to indicate that local irrigation in most parts of China did not depend on the state. State-directed water works usually served the purpose of communications and transportation, factors more of political than of economic importance.[1]

Medieval Central Asia is a much better example of state-managed irrigation networks than China. In fact, so close was the relationship then between state and irrigation in Central Asia that when the state power broke down, whole agricultural areas turned into deserts. Great empires were transient phenomena in Central Asia. They lacked the material foundation of a stable agriculture which would have provided a continuing socioeconomic basis for political power. The fact that Chinese agriculture did not need the state made it independent of

---

[1] Wolfram Eberhard, *Conquerors and Rulers: Social Forces in Medieval China* (Leiden, 1952), pp. 34 ff.

the recurrent political crises that affected the state. Thus, when dynasties fell, China did not go the way of the empires of Central Asia.

The relationship of state and village throughout the vast time span of Chinese history has been expressed by one Western scholar, John S. Burgess: "China's rulers have been only concerned with the maintenance of order and the collection of taxes; aside from demanding their submission, they have demanded no other cooperation from the people." [2] This opinion, widely shared by Chinese scholars, sees the role of the state toward the village as mainly exploitative and controlling. Implicitly it is at variance with Wittfogel's view that there is a materially defined link between state and village which necessarily gives the state a managerial role in society. However, Wittfogel admits that the traditional Chinese state never achieved total manipulation of society. Since, in his view, the state tries constantly to extend its managerial arms over society, he explains the absence of total manipulation of society through "the law of diminishing administrative returns." [3] In other words, the state could have managed all society, but beyond a certain point it did not pay.

The differences between the more common view of the traditional Chinese state as expressed by Burgess and that of Wittfogel is that the former essentially sees the role of the state as passive control, whereas the latter sees it as active management. Wittfogel's "hydraulic" thesis, which gives the state a major role in the maintenance of the irrigation systems on which village agriculture depends, necessarily leads him to such a managerial conception of the state. Management and control, as we have indicated in the preceding chapters, are different. Management means operational leadership through organization, and constant directive efforts over men to achieve goals. Control means the exercise of restraint over and the checking on human beings to make sure they are doing what is expected or are not hurting the interests of those in power. The weight of evidence from China's long history indicates that the state was far more oriented toward control than toward management of society.

Though Wittfogel's "hydraulic" and total managerial thesis is faulty, it is true that the traditional Chinese state had great capacities for organization, and during some periods of Chinese history did attempt to exercise managerial direction over Chinese society. However, the most

---

[2] John S. Burgess, *The Guilds of Peking* (New York, 1928), p. 213; see also Shimizu Morimitsu, *Shina shakai no kenkyū* (Tokyo, 1940), p. 203.

[3] *Oriental Despotism* (New Haven, 1957), p. 110.

ambitious of these attempts took place over a millenium and a half ago, during times of acute social and political breakdown. But during most of Chinese history the state let society organize itself, confined its functions to exploitation and control, and acted organizationally and managerially only for certain special purposes.

Society mostly organized itself. Villages developed various forms of cooperation based on kinship, work, religion, and other ties. Clan groups organized villages. Villages found links with the cities in the form of "native associations." Self-organization proved to be a more powerful and durable source of organization than the actions of the state. Rather than managing them, the state attempted to use these local organizations for its own interests: maintenance of control through the exercise of self-defense and judicial functions; and the facilitation of exploitation through the collection of revenues, the registration of population, and the execution of public works.

The relationship between the state and the local organizations changed from time to time. The more powerful the local organization, the greater the danger of its infringing on the interests of the state. Yet every attempt by the state to impose its own form of organization on the villages threatened to break down local organization. The state on occasion sabotaged its own interests by asserting itself excessively in a managerial direction.

Although Chinese administrative history is replete with changes, as a whole formal state administration did not reach below the level of the *hsien*. The *hsien* was an administrative unit consisting of a commercial town surrounded by an agricultural region linked by economic, political, military, social, and cultural ties. On occasion, some of these links were considered more important than others, which led to periodic redrawing of *hsien* boundaries. But the conception of the *hsien* as a basic-level administrative unit remained constant.

In the *hsien* the magistrate maintained his yamen, surrounded by clerks. In his office, one could find from time to time all the local leaders. The magistrate's office symbolized the relationship between state and society. There the leaders of civil society and the officers of government met.

Thus one can say that the predominant pattern of administration that prevailed throughout most of Chinese history was the use of the yamen as a link between the state and the local organizations. However, as mentioned earlier, during some periods of Chinese history the state tried to create local organization rather than let it develop spontaneously. The most ambitious attempt of this sort occurred during the Six

Dynasties Period (third to sixth century A.D.). This was a period of serious political and social breakdown. One of the more powerful dynasties of the period, the Northern Wei (of Turkish origin), introduced a system of village organization known as the "equal field" (*chünt'ien*) system. All land was declared to be the property of the state, and fields were allocated to the peasant on the basis of need and use. What is organizationally striking about the equal-field system is its military character. Indeed, it appears to have had its origins in an earlier form of land allocation, known as the "camp field" (*t'unt'ien*) system, which was used on China's frontier areas to settle soldiers. Under the camp-field system, the soldier became a peasant, without giving up his status as a soldier.

The equal-field system was feasible during this period of political and social breakdown. When rural stability returned during the T'ang dynasty (seventh to ninth centuries A.D.), the system was abandoned. The state once again accepted the fact that society had to organize itself. From then until the rise of the Chinese Communists, the state never again tried to change the basic nature of village organization.

Though the equal-field system marked the last attempt, until modern times, by the Chinese state to exercise total managerial direction over the village, various dynasties tried, at different times, to develop organization below the *hsien* level. This fact led some Chinese scholars, a few decades ago, to debate whether such organizations were heteronomous or autonomous, that is, whether they were created from the top down by the state, or from the bottom up by the villagers themselves.[4] In fact, they were both, as the Chinese historian Wen Chün-t'ien, has stated.[5] Tendencies toward the formation of such organization came both from within the village and from the state. Sometimes these tendencies harmonized, but more often they reflected the fundamental juxtaposition of state and village. Their nature remained dual, and the contending elements could never be completely resolved. In Chinese history, these forms of organization have appeared under various names, but are most clearly revealed in the *lichia* system of the Ming dynasty (fourteenth to seventeenth century A.D.) and the *paochia* system of the Ch'ing dynasty (seventeenth to twentieth centuries A.D.).

---

[4] The Japanese sociologist Shimizu Morimitsu expresses the following opinion: "Heteronomous self-rule (i.e., village government) basically assumed the reality of already existing human collectivities; by giving them a form suitable to the realization of the state's aims, it sought to create a cover over human relationships" (*op. cit.*, p. 203).

[5] Quoted in *ibid.*, p. 204.

Lichia and Paochia

The *lichia* system of the Ming was an essentially civil form of village organization which grouped villagers into blocks of households. The *paochia* system of the Ch'ing, while similarly grouping households, was essentially a military organization.[6] The Japanese sociologist Shimizu Morimitsu has characterized the *lichia* system as mainly concerned with taxation and corvée functions, the *paochia* system with police and defense functions.[7] However, in general, both systems were forms of organization imposed by the state on the villages for the maintenance of order, the collection of taxes, and registration of population. The latter function may be seen as instrumental, serving as the basis for the first two substantive functions, for both the system of public order and taxation presupposed a registered population. The two substantive functions can be described as control and exploitation.

Both *lichia* and *paochia* were organizations that grouped households together into units based on decimals. Under the *lichia* system, households were grouped into bodies of ten, each headed by a chief; 110 households made up a *li*.[8] The *paochia* also consisted of blocks of households organized into decimal groups. But in contrast to the *li*, the *pao*, the largest and most comprehensive unit, consisted of one thousand households.[9] The difference in size points to an important problem.

---

[6] Cf. pp. 368 ff.

[7] Shimizu, *op. cit.*, pp. 204-208. Sinologists have argued on the nature and differences between *lichia* and *paochia*. Shimizu, writing as a sociologist, differentiates them functionally, and not just historically. The fact that elements of the one could be found in the other does not challenge the idea of functional differences between them. Shimizu's arguments shed much light on the reasons for which the Ch'ing introduced the *paochia*, rather than reinforce the *lichia*. Shimizu cites the reasoning of Huang Liu-hung, the author of the *Fuhui ch'üanshu, chüan* 21, *paochia-pu, hsüan paochia-chang*, to support his point: "Each village (*hsiang*) had a headman watching over matters relating to money and grain, whereas the *pao* chief was particularly concerned with robbery and subversion, and not with other things. Under the old rules, the village headman also had to concern himself with *pao* matters. Since his tasks were not specialized, his talents were not fully used. The fact is that village headmen are chosen from among those who are older and virtuous, direct in behavior and able to persuade others; *pao* chiefs are chosen from among those who are strong and healthy, and who can lead people. Since their functions are different, different people have to be appointed, and one man cannot do both" (p. 226).

[8] *Ibid.*, p. 208; see also, Ping-ti Ho, *Studies on the Population of China 1368-1953* (Cambridge, Mass., 1959), pp. 7-11; see also, Wen Chün-t'ien, *Chungkuo paochia chihtu* (Shanghai, 1935).

[9] Shimizu, *op. cit.*, p. 229.

Shimizu argues for the essentially civil functions of the *lichia* by pointing out that, as the *lichia* declined, the tax-collecting functions of the *hsien* yamens became increasingly important.[10] Since the *lichia* was thus mainly oriented to the major civil interest of the state, namely tax collection, Shimizu states that its unit of organization was the "natural village." By contrast, the *paochia* took the "administrative village" as its unit of organization.[11]

The distinction between "natural" and "administrative" villages is important in Chinese social history. The natural village is a single ecological unit integrated by economic production and social cooperation. The administrative village is a political unit, so defined by the state. The administrative village may coincide with the natural village or it may consist of a grouping of several natural villages. That the distinctions are rarely neat is mirrored by the terminological profusion and confusion in the names for "villages" in Chinese history, and in the different regions of China. Though ecological factors formed the basis of the natural village, the political factor also acted as an integrating force, often drawing originally discrete villages together into larger units. Thus administrative villages could, in time, turn into natural villages, and, conversely, administrative villages could break up again into their component "natural" segments. The terminological complexity so marked under the Ch'ing dynasty mirrored a "fluid boundary situation" between the natural and the administrative village.

The fact that the *lichia* was oriented to the natural village and the *paochia* to the administrative village suggests a hypothesis which will be relevant to arguments to be made further along in this chapter: when the traditional state was primarily intent on strengthening its exploitation functions and attempted to use organizational means to this end, it aimed at developing organization within the natural village; on the other hand, when it was primarily intent on strengthening its control functions, it aimed at developing organization within the administrative village. Since the administrative village, in any case, was politically created by the state, it itself can be viewed as an organizational form serving control purposes.

The *paochia* system broke down as the Ch'ing government became increasingly unable to exercise political control over the countryside. But the *paochia* idea never left the minds of China's rulers. As Western ideas came into China, the old *paochia* concept became cloaked in the mantle of the democratic ideal of "local autonomy." The belated 1908

[10] *Ibid.*, p. 223.
[11] *Ibid.*, p. 231.

constitution proclaimed the ideal of local autonomy, in imitation of what was thought to be local autonomy in Japan.[12] Yüan Shih-k'ai, in 1914, announced experimental regulations for the introduction of local autonomy. And the Kuomintang, after the establishment of the Nanking government, set up an elaborate legal framework for local autonomy which was more a reflection of Western ideals than of Chinese reality.

But granting legitimacy to "local autonomy" facilitated the reappearance of the *paochia* idea in various provinces of China. Some *paochia* self-defense organizations were truly voluntary. Others were but local versions of the old state-imposed *paochia,* serving the purposes of local warlords. The voluntary self-defense organizations were often part of a pattern of village communalism, which later was called the "village cooperative movement." Those instituted by the warlords mostly served control purposes. Yen Hsi-shan, for example, warlord of Shansi, in 1917 established what amounted to a *paochia* system for Shansi. Put through as part of a system of village administration, it was based on the "village," *ts'un,* as the administrative unit. Large villages, containing up to three hundred households, were designated as "principal villages"; smaller ones known as "scattered villages," were grouped together into a single "village." Each "village" was headed by a reliable headman. The village was divided into successively smaller units which became the nuclei of the self-defense forces.[13]

Similar attempts to resurrect the *paochia* were also made in other Chinese provinces. In the years following the establishment of the Nanking government, the Kuomintang issued regulations to spur the development of local self-government. The real result, however, was not local autonomy, but the resurrection of the *paochia* system, with self-defense and policing as its central aims. In 1930, in the third campaign against the Communists in Kiangsi, the Nationalists instituted the *paochia* system in forty-three of Fukien's *hsiens.* The following year it was extended to the entire province, then to other "bandit-extermination regions": Honan, Hopei, and Anhwei. In 1933-1934, the Nanking government, perceiving the usefulness of the system, extended it to the entire country.[14]

Though the Kuomintang *paochia* served exclusively control purposes, it helped bring the hand of the state closer to the village. The

12 Wen Chün-t'ien, *op. cit.,* p. 367.

13 *Ibid.,* pp. 368 ff.

14 Matsumoto Yoshimi, "Chūgoku ni okeru chihō jiji seido kindaika no katei," *Kindai Chūgoku no shakai to keizai* (Tokyo, 1951), p. 79.

Kuomintang, unlike their dynastic predecessors, lowered the basic-level echelon of administration below the *hsien*. Under the revised administrative regulations of 1930, apparently modeled on those introduced by Yen Hsi-shan earlier into Shansi, the *hsien* were divided into "districts," for each of which a "district public office," *ch'ü kungso,* was established. Each district contained from ten to fifty "villages" (*hsiang*) and "towns" (*chen*). "Village regions" containing between a hundred and a thousand households were constituted into *hsiang*. Villages containing less than one hundred households were amalgamated into *hsiang*. Settlements of urban character with a population ranging from one hundred to one thousand households were constituted into "towns" (*chen*). Smaller settlements were simply incorporated into the surrounding *hsiang*. *Hsiang* and *chen* public offices were established.[15]

In essence, the administrative system established by the Nanking government was taken over by the Communists and remains the basic structure of rural administration in China today. The Kuomintang system made the *hsiang* or administrative village more of a reality. At least the terminological confusion of the Ch'ing period vanished. The administrative village became the basic-level echelon of state administration. Between it and the *hsien* were the districts, constituting a bridge between the two.

Though the level of state administration went down below the *hsien* to the administrative village, the Kuomintang was unable to penetrate the natural village. Though the *paochia* was intended as an instrument for village control (and for combatting Communist influence in the villages), it was never very successful. There were a number of reasons for this. It was an imposed system, not based on existing local groupings or relationships. It was linked to the administrative structure of the state, rather than to the natural village. The Kuomintang's inability to penetrate the villages and the contrasting Communist success in creating organization within the villages was a major factor in the Chinese Revolution.

CHINESE COMMUNISM AND THE VILLAGES BEFORE 1949

Village Cooperative Movements

If the *paochia* was a control-oriented organization imposed on the villages by the warlords and the Kuomintang, other forms of village

---

[15] *Ibid.,* pp. 63-64.

organization were of a different character. The most significant were the village cooperatives. Some arose voluntarily in the natural villages, and others were introduced from the outside. The revolutionary history of Chinese communism is closely linked to the peasantry; its organizational history is closely linked to the village cooperatives.

War, famine, and hardship have always prodded the Chinese peasant toward cooperation. Kinship traditionally gave him a basis for village cooperation, resulting in work organizations based on family and clan. Whereas these work organizations were permanent, other types were temporary, such as teams of neighbors for the sharing of tools and animals, pooling of labor, cooperation in planting, irrigating, and harvesting. These traditional associative tendencies within the village formed the social basis of various ambitious programs of village organization.

Throughout China, in the 1920's and 1930's, the so-called village-cooperation movement developed. The movement, as well as the term, did not come "from the bottom up" in its inception. The land problem was in the minds of both the Kuomintang and the Communists during the 1920's. The Kuomintang by 1925 had already organized 200,000 peasants in twenty-two *hsien* in Kwangtung into peasant leagues, *nung-min hsiehhui*, and in the first peasant congress held in Canton in March 1925 launched a movement to establish peasant cooperatives.[16] The later Hailufeng soviet in Kwangtung was an outgrowth of this movement, originally launched by a radical Kuomintang.

In a number of areas of China voluntary cooperative movements began to develop and reached considerable scale and size. In southwestern Honan, for example, a large cooperative movement ultimately came to encompass several *hsien*. Significantly, these cooperative movements were opposed both by the Communists and the Kuomintang, though for different reasons. The cooperatives often became tight local peasant organizations with their own self-defense forces. Radical land reform was carried out, and landlords and gentry were expelled. The more self-organization developed in these villages, the greater became the resistance to the power of the central government and to the attempts of the Communists to involve them in the revolution.

However, since the voluntary cooperatives had only limited success, they were of minor importance in the history of modern village organization in China. Of decisive importance, however, was the role of the Chinese Communists in organizing the peasantry.

Though it was the Kuomintang which originally launched the program of peasant leagues, it was the Communists, particularly after 1927,

---

16 *Chūgoku kyōsantō no nōgyō shūdanka seisaku* (Tokyo, 1961), I, 61-66.

who continued this program in force. The final break with the Kuomintang in April 1927 deprived the Chinese Communists of their urban base. Leadership of the movement passed into the hands of Mao Tsetung and Chu Teh who had created a political-military force in Hunan and Kiangsi. Mao realized that the peasantry had a revolutionary potential which could be used to achieve the aims of the Party. By using peasant revolution, Mao built up a rural Party base and created a new form of peasant leagues, namely the peasant "soviets" (that is, councils). The peasant soviets became the basis of the first organized government of the Chinese Communists, the Chinese Soviet Republic. From 1927, when the Chinese Communists began their political-military operations in Hunan and Kiangsi until 1934 when they started their Long March into Northwest China, they regarded the revolutionary peasantry as the source of their fighting capacity, and the organized peasantry as the basis for continuing power.

During this Kiangsi soviet period (1927-1934), the Chinese Communists fanned class hatreds of the peasantry which had already erupted repeatedly in rebellions of the eighteenth and nineteenth centuries. Land was confiscated, and landlords were eliminated. The disorganization of revolution was followed by new organization introduced by the Communists, namely the peasant soviets.

During the Kiangsi soviet period, the Chinese Communists carried out their first land-reform program. That program, in its early stages, consisted largely of simple confiscation of land and redistribution to the peasants; in its later stages, it took on more regularized forms expressed in land laws promulgated by the Chinese soviet government. It was in the handling of the land-reform question that the Chinese Communists gained experiences for their later more successful organizational efforts during the Yenan period.

During the early stages of land reform, land was distributed with the natural village, ts'un, as the unit. Since this was the period of revolutionary upsurge on the part of the peasantry, the natural village was the arena of struggle. However, during the later stage, the Chinese Communists changed their policy and made the hsiang, or administrative village, the unit of land distribution. They stated as their reason that the earlier policy "benefitted the rich peasants and not the poor." [17] At the same time, the Chinese Communists made the hsiang, and not the natural village, the basic-level unit of soviet government.[18]

---

[17] Ho Kan-chih, Chungkuo hsientai koming-shih (Hong Kong, 1958), p. 143.
[18] Kungfei chits'eng tsuchih chih yenchiu (Taipei, 1957), pp. 13-14.

Without going into detail, we can offer a simple explanation of this change in policy: Despite the revolutionary character of early land reform, the eventual result was renewed control over land by traditional village leaders ("rich and middle peasants"). Thus, to make sure that the poor peasants, who were a major source of support for the Communists, kept their land, administrative means imposed from the outside had to be used. The traditional political unit at the village level was the administrative village or the *hsiang*.

Such recourse to administrative means to enforce land reform indicated that the Communists were as yet unable to "penetrate deeply" into the natural village. In the early 1930's, the Chinese Communists tried a new method, namely the organization of cooperatives. In 1933, the Chinese soviet government issued an "Outline on the Organization of Labor and Mutual Aid Cooperatives," which specified that such cooperatives should be organized on the basis of the natural village, and only occasionally according to *hsiang*.[19] In 1934 the Communists started a large-scale drive to set up village cooperatives and organize spring planting. In January of that year the Chinese soviet government established the Ministry of the National Economy charged with implementing the cooperative movement. Production cooperatives, consumption cooperatives, food cooperatives, credit cooperatives were set up. The government allocated men and money to launch them. The Communists claimed that 500,000 persons had been recruited into the new cooperatives. But here again it is questionable how successful these cooperatives were, and how much of the impetus came "from below." As soviet power began to crumble, the economic crisis became more severe. Revolutionary fervor had led to considerable peasant self-organization during the early days of the soviets, but the phase beginning in 1934 seems clearly to have come "from the top down." Despite the radicalism of the Kiangsi soviet period, in many ways the revolution was imposed from above.[20] Kuomintang reconquest was aided by discontent created by the excesses of the Chinese soviet administration. Only in the Yenan period did the Chinese Communists begin to learn

---

19 *Chūgoku nōgyō shūdanka seisaku*, I, 79-80.

20 Village councils were organized in the soviet areas, but were not regarded as part of the formal apparatus of government. Article 13 of the 1931 Provisional Rules on the Organization of Local Soviets stated: "Plenary sessions of the *hsiang* soviets need not take place in a fixed location, but may move from village to village, preferably in villages where there are problems to be discussed" (cited from *Ch'ihfei fantung wenchien huipien* [n.p., n.d.] III, 705, reprinted from the Chen Cheng collection in Taiwan of captured Chinese Communist documents of the Kiangsi soviet period).

how to create organization from within a village rather than imposing it from the outside.

Cooperatives during the Yenan Period (1935-1946)

During the Yenan period the Communists began to learn the organizational techniques they have since applied throughout Chinese society. The Long March marked the end of a phase which caused the leadership sober reflection. Defeat was not simply the result of Kuomintang "bandit suppression" campaigns. The Chinese Soviet Republic never succeeded in becoming an operating entity. Radical land reform had torn up traditional social relationships in the villages, but had not substituted an effective new organization.

The United Front of the Yenan period temporarily halted the expansion of the revolution. Instead of moving "outward," the Communists began to penetrate inward and downward. The central task of the period was the organization of "revolutionary base areas." The revolutionary base areas could not function without village support. But, though the peasants might spontaneously support the Communists, organization was needed to give that support continuity. The Communists realized that such organization would have to be built up within the natural village, yet with assurance that it would be primarily loyal to the larger cause rather than to the narrower village interests. By creating a new Communist party and by training a new type of leader, the cadre, the Chinese Communists were finally able to achieve what no state power in Chinese history had been able to do: to create an organization loyal to the state which was also solidly imbedded in the natural village.[21]

The problems the Chinese Communists faced in the villages were

---

[21] Although the Yenan Period is crucial in the development of Chinese Communist theory and practice of organization, it has as yet been little studied. Chalmers Johnson has studied the period from the viewpoint of peasant mobilization against the Japanese (*Peasant Nationalism and Communist Power* [Stanford, 1962]), but without an analysis of sociopolitical conditions within the villages, one cannot grasp the full dynamic force which underlay the success of the Communists in social mobilization. Material on Yenan is available in various libraries outside of Mainland China. Even with officially published material, serious study can be launched. In 1957, the Chinese Communists published a collection of Yenan materials, largely newspaper articles, relating to the cooperative movement, under the title *Chungkuo nungyeh hotsohua yüntung shihliao (Materials on the Agricultural Cooperativization Movement in China)*. Analysis of these documents could shed considerable light on Chinese Communist organizational approaches in the villages. The Japanese publication *Chūgoku kyōsantō no nōgyō shudanka seisaku* has made extensive use of this and other Yenan materials.

much the same as in South-central China earlier, perhaps even more acute. The Shensi borderlands are among the poorest in China. Villages are small and the villagers often live close to starvation. There are few urban centers, and the population is even more illiterate than in other areas of the country. But if the problems were the same, the situation had changed. Communist military and political strength had been seriously depleted by the Long March. The United Front with the Kuomintang made the Communists agree to the formal abandonment of the soviet system. Radical land reform was halted, and the landlord class was to be reformed and not liquidated.[22] No longer could the Communists hope to impose organization on the countryside through armies alone. Their forces were scattered and, even where concentrated, concerned with other than village problems. During the first years after their arrival in the borderlands, the Communists seem to have paid little attention to the land problem. The main task was the rebuilding of the army, the creation of an efficient political party, and the consolidation and extension of their revolutionary base areas. By 1938 both Party and army had grown considerably in strength. In that year, Party membership, which had sunk to 40,000 for the entire country in 1937, was up to 70,000 in the border regions alone by 1938,[23] and to 800,000 by 1941.[24] The military strength of the Eighth Route Army had risen to 320,000 by 1940,[25] and to 440,000 by the end of 1941.[26]

But while the Communists managed to rebuild their forces, new and grave problems arose. The food situation in the border areas, always bad, was getting worse. The liberalized land policy put through in accordance with the United Front policy slowed down the program of mass organization. Dissidence became evident within the Party, as it had been earlier through the defection of Wang Ming and Chang Kuo-t'ao. And the Communists increasingly felt that pressure of the powerful Japanese and Kuomintang armies.[27]

In the hot summer months of 1941, the Chinese Communist leader-

---

[22] Even before the United Front accord, the Chinese Communists had already announced in their December 1935 theses that they were abandoning the radical land policy of the Kiangsi soviet period.

[23] Kusano Fumio, *Shina henku no kenkū* (Tokyo, 1944), p. 15.

[24] See chap. ii; also, *Chūgoku kyōsantō no nōgyō shudanka seisaku*, I, 322.

[25] Kusano, *op. cit.*, p. 177.

[26] *Chūkyō seiji keizai sōran* (Tokyo, 1962), p. 20. There is some disagreement as to the size of the Communist armed forces (see Johnson, *op. cit.*, pp. 212-213). Nevertheless, there is no doubt that there was "a very rapid increase in Communist troop strength" (*ibid.*, pp. 76-77).

[27] Kusano, *op. cit.*, p. 22.

ship launched its first "rectification" movement, designed to weed out dissident elements and harden the organizational solidarity of Party and army. Armed resistance against both the Japanese and the Kuomintang grew. But there were two pressing internal problems: the food shortage and the low state of mass organization. To resolve these problems the Yenan leaders decided during the latter part of 1942 to launch a campaign for rural cooperativization.

The cooperativization campaign started a movement that ultimately was to culminate in the great land reform of the late 1940's and early 1950's. For a proper understanding of the genesis of Chinese Communist land policy, a study of these Yenan experiments in village organization is essential. Despite the great historical importance of these experiments, no one has yet made an adequate study. Therefore, it would be unwarranted to make any definitive generalizations. However, a fair amount of documentary material is available in printed form. In the absence of such studies, we have decided to present some of this material in straight translation and follow up with some tentative remarks on the subject. The editorial presented below may be considered a classic statement on the cooperativization movement during the Yenan period. Its directness and simplicity indicates that the Chinese Communists had a keen understanding of the village problems they confronted in their efforts to organize the peasantry.

The mentioned editorial appeared on January 25, 1943, in the *Chiehfang jihpao* under the title "Let's Organize the Labor Force." In 1957 it was included in a compilation entitled *Materials on the Agricultural Cooperativization Movement in China*[28] where it was preceded by comments which we also quote below. The following two long quotations, then, are (1) introductory comments on the editorial as printed in the compilation and (2) the editorial itself:

The introductory remarks said:

"In 1941 and 1942, because of the increasingly intensive attacks of the Japanese aggressors and the Kuomintang encirclement and blockade, supplies to the Eighth Route Army and the New Fourth Army were cut off, and the liberated areas encountered extreme financial and economic difficulties. In December 1942, the Northwest Branch of the Central Committee of the Chinese Communist party called a conference of high-level cadres. In this meeting, Chairman Mao reported on 'Economic Problems and Financial Problems' and on 'A Discussion of Cooperatives'; he criticized erroneous views among the cadres which neglected the development of the economy, and the opening up of new

---

[28] *Chungkuo nungyeh hotsohua yüntung shihliao* (see n. 21).

sources of money. He proposed a policy of 'developing the economy, and assuring supplies.' At the same time, he stressed that one of the most important ways of developing the economy was the use of the mutual-aid and cooperative movement to develop agricultural production and others sectors of the economy.

"[The following] editorial in the *Chiehfang jihpao* entitled 'Let's Organize the Labor Force,' was written after the conference of high-level cadres and was based on the policy suggested by the Party Central Committee. This is an appeal to organize, made by the Party Central Committee at this time to the masses through a newspaper.

"In the spring of 1943, a production movement in the Shensi-Kansu-Ninghsia border regions burst forth under the direction of this policy. On October 1, 1943, the Party Central Committee issued a directive to all Party organizations in the liberated regions entitled 'Starting a Movement to Reduce Rents, Produce, Support the Government, and Love the People.' The directive made decisively clear the importance of organizing labor mutual aid to develop agricultural production; it demanded that Party members must carry through this policy and learn all methods relating to organizing the labor force.

"On November 26, 1943, the first labor-heroes congress was held in the Shensi-Kansu-Ninghsia border areas, in which the experiences of the previous year of the border-areas production movement were summarized and exchanged, and the policies and methods for further developing production in 1944 were fixed. Chairman Mao in this meeting gave his famous report entitled 'Let's Organize,' and indicated that organizing the popular forces was the policy for developing production. This meeting was the first in our country's history of a large-scale labor-heroes congress. The more than two hundred labor heroes and model workers who came to the congress from all areas of the border regions played an important part in raising the production enthusiasm of the masses and extending the experiences of mutual aid and cooperation."

The editorial itself said:

"Production is the central task at present in the border regions, and agricultural production is even more the center of production work as a whole. To fulfill this task, one must first of all rely on the more than 300,000-man full-time labor force and the more than 300,000-man part-time labor force of the villages in the border regions. One has only to organize these 600-700,000 people to make of them a powerful army of production, and to develop unparalleled heroic forces in them.

"But, to organize this several-hundred-thousand man labor force in the villages of the border region even better, one must make use of a number of efficient methods, among which is to carry out labor mutual aid. In the villages of the border regions, there have traditionally existed all ways for pulling together a labor force, such as the *pienkung* [a kind of labor cooperation] and *chakung* [collective hiring out of labor], which are methods rather widely used. These voluntary *pienkung* and *chakung*, though rather narrow in scope, and only restricted to relatives, friends, neighbors, are nevertheless suited to the concrete conditions of villages in the border regions. If they can be effectively utilized and directed, and organized and led in a planned way, then they can be transformed into organizations for developing productivity and raising production. To prove this point: the valuable experiences in Yenan *hsien* are worth describing. Last year in Yenan *hsien*, in all, there were organized 478 *chakung*; in addition, 4,939 workers participated in collective labor, accounting for about one-third of the total labor force, or one man in three participated in collective labor. In the opening up of new land, collective labor clearly proved to be very important. Last year in Yenan *hsien*, we had to clear 80,000 *mou* of land within 100 days, *i.e.*, 800 *mou* each day. From March 10 to April 19, we only cleared 15,000 *mou*, or 18.7 percent of the total, there remaining 65,000 to do. But already two-thirds of the time had passed. Therefore after the rain on the nineteenth we decided to attack the problem within twenty days, and in twenty days were able to do 46,442 *mou* or 58 percent of our task. If Yenan *hsien* had not promptly organized its labor force, there would have been no way to make use of the favorable time after the rain to carry through the attack, and there would have been no way to finish the 80,000 *mou* of the land-clearing plan.

"We know that it is vital in planting 'not to violate the seasons.' Whether you plant early or late can make a big difference, and harvesting late or early can also result in different yields. In order not 'to violate the seasons,' if you simply rely on individual and scattered labor, your difficulties will be compounded. But if you make use of mutual aid in labor, the situation is very different. Take the men and animals of three to five households or seven to eight families and organize them; today everyone helps you plow, tomorrow everyone helps me plow—if that plot has too many weeds, then help that family hoe first; if that family's crops ripen first, then help them to harvest first. In the *pienkung*, not only do laborers rotate with each other, but three laborers can be exchanged for the work of one oxen. Those who have labor give labor; those who have animals give animals. Those who have much give much; those who have little give little; human and animal power are put together. Thus, one can avoid violating the seasons, and is able to plow in time, sow in time, hoe in time, and harvest in time.

"Experience proves: the mutual-aid collective form of production organization saves labor power; collective labor is better than individual labor. Thus: one laborer can plow and sow fifteen *shang* of land each year. But if three laborers work together, each year they can plow and sow seventy *shang* of land, and four laborers can plow and sow one hundred *shang*. Two men and one ox can complete the task in three days; three men and one ox can complete it in two days. Not only this, a mutual-aid and collective form of production organization can greatly stimulate work enthusiasm and increase production efficiency. Because everyone works together, life is active, morale is high, and there is mutual stimulation, mutual competition, and no one wants to be behind the others. The driving pace of work is just as the masses say: 'Work for Work, Everyone Exerts Himself to the Bone.' In the end, mutual-aid collective labor organization is a true organization of the masses, but also suits our Party and the work comrades of our mass groups; it educates the masses, and increases the spirit of mutual aid and solidarity among the masses.

"Precisely because this kind of mutual-aid collective labor organization makes it possible not to violate the seasons, to put together and save man and animal power, to raise production enthusiasm, to increase labor efficiency, to develop the spirit of solidarity and mutual aid among the masses, therefore it will be sufficiently supported by the masses. Labor mutual-aid organization current among the masses is mostly of the *pienkung* and *chakung* variety, but is not restricted to these two kinds. There are some labor heroes who do not practice *chakung*, and rarely *pienkung*. They normally aid refugees in their villages, and during the busy farm season these refugees voluntarily work for them. Thus practices such as the *huoniu* [joint use of draft animals] or *huochungti* [joint tilling] all have a mutual-aid character. These forms of labor mutual-aid organization current among the masses are in content very active, concrete, and suited to real conditions. All must be promptly encouraged and broadened. We must study the example of Yenan *hsien* and get rid of negative phenomena of laissez-faire in regard to these important problems of organizing labor power, and we must take an attitude of positive leadership and encouragement. Not only must we encourage the organization of *chakung*, but we must even more universally organize *pienkung*; from the old rather narrow and small-scale organizations we must transform them into new organized *pienkung* brigades. We must, first of all, in this year's spring planting season, greatly expand this kind of labor mutual-aid organization, organize all who have labor power: healthy people, old and weak people, children, and women, in order to carry out labor mutual aid.

"But here we must take heed: labor mutual-aid organization must be grounded on a basis of voluntarism of the masses, in order to prevent formalisms, in whatever way they may arise, such as forcibly issuing orders or 'compiling name lists.' If we take people who have no clear understanding of mutual aid and forcibly organize them into *pienkung* or *chakung* brigades, make up name lists thinking that thus 'all will turn out well,' then not only will production efficiency and work morale not rise, but on the contrary will be lowered.

"Moreover, in organizing labor mutual aid we must remember that it is something active and concrete; we must absolutely give heed to concrete conditions in the areas concerned, and not regard them as uniform. Thus if we today strive to expand one kind of mutual-aid labor organization among the people, the *pienkung* brigades organized must not be too large. Neither the *hsiang* nor the administrative village must be taken as production units. Because if organization is too large, it can waste a great deal of labor power and a lot of time. It is best to take the natural village as a unit. Where there are villages which have more population and need more mutual aid, don't just organize one, but organize several [brigades]; and don't restrict them just to one village, but have them transcend the scope of the natural village, put through mutual aid between villages.

"In regard to leadership of mutual aid in labor, one must proceed through the masses and select and promote as leaders individuals who are respected by the masses, positive in production, and capable. Our village Party members and cadres must first of all play a direct part in implementing this, or they can take the Party small group as the core cadre, and organize *chakung* brigades to function as models. One can make use of this opportunity to educate the masses and solidarize them. Our village cadres, our work comrades in *hsiang* government and in mass organizations, must look upon the organization of the masses' production as their own work, as the most important task in their own work. Some comrades seem to think that 'the masses know how to do these things themselves, it's not for us to worry about them!' Such erroneous ideas must be forthwith corrected.

"Today, the 49th [day of?] is going to end, and people always say: 'When spring comes at the beginning of the 69th, then we shall start plowing.' Let us now organize a great production army, take hold of spring plowing, not miss the farming season, and complete the great tasks of agricultural production." [29]

This editorial launched the cooperativization movement of the Yenan period. The editorial hints at the lessons the Communists learned

---

[29] *Ibid.*, pp. 145-149.

from the failures of the Kiangsi period: Organization cannot simply be imposed onto the population from above; it must be woven into the existing fabric, and the power of the Party must be used gradually to transform that organization into something larger; the natural village and not the administrative village must be made the unit of cooperation; although the cadres must try to extend labor cooperation beyond the village, it is to be done carefully. In the winter of 1943, the Communists in Shensi faced production and supply problems comparable to those of the last year of their Kiangsi period. But instead of starting an ambitious program of cooperatives which could only have been implemented from above and through pressure, the Yenan cooperative movement was to start more modestly, building on existing village organization.

The task of setting up cooperatives on the basis of existing village social organization was not simple. Traditional forms of labor cooperation were so bound up with complex social relationships, such as kinship and friendship, that it was difficult for outsiders (Party cadres) to penetrate them. Moreover, rich and middle peasants usually had the greatest power and influence over labor cooperation.

These problems are discussed in detail in a report on the cooperative movement issued by the Northwest Bureau of the Central Committee. The report pointed out that traditional work cooperation was spontaneous and without leadership, thus short-termed and not continuous. Cooperation was always threatened by quarrels among members. Even larger forms of work cooperation were usually restricted to relatives, friends, and in general to a single kinship group. Given the egalitarian tendencies in this type of organization, there was no real leadership. Work discipline was not always rigorously observed. The chiefs of these traditional work organizations were usually rich or middle peasants. Furthermore, it was usually the richer peasants who were able to hire the labor of these cooperative work groups. Work cooperation was traditionally restricted largely to hoeing and weeding, and rarely used for opening up new land or for fall harvesting. Work bosses sometimes were able to get an unfair share of the money paid the team. "Senseless and superstitious habits" prevailed. In short, traditional forms of work organization reflected all the complexities of Chinese village organization.

But, said the report, perhaps the most significant element in traditional work cooperation were the strong kinship ties that determined it. "In the past, work mutual aid basically had rather good qualities in that relatively well off individuals helped poor families, and those with greater labor power helped those with less; however, this was usually restricted to relatives and friends within the same kinship group." [30] Work cooperation not based on kinship was contractual, short-termed, and inequitable, the report indicated. Permanent forms of work cooperation were usually based on kinship. This not only meant that such forms of work cooperation tended to remain small in scale and restricted to a natural village or part of it, but were not easily capable of being directed by the Party. As the report pointed out, it was important for village Party cadres to take the leadership in these movements: "Party members in villages of all areas actively take part in labor mutual aid. Some of them have become the direct leaders of labor mutual aid. Through their function as models, they have solidarized the masses, and have achieved successes in last year's harvest."[31] Only if the Party cadres could penetrate deeply into the villages and become the accepted leaders of the movement could it succeed. Administrative methods alone were not enough:

> Many village cadres still do not understand these precise work methods. On the contrary, attitudes of commandism, formalism, subjectivism are still very prevalent. They take the form of: not carrying out any propaganda toward the masses and not discussing with the masses, sitting in the *hsiang* government and compiling name registers. What they understand by propaganda is simply preaching empty homilies such as "Work cooperation is good," and once having said it they think all will turn out well.[32]

Yet, despite the stress on using existing village organization, it was clear that organization had to proceed both from the top down and from the bottom up. An article published in 1944 stated the problem:

> One must use the methods of appeals and mobilization through administrative power from the top down. But one must create a degree of volition and freedom on the part of the masses. If one only uses administrative power, power which is organized from the top down, then one cannot consolidate the system. But only to emphasize volition and freedom, and not to make use of appeals and mobilization through strong administration, to organize positively, means that work will degenerate into laissez-faire.[33]

The Communists would face this dilemma again and again. Making use of traditional forms of labor cooperation seemed a wise move. Yet the old kinship-oriented work groups were particularistic in the extreme. Once Party cadres infiltrated these groups, the latter lost their

---

[30] *Ibid.*, p. 221.
[31] *Ibid.*, p. 248.
[32] *Ibid.*, p. 264.
[33] *Ibid.*, p. 396.

particularism and much of the strength which gave them cohesion. Every intrusion of a Party member into the group represented another interference from the top down. Yet the process could not be pushed too far and too fast. A delicate balance had to be maintained between imposed and self-generated organization. It is clear how the problems of the Yenan period fostered the theory of contradictions in Chinese Communist organizational thinking.

Village Organization and the Relationship to War and Production

If the cooperative movement started modestly with the aim of increasing agricultural production, in time it became an integral part of the revolutionary struggle. The mutual-aid teams often became identical with units of the people's militia, that is, the local guerrillas of the revolutionary base areas. The peasant became a soldier and vice-versa or, as it was expressed in the slogan of the time: Unity of Work and Arms.[34] As the Communists acquired a growing organizational hold on the villages, more peasants were recruited into the regular and guerrilla armies. While militarization had proceeded during the entire Yenan period, it became more pronounced after the resumption of the civil war in 1946. Work and battle teams composed of young peasants were organized in the villages. When danger threatened, the teams marched forth to engage in battle. Work and battle committees were set up in the villages which drew all mutual aid team leaders together.

One of the most interesting things about these new forms of village organization was that everything relating to production and struggle was regarded as work. War, like work, was integrated into the pattern of daily life. Time spent in battle was reckoned as the equivalent of so many days of work in the village. Soldiers were issued "work tickets" which were later redeemed in money when the final reckoning was made. The whole population was mobilized, freeing men for military service. Women were made to do work normally done by men. When no fighting was necessary, the fighters returned to the fields to do their own work or help other peasants.[35]

The linkage between war and production based on the natural village was one of the great organizational achievements of the Chinese Communists. Through guerrilla units which worked one day and fought the next, the Chinese Communists built up their military strength. Once described, the linkage between war and production

---

[34] *Ibid.*, p. 800.
[35] *Ibid.*, pp. 904-905.

sounds simple, yet it took the Chinese Communists years of experience and defeat to achieve it. Let us therefore briefly review the organizational history of the Chinese Communists which led to these major accomplishments of the Yenan period.

By the time of the Yenan period the Communists had learned more about the theory and practice of organization than they knew during the 1920's. Despite considerable Communist success then among urban workers, the intellectual leaders of the movement hardly had a thorough grasp of the problems of mass organization. As a means of securing power, the tactics of infiltrating the Kuomintang were much more understandable to the minds of the Communist leaders of that time.

The Kiangsi period marked the beginning of large-scale Communist organization in China.[36] But again it is questionable whether the Communists ever succeeded in creating effective mass organization in the soviet areas. Peasant uprisings with all their disruptive consequences did not create fertile ground for mass organization.

It was only during the Yenan period, when the Communists realized that mass organization must be built from the bottom up, that they proceeded to create a powerful network of mass organization, grounded on the villages. To strike roots in the villages, the village had to be penetrated. It was not enough to form guerrilla units which drew strength from the villages, as the *paochia* or traditional bandit groups had done. Organization had to be created within the village itself, indissolubly linked to the village. The Communists realized that organization, to be effective, had to be linked with work. Village social organization usually involved work. Work had been the peasant's major problem for centuries, and in the course of time various forms of cooperation had arisen. In the early 1940's, the Communists began to see in these forms of cooperation the bases for the creation of their own organization in the villages.

But this was just the first step. Now the old form of organization had to be transformed from within in order to serve the new purposes of the Communist movement. This could only be done by recruiting the leaders of these village organizations into the movement. Thus

---

[36] The years 1925-1927 saw a great increase in Party enrollment, and the Communists seemed about to become a major political force on the Chinese scene. Yet it was not organized Communist strength that threatened the Kuomintang, and more specifically Chiang Kai-shek's faction, but Communist influence, acquired through infiltration, in the so-called "left wing" of the Kuomintang. The ease with which Chiang was able to destroy the urban bases of Communist power indicates that that power was not solidly grounded. The Communist threat, in an organizational sense, came when units of the Kuomintang army defected to lay the basis for the Red Army.

young peasants, native to the village and leaders in work cooperation teams, were made into "positivists," and finally taken into the Party or other mass organizations. In this way the new cadres were simultaneously village team leaders and committed members of the Party.

The last step was the link between organization, work, and war. War provides excellent opportunities for organization—a lesson which the Kuomintang never learned. Thus, as the Yenan period progressed, villages were turned into military bastions, and, accordingly, the various social forms of cooperation were linked with military forms of organization.

This "penetration of the natural village" was, in essence, the great achievement of the Yenan period. The work and battle teams had arisen on a traditional foundation of work cooperation, but, through their Party cadre leaders, had been transformed into a new type of organization that served the political-military and socioeconomic aims of the Chinese Communist party. The team was indissolubly a part of the village, yet at the same time transcended it.

Traditional forms of village military organization, such as the *paochia*, had never been integrated into village social organization. Therefore, they lacked the socioeconomic foundation which the Chinese Communist work and battle teams acquired. The military *paochia* and the civilian village traditionally remained dichotomous. The Chinese Communists discovered a new weapon for making the link: the Party. Traditional China's political weapons were restricted to army and bureaucracy, which served its major purposes of control and exploitation. But though the army could rule the village by force and the bureaucracy could exploit it by various administrative means, neither could penetrate it. The Chinese Communist party is an organizational phenomenon which never existed in traditional China. It is an organization that grew both from the top down and from the bottom up. The penetration of the natural village which we have described was the most important stage in the organizational history of the Party.

Conflict in the Village

The link between organization, work, and war, however, led to certain phenomena which help account for the radicalization during the civil-war period (1946-1949). That radicalization took the form of an increasingly violent land reform which contrasted so markedly with the more cautious emphasis on cooperatives during the Yenan period.

Radicalization after 1946 has to be understood in connection with the key role given to the young peasant cadre in the penetration of the natural village. The cadres who, during the Yenan period, led the work and battle teams were often the same types of individuals who for centuries had been recruited into the *paochia* and similar local self-defense forces. In this connection, one might cite the words of the eighteenth-century writer Huang Liu-hung on the difference between civil and military leaders in the village. Contrasting the *lichia* and *paochia* chiefs (the former organization was essentially civil and the latter was essentially military, it will be recalled), Huang noted:

Village headmen (*li*) are chosen from among those who are older and virtuous, direct in behavior and able to persuade others; *pao* chiefs are chosen from among those who are strong and healthy, and who can lead people. Since their functions are different, different people have to be appointed, and one man cannot do both.[37]

In other words, village leaders whose tasks were essentially civil were drawn from the "elders," whereas the self-defense chiefs were recruited from stronger, younger men.

The traditional village cooperation teams, as the Communists admitted in the accounts cited in the previous section (pp. 423 f.), were often dominated by older men with power and influence in the village. These were people whom the Communists would not or could not recruit into the Party. On the other hand, the Party did recruit strong, young peasants into the Party, but these were invariably individuals with little power and influence in the village. Huang Liu-hung implies a conflict between old and young village leaders which then was resolved by a division of labor: the old became the civil leaders of the village, and the young became its military leaders (through the *paochia*). Since Chinese villages had changed little since the eighteenth century, one can presume that these same conflicts existed during the 1940's.

The increasing recruitment of young peasants into the Party had two consequences: (1) it created growing conflicts between the older village leaders and the young peasant cadres, and (2) it contributed to the growing militarization of the village. Conflicts could no longer be resolved, as they had been traditionally by a division of labor, because the young cadres had acquired civil leadership positions through their command over the work teams. Since these work teams had heretofore been dominated by the older village leaders, competition and conflict arose with the young cadres. Militarization basically was caused by the intensifying civil war. However, the described processes indicate that there was a social basis to militarization as well. Since traditionally the

---

[37] Shimizu, *op. cit.*, p. 226.

young peasant cadres were primarily oriented to military activities, their coming to power in the villages enhanced the growing importance of the military element.

These facts should help explain the significant differences between the Yenan and the civil-war periods. During the Yenan period, the Communists abstained from radical land reform and stressed the formation of village cooperatives. But such an approach to the land policy meant that the traditional village leaders remained, and inevitably came to dominate the cooperatives. This had happened once before during the Kiangsi soviet period, and was to happen again in the period following 1949. Young cadres may have led the work and battle teams, but as long as the old leaders remained in power, the latter were able to exercise power and influence over the former. The traditional preference of the old village leaders was for conservatism, preoccupation with civil tasks, and hostility to external political-military involvements.

When the civil war resumed in 1946, the Chinese Communists required the total mobilization of the areas under their control, which necessitated the militarization of the villages. However, this could not be accomplished without a fundamental transformation of the authority relationships in the village. The young peasant Party cadres had to seize leadership from the old village chiefs. Unless the former acquired such leadership, the Chinese Communists could not hope to drive their organization deep into the fabric of the village, nor could the village be effectively militarized. Thus, to accomplish this, they encouraged the young cadres in their struggle with the old chiefs. Not merely ideology, but conflicts inherent in the village were important factors which led to the land reform and the revolutionary terror of the late 1940's.

Our discussion so far implies a conflict of generations between old and young. Beyond that, and more important, was the conflict between rich and poor. Ever since the Kiangsi soviet period, the Chinese Communists have regarded the distinction between rich and poor peasants as significant far beyond its manifest economic meaning. Rich peasants generally were in command of the villages, which gave them a major political role. But these same rich peasants, though often as illiterate as their poorer brethren, were also linked to the traditional rural elite, the gentry. Though they functioned as middlemen between bureaucracy and village, or between landlord and tenants, their interests coincided generally with the ruling class. Thus, what on the surface was a struggle between traditional and emerging village leaders, or between old and young, was more profoundly a part of rural class warfare. The land reform and the revolutionary terror that accompanied it did have immediate causes in these intravillage conflicts. However, the historical linkage between the rich peasant village leaders and the higher rural elite (landlords, officials, local teachers) gave the intravillage struggle a meaning that linked it to the revolutionary process which we described in the Prologue. That process finally led to the great act of class destruction which was called the land reform.

Though the Chinese Communists, ever since the time of the Kiangsi soviets, have consistently relied on the poor peasants for support, their attitudes toward both rich and poor peasants show variant patterns which have continued right down to the present. Those patterns are symbolized by the mentioned contrasts between the Yenan and the civil-war periods.

When the Chinese Communists were primarily interested in creating stable production conditions in the villages, as during the middle part of the Kiangsi period, in the early 1940's, after 1949, after the "high tide" of cooperativization in 1956, and after the agricultural disasters of the Great Leap Forward in 1961, they have tended to take more permissive attitudes toward the rich peasants. The Chinese Communists have had various ways of disguising their support of the rich peasant, such as referring to them as "prosperous middle peasants" (common in the mid-1950's). In fact, the very concept "middle peasant" is a vague conception which appears to designate a poor peasant "on his way up." A poor peasant, allowed to improve his own standard of living, would invariably start moving on the road from his status, through that of middle peasant, and hopefully to that of rich peasant. Nevertheless, since not all can be rich peasants, an explicit or implicit policy of permissiveness toward them implies a deemphasis of support for the poor peasant.

On the other hand, when the Chinese Communists were primarily interested in social movements aimed at production, battle, or socioeconomic transformation, they have appealed openly for the support of the poor peasants. This is evident during the land-reform period, during the cooperativization movement of late 1955, and during the Great Leap Forward. Land reform in the late 1940's was preceded by a sharp change in policy toward landlords and rich peasants. Along with the poor peasant, the "lower middle peasant" is usually also appealed to. In other words, it is the less advanced status of the middle peasant that is now regarded as crucial, rather than his more advanced status (as expressed in the other qualification: "prosperous middle peasant").

Our discussion suggests that internal conflict within the village was and still is a major sociological factor in Chinese rural life. Though the destruction of the gentry removed the class element from that conflict, the contending parties, rich and poor peasants, remain in competition and conflict within the village. That conflict can be regarded as an in-built contradiction within the framework of organization in Communist China today. As in so many similar contradictions, it gives the leaders in Peking leverage for moving in either conservative or radical directions. If general policy is to be conservative, a permissive policy toward the rich peasants will be adopted; if policy is to be radical, a hostile policy is adopted, paired with all-out support for the poor peasants, who form the major recruits of the rural Party organizations.

But the continued existence of such conflict does not detract from the achievement of the Chinese Communists in penetrating the natural village. By penetrating the village through the Party, the traditional Chinese village has been torn out of its centuries-old self-isolation and brought into the nation. The Party, as the link between "the leadership and the masses," has become the integrating element of the new society. It was during the Yenan period that this was first achieved, and the first stage in this process was the establishment of Party-led cooperatives within the natural village.

Land Reform and the Revolutionary Terror

The civil war which began again in July 1946 and which was to lead to complete Communist victory was mainly a struggle between rival armies. When the Kuomintang rushed to occupy the cities, the Communists withdrew into the countryside. This strategy proved effective: when the Communist counteroffensive began, the Kuomintang lost city after city, until they were driven from the mainland of China. But, at least for the Communist side, the struggle was not merely a contest of armies. As the great battles raged, the Communists intensified their revolution on the land. Social revolution and military action went together. Was the great land reform which emerged at that time the product of a peasant revolution, on whose tide the Communists swept to victory? Or was land reform manipulated by the leadership? No simple answer can be given to this question.

The Chinese Communist leaders saw land reform as an integral part of the larger struggle. They used land reform to break up traditional social organization in the villages and to lay the groundwork for new types of organization. More importantly, by giving land to the peasant, they gained his support, thus permitting wholesale recruitment of the peasants into the Communist armies.

However, at the same time, land reform had a momentum of its own. The repeated references by the leaders to "left excesses" indicate that they did not have full control over the actions of village cadres. Land reform is remembered by many persons who left China in the late 1940's and the early 1950's as a period of terror. As the military struggle became more intense, so did the radicalism of land reform. What had begun as a program of land redistribution ended as revolutionary terror in which China's traditional rural elite was destroyed.

Though, as we have said, no simple answer can be given the question whether land reform came from the top down or from the bottom up, there can be little doubt that the revolutionary terror which ensued from it had deep roots in the past, as we indicated in our Prologue, and had deep roots in the village, as we indicated in the preceding section.

On May 4, 1946, when the Communists and the Kuomintang were negotiating, the Central Committee issued a directive on land reform. Its full contents are not known. But it is clear that May 1946 marks the resumption of a radical land policy. Now it was no longer simply a question of organizing mutual-aid teams in the villages. Land was to be redistributed, and with that a decisive attack launched on traditional village social structure.[38] In September 1946, a national agricultural conference was held which passed a draft outline of a national land law.[39] In October 1947, a national peasants congress was held which formally approved the national land law.[40] This law became the basis for the land reform which was to be formally proclaimed after the establishment of the People's Republic. It decreed the confiscation of all landlord and state-owned land, the confiscation and distribution of all property above the general average. However, it allowed the free buying and selling of land distributed. The final land law implemented in 1947 manifested a further trend toward radicalism. As the official Communist historian, Ho Kan-chih has observed, "the [1947] land law, while affirming the policy directives of May 4, 1946, also made some clear changes in regard to some inconclusive elements in these directives, such as the fact that landlords received relatively more land and property than the ordinary peasants, and that the principle of rich peasants owning land should not be affected." [41]

However, the Communists were in a dilemma, for while pushing land reform in the direction of radicalism, they were also fearful of the excesses resulting therefrom. Ho Kan-chih notes that the national land law "avoided extreme leftist policies such as that 'landlords be given no land at all' and 'that rich peasants only be given poor land.' " These

---

[38] Fukushima Masao, *Jimmin kōsha no kenkyū* (Tokyo, 1960), p. 210.

[39] *Chūgoku kyōsantō no nōgyō shudanka seisaku*, p. 34.

[40] Fukushima, *op. cit.*, pp. 210-211.

[41] Ho Kan-chih, *op. cit.*, pp 319-320.

tendencies led to "the violation of the interests of some middle peasants, the destruction of industrial and commercial businesses belonging to landlords and rich peasants, and the indiscriminate beating and killing of individuals in some areas." [42] But the leftist deviations continued, as was admitted by the leadership in later years.[43] That the leaders were not fully in control of the rural cadres is revealed by the fact that in the heat of the civil war and of the land reform, they launched a rectification campaign within the Party.[44] In Party cadre meetings held early in 1948, Mao Tse-tung, Liu Shao-ch'i, and other leaders warned against leftist excesses in the implementation of land reform.

The year 1948 was decisive of war; final victory, marked by capture of the great cities, came later in the same year. All military forces of the Communists were concentrated for the great attack. But as Communist armies were being concentrated, Party cadres and their operations squads, *kungtso-tui*, were bringing land reform and revolutionary terror to the villages. The methods of these operations squads were well described in the novel *Paofeng Tsouyü* (*Hurricane*) by the Chinese Communist novelist Chou Li-po. Thus while the military battles were raging, a great struggle for power was being waged in the "liberated villages" between the traditional leaders and the Party cadres. Radicalism indeed had a mass character. The extremes of left deviation came, not from the top leadership, but from below—from the village cadres.

Ho Kan-chih, writing in the mid-1950's, admits that the top leadership was not in full control of the entire Party organization at that time. Referring to 1948, he stated that one of the major tasks was "the total unification of the Party in regard to political, military, and economic policy." Before 1948, he said, guerrilla warfare required regional "independence and autonomy." However, this had resulted in "erroneous dispersionism, lack of discipline, and anarchy in work." In many parts of the country, cadres were guilty of "free actions in political affairs, a dislike of Party leadership and supervision, a disrespect of the decisions made by the Central Committee and higher echelons," and so on. He further admitted that situations had arisen which "could not

---

[42] *Ibid.*, p. 321.

[43] Robert Carin, *Agrarian Reform Movement in Communist China* (Hong Kong, 1960), I, 23-25.

[44] Ho Kan-chih, *op. cit.*, p. 321. Rectification was apparently launched in February 1948. In April Mao Tse-tung addressed a conference of cadres in the Shansi and Suiyuan liberated areas, discussing the problem of extremism in land reform (*Chūgoku kyōsantō no nōgyō shudanka seisaku*, pp. 350, 352).

be remedied, were difficult to remedy, or if remediable had already caused great damage." [45] In January 1948, the Central Committee issued an important directive calling, in effect, for a centralization of the Party apparatus. Thus, it is interesting to see how, on the eve of final victory, the Chinese Communist leaders were acutely concerned with the organizational consequences for the Party arising out of the revolutionary terror in the country.

In March 1949, the Central Committee held its second plenary meeting since the Seventh Party Congress and announced the definitive move from the countryside to the city. The major concern of the leadership now was the restoration of order, and in particular the creation of an administrative system. It was essential that the land reform be halted, for the longer the revolutionary terror continued, the greater the threat to organization.

Late in 1949, a new land law was formulated. In June 1950, the leadership announced what amounted to an absolute ban on the revolutionary terror. Land reform was to continue, slowly and subject to central control. But the disruption of the villages in the name of class war was to cease. Liu Shao-ch'i, in a speech delivered at the Committee of the Chinese People's Political Consultative Conference on June 14, 1950, outlined the new policy.[46] Land reform was, in effect, to be halted in all areas where it had not yet started. Liu stated emphatically that even where peasants had started themselves to carry out land reform, they should be restrained from so doing. In areas where land reform had been decided on for the winter of that year (1950), every effort should be made first to complete the harvest and collect "public grain" (that is, state grain taxes and deliveries) before launching the land reform. Liu warned that if land reform should lead to " 'tendencies' which bring about confusion," it should be immediately halted. Rich peasants were not to have their land confiscated, for many had already changed their attitudes and had taken a "neutralist" position.[47] A few years before, the military situation had made heavy demands on the peasantry for military service and materials. But now conditions had changed, and it was necessary to restore and build up the rural economy. The mistakes of the previous years, Liu indicated, had to be rectified:

During the period from July 1946 to October 1947, the peasant masses and our own workers in the villages in many areas of North China, Shantung, and

---

[45] Ho Kan-chih, *op. cit.*, pp. 328-329.
[46] *T'uti kaiko chungyao wenhsien huichi* (Peking, 1951), pp. 11-28.
[47] *Ibid.*, p. 20.

Manchuria, in carrying out land reform, did not sufficiently observe the May 4, 1946, directive of the Party Central Committee not to disturb the land and property of rich peasants, but acted on their own, and simply confiscated the land and property of rich peasants. This was understandable. This was because this was a period when the Chinese people and the reactionary Kuomintang were locked in a tight and bitter struggle. It was during this period that most of the deviations occurred in land reform. Some of the interests of the middle peasants were violated, some industrial and commercial businesses in the villages were destroyed, and in some areas there arose the phenomenon of "indiscriminate beating and killing."[48]

Henceforth land reform was to be gradual, with reliance placed on poor peasants and hired laborers, but without alienating the middle peasants and the neutralist rich peasants. The peasant councils were to become "the organizational form and executive organs" of the land reform. Core cadres were to be formed by positivist elements among the peasants and by operations cadres sent down from higher echelons. Henceforth land reform was to occur in a planned manner. No decisive moves were to be made without authorization from higher echelons. Higher echelons were to be asked for instructions in carrying out land reform, and representatives sent down to aid the villages. The doors of the peasant councils were not to be closed to poor peasants guilty of some minor infraction. The poor revolutionary intelligentsia in the villages was to be welcomed, as were such "enlightened gentry who assented to the land reform." Regular courts were to be established to try offenders.

The intent of the new policy was clear. Extreme agrarian radicalism had created serious production difficulties. Therefore, though land redistribution was to continue, it was not to interfere with production. The new policy had two consequences, one social and the other political. The new land law introduced complex classifications of the peasantry: landlords, rich peasants, middle peasants, poor peasants, and laborers. Though the basic classification was based on property relations, several modifications were introduced to soften its impact. Thus landlord adherents of the revolution or landlord families constrained by circumstances to rent out land were given a special status as "small landlords," or were regarded as having dual status, as landlords and as something else. Distinctions were to be made between different members of the family. The intermediate category of "prosperous middle peasants" was introduced.[49]

---

[48] *Ibid.*, p. 21.
[49] *Ibid.*, pp. 34 ff.

The distinctions were so fine in some instances that it undoubtedly was difficult to determine exactly what social status a person held. Nevertheless the determination of social status was a significant portion of the program of total population registration. The net effect, at least in theory, was to allow the preservation of the position of the rich peasant. The new policy put a moratorium on forced social change in the village. The landlord and gentry groups had already been wiped out, thus destroying the rural elite. But the intravillage men of influence were to be tolerated, for the time being, in order to avoid further deterioration of the village economy.

The political consequence of the new policy was that the administration of the land reform was taken from the hands of the villagers. Though the peasant council, *nungmin hsiehhui,* remained the chief instrument for the land reform, it changed in character from the period of the revolutionary terror. Under the new regulations, just about all peasants in the village were permitted to join the peasants councils. Even rich peasants, assuming approval of the *hsiang* people's congress or *hsiang* peasants congress, could join. Furthermore, the basic-level peasant councils were organized around the *hsiang* or "administrative villages equivalent to *hsiang.*" This made the peasant councils large unwieldy bodies, by their size alone incapable of accomplishing much. Real power was in the hands of the peasant-council committees, made up of a small number of select cadres.[50] The old "poor-peasants bands," *p'innung-t'uan,* which had been the village equivalent of the Party operations squads were disbanded.[51] As land reform was completed, the peasant councils were transformed into *hsiang* people's congresses, and the peasant council committees into *hsiang* government.[52]

The new policies introduced late in 1949 and in 1950 halted neither land reform nor entirely the revolutionary terror which continued to break out in various parts of China, particularly in the southern regions where land reform was instituted later than in other parts. However, it attempted to transform land reform into an orderly process subject to top-level controls. The more lenient policy adopted toward the "rich peasants" meant that the Party was attempting to halt the process of exterminating all old elites in the village, a process which had come close to wrecking the rural economy.

But the inevitable counterpart of this process was the restraints put on the young "poor peasant" rural cadres who had been the main in-

---

[50] *Ibid.,* pp. 108-111.

[51] *Ibid.,* p. 115.

[52] *Kungfei chits'eng tsuchih chih yenchiu,* p. 116; hereafter referred to as *Kungfei.*

struments of the revolutionary terror. We do not know how many of these new recruits to the Party were expelled in 1950, but it was precisely they who suffered under the new Party policy of recruiting urban workers (see p. 168). Since order was to return to the village, the Communists attempted to create an effective apparatus of administration. No longer the "natural village," but the *hsiang* and the administrative villages became the focus of administration.

The magnitude of the social revolution that struck the Chinese countryside remains yet to be studied. China's vast population alone made the land reform one of the greatest social revolutions of modern times. In July 1950, the Communists announced that land reform, by the fall of 1950, would have affected 100,000,000 peasants, of whom the landlords constituted 4 percent or 4,000,000 individuals. This left another 364,000,000 peasants, according to the population calculations of the time, among whom land reform was to be carried through, and some 10,000,000 landlord elements to be eliminated.[53] Land reform in substance was said to have been completed by the end of 1952,[54] which meant presumably that the bulk of landlord and rich-peasant land had been redistributed by that time. Land reform did not lead to an economic revolution, for production patterns in the village did not change fundamentally. But as a social revolution, land reform succeeded in destroying the traditional system of social stratification in the rural areas. The old rural gentry, whether based on the villages or residing in towns, was destroyed. A social element, which had exercised leadership in the village by virtue of its status, its ownership of land, and its access to power had ceased to exist. That class which traditionally had formed a link between local society and the state—the gentry—was wiped out in the process of land reform. Land reform did not bring about complete leveling, for "rich peasants" and apparently even some former landlord elements continued to exercise power and influence within the villages themselves. But a return to the *status quo ante* was impossible.[55]

---

[53] *Ibid.*, p. 114.

[54] Union Research Institute, *Chungkung shihnien* (Hong Kong, 1960), p. 142.

[55] Liu Shao-ch'i, in his report to the Eighth Party Congress, announced that "land reform had not only destroyed the landlord class and greatly weakened the rich peasants economically, but politically had decisively overthrown the landlord class and isolated the rich peasants" (*Jenmin shouts'e 1957*, p. 11). However, because "land is little and people are many in our country's villages . . . 60 or 70 percent of the peasants in our villages are still poor peasants or lower middle peasants." This ratio, as Liu-Shao-ch'i stated, was roughly the same as in the "villages of old China." The fundamental redistribution of land therefore did little to increase the size of average

VILLAGE POLICY IN THE EARLY 1950'S

A New Administrative System

The local landlord gentry was destroyed, and in its place came the arms of the state apparatus—in the form of *hsiang* government. The drive to increase agricultural production during the early 1950's was accompanied by rapid bureaucratization at the *hsiang* levels and above. In 1950, the government issued a series of decrees outlining the structure of government at all levels of national life. The basic-level unit of administration was henceforth to be the *hsiang* or the administrative village. Late in 1950, formal rules for *hsiang* people's government were issued. In many areas, the *hsiang* people's congresses were simply the old peasant councils transformed into a more formal body. The new *hsiang* governments were staffed by rural cadres who had remained in the good graces of the leadership. As throughout China, much administration was carried out by committees, some permanent, some *ad hoc*. The formal *hsiang* people's government committee, having one head and several deputy heads, took on the following form: civil administration work committee, finance and food work committee, production cooperation committee, education and hygiene work committee, work committee for public order and security, work committee for the people's armed forces, and several *ad hoc* committees.[56]

Each *hsiang* government had attached to it units of the people's militia and a local public security-police station. In theory, *hsiang* gov-

---

peasant holdings, and consequently can hardly be seen as an economic revolution. The land reform must, therefore, be seen as a social revolution, which was aimed at two basic targets: the landlords and the rich peasants. Though classification was based on the amount and nature of landholding, in essence these two categories represented different social strata in local society. The landlords were those elements that enjoyed wealth, power, and prestige not so much in the villages themselves, but within larger local areas. They were therefore the direct competitors of any state system the Communists set up. In effect, one might say that it was the state which replaced the landlord-gentry group. However, the "rich peasants" were the leaders of the "natural village." Their power and influence were much more difficult—and dangerous—to destroy. The repeated references to "rich peasants," even during the period of communization, indicates that as an intra-village social group, they had not been eradicated. Despite its thoroughness, land reform did not succeed in bringing about a total social revolution within the villages themselves. The "natural village" remained a tough nut to crack.

56 *Kungfei,* p. 40.

ernment was subject to the *hsiang* people's congresses, which were periodically held; there, *hsiang* government officials reported on their work, announced policy, and solicited criticisms and suggestions. The different sections of *hsiang* government accurately reflected the major interests of the state in the rural areas: the maintenance of order and control, the collection of taxes, and the desire to extend the network of organization over the rural areas. The first two functions are little different from those of earlier Chinese governments, but the Communists were determined not simply to exercise control over the rural areas but to transform them.

The pace of rural reorganization was to remain slow for a number of years. The first stage in rural reorganization took the form of the creation of mutual-aid teams. By late 1952, 40 percent of China's rural households were organized in one or another form of mutual-aid teams.[57] Still, "though the mutual-aid teams were certainly organized on a massive scale, many of those, however, appeared to have produced only pro forma results." [58] Whatever the results of these early attempts to organize mutual-aid teams, the structure of *hsiang* government already reflected the intention of the leadership to concern itself with positive steps aiming at the reorganization of Chinese agriculture.

The shift toward bureaucratization which succeeded land reform and revolutionary terror gave rise to a foreseeable phenomenon: overbureaucratization. A report published in the spring of 1953 described this overbureaucratization in a large administrative village in Shantung.[59] *Hsiang* government consisted of eight regular administrative committees: civil administration, finance and food, education, relief, production, hygiene, public order, and armed forces (i.e., people's militia). In addition there were a large number of other *ad hoc* committees: arbitration, irrigation, literacy, assistance in occupational change (mostly for returned war veterans), marriage law, forestry, production technology, veterinary care, insurance, property care, people's militia investigations, recreational clubs, school construction, and Resist America and Aid Korea. There also were Chinese-Soviet friendship clubs, credit communes, statistical teams, tax teams, and publishing stations; and finally all kinds of *ad hoc* committees concerned with checking on land and property, evaluation of agricultural production, cotton-buying, food-buying, and so on.

---

57 Carin, *op. cit.*, II, i.

58 *Ibid.*, p. 30.

59 *Jen min jihpao*, May 13, 1953.

Similar reports appeared in other publications at the time. Some attempts were made by official decree to cut down on overbureaucratization in 1953, but lower-echelon local governments were still allowed to set up *ad hoc* committees where necessary.[60] Overbureaucratization soon led to a proliferation of all kinds of social and economic surveys. It was reported that the financial-economic committee of the Shansi provincial government had prepared a questionnaire "with seventy-four pages and 6,307 items." Others were equally long and complicated. "Each peasant was asked to answer eighty-three different questions." Committees and agencies issued their own questionnaires to the peasants: hygiene, taxation, banks, insurance agencies, cooperatives, all kinds of enterprises.[61] In this respect, it need only be recalled that 1953 was the year of the greatest statistical survey of all, the population census.

The shift from revolutionary to bureaucratic leadership over the masses did not imply that the state was receding from the village, such as many dynasties had done earlier. The *hsiang* not only became the nucleus of state administration, but the size of the *hsiang* was decreased to make it a smaller and more manageable unit. In 1950, when the organizational rules for district and *hsiang* government were issued, the leadership laid down criteria for determining the optimal size and extent of the *hsiang*.

Each *hsiang* was to have an average population of 2,000, and not to exceed 3,000. Districts and *hsiang* were to be set up according to ecological criteria. But the sociopolitical requisites of land reform were also taken into account. Once *hsiang* boundary lines were drawn, they were to remain relatively permanent. Article 7 of the "Principles of District and *Hsiang* Delineation" specified that "the *hsiang* was to become the basic-level organization of authority; below the *hsiang*, there are only to be 'natural villages' and no further administrative villages are to be established. If there already exist administrative villages, they are to be abolished. In the case of large natural villages or of several amalgamated natural villages, the natural village may elect a delegate chairman to carry out work. But these are not echelons of administration." [62]

---

[60] *Kungfei*, p. 33.

[61] *Jenmin jihpao*, June 27, 1953.

[62] *Kungfei*, p. 24. *Kungfei* (p. 25) also notes: "The work of reducing the size of districts and *hsiang* was of a comprehensive nature; in reality, though, in the North for example, basically there was no such thing as the *hsiang*. Below the *hsien* level, there were so and so many large and small villages or units equivalent to villages (with

It appeared to be firm Communist policy not to establish administration at the level of the natural village. Ch'i Kuang-tung, chief of the *Orgburo* of the Ministry of Interior clearly stated this policy. Ch'i said that the *hsiang* was the basic-level unit of authority, and no other level was to be below it. Consequently, formal administration at the village level was to be abolished. The existence of formal administration at the village level would impede direct contact between the masses and the *hsiang*, Ch'i said, and impose an even heavier burden on the state administration. To make liaison between the masses and the *hsiang* administration effective, every natural village was to select a "chief village delegate." [63]

The function of the chief village delegate was not much different from that of the village headmen in traditional China. He was to act as a link between government and peasantry. Though the *hsiang* would appear to be a purely political unit, at times it also appeared to have had a socioeconomic unity. G. William Skinner has suggested that there is a socioeconomic unit beyond the village, called the "standard marketing area," which may have formed the basis for drawing *hsiang* boundary lines. The standard marketing area consists of a number of villages oriented to a common marketing town. Not only economic, but social and cultural ties serve to give the standard marketing basis of unity.[64] If this is so, the *hsiang* is obviously more than what was traditionally regarded as an administrative village.

Why were the Communists reluctant to extend state administration down to the village level? During the Yenan period, they took great pains to implant Party organization within the village itself, thus indicating a determination to gain control of the village. There are undoubtedly many explanations for this reluctance. For one, the natu-

---

different designations). Even where there were *hsiang*, the population density was not as great as that in the South. Furthermore, since many of the areas in the North had long been under Communist control, basic-level government had already been established, and land reform carried out. Therefore, the main targets of district and *hsiang* reduction were the southern provinces which had fallen under Communist control rather late, where the *hsiang* and districts were quite large, and the population density greater."

In February 1953, Chou En-lai declared that people's governments had been established in the great majority of the 280,000 *hsiang* and villages of China. In September 1954, during the National People's Congress, he announced that people's governments had been established in 220,466 *hsiang* (*ibid.*, p. 39).

63 *Ibid.*, pp. 38-39.

64 G. William Skinner, "Marketing and Social Structure in Rural China," *The Journal of Asian Studies*, 24 (November 1964), 32-43.

ral villages differed in size in various parts of China and would have created uneven administrative units. More important was the need to prevent the lowest levels of the state administration from being dominated by vested interests in the villages; *hsiang* government had to remain subject to state manipulation and free from local interests. Another reason was that Party organization in most rural regions was weak. The Yenan example indicated that only the Party could control the villages, not bureaucratic administration.

VILLAGE POLICY IN THE MIDDLE 1950'S

The Creation of Agricultural Producers Cooperatives (APC's)

We have thus far described the political changes which occurred during the transition period of the early 1950's. Though, at the same time, Peking encouraged the development of mutual-aid teams and agricultural producers cooperatives, the campaign had only limited success, as we indicated earlier. Peking's main instrument for handling the villages was still bureaucratic administration exercised through the *hsiang*. However, the pace of cooperativization[65] gradually speeded up. In January 1954 the Central Committee issued a directive on "developing agricultural producers cooperatives"; by the end of the year, 114,165 APC's had been organized in the country.[66]

But the great change came in the summer of 1955 when Mao Tse-tung in his famous July speech (made public in October) "On the Question of Cooperativization in Agriculture" urged a decisive speed-up in the campaign of organizing APC's. The anger expressed in speeches and editorials which appeared in 1955 against rightist and counter-revolutionary elements, landlords, and rich peasants "who have wormed their way into the cooperatives" indicates that traditional leaders were reappearing in China's villages.[67] As happened in earlier periods of China's history, these village leaders resisted encroachments from the state. The only way the Chinese Communists saw to penetrate the fabric of village organization was, once again to do what they

---

[65] The term "cooperativization" appears as a barbarism in English, yet it is an exact rendering of the term *hotsohua*, by which the Chinese Communists designate this movement. Though the higher-stage APC's did involve collectivized property and though collectivization is a more acceptable term in English, we feel that a literal rendering of the Chinese *hotsohua* is preferable.

[66] *Chungkung shihnien*, p. 145.

[67] Carin, *op. cit.*, pp. 192-193.

had done during the Yenan period, namely make use of the Party cadre. But neglect of rural Party organization during the early 1950's had meant that there had not been enough village Party cadres to perform this task. Thus, Party recruitment policy changed. Early in 1955, before a decision to cooperativize had been made, China's leaders launched a program of building up Party organization in all rural areas of China.

During the early 1950's, the regime had succeeded in creating an administration which gradually covered the entire society. However, it was essentially oriented to the classic functions of control and exploitation. As the state intensified its exploitation of the peasantry, local administration played an ever more important role in "planned purchase" and "centralized purchase" of farm products, as well as in the task of taxation. But as exploitation functions increased, so did those of control. A rural police system was introduced in the early 1950's. Public security squads were organized. A people's militia remained on the scene, in the form of a "permanent militia" and a "supporting militia." The latter consisted of young peasants normally engaged in production, but the former was a permanent militia, either not engaged in production at all or only part of the time.[68] The combination of rural police, public security teams, and people's militia formed a kind of latter-day *paochia*, though far better organized and more effective than any known earlier in Chinese history. By 1955, the countryside was under control, and the state's mechanisms for collecting surplus were effective.

But more was needed than control and exploitation. Agricultural output had to be increased, and the policy adopted by Peking to achieve this was full-scale cooperativization. Economic considerations played an important part in the decision to speed up the pace of cooperativization in late 1955. The 1954 harvest had been bad, providing a diminished[69] surplus for industrial investment. In his July 1955 speech, Mao Tse-tung warned:

We all know that the level of production of commodities, food, and industrial raw materials in our country is very low, but the needs of the state for these materials grows from year to year. This is a sharp contradiction! If we cannot in the space of three five-year plans basically resolve the question of agricultural cooperativization, that is to say to jump from small-scale agri-

---

[68] *Kungfei*, pp. 36-37.
[69] Bernhard Grossman, *Die wirtschaftliche Entwicklung der Volksrepublik China* (Stuttgart, 1960), pp. 182-183.

culture using animal power and farm tools to large-scale management using machinery, including a large-scale movement of population to open up new land, organized by the state and making use of machinery (within the time period of the three five year plans 400 to 500 million *mou* of land is to be opened up), then we shall not be able to resolve the contradiction between needs for commodities, food, and industrial raw materials which grow each year and the presently low level of over-all agricultural production. Our task of socialist industrialization will encounter great difficulties, and we shall not be able to complete our socialist industrialization.[70]

Collectivization seemed to be the answer to the problem of increased needs for agricultural surplus. Land reform had given the peasant land, but did not lead to an improvement of the over-all agricultural situation. The average landholding of the peasant did not increase greatly as a result of land reform. The prospects for a rapid technological revolution in agriculture were not good. As Mao said, "to complete, fundamentally, the technological revolution in agriculture on a national scale, I reckon that four or five five-year plans will be necessary, or twenty to twenty-five years." [71] This meant that little capital could be diverted to agriculture during the period of intensive industrialization. Organized hand labor alone would have to be used to achieve greater agricultural output.

Mao was aware of the fact that there was widespread reluctance to intensify the pace of cooperativization, that "it goes beyond the realistic possibilities" and "goes beyond the level of consciousness of the masses." [72] True, there was the example of the Soviet Union's difficulties with collectivization, but, Mao said, the "error of 'dizziness with success' was quickly rectified." [73] Their own experience and that of the Soviet Union undoubtedly made the leadership quite aware of the adverse consequences that could ensue from collectivization. They were perhaps not aware, though, that the technological revolution could not be postponed, for as the social revolution created new forms of production organization, it also created new capital needs in agriculture.

Why did the regime decide to move so quickly and drastically on the agricultural front? Probably because there was no inevitable evolutionary process leading from land reform through mutual aid to cooperativization. Mao reported that in Chekiang "at one blow" 15,000 out of 53,000 cooperatives had been dissolved, and admitted that in

---

[70] *Shehui-chuyi chiaoyü k'och'eng ti yüehtu wenchien huipao* (Peking, 1957), I, 589.
[71] *Ibid.*, p. 595.
[72] *Ibid.*, p. 587.
[73] *Ibid.*, p. 591.

1953 there had been "the error of large-scale dissolution of coopera-tives." [74] Aside from the open dissolution of cooperatives, there was reason to question how cooperative many of the cooperatives really were. He stated:

Today in our villages there exists capitalist ownership by rich peasants and individual peasant ownership which resembles a vast ocean. We have already seen that in these last few years, autonomous capitalistic forces have been de-veloping day after day in the villages. New rich peasants have already ap-peared everywhere; many prosperous middle peasants are trying to turn them-selves into rich peasants. Many poor peasants, because of shortages of pro-duction materials, are yet in a difficult position. Some are in debt; some have sold their land; some rent it out. If we let these conditions continue to develop, the phenomenon of polarization will get more serious day by day.[75]

Mao made clear that, though land reform had done away with "feudal" forces (the landlord gentry), new "capitalist" forces (rich peasants) had arisen. During the early 1950's, Peking had decided to rule the countryside administratively, and so had retreated from the natural village. The result was a resurgence of the rich peasants who, in a manner familiar from traditional times, once again took over vil-lage leadership. Reports pointed out that in some instances rich peas-ants often refused to join the cooperatives, leaving the poor peasants in an association that had only limited land and tools. But in many other instances, landlords and rich peasants had infiltrated the coop-eratives and diverted them to the particularistic interests of the village. The greater the resurgence of traditional village leadership, the less effective the actions of the Party and Youth League cadres. Rural Party organization still suffered from the abrupt change in recruitment pol-icy in 1950. Organization was poor; cadres were of a low caliber; and central support was often lacking for a powerful organizational drive. The result of all this was growing apprehension on the part of the lead-ership that the social revolution initiated by land reform would start moving in reverse. Village self-sufficiency would reassert itself, mak-ing it increasingly difficult to crack the shell of village organization. Already "some comrades" felt that the village cadres had trouble enough organizing small-scale cooperatives; how much greater the problems in organizing them on a large scale! The leadership decided that the time had come to take a bold step to accelerate the social revo-lution.

The social revolution could be carried out in the villages only

---

[74] *Ibid.*, p. 583.
[75] *Ibid.*, p. 594.

through the Party and its auxiliary mass organizations like the Youth League. Mao declared:

> The work of establishing cooperatives and of reorganizing cooperatives must rely on the *hsiang* branches of the Party and the Youth League. Therefore, the work of establishing and reorganizing cooperatives must be closely tied together with the work of establishing and reorganizing Party and Youth League organization in the villages. Whether it is in regard to establishing or reorganizing cooperatives, cadres who are located in the villages in question must become the principal force; they must be encouraged and charged to go about this. Cadres dispatched downward from higher echelons are only supplemental forces which are to perform the function of direction and assistance. They must not do everything themselves.[76]

The message was clear enough. The social revolution was to be undertaken by cadres from the villages themselves. The old technique of sending down "operations squads," *kungtso-tui,* from higher echelons was to be used only in a limited way.

In March 1955, the "First National Conference of the Chinese Communist Party on Basic-Level Organizational Work in the Villages" was held in Peking. A program was mapped out to step up rural recruitment and to raise the quality of rural Party cadres. At the same time, the Youth League launched a similar campaign to attract more young peasants into the ranks of the League. Rural positivists, who had been discouraged after the land reform, once again emerged into the limelight. Class warfare within the village, which had abated after the land reform in favor of "more orderly procedures," erupted once again. Traditional village leadership had to be fully eliminated. The Party apparatus in the rural areas grew enormously during 1955 and 1956, judging from the sudden jump in Party membership. This time the rural Party apparatus had the full support of the central Party leadership and of Mao Tse-tung himself. The attack was to begin and not to end until complete collectivization had been achieved.

It is hardly surprising that Mao's speech was not released until October of that year. Mao announced that the plan adopted by the Central Committee in the spring of 1955 to push the number of APC's to the million figure was not ambitious enough. Mao set the figure at 1,300,000 (for China's 200,000 *hsiang*), so that each *hsiang* should have one or more "APC's of small scale and half-socialist character." This figure was to be reached before the 1956 fall harvest. Regional Party leaders were to spend the coming two months "drawing up proper plans in accordance with concrete conditions" and report to the Cen-

---

[76] *Ibid.,* p. 584.

tral Committee. Since Mao gave his speech on July 31, 1955, this meant that no action would be taken until the beginning of October, a time when the fall harvest would already have been in. The regime was not going to take the risk of unleashing the social revolution at a critical time in the farming season.[77]

Problems of Cooperativization

Reports appeared throughout 1955 and 1956 detailing experiences in the organization of cooperatives. The problems differed, as could be expected, from area to area, but certain patterns appear. I have selected one of these reports as a "case study."[78]

The report described the process of cooperativization in Talichuang *hsiang*, Chia-hsien, Honan province. The *hsiang* consisted of eight natural villages with a total of 708 households, or 3,240 individuals; there was a total of 7,705 *mou* of arable land.[79] The *hsiang* had thirty-three Party members, and eighty-three Youth League members, seven non-Party cadres in the *hsiang* administrative committee, and twelve positivists. By September 1955, there were nine APC's, with a membership of 276 households, comprising 38.9 percent of the population. Four villages had already been cooperativized; two already had cooperatives; two had none.

The report did not make clear whether the APC's corresponded to a village, a neighborhood, or something else. However, one can deduce from the facts given in this report that several natural villages had more than one APC, indicating that, at this stage of the APC's, the APC was not identical with the natural village.

The report continued by saying that cooperativization in Talichuang began in the winter season of 1953, after the completion of the fall harvest. At that time, a single cooperative was established. In the winter season of 1954, the eight other cooperatives were set up. The APC's had already achieved considerable production successes. In 1955,

---

[77] Bernhard Grossman (*op. cit.*, p. 180) feels that during the middle of 1955, the emphasis was still on the organization of mutual aid teams; only 14 percent of peasant households were organized into cooperatives, and larger-scale cooperatives were still being neglected. But by the end of 1955, the picture had changed radically: 60 percent of all peasant households were partially cooperativized by the end of 1955, and completely cooperativized a half year later. This confirms our impression that massive cooperativization only began after the assurance of the autumn harvest.

[78] *Chungkuo nungts'un ti shehui chuyi kaoch'ao* (Peking, 1956), pp. 320-328.

[79] Mao Tse-tung, in his July 1955 speech, cites a national average of three *mou* of land per person, with the average in the southern provinces going down to one *mou* or less (*Shehui chuyi chiaoyü k'och'eng ti yüehtu wenchien huipao*, p. 587). One *mou* is approximately one-sixth of an acre.

"the high tide of cooperativization" gripped the *hsiang*. Before the "high tide," in five of the villages there were still 126 eligible households not yet in the APC's. These included twenty-two poor-peasant households, seventy-six new middle-peasant households, and twenty-eight old middle-peasant households who "clamored to join." Though the "high tide" came, the *hsiang* Party organization was still unable to exercise "prompt and concrete leadership." Some of the mutual-aid teams, in the process of being transformed into APC's, recruited largely from rich and middle peasants, and were reluctant to admit poor peasants. The various teams quarreled with each other to enlist the few "core cadres and literate persons." There were quarrels as to the relative ranking of their teams. And "landlords, rich peasants, and counter-revolutionary elements acted decisively to draw peasants to their side, to use this opportunity to organize fake teams, fake cooperatives, or to carry on usurious business, and destroy the cooperativization movement." The report concluded that though "the high tide of socialist revolution" had arrived, and the class struggle had become sharper, the Party leadership still did not have full control over the new situation.

To cope with this situation, in June 1955, the *hsiang* Party branch, under the direction of the *hsien* Party committee, made a comprehensive plan for cooperativization. The first step was to acquaint all Party members with the new policy, and make it clear that it was to be carried out "gradually under Party leadership." The Party was to remain in full control of the process. The Party branch strongly criticized "erroneous views and methods that did not wish to rely on the poor peasants, favored the core cadres, the rich peasants, and did not wish to solidarize [with the masses]."

Having gone through the educational phase the Party branch laid out concrete steps for cooperativization. The villages in the *hsiang* were classified into three types. The first consisted of the four villages in which cooperativization had already been instituted. These had a total population of 250 households; five APC's already had been established, with a total of 177 households; fifty-seven households had not yet joined, excluding sixteen households of landlords and rich peasants. Because many of the remaining households were too scattered, it was decided not to set up new APC's, but expand the existing ones. The second type consisted of the two villages in which four APC's had already been set up. The total population numbered 269 households, of which 170 had not yet joined. It was decided to set up new APC's which would merge with the old ones. The third type consisted of the two villages where no APC's yet existed, and new ones had to be established.

After the plan had been formulated, the next step was to ascertain concrete conditions. Which mutual-aid teams in which villages were to serve as bases for the APC's? How many households for each APC? Which old APC's should be expanded? Which cadres and masses should be assigned to which old and which new APC's? Which mutual-aid teams should be transformed into APC's in 1955, and which in 1956?

Organizationally, as the report indicated, the situation in the *hsiang* was as follows. The entire *hsiang* had twenty-three mutual-aid teams. Seven were already capable of being transformed into APC's; the other sixteen were basically ready. There were still fifty-eight "core cadres" who were not members of any APC. Of these, eight were Party members, thirty-six Youth League members, four Party "positivists," five village cadres, and five "rather capable and strong" mutual-aid team leaders. These fifty-eight, after suitable checking and reeducation, were assigned to seven "provisional cooperatives" (*she-chiatzu*) and mutual-aid teams, according to where they lived. There were 708 households in the *hsiang*. Of these, forty-nine households of landlords and rich peasants were excluded from joining the APC's. These consisted of twenty landlord households (2.8 percent of the total population) and twenty-nine rich-peasant households (4 percent of the total population). In addition there were thirteen households of proscribed elements: former *paochia* leaders, town officials, religious leaders, men who were "objects of restriction," and "habitual bandits." The latter made up 5 percent of the population. Of the 151 middle-peasant households, sixty-three or 41.7 percent had already joined APC's. Of the 508 poor-peasant households, 213 had joined (41.9 percent). This left 383 middle and poor-peasant households still outside the APC's. Of these, 272 were said to be ideologically ready to join; fifty-nine would be ready to join in 1956; and sixteen refused to join.

It was decided to expand the eight old APC's by fifty-seven households. In the winter season, after the harvest, seven new APC's would be set up, containing 215 households. This would make a total of 548 households or 77.4 percent of the *hsiang* population. It was made clear that the proscribed households, constituting 12 percent of the population, would not be allowed to join.

One can be sure that the proscribed household constituted traditional leadership elements in the villages. The plan thus was to have ultimately fifteen APC's which would comprise a majority of the middle and poor-peasant households. Since there were only eight natural villages, it is obvious that APC and natural village were not identical. Moreover, some APC's cut across natural village lines. The report made it clear that the *hsiang* and not the natural village was to be the framework within which the APC's were to be organized. In order to smash the traditional village leadership, organization based on the natural village had to be done away with.

Once the blueprint for setting up the new APC's had been drawn up, the report continued, the Party proceeded to implement it. In typical fashion, the first step consisted of meetings organized by the Party: Party branch meetings, core cadre meetings, people's delegates meetings, and other kinds of mass meetings. After individual and collective "discussion" with the peasants, seven provisional APC's were formally established. Core cadres were nominated; the mutual-aid teams were assigned to the different APC's. In some instances, the report made clear, households were allowed to choose which APC they wanted to join.

The second step envisaged the transformation of the provisional APC's into regular APC's, as the report indicated. This step was connected with a change in production methods resulting from the amalgamation of land formerly held by the mutual-aid teams or by individuals. Here too intense propaganda and education were necessary; care was to be taken that people were not compelled to join this or that production brigade.

The change in production methods required the setting of production plans, the report stated. A three-year production plan was drawn up. To meet the expanded output goals, production materials had to be increased and improved. A program to construct new water works was launched: the original eighty-three ponds and 200 wells were to be doubled. Irrigated land was to be increased by 3000 *mou*. Farm tools were to be improved and new ones added. The number of draft and domestic animals was to be increased. Soil-improvement programs were to be carried out, so that by 1957, 1000 *mou* of land would have been covered with black earth; 200 *mou* of land were to be reinforced with dikes and trees. Above all, efforts were to be made to increase the supply of human and animal fertilizer.

Summing up the results of the new campaign, the report concluded: positivism in cooperation and production had been greatly stimulated among the masses, and new production teams and brigades had been organized; the poor peasants were brought into the APC's; the leadership of the core cadres had been strengthened; village backwardness was being eliminated; landlord elements had been attacked and crushed, and the attempts of "habitual bandits and counter-revolutionary elements" to create "fake cooperatives" had been smashed. "The enemy was further isolated." The *hsiang* chief was quoted as saying: "Our plan has led to three satisfactions: the core cadres are satisfied, the poor peasants are satisfied, and the middle peasants are satisfied!"

The process of cooperativization led to severe struggle. The report mentioned one case of a "habitual bandit" being "punished by law." Mass meetings and struggle meetings undoubtedly served to intimidate others among the 12 percent proscribed population. The elimination of the traditional leadership led to the "core cadres" coming into the APC's and assuming organizational leadership. There were 132 individuals (Party members, Youth League members, non-Party cadres, and positivists) who formed the core cadres of the *hsiang*. There were eighty-four reactionary households. Since one can presume that these latter were somewhat larger in size than the ordinary peasant household, the two groups were about evenly matched. The struggle was essentially between the old leadership and a new one. But what had the core cadres been doing before cooperativization? Many appear to have been demobilized war veterans who had returned home in 1955. Many of the Party members undoubtedly worked in the *hsiang* government. Many Youth League members were probably prominent in the work of the popular militia. As a result of the cooperativization campaign, many of these cadres moved directly down into the production brigades of the APC's. This movement may be seen as an early version of *hsia-fang*. The core cadres were young, energetic, committed to the new order. They were the same elements which provided recruits to the guerrilla armies during the social revolution of the land-reform period.

Since reports from other villages indicated a similar situation, we might draw some conclusions about village conditions at the time of the 1955 cooperativization. It must have been common expectation for years that Peking was, sooner or later, going to proceed to a higher stage of organization in the rural areas. As a result, all kinds of self-organizing activities were conducted in the villages designed to present the authorities with a *fait accompli*. The old struggle between organization imposed from the outside and village self-organization erupted once again. As the report from Talichuang *hsiang* indicates, it had been official policy to "isolate" the landlords and rich peasants. Nevertheless, it appears that these families still exercised power and influence in the village. Thus, many mutual-aid teams and pre-1955 APC's apparently once again came under the control of "reactionary elements." As the same report implies, some Party members in the villages had come under the influence of these traditional village leaders and therefore were reluctant to push through organization imposed from above.

The conflict situation described in the Talichuang *hsiang* report is similar to that which prevailed in the 1940's, except that, undoubtedly, the rich peasants were more important adversaries of the Party cadres than the landlords who had been basically eliminated by the land reform. The regime began the struggle by mobilizing the cadres, who were native to the villages concernéd, using the *hsiang* (that is, the administrative village) as a base of operations, and proceeding to the attack by organizing cooperatives which excluded the traditional village leaders and cut across the boundaries of the natural village. Once again, as in the 1940's, Peking undertook to penetrate the natural village.

APC's and Hsiang

During the 1955 cooperativization campaign, it was repeatedly made clear that the *hsiang*, or the administrative village, was to be the framework of cooperativization.[80] But the new policy also brought about a change in administrative policy toward the *hsiang*. Where it earlier had been the policy to decrease the size of the *hsiang*, the regime decided, in a directive issued on December 21, 1955, to increase their size. The directive stated: "The small districts and small *hsiang* no longer accord with the new situation created by the rapid development of agricultural cooperativization; therefore district and *hsiang* administrative regions should be gradually amalgamated." [81] It was at this time that the "districts," *ch'ü*, intermediary between *hsien* and *hsiang*, began to disappear. The following figures show the changes:[82]

1955 (spring)	218,970	*hsiang*
1956 (fall)	117,081	*hsiang*
1957 (summer)	101,730	*hsiang* and *chen* (towns)

The new directive divided the *hsiang* into three categories: (1) *Hsiang* in plains areas. Hsiang territory was to include an area of an average radius of five *li*,[83] and a population of about 10,000 people. Some *hsiang* included as many as 20,000 people. (2) *Hsiang* in hilly areas, covered territory in a radius of ten *li* and contained a population of between 5,000 and 8,000 people. (3) *Hsiang* in mountainous and border regions, where the radius was fifteen *li*, and the population 2,000-3,000, and sometimes less.[84]

In the plains regions, two or three *hsiang* were combined into one

---

[80] In his speech of July 1955, Mao cited some examples of cooperativization from "villages" (*ts'un*) in Heilungkiang. An editor added the explanatory note: "The *ts'un* in Heilungkiang are administrative units, which correspond to the *hsiang* in the main provinces; the *t'un* of Heilungkiang are not administrative units, but correspond to the *ts'un* of the main provinces" (*ibid.*, p. 596).

[81] *Kungfei*, pp. 72-74.

[82] Chou Fang, *Wokuo kuochia chikou* (Peking, 1957), p. 110. Actually, Article 53 of the Constitution had already decreed the abolition of districts below the *hsien* level, but district administration was apparently not abolished right away. See *Kungfei*, p. 72.

[83] One *li* is about 1890 feet.

[84] *Shihshih shouts'e*, VII (July 1956), 14.

new *hsiang*. In many provinces (Shansi, Liaoning, Kirin, Heilung-kiang, Shensi, Honan, Kiangsu, Anhwei, Chekiang), the number of *hsiang* decreased by one half.[85] For example, in Laiyang *hsien* (Shantung), in July 1956, the thirteen districts in the *hsien* were abolished and the 154 *hsiang* and *chen* in the *hsien* were amalgamated into thirty-five *hsiang* and *chen*.[86] In the plains areas, average *hsiang* population increased five times or more. The reasons for the new policy are not difficult to discern. The shifting down of *hsiang* government cadres to the APC's and the general policy of "administrative simplification" brought about personnel shortages in *hsiang* bureaucracy. The amalgamation of the *hsiang* made it possible to concentrate administrative personnel not affected by the shift downward of cadres.

But there was another reason. Already in 1956, the regime began to move toward an amalgamation of APC's into larger units. In many instances, effective amalgamation required the incorporation of organizational units lying outside the limits of *hsiang* jurisdiction. This made it necessary to increase the size of the *hsiang* in order to avoid jurisdictional conflicts and disputes.[87]

The Pace of Cooperativization

The year 1955 was significant in the organizational history of Communist China. It was a year of rural class struggle, even if it did not assume the violent character of the land-reform period. Organizationally, it saw the transformation of the mutual-aid teams into APC's. Once the APC's had been created, the move from an "early stage" to a "higher stage" was not difficult. Although the "early-stage" APC's did not affect property rights to the extent that the "higher stage" APC's would, the initial stage of cooperativization had introduced the principle of property amalgamation. Though there was considerable resistance to cooperativization, it appears to have mainly taken the form of passive noncompliance, withdrawal of effort, slaughter of farm animals, and the like. As a whole, however, the resistance to the APC's was far less violent than that in the Soviet Union at the time of original collectivization. The revolutionary terror was still fresh in the minds of the rural population. Neither the peasants nor the regime wished to risk a repetition of those events. Though various forms of compulsion were used, the regime was reluctant to use force which would have had a disastrous impact on production. Membership in the APC's was still

---

[85] *Ibid.*

[86] *Jenmin jihpao*, February 15, 1957.

[87] *Kungfei*, pp. 72-73.

based on voluntary assent, for even in later years the press reported instances of peasants quitting the APC's.[88]

After the fall 1955 harvest was assured, the pace of cooperativization was rapid. By the end of 1955, 75,000,000 peasant households (63.3 percent of the total peasant population) had been enlisted in one or another form of cooperative; by the end of 1956, 83 percent, and by the summer of 1957, 97 percent.[89]

Not only the speed of cooperativization but the rapidity of the conversion of "early-stage APC's" to "higher-stage APC's" were remarkable. By the middle of 1957, more than 96 percent of all peasant households were in "higher-stage APC's." These were fully socialized, and in essence comparable to the Soviet *kolkhozes*. Some writers have used the word "cooperative" to designate the earlier-stage APC's, and the word "collective" to designate the higher-stage APC's. Full collectivization meant not only the socialization of all property, but the creation of a unified village economy.[90] In its September 14, 1957, directive on the reorganization of the APC's, the Central Committee declared that "as the experiences of the previous year have shown, under most conditions, one APC per village is relatively correct." [91] Thus the transition to the higher stage involved not merely the complete socialization of peasant property, but the amalgamation of smaller APC's into larger units covering an entire village.

---

[88] See Grossmann, *op. cit.*, p. 184.

[89] The following table gives an indication of the growth of cooperativization:

Year	Early-stage APC's		Higher-stage APC's		Totals		Percent
	APC's	Households	APC's	Households	APC's	Households	
			(in thousands)				
1952	3.6	57.2	0.0	1.8	3.6	59.0	0.1
1953	15.0	272.8	0.0	2.1	15.1	274.9	0.2
1954	114.0	2,285.0	0.2	12.0	114.0	2,297.0	2.0
1955	633.0	16,881.0	0.5	40.0	634.0	16,921.0	14.2
1956	682.0	34,839.0	312.0	76,874.0	994.0	111,713.0	91.9
1957 (June)	84.0	4,497.0	668.0	113,414.0	752.0	117,911.0	97.0

SOURCE: *Chūgoku nenkan* (Tokyo, 1958), p. 229, rounded off.

[90] The criterion of property distinguishes cooperatives from collectives. In the cooperative, the peasant still owned his land. In the collective, property was owned by the APC. However, the Chinese Communists do not use the word "collective," as the Russians do ("kolkhoz" means collective economy), but speak of "higher-stage cooperatives." There is no sharp dividing line between the two stages of cooperativization, which makes it difficult to use the words "cooperativization" and "collectivization" clearly to designate the two stages. One might say that the process began with cooperativization and ended with collectivization.

[91] *Jenmin shouts'e 1958*, p. 517.

In conclusion one can say the transition from early-stage APC's to higher-stage APC's did not have the clear-cut character of the 1955 co-operativization, thus making it difficult to label the first stage coopera-tivization and the later stage collectivization. Therefore, in the follow-ing section, we shall point out some of the problems and aspects of this transition. However, the basic purpose of the regime in aiming at the higher-stage APC's is clear. As we said, full collectivization meant both the socialization of all property and the creation of a unified village economy. A higher-stage APC was to be a cooperative identical with the natural village and comprising all land, including that formerly owned by landlords and rich peasants. Such an all-village cooperative would make possible the development of a planned all-village economy, par-ticularly for the basic grains. It also would create a socioeconomic or-ganization based on the natural village, but politically responsive to the state. Thus, the early-stage APC's must be regarded as a transitional form designed mainly to break the socioeconomic power of the tradi-tional village leaders. Once their power had been broken, they and their valuable property could then, and only then, be integrated into the APC, thus permitting a transition to the higher stage.

Changes in the APC's

Cooperativization occurred rapidly, but this by no means meant that the APC's had found an organizational form which suited the re-quirements of production. During 1956 and 1957, the regime discussed the problem of the "proper size" of the APC. During the cooperativi-zation in 1955, a number of large "higher-stage" APC's had been estab-lished, some covering entire *hsiang* (*i.e.*, the earlier, smaller *hsiang*).[92] Exemplary as these early large APC's might be, the regime felt that such a large size was not practical for the country as a whole. In a di-rective issued in September 1956, the Central Committee declared:

Under present conditions the size of the APC's should be: in mountainous regions about 100 households, in hilly regions about 200 households, and in plains regions about 300. Large villages with a population greater than 300 households may also form one APC for each village.[93]

Similar prescriptions were made for the size of the production bri-gades, the nuclear units of the APC's:

At present the production brigades and teams in some areas are too large. One must adjust them in accordance with present conditions of production technology and the requisites of field work. According to the experiences of

---

[92] *Chungkuo nungts'un ti shehui-chuyi kaoch'ao*, pp. 392-393.
[93] *Jenmin shouts'e 1957*, p. 478.

various regions, under present conditions, in most areas the small-scale brigade is most suitable (on the average containing twenty-thirty or thirty-forty households) or the small-scale team (on the average containing seven-eight households) .[94]

Thus while the regime encouraged amalgamation into larger units, *pingshe*, where feasible, it also left the door open to the splitting up of APC's, if necessary. Cooperativization had led to the amalgamation of mutual-aid teams into APC's, which was fully supported by the leadership. But it also apparently led to rapid and reckless creation of large, unwieldy units. In 1957, the regime seemed to move farther away again from the prematurely large APC. In a directive issued September 1957, it declared:

Because of all kinds of peculiarities in agricultural production which now exist, as well as the low level of technology and management, concrete results from the last few years have proved that large cooperatives and large brigades do not accord with present production conditions, and have also proved that the general standards laid down by the Central Committee in September 1956 for the size of the APC's are correct. Therefore, with the exception of such APC's which are demonstrably effective, APC's which at present are too big and do not operate well, should, upon the demands of their members, be reduced. Henceforth, the scale of organization of the APC's should in general take the village of 100 households or more as its unit, and set up one APC for each village. In the case of very small natural villages, where they are close to each other, several villages can set up a single APC. Larger natural villages may set up a single APC or they may set up several. In the case of small mountain villages with only a few households, one may set up a cooperative team, or, after entering an APC, economically assume their own gains and losses. As far as the size of the production brigades is concerned, in general, twenty households or so of people who live close together is correct as to size. After the scale of the APC and the production brigades has been adjusted, a two-level administration system should be set up for production management. If there are too many layers, this is bad for getting deep into work, having liaison with the masses, and organizing production. *Once the size of the APC's and the brigades has been fixed, it should be proclaimed that there will be no further changes for the next ten years.* [My italics.][95]

The previous year, the Central Committee had also declared: "After the APC's have been set up, aside from cases where splitting up or amalgamation should be necessary, in general over the next few years, one should not lightly alter them; this will be good for allowing a consolidation of the new production relations." [96]

---

[94] *Ibid.*, p. 477.
[95] *Jenmin shouts'e 1958*, p. 519.
[96] *Jenmin shouts'e 1957*, p. 478.

The policy on reducing the size of the APC's is reflected in the macrodata. Whereas the average number of households for early-stage APC varied only slightly for 1956 and 1957 (51 and 53.5), for the higher-stage APC the figure dropped from 246 in 1956 to 169 in 1957 (calculated from data presented in footnote 89). Though conditions differed widely throughout the vast reaches of China, what the leadership really wanted was the transformation of natural villages into APC's—one cooperative for each village! The mutual-aid teams had been small intravillage cooperative groups, not always effectively integrated into the village economy. The early-stage APC's also as a whole did not include the entire population of the village. But the higher-stage APC's ultimately were to represent a dialectical transformation of the natural village. The village economy based on the integrated village once again appeared, but this time in the advanced form of a higher-stage APC.

The creation of an integrated APC based on the natural village or its equivalent meant that practically the entire village population had to be recruited—above all the proscribed groups: landlords, rich peasants, and others who had been "isolated" during the early stage of cooperativization. Since these elements often still owned the best land in the village, it was imperative that they be brought into the APC. Article 8 of the Model Regulations for Higher-Stage APC's, adopted in June 1956, made it relatively easy for former landlords, rich peasants, and penitent counter-revolutionary elements to join the APC's.[97] This policy was reconfirmed in the directives of the Central Committee issued in September. Landlord and rich peasants were presumably responsible for some cases of desertion from the APC's in 1956 and 1957, a fact which accounts for the spread of the anti-rightist campaign to the rural areas. However, aside from certain punitive actions taken against them, probably few former landlords and rich peasants were actually expelled from the APC's. The dominant organizational theme in 1956 and 1957 was consolidation and integration. Mass expulsion of former reactionary elements would not have served that policy.

In principle, the higher-stage APC was much like the Soviet kolkhoz, "based on socialist principles." According to the model regulations, "all privately owned land, draft animals, major production materials such as large-scale farm implements were to be turned over to the APC as collective property" (Article 13). The peasant could retain as private property what he needed for his own livelihood and in addition a few trees, domestic animals, small-scale tools, and tools he needed for domestic enterprises. All major water works were collectivized.

---

[97] *Ibid.,* p. 174.

Homes remained private property. If the APC had need of animals, implements, and other tools owned by members, it could purchase them from the owners and repay the owner in installments. Similar repayments by installments were to be made for other collectivized items, such as fruit and timber trees from which the owner derived income. The APC could also collectivize animal herds and compensate the original owners.

The APC required funds to invest in production and to purchase materials. These funds came in the form of "share funds," *kufen chi-chin,* which the members could "pay in the form of production goods needed by the APC." The amount of "share funds" was determined by a member's property and labor status; if he was not able to pay the requisite amount he could solicit a loan from a bank or ask the commune for a lowering of payment. The APC was authorized to set aside investment and welfare funds from its net income. If capital was still lacking, members could be asked to make additional investments.

The regulations on "share funds" (or members' share account, as it may be translated) are complex. In effect, each peasant more or less paid his share-fund allotment by the land he turned over to the APC during the early stage of cooperativization. Share funds did not bear interest, and were nonreturnable, except if the peasant left the APC. The APC member was entitled to a share in the net income of the APC.[98] Gross income in money and goods, after payment of state taxes, was subject to the following division: (1) deduction of current-year depreciation costs, laying aside of a sum for the coming year's production costs, and repayment of debts and investments on current year's production turnover; (2) a sum, from net income left after deduction of

---

[98] Gregory Grossman has pointed out to me some differences between the 1956 APC model regulations and the kolkhoz rules in the USSR. In both cases, the first deduction made from gross income is for state obligations. But whereas the Soviets distinguish between obligatory grain deliveries and state taxes, the Chinese group them both under the category of state taxes. There are no "share funds" in the kolkhozes, but there is something similar in Soviet cooperative organizations, namely, the *paevoi fond.* The Soviet kolkhoz has an "indivisible fund." But no distinction is made between "public accumulation funds" and "public benefit funds." The Chinese regulations specify that the public accumulation fund is not to exceed 8 percent of net residue after deductions of current year's depreciation costs. There is no limit set on the indivisible fund of the kolkhozes, which the kolkhoz leaders try to maximize. There is no provision in kolkhoz regulations for a public welfare fund. The Chinese regulations specify that public accumulation funds can be reduced to increase the portion for distribution to APC members.

All in all, in contrast to the kolkhozes, the Chinese regulations give the impression of liberality. This accords with the new atmosphere in 1956.

VILLAGES 459

depreciation expenses, set aside for a "public accumulation fund" and a "public benefit fund," not to exceed 8 percent and 2 percent of net income respectively; (3) the residue in goods and cash to be distributed to members according to their total number of "work days" (this includes work days in farm work, supplemental enterprise work, administrative work, and also bonus work days earned by production brigades and individuals). If the amount to be distributed was too low in some years, less could be allocated to the public investment fund. Farm products were to be distributed to members after the spring and summer harvest; cash was to be paid periodically. At year's end, a general accounting was to be held.

This is not the place to discuss the fiscal and economic aspects of APC organization, but a glance at the Model Regulations makes it easy to imagine the headaches which resulted therefrom. Given conflicting demands on an economy as primitive as that of the Chinese countryside, plus all the difficulties caused by a system that demanded that everything be planned and orderly, the resulting complications are not difficult to imagine. In effect, the peasant surrendered control of most of his land, animals, and implements, in return for a more or less guaranteed share of the crop twice a year, and a very small payment in cash. The new arrangement proved advantageous to the poorer members of the village, from whom many of the cadres were recruited. The regime promised the peasants a rise in income, and warned cadres against squeezing too much out of the peasants for investment purposes. After all, the major hope of the peasants in joining the APC's was the desire to increase personal income.[99]

The Model Regulations also make certain specifications concerning the internal work organization of the APC (Articles 30-38). All APC members were to be assigned to one of three types of organizations: (1) production brigades working on the fields, (2) production teams working in supplemental enterprises, and (3) production brigades working in supplemental enterprises. The difference between "brigade," *tui*, and "team," *hsiaotsu*, is one of size (from twenty to forty households for the former and seven to eight for the latter, but the average size was reduced in 1957 as mentioned earlier).

Specialists were also to be appointed to take charge of accounting, technical management, animal care, the preservation of public funds. "The production brigade is the basic unit of organization and work in the APC, and the membership of the production brigade should be fixed." Each brigade or team was to have its specified land and tools, al-

[99] *Jenmin shouts'e 1957*, pp. 171-172.

though on occasion reallocation and reassignment could take place. This specification would assume considerable significance a few years hence, for one of the changes that the commune system brought about was the transferability of brigade members and the flexibility with which different brigades were assigned to different tasks. Thus, despite the radical changes which collectivization brought about, the regime still attempted to preserve a traditional work order.

The APC was to specify work norms and wage standards for its members, the Model Regulations said: "Each type of work norm is to be based on the amount of work that can be done in a single day and the quality achieved by an average worker under the same conditions." The history of the Soviet Union is replete with examples of the headaches caused by calculating wages in terms of *rabochii dén'* (work day); the headaches caused by the Chinese wage system were as great. Each production brigade and supplemental enterprise work team was obliged to fulfill specified work contracts, *paoch'an*. Overfulfillment of the contract was to be rewarded by bonuses. Managerial performance was likewise to be rewarded. The APC also was to specify the number of work days of labor to be performed by each member for each season. Article 35 specified that managerial personnel "normally was not able to engage in production work," but had to contribute somewhat more work days of labor than the average worker.

The supreme administrative organ of the APC was the "members council" or "members delegates council," but in fact the APC was governed by an "administrative committee," *kuanli weiyüanhui*. The council was to meet at least twice a year and discuss and approve major policy questions relating to the APC. The administrative committee was to consist of from nine to nineteen members, depending on the size of the APC. In addition, each APC was to set up a control committee, *chiench'a weiyüanhui*, whose tasks were to check on operations in the APC. Membership ranged from five to eleven, but excluded members of the administrative committee, accountants, cashiers, and maintenance personnel. Members of the administrative and control committees were to be elected each year, but old members could be reelected. Women, minorities, and returned Overseas Chinese were to be adequately represented in the APC administration, according to the Model Regulations.

APC administration proved to be another source of difficulty for the regime, as is apparent in the Central Committee directive of September 1956. After the abolition of the districts and the amalgamation of the *hsiang*, large numbers of cadres apparently attempted to get transfers to higher echelons, thus depriving the *hsiang* government and the

APC's of leadership. More cadres had to be assigned to the lower echelons, the directive declared. Furthermore, "one had to overcome the
confusion of a lack of differentiation between Party and APC, and APC
and government." While the Party branch assumed the leadership in
the APC, "it could not involve itself in everything, and do everything
by itself." Similarly, *hsiang* government functions were to continue to
be exercised by *hsiang* government and not taken over by the APC's.
"One must change the phenomenon of Party, government, and APC
cadres holding too many positions simultaneously." The directive specified further that the Party and government had to give constant attention to disaster relief work.[100]

Model regulations are one thing and social reality is something else.
What did an APC actually look like? The organization of the APC's
undoubtedly differed from area to area, some more "socialist" than
others. But in general the higher-stage APC coincided with a "natural
village," although in the larger villages of South China, a single village
might contain more than one APC. All land in the village which traditionally had been used for the growing of staples was amalgamated and
made into the collective economy; boundary lines between plots were
eliminated. Major staples were wheat, rice, beans, cotton, and so on.
What kind of production came under the collective economy depended
on the actual production conditions in the villages. Some villages were
oriented primarily toward the growing of vegetables, and in these vege-
table growing was considered part of the collective economy. But, in
general, the typical Chinese village was oriented to the raising of basic
grains.

Each unit of land was worked by a production brigade which consisted largely of peasants living in proximity of one another and of the
land on which they worked. In general, most peasants continued working the land they had earlier owned individually. Farm implements
were assigned each production brigade. Again, in many instances, peasants simply continued to use whatever implements they originally pos-
sessed. Wealthier peasants, however, had to give up their "surplus"
tools, which were reassigned to poorer peasants. Indeed, the impact of
collectivization hit hardest the wealthier peasants, both of the rich-
peasant and of the middle-peasant categories.

Each peasant was assigned a labor quota for the collective economy.
Beyond that, he was free to do what he wanted. Indeed, as in the Soviet
Union, the "small plot" turned out to be an important source of sup-
plemental income for the peasant. The appearance of "free markets"

---

[100] *Ibid.,* p. 480.

in 1956 testifies to the productivity of home farm production. The peasant was allowed to raise domestic animals, grow vegetables, and keep small orchards for himself. These remained his private property.

At that time, women had not yet been drawn into farm work on a massive scale. Field work was still largely done by men. The peasant continued to own his own home, and the integrity of the family was still preserved. In fact, as hitherto in China, much of home production was done by women. The actual living conditions of peasants probably changed little during this period. Per-capita farm income did not rise appreciably, judging from official statements urging cadres to concentrate on convincing the peasant that joining the APC's would provide him material benefits. The loss of his land meant more to the middle and wealthy peasants than to the poorer ones who as yet did not have sufficient time to acquire strong ties of attachment to it.

Whether the stakhanovite work-day system stimulated production is difficult to say. Work patterns and methods were so traditional that there was probably not much increase in productivity. In fact, judging from reports, work performance probably declined, for agricultural work, especially in the busy season, demanded all kinds of *ad hoc* tasks, which the peasant now presumed would be taken care of by the APC. Above all, the inability of the regime to make any sizable capital investment in agriculture made it difficult and dangerous to change traditional work patterns. Like his Soviet counterpart, the collectivized Chinese peasant began to divert more of his energies to his private land and animals.

Though collectivization did not bring with it the "technological revolution" of which Mao Tse-tung talked in 1955, it did further the social revolution. A new group of young men rose to power within the village, many of them army veterans. They had by now been schooled for some time in leadership work. Many were literate or partly literate. As Party members or Youth League members, they had the support of a powerful state behind them. In 1956, they had not yet been "sent down to the front line of production." They formed the leading cadres of the APC's administrative system. Whereas organized life in the traditional village had been rather simple, it became complex in the APC's. Everything was now to be done through rational organization. Even a miniature bureaucratic apparatus now appeared in the village. The peasants, through the "APC members councils," became engaged in political and economic activities. Education was fostered. Party-led movements and campaigns became a regular feature of village life. The bright young men of the revolution superseded the "old peasants," whose work was now confined to production. Former landlords and others who earlier enjoyed status and power had been discredited, and now were reintegrated into the APC's as simple workers. Just as the cooperatives were a new form of social organization, the young cadres constituted a new village leadership. This was the social revolution in the villages which Peking aimed to bring about.

In view of the historical association of cadres with war, it is significant that the military element disappeared from village organization. In the early days after land reform, the Communists had organized a vast people's militia, which in 1953 numbered 22,000,000 members.[101] But in 1954, with the introduction of a compulsory military-service law, the people's militia began to fall into desuetude. In 1957 the regime introduced a military reserve system, *t'uiwu-chih*, which combined the earlier reserve and the remnant people's militia into a single organization.[102] Integration and stabilization were basic themes on the agricultural front in 1956. Therefore the accounts of APC organization never mention a people's militia. The young leaders who earlier had played dominant roles in the people's militia, and even earlier in the traditional *paochia*, now became the civilian leaders of the village. The problem of control was no longer as pressing as it had been in earlier years. An effective police and public-security system functioned at *hsiang* levels and above. And, most important, the regime had succeeded in creating a powerful network of Party and Youth League organization throughout the country. The higher-stage APC, unlike its successor, the commune, was an essentially civilian organization.

One can regard the period 1956-1957 as one of "two steps forward, one step backward." Within a surprisingly short period starting toward the latter part of 1955, the regime had succeeded in collectivizing the country. But once having accomplished collectivization, the regime made it clear that the process was not to go too far and too radically. The Party was to remain in firm control of the process, but in its paternalistic rather than heroic role. Order had returned to the countryside, making possible a broad-range civilianization of society. And, indeed, agricultural output made progress. If the 1957 harvest was only slightly above that of 1956, the 1958 harvest was clearly a bumper crop, though of smaller dimensions than claimed by the leadership. Even if favorable weather conditions played a part, it is also possible that a newly stabilized rural order helped to increase agricultural output. The regime had succeeded in collectivizing without plunging the country-

---

101 *Chungkung shihnien*, p. 377.
102 *Ibid.*, pp. 377-378.

side into the chaos produced in Russia by collectivization. Why then did Peking, in the summer of 1958, launch the people's communes which unsettled the countryside at a time that it had successfully come through collectivization? The answer to that question requires a look at the radical policy changes in 1957, which we have discussed in other connections in preceding chapters.

VILLAGE POLICY DURING THE GREAT LEAP FORWARD

Policy Changes Late in 1957

Two policy changes during the latter part of 1957 had a decisive influence on village policy. One was the ant-rightist movement and the other was decentralization.[103] Two aspects of the anti-rightist movement had a direct effect on the rural areas. One was the "socialist education movement" which brought about a revival of attacks on landlord and capitalist elements; the other was *hsiafang*, which saw thousands of city intellectuals sent to the villages.[104] The "socialist education movement" and *hsiafang* brought about an increasingly radicalized atmosphere in the country. Though decentralization had been planned as early as 1956, the growing radicalization during the summer of 1957 influenced the form decentralization would take. Instead of moving in the direction of a market economy, decentralization took the form of locally directed social mobilization. Instead of moving in the direction of decentralization I, as we have indicated in our chapter on government, it moved towards an extreme form of decentralization II. The revival of Mao Tse-tung's twelve-year plan for the development of agriculture early in October was the signal that a radical step forward was going to be taken in the area of land policy.

Residents in Peking at the time reported a sudden change in the atmosphere which occurred in December 1957 or January 1958. The intense, hard-driving pace of the Great Leap Forward was said to have begun at that time. It was reported that the Politburo held a secret meeting in Hangchow in December in which it decided to call for a

---

103 Cf. pp. 90 ff., 195 ff.

104 A *Jenmin jihpao* editorial of October 6 announced the beginning of *hsiafang* for Peking. However, a purely rural *hsiafang*, whereby APC cadres were transferred from their offices to the fields, had started earlier. The same editorial reported that 200,000 cadres in rural areas had been assigned to basic-level units and 100,000 to work posts.

Great Leap Forward in production and to institute a policy of amalgamating APC's into larger units. These same problems were discussed again and decided on in two later secret Politburo meetings, one in January in Nanning and the other in Chengtu in March.[105] A decision to amalgamate the APC's must have been made at the highest level, for it is hardly likely that the experimental communes, some of which dated back to the spring of 1958, could have been established without a fundamental policy decision at the top. All the more so because the basic policy in regard to the APC's, made clear as late as September 1957, had been to keep the APC's relatively small in size.

In the chapter on government, we discussed the disagreement between the "radicals" and the "conservatives" in the top leadership on the question of agricultural policy.[106] The conservatives stood for cautious development, "steps backward" every once in a while, material incentives, and use of market mechanisms. The radicals demanded that the revolution be consummated at "high speed," that social mobilization be used to bring about a technological revolution in agriculture. The power of the radicals grew from the summer of 1957 onward. Early in October, the radicals had won out in the Politburo.

The Campaign to Build Water Works

As the Great Leap Forward grew in intensity, it began to spread to the entire society.[107] What had started as a movement aimed at "overtaking England in fifteen years in industrial production" quickly became a gigantic nation-wide mass movement which affected city and country alike. The mounting *hsiafang* campaign saw millions of city people pour down into the villages to engage in agricultural work. The growing atmosphere of "high speed" also affected the villages. As 1957

---

[105] *Tsukuo* (Hong Kong), XXVI:9-10 (June 1959), 259.

[106] See pp. 195 ff.

[107] For a discussion of the genesis of the "Great Leap Forward," see *Communist China 1955-1959* (Cambridge, Mass., 1961), pp. 16-21. Two significant time points in the development of the Great Leap Forward are marked by Liu Shao-ch'i's speech, "The Significance of the October Revolution" (November 6, 1957), and his speech of May 5, 1958, entitled "The Present Situation, the Party's General Line for Socialist Construction and Its Future Tasks." The former announced many of the slogans which would become *de rigueur* during the Great Leap Forward, and in particular announced a policy of "achieving quantity, speed, quality, and economy." The latter proclaimed a Great Leap Forward already in full swing. It was presumably sometime during these six months, that the forces of radicalism won out completely, and launched the country on that experiment of radicalism and enthusiasm which would lead to the formation of the people's communes.

went into 1958, a "fermentation" was developing in the rural areas which soon would make the words of the September directives be completely forgotten.

One new policy already had a direct effect on the APC's. On September 24, 1957, a joint resolution of the Central Committee and the State Council announced a new movement to build and improve water works.[108] By the end of the year, the movement had become a "high tide" with "six hundred million people throughout the country hurling themselves into a campaign to build water works." The movement intensified as it became clear that a decision had been made to press forward with a great leap during the coming year. A large scale irrigation and water-works program had been successfully carried through during the winter of 1955 and the spring of 1956. This time an even larger program was carried out during the winter months between the fall harvest and spring plowing. Small water works were emphasized. Rather than have the work done by detailed planning, in keeping with the decentralization policy of the time, the basic planning was done at the lowest level, namely the APC's. Irrigation projects became a part of the APC's production plans. Though some support was forthcoming from the state, the APC's provided the bulk of the labor.[109]

Significantly, one of the centers of the irrigation movement was Honan, the province in which the model communes were later to develop. The irrigation movement was carried out at the village level, with the APC's as the nuclei of work organization. The projects were small in scale with "the state spending little money and relying on the masses," as T'an Chen-lin stated, one of the members of the radical group in the Politburo. Winter was a time when the peasants worked less intensely; so the regime ordered that temporarily nonworking peasants be put into water-works brigades. The projects had to be completed rapidly for in spring and summer labor would be needed once again for normal agricultural work. Furthermore spring rains would interfere with work. In fact, the construction of water reservoirs was designed to create catchment basins for spring rains and increase the amount of water available to combat possible drought. There was hardly much enthusiasm in the villages for these burdensome tasks. But by this time the whole rural Party apparatus had been mobilized to make sure that the peasants developed the requisite "positivism" for irrigation labor. The idea of mass mobilization began to grow. Irrigation labor, unlike field work, allowed for a much higher degree of organization. Workers

---

[108] *Jenmin shouts'e 1958*, pp. 533-534.
[109] *Ibid.*, p. 534.

could be formed into brigades and marched out to their work sites. Furthermore, the nature of the water pattern in much of China made purely isolated work projects carried out by the APC's alone difficult to carry through. Water projects had to be planned over broader areas which would include several APC's. This required increasing coordination and cooperation between APC's.

Changes in Work Organization

The great water-work brigades organized during the winter and spring of 1957-58 were forerunners of the production brigades that were to arise under the communes. There was an essential difference between these water-work brigades and the production brigades of the APC's. The latter were work groups that consisted largely of people who lived in the same general area and had had experiences of cooperation on more or less common land. The former were more in the nature of military units, moved from place to place as construction needs changed. The water-work brigades could be organized along lines of rational division of labor, which was difficult for the production brigades to do. The idea of mobilization and rational division of labor began to take hold in the villages, and particularly in the minds of the cadres. Methods used for the organization of water-works brigades were increasingly applied to other work sectors. As the pressures of the Great Leap Forward became more intense, the idea arose that a radical change in the organization of work must be brought about.

During the spring and summer, it became apparent that in many APC's, under the impetus of the irrigation movement, attempts were being made to create a new work order. On July 4, 1958, an article in the *Jenmin jihpao* described an APC "which was being administered like a factory." APC No. 38 in Su-hsien, Anhwei, had 1065 households, and was therefore already larger than the earlier APC's. Under the impact of the Great Leap Forward, APC No. 38 found itself caught in a number of "contradictions." First, there were the conflicting demands of agricultural work and those arising from the new policy of building small-scale industries to serve agriculture. Second, "the original simple division of labor was no longer able to satisfy the needs of the present comprehensive leap forward in agriculture." Third, original production technology was no longer adequate. And fourth, "the contradiction of a labor shortage had become particularly apparent." After considerable discussion, the cadres and masses decided that "there must be a further leap forward in work organization."

Clearly, the Great Leap Forward was beginning to make heavy demands on the peasantry. Irrigation work had already drawn off considerable labor from the fields. The drive to increase fertilizer resources demanded additional labor, as did the drive to set up small farm-servicing industries. The bumper summer crop intensified the need for labor even more. The labor shortage, occurring in an increasing mobilizational atmosphere, gave rise to the idea that the existing work order must be broken up and a new division of labor created. In retrospect now, it was at this point that the regime and its cadres were at the verge of introducing an even more profound social revolution into the village. The collectivization of land in 1955-1956 in China seems to have had a less disruptive effect on the Chinese peasant than Soviet collectivization of the late 1920's and early 1930's had on the Soviet peasant. Many Chinese poor and middle peasants did not have time to develop strong proprietary relationships to the land they received during the land reform carried out only a few years earlier. By contrast, Soviet peasants had actively seized land during the Russian Revolution. What proved to be far more disruptive in China was this attempt to transform the organization of work.

What does it mean to organize village work like that of a factory? The mentioned *Jenmin jihpao* article proceeds to describe how APC No. 38 resolved their "contradictions":

After study and trial over a certain period, APC No. 38 resolved to organize specialist brigades, divide labor and tasks, carry out specialized administration. According to the development and needs of work, the APC first of all organized irrigation brigades, brigades for opening up underground springs, vernalization, basic construction brigades; subsequently it started to set up iron and wood-implement repair shops, fodder-processing shops, noodle factories, seed-fertilizer factories, chemical-fertilizer factories, sewing shops, brick factories. According to the seasonal development of production, it also organized wet-rice-transplanting brigades, dry-field brigades, machinery brigades.

In the entire APC finally there were ten specialized brigades and seven factories. Each specialized brigade within the APC had a single uniform organization; within each specialized brigade, specialized teams and brigades were set up. Every member and cadre of the APC participated in these specialized brigades depending on each person's qualifications and work needs. Some of these specialized brigades were permanent the year round, such as the seven factories and the machinery brigades, the vernalization brigades, basic-construction brigades, and so on, which underwent little fluctuation. Some were relatively permanent, such as the wet-rice-transplanting brigades, dry-field brigades, well-digging, and garden brigades. The work of these brigades was basically permanent, though fluctuated with the seasons. Thus the wet-rice-transplanting brigades did irrigation work during the winter and spring, and in the summer they planted rice. The dry-field brigades in the winter collected fertilizer, and in the spring, summer, and fall planted dry-field grain crops. These brigades had a specialized division of labor under unified leadership.

In their farm activities, they submitted to the general needs and unified allocation of the APC. For example, during the summer season, more than 90 percent of the labor force of the entire APC participate in the summer harvest. The division of labor of these specialized brigades is clear. Each brigade assumes certain specialized tasks. Thus the sanitation fertilizer-accumulating brigade has forty-three people. All are old people, who are distributed over every production brigade of the APC. Their tasks are mainly to sweep the neighborhood and keep it sanitary, take care of the toilets, and collect manure. The vernalization brigade has forty-two people, all old people with experience in planting trees. Their tasks are to do the work of tree-planting and watching over tree sprouts. There are 1,500 people in the rice-transplanting brigades. Depending on the nature of the work, they are temporarily divided into water-drawing, ground-raking, rice-shoot-plucking brigades. Their main tasks are to plant the rice, and improve rice-planting production technology.

APC No. 38 was able to report on the excellent results of its new experiment in rational work organization which had been in effect "for several months." This was July, a month before the formal beginning of communization. Since similar reports to this effect were published from other areas of the country, it is safe to say that already in the spring of 1958, just before the summer harvest, the cadres of many APC's introduced the new principle of work organization. APC No. 38 stressed that the new system of rational allocation of labor "transformed phenomena of confusion in work organization." Thus, for example, productivity per man per day in irrigation work almost tripled after introduction of the new system. Rational organization of labor demands leadership, which the basic-level cadres were willing to provide. In APC No. 38, the committee cadres took over direct leadership of the specialized brigades. The cadres not only managed, but "penetrated deeply into each specialized brigade."

The introduction of the new work order not only meant a break with the traditional work order, but affected the entire APC. There were 1,065 households and 4,800 individuals in APC No. 38. Before the introduction of the new system, there were 2,093 full and part-time workers in the APC; later the figure rose to 2,300. The increase came from older people who "participated only little in production," but now were recruited into the sanitation, fertilizer gathering, and vernalization brigades. As yet there was no talk of a massive recruitment of female labor, as there would be when the communes were formed. But in essence the system of labor organization described in the *Jenmin jihpao* article is nearly identical with that under the communes. The communes would be larger in size, and show other features distinct from those of the APC's. However, basic to the communes was a new conception of work organization, and that conception had already become apparent in the summer of 1958. Indeed, it had its inception in the great water-works campaign launched late in 1957 and continuing in 1958.

The mobilizational system which came into prominence at that time meant for the Chinese peasant the sharpest break yet with the past. Land reform had eliminated the traditional rural elite from the scene, although the economic basis for renewed kulakization remained. The middle and poor peasants received land, but title to the land was not only "fresh" but lacked time to become institutionalized. Collectivization in 1955 and 1956 had deprived the peasant of his newly won land, yet, except for the rich peasants and the newly prosperous middle peasants, this hardly represented a serious blow to the average peasant. Though he had to give up some of his tools, he retained his home, gardens, some trees, and some animals.

The production brigades, moreover, were in many instances traditional work groups. The peasant continued to work on his land, as he had before for himself, or for his landlord. His share of the crop was probably little different from what it had been under the *ancien régime.* Indeed collectivization may have provided him a kind of security which he earlier lacked. His economic individuality could still find expression in the private land and animals he was allowed to retain. His working routine was most likely little different from what it always had been. Work was diffuse, unrationalized, and still involved a total agricultural cycle: plowing, planting, irrigating, harvesting. There was little in the way of technological improvement, but also no real interference with the work system.

But the grandiose plans of the regime, made known in its twelve-year plan for agriculture, came face to face with the realization that without a fundamental change in the "mode of production" in agriculture, output would sooner or later reach its limits and stop expanding. The only solution was the radical transformation of the technological and social basis of agriculture. But, as was stated by Mao Tse-tung, the technological revolution would have to come after the social revolution. The regime could not afford to direct great amounts of scarce capital into agriculture. The social basis of agriculture would have to be changed first, which meant only one thing: a radical transformation of the traditional system of work organization.

The life of the Chinese peasant was oriented around work and kinship. The strength of kinship ties differed from area to area in

China. Larger kinship groups, particularly those of clan type, had been weakened by years of pressure. But the nuclear family was more difficult to penetrate, and, indeed, despite some later attempts to break even the family and enter the era of familyless communism, basically the regime did not see the usefulness of trying to destroy that almost inaccessible core of Chinese social organization. But work organization was easier to change. It involved relationships that went beyond the family, and hence more accessible to transformation. Up to the spring of 1958, no attempt was made to transform the system of work organization of the peasantry. This is a decisive difference between the Chinese APC's of the 1955-1957 period and the Soviet kolkhozes, and perhaps one of the reasons for the relatively successful collectivization of the Chinese peasantry.

Concretely the radical transformation of traditional work organization meant that every peasant was recruited into a rationally designed work team which performed specialized rather than general, specific rather than diffuse tasks. He was thrown together with people with whom he had not worked, and with whom he did not maintain the informal group ties so important in any work relationships. In effect, while remaining in his home village, he was conscripted into a military force. Instead of functioning as a member of a "group," he became a member of a "squad." The bonds of rational organization, an idea still foreign to him and to which he was understandably hostile, bound him to the "squad," rather than the fuller, more diffuse ties of informal organization. For example, of the 2,300 working members of APC No. 38, 1,500 were organized into the rice-transplanting brigade; they were further broken up into water-drawing, ground-preparing, and rice-shoot-plucking brigades. This type of organization not only meant that each work team carried out the same tasks "as in a factory," but that the teams went from field to field until they had covered the arable land of the entire APC. The peasant found himself working on strange land, unfamiliar to him. The intimate knowledge of his own land meant nothing any longer. Whereas earlier he could cope with the idiosyncracies of land according to his extensive "particularistic" knowledge, now nothing but the "universalistic" methods of rationally defined work were left to him. Work became mechanistic, and subject to the commands of cadres who undoubtedly had "general" knowledge of farm processes, but could never match the intimate knowledge of the "old peasant."[110]

---

[110] After 1960, the press once again spoke in warm terms about the knowledge of the "old peasant" and the generations of experience on which he could draw.

The revolution in the organization of work preceded the actual formation of the communes, and in many ways represented the real revolution of 1958. As already stated, many rural areas faced an acute labor shortage during the summer of 1958, a shortage largely caused by the draining off of village labor for construction projects, notably water works. During his visit to Hsüshui (Hopei) early in August, Mao Tse-tung was told by the first secretary of the Hsüshui Party Committee that of 110,000 workers in the *hsien*, more than 40,000 had been diverted to water-works construction, digging wells, and operating industries, leaving only 70,000 for field work.[111] The only solution for the labor shortage was the massive liberation of women to work in the fields, and indeed Chairman Mao already observed "many women working on the land." Women in general had never done field work in North China, so the enlistment of women for this kind of arduous work represented a sharp break from tradition.

But as soon as women were engaged in field work on a large scale, a radical rearrangement in the family life of the peasant was necessary. Not only were public mess halls, nurseries, and kindergartens the rational answer to the problem of taking care of domestic needs, but the fact that fewer people were left at home to tend the private interests of the peasant family made it equally "logical" to turn over "remnant land," animals, trees, and implements to the commune for "unified management." The revolution in work organization affected the one remaining axis around which peasant life was organized: the family. Though there were few programs launched to replace private homes with dormitories, nevertheless the fact that there was no one left at home to take care of private interests and private life completed the socialization of the peasant's existence. Everything now truly became public. If the participation of women in agriculture had only been a temporary measure to be followed by reversion to the usual pattern, the consequences would hardly have been so disastrous. But by the summer of 1958, it was becoming increasingly clear that the new organization of work was supposed to remain permanent.

Amalgamating the APC's

If work was to be rationally organized, then the leadership was faced with a new limitation: the small size of the APC's. Although the average size of the APC's had grown in 1956 and 1957, as a rule the APC still was the equivalent of a "natural village" or of several small "natural villages." In fact, as we have said, in 1956 the leadership

---

[111] *Hsinhua panyüeh-k'an*, 16 (1958), 37.

discouraged the formation of excessively large APC's. This made sense as long as the traditional work order was to remain unchanged. But by the spring and summer of 1958, because of the large-scale irrigation brigades, village labor was increasingly working beyond the confines of the APC. The original directives on the organization of irrigation work had encouraged APC's to cooperate in collective efforts. As the Great Leap Forward imposed new tasks on the APC's, such as the setting up of small industries, it became increasingly obvious that the administrative framework of the APC's was too small to allow for rational management. It was necessary to establish these industries at a broader level and draw labor from several villages or APC's to operate them. When the summer harvest came and the crop was good, the labor shortage became apparent. It was even more necessary to shift work teams from village to village, and throw them into the production front as the needs arose. Crops do not ripen at exactly the same time, and there is always a slight time difference from village to village, and indeed often from field to field, in the optimal time for harvesting. It thus became common practice at this time to set up "specialized brigades" which were shifted from village to village as the need arose.

From material published at the time of the official formation of the communes, we know that a movement to "amalgamate APC's" (*pingshe*) had been in progress for some time. In its initial editorial on the communes, the *Jenmin jihpao* revealed that in Honan province the amalgamation policy had been in progress since April of that year:

This year in April, Suip'ing and P'ingyü *hsiens* started to combine small APC's into large APC's. Each *hsien* set up one large commune of 6,000-7,000 households. During May and June, the APC's of the two *hsien* gradually amalgamated into large APC's. . . . Toward the middle of July, the whole region entered the "high tide" of amalgamation and setting up people's communes. By the end of July, the amalgamation work of the 5,376 APC's in the region had basically been completed. Now 208 large-scale people's communes have been established, with an average population of 8,000 households.[112]

The amalgamated APC's were formed by combining natural villages into larger organizational units, as a whole coinciding with the *hsiang*, but in some instances comprising several *hsiang*. Since the amalgamation movement went against the cautious policy directives of the Central Committee issued in September 1957, a top-level policy decision was necessary to launch it. That decision appears to have been made in Politburo meetings held early in 1958 (see p. 142). However, since

---

112 *Jenmin jihpao*, August 18, 1958.

there were few reports on amalgamation until mid-summer of 1958, one can presume that amalgamation until then went on slowly and in piecemeal fashion.

The Emergence of the Communes

In the preceding two sections we have described two developments essential to the communes: the changes in work organization, and the amalgamation of APC's. By the early summer of 1958, it would appear that an amalgamated APC using the new principles of work organization, such as APC No. 38, Anhwei (see pp. 46 ff.), in effect already constituted a commune. However, it is significant, as will be shown, that the term "people's commune," *jenmin kungshe*, was not publicly used until August, although articles published in August and later indicated that some amalgamated APC's were called communes before that time. A further stage in the organizational process described was necessary before the communization movement could begin. But before we discuss this further stage (see p. 479), let us look at some of the developments just preceding August, the month in which the communization movement was officially launched.

From the reports on Suip'ing *hsien* and other areas of China, as we have indicated, it appears that the amalgamation movement started slowly. The *Jenmin jihpao* editorial, cited at the end of the preceding section, used the word "work" rather than "movement" to describe the first experiments in the amalgamation of APC's. However, by July, what had been "work" was transformed into a "high tide," a term used late in 1955 to describe the most intensive period of cooperativization. Reports indicate that the "high tide" came in Honan and Manchuria in July 1958. From articles published later, it is apparent that the amalgamated APC's in these regions were referred to as people's communes.

Thus, from July 29 to August 5, the Party committee of Hsinyang *hsien* (Honan) met in the new Sputnik Commune "to consolidate the people's communes and further develop production."[113] This presumably meant that the commune was already in existence before the Party committee had met. People's communes had also been established in Heilungkiang province late in July, where incidentally there had been heavy floods during the middle of that month.[114] In fact, water problems were among the major reasons for setting up the communes in

113 *Jenmin jihpao*, August 21, 1958.
114 See Carin, *op. cit.*, III, viii.

Shangchih *hsien* (Heilungkiang).[115] Similarly, late in July, the large APC's which had arisen in Liaoning province as a result of amalgamation were called people's communes.[116] Thus the month July appears to mark the time when the word commune was first applied to the new formations.

If we know, on the basis of subsequently published reports, that the term "people's commune" was beginning to be used in July, we also know that it was not used publicly in the newspapers until the following month. The first published mention of the term I have seen is a passing reference in an account published on August 11, 1958, concerning Mao Tse-tung's visit to Hsüshui (Hopei). Mao paid a short visit to Hopei after a three-day visit to Honan, lasting from August 6 to August 8. The report states: "Communes which earlier had been 'fermenting' in Tassukochuang village were formally established that evening; all trees were to be collectivized; homes were also to be uniformly allocated by the commune, and the members carry out a wage system." [117]

This report was published a week before the formal announcement of communization. On the following day, the *Jenmin jihpao* published a report of Mao's trip to Honan. There it is stated for the first time that he visited a commune, the Ch'iliying People's Commune. At that time, the following curious conversation was reported:

> Chairman Mao smiled and said to Wu Chih-p'u [first secretary of the Honan Province Party Committee and governor of the province]: "Secretary Wu, you really have hopes. You in Honan all seem to be as good as this!" Wu Chih-p'u said: "If there is one commune like this, then we don't have to worry about many other communes like this." Chairman Mao said: "Correct. If there is a commune like this, then there can be many of them!"

This was the first time that tours throughout China of its great leaders were reported in such detail. One gets the impression that the leaders were receiving information rather than handing out suggestions and policy statements. If the communes in Honan were indeed formed in July, then they arose before Mao's visit. We should like to suggest that the July "high tide" may have erupted in Honan, Manchuria, and a few other areas without an explicit order to that effect from Peking. If so, it would explain these far-ranging visits of almost all the top leaders in Peking. Ever sensitive to the delicate agricultural

---

115 *Hsinhua panyüeh-k'an*, 17 (1958), 71.

116 Carin, *op. cit.*, III, 67.

117 *Hsinhua panyüeh-k'an*, 16 (1958), 37.

situation, they apparently wanted to see with their own eyes what was transpiring. What they saw evidently pleased them.

Communization was formally launched by what was called the August-29 Communique of the Central Committee. However, it was not the Central Committee, but an "enlarged meeting of the Politburo" which met from August 17 to August 30 in the resort town of Peitaiho (see p. 147). The Peitaiho meeting was larger than a Central Committee plenum. Present were the entire Central Committee, Party first secretaries from all provinces, autonomous districts, and directly attached cities, as well as cadres from Party fractions in key government ministries. The length of the meeting indicates its serious character and possibly also disagreements. However, the fact that it was not officially labeled a plenum indicates that policy decisions had not yet been worked out to the point that they could have been presented to a Central Committee plenum for operational discussion.

Previously, the Central Committee had met in its fourth and fifth plenary sessions in May at the time of the second session of the Eighth Party Congress. Its sixth plenary session was to be late in November and early December. We have no record of any Politburo or Central Committee meeting between May and the time of the Peitaiho meeting. We are certain that the decision to amalgamate the APC's had been made early in 1958. Undoubtedly that decision was approved by the second session of the Eighth Party Congress, when it ratified the twelve-year program for the development of agriculture. However, if one recalls the situation during the summer of 1955, when cooperativization had been approved in principle but was not implemented until the fall, when news of the good harvest was in, it is difficult to regard the May decisions as a definitive go-ahead signal for communization. In May, the summer harvest was not yet in. In July it was, and Peking became aware of its magnitude.[118] Early in July, Liu Shao-ch'i set out on his grand tour, shortly to be followed by the other leaders.

Given these circumstances, it would seem that the final decision to launch communization was not made until the July visits of the leaders had been climaxed by Mao's personal visits to some of the most important areas of communization. This would therefore indicate that the Peitaiho meeting, as a Politburo and not a Central Committee meeting, was convened to discuss rather than simply implement a decision.

If the Peitaiho meeting made the decision to launch communization, this could only mean that communization had been started in some areas without an explicit decision by the highest bodies of the Party.

---

[118] *Ibid.*, 14, 55.

What, in the spring of 1958, had been piecemeal amalgamation of APC's, in July turned into a full-scale "amalgamation movement." Honan, parts of Hopei, and Liaoning seem to have been the epicenters of the movement. This suggest 'hat regional Party cadres in these areas had launched the movement on their own, undoubtedly with the powerful support of the radical wing of the Party, but also without the unanimous approval of either the Politburo or the Central Committee. When Mao visited Honan, communization was already in full swing. It was a movement led by Party First Secretary and Governor Wu Chih-p'u, one of Mao's most loyal regional supporters. Given the great power of the regional Party apparatus, it is possible that regional Party cadres, notably in the mentioned provinces, started the movement and so gave Mao Tse-tung and Liu Shao-ch'i a *fait accompli* finally to force through a decision in the Politburo.

On August 18, one day after the Peitaiho meeting began, the *Jenmin jihpao* made the first announcements about the new people's communes. Since Mao only returned to Peking (which is not far from Peitaiho) a week before, the decision on communization presented to the Peitaiho meeting must have been hurriedly made.

Let us return to a consideration on the word people's commune and its significance for that further stage in the organizational process alluded to in the opening paragraph of this section. Though the first published reference to a people's commune was made on August 11, the word "commune," in a more general sense, was used well before then. In the July 1958 issue of *Hungch'i*, the recently established official organ of the Central Committee, there had appeared a significant article by Ch'en Po-ta, chief editor and a long-time, intimate associate of Mao Tse-tung. Ch'en's article (entitled "Under the Banner of Comrade Mao Tse-tung") urged that industry, agriculture, commerce, education, and militia should be combined "into single large communes." He found support for this—in spirit, at least—in Mao's report on the general line for the building of socialism which has been delivered to the Second Plenum of the Central Committee in November 1956. Ch'en Po-ta said:

In this kind of commune, industry, agriculture, and exchange are the people's material life; culture and education are the spiritual life of the people which reflects their material life. The total arming of the people is to protect this material and spiritual life. Such an arming of all the people is necessary as long as in the entire world the system of exploitation of the people by other people is not decisively destroyed. Mao Tse-tung's thoughts on this kind of commune are the conclusions he has derived from the experiences of real life.[119]

---

[119] *Hungch'i*, 4 (July 1958), 8-9.

The word "commune" has a specific history in Marxism. In the Paris commune, the Russian war communes, and the Canton commune the word referred to totally organized living and working communities, dominated by the armed proletariat. It is clear from Ch'en Po-ta's speech, that it was the militarization of the community which made it into a "commune."

The reference to Mao Tse-tung's report to the Second Plenum is obscure. Ch'en quotes Mao on the unification of industry, agriculture, commerce, education, and militia, but does not quote him directly on the word "commune." Perhaps Mao Tse-tung already referred to the establishment of communes late in 1956 but since the report was never published, we do not know. In view of the fact that the Second Plenum was held just after the Hungarian rebellion, at a time when thoughts were being directed to "contradictions among the people," it is doubtful that Mao, at that time, sketched out a plan for the organization of the peasantry into armed units.

The use of the term people's commune was thus not simply the adoption of a convenient name for the new formations, in view of its clear-cut connotation of an armed population. In Hsüshui, for example, Mao was informed that "they had carried out militarization; the APC's in the entire *hsien* had set up more than 90 battalions and more than 200 companies." When Peking announced communization, at the same time it also announced that the people's militia was to be revived. So rapid was the recruitment into the people's militia that by the end of 1959, more than 220,000,000 people had been enlisted; of these, 30,000,000 were armed.[120] The transformation of the large APC's into communes sometime late in July thus must have been tied in with the arming of the peasantry. Industrial, agricultural, commercial, and educational functions were already being integrated within the amalgamated APC's. This fact has led observers of the communization movement, such as A. V. Sherman, to point out that many of the elements making up the communes were already in existence well before 1958.[121] However, before July, there is no evidence of an arming of the peasantry. Thus, we may conclude that the arming of the peasantry in July constituted the last stage in the organizational process leading to the formation of the communes. The true meaning of the "high tide" which was said to have erupted in July now becomes clear.

---

[120] *Chungkung shihnien*, p. 378.

[121] A. V. Sherman, *The Chinese Communes: A Documentary Review and Analysis of the "Great Leap Forward"* (special issue of *Survey*), (London, 1959).

The Militarization of the Peasantry

To see what was meant by the militarization of the peasantry, let us quote from an August editorial in *Red Flag*:

The broad working people have unfalteringly accepted the organizational forms of the people's commune, and have unfalteringly transformed many antiquated production relationships. . . .

The working people in their drive forward have advanced the following slogans which fulfill the revolutionary spirit: Militarize Organization, Turn Action into Struggle, Collectivize Life! What is meant by the militarization of organization of course does not mean that they are really going to organize military companies, and even less does it mean that they want to give themselves officers' ranks. The rapid development of agriculture simply demands that they greatly emphasize their own organizational character, demands that in their work they act faster, in a more disciplined and efficient way, that they can better be shifted around within a broad framework, like the workers in a factory or the soldiers in a military unit. Thus they have recognized that their organization requires militarization.

It is possible that the leaders of the peasants who have raised these slogans are not aware of the fact that Marx and Engels long ago in the Communist Manifesto set out a general program "of forming production armies, particularly in agriculture." However, they and the broad peasant masses during the prolonged armed struggle of the people's revolution know perfectly that there is nothing to fear in militarization. On the contrary, the total arming of the people carried out in order to repel imperialist aggression and their running dogs, is quite natural for them.

Though militarization in agricultural work is not for the purpose of repulsing the enemies of mankind, but for the purpose of carrying on the struggle with nature, it makes it easy to transform one of these two kinds of struggle into the other. The people's commune which combines the industrial, agricultural, commercial, educational, and military, at a time when there are no attacks from external enemies, is an advancing army [fighting] against nature, [fighting] for the industrialization of the village, the urbanization of the village, and for the happy future of communism in the villages. But if an external enemy should dare to attack us, all the people can be mobilized and armed, and made into an army decisively, resolutely, thoroughly, and completely to destroy the enemy.[122]

The message is clear. The militarization of organization in the first instance signified the revolution in the organization of work. The profound changes in work organization which we have described in an earlier section meant a great change in the traditional working habits

---

[122] *Hungch'i*, 7 (August 1958), 14-15.

of the peasant. If the changes in property relationships brought about by cooperativization mainly affected the rich and middle peasants, the changes in work organization directly affected the poor peasants. Ever since the launching of the water-works campaign late in the winter of 1957, the peasant had been conscripted into production brigades. Since the amalgamation movement was launched, these production brigades had been used for agricultural work. Corvee labor has a long history in China. Traditional corvee labor was always temporary, for as soon as the work was done, the peasant could return to his fields. However, communization aimed at making the brigade and team system into something permanent, something which would entirely replace traditional ways of working. Only thus could the village be made into a factory, as the *Red Flag* editorial put it.

No revolution can be carried out without ideology. Since the revolution in work organization was one of the most ambitious stages in the rural revolution undertaken by the Communists, it demanded an ideology of particular force. As we have indicated in our chapter on ideology, communization was accompanied by an excited utopianism which promised the peasants a rapid transition into communism. Three years of suffering would be followed by a thousand years of happiness, the peasant was told. If the ideal of communism was the pure ideology of communism, its practical ideology was militarization. The methodology of the revolution was the militarization of the peasantry.

The period beginning in July 1958 was the most militant since the Korean War. The fact that the people's militia was revived and that arms were actually distributed to the young men and women who made up the militia indicates that militarization had military as well as civil purposes. Since Peking was in full control of the country at that time, the question arises whether the military aspects of militarization had something to do with the international situation.

In August, gunfire broke out again in the Taiwan Straits, leading to the Quemoy-Matsu crisis. Mass demonstrations had been held before that protesting American imperialism in the Middle East, notably the landing of troops in Lebanon. These demonstrations were on a scale comparable with any that had been held before that time in China. The Chinese Communists, moreover, were urging the Soviets to take a more active role in the Algerian fighting. Given this marked Chinese belligerence toward the outside world, one may ask what the relationship between internal militarization and external belligerence might have been.

The dates of significant events internal and external during the summer of 1958 generally appear to coincide. Communization began in July; arming of the peasantry, particularly in Honan, Fukien, and Manchuria, also began in July;[123] the important visits of the top leaders again also took place in July or early in August; the Peitaiho meeting covered the latter half of August. As far as external events were concerned, the Iraq and Lebanon crises, which produced violent reactions in China, broke out in July; on July 29, Communist and Nationalist planes clashed in force over the Taiwan Straits; at the end of the month, Khrushchev arrived in Peking, presumably to warn Mao against becoming too belligerent; on August 23, while the Peitaiho meeting was underway, the bombardments of Quemoy and Matsu started. Chronology alone, therefore, cannot be used to indicate whether foreign policy derived from internal policy, or vice versa.

Our discussion has indicated that the arming of the peasantry was a last stage before communization. Undoubtedly the bountiful summer harvest, known by July, made Mao Tse-tung and his supporters, not only in Peking but in the provinces, conclude that the time had come to consummate the social revolution which Mao had preached ever since he first drafted the twelve-year program for the development of agriculture early in 1956. The visits of the leaders to the provinces must have convinced them that the entire country was solidly behind the revolution. What counts in foreign policy is action. The great demonstrations in July did not qualify as action. The Chinese Communists have often held mass demonstrations over foreign developments which they had no power whatsoever to influence, such as events in Panama, Brazil, and the Dominican Republic. At other times they have acted, as in the attack on the Indian border armies, without holding mass demonstrations. Though the first act may be said to have been the air clash with the Nationalists late in July, the real Quemoy-Matsu crisis did not begin until later in August. The tentative conclusion would emerge that the decisive internal events had been underway before the decisions were made to act externally.

During the civil war period (often referred to during the Great Leap Forward), the Communists launched radical land reform in May 1946, two months before the final break with the Nationalists. As we have indicated earlier in this chapter, one of the purposes of land reform

---

[123] The final general policy decision to "arm the entire people" was only made in September; see *Hsinhua panyüeh-k'an*, 18 (1958), 47. The general policy decision of September served the purpose of coordinating a movement already in progress, rather than launching one.

was to elicit the support of the peasantry and use it to recruit peasants into the armies. In a sense, the 1958 militarization of the peasantry had a similar purpose. Both land reform and communization were profound social revolutions, but they also created internal energy which the Chinese Communist leaders considered vital for final victory. It is possible that Mao, seeing the success of communization, felt that the moment had come to use the energies liberated by it to achieve his one supreme foreign policy goal, the resolution of the Taiwan question.

ORGANIZATION OF THE PEOPLE'S MILITIA

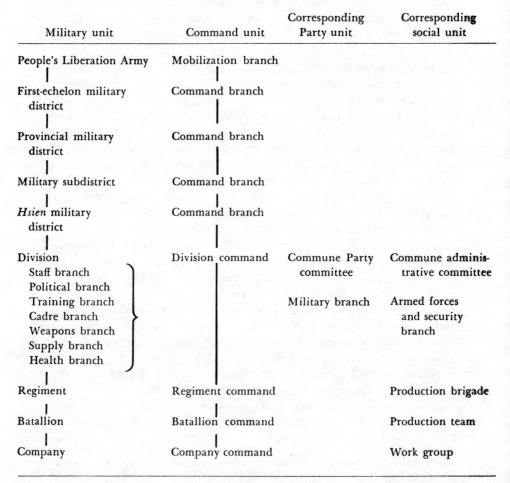

Military unit	Command unit	Corresponding Party unit	Corresponding social unit
People's Liberation Army	Mobilization branch		
First-echelon military district	Command branch		
Provincial military district	Command branch		
Military subdistrict	Command branch		
Hsien military district	Command branch		
Division Staff branch Political branch Training branch Cadre branch Weapons branch Supply branch Health branch	Division command	Commune Party committee Military branch	Commune administrative committee Armed forces and security branch
Regiment	Regiment command		Production brigade
Batallion	Batallion command		Production team
Company	Company command		Work group

SOURCE: Furuta Tokio, "Jimmin kōsha no soshiki to unyō," in *Chūgoku jimmin kōsha no soshiki to kinō* (Tokyo, 1961), p. 113.

The Nature of Commune Organization

What was the commune as social organization? Since communes differed widely from area to area, it is difficult to point to a single "ideal type." Nevertheless, general organizational policy was uniform throughout the country. In some instances, the amalgamated APC's were totally transformed along the new lines. In other cases, amalgamation meant little more than the creation of a new overarching administrative framework over the discrete APC's. The official literature of the period singled out the advanced communes as models for others to follow.

But no matter how radical the reorganization, the communes did not represent a completely new creation. There was an existing social organization with which the cadres had to reckon. In fact, there are indications that the regime was concerned over the tendency of the local cadres to move too fast and too radically in transforming existing social organization. The communiqué of the Central Committee on the establishment of communes which was issued on August 29 but not published until September 10,[124] is a surprisingly cautious document full of advice not to do this and that. The communiqué warns the cadres not to go too far in tampering with existing organization and not to jeopardize agricultural production, as is evident in the following paragraph: "One must combine the amalgamation of large APC's into communes with existing production [conditions]. Not only must it not adversely affect existing production, but this movement must be made into a great force to bring about an even greater leap forward in production. Therefore, in the early period of amalgamating APC's it is well to adopt the policy of 'moving at the top but not at the bottom.' "[125]

It is apparent that the leadership was already worried over the radicalism of the communization movement. The fall harvest was impending, and the leadership was not willing to risk jeopardizing what promised to be another bumper crop. The policy of "moving at the top and not at the bottom" meant that the cadres must not go too far in disturbing existing social organization. Better to move radically at the commune level and more carefully at the village level. The August-

---

[124] The commune movement must have aroused considerable misgivings among many members of the Central Committee, as indicated by the length of the sessions and by the cautious nature of the communiqué. The quick retreat beaten only a few months later indicates that the "conservatives" scored a point, although the radicals were still in firm control of policy.

[125] *Hsinhua panyüeh-k'an,* 18 (1958), 2.

29 communiqué made clear that the communes must take as their nuclear elements the preexisting APC's.

At that time references appeared to the "three-level system of organization in the communes." The three-level system meant that each commune consisted of a number of large production brigades which in turn consisted of a number of small production brigades (later called "teams").[126] Although the official literature always speaks in terms of brigades and never of villages, it is apparent that, even in the early days of communization, these organizational units bore some relationship to real social entities. The official literature indicated that the large production brigades as a whole corresponded to "the original small APC's," and the small production brigades corresponded to "the original production brigades." [127] However, we know that most of the so-called small APC's (the original higher-stage APC's) were identical with larger natural villages or groupings of contiguous small natural villages; the former production brigades were equivalent to the early-stage APC's, that is, small villages, or sections of larger villages. The phrase "three levels of organization" was not often used during the early days of communization, but came to be used more frequently as conservative tendencies set in. Since the phrase came later to be associated with conservative rather than radical policies towards the communes, we may infer that its appearance in the August 29 communique already reflected concern that communization may have gone too far. The use of the phrase, as well as the references to the APC's, indicates that the new commune organization was to be based on real social entities rather than on artificial ones.

Communization, however, aimed at something broader than the creation of a larger administrative framework for the APC's. As we have said, communization was meant to revolutionize the entire conception of agricultural work. Mobilization was to become a permanent part of village life. The degree of permanent mobilization differed from village to village, but the essence of commune organization was mobilization.

What did permanent mobilization mean? The following description of a commune in remote Chinghai Province describes mobilization in one multinational commune:

The Red Flag people's commune [of Lotu *hsien* in Chinghai Province] was formed out of seven APC's. . . . Now it has 524 households and 3,003 individuals. Among them there are 408 Han households, or 2,494 individuals, 113

---

126 *Ibid.*, p. 19, 85.
127 *Ibid.*, p. 103.

households of local peoples or 500 individuals, and three households of Tibetans with nine individuals. There are 12,000 *mou* of land consisting of 700 *mou* of high mountain land, 4,400 *mou* of mountain stream land, and 6,900 *mou* of shallow mountain dry lands. Each laborer on the average was able to take responsibility over twelve *mou* of land; there were somewhat over a thousand workers, male and female. In addition there were 3,000 head of sheep, some fifty fruit trees (apricot, *shakuo*, pear). Geographically, there are stream areas, stream lands. From east to west the commune covers more than thirty *li*. . . .

Before the commune was established, the seven APC's had an average of twenty-thirty households. The largest hardly numbered a hundred. The population was scattered, and there was a shortage of labor. Though irrigation was practiced, land was leveled, schools and factories were set up—all was difficult. The land was fragmented into small parcels. It was impossible to use machinery to till the land, nor was it possible to use large implements. The local people who lived in the mountain regions subsisted on millet and were never able to eat wheat. The Han people living in the stream regions found it difficult to consume milk. As long as production materials such as forests, fruit trees, houses, sheep, small plots of land were still under private ownership, it was impossible to carry out unified planning and unified use, something which affected the development of production and construction. Private ownership of these production materials and small collectivity ownership (the small APC's) came into contradiction with productive forces which since the Great Leap Forward have demanded rapid development. The setting up of a people's commune was the best way of resolving these contradictions.

The Red Flag Commune can prove this point. Since the commune was established, within the short space of one month, there came about a great change. Through the unified allocation of the work force, when wheat was being harvested in the stream areas, more than 200 people were recruited from among the local hill people to assist. Work which before took twenty days to do was accomplished in five days. Now when the millet ripens in the hills, the commune members in the stream areas take their tents to the hills.

Recently several specialized brigades have been set up which operate industry, agriculture, and supplemental enterprises, and work with a division of labor. Since the forests now belong to the commune, the lumber problem for building a wood track railroad has been resolved. Recently iron and coal ore have been found in the hills, making it possible for the commune to smelt iron. The iron foundries, wine-making plants, medicine-processing shops, red-and-expert school, after-hours middle school, clinic, maternity room, nursery, mess hall, barber shop, sewing teams which have been set up by the commune—all are unifiedly run by the commune.[128]

The Red Flag Commune of Lotu *hsien* was different from the usual Chinese commune. Since Chinghai province has a large minority population, the commune was ethnically mixed, in contrast to the popula-

---

[128] *Jenmin jihpao*, September 13, 1958.

tion of the usual commune solidly Han. The settlement patterns in Lotu *hsien* were typical of areas of ethnically mixed habitation in China. The Han peoples occupied the lowlands adjacent to the streams; the aboriginal peoples lived in the hills. Traditionally, the different races did not mix. Though there always were exchange relationships between them, social organization never united Han and non-Han. The original APC's in Lotu *hsien* had been set up along ethnic lines. But the new commune aimed at uniting something that tradition had kept apart. Thus, Chinese were sent into the hills to help the local people harvest millet, and local people were mobilized to help the Chinese with their wheat harvest.

The Red Flag Commune provides an example of what communes throughout China tried to do, namely to break through the barriers of traditional and territorial limitations—break through from the village to the *hsiang* to the *hsien* and link up with the larger world. Here in Chinghai not only territorial limits were broken through but traditional ethnic boundaries.

The introduction of new work organization made another fateful step inevitable: the collectivization of private holdings. Whatever the peasant retained to maintain his private social and economic identity was now handed over to the commune. Throughout China one reads of mass meetings in which the peasants "handed over their private property." In the Lotu *hsien* Red Flag People's Commune, it was reported:

One day when small brigade No. 12 in this commune held a meeting, the commune members registered their orchards, houses, sheep, household chairs, tables, boards, benches, pots, and stoves, together with their production materials and subsistence materials, and wholeheartedly handed them over to the commune. We asked some commune members: now that you have given all these subsistence goods to the commune, how shall you later be able to buy such goods as radios, watches, and the like? If you can, will they be considered the commune's? They didn't hesitate to answer: whatever belongs to the commune and whatever belongs to private individuals must be considered from the point of view of whether it is useful to the development of production.

The picture described for the Red Flag People's Commune in Lotu *hsien* was repeated thousands of times throughout China. In the fever heat of communization, the cadres pressed for the collectivization of almost all private property. Indeed, it was often largely due to restraining admonitions from higher echelons that some concessions were made toward private property. But even though the leadership shrank from total collectivization and announced that some possessions should remain in private hands, the damage had been done. As in the Soviet

Union, it had been the private lands and animals that produced a disproportionately large share of farm produce, particularly in the category of what the Chinese call "supplemental food items": vegetables, meats, edible oils, and so on. So much labor had been mobilized into production battalions that little labor and time were left for "supplemental food production."

SOCIAL ORGANIZATION OF A PEOPLE'S COMMUNE (1958)

Commune = Administrative village *(hsiang)*

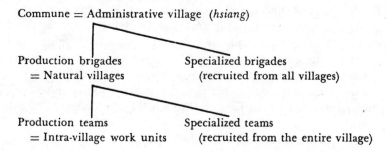

Production brigades   Specialized brigades
  = Natural villages   (recruited from all villages)

Production teams   Specialized teams
  = Intra-village work units (recruited from the entire village)

Amalgamation of State and Society

In addition to the revolution in the organization of work, there was another revolutionary development: an attempt to amalgamate state and society. Throughout China, most communes not only became coextensive with the *hsiang,* but merged with the *hsiang.* Social organization in the form of the commune merged with political organization in the form of the *hsiang.* This was hailed at all levels as the first step toward communism, toward the narrowing of the gap between state and society. Communes originally were of different dimensions, but in time they became equivalent to the *hsiang*—either the old *hsiang* or new ones created along the framework of the communes. The August-29 communiqué of the Central Committee spelled out the new policy:

As far as the organizational dimensions of the communes are concerned, it can be said that at present as a whole it is suitable to have one *hsiang* equal to one commune, with about 2,000 households. The limits of some *hsiang* are rather broad and the population is relatively small; in this case there may be fewer than 2,000 households, and one *hsiang* may have several communes. In some areas, depending on natural conditions and the needs of production development, several *hsiang* may be combined into one *hsiang,* and a single commune set up, with six or seven thousand households. As far as communes with ten or twenty thousand households are concerned, one should not oppose them, but also at present not encourage them.

The communiqué clearly reveals skepticism about some of the vast communes of the Liaoning type which had been set up, but the new policy was clear: commune administration and *hsiang* government were to merge.

Apparently already during the cooperativization in 1955, some large-scale APC's had been established in which a *de facto* merging of APC administration and *hsiang* government occurred.[129] But these were isolated instances. In the summer of 1958, the merging of commune and *hsiang* became official policy. It is significant, however, that this merging has never been ratified by the National People's Congress. Thus, though commune and *hsiang* are *de facto* identical, for the most part, they have never been made *de jure* identical. The merging was in the spirit of "impending communism," and seemed to be the first step in the final amalgamation of state and society. State and society had already come closer together through decentralization—so it seemed. Now the gap narrowed even further through the establishment of the communes.

The unification of commune and *hsiang* was facilitated because the Party played the dominant role in administration. Once the *hsiang* Party committee and the commune Party committee were identical, amalgamation of the formal structures became a relatively simple matter. Real power rested with the Party. The Party made the decisions in regard to all major activities of the *hsiang* and the commune. Administrative work and production work were combined into a single activity, just as administrative cadres were sent down to the production lines. What this meant concretely is described in the following words:

(1) After the unification of administration and commune, *hsiang* government, which had been a simple administrative structure, was transformed into a unit of economic accounting, which held supreme economic authority over *hsiang* production, finances, allocation, distribution of materials, and allocation of labor. . . . (2) Since *hsiang* government was at the same time the administrative structure for the commune . . . it no longer was necessary to go through the various scattered small APC's indirectly to carry out work. . . . Thus for example, the task of tax collection which in the past cost so much effort, the purchase of agricultural goods (*i.e.*, state deliveries), the repayment of loans and other financial tasks could be carried out by cadres who unifiedly administered the financial work of *hsiang* and commune; under the unified leadership of *hsiang* and commune, this could be arranged quickly according to the income and expenditure conditions of the commune. . . . (3) After the unification of administration and commune, organizational structures were simplified. The number of nonworking cadres in the entire

---

129 *Hsinhua panyüeh-k'an*, 19 (1958), 104.

hsiang was reduced by twenty men. . . . (4) The broad majority of cadres and masses experienced a great increase in the ideology of collectivism; it was possible now to consider the interests of the people in the entire *hsiang*.[130]

One of the most important changes resulting from the merging of *hsiang* and commune was the emergence of *hsiang* government as a unit of economic accounting. It was no longer a government agency operating with a budget, but a unit of production operating with its own funds. As a production unit, it enjoyed greater operational autonomy from higher-echelon administration than it did as a government agency.

ADMINISTRATIVE ORGANIZATION OF A PEOPLE'S COMMUNE
(1958)

Top level: Commune Administrative Committee=
              Hsiang People's Committee[a]

Middle level: Administrative areas=   ← Factories   Specialized shops
              Large production brigades[b]

Basic level: Small production brigades[c]   ← Factories   Specialized brigades

[a]Office	[b]Tractor brigades
Agriculture branch	Purchase-sales sub-branches
Water works branch	Credit sub-branches
Planning branch	Post offices
Animal husbandry branch	Clinics
Industry-communications branch	
Public security and armed forces branch	[c]Dining halls
Finance and food branch	Stores
Credit branch	Credit offices
Purchase-sales branch	Servicing stations
Culture and education branch	Health stations
Civil administration branch	Maternity stations
Livelihood and welfare branch	
Planning committee	
Science and research committee	

SOURCE: Furuta Tokio, "Jimmin kōsha no soshiki to unyō," in *Chūgoku jimmin kōsha no soshiki to kinō*, (Tokyo, 1961), p. 98.

---

[130] *Ibid.*, pp. 104-105.

In the light of our discussion earlier in this chapter, it must also be noted that the attempted amalgamation of state and society was, in effect, a leveling of the differences between natural and administrative villages. The administrative village, *hsiang,* had been transformed from a purely political unit into a socioeconomic unit, the commune. As such, it was to supersede the earlier socioeconomic unit, the natural village.

It is fitting that we end our discussion of communization with re-marks on the amalgamation of state and society. The withering away of the state has been an old Marxist dream. For a few brief months in the summer of 1958, the Chinese Communists thought that they could achieve this. Ever since late 1957, they had been dismantling bureaucratic structures and turning administrative powers over to the Party. This process reached its extreme in the communes where Party committees literally displaced the state administration. Some, at that time, envisaged the whole society being administered by the Party alone. Party-led production units, both in cities and in villages, would administer themselves, subject only to general policy and discipline from the leaders in Peking.

Great social revolutions may be inspired from above, but the energy comes from below. The utopian dream of escaping from a peasant ex-istence came from the local cadres, and probably was shared by a large segment of the peasantry itself.[131] As we indicated in our Prologue, one of the traditional enemies of the peasant was the official. It is not im-possible that the utopian ideal of the withering away of the state, so widely talked about for a short period of time in the summer of 1958, may have released the revolutionary energies of the peasant once again. It is significant that the August-1958 communiqué already revealed concern on the part of the leaders that the movement may have gone too far. The first retreat came only a few months later, in December.

The Retreat

The great assault on agricultural production lasted only to the end of 1958. From November 28 to December 10, 1958, the Central Committee held its Sixth Plenum on the Wuchang side of the triple city of Wuhan. The communiqué issued marked the first step in the retreat from the extremes of the summer before. It called for modera-

---

131 See Richard Crossman, "The Chinese Communes," *New Statesman* (London), January 10, 1959, pp. 34-35; see also, Anna Louise Strong, *The Rise of the Chinese People's Communes, and Six Years After* (Peking, 1964), pp. 220-221.

STAGES IN RURAL COMMUNIZATION

Period	Aims	Units of operation
Spring 1958 - July 1958	Amalgamation of APC's	Administrative village (*hsiang*)
July 1958 - November 1958	Militarization of the peasantry Formation of the communes	Administrative village (*hsiang*)
November 1958 - August 1959	Consolidation around the production brigade	Natural village (*ts'un*)
August 1959 - Summer 1960	Renewed production drive through mobilization	Natural village (*ts'un*)
Summer 1960 - Spring 1961	Final retreat; decentralization to the production team	Intra-village work

SOURCES: Philip P. Jones and Thomas T. Poleman, "Communes and the Agricultural Crisis in Communist China," *Food Research Institute Studies*, III:1 (February, 1962), 1-22; Peter S. H. Tang, *The Commune System in Mainland China* (Washington, D. C., 1961), pp. 18-26.

tion and consolidation in implementing communization. During the spring and summer of 1959, repeated reference was made to the "three-level system of ownership" in the communes (see p. 484). These references indicated, as we can now say in retrospect, that Peking was increasingly adopting a policy of retreat from the extremes of commune centralization during the summer of 1958. The Seventh Plenum, held April 1959 in Shanghai, discussed the communes but did not issue any definitive policy statement. The communiqué of the Eighth Plenum, held in Lushan from August 2 to 16, 1959, made the now famous admission of the exaggeration of the 1958 crop figures. It also made clear that the basic unit of ownership in the communes was the brigade, that is, the second of the three levels of ownership. Though the Eighth Plenum was followed by a partial return to the mobilizational policies of 1958, by the summer of 1960 it became clear that Peking was continuing its retreat. On November 20 and 25, 1960, the *Jenmin jihpao* published two major policy editorials on the communes, which, in effect, made the team (that is, the third or the smallest of the three levels) the *de facto* unit of ownership. Although the editorial made clear that the legal ownership rights remained within the brigade, it differentiated between rights of ownership and rights of use. The team was given full rights of use over labor, land, animals, tools, and equipment. It was formally made the basic-level unit of accounting in the commune. In January 1961, the communiqué of the Ninth Plenum of the Central Committee announced a far-reaching reversal of economic policy which ended the Great Leap Forward and inaugurated a period of economic consolidation and liberalization.[132]

Retreat would thus appear to have begun in December 1958, only a few months after the communes were launched. However, in view of the cautious notes already evident in the Peitaiho communiqué of late August, one might even suggest that the retreat started at the very time that communization was launched. By the summer of 1959, Peking, for all practical purposes, had gone back to the old higher-stage APC's which were the same as the large production brigades of the communes. By autumn 1960, it had retreated even further. Since the small production brigades or teams were the equivalent of the early-stage APC's, that is, parts of the natural village, Peking had even abandoned the idea of an operationally unified natural village. Of course, the all-village collective economy was still directed at the brigade level. However, the teams, though they were required to contribute labor to the collective economy, had full rights of disposition over ways to do so.

Liberalization set in in force after the great policy reversal of early 1961. On the one hand organizational pressure on the peasant was reduced—for example, by expanding the free market. On the other hand, both heavy and light industry were reoriented to fulfilling some of the consumer needs of the peasant. Peking, at that time, abandoned its policy of social mobilization on the land and tried a campaign of selective capital investment in agriculture. Since then, the food situation has gradually improved until, at present, most food items appear to be plentifully available in the cities. Peasant income has apparently risen, and peasant life, particularly in the vicinity of the great urban and industrial areas, has improved. The main beneficiaries of the new land policy have been the more productive peasants, just as the professionals have gained from the new policy toward industry. Rich peasants are appearing again, which suggests that "kulakization" may be endemic to an imperfectly collectivized rural economy such as that of China.

---

[132] See Philip P. Jones and Thomas T. Poleman, "Communes and the Agricultural Crisis in Communist China," *Food Research Institute Studies* III:1 (February 1962), 1-21; H. F. Schurmann, "The Communes: A One-Year Balance Sheet," *Problems of Communism*, VIII:5 (September-October 1959), 7-14; and "Peking's Recognition of Crisis," X:5 (September-October 1965), 5-14.

NUMBER AND POPULATION OF RURAL PEOPLE'S COMMUNES

Period	Number of communes	Peasant population in communes (million households)	Percentage of total peasant population	Average number of households per commune
August 1958 (end)	8,730	37.78	30.4	4,328
September 1958 (early)	12,824	59.79	48.1	4,662
September 1958 (middle)	16,989	81.22	65.3	4,781
September 1958 (end)	26,425	121.94	98.0	4,614
December 1958 (end)	26,578	123.25	99.1	4,637
1959	24,000			5,000
Since 1960-61	more than 70,000			(less than 2,000)

SOURCES: *Weita ti shih-nien* (Peking, 1959), p. 36. For the 1959 figure. See *1960-nen no Chūkyō* [*Communist China in 1960*], (Tokyo, 1960), p. 209. The 1960-61 figure was revealed by Liao Lu-yen, Minister of Agriculture, in an article entitled "Acerca de la colectivización de la agricultura en China," *Cuba Socialista* (October, 1963), p. 41.

Yet the ebb and flow of policy continues, and so one sees today an intensification of political and ideological pressures. Since the late summer of 1962, a new socialist education movement (the first, it will be recalled, was launched in August 1957 as a part of the anti-rightist campaign) has been in progress. It differs from the earlier campaign in that the movement is not marked by peaks of political intensity. It has now been going on for three years with a steady drumfire of ideological indoctrination. There have been the expected attacks on "capitalistic vestiges," which is to say attacks on the wealthier and more individualistic peasants. But, so far, "socialist education" has not been followed by concrete action. As in so many other areas of life in China, a gap between ideology and organization has been developing.

In the face of this new situation, what is the state of social organization on the land? It is now certain that Peking has given up its attempts to create a rural economy transcending the limits of the natural village. The peasant may still be called on to do labor outside of his village, but it is usually for emergency tasks, such as flood control. For the most part, he works within the confines of his village, as he always has done. The real social unit appears to be a small team of twenty or thirty households who live close to each other; given the nature of Chinese villages, they may be related to each other by kinship. Though the team must contribute to the collective economy of the village, it devotes a considerable part of its labor to the raising of "supplemental crops." What is left of the peasant's time is given to his private holdings which, as in Russia, constitute an important part of the rural economy. The state pays better prices for farm output, thus increasing the income of the peasant. A portion of the collective output is left to the peasants to be disposed of on the now legal open market. Peasants who live close to cities bring in their produce and sell it individually to urban consumers. The official literature indicates that "old peasants" have again assumed leadership in the villages. The "old peasants" are not the young Party cadres who led the Great Leap Forward. Some are probably new rich peasants; others are probably peasants who enjoy local prestige for traditional reasons.[133]

The popular militia remains, and is important for maintaining public order; in the exposed coastal regions, it has been a major instrument for capturing subversives landed from abroad. The young cadres have an unchallenged part to play in the popular militia. Party cadres continue to exercise power and influence at commune and village administrative levels, though, under the new policy, they have been instructed not to lead or dominate the work life of the peasant. The communes remain as an administrative framework—not surprising since they are the latter-day version of the earlier *hsiang* administration. If the *hsiang* is indeed the equivalent of a standard marketing area, as G. William Skinner has suggested (see p. 441), then the commune has an important role to play in rural trading. The communes continue to operate some of the small industries that are still functioning. And, most important, the commune directs disaster relief and emergency work. The natural village has come into its own again; it is the unit of the collective economy. Party cadres still sit in the committee of the production brigade, but they may no longer impose plans from above. Procurement plans for farm products are worked out as a compromise between the state's demands and the peasant's capabilities. The state persuades rather than commands the peasants to raise crops which the state needs.

The Commune in Historical Perspective

Earlier in this chapter, we suggested that traditionally the state had two main interests in regard to the village: exploitation and con-

---

133 John Wilson Lewis, "The Leadership Doctrine of the Chinese Communist Party: The Lesson of the People's Commune," *Asian Survey*, III (October 1963), 457-464.

trol. If the state could collect its taxes and if the peasants kept peaceful, Peking hardly cared what went on otherwise. However, to enforce exploitation and control, Peking periodically used its organizational powers to create civil and military organization at the village level. The essentially civil *lichia* and the essentially military *paochia*, of the Ming and Ch'ing dynasties respectively, have been discussed early in this chapter as major historical instances.

However, by Ming and Ch'ing times, the state had realized that village-level military and civil functions could not be combined into a single organization. A thousand years earlier, the state had tried to accomplish such a combination by a militarization of the peasantry. The camp-field system made the soldier into a peasant as well. Under the equal-field system, the village was organized along military lines, even though the peasant did not bear arms. The early T'ang dynasty continued to apply the equal-field system, but paired it with an army-reserve system, known as the *fuping*, in which the peasant was made liable to military duty when the state needed him. Though the state's hope of creating village organization which combined the functions of peasant and soldier ended during the middle of the T'ang, it was temporarily revived during the Sung. Wang An-shih, the dictator of the Northern Sung dynasty, fearing barbarian conquest in the face of a routinized society, first created the *paochia*, which we have discussed in its Ch'ing form. The Sung *paochia* differed from earlier peasant-soldier organizations in that the peasant acquired a dual organizational identity. In his village he remained a peasant, but in the *paochia* he became a soldier. Wang An-shih was in power only a short time, and his *paochia* collapsed with him.

Since that time, the state realized that, organizationally, military and civil functions had to be kept separate. Philosophically, this was traditionally expressed by Confucian teaching on the fundamental differences between *wen*, the civil, and *wu*, the military. During the early Sung, this realization led the state to put its reliance on professional rather than popular armies. Under the impact of the Mongol conquest in the thirteenth century, the trend toward professional armies became even stronger. Both the Ming and the Ch'ing followed this practice. Though the Ch'ing *paochia* had some civil functions, such as aiding in the registration of population, its main purpose was military. It was seen as a local militia to aid the professional military forces maintain law and order. The Kuomintang *paochia* served essentially the same purposes as the Ch'ing *paochia*.

The traditional concern with exploitation and control rested on a basic assumption that peasant society would not or could not change.

Despite lofty pronouncements on the subject of land reform, the Kuomintang basically shared this assumption. The Communists, on the other hand, coming to power through the Chinese Revolution, added a third and new concern to the traditional two. Though their needs for exploitation (to provide savings for industrialization) and control (to assure law and order in the wake of chaos) were even greater than those of their predecessors, their commitment to a fundamental transformation of rural society was absolute. Thus they added change to the other two as a fundamental concern of the Chinese state. Though this concern has deep ideological roots, it also springs from the realization that a traditional agriculture which has exhausted its developmental potentiality cannot meet the increasing needs of a growing modern economy.

The Communists' commitment to change is fundamental for understanding the three stages of China's social revolution on the land which we shall discuss in the next and concluding section of this chapter. Here, we should like to reexamine the communes in the historical perspective sketched out.

Communization constituted a militarization of the peasantry. The Communists believed that the social revolution had so weakened or changed the traditional social organization of the peasantry that a new form of organization, based on military and industrial principles, could be introduced. In this respect, similarities may be noted to the organizational systems of the Six Dynasties period. Then too, China's peasant population, particularly in the North, had experienced severe social breakdown, after foreign and domestic wars. Moreover, the Communists regarded militarization as an instrument of change. They felt that, through militarization, fundamental social transformation so necessary to the technological revolution could be brought about.

The Chinese Communists, at that time, did try to combine the *wen* and the *wu*; they deprofessionalized their modern armies, and set up a people's militia; they tried to make the villager into a peasant-soldier, in a manner reminiscent of a time many centuries earlier.

If the psychological aim of militarization was to transform the peasant into a modern producer, its political aim was to make the village an indissoluble part of the body politic. The commune, as a new socioeconomic unit built on the foundations of an older political-administrative unit, was to become the bridge on which state and society would meet and merge. The Chinese Communists are the first state power in Chinese history convinced that it has the means of managerially directing all of society. What Karl A. Wittfogel attributed to "oriental despotisms," thus has been true only of the modern Communist state, and specifically that of China.

The people's commune could never have come into being without the Party. And the Party, as we have indicated, is a modern organization, unknown before in Chinese history. Its basic ideological orientation is "struggle," that is, a positive commitment to change. The Party arose from the changes in Chinese society brought about by the Chinese Revolution with its roots in the past. But once it existed, it itself became an instrument of change.

However, militarization did not last long, and the communes that remain today are far different from what they were in 1958. The lessons of history appear to indicate that the *wen* and the *wu* cannot be combined. But, if that is the case, it also indicates that the state, even with modern organization, cannot become a true "oriental despotism" with total managerial control over society. The present state in China does more than just exploit and control, but it also does not manage totally. In our chapter on management, we discussed the policy-operations dichotomy. Clearly, the state has absolute control over policy. But just as clearly it does not have absolute control over operations. If it did, it would be a total managerial state. The failure of the communes indicates that Peking is still far from that goal.

REFLECTIONS ON THE SOCIAL REVOLUTION

The social revolution in China's villages consisted of three stages: land reform, cooperativization (or collectivization), and communization. The first destroyed the traditional elite, the official-landlord gentry, and gave land to the peasant. The second weakened the rich peasants, integrated their property into the APC's, and created an all-village collective economy based on the natural village. The third tried fundamentally to transform the traditional work organization of the peasantry; it aimed primarily at the poor peasant. In the light of the preceding discussion, one may ask: what have been the lasting effects of these three stages of the social revolution?

The land reform scored the most decisive success of the three. Despite occasional references to "landlord remnants," the gentry has disappeared from the rural life of China. As we pointed out in the Prologue, its economic power was based on land ownership, its political power was based on its relationships to the state bureaucracy, and its social power was based on its traditional status. All three sources of power have vanished. The Party has replaced the gentry as the dominant elite in the rural regions.

Cooperativization has taken roots in the Chinese village. Though rich peasants continue to exist, they cannot recreate what had been the basis of their earlier power, namely ownership of property. All village land remains under collective ownership, which means ownership by the production brigade. Moreover, collective ownership continues to have concrete form in the all-village collective economy. Nevertheless, the fact that the production teams have basic rights of usage over land gives the rich peasant an opening for acquiring *de facto* control over portions of land greater than that officially allotted to him. The production brigade now appears to be an arena where Party cadres, loyal to the state, and "old peasants" (most likely, rich and wealthy middle peasants), loyal to village interests, struggle with each other. The present-day procurement plan for the village, for example, may be regarded as a continuing product of compromise in this basic conflict.

To use a Chinese Communist term, we might say that the second stage of the social revolution was "basically successful." "Basic" means "not quite." It is this "basic success" that is manifested by the fact that the present stage of village social organization appears to be at the point of the early-stage APC's, a stage that had advanced beyond land reform but had not yet reached full collectivization.

The third stage or communization would seem to have been unsuccessful. There is little evidence that the fundamental work organization of the peasantry as a whole has changed. Rather, all evidence indicates that the demilitarization of the villages was followed by a return to traditional work patterns. Since the essence of the commune was military-industrial organization (see p. 467), the abandonment of that type of organization must be regarded as equivalent to the abandonment of the commune system. The fact that the commune remains as an administrative unit testifies to the failure rather than to the success of communization. Moreover, since the militarization of work hardly lasted beyond the winter of 1958, the revolution in work organization could not have been very thorough. This even suggests that the communes were phantasms rather than real things.

The fact that Peking has now proceeded to use purely "educational" approaches toward the peasant, particularly the poor peasant, might indicate that communization must be viewed as a spiritual rather than a material revolution. Perhaps the shock effect of communization was necessary to tear the peasant from his traditional spiritual isolation in the villages. In a world where new nations are clamoring for the transformation of agriculture, it is sometimes overlooked that to make the traditional peasant into a modern farmer, he must be spiritually as well as materially liberated from the conditions that have bound him to the soil.

If this is true, Peking, through communization, may have created a spiritual infrastructure whose material payoff in the form of a technological revolution in agriculture will not come for years and even decades.

There can be no further phase to the social revolution. The three phases, each of which was aimed at one of the key social groups on the land (landlords, rich peasants, and poor peasants), have exhausted their revolutionary targets. The only revolution that can now follow is the economic revolution which will transform the technological basis of agriculture. However, as we have indicated in the Prologue, economic revolutions take time; they cannot be imposed at one blow.

STAGES IN THE SOCIAL REVOLUTION ON THE LAND

POLICY		AIMS	TARGETS
Land reform		Elimination of landlords Distribution of land	Landlords
Cooperativization	Early stage	Elimination of rich peasants Consolidation of land	Rich peasants
	Higher stage	Collectivization of property Creation of an Integrated Village Economy	
Communization		Mobilization of the peasantry Transformation of work organization	Poor peasants

The thread that goes through this book is the theme of contradictions. Fundamental contradictions remain in the Chinese village, as they do in all of Chinese society. Though some of these contradictions have existed in Chinese society for a long time, others have arisen in the wake of the social revolution, before and after 1949. It is these old and new contradictions that make Communist China into a polylithic structure where power has gradually diffused to different parts of the organization. As institutionalization inevitably sets in, Communist China may be making the transition from organization to system. Though the ideology proclaims that the revolution has not yet ended, that China has not yet been fully constituted as a nation, and though the economic revolution has only begun, the final phase of the social revolution may have opened the door to institutionalization.

At the beginning of the Prologue, we said that the Chinese Revolution is for the latter half of the twentieth century what the Russian Revolution was for the first half. Russia only emerged as the great rival of the United States after World War II, having gone through three decades of political-social organization and technical-economic development. What we have attempted to describe in this book is a comparable process of political-social organization in China; the story of its technical-economic development must be told by the economists.

China has experienced the acts of political and social revolution before it has fully entered the process of economic revolution. It is fitting that our last chapter deals with the peasantry and agriculture, for their economic and technological transformation remains the supreme challenge facing the leaders of China in the coming years. Earlier committed to the policy of social mobilization to bring about that transformation, the leaders of China seem now to realize that economic revolution can only be accomplished by economic means. If they succeed, they will have shown that the world's largest underdeveloped country, bearing the burden of a massive peasantry and a primitive agriculture, can achieve what hitherto has only been achieved by the Western countries and that one remarkable exception in the ranks of the non-Western countries, Japan.

Though technically and economically China has a long way to go before it can rival Russia or the United States, politically and socially it has achieved a unity and undergone a transformation which are the foundations of its further technical and economic development. When its economic power will finally have matched its political power, it will inevitably become the dominant power in Eastern Asia.

SUPPLEMENT

INTRODUCTION

THIS supplement covers ideology, organization, and society in China from 1961 to 1967; the first edition covered essentially the 1950's. Although the period from 1961 to 1967 is divided by the beginning of the Cultural Revolution in May 1966, I have discussed it as a continuum. The currents which erupted during the Cultural Revolution have their origins in the early 1960's. Since these currents, however, only became clear during the Cultural Revolution, the discussion will often refer forward to elucidate a point for an earlier time.

Periodization invites naming. Although I have no hesitation in calling the second period the Cultural Revolution, the first period is more difficult to characterize. Those Western observers who have seen the Cultural Revolution as an assault on the pragmatism followed since 1961 would readily call it the period of pragmatism. But I am not prepared to do so. True, the period began dramatically in January 1961 with a resort to pragmatic policies in society and economy. However, by the summer of 1962, a new theme emerged: the rebuilding of Party organization, control, and discipline. That theme, and not the one of pragmatism I regard as the chief characteristic of the period between 1962 and 1966. As is clear now, throughout the entire period from 1961 to 1966, a great ideological and political struggle was waged at the highest levels of power. Since that struggle surfaced during the Cultural Revolution, we now know much about it. Had there been no

Cultural Revolution, that struggle probably would have gone un-
noticed, except as another of the contradictions inherent in Chinese
state and society.

This supplement consists of three parts: (1) ideology, (2) organization, and (3) society. They correspond, respectively, to Chapter I,
Chapters II-V, and Chapters VI-VII. I have generally made use of the
same analytical tools as in the body of the book but there are differences in emphasis. Ideology and Party remain prominent in the period
1961-1967, but the prominence of army and government is reversed. In
the 1950's, the army was basically segregated from society in China,
and hence a detailed study of the army was not necessary to explain
the workings of organization. Conversely, the relationship of government to society was important. In the 1960's, the army has become an
integral part of society, whereas government's relationship to society
has become quietly administrative. So I say much about the army, but
little about government. The part on society discusses mainly the intellectuals, and specifically the role of the students in the Cultural
Revolution. Perhaps if I had done more research, I could have expanded my comments on workers and peasants. Yet the official material is singularly barren on both, and not enough interview material
is available to sketch an adequate picture of developments within these
two classes. Despite this, evidence indicates that the forces of Chinese
society are equally as important as those coming from the structure of
state power. I do not believe that this indicates a resurgence of the old
social system, but rather that China's major social classes (workers,
peasants, intellectuals) exert great pressure on the ideology and organization which direct that country. If revolution makes ideology and organization necessary to refashion society, the passage of time leads to a
resurrection of the forces of society. Thus, for example, in the Cultural
Revolution, I believe that, no matter how much the students were
guided from above, they basically expressed forces deriving from their
own social class. That Mao knew how to use such forces testifies to his
intelligence as a political leader.

If I were to give the book a new title today, I would call it *Ideology,
Organization, and Society in China*. The original title testifies to the
weight I assigned ideology and organization, and to China's Communist character. However, due weight must now be given to the resurgence of the forces of Chinese society. The adjective "Communist" must
also be dropped. This does not mean that China has ceased to be Communist, but that its communism has undergone a major transformation as the result of the Cultural Revolution. As is evident in the dis-

cussion, the conflict between the Soviet and Chinese conceptions of ideology and organization is so basic that we can no longer easily regard both simply as "Communist.' But that is only one reason for dropping the adjective Communist. China is today more its national self than ever before in the history of the People's Republic. In its stance it is proudly nationalistic, and in its internal constitution its Chinese character is more than ever evident.

But as it has become more Chinese, China has also become more remote from the world. It stands as a proud lonely giant indifferent to what the remainder of the world thinks of it. Its leaders strongly identify with the revolutionary poor throughout the world, and with all young people. But lines of communication have broken down. Thus the Cultural Revolution has appeared to most people in the world, including third-world radicals, as a strange Chinese theater of the absurd. It can be understood, but no one in China has done much to help friendly outsiders understand it. In Eastern Europe, many fear China as a new Stalinist power. Though nothing could be more different than Mao's beliefs in "daring to rebel" and Stalin's obsession with control, there are some similarities between Stalin's Russia and Mao's China. In the 1930's Russia withdrew into itself with a deified leader at its helm. Like China today, Russia awaited an "almost inevitable war," as Ch'en Yi puts it in regard to China's present fear of American attack.

Yet for all her remoteness, China, in my mind, is a country that has experimented on a broader and deeper scale with the problems of modernization and industrialization than any other country in the world. Even if the Chinese themselves will not explain it, China, with all its successes and failures, its good and evil, remains a model which the world could well study.

CHAPTER I

IDEOLOGY

THE drama of China in the years since the end of the Great Leap Forward has been ideological and political, not social or economic. The currents in society and economy have been slow and deep compared to the frenzy in ideology and politics. When the Ninth Plenum of January 1961 loosened ideological and political controls on the social and economic behavior of the people in order to stimulate recovery from the great crisis, it initiated a growing separation of state and society. Ideology and politics, being in the realm of the state, took on an autocephalous character. Unlike in earlier years, one cannot find evident linkages between ideological-political policies and concrete socioeconomic problems. In fact, in the 1960's, it is hard to find any socioeconomic policies introduced by the leadership comparable to those of the 1950's. New socioeconomic policies in the past were always preceded by major institutional changes. In the 1960's, there were few such changes, and those which did occur were not of great moment. One great exception is the field of education, where the Cultural Revolution struck particularly hard and brought about major changes. But education, more than any other activity in society, is intimately related to ideology, and, given the higher schools' cadre-training functions, equally related to politics. As ideology and politics became more removed from concrete socioeconomic concerns, the great struggles took on the quality of a storm, feeding on itself, finally turning into the hurricane of the Great Proletarian Cultural Revolution.

The growing gap between state and society inevitably brought about a separation of the pure and practical ideologies. China's leaders no longer prescribed specific work methods, but rather stressed correct individual attitudes. According to *The Thought of Mao Tse-tung*, anything could be accomplished if individuals were inspired by his writings: nuclear bombs detonated, Mt. Everest scaled, a new automobile produced, a bumper harvest achieved. Yet Chairman Mao had nothing to say about the methods used in such successes. In the famous little red book, *The Sayings of Chairman Mao*, there is not a single practical, operational prescription. And so it is not surprising that the technical success of China has used standard international methods, and that the bumper harvest of 1967 has not been attributed to any particular method. Since no modern society can operate without a practical ideology, be it that of a Galbraithian technostructure,[1] it would appear that the growing silence on a specifically Communist practical ideology means that the methods used in China for science, technology, and production have become those of "expertise" — that is, methods used throughout the world to achieve modernization and industrialization. I have already suggested that, during the 1950's, two practical ideologies were in competition (red and expert; see pp. 51-53) , and so the demise of a red practical ideology has left the leadership with no choice but to accept that of the experts.

The practical ideology discussed in the earlier part of this book is closely related to organization. The methods of management and control, of the mass line, of the communes could not have been implemented without the Party. The Party was, in fact, the embodiment of the practical ideology. As is clear now, after the turbulence of the Cultural Revolution has passed, the Party, its organizational structure and nature, and its key people have been the chief victims of the storm. For Chairman Mao and his colleagues, something was so profoundly wrong with the Chinese Communist Party that he had to unleash a *revolution* to transform it from top to bottom. Clearly this meant that the basic work methods of the Party had to be likewise transformed. This can be illustrated in the controversy over the "work teams," *kungtso-tui* (or operations squads, as I preferred to translate the term) which erupted during the Cultural Revolution. The work team was a favorite method of the Party to organize communities. It consisted of a

---

[1]John Kenneth Galbraith, *The New Industrial State* (Boston: Houghton Mifflin Company, 1967) , pp. 60 ff. In Chinese Communist terminology, Galbraith's practical ideology would be one of "expertise"; more specifically, a practical ideology of "white and expert."

small group of cadres who moved into a target community, organized local cadres, educated the population, and, after a suitable period of preparation, launched a new policy. Work teams were widely used during the revolutionary land reform (see p. 433) .[2] Assuming a revolutionary situation, in which the masses were spontaneously ready to bring about social change, the work team introduced organization, control, and centralization into the process. During the Cultural Revolution, Liu Shao-ch'i was violently accused of having used the work-team method in the early summer of 1966 to channel the developing Cultural Revolution in the universities in directions which could be controlled by the Party.[3] Therefore, the work-team method was branded as fundamentally wrong, and rejected for all time. The correct method, according to the Maoists, was to rely on the spontaneity of the masses (on "democracy" rather than "centralism," though the writings of the Cultural Revolution never put it quite in those terms) . In repudiating the work-team method, the "revolutionary rebels," in fact, did away with one of the key devices of the Chinese Communist party's organizational handbook.

The repudiation of the work-team method climaxed an erosion of the Party's practical ideology which had been going on during the early 1960's. There were great conflicts over political methods, evident in the dissension over the correct way to carry out the "socialist education" and "four clean" movements.[4] These conflicts made it impossible for the leadership to agree on operational methods of organization; by contrast, such agreement had always been achieved during the 1950's. The struggles over the practical ideology were only obscurely reflected in the mass media; the documents of the Cultural Revolution have given us some insight into their nature.

------

[2] William Hinton, *Fanshen: A Documentary of Revolution in a Chinese Village* (New York and London: Monthly Review Press, 1966) , pp. 259 ff.

[3] See Gene Hsiao, "The Background and Development of 'The Proletarian Cultural Revolution'," *Asian Survey* VII: 6 (June, 1967) , 401. In his confession, which reached the outside world through Japanese translations of Peking wall posters, Liu dwelt at length on his "errors" in having sent work teams into the universities to bring the Cultural Revolution under control; see *Mainichi Shimbun*, January 28-29, 1967; see also *Asahi Shimbun*, December 27, 1966.

[4] See Richard Baum and Frederick C. Teiwes, Ssu-ch'ing: *The Socialist Education Movement of 1962-1966 (China Research Monographs*, No. 2, Berkeley: Center for Chinese Studies, 1968) ; see also Wang Hsiao-t'ang, "The 'Four Cleans' and the 'Cultural Revolution' of the Chinese Communists," *Feich'ing Yenchiu* [*Studies on Chinese Communism*], I: 1 (Taipei, January, 1967) , 23-31. The issue of the "socialist education" and "Four Clean" movements is so complex that I can only attempt a brief explanation here.

The drama of the 1960's evident in the mass media was in the realm of pure ideology. We can discern two great currents in this drama: (1) the unfolding of China's *Weltanschauung,* particularly as expressed in the polemics with the Soviet Communist party, and (2) the development and final triumph of *The Thought of Mao Tse-tung.* Beginning in the spring of 1960, the Chinese started to issue a growing torrent of documents, written in fine Marxist-Leninist style, analyzing the world political situation, attacking revisionism, and prescribing the proper course for socialist countries to take, both at home and abroad.[5] All

----

The Tenth Plenum, of September 1962, announced a new policy to combat capitalistic tendencies in agriculture. During the early months of 1963, the leadership proceeded cautiously with its program to use the Party machinery to combat these tendencies and strengthen political control on the land. By the summer of 1963, it became public that a "socialist education" movement was underway. The movement was subject to significant vagaries due to disagreements among the leaders about the methods for carrying out the movement. However, the movement gradually gained in intensity, reaching a high point in the autumn of 1964. In January 1965, the movement slowed down. The term "Four Cleans" first appeared in 1963 and designated a campaign to rectify largely economic wrongdoings among the rural cadres. However, as the "socialist education" movement intensified, so did the objectives of the "four cleans" expand: the cleaning now aimed at all kinds of wrongdoing on the part of the cadres.

The vagaries of the movement are marked by key documents which, since the revelations of the Cultural Revolution, have become identified either with the Mao or the Liu forces. The first key document was issued in May 1963 and has since become known as the "former ten points." They have now been officially labeled as pro-Mao (see *Jenmin jihpao,* November 23, 1967—the word "former" has been dropped). Baum and Teiwes regard this document as "optimistic" because of "a more tolerant view of cadre foibles and shortcomings." In September, 1963, a second document, labeled the "later ten points" was issued which now is considered as pro-Liu (*ibid.*). Though Baum and Teiwes also regard it as optimistic, it is noteworthy for its emphasis on the work teams. In September, 1964, a third document was issued which also has been labeled as pro-Liu. Baum and Teiwes regard this as "pessimistic." The fourth and last document was issued in January 1965, the "twenty-three points." It is now considered officially to be pro-Mao; Baum and Teiwes see it as moving ambiguously in an optimistic direction. But, most importantly, after January 1965, criticism of rural cadres was no longer reported in the press.

The conclusion which emerges from a study of these documents is that it was Liu who advocated a tough line toward the rural cadres and Mao who advocated a more tolerant approach.

[5]Most of these documents were published in the *Peking Review.* Many are presented in William E. Griffith, *The Sino-Soviet Rift* (Cambridge, Mass.: The M.I.T. Press, 1964), and in *Diversity in International Communism: A Documentary Record, 1961-1963* (ed. by Alexander Dallin), (New York and London: Columbia University Press, 1963).

documents were issued by the highest circles of the Chinese Communist party. We can call this current "Marxist-Leninist." The second current began in the fall of 1960, when Volume IV of Mao Tse-tung's *Selected Works* was published. The prominent attention given to an article by Lin Piao on the issuance of Volume IV and the convocation of a special ideological meeting of the Military Affairs Committee of the Central Committee under Lin Piao's direction indicates that the source of this second current was the army. Subsequently it became increasingly clear that the chief proponent of the campaign to study *The Thought of Mao Tse-tung* was the army. This became evident when the first copies of the famous red book, *The Sayings of Chairman Mao,* were published under the auspices of the General Political Department of the People's Liberation Army. We can call this current "Maoist."[6]

These two ideological currents are related to the struggle between the Party and the army, which reached a climax with the Cultural Revolution. One of the key issues in that struggle was who should exercize command over policy and operations: Chairman Mao or the collective body of high-ranking Party leaders. In his rare articles, Lin Piao never failed to point out that all successes of war, revolution, and construction were due to the personal command of Chairman Mao.[7] The Cultural Revolution not only launched a great campaign to study the works of Chairman Mao, but made it clear that it was Mao who exercized direct command over all policy and operations in China. The constant publication of pictures of Chairman Mao, particularly on the covers of *Red Flag* and the first page of the *People's Daily* served to drive that point home. Mao was henceforth always referred to as chairman and not as comrade, as had been done earlier. Thus the Maoist current can be seen as an expression of a political force seeking to restore Mao Tse-tung to direct and personal command of the country.

First one might note that the Marxist-Leninist current dealt almost entirely with the *Weltanschauung*. It began with a glorification of Lenin, and, already in the summer of 1960, was characterized by the publication, in many languages, of key works of Lenin. The term Marxism-Leninism was widely and prominently used, and, as the Sino-Soviet split worsened, the Chinese began to refer to themselves and

---

[6]The Chinese still do not use the term "Maoism," whereas it has been adopted by the Soviets (see "Party," note 1).

[7]As early as the fall of 1959, Lin Piao, listing a series of basic economic and military policies, said "there is not one which has not been the result of Comrade Mao Tse-tung's direct leadership." *Hungch'i* 19 (October, 1959), 24.

those parties who sympathized with them as "true Marxist-Leninist." The Maoist current dealt mostly with the question of thought *(szuh-siang)*, and specifically the thought of Chairman Mao. Significantly, this current also began with the publication of classics, namely Volume IV of Chairman Mao's works. Comments on the world situation were much rarer in this current (except for the increasingly bitter attacks on the "revisionist decadence" of the Soviet Union). Conversely the stress was on the spiritual importance of *The Thought of Mao Tse-tung* in bringing about correct attitudes in individuals. The *Sayings* eventually became the quintessence of this current: a set of maxims for each individual to learn all aspects of being a revolutionary. The writings of the Maoist current were not particularly theoretical, generally written in simple language, exhortative rather than argumentative. The Red Guard publications further developed this current in the form of news tabloids, often written in the style of the *New York Daily News,* devoid of Marxist-Leninist language, and colloquially Chinese in tone. The Marxist-Leninist current, by contrast, set new standards for international Marxist prose, and was widely admired in the international Marxist world, even by those who disagreed with the Chinese position.

The struggle between theory and thought ended with the triumph of thought. Today there are still references to Marxism-Leninism in the Chinese literature, but overwhelmingly it is Mao and his writings that are quoted, though occasionally references are made to Marx, Engels, Lenin, and Stalin. A clear reversal has taken place in the counterpoint of the two themes of *The Thought of Mao Tse-tung* and Marxism-Leninism. Before the Cultural Revolution, *The Thought of Mao Tse-tung* always followed Marxism-Leninism as a derivative system (see pp. 26-27); subsequently it became the dominant theme, with Marxism-Leninism remaining as a distant echo. Yet, despite the remarkable disappearance of the language of Marxism-Leninism, nothing in the literature has suggested a turning against this tradition. Marxism-Leninism remains a subordinate theme, but one which, under the appropriate circumstances, could again be revived. It was revived in and after the civil war, although the statements of the Seventh Party Congress showed a strong trend toward nationalism, toward the glorification of Chairman Mao, and toward nonideological realism.

Lin Piao, since praised as Chairman Mao's closest comrade in arms, expressed this reversal of themes in his article "Long Live the Victory of the People's War" of September 3, 1965:

The whole series of Comrade Mao Tse-tung's theories (*lilun*) and policies (*chengts'e*) have creatively enriched and developed Marxism- Leninism.[8]

Even more significant is Lin Piao's references to Mao's "theories," which indicates a push toward an even higher plane in the ideological pantheon—one which would not be consummated until the Cultural Revolution. During the Cultural Revolution, Chairman Mao has been proclaimed the true successor to Lenin and Stalin (although no images of the new quinquevirate have yet appeared). His writings, or more specifically his "thought," are stated to be valid for all revolutionaries (evident in the great international campaign to distribute the *Sayings*). Mao has laid down the basic principles, but has himself formulated the key policies which led the Chinese revolution to continuing successes. *The Thought of Mao Tse-tung* propounds both theory and thought, both theory and policy, both theory and practice. It is thus no longer valid to say that theory is pure ideology and thought is practical ideology, for *The Thought of Mao Tse-tung* now subsumes all of them (see p. 23).

Yet if, as I have said above (see p. 507), practical ideology is closely related to organization, then only the appearance of new organizational forms to supersede those rejected in the Cultural Revolution would make it valid to speak of *The Thought of Mao Tse-tung* as practical ideology. New organizational forms were clearly in the process of being built during the Cultural Revolution, particularly those modeled on the Paris Commune: revolutionary committees representing the masses to rule the Party, periodic reelection of Party members, the "triple alliance" of revolutionary rebels, soldiers, and cadres. However, the ebb and flow of the struggle, the apparently inconclusive nature of the reorganization, and the absence of clear-cut directives announcing new operational policies indicate that Chairman Mao and his colleagues have, so far, been unable fully to implement their ideas. Furthermore, the abstract nature of the maxims of the *Sayings* and Lin Piao's repeated praise of Mao Tse-tung's flexibility in methods,[9] suggest that new operational norms, the crux of any practical ideology, have not been worked out. Thus, in the absence of a new "red" practical ideol-

---

[8]*Jenmin jihpao*, September 3, 1965; see p. 28, n. 7.

[9]For example: "The many military principles which Comrade Mao Tse-tung proposed, as they were concretely applied during the entire course of the war, were never unchanging, but rather evolved constantly in accordance with the development of the situation" (*Hungch'i* 19 [October, 1960], 9).

ogy, it would appear that the *de facto* practical ideology is that of the "experts."[10]

Nevertheless, it would be wrong to conclude that the absence of a new red practical ideology means that the ideological drama had no significance other than as an expression of the political struggles. The immense volume of writing alone, the intensity of argumentation during the Cultural Revolution, and the all-pervasiveness of ideology reported by foreign travellers—these alone would indicate that something important was occurring in the minds of men. Everyone in China today is urged to read, recite, and use the maxims of the *Sayings*. Throughout the country, small groups of people can be seen studying the works of Chairman Mao. The *Sayings* have become a Bible or breviary which each person is expected to carry with him all the time. What Mao hopes to achieve is such a spiritual transformation of man that the new revolutionary attitudes and behavior will continue beyond his death. Han Suyin, in her book *China in the Year 2001,* has described Mao's approach as one "to change the content of motivation, to provide through continuous and painstaking socialist education, through rectification campaigns and movements, a change in behavior, 'within the soul of man'." She adds: "This conversion has been attempted before, in religious systems, but not with the thoroughness of a science, which is Mao Tse-tung's treatment of this psychological remarking."[11] Given the mystery and intractability of human nature, regardless of race, color, or creed, a scientific campaign to change the soul of man seems to be a task which normally only God would set himself to accomplish.

The glorification of Chairman Mao in China has by now reached such proportions that he seems at times to be as much God as any living human being could aspire to be. There are undoubtedly sociopolitical reasons for this glorification, not dissimilar to those which led to the glorification of Stalin during the height of his power. Elements of irrationality and madness in this phenomenon cannot be excluded, particularly considering that the Cultural Revolution struck at the core of the organization which had been the mind, body, and soul of the country, the Communist Party. Yet the explanation of madness

---

[10]In January 1968, Foreign Minister Takeo Miki of Japan, a nation with close economic ties to China, stated ". . . particularly in the economic field, [the Chinese] are still following Liu Shao-ch'i's line" (*Hsingtao jihpao* [Hong Kong], January 19, 1968). The reference to Liu aside, this means that the Chinese are still following pragmatic economic policies.

[11]Han Suyin, *China in the Year 2001* (New York: Basic Books, 1967), pp. 185-186.

must always be left as the last resort, when all other attempts to explain have failed. There are consistent patterns in this great campaign of soul-remaking which can be discerned in the way it is being carried out and in the policies which initiated it—policies which, we are told, derive directly from Chairman Mao.

A quotation in the *Sayings* gives us Chairman Mao's ideas on "correct thought," the source of proper motivation:

> Where does man's correct thought come from? Does it fall down from Heaven? No. Is it imbedded in his own mind? No. Man's correct thought only can come from social reality, only can come from three realities: production struggles in society, class struggles, and scientific investigation.[12]

If one reads Liu Shao-ch'i's lengthy treatise "On the Training of a Communist Party Member," prominently republished on August 1, 1962, and bitterly denounced during the Cultural Revolution,[13] it is apparent that for Liu, the Party theorist, correct thought could only come from the correct resolution of struggles within the Party which, in turn, are a reflection of the external social reality, particularly the class struggle. Both Mao and Liu have written extensively on "correct behavior," but the now evident conflict between the two has revealed that their ideas have not been identical. Earlier I wrote that the individual could only create and maintain his commitment within organization, and that the instrument for eliciting such commitment was the practice of thought reform (see pp. 50-51). That, it now seems, was Liu's approach. For Liu, the Party is the key instrument in the psychological transformation of men. Men have varying degrees of correct consciousness, but it is only within or through the Party that men can be remade and become the true bearers of the revolution and of revolutionary construction. The current ideology says nothing about the kind of thought reform described above (pp. 45 ff.) that assumes the key role of organization. Mao says, in effect, that correct thought can only come about through open struggle in the social arena. Liu, on the other hand, says that correct thought must be cultivated through struggle and persuasion within the confines of the Party. Mao, more confident than Liu in the forces of society, welcomes the upsurge from below, for in the struggles of that upsurge men will inevitably develop

---

12Section 22; the date is May, 1963, when Mao's struggle with Liu was apparently already underway.

13Republication on August 1, China's Army Day, suggests, in retrospect, the Party-Army struggle. Liu's vigorous criticism of "left opportunism" again implies opposition to Mao.

a true revolutionary consciousness. Liu, in the fashion of the rulers of the Soviet Union, believes that such an upsurge can only be destructive. He believes that true revolutionary consciousness can only develop through ideologically and organizationally controlled thought reform.

Throughout the literature of the Maoist current goes the theme of class struggle. Already before the eruption of the Cultural Revolution, voices of the Maoist current warned that unless China underwent further class struggles, the revolution would be lost and China would "change color," that is, return to capitalism. When the Cultural Revolution first began, it was called "socialist," but after the defeat of the Liu faction, the name changed to "proletarian." As H. C. Chuang has said in his researches on the terminology of the Cultural Revolution: "to Mao and the Maoists [proletarian] was more distinctive, striking, and, above all, clearly class-oriented."[14] "Proletarian" implies, not so much working class, but an element in the contradiction of "proletarian" versus "capitalist." Now that the Liu Shao-ch'i faction has been officially denounced as "capitalist," whatever is in opposition to it is "proletarian." Thus, whoever the revolutionary rebels be, they are, by the laws of contradiction, proletarian. But who are these new "capitalists"? In the official terminology, they are "the authoritarian clique who are following the capitalist road," namely the revisionists. Today Liu Shao-ch'i is not referred to by name in the official literature (though he is openly named in the Red Guard newspapers and posters), but as the "Chinese Krushchev"—Krushchev, for the Chinese, being, of course, "the" arch-revolutionist.[15] But "authoritarian clique" means people in power, namely those in the highest ranks of the Party. Since they are capitalists, they are therefore a class, and those opposed to them are likewise a class. The literature of the Cultural Revolution has stated, in effect, that a capitalist class (or, more specifically, revisionists turning into capitalists) took over the Chinese Communist Party. That being the case, as in all class struggles, only a revolution can dislodge them and return power to the proletariat.

Leaving aside the power-political struggles in the Cultural Revolution, the intent of Mao's ideological method now becomes clear. If

---

[14]H. C. Chuang, "The Great Proletarian Cultural Revolution," *Studies in Chinese Communist Terminology*, No. 12 (Berkeley, California: Center for Chinese Studies, 1967), p. 5.

[15]See, for example, the critique of Liu Shao-ch'i's "On the Training of a Communist Party Member" in *Hungch'i* 6 (May, 1967), 3-9. The article plays on the word *hsiu* (a word in the binom "training," *hsiuyang*, but also in the word revisionism, *hsiucheng chuyi*).

correct thought—that is, the spiritual transformation of man—can only come through social struggles, then those struggles must be class struggles (see *Sayings*, Section 2). By implication, therefore, no amount of thought reform, no amount of training and cultivation of cadres, can ever bring about the spiritual transformation of man. Obviously, when classes cease to exist, struggle will cease, and also the need for spiritual transformation. But as all in China, including the Liu faction, agree, the revolution has not yet been completed (see p. 118). Therefore, classes continue to exist, and so also class struggles, whether latent or manifest. But if man is to be spiritually transformed, then class struggles must again and again be aroused. Mao Tse-tung has several times stated that repeated rectification movements would be necessary before China could fully make the transition to socialism. For Liu, such rectification meant intra-Party struggles, and socialist education and criticism among the masses. For Mao, rectification has to mean class struggle. In his works, Liu argues for painstaking work to bring about correct attitudes in people. Mao, on the contrary, urges that man "dare to struggle, dare to win." During the Cultural Revolution, the Red Guards cried out: "Dare to rebel."

During the Cultural Revolution, thousands of incidents of mainly verbal but sometimes physical fighting erupted in China. Many Western observers saw China on the verge of civil war, and even collapse. Foreign journalists freely reported instances of fighting to their news media. Puzzling was the fact that the Red Guard publications and even the official newspapers often greatly exaggerated the scope of the fighting. Whole provinces appeared to have broken away from Peking, and then, only a few days later, quiet reigned. It may never be possible to determine the true nature of the turmoil. But there can be no doubt of the intense struggle waged, particularly in schools and Party committees. If we had to interpret this in ideological terms alone, we would have to say that, for Mao, the more intense the struggle, the better.[16] Just as the peasantry achieved a new revolutionary consciousness through the revolutionary land reform, so now the "proletariat" has achieved a new revolutionary consciousness and spiritual transformation through its struggle against the "capitalists"—that is, the authoritarian clique which dominated the Party.

------

[16]Despite the intensity of the struggles of the Cultural Revolution, they have remained essentially "nonantagonistic," that is, they have been contained within a larger framework of unity. As of January 1968, nothing indicated that the struggles ever reached the point of endangering the unity of the country. That larger framework of unity has been guaranteed by the army, which played the key role to make sure that the struggles did not get out of hand.

What I earlier regarded as only a remote possibility, namely a contradiction between Party cadres and the masses (see p. 98) now came into being. Since the Cultural Revolution swept away almost an entire layer of leading Party cadres, this means, in the logic of Chairman Mao, that revisionists, a new emerging capitalist class, had seized power and so stood in opposition to the bulk of the people. Milovan Djilas' designation of the Party élite in Communist countries as a "new class" squares entirely with Mao's ideas. Since the Party is the heart and soul of the country—the very first sentence of the *Sayings* reads: "The Chinese Communist Party is the core force which directs our operations"— revisionism in the Party means eventual revisionism in the country, leading to a "capitalist restoration." In the welter of accusations against Liu Shao-ch'i, his permissiveness toward the reappearance of private ownership and operations in agriculture have been more intensely denounced than anything else. To prevent that, the masses had to be aroused to revolutionary class struggle against the Party cadres. The struggle will remove the new class from power, but it will also bring about the spiritual transformation of the masses, particularly the new cadres who take over from the old.

I noted earlier that two new élites appeared to be developing in China: the educated professionals and the red cadres (p. 51). That phenomenon is the crux of Mao's vision of a China reverting, through revisionism, to capitalism. But it has not been the educated professionals so much as the red cadres who have borne the brunt of the accusations of becoming a new ruling class. From the first days of Communist rule in China, repeated rectification movements had effectively separated the professionals from political power; the elimination of a professional officer corps in the army was the last stage in turning the professionals into technical experts, critical for the development of the country but removed from the arena of political decision-making. But the red cadres ruled the country, for it was they who dominated the key organizational structure of the country, the Communist Party. Mao knows well the history of his country. Time and time again, new ruling élites arose in the wake of great socioeconomic changes. But as long as the economic and the scientific-technological revolutions have not been completed, the formation of a new ruling class can only mean that stabilization comes too quickly to China. Only revolution can accomplish change, and all ruling classes are enemies of revolution. And revolution can only be accomplished by the masses. But Mao, both as a Marxist and a Chinese, knows that a new ruling class will impose its ideology on the masses. If that ideology is revisionist, so then will the ideology of the masses become revisionist.

The spiritual transformation of the masses, therefore, is insepar-able from the class struggle. The new class struggle, however, was di-rected against those who held the instruments of state power, the new class of red officials. Perhaps in all this we can see a modern reappear-ance of a perennial Chinese revolutionary struggle against the officials, already apparent in the Later Han Dynasty in the Yellow Turban re-bellions and, of course, prominent in the Taiping smashing of the of-ficials (see p. xxxi). We can also see a reappearance of a deep anarch-ist strain in the Chinese Communist tradition. For the Chinese anarch-ists who became a strong political force after the May Fourth move-ment, the state was the enemy; for the Marxists, the enemy was that class which held economic power, chiefly the landed gentry. The class struggle on the land, which reached considerable intensity during the "socialist education movement" (1962-1965), ended in 1965 and did not erupt during the Cultural Revolution. The Cultural Revolution went, for a time, into the factories, but did not go into the villages (though it may again, now that the political phase appears to have passed). The fight was entirely one between the political élite and a rising generation of new "revolutionary rebel" cadres, mainly students.

I stated earlier that the primary purpose of thought reform was the creation of a political élite of cadres (see p. 51). We can now conclude that the primary purpose of the great ideological drama which cul-minated in the Cultural Revolution was to create a new generation of political leaders, not through a Party-guided ideological indoctrination but through a class struggle waged against those who controlled the Party. In many ways, removal of an entire stratum of a ruling political élite during the Cultural Revolution is similar to Stalin's purges of the 1930's (though the Chinese accomplished this without the physical liquidations that made the Stalin purges so terrible). How-ever, Stalin was incapable of conceiving a spiritual transformation of the new political generation. New aspirants simply filled the vacancies created by the purges, attracted by the lure of power and prestige. But Mao is not Stalin. Stalin, throughout his life, believed in the power of organization, of the state. Mao, on the contrary, believes that organiza-tion alienated from the masses ultimately means its own doom.

It is now possible to state that one of the central contradictions I have described in this book, that of democracy and centralism (see p. 54), marks the clash between the two great ideological currents of the 1960's—that identified with Mao Tse-tung and the other now identi-fied with Liu Shao-ch'i. Though both Mao and Liu accept the notions of democracy and centralism as crucial to proper organizational func-tion, Mao stresses the primacy of democracy and Liu the primacy of centralism. For Mao, democracy means a populist upsurge of the masses, a spiritual liberation that unleashes their creative energies (see p. 88). For Liu, centralism meant the rule of organization, specifically that of the Party. These two currents apparently already clashed during the Great Leap Forward. The spontaneous upsurge of the peasants to form the communes would seem to have followed Mao's approach, but the Party-led centralization of the communes followed the organizational line of Liu Shao-ch'i. A more evident clash occurred during the "Four Clean" movement of late 1964. According to the revelations of the literature of the Cultural Revolution, Liu advocated the use of work teams to cleanse and strengthen the rural Party apparatus. Local cadres who had gained acceptance in the communes were to be replaced by men completely loyal to the Party. Mao, on the contrary, called for reliance on the creative energies of the poor and lower middle peasants. That meant relying on those local cadres whom Liu's policies wished to eliminate.[17] Obviously, political methods as well as ideological principles were involved. Liu argued that the Party must be the instrument to rectify itself. Mao called directly on the peasants to attack corrupt Party cadres. Lin Piao in his essay on people's war said that "all imperialists . . . are strengthening their state machinery."[18] The Mao forces accuse their opponents, "the authoritarian clique," of doing precisely that, and demanded rectification from below to prevent that from happening. The Liu forces, following the Soviet tradition, worked for the strengthening of the state machinery and for absolute control of that machinery through a centralized Communist Party.

In the original introduction, I asserted a theoretical difference between organization and social system (see pp. 3-6), comparable to the more common distinction between state and society. I further asserted that the Chinese revolution had so destroyed the traditional social system of China that organization had become its functional equivalent in

----

[17]For a major attack on the "work teams," see *Hungch'i* 5 (March, 1967), 26-30. One of the most extensive accounts of Liu Shao-ch'i's policies in the "Four Clean" movement was given in an article entitled "The Phony 'Four Cleans' and the True Restoration," *Jenmin jihpao,* September 6, 1967. This was an account of Wang Kuang-mei's (Liu Shao-ch'i's wife) expedition to the famous "peach garden brigade" (already widely publicized in the Red Guard press). She is portrayed as an old-time magistrate entering into "enemy territory" surrounded by police guards. To establish "the dictatorship of the work teams," she recruited the worst elements in the village into the Party, while conniving to get rid of fine poor peasant cadres who had long been admired by the peasants as leaders.

[18]See A. Doak Barnett, *China After Mao* (Princeton, N. J.: Princeton University Press, 1967), p. 238.

the new China. Social systems, I said, take time to build up; once destroyed, long periods of time must elapse before one can say that a new social system has arisen (see pp. 7-8). If power is the key element in organization, authority is the key element in a social system. The formation of authority, however, goes hand in hand with the development of a new status group. Clearly, the leaders of China do not believe that all vestiges of the traditional social system have been destroyed, given the repeated attacks on bourgeois, landlord, rich peasant survivals in China. However, no recent campaign against traditional social vestiges compares with the violence of the onslaught against the "authoritarian clique" which had seized power in the machinery of the state. That clique, in the eyes of the Mao forces, was rapidly becoming a new status group and had to be smashed before it consolidated itself into a new ruling class. In Mao's thinking, a premature transition from organization to social system meant the failure of the revolution.

Mao's emphasis on the masses, on the importance of class struggle, reveals his deep belief that the forces of society control the state, and not the reverse. Concretely this means that it is of enormous importance that the right class control the instruments of the state, of organization. In the villages, it must be the poor peasants who control the communes. In the cities, it must be the "proletariat," mainly, the young generation of rising cadres. At times, it seems as if Mao conceives of the two classes, "capitalist" and "proletarian," in generational terms. The former are those "over forty" who have held power for a long time and so have acquired authority. The latter are the young who have no power.[19] Liu's emphasis on the primacy of the Party as organization implicitly denies what Mao emphasizes. In this sense, accusations of "revisionism" against Liu are correct, for his advocacy of careful, painstaking buildup of the Party follows the Soviet approach, where the Party has become a sacred, untouchable entity. In this sense, Mao is more Marxist than Leninist, and Liu is the true follower of Leninism in China. We might remember that it has been Mao who espoused the notion of remaking the Party along the lines of the Paris Commune based on the classic descriptions of that revolution by Marx and Engels. On the other hand, it was during the years of Liu's dominance in the Party that the writings of Lenin were widely propagated.

The struggle of these two ideological currents has significance far beyond China. Everywhere in the world, rapid economic and scientific-

---

[19]On the issue of "over forty," see pp. 545-551. Mao's open identification with young people during the Cultural Revolution indicates that the generational issue was an important political factor in the struggles.

technological development is leading to political centralization, to the growth of state power. Far more than most Americans are aware, this is true of the United States. We now have in the United States, as Galbraith has written, a new industrial state. But the more powerful the state becomes, the more alienated it becomes from society, from the classes which compose society, from the people who make up its living human beings. The United States has only recently begun to realize the consequences of this alienation: insurrections in the black ghettoes, dissidence among the educated, racism within the middle and working classes, apathy among the bulk of the population to the great political and social issues of the day. The doctrines of "liberal" ideology in America have, in fact, accepted much of the *de facto* ideology of the Soviet Union, namely that a benevolent state power dominated by technical élites, can assure peace and tranquility for all.[20] There is thus not only a systemic convergence between the United States and the Soviet Union, but also an ideological convergence. There is much truth to the oft-heard comment among American conservatives that the Russians are getting more capitalist and the Americans more socialist. Thus it is not surprising that in the struggle between Mao-Tse-tung and Liu Shao-ch'i, the sympathies of the West gravitated quickly to Liu, who was seen as a "pragmatist," in contrast to the "adventurist" Mao. We can even hear justifications of the Vietnam War on the grounds that it is a struggle to allow the experts to come to power throughout Asia, including China. Mao would agree with that analysis, except that it is not the experts who would come to power but a red, revisionist élite. Mao's answer is that any alienation between state and society will lead either to tyranny or to a revolt of the masses. The Chinese, again and again, predict that the Russian people will some day overthrow their revisionist rulers. The possibility seems remote now, but one must remember the Hungarian rebellion, which made a profound impact on Mao—his February 1957 speech on internal contradictions among the people was inspired by that rebellion. When the Russians say that their revolution was over by 1920, they fully accepted the notion that the state constituted the functional equivalent of society, and that society would be created anew through the state. Mao argues flatly that the revolution is not over, that society continues to function, and that the state can never functionally replace society. There may be madness in China today, yet the issues of the Cultural Revolution, of the great ideological and political drama, are of the deepest significance for all of mankind. They have been fought

---

[20]Galbraith, *op. cit.*

out time and time again during all of man's civilized history.

The elevation of *The Thought of Mao Tse-tung* to the highest planes of pure ideology has obviously had political and organizational purposes. As once before, in the Great Leap Forward, the leaders used pure ideology to appeal to the masses over the heads of the professionals who exercized constraints on the policies of the leaders (see p. 72). In late 1957 and 1958, however, the leaders were Mao Tse-tung and Liu Shao-ch'i, backed by the bulk of the Party. The professionals were bureaucrats and administrators who dominated positions in the State Council. In 1966, the leaders who launched the Cultural Revolution were Mao Tse-tung and Lin Piao, and the professionals of the organizational middle tier whom they attacked were the bulk of the Party. Judging from the role played by Chou En-lai, who commanded the State Council, the bureaucrats and administrators this time threw their support behind Mao and Lin. What we earlier said about men of the middle tier of organization being insensitive to pure ideology and predominately receptive to practical ideology (see p. 72) seems, now too, to be true for the Liu group. They were the men of China's hitherto dominant practical ideology, namely the organizational ideology of the Chinese Communist Party. We also stated that when leaders at the top appealed to the masses in terms of pure ideology, that ideology tended to take on utopian forms (see p. 71). Has this been true for the ideology of the Cultural Revolution?

In one sense this has been so, but in another it has not been. It is hard to find much of the positive side of utopianism, namely the promise of a bright future just in the offing, in the literature of the Cultural Revolution. In 1958, the cadres told the peasants that three years of suffering would lead to a thousand years of happiness. Now, the promise of the future appears to be one of long, arduous work and suffering. The morality tales, such as those about the soldier-hero Lei Feng or about the self-sacrifice of Dr. Norman Bethune, have become a prominent part of the preachings of *The Thought of Mao Tse-tung*. Lei Feng and Dr. Bethune suffered for the Chinese people whom they loved, but they died long before victory was achieved. In fact, the literature of the Cultural Revolution has been singularly barren of any indication of what would follow after the revolution had been completed. The most concrete indication was a short-lived propagation of the notion of reorganizing the Party along the lines of the Paris Commune, but that theme was quickly dropped in favor of a more coalitionist approach, namely the "triple alliance" which would bring soldiers, new and old cadres together into new Party committees. The conception of the Paris Commune applied to China has remained still-born. There has been much talk about the reorganization of education, and indeed new curricula, new methods, new forms of learning have been announced in the press. But these are practical rather than utopian. Particularly notable in the education reforms is the stress on practical training. In the fall of 1967, the press began a campaign against capitalist survivals in the rural areas, blaming their reappearance on Liu Shao-ch'i. But the slogan was *tou-szu p'i hsiu* ("struggle against privatism and criticize revisionism") which an editorial in *Red Flag* defined as "using *The Thought of Mao Tse-tung* to rectify oneself, breaking decisively with word 'private' in one's thoughts, establishing *a spirit of no benefit to oneself and all benefit to others,* and establishing a proletarian world view."[21] Here again one finds the typical Mao stress on spiritual transformation, but no implication of a new and better life for society as a whole.

But it is the negative side of utopianism, its hostility against an existing order (see p. 72), which is clearly present in the ideology of the Cultural Revolution. From the first violent eruption of the Cultural Revolution (May 1966) to the fall of 1967, the predominant theme has been the attack on "the authoritarian clique who are following the capitalist road" (with a related theme directed against a "counterrevolutionary black gang" who had actually betrayed the interests of China). By the fall of 1967, the attack concentrated almost entirely on Liu Shao-ch'i, or the "Chinese Khrushchev," as he is always called in the press. Liu appears as anti-Christ, as the devil locked in mortal struggle with God. Whether the Liu faction retains any power seems immaterial to the great ideological drama where the forces of Mao struggle with those of Liu, like the combat of the elements of light and dark in Manichaeanism. The forces of Mao will and must win, but the struggle will be long and hard, and may, in fact, go on for decades.

The absence of this positive aspect of utopianism could possibly be explained by the different nature of the "masses" in the Cultural Revolution, contrasted to the Great Leap Forward. During the latter, the "masses" were the peasants who were asked to break with tradition and form new institutional structures, namely the communes. The issues were real in the sense that the communes were to accelerate production and create a new social order in the villages. On the other hand, the "masses" in the Cultural Revolution have been overwhelmingly students and teachers, namely the emerging intellectuals of China. Students have their socioeconomic fulfillment in the future, not in the

---

[21]*Hungch'i,* 15 (October, 1967), 21; italics in original.

present. In school they learn but do not participate in the real life of society. Eventually they go forth and become participants in social life. Mao Tse-tung urged the students to "rebel," but he could not prescribe a new institutional road for them to follow. In many ways, the negative utopianism of the Cultural Revolution is similar to that of student movements throughout the world, whether nationalistic or social revolutionary in the poor countries or antiauthoritarian in the advanced countries. Such movements attack social orders but are incapable of projecting a new order. That is because students are not yet part of society. So far as education is part of the superstructure of a nation, if one may speak in Marxian terms, it is tied more closely to the state than to society. Students are thus an element, albeit a lowly one, in the structure of the state, and their rebellion is ultimately directed against the state. Mao Tse-tung understands this well, and knew that the students were the key ideological instrument for his attack against his enemies who wielded power at the highest levels of the state.

Why has the Maoist ideological current led to a cult of personality which often makes that of Stalin pale in comparison? Chairman Mao is the reddest of all suns, the helmsman, the commander-in-chief of the Chinese people and of all revolutionary people in the world. Lin Piao may be his closest comrade in arms, and Chou En-lai his staunchest supporter, but these two men pale in the dazzling light of Chairman Mao. Chairman Mao is the leader, the sole leader—that is the message which, day upon day, is broadcast forth from China. That Chairman Mao recovered leadership from a Politburo which, though acting in his name, carried out their own policies, is apparent from the political drama of the Cultural Revolution. But the intense emotional adulation must be explained in other terms. Chairman Mao has indeed become a charismatic leader, in the full religious sense of that much-abused term. Many explanations are possible, but I should like to offer one of my own.

One of the remarkable transformations which occurred in China as a result of the Cultural Revolution was the disappearance of that organizational impersonality which had been so characteristic of Communist parties throughout the world. Men and women with real names and faces began to appear on the political scene. Young students who before would have been but part of the masses now argued in their own names on national and local platforms. The Red Guard newspapers began to print extraordinary details about the personal lives of the disgraced leaders. Chairman Mao walked among the masses; Lin Piao chatted with students and soldiers; Chou En-lai led them in song. Wives came onto the scene: Chiang Ch'ing, as the faithful spouse of the Chairman, and Wang Kuang-mei as the scheming partner of the Chinese Khrushchev (thus, Christ and anti-Christ had their female counterparts). The *Sayings* were issued with photographs of a human (and not god-like) Chairman Mao on the back cover. With collective leadership replaced by individual leadership, the personality of the leader came fully into prominence. *The Thought of Mao Tse-tung* stresses the importance of the ideological transformation of the individual (see pp.30-37), and so it follows that the individual, as well as the class, has a unique significance in the ideological-political realm. In the crisis of organizational breakdown, what remained were the forces of society, namely classes. However, classes, unlike organizations, cannot act; only individuals can act. Thus what replaced organization in the days of the Cultural Revolution were individuals who, however, correctly expressed their class interests. What guaranteed that the individual did so was the intensive study of the works of Chairman Mao. The revolutionary rebel committees which arose in the wake of the struggle against the Party throughout China were collections of individuals. Their composition changed constantly in the heat of the fray; some revolutionary rebels were denounced subsequently as disloyal to Chairman Mao and others then emerged as his true disciples.

At the top, the Cultural Revolution portrayed the struggle between Chairman Mao and his few loyal followers against the concentrated power of the authoritarian clique. In the same way was the struggle portrayed in thousands of lower-level Party committees. In that struggle of individuals against organization, Chairman Mao emerged as the supreme individual.

Yet in all the glorification of Mao Tse-tung as the individual leader, there is no real personalization of Mao. No biographies have been issued telling the story of this dedicated revolutionary from his early years. There has been no large-scale rewriting of history, although the past activities of many men have been bitterly criticized (even of Chu Teh and Ch'en Yün, who are back in favor). Mao, for all his individuality, remains remote as a personality. The people are urged to study the writings of Chairman Mao. No one instructs them to emulate the life of the Chairman. Hero models held up for the people to follow are ordinary men, such as Lei Feng and many others who have since then been glorified in the press. It is the wisdom of Chairman Mao which counts, and not so much his personality. That wisdom, unlike his own corporeal self, has an immortality which cannot be destroyed. The man himself must some day pass away. Chairman Mao individually personifies the ideology, an achievement toward which all in society must aspire.

Weltanschauung

From 1960 until 1966, the leaders of China, in an extraordinary torrent of publication, developed their Marxist-Leninist vision of the forces of world history. Almost without exception, each of these documents was directed toward the Soviet Union; the major ones were, in fact, public exchanges of letters with the Soviet Communist Party. The general theme of these documents was that the key contradiction in the world was that between socialism and capitalism, that United States imperialism was embarked on an aggressive path to seize control of the world and challenge the socialist countries, that the rise of national liberation movements in the poor countries was increasingly thwarting the expansive efforts of imperialism. The Chinese prescription for action was: monolithic solidarity of the entire socialist camp, particularly of the Soviet Union and of China, and maximal aid to all national liberation movements. The Soviet response, though not always direct, was to proclaim peaceful coexistence—that is, a détente with the United States, which would banish the threat of nuclear war, as the top priority policy to be followed by all socialist countries and movements.

What I have said earlier about the Chinese *Weltanschauung* (see pp. 38-45) is true of this current. But, we have seen that a second Maoist current had been developing during the 1960's which, in the Cultural Revolution, became the dominant theme of the pure ideology. The two currents considerably overlap in their view of the forces of world history, but they differ profoundly in regard to one key point: the nature and role of the Soviet Union. Despite the violent attacks against Soviet revisionism, the Marxist-Leninist current still clung to the hope that the Soviet Union would some day turn against revisionism and resume its fraternal alliance with its friend and ally China. In the last Chinese letter to the Soviet Communist Party in March 1966, turning down an invitation to attend the Soviet Twenty-third Party Congress, the Chinese appeared to be desperately pleading with the Soviets to change their ways.[22] After that the Soviet Union rapidly became a full-scale enemy of China, plotting with the United States to

---

[22]At the time, the power struggle which led directly to the eruption of the Cultural Revolution, was in full swing. The poor prose of the Chinese letter, in such startling contrast to the brilliance of their earlier documents in the exchange, suggests strongly that the contending factions were unable to achieve unanimity.

create a "holy alliance" to encircle China. The Soviet Union was bitterly denounced in the Cultural Revolution as a degenerate socialist state well on the way to a restoration of capitalism. Everything Russian was derided, and Soviet citizens were maltreated. All party-to-party communications ceased, and the two countries spoke to each other only through their foreign offices (as of February 1968, their respective embassies and a few foreign correspondents still remain in Moscow and Peking). China and Russia thus appeared to have turned simply into two countries no longer bound by the common tie of ideology. For if revisionism be the road to capitalism, then it no longer has anything to do with Marxism-Leninism. For that second Maoist current it is no longer true to say that the conception of the Soviet Union plays a key role in its pure ideology (see pp. 43-44).

The attacks on Soviet revisionism, however, cannot be attributed solely to the second current. In fact, the chief attacks have come from the first. What started in the late 1950's as a criticism of Yugoslav revisionism and the Tito clique (surrogates for Soviet revisionism and the Khrushchev clique) reached a crescendo in July 1964 with the publication of the document entitled "On Khrushchev's Phony Communism."[23] Except for the accusation that the Soviet Union was deliberately plotting with the United States to destroy China, that document exposed the degeneracy of the Soviet Union in terms which could hardly be exceeded in the Cultural Revolution. Nevertheless, in this as well as in later documents, the hope was still expressed that the Soviet Union would reform itself. And indeed, the fall of Khrushchev some months later encouraged the Chinese, for a while, to think that this might happen.

The conflict between these two currents of pure ideology over their views of the Soviet Union and of revolutionary struggles in the third world, can also be put in terms of the primacy of organization or of social classes and struggles. In their view of the revolutionary forces in the third world, both currents stressed the importance of national liberation movements. Yet whereas the Marxist-Leninist current strongly emphasized the leadership role of the "proletarian parties" (i.e., Communist parties), the Maoist current emphasized the role of the united front, guerrilla warfare, and the creation of revolutionary base areas.[24] For the Marxist-Leninist current, the key factor in the na-

---

[23]See Barnett, op cit., pp. 121-195.

[24]These divergences are apparent in a comparison of two key documents: "Proposal Concerning the General Line of the International Communist Movement" (June 14, 1963), and Lin Piao's famous treatise "Long Live the Victory of the

tional liberation struggle is a Communist party, "true Marxist-Leninist," of course. For the Maoist current, the key factor is the class struggle which must take the form of armed uprisings in the rural areas. That these were not just words can be illustrated by the different policies pursued toward the revolutionary movements of the third world for the periods 1960 to 1966, and 1966 to the present. During the first period, the Chinese everywhere encouraged the organization of revolutionary movements, supported antirevisionist Communist parties, sought alliances in the Afro-Asian world. Particularly close to China at that time was the Indonesian Communist party, the second largest in Asia and one of the most pro-Chinese. Many foreign observers were convinced that the Chinese were moving in the direction of proclaiming a new Communist Internationale. Since 1966, however, China appears to have withdrawn into herself. No new Internationale is talked about. Many Communist parties once close to the Chinese have moved away (including the supposedly pro-Peking left-wing Communists in India). Except for Albania, more a national than an organizational friend of the Chinese, the Chinese appear to have become disinterested in European radical leftism.

———

People's War" (September 3, 1965). Assigning these two documents respectively to the Marxist-Leninist and the Maoist currents seems dubious in view of the statements of the communiqué of the Eleventh Plenum that the former "was decided on under the personal leadership of Comrade Mao Tse-tung" (*Hungch'i* 11 (August, 1966), 5. The first document stated the Chinese position expressed in the July Sino-Soviet talks of July 1963; the Chinese delegation headed by Teng Hsiao-p'ing and P'eng Chen, both subsequently purged, tried to convince the Soviets not to sign the test-ban treaty. Despite the Eleventh Plenum's endorsement of this document, its approach is sufficiently different from the second to warrant placing it into the Marxist-Leninist current. So doing does not imply that Mao Tse-tung was then opposed to it. The "proposal" stresses the contradiction between the socialist and the imperialist camps, but also the revolutionary movements within capitalist countries, the national liberation struggles, and the possibility of war among capitalist nations themselves. Lin Piao, on the other hand, indicates that the main contradiction, "the main battlefield of the fierce struggle between the people of the world on the one side and U. S. imperialism and its lackeys on the other is the vast area of Asia, Africa, and Latin America." Whereas the "proposal" calls for a strengthening of the international Communist movement by combatting revisionism within the socialist camp and building Communist parties in the poor countries, Lin Piao says nothing about the international movement, and argues, in effect, for revolutionary armed movements politically based on a broad coalition of forces. Since the Eleventh Plenum also endorsed Lin Piao's treatise, both these contradictory documents therefore remained in effect as guidelines for China's foreign policy. I interpret this as an indication that Mao Tse-tung, despite his bitter antipathy to the Soviet Union, had not yet completely ruled out the possibility of collaboration with it, specifically over the issue of Vietnam.

The concrete implications of these two approaches are different. If organization be the key to launching national liberation movements, this means primarily building up a Communist party. On the basis of the Communist party, party-to-party international linkages are possible, and so an international Communist movement. But if class struggles be the key to launching national liberation movements, this means arousing uprisings among the oppressed classes. Concrete class struggles, as Mao points out, are the result of particular contradictions, that is, the conditions for such struggles differ from region to region, Self-reliance, as Lin Piao says in his treatise on people's war, is critical for developing the movement; furthermore, the movement must seek a united front with all oppositional elements. If that is so, the organization of a Communist party with its internationally shared ideology and organization is not the key factor in launching national liberation movements. Thus the class struggle approach appears almost to exclude the importance of the international Communist movement. That, of course, has key implications for the conception of the Soviet Union in these two currents of the pure ideology.

Lin Piao, whose treatise can be accounted the only lengthy recent exposition of Mao Tse-tung's view of the forces of world history, states flatly that the revolutionary forces of the contemporary world come from its "villages," that is, the poor countries, and not from its "cities," that is, the advanced countries. Since he states openly that "the proletarian revolutionary movement has for various reasons been temporarily held back in the North American and West European capitalist countries," we can presume that he includes the Soviet Union in the category of the "cities." Thus, in effect, Lin Piao contradicts the adherents of the Marxist-Leninist current who argued that the forces of socialism in the Soviet Union would one day rescue that country from revisionism. If there is no hope for the class struggle in the Soviet Union, then nothing any longer binds Russia to China—except the dictates of concrete commitment to support the Vietnamese against the United States.

I wrote earlier that the Chinese Communists' conception of the United States gave content to their conception of the Soviet Union, that in their state of weakness only the Soviet Union could protect them against the American threat (see p. 44). This statement is no longer valid. The erosion of the Soviet nuclear shield, China's main protection against the American threat, began with the June 1959 Soviet renunciation of their nuclear-sharing pact concluded with China in October 1957. The erosion appeared complete when the Soviet Union and the United States concluded their partial test-ban treaty in late July 1963. The Chinese sent a high level Party delegation to dissuade the Russians from concluding the agreement, but they failed.[25] The explosion of the first Chinese atomic device in October 1964 marked the beginning of the development of an independent Chinese nuclear deterrent against the United States. The repeated Chinese stress on the need for "self-reliance" obviously now applies to the nuclear field as well. With China committed to developing her own resources to protect her national security and with the ideological triumph of the Maoist current over the Marxist-Leninist, the repudiation of the Soviet Union appears to be complete.[26]

According to the Marxist-Leninist current, ideological conceptions of the United States and the Soviet Union had to be related. In fact, the contradiction between the socialist camp and the imperialist camp was considered the key contradiction in the temporary world.[27] That meant, concretely, that World War III between the United States and the Soviet Union was still a possibility (see p. 42). In the wake of the developing Soviet-American détente, Mao Tse-tung appears to have concluded that this might not be so. That means China will have to confront the United States alone.

The *Weltanschauung* of the Maoist current is contained in the essay of Lin Piao on people's war. But the attitude toward the United States is contained in one short section of the *Sayings*: imperialism and all reactionaries are paper tigers—despise them strategically but respect them tactically. In short, China will eventually win, but it must be careful.

The Soviets have now fully reciprocated the Chinese repudiation of

------

[25]The delegation was led by Teng-Hsiao-p'ing and P'eng Chen, and included K'ang Sheng, Yang Shang-k'un, Liu Ning-i, Wu Hsiu-ch'üan, and P'an Tzu-li. Since the latter two men can be regarded as "experts" on Soviet affairs, the other five are the true political delegates. Three of the five (Teng, P'eng, and Yang) were purged during the Cultural Revolution and have been bitterly denounced; P'eng and Yang were singled out as counterrevolutionaries.

[26]The purges have struck deeply at men who, at one time or another, could have been considered pro-Soviet. The attacks on P'eng Te-huai, for example, who was dismissed in the summer of 1959, clearly are directed against those who advocated some kind of reliance on the Soviet Union; P'eng Te-huai, in particular, advocated continuing reliance on the Soviet deterrent, apparently even in the face of the breaking of the nuclear sharing agreement. P'eng Te-huai's pro-Soviet approach is indicated in the usual manner through historical analogies to known pro-Soviet figures such as Li Li-san, Wang Ming, and Kao Kang; see *Jenmin jihpao*, August 16, 1967.

[27]See Schurmann and Schell, *Communist China*, p. 48. Vol. III of *The China Reader* (New York: Vintage Books, Random House, 1967).

themselves. Mao Tse-tung and his clique are denounced as "the mouth-piece of great power chauvinism and petty-bourgeois adventurism." The Cultural Revolution is denounced as an onslaught against the Communist party itself. If the Chinese see a capitalist restoration in the Soviet Union, the Russians say the same for China. They accuse Mao of having abandoned working-class leadership of the Communist party and so having turned against a program of rapid industrial development. Instead, China is to be kept poor so that Mao can pursue his expansionist schemes in Southeast Asia and incite the world to World War III. The Soviets appear to be making a stronger case for the containment of China than even the United States.[28]

Only the commitment of both countries to the struggle of the Vietnamese now holds them together. As of our writing, new war clouds are gathering in Korea, again a country to which both Russia and China are committed.

Yet despite the deep erosion of Marxism-Leninism in China, its theme remains, albeit a subordinate one. The contradictory nature of things in China which we have described in the body of the book still remains. Marxism-Leninism remains an option which, some day, could be revived. During the latter part of 1967, the Chinese were moving to consolidate the Cultural Revolution and restore the Party. Since *The Thought of Mao Tse-tung* has not been able to generate its practical ideology, it may, once again, have to take recourse to the methods elaborated during the decades of its history, namely those of Marxism-Leninism. But China is now at a crossroads. If peace should prevail in the world, China's development will be very different from that which will occur if war should come to its shores. The practical ideology of *The Thought of Mao Tse-tung*, which developed during the years of struggle with the Japanese and during the civil war, seems more appropriate for war conditions than for peace-time development. Similarly, if the practical elements of Marxism-Leninism are not revived, its pure elements possibly could. Once again China would be prepared to seek ideological linkages with parties beyond her borders. The possibility of a drawing together of the two Communist giants cannot be ruled out, even at a time when the split is so deep that it seems more likely that Russia might join the United States in a containment of China—even in war against China.

---

[28]M. Sladkovskii, "Ugroza ekonomicheskim osnovam sotsializma v Kitae" ["Danger to the Economic Foundations of Socialism in China"], *Kommunist* 12 (August, 1967), 93-108, especially pp. 104-108; P. Fedoseev, "Marksizm i Maotsedunizm" ["Marxism and Maoism"]. *Kommunist* 5 (March 1967), pp. 107-122.

CHAPTER II

ORGANIZATION

As A RESULT of its revolution, China became a land of organization. Everywhere people became members of some unit of organization—factory, school, office, production brigade or military company—which determined the course of their lives. As has been shown, the Chinese Communist party determined the character of organization. It was the leader, the model, the heart and soul of the nation. The state seemed to have become a functional substitute for society, and the Party was the dominant element in the state. This was the situation in China during the 1950's.

During the 1960's, however, it became apparent that a trinity of state power was developing in which party, army, and government formed the key organizational structures. The organizational history of China in the 1960's is marked by a transition from Communist party domination of the state to a new partnership between Party, army, and government, the exact forms of which are as yet unclear.

In the 1960's as in the 1950's, the Party dominated the decision-making command posts of the state and exercized leadership throughout society. Similarly, the government controlled the operational spheres; it was responsible for carrying out policies and decisions made by the Party. While the functions of Party and government remained essentially the same, the functions of the army changed. What had been essentially a professional military force segregated from organization and society, became an integral part of both. Whereas earlier the army still performed the classical functions of assuring national security, maintaining law and order, and carrying out certain large-scale and otherwise strategic public works, in the 1960's it gradually became the chief vehicle for implanting the ideology of Mao Tse-tung in the people, particularly the young generation. As its ideological role grew, so did its importance for policy and operations. Military influence on political decision-making became increasingly apparent, bringing about an inevitable clash with the Party. Military participation in governmental operations likewise became apparent, particularly through the formation of "political departments" in units of economic administration and management (see p. 575). However, contrasted with Party-army relations, those between army and government appear to have been harmonious. As a result, a kind of alliance has grown up between the military and the government, symbolized by Lin Piao and Chou En-lai, Chairman Mao's two chief supporters during the Cultural Revolution. With Chairman Mao as the leader of the Communist Party, we can say that the trinity of state power is symbolized by the triumvirate of these three men.

Has this trinity of state power altered the nature of organization in China? The very term Cultural *Revolution* implies profound change; not since the land reform of the late 1940's had the word revolution been applied to any social process in China. The ideological attack on the authoritarian clique implied that the entire top stratum of Party leaders had become hopelessly corrupted. The Soviets have directly accused Mao Tse-tung of smashing the Party and replacing it with army rule.[1] Since the Party had been the heart and soul of the organizational structure which ruled China, an answer to the question depends on whether the nature and function of the Party has changed in some fundamental way. During the 1950's, the key problems of state power revolved around relations between the Party and the government: thus I chose to analyze these two structures. However, in the 1960's, the key problems of state power revolved around relations between the Party and the army. Just as the army developed somewhat independently during the 1950's, so the administrative system appeared to go its own way during the 1960's, which helps account for the remarkably little effect the Cultural Revolution has had on it. Let us proceed therefore in terms of a discussion of Party, army, and government.

———

[1] See P. Fedoseev, "Marksizm i Maotsedunizm" ["Marxism and Mao Tse-tung'ism"]; *Kommunist* 5 (March 1967), p. 117: "Mao Tse-tung's group has made widespread use of the army for the smashing of the organs of Party and state."

PARTY

From 1959 to 1961, the Chinese Communist party recruited three million new members, a greater quantitative jump than at any other period of its history. Since then no new figures on Party membership have been announced. We can be certain that these three million were recruited before the winter of 1960/61, for at that time, in the midst of China's terrible economic crisis, the leadership began a basic-level rectification movement within the Party. The movement, announced by Li Fu-ch'un in the January 1961 communiqué of the Ninth Plenum, spread "in bits and stages" from province to province. Party cadres who had become virtual military commanders in the communes were severely criticized.[2] Not having the publicity given other rectification movements, it was not widely noticed at the time. However, the movement, coinciding with the loosening of controls over the population to spur recovery, resulted in a loss of power on the part of Party cadres throughout the country. Articles appeared warning cadres not to interfere in production, indicating that "old peasants and those experienced in production" should take charge of the teams.[3] The shift clearly was from red to expert, and no one expressed it as clearly as the outspoken foreign minister of China, Ch'en Yi.[4] At all levels of organization, power appeared to pass from the Party to the experts, were they government administrators, factory managers, or old peasants experienced in production.

This sudden decline in Party power was undoubtedly connected with the economic crisis. Right into the winter of 1960/61, Party cadres had been driven to push the population for one last heroic effort to save the country, but the food crisis showed their efforts to have been in vain. The law of contradiction thus turned against them, and they paid the price in power.

Nevertheless, power struggles at the highest level also played a major role in this loss of Party power. Mao Tse-tung's resignation from the chairmanship of the republic in December 1958 is, through the revela-

---

[2]See *China News Analysis* 399, Hong Kong (December 1, 1961), 3-4.

[3]*Jenmin jihpao*, January 1, 1961.

[4]Ch'en Yi made some statements in his famous talk to the students of Peking University in September 1961, which he would later rue, though, being an expert, he politically survived the Cultural Revolution. For example: "Now take me for example. My individual thoughts are exceedingly complex. I have Communist thoughts, but I also have Confucian and Mencian thoughts, and even some bourgeois thoughts. Though I've taken part in the Revolution for forty years, I can't say I'm 'Communist through and through'." *Chungkuo ch'ingnien* 17 (1961), 4.

tions of the Cultural Revolution, known to have been a defeat for him and a victory for his rival Liu Shao-ch'i. Though the pace of communization and of the Great Leap Forward slackened in the spring of 1959, the Party tightened its grip over the countryside. In September 1959, a major purge took place in the army with the dismissal of P'eng Te-huai, Huang K'o-ch'eng, and others associated with pro-Soviet positions (and now with Liu Shao-ch'i). By the autumn of 1960, when Mao Tse-tung's fourth volume of selected works were published and Lin Piao wrote the key eulogies on them, it was apparent that the army was beginning to enter the domestic political scene in force. The revelations of the *Work Bulletins (Kungtso t'unghsün)* show that, during the time of deepest crisis, social disorganization and even armed uprisings had occurred in many parts of the country.[5] Liu Shao-ch'i's visit to Moscow in October 1960 must have eroded his position, for the joint declaration adopted by the assembled Communist parties, and even more importantly Khrushchev's utterances, showed few Soviet concessions to the Chinese position.[6]

The "Hundred Flowers" spirit which prevailed during 1961 and much of 1962 appeared to indicate a return to the policies of 1956. Intellectuals in the sciences and the arts wrote more freely than they had in years. The publication of economic debates showed that experts were allowed to express their different views on the future development of the country. The adoption of Ch'en Yün's 1957 program of decentralization (see pp. 196ff.) appeared to launch a trend toward broader distribution of political power in the country. The Party had clearly lost some of its power which flowed to the government and the army, but also to managers and peasants in the units of production.

From early 1961 to the middle of that year, each of the three elements in the trinity of state power were strengthening their own spheres of operation. Many governmental departments were recentralized in the wake of the chaos. The Party appeared to be strengthening its hold on the province-level apparatus, which eventually led to the formation of entrenched political machines,[7] only uprooted by the Cultural Revolution. But it was in the army where the most significant developments were taking place. Under the leadership of Lin Piao, a

––––

[5]See John Wilson Lewis, "China's Secret Military Papers: *'Continuities' and Revelations',*" *The China Quarterly* 18 (April-June, 1964), 73-77.

[6]See Harry Gelman, "The Sino-Soviet Conflict," in Schurmann and Schell, *Communist China,* pp. 280-281.

[7]See Frederick C. Teiwes, *Provincial Party Personnel in Mainland China, 1956-1966* (Occasional Papers of the East Asian Institute, Columbia University, New York, N. Y., 1967).

widespread education campaign was undertaken, beginning in the summer of 1961, to turn the army from a professional fighting force into a people's army in close contact and cooperation with society, particularly with the youth. It appears to have been at the ideological level that the first serious conflicts erupted between Party and army. Obviously, the question of who dominated the army was the main political issue in this ideological struggle.

In 1962, the Party began its comeback. The publication on August 1, 1962 (China's army day) of Liu Shao-ch'i's "On the Training of a Communist Party Member" marked a major step forward in the Party's attempt to preempt the ideological field for itself. Pictures of Liu Shao-ch'i appeared everywhere, usually alongside those of Mao Tse-tung. It was widely presumed that Liu had been designated as Mao's successor. From September 24 to 27, 1962, the Central Committee held its Tenth Plenum. If, as I have said, plenums are only held when policy decisions have already been made and operational implementation is to be discussed (see p. 143), then the short duration of the Tenth Plenum would appear to indicate broad agreement on major problems. Despite the trouble on the Sino-Indian frontier and the first flickers of a new Cuban crisis, the international scene was calm; the formation of a coalition government in Laos, supported by the Chinese, appeared to augur well for the stabilization of Far Eastern tensions. That and the relatively short amount of space given international problems in the communiqué indicated that domestic problems received top priority. The key decision was to launch a socialist-education movement in the rural areas, to serve the purpose of rooting out capitalistic influences that had crept back in the countryside. Regardless of the political differences between Mao Tse-tung and Liu Shao-ch'i, they must have agreed that the 1961 loosening of controls had gone too far. The stress on accumulation to accelerate economic development necessitated the imposition of new rural policies to assure the needed flow of savings from the agricultural to the industrial sector. But Mao and Liu did not agree as to the methods by which the movement should be carried out. Mao, as would be evident in his support for the poor and middle peasant associations in the following year, once again favored an upsurge from below. However, Liu, the apostle of organization, regarded the movement as a way of once again imposing Party control on the countryside. That the dominant power of the conference was Liu's is indicated by the fact that out of three men elected to the Party secretariat, two were loyal to him: Lu Ting-i and Lo Jui-ch'ing. Only K'ang Sheng can be accounted a follower of Mao Tse-tung.

The Party-army struggle is apparent in the replacements announced for the Secretariat (the dismissed Huang K'o-ch'eng and T'an Cheng were prominently associated with P'eng Te-huai). However, a curious statement suggested another facet to the struggle: "The Chinese People's Liberation Army and the Public Security Forces are the main firm and reliable people's troops." Given his long association with the secret police, Lo Jui-ch'ing thus brought the power of the secret police into the army, which he was well able to do since he was chief of staff of the army as well as secretary of the Military Affairs Committee. Using the secret police to gain control of the army was an old organizational device, well known to the Chinese from the history of Stalin's Russia. Lo, whose ties linked him to the Party, to the army, and to the secret police, thus symbolized the emergence of a new power thrust—one which Mao Tse-tung and Lin Piao clearly feared.[8]

During 1963 and 1964, the socialist-education campaign in the rural areas assumed an ever greater intensity reaching a climax with the "four clean" movement in the fall of 1964 (see p. 508, note 4). Since the disputes between Mao and Liu over these movements now figure prominently in the literature of the Cultural Revolution, it is no longer easy to ferret out the truth. Liu—and particularly T'ao Chu, who was then responsible for agricultural policy—are denounced as revisionists who wished to permit a full restoration of capitalism in the countryside. What seems more likely is that both Mao and Liu agreed that the liberalization allowed in January 1961 to get out of the economic crisis had to end. Warnings that bad elements were worming their way into leadership positions of the Party were voiced by men now known as supporters of Chairman Mao as well as by those now known as his opponents.

Since the Yenan period, China had undergone three great upheavals on the land: the revolutionary land reform, collectivization, and finally communization. In all three cases, implementation of these revolutionary policies was preceded by thorough-going organization of the peasantry. The period of the socialist-education movement can be regarded as one of these preparatory organizational periods. Organization among the peasants had broken down, and had to be built up again. But the question was: how. The policies advocated by Mao Tse-tung and Liu Shao-ch'i diverged. While Liu was committed to restoring the primacy of the Party, Mao put his emphasis on the masses, particularly the poor and the lower middle peasants. In May 1963,

---

8On Party, army, and secret police in Stalin's Russia, see Merle Fainsod, *How Russia is Ruled* (Cambridge, Mass: Harvard University Press, 1958), pp. 408-414.

Mao temporarily had his way when the Central Committee adopted his "ten-point program." Thus for a time during the summer and early fall of 1963, the press printed items about the formation of poor and lower middle peasant associations. However, in September, Liu counterattacked and prevailed upon the Central Committee to adopt his own "ten-point program" (since then these two programs have been known respectively as the "earlier" and "later" ten points). All references to poor and lower middle peasant associations were dropped. Then in January 1965, Mao Tse-tung, once again, counterattacked and got the Central Committee to adopt his "twenty-three-point program." So, on the eve of the escalation of the Vietnam war, Chairman Mao's rural policy appears to have won out in the struggle.[9]

All this sounds abstract, and, even with the franker revelations of the documents of the Cultural Revolution, it is difficult to discern what actually occurred. Yet reports which came out of China in 1963 and particularly during the Four Clean movement in the fall of 1964 indicated that more than ideological verbiage was at stake. The Four Clean movement turned out to be the biggest purge among rural cadres since the rectification movement of the winter of 1960/61. In order to penetrate the ideological fog, let us cite some items from the documents of the Cultural Revolution. First, Liu Shao-ch'i is quoted as having said the following in September 1964, during his tour of areas undergoing the Four Clean movement:

> In my view, leadership power in one third of the entire country rests in the hands of the enemy. . . . The year I went to Hunan to link up with the basic-level cadres (cha-ken ch'uan-lien), they chased me away. . . . While we have had some success in the past Four Clean movement, we still haven't gone deep and thorough enough—we're still outside the gate.[10]

Liu's wife, Wang Kuang-mei, was even more explicit, as indicated in remarks attributed to her by a Red Guard publication:

> When Wang Kuang-mei went to Paoting in 1964, she sang the same old song as Liu Shao-ch'i. She called the class formations of the village blackguards and ruffians. Analyzing the poor and lower middle peasant formations in Kaochen, she said: "Here they're all Wang Feng-kan's old gang —a lot of them were with him in the puppet army. There are also a lot of them who used to be bandits and with secret societies. Too many people have defects about their personal history. No matter how much

---

[9]See p. 508, note 4.

[10]*Chanpao* (Peking, a Red Guard tabloid), January 9, 1967.

you teach the poor and lower middle peasants, hardly any of them lacks defects. The only pure ones are a few young people. . . . Bandits, KMT's, puppet army men, big Buddhists, old priests—there's hardly any one over thirty-five who is any good. . . . Try as you will, you can hardly find any poor and lower middle peasants who are without defects. You can't find any core cadre who works well, whose social origins are right, and who is respected." Wang Kuang-mei, herself of capitalist origins, poisonously and contemptuously speaks of "thieves and crooks among the poor and lower middle peasants."[11]

If Liu and his wife were correct, this must mean that traditional peasant elements, "old peasants and those experienced in production" who were openly praised in the wake of the economic crisis, had achieved widespread power within the villages. Liu states that, in 1964, the Party had lost control of one-third of the rural areas of the country. That fact alone would account for the enormous effort made by the Party to reestablish its authority, evident in the intensity of the Four Clean movement. But the disagreement between Mao and Liu was whether control should be imposed from below (by mobilizing the poor and lower middle peasants) or from above (by using the instruments of the Party). On which method was correct hinged a key judgment: was or was not the bulk of the peasantry reliable? Mao's judgment is apparent from the articles of the "twenty-three-point program," now officially attributed to him.[12] He calls for "relying on the working class, the poor and lower middle peasants, on revolutionary cadres, revolutionary intellectuals, and other revolutionary elements, and paying particular attention to solidarizing more than 95 percent of the masses, more than 95 percent of the cadres."[13] The document explicitly calls for leniency to cadres who have mended their ways, but warns that one must struggle against people who have taken the capitalist road at all levels of organization, including the Central Committee itself. In other words, Mao says simply that, whatever shortcomings the peasantry may have, it is basically reliable. By strong implication, what is unreliable is the organizational structure, namely the Party, which has been infiltrated by alien elements. Liu's judgment appears to have been exactly the opposite. The rot within the peasantry had gone so far that drastic measures were needed to root it out. Rectifica-

---

[11] *Tungfang-hung* (Peking, a Red Guard tabloid) , May 7, 1967.

[12] "The Struggle Between the Two Roads in the Chinese Village," *Jenmin jihpao,* November 23, 1967. This is a major official attack on Liu Shao-ch'i's rural policies.

[13] Although the "twenty three point program" has not yet been officially published, this passage has been repeatedly cited; see *Jenmin jihpao,* November 23, 1967.

tion could only be carried out by proper methods, and that meant work teams dispatched from central points out to the rural areas.[14]

It has become commonplace in the West (and in Eastern Europe) to brand Mao the adventurist and Liu the pragmatist. Mao is regarded as fanatically committed to revolution, willing to plunge his country and other countries into turmoil in order to keep the revolution going (Trotzkyism, in short). Liu, on the other hand, is seen as the man who is committed to the careful, painstaking development of China to true great power status. That image has been greatly fostered by the Chinese themselves; if Liu Shao-ch'i is indeed the "Chinese Krushchev," then, given the Western view of Khrushchev, Liu must indeed have been the pragmatist. The fragmentary evidence from the Four Clean movement suggests that such a conception is not correct. In fact, it appears to have been the forces of Liu Shao-ch'i which, in the fall of 1964, pushed the movement to new heights of intensity, and it was Mao Tse-tung, speaking through the "twenty-three-point program," who urged a calming down of the movement. In fact, from January 1965 on, the socialist-education movement in the countryside slackened and finally appears to have ended. Furthermore, there is no evidence that the Cultural Revolution ever erupted in any large-scale way in the villages. Red Guards streamed through the countryside by the millions in 1967, yet without inciting the poor and lower-middle peasants to rebellion against their class enemies. China's 1967 bumper crop can, to a large extent, be attributed to the fact that the countryside remained quiet while the cities were in turmoil. Perish the thought that it might, after all, be Chairman Mao who turned out to be the pragmatist in regard to rural policy!

To press the argument further, we might note another curious operational principle which was voiced during the fall of 1964, mainly by men who were purged during the Cultural Revolution. For example, Wei Wen-po, an East China agricultural cadre:

> There still are some comrades who say that for class struggle you rely on poor and lower-middle peasants, but you can't rely on them for the production struggle. They say: "for struggle you must follow the class road; for production you must follow the work road . . . for land reform you rely on the poor peasants; for production you rely on the middle peasants."[15]

------

[14]Liu and his wife have been derided for advocating a method of "squatting on a spot" (*tun-tien*), i.e. sending a cadre out to some village to organize them properly.

[15]*Hungch'i* 18 (September 1963), 36.

The same was said by Chang P'ing-hua, a Hunan Party cadre who was bitterly attacked during the Cultural Revolution.[16] Both men derided this notion as an insult to the poor and lower-middle peasants. We have already noted that the term "middle peasant" is relative. When the Communists were interested in social movements, and therefore aroused the poor peasants, they stressed the "lower" quality of the middle peasants. When they were interested in stability on the land, they stressed their "prosperous" quality (see pp. 199, 430). In other words, if the leadership wanted political struggle on the land, it had temporarily to sacrifice production, because struggle would alienate a large portion of the middle peasants whose talents and experience were crucial for bring the harvest in. On the other hand, if the leadership wanted a good harvest, gave the economic front priority, then it had to stabilize the social situation, which meant conciliating the middle peasants. This notion of the mutually exclusive character of class struggle and production appears close to what was advocated by Ch'en Yün and his fellow pragmatists during the 1950's. (Ch'en Yün, one might note, has prominently reappeared during the Cultural Revolution.) If Chang P'ing-hua reflected Liu's ideas, then it cannot be maintained that Liu was the pragmatist who, above all, sought the increase of agricultural production through rural social stability. The "twenty-three-point program" takes a very conciliatory approach, not only to middle peasants, but even to landlords, rich peasants, counterrevolutionaries, and "bad elements" who had mended their ways. Wei Wen-po, on the other hand, speaks in the same vein as Liu Shao-ch'i and Wang Kuang-mei in the statements cited above: "in the villages of East China . . . these demons and monsters . . . carry out all kinds of activities, open and secret, hard and soft; there is nothing they don't use, no hole they don't crawl into."[17] It seems evident, therefore, that Liu Shao-ch'i was as much determined to struggle with the peasants as Mao Tse-tung. The question was not one of struggle versus production, but one of methods how to carry out the struggle.

Chang P'ing-hua makes clear how he saw the struggle: "The Party and the poor and lower-middle peasants are bound together like blood and flesh. They must not be split. They cannot be split."[18] How are they to be organized? In the classic method of linking up with basic-level cadres (cha-ken ch'uan-lien): "Arouse them one by one; arouse them bit by bit; establish their power team by team; establish their power

---

16 *Jenmin jihpao*, November 2, 1964.

17 *Hungch'i* 18 (September 1963), p. 32.

18 *Jenmin jihpao*, November 2, 1964.

commune by commune." In others words, Chang P'ing-hua outlines the old work-team method of carefully organizing the struggle from the top. He warns that unless one is willing to do this painstaking mass-level work, and just is satisfied with "a superficial upsurge," then the masses cannot be organized. He subsequently admits that poor and lower-middle peasant associations have to be set up, but urges that the Party "from the provincial committees to the branches" give them sufficient attention, help, and support. Mao Tse-tung, speaking through the "twenty-three-point program," argued for an approach which would conciliate as many people as possible, for the organization of poor and lower-middle peasant associations not identical with the Party, and for a movement which would span six or seven years.

What Mao Tse-tung advocated appears very much in accord with Lin Piao's program for revolutionary development in the "villages" of the world: the development of self-reliant base areas, reliance on the forces of the peasantry, and a broad united front policy among all progressive elements. It is Mao in effect who argues that the peasantry must be respected for what it is, that it cannot be manipulated organizationally to fit into a mold imposed by the Communist Party. Organization must come from below, not from above. Just as revolution cannot be exported from abroad, so organization cannot be imposed from an outside area onto the village. Just as during the Yenan period, when Mao's ideas were triumphant, now too Mao argued that Party organization had to be based on the reality of the village. The Party could not remake that reality to conform to its own wishes.

Yet while Mao appears to be more of a realist and pragmatist in regard to organization than his Party-oriented opponent Liu, the reverse seems to be true in the realm of ideology. The documents accusing Liu of revisionistic practices in the economy have reached mammoth proportions. One of the key issues of the Cultural Revolution has been that of moral versus material incentives.[19] The "revolutionary rebels" have accused the authoritarians of following the capitalist road, of seeking a capitalist restoration by a return to material incentives. Liu is accused of having introduced free, private, and capitalistic policies in agriculture—particularly the free market, the private gardens, independent accounting, and allowing individual peasant households to make production contracts.[20] Since these are similar to the reformist economic policies advocated by the Soviet leaders, Liu Shao-ch'i thus is clearly a revisionist. Furthermore, since these are the real policies

---

[19]See Han Suyin, *China in the Year 2001* (New York: Basic Books Inc., 1967), pp. 88-91.

which prevailed in agriculture since the volte-face of January 1961, Liu now is adjudged to be the man chiefly responsible for them. The conclusion thus seems inescapable, and has been made by many Western China-watchers, that China is on the verge of a new radicalization of the rural scene. As Philip Bridgham puts it: ". . . the outlook in Communist China in the years ahead is for the unfolding of a program of economic and social development featuring increased tension and conflict and patterned increasingly on the Stalinist model of forced-draft economic development of a generation ago."[21]

Given the unpredictability of events, no one can dispute that forecast. After all, the Cultural Revolution came as a great surprise to the students of China. There is a growing austerity theme in China, coupled with calls for a new collectivism to replace an individualism which had run rampant in previous years. The mood in China today cannot and must not be separated from the considerable chances that war may spread to China in the not too distant future. Han Suyin has argued, from first-hand knowledge, that the Cultural Revolution is in great part a preparation of the country for war. Obviously if war comes, China will wish to attain that remarkable level of popular solidarity and collectivism that marks North Vietnam's resistance to the air war imposed on it. That solidarity, as the Chinese well know, was not imposed by organization coming from the top, but by the spontaneous rallying of the people around their leaders. War, as we should realize, is a great unifier for those under attack.

As the date for the beginning of the Third Five-Year Plan was approaching (January 1, 1966), the importance of the agricultural sector to provide savings for the industrialization program had grown. No longer could the pragmatic permissiveness of the early recovery period be tolerated, else the accumulation targets could not be met. Liu Shao-ch'i appears to have advocated classical methods of strengthening control through the Party as the necessary prelude for increasing pressure on the peasantry. Party control, however, did not exclude retention of many of the economic policies of the recovery period, such as the free market. Nor does Party control exclude a new leap forward in agriculture. If a powerful Party deeply imbedded in the villages was traditionally seen as an indispensable instrument for carrying out whatever policy was decided on by the leadership, then Mao's enaouragement of the poor and lower-middle peasant associations must have been seen as

---

[20]*Jenmin jihpao,* November 23, 1967.

[21]Philip Bridgham, "Mao's 'Cultural Revolution': Origin and Development," *The China Quarterly* 29 (January-March, 1967), 35.

working squarely against this policy. Surely Mao Tse-tung must have realized that these village and not Party-based organizations were far less capable of central manipulation than strong Party branches: the stronger the village, the greater its powers of resistance against the state. If the situation was as bad as Wang Kuang-mei described it, then Mao's program would only strengthen the grip of these traditional elements over the village. Under these conditions, the leadership would lose much of its ideological and coercive power over the villages, and have no alternative but to turn to material incentives: the lure of gains to the peasants through the exchange of their products with the state or on the free market. Since the little information we have on the villages during the period of the Cultural Revolution indicates an unbroken continuation of the policies pursued during the recovery period, it would appear that it is material incentives which prevail. In the latter part of 1967, the press began a campaign denouncing "private" tendencies in the country, and this could indicate a new campaign against capitalist survivals in the village. But where are the organizational instruments for carrying out the new policy? With the weakening of the central and provincial Party apparatuses during the Cultural Revolution and the continuing reappearance of traditional elements in the villages, it does not seem likely that the rural Party cadres can lead such a campaign, such as their predecessors did during collectivization and communization.

There may be only one answer to the question why Mao advocated an approach which only reduced the scope of political control over the villages: he truly believed that the collectivist forces of the peasantry, aroused by education and indoctrination, and not by political coercion through the Party, would win out over individualist and kulak trends and make the commune ideal a reality. Mao was willing to loosen controls in the belief that the impulses from below would work out correctly. Liu, the orthodox Communist, believed that any loosening of controls would lead to chaos and disaster. Thus we truly could say that Mao is the adventurist and Liu the pragmatist, but it is Liu who advocated reliance on that machine of centralized organized power which, in earlier times, Western writers have denounced as Communist totalitarianism.

The Four Clean movement of the fall of 1964 marked the most ambitious attempt of the Party leadership, apparently controlled by Liu Shao-ch'i and Teng Hsiao-p'ing, to establish its power throughout the country. As An Tzu-wen, director of the Central Committee's organization department, said in September 1964: ". . . this is the most far-reaching, most profound socialist revolutionary movement since the

Party took power; it is the finest school for educating and tempering the cadres, for cultivating successors in the task of proletarian revolution."[22] An Tzu-wen was denounced, during the Cultural Revolution, as one of China's "great renegades."[23] The movement was complex, and its zigzags were obviously a reflection of the struggle between the two great ideological-political currents. It began rather modestly as a rectification movement to root out corrupt cadres in the rural areas, but eventually turned into a "hurricane" to cleanse the political, economic, organizational, and ideological attitudes of the cadres.[24] Undoubtedly, Liu and Teng believed that whoever controlled the villages, controlled China. Mao Tse-tung's comeback in the winter of 1964/65 indicates that the attempt did not succeed.

In 1964, many articles appeared on the issue of the "successor generation"—the "next generation" of cadres. At first this appeared to be an indirect way of discussing the successor to Chairman Mao, who was getting old and would soon pass from the scene. However, it has since become clear that the issue was precisely what it was stated to be: who was to succeed to the millions of cadres who had been in power much over a decade and were getting old? I have already noted the low attrition rate of Party members (see p. 133); that meant Party cadres once in power tended to stay there. In late July 1964, an obscure editorial appeared in the official Party organ *Red Flag* which first brought up the issue of cadres over forty years of age. Since Ch'en Po-ta, now a close collaborator of Mao, was the editor of *Red Flag* and given the obscure placing of the editorial, it would appear that the editorial reflected the views of Chairman Mao. The editorial stated:

Just as all things in the cosmos accept the new and reject the old, so also for our revolutionary troops the young generation must replace the old. Only so can we forever preserve and strengthen our powers of struggle; only so can we have the unlimited force of life. Revolutionaries must self-consciously follow this law of nature, positively cultivate the superior forces in the new generation, thus constantly replenishing the troops of Party members and cadres, replenishing our leadership capacities with new blood and bones. Now, the average age of leadership groups in many basic level units . . . is over forty. Party cadres over forty

---

22*Hungch'i* 17-18 (September 1964), 12.

23*Jenmin jihpao*, November 23, 1967. It makes sense that An Tzu-wen, the old master of organization, should be closely linked with Liu Shao-ch'i.

24For a reasonably good description of the movement, see Wang Hsiao-t'ang, "The 'Four Cleans' and the 'Cultural Revolution' of the Chinese Communists," *Feich'ing yenchiu* [*Studies on Chinese Communism*] I:1 (Taipei, January, 1967), 23-31, especially p. 26

years of age already form the majority. Of course, forty years is still a vigorous age, and people still have much latent force for work. But what happens "ten years, twenty years later"? As we see it, cultivating successors, adding new blood is something we must begin to consider, is a question we must urgently resolve.[25]

An Tzu-wen's article cited above makes no mention of the problem of cadres "over forty years of age."

The *Red Flag* editorial also warned that "new and old capitalistic elements . . . are trying to pull the young generation into non- and antirevolutionary directions." It is not difficult to conclude that a great struggle for the allegiance of the youth was being waged between the followers of Mao Tse-tung and of Liu Shao-ch'i. Thus we can see the political background to the ideological struggles described in the earlier section. Ideology may not have been important to the power struggles waged at the highest levels of power, but it was crucial for capturing the minds and hearts of the young people. But the protagonists in the struggle were not only two different currents in the Party, but also the Party and the army. In 1964, a vast campaign was begun to "learn from the People's Liberation Army" and spread *The Thought of Mao Tse-tung*. The army was the incarnation of youth, and its heroes, like Lei Feng, were young soldiers. Unlike the Party, where membership conferred life-time tenure, conscription kept the flow of new and old going in the army. The fight against a professional officer corps, waged by Lin Piao ever since the ouster of P'eng Te-huai in 1959, guaranteed that new blood would keep flowing, even into the higher ranks of the armed forces. Thus the army, by its nature, had powerful advantages over the Party in the struggle for the youth. What made it difficult for An Tzu-wen even to mention the question of cadres "over forty" was the fact that the higher the echelon in the structure of Party organization, the older the average age of the cadres. Thus the issue of age was not so important at the basic level, where cadres undoubtedly were younger anyway, but at the intermediate and higher levels of organization. We know now that the Cultural Revolution hit hardest and predominantly at the higher levels of the Party. The elimination of those "over forty" in the Party thus paralleled the campaign against the "professionals" in the army. We can thus see that the army, already in 1964, formed the spearhead of this campaign.

But the forces of Liu Shao-ch'i were not unaware of the importance

---

[25]*Hungch'i*, 14 (July, 1964) , 36. See John Wilson Lewis, "Revolutionary Struggle and the Second Generation in Communist China," *The China Quarterly* 21 (January-March, 1965) , 126-147.

of gaining the adherence of the youth. Wang Kuang-mei's remarks about people over and under thirty-five ("the only pure ones are a few young people") indicate that, in the villages, the Party was determined to recruit the new young leadership forces into its ranks, just as it had done in the precollectivization period of 1954 and 1955. We know from the bitter struggles in the higher schools during the Cultural Revolution that the allegiance of the majority of the youth was a major prize. However, in the schools, the Red Guards emerged as a competitor organization which finally succeeded in wresting power away from the Party structure. Similarly, the Party structure in the rural areas faced another competitor: the people's militia. In November 1964, a time when the Four Clean movement was in full swing, the General Political Department of the People's Liberation Army held a supreme conference under the personal leadership of Chairman Mao; judging from the list of participants, Mao's forces were in the majority.[26] The directives issued from the conference made clear that the militia had to be directly engaged in production. What that meant was that the militia was to be a vital part of the everyday life of the village. Provincial, military district, and county armed forces were directed to dispatch cadres down to the village to take part in the socialist education movement (i.e., the Four Clean movement). True, they were ordered "to follow the unified leadership of the local Party committees and work teams," but their lines of command went through the army.[27] This suggests that the stress on organizing poor and lower-middle peasant associations may have meant more than arousing a social movement among the peasants. Perhaps it was the rural militia, composed entirely of young people, which was intended to be the organizational form of these associations.

The discussions above indicate that the Party and the army were moving toward a clash, both in the ideological and the organizational arena. Whichever won would select the new generation of cadres to govern China in the future. Yet though there were deep currents of struggle which led to the Cultural Revolution, politics always concerns immediate and real issues. Such issues may often be only the peaks of the iceberg below, yet this does not diminish their importance. I have already noted the political upheaval indicated by the word "revolution" applied to the events of 1966 and 1967. We also know that the Cultural Revolution finally broke that extraordinary solidarity of the

---

[26]The length of the meeting (15 days) indicates that debate must have been acrimonious.

[27]*Jenmin jihpao,* November 17, 1964.

top leadership group of China which had persisted since the earliest days of the Communist movement. Debates, disagreements, purges among the top leadership have marked the entire history of Chinese communism, but always the contending factions came together again. He who lost out today had a chance of coming back tomorrow. Clearly a cleavage of such magnitude had come into being that Chairman Mao had to resort to the most extreme measures to implement his point of view. The Cultural Revolution made it evident that Chairman Mao is the one and only, the undisputed *leader* of the country. Since Chairman Mao's political role appears to have been of such central importance in this struggle, let me quote at length the introductory paragraphs of an important speech he made on October 26, 1966:

> I would like to talk about one or two questions. First I shall talk about the history of struggles within the Party. For seventeen years there has been a question that has not been well spoken about, namely that of the first and second line. In view of our country's security considerations and in view of what happened in the Soviet Union [under Stalin], we divided the Standing Committee of the Politburo into a first and second line, and set up the Secretariat. I retreated into the second line; Liu Shao-ch'i and Teng Hsiao-p'ing were in the first line. Liu, as vice-chairman, managed a portion of the important meetings, and Teng handled every-day affairs. As a result, this strengthened dispersionism over the last seventeen years, and led to the formation of many "independent kingdoms." Therefore, at the Tenth Plenum [should read Eleventh Plenum], we abolished the second line.[28]
>
> When I was in the second line, I did not handle every-day affairs, and left them to other people. I did this in order to give them confidence, because I expected to see God soon,[29] and because I did not expect any great changes in the country. When we discussed these things in the Party center, all members approved. Thereafter there were a lot of bad things about the comrades in the first line (because of dispersionism they made mistakes, and did not do the important things).
>
> It is not right just to blame those in the first line. First it was I who suggested the division of the Standing Committee into a first and second line, and the setting up of the Secretariat; they all agreed. Second, overly trusting these other people, it was only when the "twenty-three-point program" was adopted that I became aware of something funny going on. In Peking, "because of P'eng Chen," I couldn't get a needle

---

[28]An English translation in *Joint Publications Research Service* (Washingnton, D.C.) says Eleventh Plenum (August 1966).

[29]The same phrase appears in Edgar Snow's January 1965 interview with Mao Tse-tung. This argues for the authenticity of the speech. See *New Republic,* January 20, 1965.

in edgewise. There was nothing either I or the Party center could do.

At the time of a meeting of the Party center in September-October 1965, I asked: "What are we going to do about revisionism which has cropped up in the Party center—we must overturn revisionism in the provinces." At that time I could not carry out my ideas in Peking. The reason I launched the criticism of P'eng Chen in Shanghai away from Peking was that I knew anything I proposed would not be carried out by P'eng Chen. Now we have already resolved the problem of Peking.[30]

Although the text of the speech has come to us through indirect sources (Red Guard tabloids quoted by Japanese correspondents in Peking), the style (reminiscent of interviews Mao has given foreigners) and the substance argue for its authenticity. In this speech, Mao Tse-tung has suggested answers to some problems of top-level leadership and decision-making which I have discussed earlier (see pp. 143-147). Mao confirms, in effect, that the Secretariat headed by Teng Hsiao-p'ing (P'eng Chen was deputy chairman) had operational control of the Party. Since policy is not automatically converted into operations (see pp. 223-225), this meant that Mao could have no assurance that, even if his decisions were adopted at the policy level, they would be translated into corresponding action at the operational level. However, Mao admits further that, even at the policy-making level, he had abdicated a portion of his power. If Liu "managed a portion of the important meetings," this presumably meant that Liu would be responsible for the making of specific policies, but in the event of a major situation or crisis, the second line would be summoned, much as the National Security Council is supposed to be summoned for similar cases in the United States. Mao clearly said that, even when major policy issues were considered, the second line was not summoned. Thus it would appear that with Liu Shao-ch'i in control of the policy-making machinery and Teng Hsiao-p'ing in control of the operational sector, it was impossible for Chairman Mao to exercize leadership, no matter how revered he was as the maker of the Chinese Revolution and the giver of its ideology.

From widespread publicity given Liu Shao-ch'i and P'eng Chen in the official press during the fall of 1964, and from what is known of the Four Clean movement, we can presume that, indeed, Mao Tse-tung had lost *de facto* control of the Party at that time.[31]

––––

[30]This version is taken from *Yomiuri*, a Tokyo newspaper, January 7, 1967. The translation was presumably made from a Chinese original copied by Japanese correspondents in Peking.

[31]Both Liu Shao-ch'i and P'eng Chen were prominently featured in connection with the 1966 missions of the Japanese Communist party, headed by Miyamoto Kenji.

It was also then that Mao granted interviews to a number of foreign bourgeois visitors, notably a French delegation and Edgar Snow (in January 1965) ; perhaps he wished to transmit messages, as American presidents have been known to do, to the external world without being blocked by his own bureaucracy. Nevertheless, Mao appears to have had one organizational channel for conveying his opinions, namely the military. The meeting on activities of the people's militia mentioned above was held under the aegis of the General Political Department of the army. Yet even there, the active presence of so many men later purged (e.g., P'eng Chen, Lo Jui-ch'ing, and others) indicates that Mao's control did not penetrate effectively. Thus, as Branko Bogunovic, the veteran Yugoslav reporter in Peking, noted during the Cultural Revolution, Chairman Mao was, in fact, "the opposition minority" who stood up against the majority.[32]

But Mao had to struggle hard to win the army to his side, and as late as 1968 it was not certain that he had yet done so.[33] Lin Piao was long reputed to be in bad health. Lo Jui-ch'ing, later revealed as an arch counterrevolutionary, dominated the critical Military Affairs Committee. The General Political Department, an important link between the Party and the army, was obviously an arena of struggle between the two forces. I noted earlier that it was strange that the new political departments in economic administration and management had not been put under the jurisdiction of the operational departments of the Central Committee (see p. 144, 575). We can now see this as part of an effort to shift policy and operational powers from the Party to the army. That struggle must have gone on with ever increasing intensity during 1965 and the early part of 1966. When the army began its open attack on the Party in April 1966, leading quickly to the violent eruption of May 1966, Mao Tse-tung must have felt assured that, at least in the army, his leadership was supreme. Such confidence must have come to him when he succeeded in purging Lo Jui-ch'ing, reputedly in November 1965.

Those missions related directly to the question of Vietnam, Sino-Soviet relations, and to the most basic issues of Chinese foreign policy. On August 6, 1967, the *Jenmin jihpao* published a sharp attack on Miyamoto, accusing him of loudly advocating "united action" to oppose the United States and help Vietnam, while attacking China.

[32]"The Status and Future of Mao Tse-tung," *Oakland Tribune* (Oakland, Calif.), September 3, 1967.

[33]See Chalmers Johnson, "China: The Cultural Revolution in Structural Perspective," *Asian Survey* VIII:1 (January, 1968), 15.

The subsequent events of the struggle between Mao and Liu, between the army and the Party, form part of the drama leading to the Cultural Revolution, most of which is still wrapped in obscurity. Although the Chinese themselves today present the struggle in a theatrical, Manichaean way, as one between the forces of light (Mao) and those of darkness (Liu), it was obviously more complicated. From the fragmentary evidence available, it appears that the anti-Mao forces were divided into at least three groups: (1) one centering in P'eng Chen, Lo Jui-ch'ing, Lu Ting-i, and Yang Shang-k'un, (2) another centering in Liu Shao-ch'i, and (3) a third one centering in Teng Hsiao-p'ing. The first four have been openly called counterrevolutionary traitors, which thus makes them liable to the severest punishment (they were publicly pilloried with denunciatory placards hung around their necks). The Liu and Teng groups are officially called "the authoritarian clique following the capitalist road," terrible enough but not implying crimes as heinous as those attributed to the first group.

The first to be attacked and the first to be purged were P'eng, Lo, Lu, and Yang. We know that Mao Tse-tung used the Shanghai Party organization to launch his attack on P'eng Chen, who controlled Peking. Since Shanghai was subject to the jurisdiction of the Party Secretariat, headed by Teng Hsiao-p'ing, one could presume a temporary alliance between Mao and Teng. Indeed Teng, and some of his chief adherents, such as T'ao Chu, achieved prominence during the early months of the Cultural Revolution (the latter part of 1966). Thus Mao appears to have followed the classic principle of *divide et impera*. Between the four of them, these men controlled some of the most important apparatuses of the structure of state power: P'eng, through the Peking Party organization, wielded power over the state administration; Lo, as secretary-general of the Military Affairs Committee and chief of staff of the army, was Lin Piao's main competitor for control of the army; Lu headed the Propaganda Department of the Central Committee and so controlled the all-important sector of the mass media; Yang headed the General Office of the Central Committee, which position gave him control over all top Party personnel.[34] All four men were with long experience in the Party, and knew the importance of gaining operational control at the second echelon as a way of gaining policy control at the first echelon. The purge of these four men must be seen as a campaign by the forces of Mao Tse-tung to

----

[34] On the importance of personal control, see p. 258. See also, A. Doak Barnett, "Social Stratification and Aspects of Personnel Management in the Chinese Communist Bureaucracy," *The China Quarterly* 28 (October-December, 1966), 8-39.

wrest control of key organizational sectors away from men whom he regarded as his enemies. Only one aspect of this campaign, that against the mass media, specifically the *People's Daily*, is fairly well known. The first targets of the attack by the army in April 1966 were the mass media (e.g., the attacks on Teng T'o). That battle can be adjudged to have been won in June 1966, when the *People's Daily* dramatically changed its front-page format. I have already discussed the importance of the communications system for organization in China, and need not repeat the arguments (see pp. 58-68). He who controls the mass media, determines which ideological current shall dominate. Mao Tse-tung well understood that principle. One of his key supporters has been Ch'en Po-ta, editor of *Red Flag*, who replaced Lu Ting-i as the chief propagandist of the country.

During the Cultural Revolution, Red Guard wall posters appeared which accused the four of plotting a "February [1966] coup" to seize power.[35] Whether true or not, Mao Tse-tung and his followers had obviously made up their minds to "open fire" on the four leaders of the "counterrevolutionary black gang." P'eng Chen last appeared publicly late in March 1966, at a farewell for Miyamoto Kenji, the Japanese Communist leader. Early in June, he was formally ejected from his post as Party first secretary for Peking. In April Liu Shao-ch'i was out of the country.

In May, the first great outbursts of the Cultural Revolution began in the universities of Peking. However, it appears that it was Liu Shao-ch'i who assumed power in Peking. In his alleged confession, Liu stated that he had been in charge of the Cultural Revolution in Peking "for more than fifty days," starting on June 1, 1966; he was in charge of "everyday affairs" (i.e., operations) of the Central Committee.[36] Mao did not return to Peking until July 18; the previous day, he had just completed his phenomenal swim in the Yangtze, which, however, was not publicized until July 25. As in the supposed "February coup," reports later appeared about a "July coup" led by Liu Shao-ch'i. The coup failed, allegedly because Teng Hsiao-p'ing eventually threw in

----

[35]*China Topics* of Hong Kong (May 11, 1967) translated two of these posters: one of January 18, 1967 (published in *Chanpao*, a Red Guard tabloid), and the other April 17, 1967. A lengthy introduction casts doubt on these revelations. According to a May 7, 1967, report in *Chanpao*, Chou En-lai denied the existence of a "February coup." Nevertheless, there are grounds for believing that a major political struggle occurred in China in February and March 1966.

[36]See Liu Shao-ch'i's confession, *Asahi Shimbun*, December 27, 1966.

his lot with Mao and Lin.[37] From August 1 to 12, the Central Committee met in its Eleventh Plenum. The session must have been stormy, judging from the admitted presence of students from Peking's higher schools. It appears to have been a general triumph for Mao: his "[former] ten-point program" of May 1963 and, especially, his "twenty-three-point program" of January 1965 were officially accepted. "The entire plenum completely agreed with all the brilliant policy decisions made by Comrade Mao Tse-tung during the previous four years."[38] But Mao may have felt that, again, he had gained only verbal compliance. On August 18, a gigantic rally was called on T'ienanmen Square. As Mao Tse-tung, Lin Piao, and Chou En-lai appeared among the masses, the Red Guards surged forth and took charge of the political drama. From then until the end of 1967, the Red Guards were the chief instrument of Chairman Mao in the struggle against his enemies in the Party.

By August, 1966, Mao appeared well on the way to having captured the operational sectors of organization in Peking, as well as the top policy-making positions in the Central Committee. Thus, of the three groups singled out above, two were well on the way to complete elimination by this time. The turn of the third was yet to come. By the end of the year, Teng Hsiao-p'ing fell from his sudden rise to prominence, and a large-scale purge of the entire provincial Party apparatus began, that is, the organizational sector controlled by Teng. Men like T'ao Chu, Ulanfu, Li Ching-ch'üan, Liu Lan-t'ao, Ts'ao Ti-ch'iu, and many others, who had for years built up their power in the provinces (greatly aided by the operational autonomy gained by the provinces as a result of decentralization) were blasted from their positions by the Red Guards. In October 1967, *Agence France-Presse* reported from Peking that "the nation is almost entirely under military control. . . . In 26 of the 27 regions the leaders are new men, often military officers and often previously unknown."[39]

Early in 1967, it became apparent that Mao Tse-tung and his followers were making attempts to restore the organization that had been shattered during the Cultural Revolution. Early in February, Heilungkiang Province announced the formation of a "temporary supreme

---

[37]See Hsiao, "The Background and Development of 'The Proletarian Cultural Revolution'," p. 400. An article in the January 23, 1967 issue of the *Far Eastern Economic Review,* allegedly from a Yugoslav correspondent in Peking, claimed that Teng's switch played a decisive role in the events of July 1966. The article was widely reproduced in the Japanese, Taiwan, and French press.

[38]*Hungch'i,* 11 (August, 1966) , 3.

[39]*New York Times,* October 9, 1967.

power structure" to replace the old Party committee which had been smashed. This new structure was based on a "triple alliance" of revolutionary rebels, military leaders, and revolutionary leadership cadres (i.e., old Party cadres who had rallied to Mao). The reappearance of P'an Fu-sheng who had been purged in 1957 (see p. 215) and of Sung Jen-ch'iung, an old army man, in prominent leadership positions suggested a return to power of men who had lost out in earlier struggles.[40] Indeed, subsequently, a number of old-timers reappeared in prominent public places.[41] However, it is doubtful that these men exercize any real power today. New men are coming into political power throughout China. However, the Cultural Revolution seems to have succeeded finally in breaking the grip of those "over forty" on the key organization of the country, the Communist Party.

In January 1968, it was reported from Peking that the leadership had stepped up its drive to rebuild the Communist Party apparatus and had ordered the cessation of all Red Guard publications.[42] As has happened before in the Party's history, centralism is again returning. The Communist party has not disappeared, but it is too early to say whether the nature and structure of its organization have been basically changed by the Cultural Revolution. Perhaps Mao will try to implement his "Paris commune" model with periodic elections of Party members. But it is equally possible that the Party will gradually resume the form it had prior to the Cultural Revolution. As happened with Stalin's purges in Russia, an entire leadership stratum has been swept away, but this does not mean that the essence and dynamics of that organization have changed.

It will probably never be possible to arrive at a fully satisfying explanation why contradictions became so acute that they led to this upheaval. After all, the leadership had weathered intense storms of contradictions many times in the past without splitting asunder. Prominent leaders had many times in the past dropped from leadership (e.g., P'eng Te-huai) without provoking such storms. That there were deep currents of conflict between the various elements in the trinity of state power is obvious from our discussion, but why did these conflicts not go on in the way they had in the past? The simplest explanation is

---

40*Jenmin jihpao*, February 2, 10, 1967.

41For example, on October 1, 1967, China's national day: Chu Teh, Ch'en Yün, Soong Ching-ling, Tung Pi-wu, Fu Tso-i (KMT general who surrendered Peking), and Li Tsung-jen (former president of China who returned to Communist China from America a few years before); see *Jenmin jihpao*, October 2, 1967.

42*New York Times*, January 20, 1968.

that Chairman Mao knew that he would soon "face God," and wished to refashion the country according to his vision before he disappeared from the scene. This would explain his support of the army against the Party. But Mao has often spoken of the revolution in China as a matter of decades and even centuries. Given his belief in the forces of society, he must have known that the politics of the superstructure, that is, the state, alone could not determine the movements of the substructure—society. What must be explained, I believe, is the urgency, the sense of crisis which impelled Mao to act so violently in the spring and summer of 1966.

The Red Guard wall poster which described the alleged "February coup" claimed that "from May 1965 to the beginning of 1966 the coup clique have been trying to make public opinion believe that war was on the point of breaking out."[43] Early in May, 1965, Lo Jui-ch'ing wrote a major article, advocating "active defense" as a policy to be pursued against China's enemies. Those enemies, chiefly the United States, then were intensively bombing North Vietnam; on May 4, 1965, President Johnson reported to Congress that in April the United States had flown 1,500 strike sorties against North Vietnam as against 160 in February.[44] On January 31, 1966, the United States resumed heavy bombing of North Vietnam after a thirty-seven-day pause; the new bombing campaign reached an unprecedented point of intensity in April.[45] On June 29, 1966, the United States bombed the oil storage depots in the suburbs of Hanoi and Haiphong.[46] It is inconceivable that the issue of the Vietnam war expanding to China did not enter the minds of the men who were struggling for power in Peking.

On July 22, 1966, the Chinese government, under the name of Liu Shao-ch'i, issued a major declaration on Vietnam, stating China to be the "rear area" (houfang) of North Vietnam. Since North Vietnam considers itself officially to be the "rear area" for South Vietnam, the statement promised an analagous relationship to North Vietnam on the part of China.[47] That statement was quickly withdrawn from Chinese publications destined for foreign readers, and so, by implication, remained null and void. Three days later Chairman Mao's swimming feat in the Yangtze River was prominently (but belatedly) featured in the press. The message was clear: Chairman Mao and no one else is in

---

[43]See n. 36.

[44]*New York Times,* May 5, 1965.

[45]Franz Schurmann, Peter Dale Scott, Reginald Zelnik, *Politics of Escalation* (New York: Fawcett, 1966), pp. 129-131.

[46]*Ibid.,* p. 139.

[47]*Jenmin jihpao,* July 22, 1966.

command. The Vietnam statement was Liu Shao-ch'i's last official act. We know furthermore that P'eng Chen played a key role in the mission of the Japanese Communist party, headed by Miyamoto Kenji; that mission, traveling to North Vietnam and North Korea as well as China, obviously was concerned with the relationship of the Communist countries and movements to the Vietnam war.

In my opinion, the issue of policy toward the Vietnam war and, closely related to it, the issue of the relationship with the Soviet Union, were the sparks which set off the storm, whose deeper currents, however, had been building up for years and dealt with fundamental conflicts within the entire political structure.[48]

In this book, I have only discussed foreign policy incidentally, although, from the founding of the Chinese Communist party, its relationship to foreign countries and movements, notably the Soviet Union has had a profound influence on the Party's ideology and organization. The Soviet Union and China were in close alliance during the 1950's. That alliance turned to bitterness, hatred, and finally open hostility in the 1960's. Until February 1965, the Soviets and the Chinese were still able to argue about peace, war, and revolution in abstract terms. But when American planes began systematic warfare against North Vietnam, China's national security was directly and immediately threatened. Since the Soviets too were deeply involved in Vietnam, the Sino-Soviet polemic ceased being abstract. Policy toward Vietnam, in fact, became the one key issue in the Sino-Soviet relationship. Whatever decisions China made regarding that conflict would affect its future for years to come. That being the case, Chairman Mao could not allow others to make the decisions. He believes profoundly that his course is correct. Of those purged, all were deeply involved in the making of foreign policy. Lo Jui-ch'ing appears to have advocated a strong line on Vietnam. P'eng Chen was closely linked to the pro-Peking segment of the international Communist movement, and undoubtedly shared many of its views; in the spring of 1966, the North Koreans and the Japanese Communists, for example, argued that help for Vietnam and resistance to American imperialism should be the

----

48I have expressed these views more fully in two articles: "What is Happening in China," *The New York Review of Books,* October 20, 1966, and "An Exchange on China," *ibid.,* January 12, 1967. For a similar view, see Uri Ra'anan, "Rooting for Mao," *New Leader,* March 13, 1967, pp. 6-10; see also, *The Economist* (London) , February 25, 1967, p. 722. The best discussion on Peking's hawks and doves can be found in Donald Zagoria, *Vietnam Triangle* (New York, N.Y.: Pegasus, 1967) , pp. 63-98.

priority concern of all Communists. Liu probably came to share P'eng's views. If these men had brought China into the war, it is doubtful that Chairman Mao could have launched the Cultural Revolution, for wars tend to put a moratorium on political activity in the interest of national unity. If, indeed, these men, at various times, were contemplating moves leading to war, Mao had to act fast to prevent them from creating a fait accompli. He acted fast in July 1966.

ARMY

WHEN we speak of the army (all Chinese armed forces are designated as the People's Liberation Army) as a party of the trinity of state power, we not only indicate its great political importance but imply as close a relationship to society as for Party and government. In the advanced Western countries, people see the armed forces as bodies which are essentially segregated from society. Soldiers are governed by special law. They live in isolated bases. Only in cases of extreme emergency do they interfere in the activities of society. As organizations, the armed forces are regarded as the special instruments of the government to implement its foreign policy. Though they are given substantial sums from the revenues coming into the government, they are not supposed to constitute a part in the network of normal civil economic activity. Separate not only from society, they are also supposed to be separate from the normal constitution of the state. Their uniforms symbolize this separation both from society and from state.

Yet, since the end of World War II, armed forces, throughout the world, have played an increasingly important role in state and society. In many backward countries, military dictatorships have come to power. In some countries (e.g., Israel) armies play important roles in the education of the people. But particularly in the United States military organization has come to form an important element in state power, and so to develop increasingly close relationships to society. The importance of defense spending for the American national economy is obvious. The importance of the military in the making of foreign policy has been growing. With the outburst of urban unrest in American cities, the military is gradually coming to assume tasks of maintaining law and order in civil society. The traditional segregation of military and civil sphere is beginning to disappear.

In traditional China, Confucian scholars always argued that the civilian should take precedence over the soldier, and that the military sphere should be separate from the civilian. In fact, from the Sung Dynasty (960-1279) to modern times, military and civil officials were segregated. But the segregation that the Sung achieved came after centuries of experimentation with military systems which joined the two. During the three centuries of turbulence following the collapse of the Han Dynasty (221 A.D.), various dynasties, trying to reunite China and stabilize its society, introduced military systems which combined soldier and peasant. Every peasant was made a soldier and was liable to military service whenever the government called on him. These soldier-peasant military systems were usually connected with land-reform policies, namely the "equal-field" system which prohibited large-scale land ownership and guaranteed each peasant land to till. The soldier-peasant system thus served sociopolitical as well as military purposes. The state, through nationalization of the land, gained control of the villages, was able to exercize pressure on the landed gentry from below, and increased its tax-gathering capabilities. The soldier-peasant system helped reestablish law and order in the villages and provided the state with a steady flow of military manpower. But it had two main defects. Militarily, it restricted the manipulability of the army, for the soldier-peasants were reluctant to leave their home regions. Economically, it inhibited economic development which was spurred by private, and hence large-scale, ownership of land. When the great T'ang Dynasty came to power (618 A.D.), its centralizing government was determined to continue both the equal-field and the soldier-peasant systems (then called *fuping*). However, the growth of regionalistic military forces and the growing power of the landed gentry finally forced the T'ang to abandon both. After the short-lived but destructive An Lu-shan rebellion (755 A.D.), the country degenerated into warlordism. Local military commanders allied with local gentry acquired powerful armies with which they resisted the power of the central government. For two hundred years China was racked by civil war, which the first Sung emperor managed to end. He created a fine professional army under the direct command of the emperor. Splitting his enemies, he reestablished the power of the central government in the local areas by seizing control of the fiscal system, thus separating local gentry from local military commanders. What remained of local military forces, henceforth also recruited on a professional basis, served mainly to maintain law and order. Professionalization led to considerable emphasis on advanced techniques of war; for example, the Sung were the first to create a modern Chinese navy. The Sung thus finally achieved what the Confucians had been preaching for centuries: the military and civilian spheres were segregated, and the military, under the firm command of the emperor, became the instruments of the civil authorities (though not of the bureaucracy) .

The key method adopted by the Sung was the professionalization of the armed forces. Men were recruited by enlistment, not by conscription, as in the past. Soldiering became a life-time career. However, even this new system soon revealed itself to have severe drawbacks. As the barbarian encroachments intensified, the Sung suffered severe shortages of manpower. This led to a series of foreign conquests of China, culminating in a century of Mongol rule. When the Ming acceded to power in 1368, riding the crest of popular revolt against the Mongols, they tried, unsuccessfully, to return to a soldier-peasant system; similarly, like their earlier predecessors, they tried to reassert government control over the villages. The Manchus, foreign conquerors of the Ming, returned to the notion of professional armies. Their only move in the direction of a soldier-peasant system was the creation of village-based police forces, the *paochia* (see pp. 409-412) .[1]

The importance of armed forces for revolutionary warfare is obvious. From 1927 to 1949, the Chinese Communists waged a military struggle of great ideological, political, and organizational brilliance against their enemies. However, in 1950, their whole way of life, evolved for two decades, changed radically: they won. Victory may have been more of a spiritual trauma for the Chinese army than all the battles they fought earlier. With no military enemies left to fight, except mopping up operations, their very reason for being changed. What was to be their task during the period of construction and growth?[2]

We must make one fundamental assumption about Mao Tse-tung and other Chinese Communist leaders: like all men of learning in China, they have a deep knowledge of their country's history from ancient to modern times. Mao knows the history of rebellion and revolution in China, and has drawn many lessons from it. But he also knows the history of the military-civil relationship in China during times of peace. The history we have briefly described above he knows well, and in detail. Men may or may not learn lessons from history, but history teaches them what the problems are. Mao's views on the relationship of military and civil authority are shown in two famous sayings of his:

————

[1]See Chang Ch'i-yün, *Chungkuo chünshih shihlüeh* [*Brief Military History of China*] (Taipei, 1956) .

[2]See pp. 246, 321 for some of the problems of transition from war to peace.

Every Communist must understand this truth: "Political power grows out of the barrel of the gun."

Our principle is that the Party commands the gun; we must never allow the gun to command the Party.[3]

Put in different terms, these two maxims say that armed forces always generate political power; unless the civil retains firm control, the military will assume independent power.

Since military questions relate to national security, much of the organizational history of the army is unknown to us. If Party and government, at times, reveal their activities in some detail, the army discusses its problems in general terms. But even the little we know permits us to make some assessments and analyses of its part in the trinity of state power.

In October 1950, the Chinese entered the Korean War. Barely one year after the triumph of the Chinese Revolution, Chinese soldiers were again engaged in battle. However, this time they fought on foreign soil. During that war, the Chinese decided to adopt Soviet techniques and pursue a policy of building a modern, professional army. Despite the technological inferiority of the Chinese, the fight in Korea was between two modern armies. As Alexander L. George has said, the Chinese made the transition from "a revolutionary to a professional army."[4] Since the Chinese were universally emulating Soviet methods, it was not surprising that their army too was sovietized; even the "human wave" attacks, used so widely in the Korean War, were more reminiscent of Russian tactics in both World Wars than the revolutionary warfare tactics used by Lin Piao during the civil war. The decision to modernize and professionalize the army had profound effects: it meant concentration on the development of modern military techniques, the development of a professional officer corps, the introduction of conscription, and, above all, a policy of reliance on the Soviet Union.[5] Just as Stalin, in the 1930's, decided to turn the Red Army into a professional body, his Chinese emulators, in the early 1950's, decided to follow a similar policy. Soviet uniforms became standard in the Chinese army, as did

---

[3]*The Sayings of Chairman Mao* (Peking: General Political Department of the People's Liberation Army, 1966) , sections 5, 9.

[4]Alexander L. George, *The Chinese Communist Army in Action* (New York: Columbia University Press, 1967) , pp. 199-205.

[5]See Ellis Joffe, *Party and Army: Professionalism and Political Control in the Chinese Officer Corps, 1949-1964* (Cambridge, Mass.: Harvard University Press, 1965) , pp. 1-45.

Soviet-style military decorations. The distinction between officers and men was emphasized.[6]

Modernization and professionalization also meant organizational centralization. In 1954, the Ministry of National Defense became one of the most powerful bureaucracies in the central government. Like the Department of Defense in the American government, the Ministry of National Defense wielded supreme command over all armed forces of the country. P'eng Te-huai, commander in chief of Chinese forces in Korea and leader in the modernization drive, became minister, a post he held to his purge in September 1959. There can be no doubt that the military played a key role in the program of economic development, and that it strongly supported rapid development of a modern, heavy industrial base.[7] P'eng Te-huai's association with Kao Kang on China's first State Planning Commission in 1952 already suggested the army's commitment to a program of heavy industrialization, from which it would eventually acquire needed modern weaponry (see p. 333). Here again the Chinese army was following the Stalinist approach to heavy industrialization, which closely linked heavy industry with the development of a modern military potential. Given the immense power of the military in the economic sphere, it is obvious that no economic policies could be adopted without the agreement and support of the military.

A counterpart of the program of modernization and professionalization was a decline of the People's Militia *(minping)*. The militia numbered 22,000,000 individuals in 1953, but, with the introduction of conscription to replace the volunteer system previously in effect, the militia was gradually amalgamated with the military reserves. From 1953 to 1958, little was said about the militia. With communization, however, the militia, once again, became an important force on the local political scene (see pp. 478 ff.) [8]

The adoption of the Military Service Law in November 1954 which provided for conscription and a system of trained reserves thus signaled formal adoption of the program advocated by P'eng Te-huai. The inevitable consequences of that policy was the demobilization of the huge standing armies the Chinese had built up during the Korean War. By

---

6*Ibid.*, pp. 72-79; see *Chungkung shihnien,* p. 377.

7Explicitly stated by then Deputy Minister of National Defense T'an Cheng, whom the attacks of the Cultural Revolution have linked to P'eng Te-huai; see *Kuangming jihpao,* October 1, 1955.

8*Chungkung shihnien,* pp. 377-378. The compilation *Source Book on Military Affairs in Communist China* (Hong Kong: Union Research Institute, 1965) presents no documents on the militia between 1952 and 1958.

December 1955, 4,510,000 soldiers had been demobilized from the army.[9] Conscription provided for about 700,000 men to be drafted each year for a three year period of service.[10] The army thus was to become a tight, compact streamlined military force.

Seen in historical perspective, P'eng Te-huai's policy followed the military course pursued by the Sung Dynasty. As during the Sung period, such a policy limited the availability of active service personnel at the disposal of the government. We know that there was strong dissent from this policy during the mid-1950's. Generals Liu Po-ch'eng and Yeh Chien-ying (the latter has risen to prominent position during the Cultural Revolution) argued against reduction of the armed forces and for "immediate development of well-trained and well-equipped forces-in-being, a strong air force, and an adequate air-defense system."[11] The policies advocated by Liu and Yeh appeared to be even more "expert" than those advocated by P'eng.

There can be little doubt that the chief advocates of the People's Militia were Mao Tse-tung and Lin Piao, and that the reintroduction of the militia system in 1958, simultaneous with communization, expressed the policies advocated by Mao. The reserves and the militia recruited the same people: young men who were not conscripted and veterans. But the nature of service was different. A member of the reserves was always subject to call-up; he could be sent anywhere the military authorities decreed. A member of the militia, however, served for the defense of his village or his local area; he could not be sent away to distant areas. Again, in historical perspective, we can say that Mao Tse-tung advocated a soldier-peasant military system, similar to that which had been in effect in periods before the Sung Dynasty.

The Sung system was based on a segregation of the military and civil spheres, and the same was implied by P'eng Te-huai's policies. However, the Sung system also assumed civil control of the economy; through the instrument of the bureaucracy, the state gained control over the fiscal system. The counterpart of that in the mid-1950's was Party control over society. I have already pointed out that the demobilized veterans in 1955 formed a nucleus for Party build-up in many villages where Party organization had not yet been established (see p. 135). The establishment of Party control at the village level through-

---

[9]Peter Tang, *Communist China Today* (2nd ed., Washington, D. C., 1961), p. 403.

[10]Joffe, *op. cit.*, p. 39.

[11]Alice Langley Hsieh, *Communist China's Strategy in the Nuclear Era* (Englewood Cliffs, N. J.: Prentice-Hall, 1962), p. 40.

out China made possible the collectivization of 1955/56. However, even if veterans formed a major part of the Party cadres, their simultaneous status as members of the reserves did not conflict with their essentially civil roles as Party members. On the other hand, the militia had the potential for creating another kind of organization at the village level which could conflict with the Party. There are grounds for believing that this is what Mao advocated in 1964 (see p. 547). With recent attempts to link P'eng Te-huai with Liu Shao-ch'i in the official press,[12] I could be exaggerating the compatibility of their policies in the 1950's. However, my argument would indicate no real conflict between P'eng's stress on a small professional army and a system of trained reserves and Liu's commitment to maximizing the Party's organizational control.

What was the rationale behind P'eng's policies? Alice Hsieh indicates that "this approach permitted him to support a decrease in Chinese defense expenditures through a reduction in the standing army and greater dependence on trained reserves, and to argue that the saving in military expenditures should be applied to economic development."[13] We know from the example of many underdeveloped countries that they must make a clear-cut choice between "butter" (i.e., economic growth) and "guns" (i.e., military might). In the 1950's, China made the decision for economic growth at the expense of maximal military preparedness. However, this policy made one basic assumption: that China's national security would be guaranteed by the Soviet nuclear shield and that her requirements for modern weaponry, till a time that she could produce them herself, would be supplied by the Soviet Union. That assumption was shattered in June 1959 when the Soviets broke their nuclear-power-sharing agreement with the Chinese; one month later, P'eng Te-huai was dismissed. The Soviets, one might add, have been attacking Mao Tse-tung on the grounds that he seeks Chinese military might at the expense of economic development. What they fail to note is that China could only have continued on the path laid out by P'eng Te-huai if she had absolute assurance of the Soviet nuclear shield and absolute assurance of Soviet military support.

---

[12]See the editorial "From the Defeat of P'eng Te-huai to the Bankruptcy of the Chinese Khrushchev," *Jenmin jihpao*, August 16, 1967. The editorial and lead article focus on the Lushan meeting of July, 1959. They accuse both P'eng and Liu of opposition to the Great Leap Forward, of opposition to Chairman Mao, and of trying to worm their way into Party and army.

[13]*Op. cit.*, p. 37.

We must also note that P'eng was opposed not only by Mao Tse-tung but from influential fellow "professionals," notably Liu Po-ch'eng, Yeh Chien-ying, and Su Yü. Though Liu now seems out of favor, both Yeh and Su are among the top leadership group in China.[14] All argued, against P'eng, for "interim defense measures," that China must ever be prepared against "sudden attack" by the United States, wanted a step up in military preparedness, and, implicitly, put less reliance on the Soviet shield.[15] As the Sino-Soviet split worsened, the military policies of these men increasingly prevailed. The launching of China's nuclear program closely follows their view that China must create her own modern defense potential. The rapid build-up of China's military industry during the early 1960's likewise reflects their "professional" views. Just as the Cultural Revolution did not disturb Chinese nuclear tests, so these men, and many other "professionals," remained outside the political arena. Significantly, Nieh Jung-chen, the leader of China's research and development program, is today among the top leaders of the country. Some Western observers have argued that Mao Tse-tung and Lin Piao wished to turn the Chinese army back to its guerrilla past. Nothing could be farther from the truth. The Chinese army, despite (and possibly even because of) the Cultural Revolution is rapidly becoming a modern fighting force. Any attack will be met with more than rifles and grenades.

Compared with these men P'eng Te-huai appears more political than professional. Many Western scholars have interpreted the struggles within the Chinese leadership during the 1960's as between the revolutionaries and the professionals, between the reds and the experts.[16] This view implies that the professionals and the experts are identical, that expertise leads to professionalism. I have, in fact, said the same in speaking of expert professionals and red cadres (see p. 72). However, closer examination of these political struggles forces me to revise my views. In the immense quantity of documents which have come out of the Cultural Revolution, the phrase "red and expert" has hardly appeared. P'eng Te-huai has been bitterly attacked for trying to usurp power in Party and army, but not for advocating "expertise."[17] A major article published by the army's newspaper *Liberation Army Daily* of August 1, 1966 accused the enemies of Mao Tse-tung (P'eng Te-huai

---

[14]They are listed among the top twenty-one leaders at the October 1, 1967 celebrations; see *Jenmin jihpao*, October 2, 1967.

[15]See Hsieh, *op. cit.*, pp. 38 ff.

[16]See, for example, A. Doak Barnett, *China After Mao* (Princeton, 1967), pp. 25 ff.

[17]See *Jenmin jihpao*, August 16, 1967.

was clearly meant) of advocating the "regularization and moderniza-tion" of the armed forces and urging the copying of foreign (i.e., Soviet) methods. However, again, no accusation of advocating "ex-pertise" over "redness" was made.[18] The reasons for this important ommission are clear. High-ranking leaders who have come out in support of Mao have been the experts in the military (such as Nieh Jung-chen, Yeh Chien-ying, and Su Yü) and the experts in the govern-ment (for example, Li Fu-Ch'un, Li Hsien-nien, Ch'en Yi and many others). In fact, the August 8, 1966 resolution of the Central Commit-tee (confirmed by the Eleventh Plenum) which became the guidelines for the great popular outburst following August 18, exempted scientists and technicians from the struggle.[19] If the Cultural Revolution there-fore, was not directed against the experts, then expertise could not have been the key issue in the struggles which led up to it.

I suggest that a distinction must now be made between professional and expert. Expertise means a technical capacity (e.g., in science, technology, or administration), but professionalism means commit-ment to an occupational position. I have noted that two élites ap-peared to be developing in China: the body of organizational leaders with political status deriving from ideology, and the professional in-tellectuals with status deriving from education (see p. 8). If occupa-tional position gives rise to status, then professionalism will lead to the formation of élites. The accusations directed against "the authori-tarian clique following the capitalist road" have aimed at their élite status, and not at their expertise. That has also been at the root of the attacks on the tendencies for a professional officer corps to develop.[20] The intellectuals are the men of expertise in China, its scientists, tech-nicians, and administrators. There have been and undoubtedly will continue to be tendencies toward the formation of an expert élite. However, since the brunt of the attack of the Cultural Revolution was on the Party, of gravest concern to Mao Tse-tung and his followers was the emergence of a professional red élite—that is, an élite whose power and status derived from Party position.

The attacks on P'eng Te-huai can thus been seen as the beginning of a struggle by the forces of Mao Tse-tung against an emerging élite of political professionals whose power centered on the Party. Ellis Joffe has noted that Lin Piao and his supporters intervened in the Cultural Revolution as part of a political élite and not as representatives of the

---

18*Peking Review*, August 5, 1966; see also Schurmann and Schell, *Communist China (The China Reader*, Vol. III), (New York: Random House, 1967), p. 625.

19*Hungch'i* 10 (August, 1966), 8 (point 12 of the 16-point resolution).

20Joffe, *op. cit.*, pp. 72 ff.

military, adding that there is no indication that the army, as an organization, has played a role in the Cultural Revolution.[21] Judging from the scope of the purges, Lin Piao's "political élite" was far inferior in numbers to the political élite which was being attacked. Whether Joffe's observation that the army, as an organization, played no major role in the Cultural Revolution is correct could be argued from various points of view. The army did intervene, from time to time, to put down disorder and mediate between contending factions; army officers have played a major role in the emerging group of new "triple alliance" leaders; there were apparently instances of resistance to Peking by local military commanders (e.g., Ch'en Tsai-tao in Wuhan, and the reported resistance of Wang En-mao in Sinkiang). However, there is no evidence that struggles comparable to those which erupted within the Party occurred in the army. The key struggle was to capture the policy and decision-making positions within both the Party and the army, and that struggle was fought between a red revolutionary and a red professional current. A third current might be called that of the pure experts, symbolized by Yeh Chien-ying, Nieh Jung-chen, and Su Yü. Apparently not aspiring to policy-making positions or having rallied to Mao or simply having waited on the sidelines to see who would win, this current, like that of their expert counterparts in the government administration, stood apart from the Cultural Revolution.

The pure experts appear to have had one main concern: that the army be provided with the most modern defense capabilities. Where they differed from such red professionals as P'eng Te-huai was in their judgments over reliance on the Soviet Union to supply this weaponry. By 1960, when the Soviets withdrew their technicians from China, this question became academic. Either China developed its own strategic industry or it would not have a modern defense capability. Since all protagonists in the political struggles favored the most rapid development of strategic industry, one can presume that the pure experts were not directly involved in those struggles since 1960. Could one then speak of a conflict between the Party and the army during this period? If we remember that the red professionals had their base in the Party, then we can presume that they sought to gain policy and decision-making control over the army from that base. Conversely, the red revolutionaries, led by Mao Tse-tung and Lin Piao, sought to use their power and influence within the policy and decision-making posi-

---

[21]"The PLA in Politics and Politics in the PLA, 1965-1966," Columbia University Seminar on Modern East Asia, November 30, 1966), p. 1.

tions in the army to exercize pressure on and, eventually, acquire control over the Party.

As I have already indicated, one of the key issues of contention between Mao Tse-tung and P'eng Te-huai was over the question of the People's Militia. In the denunciations of P'eng Te-huai, he was accused of trying to "abolish the local armed forces and the militia." This was in 1959. However, during the summer of 1958, Mao Tse-tung had won out; the peasants were militarized and the militia was resurrected. But the opposition to Mao must have been strong, for the decision was only made after the Military Affairs Committee of the Central Committee had met for over a month (May-July, 1958) .[22] Since we know that Mao had suffered a defeat in December 1958 and had resigned as chairman of the republic, we can presume that P'eng Te-huai, during the time between December 1958 and September 1959, when he was dismissed, had tried to reverse the process of militia formation. That this happened was confirmed by documents in the *Work Bulletins* (*Kungtso t'unghsün*): "Some [Party] leaders and cadres . . . indiscriminately kicked out all militia organizations, and reorganized them without exception; they withdrew all militia arms."[23] P'eng's dismissal in 1959 prepared the way for Lin Piao's rise to power in the army and renewed attempts to implement the militia system on a nation-wide scale. Progress appears to have been slow until 1963, when the "Learn from the People's Liberation Army" campaign was launched. By 1964, the campaign was in full swing. By then it was clear that the militia was to become one of the most important basic-level organizations in the Chinese village.

The original militia campaign launched during the Great Leap Forward followed the slogan: "Everyone a Soldier." That this was not an empty phrase is indicated by an important article on the militia contained in the *Work Bulletins:* Honan province had about twenty million militia members, constituting 39 percent of the entire population.[24] Obviously such a vast organization could not become effective in a short period. The mentioned article notes that, throughout Honan, bad elements had assumed command positions in the militia. Militia members were guilty of serious crimes, and were bitterly hated by large elements of the population.[25] The sudden distribution of arms to the militia in the summer of 1958 (a policy opposed by the red

---

22See n. 19. See also *Jenmin jihpao*, August 1, 1958.

23*The Politics of the Chinese Red Army* (ed. by J. Chester Cheng) , (Stanford, Calif.: Hoover Institute Publications, 1966) , p. 566.

24*Ibid.*, p. 117.

25*Ibid.*, p. 119.

professionals) created new sources of village power. As Mao Tse-tung said, "political power grows out of the barrel of the gun." But aside from the wrongdoings committed by the militia men, the most serious problem was that the militia came to constitute a competitor for local power with the village and commune Party organizations. Thus, that same Party-army struggle which one could observe at the highest levels of the state was being repeated at the village level.

As I have indicated earlier (see p. 542), Mao Tse-tung appears to have had more confidence in the basically reliable qualities of the peasants who made up the militia than Liu Shao-ch'i. Nevertheless, Mao knew from the history of the *paochia* during Ch'ing times and of the village self-defense brigades of Kuomintang days that more was necessary than putting arms in the hands of the peasants. Leadership was all-important, and correct leadership could only come about through training. Such training could only be carried out by the army.

The important role played by veterans in village political organization is indicated by the following report on Shantung from January 1963, a time when the "Learn from the People's Liberation Army" campaign was launched:

> In the entire province of Shantung there are 700,000 veterans and soldiers wounded during the revolution. The great majority received training and experience during the revolutionary war. After they returned to their villages, they constituted an important core cadre force in the development of a collective economy through the communes. Now veterans and wounded soldiers have been elected to basic-level cadre positions in the villages; they constitute 30 percent of all commune and brigade cadres in the province. In the old revolutionary base areas, they constitute more than 60 percent.[26]

These old veterans of the revolutionary wars became cadres in the villages. However, rotation of conscription also returns large numbers of new veterans back to the villages each year. Since the great majority of new veterans had been recruited into the Party or the Youth League during their military service, they already had cadre status when they returned home.[27] Probably there was generational conflicts between those "over forty" and the young people. But perhaps more significant, these new veterans assumed leadership roles in the militia where youth predominated.

Both as members of the militia and of the Party, the veterans were

---

26 *Jenmin jihpao,* January 17, 1963.

27 See China News Analysis 581 (September 17, 1965), p. 3; see also A. Doak Barnett, *Cadres, Bureaucracy and Political Power in Communist China* (New York and London: Columbia University Press, 1967), p. 181.

subject to channels of ideological influence and political power. But because of the struggles then being waged at the highest levels of leadership, the messages coming from these two channels could not have been identical. The Party, of course, controlled its own education, but education in the army was under the jurisdiction of the General Political Department of the army. The General Political Department formally was an organization on a par with the General Staff; both were under the jurisdiction of the Ministry of National Defense. However, as a political body it was also subject to the jurisdiction of the Military Affairs Committee of the Central Committee.[28] That there were two distinct channels of power and influence was stated explicitly by Hsiao Hua, director of the General Political Department, in January 1966: "We must resolutely implement dual rule over the army by the military system *(hsit'ung)* and the regional Party committees under the unified leadership of the Party Central Committee."[29]

During the 1960's, the Military Affairs Committee and the General Political Department were the arena of the great political struggles which led to the Cultural Revolution. T'an Cheng, director of the General Political Department from 1956 to September 1964, was openly implicated with P'eng Te-huai; it is likely that his influence declined after the ouster of P'eng in 1959. In September 1964, Hsiao Hua replaced him. Hsiao Hua's commitment to the Maoist ideological and political current is clear from a major article he wrote in the summer of 1963 under a thinly disguised pseudonym.[30] Mao's greatest foe, however, was Lo Jui-ch'ing, secretary general of the Military Affairs Committee since 1961 (see p. 550). How long it took Mao and Lin Piao to assure their command over the Military Affairs Committee is difficult to say. The meeting of the General Political Department in November 1964 already suggested a pro-Mao majority (see p.547). However, by the summer of 1966, their command was absolute. Point fifteen of the sixteen-point resolution of August 8, 1966, on the Cultural Revolution stated: "The Cultural Revolution and socialist education movements in the army will take place according to directives from the Military Affairs Committee of the Central Committee and from the General Political Department."

The sixteen-point resolution, in effect, eliminated the dual rule of

----

28See pp. 144, 150; see, also, *Current Scene* IV:15 (Hong Kong, August 8, 1966) .

29*Jenmin jihpao,* January 25, 1966. On "dual rule," see pp. 188 ff. On the special significance of the word "system" *(hsit'ung),* see Barnett, *op. cit.,* pp. 6 ff. "System" appears to be the word now used in China to refer to what I have called branch-type organization (see p. 89) .

30*Hungch'i* 15 (August, 1963) , 14-23.

which Hsiao Hua had spoken in January of the same year. Henceforth, there was to be only one line of policy and decision-making command in the army, from the highest levels down to the militia. Lin Piao now stood undisputed at the head of that chain of command. That triumph was also indicated by the prominence over the *People's Daily* of the *Liberation Army Daily,* the organ of the army. Since Mao and Lin had first assured their command over the army before attacking the Party, the army newspaper became the organ of their ideological and political current. So also in the important arena of the mass media, one could see the two channels of influence and power.

When the militia was revived during the Great Leap Forward, it was intended to serve as a popular arm of the army; of course, channels of command went from the army to the militia (see p. 482). However, as I have already noted, the militia system never was effectively implemented. A. Doak Barnett's study of county organization does not indicate that the militia played an important role in the political life of the county. In fact, "in the early 1960's . . . militia work slipped temporarily into the background."[31] Contact with the army does not appear to have been active; moreover, the regular army troops were "isolated to a fairly high degree from the general population."[32] Barnett's study shows that the Party dominated organizational life in the county. However, the conditions described in that study apply mainly to the early 1960's. By 1964, a determined effort was being made to strengthen the militia system. The November 1964 meeting of the General Political Department under Mao Tse-tung's personal leadership indicated that "in recent years, under the leadership of the Party Central Committee, the Military Affairs Committee, and the regional Party committees, militia work had achieved great success."[33] However, it is hardly likely, in view of the "Four Clean" campaign then in process, that the regional Party committees were enthusiastic about advancing militia work. But, by this time, Mao had another weapon to implement his policy. The "Learn from the People's Liberation Army" campaign which began in 1963 was designed precisely to overcome that isolation of the army from the general population, which Barnett noticed in the county he studied. Thus we can presume that the army began to exercize that chain of command over the militia which was originally intended during the Great Leap Forward. But in addition to command, the army was able to exert ideological and political in-

---

[31]Barnett, *Cadres,* p. 248.

[32]*Ibid.,* p. 249

[33]*Jenmin jihpao,* November 17, 1964.

fluence over the young militia men through the military Party committees which were controlled by the General Political Department.

During the Cultural Revolution, the villages of China, so far as could be gathered, remained quiet. Whether that was due to the successful implementation of the militia system is hard to say. Nevertheless, with the disarray of the Party as a result of the Cultural Revolution, the militia under the direction of the army must be accounted one of the major stabilizing forces on the land.

From the 1950's to the present, Mao Tse-tung must be seen as the prime mover in the campaign to implement the militia system. It is a soldier-peasant system—"everyone a soldier," as the slogan went. It had been implemented in China centuries before when strong central governments wanted secure control over the villages, exercize pressure on the landed gentry from below, and increase their tax-gathering capabilities (see p. 558). The soldier-peasant system generally went hand in hand with land reforms based on equal ownership and periodic rotation of land. Similarities between these ancient soldier-peasant systems and Mao Tse-tung's program for the peasantry seem evident. Mao's advocacy of the militia is always linked to his defense of the commune system. However, there is another important similarity. The ancient soldier-peasant and equal-field systems were directed against the local landholding gentry whose power formed a wedge between the government and the peasants. The stronger the gentry, the less able was the government to carry out its will. Specifically, a strong gentry impeded the government's ability to collect taxes. When the T'ang finally abandoned the soldier-peasant and equal-field systems, it was because the strength of the local landholding gentry had become so great that the government had to come to terms with it. An analagous situation seems to have existed in China in the early 1960's. The implementation of decentralization II in 1957 (see pp. 175-1756, 195 ff.) greatly increased the power of the regional Party organizations. Decentralization I instituted in 1961 temporarily reduced the powers of the regional Party organizations, but I have already noted that they had begun to recover some of their lost powers (see p. 219). If, in general, the Party can be seen as a functional equivalent to the gentry (see p. 8), then, like its ancient predecessor, it began to develop its greatest strength at the regional level.[34]

---

[34] I have elsewhere discussed the tendency of all Communist parties to develop their greatest strength, as organizations, at regional rather than national levels; see my article "Politics and Economics in Russia and China," in Donald Treadgold, ed. *Soviet and Chinese Communism: Similarities and Differences* (Seattle: University of Washington Press, 1967), p. 317.

The power of the traditional gentry was based on ownership of land, solidarity of kinship, and participation in the regional and national political systems. Education, formally attested by the holding of a patent gained by passing state examinations, was the ideological-political bond which held the entire class together from one end of the country to the other. Granted the differences between the traditional gentry and the Communist party of China, Mao Tse-tung perhaps thought that the Party might have been turning into a neo-gentry. As Barnett points out for the county he studied, "to a large extent, a small group of these men [i.e., "old cadres"] had dominated the power apparatus in this area ever since Communist takeover."[35] If this was true at the local level, it was even more true with the provincial Party organizations where men like T'ao Chu were able to build Party machines, from which base they came to exert great power and influence at the national level.[36]

If ancient patterns were being repeated, then perhaps the accusations against "the authoritarian clique" that they favored a capitalistic restoration on the land may have some truth to them. Private ownership of land *per se* was never a goal of the gentry. In old China, the gentry acquired a tight grip on the local economy through large-scale accumulation of land, and so was able to force the government to come to terms with it. In Communist China, economic decentralization enhanced regional Party power; Party control of the communes brought its grip right down to the village level. Like its gentry predecessor, the regional Party apparatus was thereby in a position to control the local economy.

That the commune system is critical for the survival of a revolutionary China is one of Mao's basic beliefs. However, Mao believes also that the communes can only survive if they are controlled by the peasants themselves. That will only be assured if "democracy"—that is, the ability of the peasants to make their own decisions—is fully implemented (see pp. 85 ff.). Mao's advocacy of the formation of poor and lower-middle peasant associations in 1963 indicates his concern that control of the communes be "democratic" and not "centralized," that is, controlled by an external Party apparatus. The failure of these associations to materialize in 1963/64 explains why Mao put so much emphasis on the militia: through the militia, educated along the same

---

[35]Barnett, *Cadres*, p, 130.

[36]See Michel Oksenberg, "Paths to Leadership in Communist China," *Current Scene* III:24 (August 1, 1965). See also, Teiwes, *op. cit.*

democratic lines as the army,[37] "democracy" would be implemented in the communes.

The "democracy" advocated by Mao for the communes is much more compatible with decentralization I than with decentralization II (see pp. 175 ff.). This may explain the prominent reappearance during the Cultural Revolution of Ch'en Yün who, as I have indicated, was the chief advocate of decentralization I during the mid-1950's (see pp. 195 ff.). It may also explain the fact that, in essence, the practical policies introduced into the countryside in 1961 are still in effect. On the other hand, we must remember that, in ancient China, egalitarian land systems were implemented by strong centralized governments in order to enhance their tax-gathering capabilities. This suggests that the policies advocated by Mao may result in an even greater nation-wide centralization. Mao makes it clear in his *Sayings* that he believes both in democracy and centralism. If that is so, then the army may indeed be the true model on which the new organizational structure of China is to be developed.

The Chinese army operates on a principle of centralized and co-ordinated command, but has also considerable autonomy for basic-level units to act on their own. During the guerrilla war against the Japanese, Communist units operated with great autonomy in thousands of local actions. Yet, due to a remarkable communications system, to ideological and political unity, and to coordinated leadership, the People's Liberation Army was able to function as a single armed force. By contrast, its chief enemy, the Kuomintang, was bedeviled by war-lordism and vested interests at intermediate levels of organization, a phenomenon which, in the end, sapped its unified fighting capabilities.

In the struggle between Mao and Liu, between the army and the Party, we must not forget that Mao is convinced that China will one day be attacked by foreign enemies, notably the United States. China is preparing for war, as Han Suyin tirelessly points out. The escalation of the Vietnam war in 1965 increased the urgency of the internal struggles. Time was running out, both for Mao as a man and for China as a country. The changes which Mao deeply believed had to be implemented to prepare China for war could not be delayed. I have no doubt that, were it not for the developing war crisis, the Cultural Revolution would never have attained the furor that it did.

Mao Tse-tung used the army, not just to attack the Party but to cleanse it. The Party remains, and now, early in 1968, is in the process of being rebuilt. The Party will continue to be the corps of the coun-

---

[37]See Joffe, *op. cit.*, pp. 30 ff., 72 ff.

try's cadres. It had been turning into an élite of red bureaucrats. By contrast, the army had been becoming increasingly democratic: ranks and insignia were abolished, officers and men came closer together, soldiers and people joined. During revolutionary days, Party and army were alike. Subsequently, they diverged. Mao is determined to make the Party once again the fine egalitarian, democratic, flexible, revolutionary instrument it was in the days of the war against the Japanese and the Kuomintang.

GOVERNMENT

OF the three structures in the trinity of state power, the government, in the period since 1961, has been least visible. Aside from occasional announcements of administrative changes, the press has reported almost nothing about the operations of China's administrative system. When the Cultural Revolution began, what little news there had been about the government disappeared all together. Yet, despite this silence, the government has been going about its business. Indeed, business—that is, the management of the economy—is the chief concern of the government (see p. 182). One of the great surprises to many Western observers was that, despite some setbacks, the Chinese economy survived the Cultural Revolution intact. A good crop came in 1967, and food supplies were plentiful in the cities. Moreover, foreign trade remained active. Since disruption of the administrative system in 1958 was one of the contributing causes to the economic crisis of 1960/61, it would appear that the Cultural Revolution did not lead to a similar disruption.

Considering the close interpretation of Party and government, it is surprising that such a shattering attack on the Party at its highest levels did not result in chaos within the administrative system. I can only offer one tentative explanation: the leadership, whatever the differences among itself, had succeeded in separating policy from operational functions (see pp. 110-111, 223-225). Thus, in the absence of new policy directives, the leaders and workers of the state administrative system just kept on doing what they had been doing. Often, in articles on administrative problems, one comes across the word *yehwu*, "business" or "operations." *Yehwu* refers to the technical and specialized tasks of an administrative body.[1] Since these tasks are determined

---

[1] See A. Doak Barnett, *Cadres, Bureaucracy, and Political Power in Communist China*, p. 22.

by previous history and cannot easily be changed, we can presume that, as the turmoil of the Cultural Revolution intensified, the administrators simply kept to their business and operational tasks.

Yet the official silence on the government did not mean that the contending parties in the struggle were not making efforts to assure themselves command over the key positions in the government. Liu Shao-ch'i, Teng Hsiao-p'ing, P'eng Chen and other leading Party figures of the time exercised great power over the government. However, the forces of Mao and Lin disputed that power. In the summer of 1964, formations called "political departments' *(chengchih-pu)* were set up in various branches of economic administration, both at central and at regional levels.[2] Aside from a few other references to these political departments, little is known about them. However, not only the admonition to them to study the works of Chairman Mao and emulate the army, but their very name suggested a military character. To that time, the only "political departments" in China were in the army. At the head of the military political departments stood the General Political Department which, as we have seen, was the body through which Mao and Lin sought to implement their control over the army. By implication, therefore, these economic "political departments" were under the command of the army, and not of the Central Committee of the Party. The association of Li Hsien-nien who, despite some attacks against him by the Red Guards, is among the top leaders of the country, suggests that Li was instrumental in swinging the loyalty of a major segment of the government to Mao.

Perhaps even more important, the establishment of "political departments" at lower levels of the administrative system helped create a parallel chain of command which bypassed the Party. Thus when the Party lines of command broke down during the Cultural Revolution, alternate chains of command could be immediately implemented. The success of the administrative system in weathering the storm may indicate that this new system had, by 1966, become effective.

Above all, the institutionalized separation of Party and government made it possible for the political departments to succeed. Since government channels served to relay technical commands, they were not affected by the move of the political departments into the channels of policy commands. Thus army and party could struggle over policy, while government continued to function.

----

[2]*Jenmin jihpao,* June 7, 1964; see also, *China News Analysis* 581 (September 17, 1965), pp. 3-7.

CHAPTER III

SOCIETY

WHEN Mao speaks of Chinese society, he means essentially China's social classes. In the chapters on cities and villages, where I discussed developments in the 1950's, the force of social class was not entirely clear. True, Mao spoke of all kinds of social contradictions in 1957, but organization was so all-powerful that it appeared able to manipulate class forces at will. Its neglect of class forces was indicated by silence on the subject of class criteria for Party membership in the 1956 Party Rules. However, no analysis of developments in China in the 1960's can overlook the rising force of social class. Chinese society is thus reasserting itself and seeking a new relationship to the state. This is particularly true of the intellectuals who, in the form of the students played the major sociopolitical role in the Cultural Revolution, and of the peasants who, through the poor and lower-middle peasants, are asserting themselves in the villages.[1] But the most important indicator of the reassertion of class forces has been the Cultural Revolution itself. The "authoritarian clique" has been attacked as a newly emerging capitalist class, and the instruments of the attack, the students, are the vanguard of China's intellectual class.

As in the past, the intellectuals and the peasants seem today to be the key social classes of China. The intellectuals, the products of high-

---

[1]The poor and lower-middle peasant associations which Mao tried but failed to organize in 1963 now appear to be coming into being. See *Tsukuo* [*China Monthly*] 33 (December, 1966), 41.

er education, are the future leaders of China. Young people now in school will eventually go into Party, army, and government to become political and technical cadres. The peasants control agriculture, the keystone to China's still backward economy. The Soviets have openly accused Mao of destroying the leadership role of the industrial proletariat in Chinese society.[2] Despite widespread use of the term "proletarian," there is substance to this accusation. Since the late 1950's, praise of the industrial worker as the model for the future has waned. If his role in Chinese society reflects the position of heavy industry in the list of economic priorities (since 1961, the official rank order has been: agriculture—light industry—heavy industry), then it is not a leadership role. We might again note that Mao's writings are preoccupied with only two of these three social classes, the peasants and the intellectuals (see p. 90).

WORKERS AND PEASANTS

SINCE the industrial worker symbolizes the city and the peasant symbolizes the village, their history since 1961 should constitute our supplemental chapter on cities and villages. But not enough is known to write a full chapter. Except for the Cultural Revolution, the cities have been quiet. Food shortages of the 1960/62 crisis period have disappeared. Industry has recovered and output is again rising. The on-the-spot researches of Barry Richman indicate a variegated pattern of industrial management and a considerable degree of industrial effectiveness.[3] As is obvious from China's growing foreign trade and its changing components (growing share of factory products in exports), Chinese industry has been developing quantitatively and qualitatively. However, there is no evidence of new social experiments in the cities. During the winter of 1966/67, the issue of "economism"—emphasis on material rewards—was widely raised in the press. Many Party officials, it seems, attempted to secure the loyalties of workers by raising wages and granting bonuses. Thus in the conflict over moral versus material incentives, the enemies of Chairman Mao were portrayed as proponents of material incentives. Clearly the triumph of Chairman Mao presages a new program of austerity for China. Nevertheless, as of

---

[2]M. Sladkovskii, "Ugroza eknomicheskim osnovam sotsializma v Kitae" ["Danger to the Economic Foundations of Socialism in China"], *Kommunist* 12 (Moscow, 1967).

[3]Barry Richman, *A Firsthand Study of Industrial Management in Communist China* (Division of Research, Graduate School of Business Administration, University of California at Los Angeles, 1967). A larger manuscript is in preparation.

January 1968, no hint has been given in the press about any institutional changes proposed for the factories. Workers in many parts of the country organized in opposition to the Red Guards. These were called *ch'ihwei-tui;* though also translatable as red guards, this term has always been used to refer to the classic worker red guards who emerged in Russian cities after the October Revolution. The Russians, understandably, have refused to call the *hungwei-ping* Red Guards and either use the Chinese term directly or call them "Mao Tsetung'ists." The *ch'ihwei-tui,* however, did not last long. Therefore one can conclude that the *hungwei-ping,* throughout the Cultural Revolution, was essentially a student movement.[4]

Much more information is available about the peasantry, but here too the lines of development are not clear. We now have available the research results of G. William Skinner on villages, communes, and marketing, and on the power cycle in the villages of Communist China. These researches indicate a far greater reappearance of traditional patterns than was previously suspected. Thus it appears that, by and large, the traditional natural village has reasserted itself in the form of the production brigade, and what Skinner calls the standard marketing community (a traditional local network of economic and social interrelationships) has reasserted itself in the form of the communes.[5] If Skinner's conclusions are correct, then it may be far more difficult for the Chinese leaders to impose new institutional changes on the villages and the communes than at any time since their rise to power. In the early 1950's, the villages still were upset by the turmoil of decades of war. Now they have not only enjoyed several years of peace, but the institutional formations now in existence are strengthened by their correspondence with traditional socioeconomic patterns.

Skinner has also advanced a thesis on the alternation of power and compliance cycles in the village. This somewhat dialectical thesis sug-

---

[4]On the worker *ch'ihwei-tui,* see *Hungch'i* 2 (January, 1967), 4-6. Andrew Watson comments on the worker-student relationship: "The second point is the division maintained throughout the revolution between workers and students. There is certainly strong animosity between workers and students now. The workers have been cautious and practical. The students have been extreme and idealistic. Before I left a worker told me that the students are so cocksure and arrogant that you cannot speak to them. This division indicates that all attempts to unite the intellectuals and proletariat have as yet been unsuccessful." ("Armageddon Averted," *Far Eastern Economic Review* [May 25, 1967], p. 452).

[5]G. William Skinner, "Marketing and Social Structure in Rural China," *Journal of Asian Studies* XXIV:1 (November 1964), 3-43; XXIV: 2 (February 1965, 195-228; XXIV:3 (May 1965), 363-399. Part III deals with Communist China. See particularly, n. 277, p. 398.

gests that Communist policy toward the village has gone through a set of cycles, each containing similar stages. These stages occur when a certain policy produces a predictable response on the part of the peasantry, which in turn impels the leadership to resort to a new policy to achieve its goals. The succession of these predictable policies constitutes the stages of the cycle. Skinner distinguishes three types of policies: normative (i.e., essentially ideological, with emphasis on moral incentives); coercive (i.e., the use of force to gain compliance from the peasants); and remunerative (i.e., the use of material incentives). Peasant response moves from "calculative commitment" to normative policies, then to ambivalence and alienation toward coercive policies, and finally to "calculative disengagement" to remunerative policies.[6] The thesis is predictive for it suggests that each stage must, sooner or later, be followed by its successor.

Skinner distinguishes five stages in each cycle: (1) mobilization, (2) the "big push," (3) crisis, (4) retrenchment, and (5) respite or "normalcy." Looking at the period since the Great Leap Forward, one can certainly see a succession of these stages. However, the last stage appears to have been in effect for several years now. In March 1962 a professor of political economy wrote in the *People's Daily:*

> The government can only include major and important commodities directly into its plan; it cannot include the thousands of minor commodities into its plan. Therefore it must make use of economic contracts, based on the unified state plan and the general [material] balances, as an important supplemental method.[7]

Evidence indicates that the government has made widespread use of the contract system in concluding procurement agreements with the communes and the brigades. Since such contracts assume back-and-forth negotiations between state and commune officials, we can presume that the villagers have the capacity to defend their interests. As far as the peasant is concerned, his main interests are presumably the assurance of maximal material rewards from the agreement. Since Skinner's last stage leads to "calculative disengagement" on the part of the peasant, this means that the government's power to maximize procurement from the agricultural sector becomes constrained. Thus,

---

[6]G. William Skinner, "Compliance and Leadership in Rural Communist China," paper delivered for the 1965 Annual Meeting of the American Political Science Association, Washington, D. C., September 8-11, 1965.

[7]*Jenmin jihpao,* March 9, 1962.

sooner or later, it must recommence the cycle—that is, institute mobilization with a characteristic power mix of normative and remunerative policies.

The period of the socialist education movement in the villages (1963-1965) suggests a mobilizational approach. Nevertheless, one of the key conditions for the cycle was absent: a unified political leadership. Mao Tse-tung and Liu Shao-ch'i, as we have seen, differed sharply over the methods to be used toward the villages. Mao advocated the formation of poor and lower-middle peasant associations and the strengthening of the militia. Liu advocated strengthening the grip of the Party over the village. Both mobilizational policies could not be implemented simultaneously. However, now that Mao has won out in the struggle, many observers are predicting another "big push." The stress on ideological themes, on moral incentives, the attacks on capitalistic vestiges in the villages, the vigorous defense of the 1958 commune system—all these suggest that another stage in the cycle may be approaching.

In my discussion of the soldier-peasant systems of traditional China, I already noted some similarities between the government-gentry-peasant relationships in earlier periods and the government-party-peasant relationships of the present day. Skinner has also noted these similarities. He moreover sees a similarity between the alternating styles of Communist policy toward the peasants and likewise alternating styles of the imperial bureaucrat and the local gentry in traditional China.[8] If Liu Shao-ch'i's policies had been leading to a reassertion of the power of provincial and local Party cadres, then Skinner may be right. However, there are dangers in drawing too close an analogy between the situation in late imperial China and that prevailing today. Then the peasantry was still governed by traditions which had been operative for at least a thousand years. Today the peasantry is emerging from one hundred years of revolution. Then the local lineage systems on which gentry power was based still exerted a powerful force on the peasantry. I doubt that these lineage systems still play a major role in rural China. The attacks on the Liu Shao-ch'i line concentrate on the issue of "rich peasants," in other words kulak tendencies on the land.[9] It is the peasant as an independent producer (tankan) seeking material gain who is denounced, not the peasant as a passive member of a feudal social system based on kinship. Revolution has turned the inert

---

[8]See Skinner, "Compliance and Leadership in Rural Communist China."

[9]See *Jenmin jihpao*, November 23, 1967.

peasantry of imperial China into an active force with which the leaders of the state must come to terms.

The traditional patterns which have reappeared in village and commune organization are essentially economic. But if economic patterns and social system were closely linked in the past, this does not mean that they are today. The traditional social system was a network of human relationships based on a particular type of authority. The gentry, as a social class, was the key to that authority. The Party may have gradually been evolving into a neo-gentry. But unlike the gentry's kinship based solidarity, the local "old cadres" have not had sufficient time to institutionalize their developing authority, nor is there much evidence that kinship has played a role in their solidarity (though there are hints of some kinship-based politics in the denunciations of Liu Shao-ch'i's Four Clean policies). Nevertheless, a Marxian approach would suggest that a certain type of economic patterns necessarily gives rise to corresponding social-political patterns. Therefore, if, as Skinner has convincingly shown, traditional economic patterns have been reappearing in the countryside, then this would, eventually, give rise to traditional social-political patterns. Mao Tse-tung would, I think, agree.

The supreme challenge facing the leaders of China in the coming years is the economic and technological transformation of its agriculture. I have indicated my belief that these leaders now realize that this transformation must be brought about by economic means, no longer through social mobilization (see p. 500). Writing in February 1968 I can no longer say this with such confidence. Economic means will not be adequate for such a transformation for a long time to come. However, Mao Tse-tung believes profoundly in the reality of the revolution on the land, and in the awakened revolutionary consciousness of the peasant. He believes that education of the peasant can become a major instrument in his modernization; that a militia made up of poor and young peasants has a major role to play in this process; that the institutional form of the communes will hasten that transformation.

A few years from now we shall know whether the Cultural Revolution was the forerunner of a big push in the rural sector or a phenomenon concerned mainly with the nature of state power. So far Chinese society, except for the intellectuals, has been largely unaffected by the Cultural Revolution. But we must remember the great antirightist movement of 1957/58 which was the precursor to the Great Leap Forward. Skinner's cyclical theory may be correct, and China so must undergo a repetition of this cycle until the economic transformation of the land has been completed.

THE GREAT PROLETARIAN CULTURAL REVOLUTION

I HAVE mentioned the Cultural Revolution several times; I have discussed the ideological struggles between the two currents of the pure ideology; I have discussed the struggle between Mao Tse-tung and the old leaders of the Party, between the army and the Party; now I shall discuss it as social struggle. That struggle took the form of a gigantic student movement which brought virtually every student, from higher and middle schools, into the political arena. However much it was manipulated from above in the interests of the power struggle, the Cultural Revolution must be accounted the greatest student movement in history.

The importance attached by the Chinese Communists to ideology is reflected in their acute concern with education, because education is the instrument for inculcating the ideology into the minds and hearts of the people, particularly the young. Since the Chinese have traditionally regarded the school as the center of the educational effort, the leaders of the country have always been deeply concerned with the manner in which the schools carried out their tasks. Education can be dispensed through the mass media, but the schools combine education with personal influence. Friendships formed in schools last a lifetime. The values and norms a young man has acquired in school have a deeper impact on him than any other kind of educational experience. Moreover, since the schools are the training grounds for the future cadres, what they have learned and the friendships they have made in school will go with them into their subsequent careers. Thus it could be said that whoever controls the schools determines the character of the "successor generation." As the political struggle became more acute, the issue of who controlled the schools became critical.

When the Cultural Revolution began in the late spring of 1966, the Party had been in firm control of all schools in China. Within a few months, that structure of Party control was well on the way to being destroyed. The apparent issues of the struggle seemed to center on recruitment. School officials were charged with discrimination against students of worker, peasant, and soldier origins.[10] To rectify this situation, all enrollment and examinations were suspended until new procedures could be worked out. Thus the struggle appeared to be a revolt of the poor against the privileged in the schools. It is true that

---

[10]See *Peking Review* (June 24, 1966), 15-17; see also, Schurmann and Schell, *Communist China*, pp. 619-622.

a disproportionate number of students had always come from bourgeois families, but it is difficult to believe that more than a decade of attempts to recruit the children of poor parents did not have a high degree of success. But the apparent issues were not the key elements in the attack. Simply, the students were rebelling against the school authorities who were all leading members of the Communist party.

In May 1957, China experienced a student outburst in many ways similar to the Cultural Revolution. In February of that year, Mao Tse-tung made his long speech "On the Correct Resolution of Internal Contradictions Within the People." The speech was distributed throughout China on tape; a heavily edited version was published in June. As I have already noted, its theme was that, despite the triumph of the revolution, Chinese society was still rent by deep contradictions (pp. 74 ff.). A factor in prompting Mao to make this speech was the Hungarian Rebellion—an urban population led by students and workers rising against the Communist party and the state machinery, destroying it, and then only being put down by the intervention of Soviet armed force. The events of 1956, beginning with Khrushchev's de-Stalinization speech of February, the Polish and then the Hungarian uprisings, threatened Communist rule, not from abroad but from internal discontent. If Mao feared that a similar uprising could occur in China, he concluded that it could only be prevented by allowing the discontent to flare into the open. Thus, in April, a rectification movement was launched in the cities. People were urged to criticize the shortcomings of cadres. As has happened during the Cultural Revolution, wall posters appeared in large numbers. However, the initial phase of the rectification was led by the Party itself—the Party thus was the instrument of its own self-criticism. The same thing happened during the Cultural Revolution. During the initial phase, Party "work teams" *(kungtso-tui,* operations squads) carried out the Cultural Revolution in a planned and disciplined manner. The careful April 1957 rectification, however, got out of hand. In May a new kind of wall poster appeared, attacking the fundamental principles on which Communist rule was based. They first became evident in the National Aviation University (during the Cultural Revolution a key center of the Red Guards), and then spread to Peking University. The Party was accused of being despotic, totalitarian, Stalinist. The students urged Mao Tse-tung to lead China toward a new era of freedom and democracy. For weeks, Party cadres were the targets of bitter attack. It was reported that the Politburo was in a state of paralysis. Classes were suspended. Students everyday mounted soap boxes and harangued their fellow students.

Suddenly, on June 8, 1957, an editorial appeared in the *People's*

Daily demanding an end to the movement. The Party pulled itself together and went on a counterattack, launching the antirightist movement. By the winter of 1957/58, thousands of students, professors, administrators, technicians, and scientists had been attacked, purged, and sent down *(hsiafang)* to the "front line of production."[11]

In 1957 large segments of the student population emerged as bitter critics of the Communist party. The universities, where the severest battles took place, were divided between supporters and opponents of the Party. The Party was what it was supposed to be: a tight unified organization which controlled virtually the entire life of the university. The critics were largely individuals who banded together into loose groups (not so dissimilar from the later Red Guards). The Party demanded order and discipline, but the students demanded freedom. Though there were undoubtedly real bourgeois rightists among the students (not surprising in view of the bourgeois social origins of many of them), the majority of the critics were loyal to the revolution, but they believed that the Communist party was deviating from the true goals of that revolution. Among the most vehement of the critics were some of the most talented students in China: those studying in the scientific-technical faculties of China's finest universities.

Student movements have played an important role in the Chinese Revolution. The great May 4, 1919, movement played a major role in the formation of the Chinese Communist party; its founders were student products of that movement. In the 1930's, student movements fanned Chinese nationalism and helped propel a reluctant Kuomintang into resistance against the Japanese. In the later 1930's and 1940's, the universities were important recruiting grounds for cadres who went into the hills to join the Communists. The Chinese universities, like those in many other lands, were the breeding grounds of a new idealism. Students saw themselves as the carriers of the most fundamental ideals of their society. At the same time, they saw those ideals violated by a corrupt power structure whose arms reached directly into their universities. Thus student opposition often tended to take on an anarchist character—the enemies were the holders of state power, and so the students often demanded the leveling of all state power. This anarchistic strain they shared with the peasants, for already the Tai-

---

[11]See Dennis Doolin, *Communist China: The Politics of Student Opposition* (Stanford, Calif.: Hoover Institution, 1964); also, Schurmann and Schell, *Communist China*, pp. 148 ff. On *hsiafang*, see Rensselaer W. Lee III, "The *Hsia Fang* System: Marxism and Modernization," *The China Quarterly* 28 (October-December, 1966), 40-62.

ping Rebellion had revealed the deep strain of peasant hostility to all officialdom (see p. xxxi) .[12]

During the Cultural Revolution, some suggested that in the events of 1957 it was Mao Tse-tung who had urged the rectification, but that it was Liu Shao-ch'i who insisted on reimposing Party controls. Whether true or not, Mao's concern for "democracy" certainly was closer to the students' cries for freedom than Liu's commitment to "centralism."

Since I have already discussed the ideological and political origins of the Cultural Revolution, I need not go into them again in detail. Suffice it to say that in November 1965, a Shanghai newspaper, later identified as an organ of Mao Tse-tung, attacked a leading Party cadre identified with the Peking Party committee controlled by P'eng Chen—this can be said to have been the direct origin of the current which led to the explosion of May 1966. When articles from the *Liberation Army Daily* began appearing in authoritative places in the *People's Daily* around the middle of April, this indicated Mao's growing control over the country's mass media. When he launched the attack in May, Mao could count on the army and on the mass media. But why did he decide to unleash a new student movement? One generally accepted explanation has been that, unlike the army, the students could be construed as a nonviolent instrument with which politically, but not physically, Mao could attack his opponents. Certainly the preponderance of verbal over physical violence during the course of the Cultural Revolution suggests that this was so. Yet, as Joseph R. Levenson has suggested, there were real cultural issues in the Cultural Revolution.[13] The intensity with which the students of China participated in the movement went far beyond anything which would have been achieved with mere manipulation from the top down. Moreover, the striking similarity with the student outburst of May 1957 indicates that a great accumulation of student grievances surfaced to the top in May 1966. As in 1957, classes were suspended, meetings held, students everywhere argued, posters were plastered all over the walls of the universities and other schools. Since the Chinese often pair the terms culture and education *(wen-chiao)*, we can assume that the Cultural Revolution related to some of the most basic educational problems in China. The

----

[12]On Chinese student movements, see Chow Tse-tsung, *The May Fourth Movement* (Cambridge, Mass.: Harvard University Press, 1960) ; John Israel, *Student Nationalism in China, 1927-1937* (Stanford, Calif.: Stanford University Press, 1966) .

[13]Joseph R. Levenson and Franz Schurmann, "An Exchange on China," *The New York Review of Books* VII:12 (January 12, 1967) , p. 31.

intensity of the student movement indicates that the students felt that way about it too.

What these educational problems and student grievances were is not easy to discover. Despite the welter of documentation which has come out of the Cultural Revolution, there is little straight-forward talk by the revolutionary rebels about the real issues. Andrew Watson, a British teacher who was in Sian during the Cultural Revolution, noted this:

> Throughout the movement one never saw a clear analysis of the "bourgeois line." . . . For the ordinary man on the street the "black line" was mainly described in rumor and swear words. The general level of political argument and analysis was for the most part very low.[14]

Such reticence contrasts sharply with the eloquence in May 1957, and tends to indicate that students were warned to stay away from certain subjects. Vietnam, for example, was almost never mentioned during the Cultural Revolution. Nevertheless, no matter how much theatrical and absurdist the Cultural Revolution often appeared to be, there must have been important substance to it relating directly to educational and cultural problems.

The term "cultural revolution," often used by Mao Tse-tung in his writings, came again into prominence in 1964. In his report to the National People's Conference late in December 1964, Chou En-lai announced that "the goals of our cultural revolution are to workerize our intellectuals and to intellectualize our workers." Specifically this meant once again introducing half-study, half-work programs throughout all of China's educational system. Curious, however, was Chou's statement that this was to be carried out "according to the directives of Chairman Liu Shao-ch'i."[15] Clearly, a far-reaching new program of educational reform was in the making.

The educational liberalization which had been announced by Ch'en Yi's speech to the higher schools of Peking in September 1961 and affirmed in the Seventy Articles Concerning Education and Cultural

---

14Andrew Watson, "Embattled Armies," *The Far Eastern Economic Review* (April 27, 1967), p. 233. Watson's five articles which appeared in the issues of the *Review* from April 20 to May 18, 1967 are among the best first-hand reports on the student movement. Equally good is Neale Hunter's "Three Cadres of Shanghai," *Far Eastern Economics Review* (Hong Kong, June 1, 1967), pp. 491-495.

15*Jenmin jihpao*, December 31, 1964.

Affairs was coming to an end.[16] One of the most significant aspects of that educational liberalization had been clear-cut admonitions to Party cadres not to interfere with the studies of the students, not to attack professors and students, not to force the students to do too much physical labor, not to interfere with their private lives, and to allow them to become proficient in their studies.[17] In 1963, as the socialist education campaign got under way, thousands of students were sent to the countryside and to distant provinces to mingle with the masses. This new *hsiafang* provoked considerable discontent among the students as is clear from the official press.[18] Most remembered the great *hsiafang* of 1957/58 and the hardships which it entailed for the city-bred youth. As the new educational policies unfolded, what Ch'en Yi had promised the students in 1961 quickly was forgotten.

As one reads the accusations leveled against the "bourgeois line" in the universities in June 1966, the issue of students being sent to the countryside comes up repeatedly. For example, there was the story of one poor history student of excellent social origins (of Chuang nationality, poor peasant, revolutionary soldier, and Party member) but who could not make it academically. Despite repeated appeals by his history professor to President Lu P'ing (the chief target of attack by the Red Guards), he was not allowed to remain in school. Finally, "under the pressure of the anti-Party black gang, he left Peking University and went back to his village production brigade to tend cows." Worse even, "the school was supposed to find work for him . . . but once he left school, the school neither cared nor asked about him."[19] There was another student who, in January 1965 (when Mao's "twenty-three-point program had been adopted), proposed to the Party: "to carry out the [socialist education] movement in our school [Peking University], and decisively to give a good foundation to Peking University, send back the teachers and students who have been participating in the village socialist education movement; first carry out the movement well in school, and then send them back to the villages."[20] These and many similar examples suggest that the Party was implementing a policy of taking the poorer students in the schools and sending them out to the

16On Ch'en Yi's speech, see *Chungkuo ch'ingnien* 17 (September, 1961), 2-4. The Seventy Articles were promulgated in December, 1961, but never officially published. A fairly complete text, however, was published in *Tsukuo* [*China Weekly*] 520 (December 24, 1962), 308-311.

17*Ibid.* See articles 20, 23, 35, 39, 40, 41, 42, 54, 55, 58, 59.

18See Schurmann and Schell, *Communist China*, pp. 456-457.

19*Jenmin jihpao*, June 23, 1966.

20*Ibid.*, June 20, 1966.

villages. Since the bulk of the poor students most likely came from peasant and worker origins, this would correctly be construed as discrimination against people of lower class origins. However, it also suggested resistance on the part of the students in general to being sent out to the villages forever.

Let us remember that May just preceded the summer vacations. Under the *hsiafang* policies then in effect, presumably millions of students would have been assigned by Party authorities to do work in the villages. Many others probably faced permanent assignment to the villages, largely on grounds of poor academic performance. The *hsiafang* campaign of 1963 undoubtedly was designed to alleviate the burdens caused by China's rapidly growing academic proletariat. However, the campaign also served Party purposes. Being educated, many would go as cadres and help in the program of rebuilding the Party in the villages.

This fragmentary evidence, together with Chou En-lai's reference in 1964 to "the directives of Chairman Liu Shao-ch'i," suggests that the students were deeply discontented with the *hsiafang* policy with which the Party had become closely identified. *Hsiafang* symbolized the life-and-death power which the Party wielded over the students. When suddenly in May, the *People's Daily* began attacking the "black gang," the students began to react, though slowly at first. When Nieh Yüan-tzu, a girl philosophy student at Peking University, mounted her famous May—25 poster, the country knew that a new movement was afoot, one with explicit support from the highest levels. Nieh made clear whose support in her cries: "Protect the Party Central Committee; protect *The Thought of Mao Tse-tung;* protect the proletarian dictatorship." The enemies and their methods were also made clear: "Lu P'ing with his status as 'Party committee secretary' of Peking University and in the name of 'organization' has been threatening students and cadres who want to start a revolution. He says anyone who doesn't obey the commands of this small handful of people is violating discipline and is therefore anti-Party."[21] Revolutionary rebels, called Red Guards, began to form in university after university to "open fire" against the "black gang."

The universities in June 1966 became the first open arena where the same struggles were being fought out as at the highest levels of the political structure. The Party counterattacked, and, using the old work-team method, tried to bring the revolution under its control. As Andrew Watson points out, until early August, the revolutionary

---

[21]*Ibid.*, June 2, 1966.

rebels were in the minority. However, by then the work teams had been defeated, and the rebels gradually became the majority.[22] Undoubtedly the see-saw struggle in the schools reflected a similar ebb and flow of political power at the top. By early August, the forces of Mao came into ascendancy, both at the top and at the bottom.

On August 18, 1966, six days after the termination of the Eleventh Plenum, Mao Tse-tung and Lin Piao called out the Red Guards in a gigantic demonstration on Peking's T'ienanmen Square. A million people were present, but the young dominated (soldiers and students in the majority). Another nine such mass demonstrations were held in Peking, each featuring Mao himself—happy, fit, alert, waving to the masses. The message was clear: Chairman Mao now personally directed state power.

When the students saw Mao on August 18, they knew immediately that a major change had taken place in the leadership: Liu Shao-ch'i, heretofore referred to as chairman along with Mao Tse-tung, had fallen to eighth place. Realizing that Mao himself had chosen them as the instrument of the revolution, the students turned with anger against the Party. Although, in the beginning, many Red Guards took seriously the talk of rooting out old habits, and defaced historical monuments, beat old people, attacked bourgeois and Overseas Chinese, that was but a temporary phase which soon ended. It quickly became clear that the true "capitalists" were the Party cadres who dominated organization. The attacks on school officials, already violent, became even more so. "Open fire against the Party committee" was a cry heard in every Chinese city. Party officials, who for years had commanded their city domains, were paraded with dunce caps on their heads through the streets. Students broke into Party offices. More and more their fire was leveled at high officials. Mayors, governors, Party first secretaries were forced to attend meeting upon meeting, where they were subjected to humiliating criticism. Just about every leading official, at one time or another, was subject to attack. Even those who survived to resume their leadership positions were attacked. The emerging new leaders also underwent criticism and had to spend hours patiently talking with the students. Refusal to talk was immediately followed by torrents of abuse. Every wall was covered with posters. Tabloids, written in earthy Chinese, were published everywhere. Boys hawked these tabloids as they do in bourgeois countries. Thousands of Red Guard organizations formed, generally without much internal organization. Some, while professing to be Maoist, actually were the

---

[22]Watson, *op. cit.*, pp. 125, 231.

creations of old Party cadres. Others again were little more than mobs of hooligans intent on making trouble. Others still were idealistic. Twenty million students left their schools and began marching throughout the country. Except for scientific-technical instruction, all classes were suspended for the academic year 1966/67. Ten million young people made the pilgrimage to Peking to catch a glimpse of Chairman Mao. The catchword "rebellion" (tsaofan) began to spread: rebel against the despotic Party committees which for years had oppressed the people. Rebellion would save the revolution and prevent China from reverting to capitalism.

The similarities between the outbursts of May 1957 and of May 1966 are unmistakable. In both cases, it was an uprising of students, the vanguard of the intellectuals, against the Party.[23] Although such obviously pragmatic figures as Ch'en Yi and Li Hsien-nien were attacked (both again in high favor), the targets were the leading red organization men of the Party. As one reads the documents, one sees that the accusation "capitalistic" meant more than wanting profits or private ownership: it meant authoritarianism, a love of power.

The August 18, 1966 demonstration launched a year of intense, emotional activity. Early in 1967, it appeared that China was on the verge of civil war. In many places, physical violence occurred. Red Guard groups attacked each other and struggled to achieve command in the new revolutionary committees. However, somehow, hidden behind the din, was a framework which did not break. The army, into whose hands power had passed, assured the continued unity of the country. By the autumn of 1967, the schools were reopened and the students were urged to go back to their classes and carry out the revolution in the places where they belonged. In fact, the notion of belonging to a place and group was important throughout the Cultural Revolution: as with army teams, classmates sallied forth to wander together throughout the countryside, in contrast to the atomisation of hsiafang. Foreign opinion, and not in the least Soviet, was appalled by the wild behavior of the Red Guards, but visitors to China reported the exhiliration it produced in the people, particularly the young.

In this brief review of China's history since 1961, one theme has gone through the entire discussion: the attack on the nature and structure of the Chinese Communist party. I have pointed out the erosion of its practical ideology, how its leading organization men have been

---

[23]Watson notes that a Sian university president likened the rebels to the rightists of 1957; op. cit., p. 123.

purged, how the army has come to play a major role in the trinity of state power. But my brief discussion of Chinese society, notably of peasants and intellectuals, also suggests that social classes have become less manipulable by organization, that they are becoming forces in their own right. However people interpret the word "democracy," it has to mean the power of the people. Mao Tse-tung has not only preached the importance of his "democracy,' but has allowed popular protest to vent itself. True, he has used the force of the poor and lower-middle peasants, and of the students to advance his own goals; true, he has always made certain that social forces did not get to the point of endangering the unity of the country; true, he may have created conditions for a new type of top-down control: by a centralized governmental bureaucracy and a tightly organized military machine; true also, he may yet again permit the renewed development of a classical Communist party organization which would return to the practical ideology and organization I have described in this book. Yet that extraordinary fabric of sociopolitical control that enabled the Communist party to penetrate every corner of society has been rent. Officials and soldiers can not control people as effectively as members of a Communist party. But then we ourselves may have fallen victim to the obsession with control. Why must state power or any managerial-administrative body have control over the people it rules? Is it because otherwise they would fall apart, fight each other, degenerate into anarchy? Such ideas are heard increasingly in the United States, the home of Western democracy. Thus when control seemed to break down in China, many Western observers immediately predicted collapse, civil war, disintegration. It is always said that Mao Tse-tung has faith in the masses. He may or may not be right. In the Cultural Revolution, he risked an enormous experiment. Years from now we shall see whether his gamble paid off.

When I finished the first edition, peace seemed assured in the world, and so I looked forward to China's continued economic growth. Now, it is uncertain whether, in the near future, the world will be at peace or at war. Whichever it be, it will determine China's future history. I agree with Han Suyin that one of the key factors in the Cultural Revolution was the expectation that China would soon again be at war. China's Communist party must be given credit for the extraordinary socioeconomic development that country has experienced. Thus, if peace were to prevail, the Russians may be correct in their accusations that Mao has wrecked China's key instrument for its economic development. On the other hand, if war comes, then the Cul-

BIBLIOGRAPHY

BOOKS

Aird, John S. *The Size, Composition, and Growth of the Population of Mainland China*. Washington, D. C.: Bureau of the Census (Series P-90, no. 15), 1961.

Ajiya keizai kenkyūjo アジア経済研究所 [Institute of Asian Economics] *Chūgoku jimmin kōsha no soshiki to kinō* 中国人民公社の組織と機能 [*Organization and Function of the Chinese People's Communes*]. Tokyo, 1961.

An Tzu-wen 安子文. *Chunghua jenmin kunghokuo san-nien-lai ti kanpu kungtso* 中華人民共和國三年來的幹部工作 [*Cadre Operations in the People's Republic of China Over the Last Three Years*]. Peking, 1952.

Apter, David E. "Ideology and Discontent," in David E. Apter, ed., *Ideology and Discontent*. New York: The Free Press (Macmillan), 1964.

Barnard, Chester I. *Functions of the Executive*. Cambridge, Mass.: Harvard University Press, 1938.

Barnett, A. Doak. *Cadres, Bureaucracy and Political Power in Communist China*. New York and London: Columbia University Press, 1967.

———. *China After Mao*. Princeton, N. J.: Princeton University Press, 1967.

594 BIBLIOGRAPHY

Bauer, Raymond, Alex Inkeles, and Clyde Kluckhohn. *How the Soviet System Works*. Cambridge, Mass.: Harvard University Press, 1957.

Baum, Richard and Frederick C. Teiwes. *Ssu-ch'ing: The Socialist Education Movement of 1962-1966.* Berkeley, Calif.: Center for Chinese Studies, University of California, 1968 *(China Research Monographs,* No. 2) .

Bendix, Reinhard. *Max Weber, An Intellectual Portrait*. Garden City, N. Y.: Doubleday Anchor Book, 1962.

———. "The Cultural and Political Setting of Economic Rationality in Western and Eastern Europe," in Gregory Grossman, ed., *Value and Plan—Economic Calculation and Organization in Eastern Europe*. Berkeley and Los Angeles: University of California Press, 1960.

———. "The Age of Ideology: Persistent and Changing" in David E. Apter, ed., *Ideology and Discontent*. New York: The Free Press Macmillan), 1964.

Berliner, Joseph S. *Factory and Manager in the USSR*. Cambridge, Mass.: Harvard University Press, 1957.

Bienstock, Gregory, Salomon Schwartz, and Aaron Yugow. *Management in Russian Industry and Agriculture*. London, New York, and Toronto: Oxford University Press, 1944.

Blau, Peter, and Richard W. Scott. *Formal Organizations*. San Francisco: Chandler Publishing Company, 1962.

Burgess, John S. *The Guilds of Peking*. New York: Columbia University Press, 1928.

Carin, Robert. *Agrarian Reform Movement in Communist China*. Hong Kong, 1960. Vol. I.

Chang Ch'i-yün. *Chungkuo chünshih shihlüeh [Brief Military History of China]*. Taipei, 1956.

Cheng, J. Chester, ed. *The Politics of the Chinese Red Army*. Stanford, Calif.: Hoover Institute Publications, 1966.

Chungkuo nungts'un ti shehui-chuyi kaoch'ao 中國農村的社會主義高潮 *[The High Tide of Socialism in China's Villages]*. Peking, 1956.

Chengfeng wenhsien 整風文獻. *[Documents on Rectification]*. Hong Kong: New Democracy Publishers, 1949.

Chou En-lai 周恩來. *Kuan yü chihshih fentzu went'i ti paokao* 關於知識分子問題的報告 . *[Report on the Question of Intellectuals]*. Peking, 1956.

Chou Fang 周方 . *Wokuo kuochia chikou* 我國國家機構 *[The State Structure of Our Country]*. Peking, 1955 (1st ed.), 1957 (2d ed.).

Chou Li-po 周立波. *Paofeng tsouyü* 暴風驟雨 *[Hurricane]*. Peking: 1961 (third printing).

Chow Tse-Tsung. *The May Fourth Movement.* Cambridge, Mass.: Harvard University Press, 1960.

Chuang, H. C. "The Great Proletarian Cultural Revolution," in *Studies in Chinese Communist Terminology,* No. 12. Berkeley, Calif.: Center for Chinese Studies, University of California, 1967.

Chūgoku jimmin kōsha no soshiki to kinō. See Ajiya keizai kenkyūjo.

Chūgoku kyōsantō no nōgyō shūdanka seisaku 中國共產黨の農業集團化 [*Agricultural Collectivization Policies of the Chinese Communist Party*]. Tokyo, 1961.

Chūgoku seiken no genjō bunsetsu. See Nippon gaisei gakkai.

Chūkyō no zaisei 中共の財政 [*Finance in Communist China*]. Tokyo, 1961.

Chungkuo kungch'antang changch'eng chiaots'ai 中國共產黨章程教材 [*Teaching Materials on the Party Rules of the Chinese Communist Party*]. Canton, 1957.

Chungkuo nungyeh hotsohua yüntung shihliao. See Shih Ching-t'ang.

Cohen, Arthur A. *The Communism of Mao Tse-tung.* Chicago and London: The University of Chicago Press, 1964.

Communist China 1955-1959. Cambridge, Mass.: Harvard University Press (Center for International Affairs. East Asian Research Institute), 1962.

Dallin, Alexander, ed. *Diversity in International Communism, A Documentary Record, 1961-1963.* New York and London: Columbia University Press, 1963.

Doolin, Dennis. *Communist China: The Politics of Student Opposition.* Stanford, Calif.: Hoover Institution, 1964.

Drucker, Peter F. *The New Society.* New York: Harper Torchbook, 1962.

Eberhard, Wolfram. *Conquerors and Rulers: Social Forces in Medieval China.* Leiden: E. J. Brill, 1952.

Engels, Fredrick. *Origins of the Family, Private Property, and the State.* New York: International Publishers, 1942.

Etzioni, Amitai. *A Comparative Analysis of Complex Organizations.* Glencoe, Ill.: The Free Press, 1961.

Fainsod, Merle. *How Russia is Ruled.* Cambridge, Mass.: Harvard University Press, 1958 (2d ed.).

———. *Smolensk Under Soviet Rule.* Cambridge, Mass.: Harvard University Press, 1958.

Feuerwerker, Albert. *China's Early Industrialization.* Cambridge, Mass.: Harvard University Press, 1958.

Fukushima Masao 福島正夫. *Jimmin kōsha no kenkyū* 人民公社の研究. [*Study on the People's Communes*]. Tokyo, 1960.

Galbraith, John Kenneth. *The New Industrial State*. Boston: Houghton Mifflin Company, 1967.

George, Alexander L. *The Chinese Communist Army in Action*. New York: Columbia University Press, 1967.

Gouldner, Alvin J. "Organizational Analysis," in Robert K. Merton, Leonard Broom, and Leonard S. Cottrell Jr., editors, *Sociology Today*. New York: Basic Books, 1959.

Granick, David. *The Red Executive*. Garden City, N. Y.; Doubleday Anchor Book, 1961.

Griffith, Samuel B. *Mao Tse-tung on Guerrilla Warfare*. New York: Praeger, 1961.

Griffith, William E. *The Sino-Soviet Rift*. Cambridge, Mass.: The M. I. T. Press, 1964.

Grossmann, Bernhard. *Die wirtschaftliche Entwicklung der Volksrepublik China*. Stuttgart: G. Fischer, 1960.

Han Suyin. *China in the Year 2001*. New York: Basic Books, 1967.

Hegel, Georg Wilhelm Friedrich. *Sämtliche Werke*. Vol. III: *Grundlinien der Philosophie des Rechts*. Stuttgart: F. Frommann, 1952.

Hinton, William. *Fanshen: A Documentary of Revolution in a Chinese Village*. New York and London: Monthly Review Press, 1966.

Ho Kan-chih 何幹之. *Chungkuo hsientai koming-shih* 中國現代革命史. [*Modern Revolutionary History of China*]. Hong Kong: Sanlien, 1958.

Ho, Ping-ti. *The Ladder of Social Success in Imperial China*. New York and London: Columbia University Press, 1962.

———. *Studies on the Population of China 1368-1953*. Cambridge, Mass.: Harvard University Press, 1959.

Homans, George C. *The Human Group*. New York: Harcourt, Brace, and Co., 1950.

Houn, Franklin. *To Change a Nation, Propaganda and Indoctrination in Communist China*. Glencoe, Ill.: The Free Press, 1961.

Hsia, T. A. *The Commune in Retreat as Evidenced in Terminology and Semantics*. Berkeley, Calif.: Center for Chinese Studies, University of California, 1964.

Hsieh, Alice Langley. *Communist China's Strategy in the Nuclear Era*. Englewood Cliffs, N. J.: Prentice-Hall, 1962.

Hsienfa went'i ts'ank'ao wenchien 憲法問題參考文件. [*Reference Materials on the Question of the Constitution*]. Peking, 1954.

Hsü Ti-hsin 許滌新. *Kuanliao tzupen p'ip'an* 官僚資本批判 [*Critique of Bureaucratic Capital*]. Nanking, 1948.

Hsüehhsi "Mao chuhsi lun chih-laohu" wenhsien 學習"毛主席論紙老虎"文獻 [*Study of the Document "Chairman Mao Discusses the Paper Tiger"*]. Hong Kong: Sanlien, 1958.

Hughes, T. J. and D. E. T. Luard. *The Economic Development of Communist China 1949-1958.* London and New York: Oxford University Press, 1959.

Inkeles, Alex A. and Raymond A. Bauer. *The Soviet Citizen.* Cambridge, Mass.: Harvard University Press, 1959.

Ishikawa Shigeru 石川繁 *Chūgoku ni okeru shihon chikuseki kikō* 中國に就ける資本蓄積機搆 [The Structure of Capital Accumulation in China]. Tokyo, 1960.

———. *Chūgoku keizai hatten no tōkei-teki kenkyū* 中國經濟發展の統計的研究 [Statistical Study of China's Economic Development]. Tokyo, 1962. 3 vols.

Israel, John. *Student Nationalism in China, 1927-1937.* Stanford, Calif.: Stanford University Press, 1966.

Janowitz, Morris. "Hierarchy and Authority in the Military Establishment," in Amitai Etzioni, ed., *Complex Organizations.* New York: Holt, Rinehart, and Winston, 1961.

Joffe, Ellis. *Party and Army: Professionalism and Political Control in the Chinese Officer Corps, 1949-1964.* Cambridge, Mass.: Harvard University Press, 1965.

Johnson, Chalmers. *Peasant Nationalism and Communist Power.* Stanford, Calif.: Stanford University Press, 1962.

———. *Revolution and the Social System.* Stanford, Calif.: Hoover Institution Series, 1964.

Kokusai zenrin kurabu 國際善隣倶樂部 [*International Friendship Club*]. [*Communist China*] (1958 through 1961), (in Japanese). Tokyo, 1958-1961.

Kungfei. See Kuo Shou-hua, or Li Chen-tsung, or Tai Ting.

Kuo Shou-hua 郭壽華. *Kungfei kungan tsuchih yü jenmin chingch'achih* 共匪公安組織與人民警察制 [*The Public Security Organization and People's Police System of the Communist Bandits*]. Taipei, 1957.

Kusano Fumio 草野文男. *Chūkyō keizai kenkyū* 中共經濟研究 [*Studies on the Chinese Economy*]. Tokyo, 1962.

———. *Shina henku no kenyū* 支那邊區の研究 [*Studies on the Border Areas of China*]. Tokyo, 1944.

Landes, David. *Bankers and Pashas.* Cambridge, Mass.: Harvard University Press, 1958.

Lenin, V. I. *Selected Works.* Moscow, 1952.

———. *Sochineniia* [*Collected Works*]. Moscow, 1941-1962.

Levenson, Joseph R. *Confucian China and Its Modern Fate.* Berkeley and Los Angeles: University of California Press, 1958 and 1964. 2 vols.

Levy Jr., Marion J. *Family Revolution in Modern China.* Cambridge, Mass.: Harvard University Press, 1949.

———. *The Structure of Society.* Princeton, N. J.: Princeton University Press, 1952.

Levy Jr., Marion J. and Shih Kuo-heng. *The Rise of the Modern Chinese Business Class.* New York: International Secretariat, Institute of Pacific Relations, 1949.

Lewis, John Wilson. *Leadership in Communist China.* Ithaca, N. Y.: Cornell University Press, 1963.

Li Chen-tsung 李振宗. *Kungfei jenshih ts'oshih chih yenchiu* 共匪人事措施之研究 [*Study on Personnel Programs of the Communist Bandits*]. Taipei, 1957.

Li, Choh-ming. *Economic Development of Communist China.* Berkeley and Los Angeles: University of California Press, 1959.

———. *The Statistical System of Communist China.* Berkeley and Los Angeles: University of California Press, 1962.

Li Ta 李達. *Chunghua jenmin kunghokuo hsienfa chianghua* 中華人民共和國憲法講話 [*Remarks on the Constitution of the Chinese People's Republic*]. Peking, 1956.

Lifton, Robert J. *Thought Reform and the Psychology of Totalism.* New York: Norton, 1961.

Liu, T. C. and K. C. Yeh, *The Economy of the Chinese Mainland: National Income and Economic Development, 1933-1959.* Santa Monica, Calif.: The RAND Corporation, 1963. 2 vols.

Liu Shao-ch'i 劉少奇. *Tsuchih-shang ho chilü-shang ti hsiuyang* 組織上和紀律上的修養 [*Training for Organization and Discipline*]. Stanford, Calif.: Hoover Institution for War, Revolution, and Peace, Chinese Collection, No. 4292.52 7294.2

———. *Lun-tang* 論黨 [*On the Party*], Peking, 1950.

———. *Lun kuochi-chuyi yü mintsu-chuyi* 論國際主義與民族主義 [*On Internationalism and Nationalism*], Hong Kong: New Democracy Publishers, n.d. (presumably 1949).

Mannheim, Karl. *Ideology and Utopia.* New York: Harcourt, Brace, and Co., 1949.

———. *Man and Society in an Age of Reconstruction.* New York: Harcourt, Brace, and Co., 1954.

Mao Tse-tung 毛澤東. *Mao Tse-tung hsüanchi* 毛澤東選集 [*Selected Works of Mao Tse-tung*]. Peking, 1951-1960. 4 vols. Notably "Lun jenmin minchu chuancheng," 論人民民主專政 ["On the People's Democratic Dictatorship"], in Vol. IV of *Selected Works of Mao Tse-tung*; "Maotun-lun" 矛盾論 ["On Contradiction"], in Vol. I; "Shihch1en-lun" 賈踐論 ["On Practice"], in Vol. I; "Wei chengch'ü ch'ien-pai-wan ch'ünchung chinju k'ang-jih t'ungyi chanhsien erh toucheng" 為爭取千百萬群眾進入抗日統一戰綫而鬥爭 ["Fight for the Participation of the Masses in the Unified Struggle Against Japan"], in Vol. I.

————. *The Sayings of Chairman Mao.* Peking: General Political Department of the People's Liberation Army, 1966.

Matsumoto Yoshimi 松本善美. "Chūgoku ni okeru chihō jiji seido kindaika no katei" 中國に就ける地方自治制度近代化の過程 ["The Modernization Process of Local Autonomy in China"] in *Kindai Chūgoku no shakai to keizai* 近代中國の社會と經濟 [*Society and Economy in Modern China*]. Tokyo: 1951.

Merton, Robert K. *Social Theory and Social Structure.* Glencoe, Ill.: The Free Press, 1957.

Monas, Sidney. "The Political Police: The Dream of a Beautiful Autocracy," in Cyril Edwin Black, ed., *The Transformation of Russian Society.* Cambridge, Mass.: Harvard University Press, 1960.

Moore Jr., Barrington. *Political Power and Social Theory.* Cambridge, Mass.: Harvard University Press, 1958.

Mu Fu-sheng. *The Wilting of the Hundred Flowers.* New York: Praeger, 1963.

Nippon gaisei gakkai 日本外政學會 [Japan Foreign Affairs Association]. *Chūkyō seiken no genjō bunseki* 中共政權の現狀分析 [*Current Analysis of Chinese Communist Politics*]. Tokyo, 1961.

Orleans, Leo A. *Professional Manpower and Education in Communist China.* Washington: U. S. Government Printing Office, 1960.

Osnovy marksistskoi filosofii [*Foundations of Marxist Philosophy*]. Moscow, 1958, 1959, 1962 editions.

Parsons, Talcott and Neil J. Smelser. *Economy and Society.* Glencoe, Ill.: The Free Press, 1956.

Parsons, Talcott. *The Structure of Social Action.* Glencoe, Ill.: The Free Press, 1949.

————. *The Social System.* Glencoe, Ill.: The Free Press, 1951.

Pfiffner, John M. and Frank P. Sherwood. *Administrative Organization.* New York: Prentice-Hall, 1960.

Polanyi, Karl. *The Great Transformation.* Boston, Mass.; Beacon Paperback, 1957.

Richman, Barry. *A Firsthand Study of Industrial Management in Communist China.* Los Angeles: Division of Research, Graduate School of Business Administration, University of California, 1967.

Riecken, Henry W. and George C. Homans. "Psychological Aspects of Social Structure," in Gardner Lindzey ed., *Handbook of Social Psychology.* Reading, Mass. and London: Addison-Wesley, 1954. 2 vols.

Sampson, Robert C. *The Staff Role in Management.* New York: Harper, 1955.

Scheele, Evan D., William L. Westerman, and Robert J. Wimmert. *Principles and Design of Production Control Systems.* New York: Prentice-Hall, 1960.

Schram, Stuart R. *The Political Thought of Mao Tse-tung.* New York: Praeger, 1963.

Schurmann, Franz. "Politics and Economics in Russia and China," in Donald Treadgold, ed., *Soviet and Chinese Communism: Similarities and Differences.* Seattle: University of Washington Press, 1967.

———, and Orville Schell. *The China Reader.* 3 vols. New York: Vintage Books, Random House, 1967.

———, Peter Dale Scott, and Reginald Zelnik. *Politics of Escalation.* New York: Fawcett, 1966.

Schwartz, Harry. *The Soviet Economy Since Stalin.* Philadelphia and New York: Lippincott, 1965.

Selznick, Philip. *The Organizational Weapon, A Study of Bolshevik Strategy and Tactics.* New York, Toronto, and London: McGraw-Hill Book Co., Inc., 1952.

———. *Leadership in Administration.* Evanston, Ill.: Row, Peterson, and Co., 1957.

Sherman, A. V. *The Chinese Communes: A Documentary Review and Analysis of the "Great Leap Forward"* (special issue of *Survey*). London: Congress for Cultural Freedom, 1959.

Shih, Anderson. "Urban People's Commune" (mimeographed). Hong Kong: Union Research Institute, no date.

Shih Ching-t'ang 史敬棠, ed. *Chungkuo nungyeh hotsohua yüntung shihliao* 中國農業合作化運動史料 [Materials on the Agricultural Cooperativization Movement in China]. Peking, 1957. 2 vols.

Shimizu Morimitsu 清水盛光 *Shina shakai no kenkyū* 支那社會の研究 [Studies on Chinese Society]. Tokyo, 1940.

Sloan Jr., Alfred P. *My Years with General Motors.* Garden City, N.Y.: Doubleday, 1964.

Source Book on Military Affairs in Communist China. Hong Kong: Union Research Institute, 1965.

Stalin, Joseph. *Problems of Leninism.* Moscow, 1954.

Strong, Anna Louise. *The Rise of the Chinese People's Communes— And Six Years After.* Peking: New World Press, 1964.

Tai Ting 戴鼎, *Kungfei chits'eng tsuchih chih yenchiu* 共匪基層組織之研究 [*Studies on Basic-level Organization of the Communist Bandits*]. Taipei, 1957.

Tang, Peter S. H. *The Commune System in Mainland China.* Washington, D.C.: The Research Institute on the Sino-Soviet Bloc, 1961.

———. *Communist China Today.* Washington, D.C.: Research Institute on the Sino-Soviet Bloc, 1961. 2d ed.

Teiwes, Frederick C. *Provincial Party Personnel in Mainland China.* New York: Occasional Papers of the East Asian Institute, Columbia University, 1967.

Union Research Institute, ed. *Chungkung shihnien* [*Ten Years of Communist China*]. Hong Kong: Union Research Institute, 1960.

Wales, Nym. *Notes on the Chinese Student Movement, 1935-1936.* Stanford, Calif.: Nym Wales Collection on the Far East in the Hoover Institution on War, Revolution, and Peace, 1959.

Weber, Max. *The Protestant Ethic and the Spirit of Capitalism.* New York and London: Scribner, 1930.

———. *Essays in Sociology.* New York: Oxford University Press, 1946.

———. *The theory of Social and Economic Organization.* Glencoe, Ill.: The Free Press, 1947.

———. *The Religion of China.* Glencoe, Ill.: The Free Press, 1951.

Weita ti shih-nien 偉大的十年 [*The Ten Great Years*]. Peking, 1959.

Wen Chün-t'ien 聞鈞天. *Chungkuo paochia chihtu* 中國保甲制度 [*The Paochia System in China*]. Shanghai, 1935.

Whiting, Allen S. *China Crosses the Yalu.* New York: Macmillan, 1960.

Wiles, P. D. J. *The Political Economy of Communism.* Cambridge, Mass.: Harvard University Press, 1962.

Wittfogel, Karl A. *Oriental Despotism.* New Haven: Yale University Press, 1957.

Wu Ch'ing-yu 吳清友. *Sulien ti kungyeh kuanli* 蘇聯的工業管理 [*Industrial Management in the Soviet Union*]. Shanghai, 1950.

Yang, C.K. *Religion in Chinese Society.* Berkeley and Los Angeles: University of California Press, 1961.

Yu, Frederick T. C. *Mass Persuasion in Communist China.* New York and London: Praeger, 1964.

Zagoria, Donald. *Vietnam Triangle.* New York: Pegasus, 1967.

ARTICLES

Barnett, A. Doak, "Social Stratification and Aspects of Personnel Management in the Chinese Communist Bureaucracy," *The China Quarterly* 28 (October-December, 1966), 8-39.

Boorman, Howard L. "Liu Shao-ch'i: A Political Profile," *The China Quarterly*, 10 (April-June 1962), 1-22.

Bridgham, Philip. "Mao's 'Cultural Revolution': Origin and Development," *The China Quarterly*, 29 (January-March 1967), 1-35.

Chang Hsing-fu 張興富. "Wokuo kungyeh-hua ti taolu ho fangfa" 我國工業化的道路和方法 ["Directions and Methods of Industrialization in Our Country"], *Jenmin shouts'e 1958*, pp. 446-448.

Chao Kuo-chün. "Leadership in the Chinese Communist Party," *The Annals of the American Academy of Political and Social Science*, 321 (1959), 40-50.

Chuang, H. C. "The Great Proletarian Cultural Revolution," in *Studies in Chinese Communist Terminology*, No. 12. Berkeley, Calif.: Center for Chinese Studies, University of California, 1967.

Cohen, Jerome A. "The Criminal Process in China" (unpublished paper, February, 1965, Harvard Law School).

Crossman, Richard. "The Chinese Communes," *New Statesman* (January 10, 1959).

Doolin, Dennis J. and Peter J. Golas, "*On Contradiction* in the Light of Mao Tse-tung's Essay on 'Dialectical Materialism,'" *The China Quarterly*, 19 (July-September 1964), 38-46.

Fedoseev, P. "Marksizm i Maotsedunizm" ["Marxism and Maoism"], *Kommunist*, 5 (March 1967), 107-122.

Fukushima Hiroshi 福島裕. "Toshi jinmin kōsha" 都市人民公社 ["Urban People's Communes"]. *Chūgoku kenkyu geppō*, 151 (November 1960), 1-37.

———. "Kigyō no takaku keiei to rengōka" 企業の多角經營と連合化 ["Management and Merging of Multiple-Operation Enterprises,"] *Ajiya keizai junpō*, 462 (March 1961), 1-10.

Gelman, Harry, "The Sino-Soviet Contflict" in Franz Schurmann and Orville Schell, editors, *The China Reader*, Volume III, pp, 267-289.

Grossman, Gregory. "The Structure and Organization of the Soviet Economy," *Slavic Review*, XXI:2 (June 1962), 203-222.

Ho Kuei-lin 何桂林. "'Shehui-chuyi shengch'an chiako-lun' ti shih-chih" 社會主義生產價格論'的實質 ["The Real Substance of

'The Theory of Socialist Production Value' "], *Chingchi yenchiu*, 1 (January 1965), 20-25.

Hoeffding, Oleg. "The Soviet Industrial Reorganization of 1957," *American Economic Review*, XLIX:2 (May 1959), 65-77.

Hoffmann, Charles. "The Basis of Communist China's Incentive Policy," *Asian Survey*, III:5 (May 1963), 245-257.

———. "Work Incentives in Communist China," *Industrial Relations*, III:3 (February 1964), 81-97.

Holubnychy, Vsevolod. "Mao Tse-tung's Materialistic Dialectics," *The China Quarterly*, 19 (July-September 1964), 3-37.

Hsia, T. A. "Heroes and Hero-worship in Chinese Communist Fiction," *The China Quarterly*, 13 (January-March 1963), 113-138.

Hsiao, Gene. "The Background and Development of 'The Proletarian Cultural Revolution,'" *Asian Survey*, VII:6 (June 1967), 389-404.

———. "Legal Institutions in Communist China," *Problems of Communism*, XIV (March-April 1965), 112-121.

Hsüeh Mu-ch'iao 薛暮橋. "Tui hsienhsing chihua kuanli chihtu ti ch'upu ichien" 對現行計劃管理制度的初步意見 ["Preliminary Opinions on the Current System of Plan Management"], *Chihua chingchi*, 9 (September 1957), 20-24.

Hunter, Neale. "Three Cadres of Shanghai," *The Far Eastern Economic Review* (June 1, 1967), 491-495.

Ishikawa Shigeru. "Choice of Technique in Mainland China," *The Developing Economies*, 2 (Tokyo: September-December 1962), 23-56.

Johnson, Chalmers, "China: The Cultural Revolution in Structural Perspective," *Asian Survey* VIII:1 (January, 1968), 1-15.

Jones, Philip P. and Thomas T. Poleman, "Communes and the Agricultural Crisis in Communist China," *Food Research Institute Studies*, III:1 (February 1962), 3-22.

Karnow, Stanley. "The G. I. Who Chose Communism," *Saturday Evening Post*, November 16, 1963.

Lee, Rensselaer W., III. "The *Hsia Fang* System: Marxism and Modernization," *The China Quarterly*, 28 (October- December 1966), 40-62.

Levenson, Joseph R. "The Place of Confucius in Communist China," *The China Quarterly*, 12 (October-December 1962), 1-18.

Levenson, Joseph R. and Franz Schurmann. "An Exchange on China." *The New York Review on Books*, VII: 12 (January 12, 1967).

Lewis, John Wilson. "The Leadership Doctrine of the Chinese Communist Party: The Lesson of the People's Commune," *Asian Survey*, III (October 1963), 457-464.

———"Revolutionary Struggle and the Second Generation in Communist China," *The China Quarterly* 21 (January-March, 1965), 126-147.

Liao Lu-yien (= Liao Lu-yen 廖魯言). "Acerca de la colectivización de la agricultura en China," *Cuba Socialista*, (October 1963), 40-61.

Lifton, Robert J. "Thought Reform of Chinese Intellectuals, A Psychiatric Evaluation," *The Journal of Asian Studies*, XVI:1 (November 1956), 75-88.

———. " 'Thought Reform' of Western Civilians in Chinese Communist Prisons," *Psychiatry*, XIX:2 (May 1956), 149-172.

Ling Piao 凌飆. "Chungkung yu-kuan ch'engshih chengts'e falü" 中共有關城市政策法律 ["Chinese Communist Policies and Laws on the Cities"], *Tsukuo*, 6 (Hong Kong: September 1964), 17-23.

Ma Wen-kuei 馬文桂. "Shehui-chuyi kungyeh ch'iyeh chihua ti t'etien, jenwu, ho fangfa" 社會主義工業企業計劃的特點任務和方法 ["Concerning Special Aspects, Tasks, and Methods of Planning in Socialist Enterprises"], *Chingchi yenchiu*, 7 (July 1964), 8-17.

Niida Noboru, "The Industrial and Commercial Guilds of Peking and Religion and Fellow-countrymanship as Elements of their Coherence," *Folklore Studies*, IX (1950), 179-206.

Oksenberg, Michel. "Paths to Leadership in Communist China," *Current Scene*, III:24 (August 1, 1965).

Perkins, Dwight H. "Centralization and Decentralization in Mainland China and the Soviet Union," *Annals of the American Academy of Political and Social Science*, 349 (September 1963), 70-80.

———. "Centralization and Decentralization in Mainland China's Agriculture 1949-1962," *The Quarterly Journal of Economics*, LXXVII (May 1964), 208-237.

Ra'anan, Uri, "Rooting for Mao," *New Leader*, March 13, 1967.

Schein, Edgar H. "The Chinese Indoctrination Program for Prisoners of War," *Psychiatry*, XIX:2 (May 1956), 149-172.

Schram, Stuart R. "Chinese and Leninist Components in the Personality of Mao Tse-tung," *Asian Survey*, III:6 (June 1963), 259-273.

Schurmann, Franz. "Organization and Response in Communist China," *Annals of the American Academy of Political and Social Science*, 321 (January 1959), 51-61.

———. "The Communes: A One-year Balance Sheet," *Problems of Communism*, VIII:5 (September-October 1959), 7-14; "Peking's Recognition of Crisis," X:5 (September-October 1963), 5-14.

————. "China's 'New Economic Policy'—Transition or Beginning?" *The China Quarterly*, 17 (January-March 1964), 65-91.

————. "What is Happening in China," *The New York Review of Books*, October 20, 1966.

Skinner, G. William. "Marketing and Social Structure in Rural China," *The Journal of Asian Studies*, XXIV:1 (November 1964), 3-43, XXIV:2 (February 1965), 195-228, XXIV:3 (May 1965), 363-399.

Sladkovskii, M. "Ugroza ekonomicheskim osnovam sotsializma v Kitae" ["Danger to the Economic Foundations of Socialism in China"], *Kommunist*, 12 (August 1967), 93-108.

Snow, Edgar, "Interview with Mao," *New Republic*, January 20, 1965.

Tien, H. Yuan. "Induced Abortion and Population Control in Mainland China," *Marriage and Family Living*, XXV:1 (February 1963), 35-43.

Ubukata Naokichi 幼方直吉. "Chū-shi no gōko ni kansuru sho-mon-dai" 中支の合股に關する諸問題 ["Problems Concerning the 'Ho-ku' (Companies) in Central China"], *Mantetsu chōsa geppō*, XXXIII:4 (1943), 91-116.

Wang Hsiao-t'ang. "The 'Four Cleans' and the 'Cultural Revolution' of the Chinese Communists," *Feich'ing yenchiu* [*Studies on Chinese Communism*], I (January 1967), 23-31.

Wang Hu-sheng 王琥生. "Kuan yü chung-kungyeh ho ch'ing-kungyeh huafen ti chiko went'i" 關於重工業和輕工業劃分的幾個問題 ["Questions on the Differentiation Between Heavy and Light Industry"], *Chingchi yenchiu*, 4 (April 1963), 16-26.

Watson, Andrew, "Revolution in Sian," *Far Eastern Economic Review* (April 20, 1967), 123-126; "Embattled Armies," *ibid.*, (April 27, 1967), 231-233; "Scarlet and Black," *ibid.* (May 4, 1967), 265-269; "Showdown in Sian," *ibid.* (May 18, 1967) 403-406; "Armageddon Averted," ibid. (May 25, 1967), 449-452.

Wright, Arthur F. "Struggle vs. Harmony—Symbols of Competing Values in Modern China," *World Politics*, VI:1 (October 1953), 31-44.

Wu Yuan-li. "The Pattern of Industrial Location and its Relation to Railway Transportation" (unpublished paper for the first research conference of the Social Science Research Council Committee on the Economy of China, Berkeley, California, January 31, February 1-2, 1963).

Yang Ying-chieh楊英傑. "Lun ts'ung liu-i jenk'ou ch'ufa" 論從六億人口出發 ["Let's Talk About Starting With Six Hundred Million People"], *Chingchi yenchiu*, 6 (June 1958), 39-46.

Yo Wei兵魏 . "Kuan yü kuomin chingchi tsungho p'ingheng ti chiko went'i" 關於國民經濟綜合平衡的幾個問題 ["On Some Problems of Comprehensive Balance in the National Economy"], *Chingchi yenchiu*, 7 (July 1964), 1-17.

NEWSPAPERS

Anhwei jihpao [*Anhwei Daily*], **Hofei, Anhwei Province.**

Asahi Shimbun (Tokyo)

Ch'angchiang jihpao [*The Yangtze River Daily*], **Hankow, Hupei Province.**

Chanpao [*Combat*], Peking.

Chiehfang jihpao [*The Liberation Daily*], **Shanghai.**

Fukien jihpao [*Fukien Daily*], **Foochow, Fukien Province.**

Hopei jihpao [*Hopei Daily*], **Paoting, Hopei Province.**

Hsingtao jihpao [*The Hong Kong Daily*], **Hong Kong.**

Hsinhua jihpao [*The New China Daily*], **Chungking, Szechwan Province.**

Jenmin jihpao [*The People's Daily*], **Peking.**

Kiangsi jihpao [*Kiangsi Daily*], **Nanchang, Kiangsi Province.**

Kirin jihpao [*Kirin Daily*], **Kirin, Kirin Province.**

Kuangchou jihpao [*Canton Daily*], **Canton, Kwangtung Province.**

Kuangming jihpao [*The Enlightenment Daily*], **Peking.**

Kungjen jihpao [*The Workers Daily*], **Peking.**

Kweichow jihpao [*Kweichow Daily*], **Kweiyang, Kweichow Province.**

Liaoning jihpao [*Liaoning Daily*], **Mukden, Liaoning Province.**

Nanfang jihpao [*The Southern Daily*], **Canton, Kwangtung Province.**

New York Times (New York).

Shenyang jihpao [*Mukden Daily*], **Mukden, Liaoning Province.**

Szechwan jihpao [*Szechwan Daily*], **Chengtu, Szechwan Province.**

Takungpao [*The Impartial Daily*], **Peking edition, Tientsin edition, Hong Kong edition.**

Tientsin jihpao [*Tientsin Daily*], **Tientsin, Hopei Province.**

Tsingtao jihpao [*Tsingtao Daily*], **Tsingtao, Shantung Province.**

Tungfang-hung [*The East is Red*], Peking.

Tungpei jenmin jihpao [*Manchurian People's Daily*], **Mukden, Liaoning Province.**

Wenhuipao [*The Cultural Contact Daily*], Shanghai edition, Hong Kong edition.

Wuchou kungjen jihpao [*The Wuchow Workers Daily*], Wuchow, Kwangsi Province.

Yomiuri Shimbun (Tokyo).

PERIODICALS

Ajïya keizai junpō [*Trimonthly of Asian Economics*], Tokyo.

American Economic Review, Stanford, California.

Annals of the American Academy of Political and Social Science, Philadelphia.

Asian Survey, Berkeley, California.

Chihua chingchi [*Planned Economy*], Peking.

China News Analysis, Hong Kong.

The China Quarterly, London.

China Monthly. See *Tsukuo*.

Chingchi yenchiu [*Economic Studies*], Peking.

Chūgoku kenkyu geppō [*China Studies Monthly*], Tokyo.

Chungkuo ch'ing-kungyeh [*Chinese Light Industry*], Peking.

Chungkuo ch'ingnien [*Chinese Youth*], Peking.

Cuba socialista, Havana.

Current Scene, Hong Kong.

The Developing Economies, Tokyo.

Folklore Studies, Tokyo.

Food Research Institute Studies, Stanford, California.

Hsinhua panyüeh-k'an [*New China Semi-monthly*], title changed from *Hsinhua yüehpao* [*New China Monthly*] in 1956, Peking.

Hsinhua yüehpao. See *Hsinhua panyüeh-k'an*.

Hsin kuanch'a [*New Observer*], Peking.

Hungch'i [*Red Flag*], official organ of the Central Committee of the Chinese Communist party, Peking.

Industrial Relations, Berkeley, Calif.

Journal of Asian Studies, Ann Arbor, Mich.

Journal of Economic History, Seattle, Washington.

Mantetsu chōsa geppō [*Investigation Monthly of the South Manchuria Railway Company*], Dairen.

Marriage and Family Living, Minneapolis, Minn.

Nankai Social and Economic Quarterly, Tientsin.

Peking Review, Peking

Problems of Communism, Washington, D.C.
Psychiatry, Washington, D.C.
Quarterly Journal of Economics, Cambridge, Mass.
Slavic Review, Seattle, Washington.
Tsukuo [China Monthly], Hong Kong.
World Politics, Princeton, N.J.

MISCELLANEOUS

DOCUMENTS

Ch'ihfei fantung wenchien huipien 赤匪反動文件彙編 Reprinted from the Ch'en Ch'eng collection of captured Chinese Communist documents of the Kiangsi soviet period. n.p., n.d.

Chungkuo kungch'antang tipatz'u ch'üankuo taipiao tahui wenchien 中國共產黨第八次全國代表大會文件 [*Documents of the Eighth National Congress of the Communist Party of China*], Peking, 1957.

Hsienhsing paochia faling huipien 現行保甲法令彙編 [*Current Laws and Decrees on the Paochia*], August 13, 1940, n. p., presumably published in Japanese occupied China.

Kungtso t'unghsün 工作通訊 [*Operations Bulletin*], Chinese Communist regimental bulletins released by the United States State Department. n.p., n.d.

Shehui-chuyi chiaoyü k'och'eng yüehtu wenchien huipien 社會主義教育課程閱讀文件彙編 [*Collection of Documents for Course Reading in Socialist Education*], Peking, 1957 (Vol. I), 1958 (Vols. II and III).

T'uti kaiko chungyao wenhsien huichi 土地改革重要文獻彙集 [*Collection of Major Documents on Land Reform*], Peking, 1961.

YEARBOOKS

Chūgoku nenkan 中國年鑑 [*China Yearbook*], now renamed *Shin-Chūgoku nenkan [New China Yearbook]*, Tokyo.

Jenmin shouts'e 人民手册 [*People's Handbook*], Peking.

Shanghai nienchien 上海年鑑 [*Shanghai Yearbook*], Shanghai.

Shihshih shouts'e 時事手册 [*Current Affairs Handbook*], Peking.

World Strength of Communist Party Organizations, U.S. Department of State, Washington, D.C.

DICTIONARIES AND ENCYCLOPEDIAS

Bolshaiia sovetskaiia entsiklopediia, Moscow, 1950-1958. 51 vols.

Chūkyō seiji keizai sōran 中國政治經濟綜覽 [*Lexicon of Chinese Communist Politics and Economics*], Tokyo, 1962.

Gendai Chūgoku jimmei jiten 現代中國人名辭典 [*Lexicon of Persons in Present-day China*], Tokyo, 1957.

Gendai Chūgoku jiten 現代中國事典 [*Lexicon of Present-day China*], Tokyo, 1959.

Hsin mingtz'u tz'utien 新名詞辭典 [*New Name Dictionary*], Shanghai, 1951.

Iuridicheskii slovar', [*Juridical Dictionary*], Moscow, 1956, 2 vols.

Kuoyü tz'utien 國語詞典 [*Dictionary of Mandarin*], Hong Kong, 1961.

DISSERTATIONS

Chen, Joseph T. "The Shanghai May Fourth Movement" (unpublished doctoral dissertation, University of California, Berkeley, Calif.).

Townsend, James. "Mass Political Participation in Communist China" (unpublished doctoral dissertation, University of California, Berkeley, Calif.).

OTHERS

"Ch'iyeh kuanli chich'u chihshih chianghua" 企業管理基礎知識講話 ["Remarks on Basic Knowledge Concerning Industrial Management"], *Chungkuo ch'ing-kungyeh* 18 (1958) to 12 (1960). See Periodicals.

"Shanghai chingchi hsüehhui 1962-nien nienhui t'aolun ti chuyao went'i tsungshu" 上海經濟協會1962年年會討論的主要問題綜述 ["Summary of the Major Problems Discussed at the 1962 Annual Meeting of the Shanghai Economic Association"], *Chingchi yenchiu*, 4 (April 1963), 62-70. See Periodicals.

Yang Jun-jui and Li Hsün 楊潤瑞,李勳. "Shih-lun ch'iyeh kuanli ti chingchi hosuan" 試論企業管理的經濟核算 ["Experimental Discussion of Economic Accounting in Industrial Enterprises"], *Jenmin jihpao*, July 19, 1962. See Newspapers.

"Che shih wei shenmo?" 這是爲甚麼 ? ["Why Is This?"], *Jenmin jihpao*, June 8, 1957.

COMMUNIQUES, SPEECHES, AND REPORTS (chronological)

Party Rules of the Seventh Party Congress. See Liu Shao-ch'i, *Luntang.*

Central Committee of the Chinese Communist Party, "Directive On Carrying Out Land Reform Operations in the Old Liberated Areas and on Party Rectification Operations," February 22, 1948, *Much'ien hsingshih ho women ti jenwu* [*The Present Situation and Our Tasks*] (Hong Kong: Commercial Press, 1949), pp. 72-81.

Mao Tse-tung, "Lecture to a Meeting of Cadres from Shansi and Suiyuan," April 1, 1948, *ibid.*, pp. 82-95; also in *Selected Works of Mao Tse-tung*, IV, 1303-1315.

Central Committee of the Chinese Communist Party, communiqué of the Fourth Plenum, February 17, 1954, *Jenmin jihpao*, February 18, 1954.

National Delegates Meeting of the Chinese Communist Party, resolution on the anti-Party league of Kao Kang and Jao Shu-shih, March 31, 1955, *Jenmin jihpao*, April 5, 1955.

Mao Tse-tung, "On the Question of Agricultural Cooperativization," July 31, 1955, *Jenmin shouts'e 1956*, pp. 80-86.

National Program for the Development of Agriculture from 1956 to 1967 (draft), with an address by Mao Tse-tung to a Supreme State Meeting, January 25, 1956, and the annotation: "Presented by the Central Politburo on January 23, 1956" published as a pamphlet in Peking, February, 1956.

Reports to the Eighth Party Congress, September 15 to 27, 1956 (in *Chungkuo kungch'antang tipatz'u ch'üankuo taipiao tahui wenchien*) Mao Tse-tung, pp. 7-10; Liu Shao-ch'i, pp. 11-72; Teng Hsiao-p'ing, pp. 73-100; Lo Jui-ch'ing, pp. 272-286; Ch'en Yün, pp. 326-336; Teng Tzu-hui, pp. 352-364; Li Hsien-nien, pp. 386-396; Li Fu-ch'un, pp. 447-456; Li Hsüeh-feng, pp. 457-464; Huang Ching, pp. 535-542; Ch'ien Ying, pp. 708-711.

Rules of the Chinese Communist Party, *ibid.*, pp. 821-841; membership of the Central Committee of the Chinese Communist party, *ibid.*, pp. 860-861.

Mao Tse-tung, "On the Question of Correctly Resolving Contradictions among the People," *Jenmin shouts'e 1958*, pp. 9-20.

Central Committee of the Chinese Communist Party, directives on consolidating the Agricultural Producers Cooperatives, September 14, 1957, *Jenmin shouts'e 1958*, pp. 517-520.

Central Committee of the Chinese Communist party, communiqué of the Third Plenum, September 20 to October 9, 1957, *Jenmin shouts'e 1958*, p. 182; report of Teng Hsiao-p'ing, *ibid.*, pp. 33-41, report of Teng Tzu-hui, *ibid.*, pp. 520-523.

Liu Shao-ch'i, speech at a mass meeting in Peking honoring the fortieth anniversary of the Russian Revolution, November 6, 1957, *Jenmin shouts'e 1958*, pp. 297-301.

Liu Shao-ch'i, report to the second session of the Eighth Party Congress, May 5, 1958, *Jenmin shouts'e 1959*, pp. 17-26.

Enlarged Meeting of the Politburo of the Central Committee of the Chinese Communist party, communiqué of the Peitaiho meeting, August 29, 1958, *Jenmin jihpao*, September 10, 1958.

Central Committee of the Chinese Communist Party, communiqué of the Sixth Plenum, December 10, 1958, *Jenmin jihpao*, December 18, 1958.

Central Committee of the Chinese Communist Party, communiqué of the Ninth Plenum, January 20, 1961, *Jenmin jihpao*, January 21, 1961.

Central Committee of the Chinese Communist Party, communiqué of the Tenth Plenum, September 28, 1962, *Jenmin jihpao*, September 29, 1962.

Joffe, Ellis, "The PLA in Politics and Politics in the PLA, 1965-1966," Columbia University Seminar on Modern East Asia, November 30, 1966.

Skinner, G. William. "Compliance and Leadership in Rural Communist China," paper delivered for the 1965 Annual Meeting of the American Political Science Association, Washington, D.C., September 8-11, 1965.

INDEX FOR MAIN TEXT

Chinese Communist leaders are identified, first, by their present position according to *Chūka jimmin kyōwakoku genshoku jimmei jiten* [*Dictionary of Office-holders in the People's Republic of China*] (Ajiya keizai kenkyūjo: Tokyo, 1964), and, if different, secondly, by their major positions discussed in this book.

bureaucratic centralization of Manchuria, 267 ff.; abolition of, 284 ff.; economic control as weapon against, 313, 325, 339

Operations: definition of, 224, 224 n.; translation of policy into, 68; as function of staff-and-line, 69; operational functions of agenices of the Central Committee, 143, 145, 166; operational functions of branch-type organizations, 175; the policy-operations dichotomy, 224 ff., 257 n., 279, 287 ff., 297 ff.; Party acquires control over policy and, 216, 234; the policy-operations dichotomy in Chinese business before 1949, 223 ff.; unity of policy and, through one-man management, 246, 248, 254, 259; "independent operational authority," 297 ff.

Opinion, as element in intra-organizational "discussion," 54-56, 196; groups, 55-57, 196 ff.; opinions of the masses, 256, 316, 317, 376

Opium War, xxxii

Organ: definition of, 159. See also Agencies

Organization: as means of reuniting society after revolution, xxxiii, 178 ff., 438 ff.; recruitment of traditional elites into, xxxiv, 5, 6, 167 ff., 231; need of consciousness in, xlii, 45 ff., 234; Chinese Communist concern with, xxxviii, xlii, xlvi, 54, 416 ff.; function of elites in, xxxviii, xxxix, 4-6, 167 ff.; a small group as core element in, xli, see also Group, Production team; ideology as an instrument for creating and using, xlii, 14, 18 ff., 45 ff.; contradictions as functional element in, xlv, 53 ff., 73 ff., 188 ff.; contrasted with institution, xlv, 226 ff.; definition of, 3, 4; distinctions between, and social system, 4-6; the particular importance of practical ideology for, 23, 68 ff.; ideology of, as contrasted with class and individual ideologies, 18 ff., 30, 31, 33; regarding all organization as essentially consisting of three tiers, 68 ff., see also Three-tiered conception of organization; pure ideology as a means of by-

passing the middle and arousing the lower tier of, 71-73; the Communist party as, 105 ff.; principles of, 53 ff., 85 ff., 173-178; unity in, 225 ff.; technical and human, 231 ff., see also Human organization, Technical organization; control in, 309, 310; middle levels of, 69-72

See also Administration, Branch-type organization, Centralization, Committee-type organization, Communist party of China, Control, Decentralization, Dual rule, Government, Human organization, Leadership, Management, One-man management, Technical organization, Three-tiered conception of organization, Vertical rule

Orleans, Leo A., 137 n.

"Outsider," 57, 216, 305, 313, 314, 326 ff., 332, 336, 339, 343, 349, 423

P'an Chen-ya, deputy governor of Kiangsi province; deputy head of the Ministry of State Control, 329, 364

P'an Fu-sheng, Acting chairman of the All-China Federation of Supply and Marketing Cooperatives; first secretary of the Honan provincial committee of the CCP, 215

Panama, 481

Pao system, 294, 460

Paochia: rural, 408 ff., 426-428, 443, 463, 495; urban, 369-372, 374, 376

Paris, xxxvi

Parsons, Talcott, 2 n., 39 n.

"Party life," 48, 49, 66

Pater familias. See *Chiachang*

Pat'ou. See Foreman

Peasants, peasantry, Chapter VII; and revolution, xl, xli, xlii, 40, 425 ff.; as cadres, xliii, 52, 168-172, 423 ff.; as class in Chinese society, 16, 119, 120; in land reform, 32, 431 ff.; as emerging proletariat, 40, 41; hostility to officials, xxxi, 72; contradictions affecting the, 75, 90, 92-96, 102; Party membership of, 132, 133; material incentives and, 198, 199, 201, 494; migration of, into cities, 382, 401, 402; organization of, in Traditional China, 405 ff.; cooperative movement among, 412 ff.

Individual peasants, 204 n.

Middle peasants, 199, 430, 433, 435, 437 n., 445, 448-450, 461, 462, 468, 470

"Old peasants," 471, 494, 498

Poor peasants, 415, 429-431, 435-437, 445, 448-450, 461, 462, 468, 470, 480, 497, 499

Rich peasants, 206, 414, 415, 423, 429-438, 442, 445, 448-451, 455, 457, 461, 462, 470, 492, 494, 497, 499

Peasant councils, 435, 436, 438

Peasant leagues, 413

Peitaiho, 146, 147, 476, 477, 481, 492

Peking, xxxviii, 6, 139 n., 140, 147, 149, 178, 208, 215, 257, 259, 267-271, 277, 303, 319, 320, 323, 332, 333, 339, 342, 345, 385, 394, 395 n., 464

P'eng Chen, first secretary of the Peking city committee of the CCP, mayor of Peking, member of the Politburo, 333, 362

P'eng Ta, deputy bureau chief of the Ministry of State Control, 353 ff.

P'eng Te-huai, member of the Politburo, deputy chairman of the National Defense Council; head of the Ministry of National Defense, 56 n., 144, 187, 333

"People," 110, 111, 115, 118-122, 179

People's Democratic Dictatorship, 119, 124

People's Liberation Army. See army

People's Revolutionary Military Council. See National Defense Council

Perkins, Dwight H., 206 n.

Personnel, 207, 258, 260, 292, 343, 344

Petrograd, xxxvi

Pfiffner, John M., 222 n., 224 n.

P'ingyü hsien (Honan), 473

Planning: agencies denounced as conservative, 70, 238, 295, 296; contrasted with Mao Tse-tung's vision, 74; long- and short-range, 84, 181; under socialism and communism, 113; co-ordinative function and committee-type organization of, agencies, 175, 189; as envisaged under the decentralization program advocated by Ch'en Yün, 197; how the 1957 decentralization affected,

207, 208; regional, 210, 217; criticism of Soviet-type, 242, 285, 286, 363; at factory-level, 249-251, 286, 292, 298; one-man management as requisite to, 253, 254; design, 302, 306 n., 307 n.

Po I-po, Chairman of the State Economic Commission, alternate member of the Politburo, 83, 333, 352, 358 n.

Poland, 117, 138

Polanyi, Karl, 2 n., 3 n.

Police. See Public security

Policy: in sense of practical ideology, 28 n., struggles in Politburo, 56; public communication of, 60, 61, 63-66; definition of, 86, 86 n., 87 n., 238; separation of, and operational functions between Party and state, 110, 111; "line and policy" announced at Party congresses, 140; policy-making agencies, 143, 145, 146, 175, 180, 195; translation of policy into operations by regional agencies, 154, 216; and operations, 134, 223 ff., 246, 248, 257 n., 258, 259, 278, 287 ff.

Political Affairs Conference, 178. See also Chinese People's Political Consultative Conference

Political departments (army), 144. See also Communist Party of China, political departments

Political-legal departments, 151, 310, 350 n.

Political revolution, xxix, xxx, xxxiii, 500

"Politics Takes Command," 154 n., 156, 206, 209, 279, 305

Population: growth in 18th century, xxxv; as reason for labor-intensive policies of the Great Leap Forward, 83, 380-382; Party membership and, 135-139; intellectual, 130, criteria for Party organization, 153; of cities, 365, 380-382; affected by land reform, 438; in mutual-aid teams, 440; in APC's, 454; in communes, 156, 493

Port Arthur (Lüshun), 242

Positivist: ideological and organizational activists who are potential Party members, 168, 170, 246, 247, 373-375, 427, 446

Power: wealth, and prestige as criteria

INDEX FOR SUPPLEMENT